Ideology and Private Law: Polish Experiences in the Long 20th Century

Legal History Library

VOLUME 74

The titles published in this series are listed at *brill.com/lhl*

Ideology and Private Law: Polish Experiences in the Long 20th Century

By

Anna Machnikowska, Michał Gałędek, and Rafał Mańko

BRILL | NIJHOFF

LEIDEN | BOSTON

This publication was prepared as part of the 'Between modernization and national character. Ideology and axiology of the drafters of Polish private law in 20th century' project financed by the National Science Centre (Narodowe Centrum Nauki) on the basis of decision no. DEC-2016/21/B/HS5/03221.

Cover illustration: Depiction of the emblem of the Second Polish Republic, featuring symbols of the USSR and European Union to represent the sources of inspiration for later modification to Polish private law. Kaja Mucha, 2024.

The Library of Congress Cataloging-in-Publication Data is available online at https://catalog.loc.gov
LC record available at https://lccn.loc.gov/

Typeface for the Latin, Greek, and Cyrillic scripts: "Brill". See and download: brill.com/brill-typeface.

ISSN 1874-1793
ISBN 978-90-04-72999-5 (hardback)
ISBN 978-90-04-73002-1 (e-book)
DOI 10.1163/9789004730021

Contents

Acknowledgments

The authors extend their cordial thanks to Professors Anna Chełmońska-Soyta, Ewa Łętowska, Leszek Leszczyński, Andrzej Mączyński, Jerzy Pisuliński, Zbigniew Witkowski, Doctor Sybilla Stanisławska-Kloc, Anna Chrabąszcz and Aleksandra Matysiak for their invaluable assistance in the search for illustrative material for this book.

Figures

Abbreviations

AAN	Archiwum Akt Nowych [Central Archives of Modern Records in Warsaw]
ABGB	*Allgemeines Bürgerliches Gesetzbuch* [Austrian Civil Code of 1811]
BGB	*Bürgerliches Gesetzbuch* [German Civil Code of 1896]
BMS	*Biuletyn Ministerstwa Sprawiedliwości*
BP KC PZPR	Biuro Polityczne Komitetu Centralnego Polskiej Zjednoczonej Partii Robotniczej [Politbiuro of Polish United Workers' Party Central Committee]
CPH	*Czasopismo Prawno-Historyczne*
DPP	*Demokratyczny Przegląd Prawniczy*
Dz.U.	*Dziennik Ustaw* [Journal of Laws of the Republic of Poland / Polish Peoples' Republic]
GSW	*Gazeta Sądowa Warszawska*
KPCiK	*Kwartalnik Prawa Cywilnego i Karnego*
KPP	*Kwartalnik Prawa Prywatnego*
MS	Ministerstwo Sprawiedliwości w Warszawie [Ministry of Justice in Warsaw]
OSN	*Orzecznictwo Sądu Najwyższego* [Decisions of the Polish Supreme Court]
OSNC	*Orzecznictwo Sądu Najwyższego Izba Cywilna* [Decisions of the Polish Supreme Court – Civil Law Chamber]
OSNPC	*Orzecznictwo Sądu Najwyższego – Izba Cywilna/Pracy* [Decisions of the Polish Supreme Court – Civil/Labour Law Chamber]
PiP	*Państwo i Prawo*
PZPR	Polska Zjednoczona Partia Robotnicza [Polish United Workers' Party]
RPEiS	*Ruch Prawniczy Ekonomiczny i Społeczny*
ZGB	*Zivilgesetzbuch* [Swiss Civil Code of 1907]

Instrumentalization of Polish Private Law in the 20th Century

1 The Universal Dimension of the Problem of Ideologization of Private Law

Historico-legal literature available in international circulation – which is essentially coterminous with its availability in at least one of the English, French, German or Spanish languages – has a dearth of studies tracing the development (especially codification) of modern positive law in the various countries of Central and Eastern Europe. Only recently has the situation slowly begun to change with regard to studies on private law in this part of Europe, for the most part thanks to the research initiated and conducted by Martin Löhnig and Anna Moszyńska.[1] Only precious few satisfactory cognitive results can be found when it comes to legal developments in the eastern part of the continent. Certain important cognitive threads have not yet gained currency in international academic circles. They do not enjoy wide-scale publicity, or they are simplified or even misrepresented. This contrasts with the familiarity of the legal history of Western Europe.

Moreover, the problem of the ideological framework underpinning the reforms of Polish private law implemented throughout the 20th century has not yet been made the subject of study, or at least not from the classical perspective of theories of modernization and dependence. This is due above all to the fact that private law is mainly studied with the use of formal-dogmatic methods (doctrinal research), which is also applied to historical studies in private law (the *Dogmengeschichte* method analysing the historical evolution of individual institutions of private law). What is definitely lacking is more profound reflection on the long-term social, economic and political role played by private law, its principles and institutions in Polish socio-economic reality, together with desirable directions of transformation.

1 See e.g. Martin Löhnig, Anna Moszyńska (eds), *Laboratorium für internationale gesetzgeberische Arbeit. Die Geburt der polnischen Rechtsordnung der Zwischenkriegszeit im europäischen Kontext*, Böhlau Verlag, Wien, 2021.

 | DOI:10.1163/9789004730021_002

This lack of reflection has become even more prominent nowadays, when – two decades after Poland's accession to the European Union – differences between the respective axiologies of Polish and EU private law are coming under the spotlight, which should certainly be analysed from historical and ideological perspectives.

Our book intentionally breaks with certain standards of a classic work in the discipline of legal history. The point of departure here is the premise that legal history should deliver something more than just the description of a legal system as it stands at a given point in history. With this goal in mind, we constantly endeavoured to examine the ideas motivating the introduction of specific solutions into private law, shaping its principles and institutions. We embarked on an analysis of the constituent parts of the system of private law, observing them through the lens of instruments designed to serve specific ideological and axiological purposes. On the one hand, there are postulates formulated already in the 19th century by a nationalist ideology calling for a codification of private law adapted to the allegedly unique characteristics – psyche, spirit and customs – of a specific nation. On the other hand is the perception of modernization as a positive value. The socialist and communist ideology invoked ideals of social solidarism, leading to the *de facto* disintegration of this concept. The liberal (or, more modernly, neo-liberal) ideology manifests itself through modern private law grounded in ideals of individual autonomy.

The ideological questions relating to private law can be addressed on three levels. The first, external level is composed of extralegal ideologies (liberalism, nationalism, socialism or conservatism) falling more or less in line with modernization or traditionalism. The second level – internal and spanning the entire legal system – represents ideologies such as legal positivism, normativism or legal modernism. The third level groups ideologies founded on the paradigms of the previous two ideological levels on the one hand and profiled by the current requirements of time and place on the other hand. Our work concentrates on inquiries pertaining to this third level.

While extralegal ideologies are well-described by political scientists and historians of political ideas, general intralegal ideologies are the field of study of historians of legal ideas, legal theoreticians and philosophers, in whose fields 'current' legal ideologies are usually more difficult to identify. On the third level, the legal ideology is often hidden behind a veil of simulated or seemingly but not truly neutral legal institutions. Legal institutions such as legal personality, the principle of *pacta sunt servanda*, the concept of tort liability or inheritance by family members are natural, and they are neutral to the point that it is difficult to decode whatever ideological content they might possibly carry. All, however, correspond to a certain normalized vision of social reality, which is ultimately an ideological construct.

2 Research Objectives

The authors intended to explore and explain the premises guiding the development of the Polish system of private law in the 20th century. This includes trying to answer the question of what reasons dictated the choice of one regulatory solution over the other, also affecting private law course of development as a whole, as well as what goals the various groups of legal experts working on all the drafts and blueprints (with particular emphasis on codification commissions)[2] had in mind; lastly, and to a lesser degree, how such blueprints were realized in specific statutes and especially how those were interpreted by legal scholars and judges.

Among the aforementioned objectives, there are some far-reaching ones that were also ideological in nature, driven by a long-term vision and belief that the law can be used as an efficient instrument of social engineering and can become the vehicle of change in the chosen direction, so as to materialize a specific ideological vision or axiological precept. A distinction must here be drawn between the goals thus defined and any short-term changes of direction – sometimes unintentional – occurring for simpler reasons, without being accompanied by any desire for a more durable effect, as well as strictly functional and technical changes aimed only at streamlining the operation of the system. Our analysis, therefore, focuses on the instrumental use of private law in pursuit of a certain consciously chosen and followed political line, in connection with the ideological and axiological tenets professed by the initiators of such changes.

The study is grounded in the assumption that the fundamental elements of the private-law system – including a number of principles and regulatory solutions constituting the foundation of private law – have not as yet been modified. Notwithstanding the changes occurring in civil law, civil procedure or

2 Stanisław Grodziski: *Prace nad kodyfikacją i unifikacją polskiego prawa prywatnego (1919–1947)* [The process of codification and unification of Polish private law (1919–1947)], KPP 1 (1992)/1–4, 9–56; Stefan Grzybowski: *Zagadnienia kodyfikacji polskiego prawa cywilnego (Organizacja i wyniki pracy 1919–1992)* [Codification of Polish civil law: Work organization and products 1919–1992], KPP 1 (1992)/1–4, 91–114.

commercial law, the original work product of the interwar Codification Commission (1919–1939) in the form of its various codes and unrealized drafts, as well as principles and institutions stipulated by their provisions, has continued to supply the main point of reference for and inform the direction taken by the development of Polish law until – as we assume and go on to verify – the present day.

The above does not change the fact that the 20th century, in a contradiction to most other periods of history, was not a homogeneous era. From a Polish and wider European perspective, the conditions in which Poland's private law was given shape varied dynamically. The key turning points were the two successive fundamental transitions of the political system: the building of a socialist state after World War II and of a liberal democracy after 1989. Each caused an upheaval of the entire social, economic and political reality, as well as the legal reality of its time. According to a commonly held conviction, which we set out to verify in this book, the ideological goals espoused by those in power were entirely redefined. All this could not but have a strong impact upon the legal system previously in existence, including the sphere of private law.

Nevertheless, it was hypothesized and subsequently verified in the course of our research that the stability of the system of private law, expanded upon by the interwar Codification Commission, was not irretrievably shaken up. Admittedly, during the period of the building of a socialist legal system, certain important structural elements of private law – especially commercial law – underwent fundamental changes. Nevertheless, we proceeded from the hypothesis that the systemic skeleton expanded upon in the interwar period had been retained. As a result, also the subsequent systemic transformation of 1989 did not necessitate – and this constituted a further hypothesis advanced in this study – a complete overhaul of the system of private law; whatever reforms were undertaken essentially came down to the restoration of ideas, principles and legal institutions already designed in the interwar period.

In other words, we set out to determine whether the scope and form of the systemic regulatory solutions designed during the interwar period and adopted at that time or adopted without major changes just after World War II (1945–1946) could have been rescinded in the course of the major legal reform carried out in the process of 'socialism-building' (the three codes of 1964: Civil Code, Code of Civil Procedure, Family and Guardianship Code). The surviving underpinning solutions from the interwar era made it a relatively easier task to achieve the restoration the old legal order amid the systemic transformation executed after 1989 (on the wave of which the codes of

1964 were not repealed).[3] Moreover, also at a later time, despite the emerging trend of harmonization of private law in the European Union, even the transposition of EU directives did not lead to any weakening of the foundations of private law developed, or developed upon, by the Codification Commission almost a full century prior.

Our research focused on the ideology (premises and goals) of the actors influential in the development of private law throughout the legislative reforms of the 20th century. We distinguished three major eras:

1. The interwar period (1919–1939) in which we focused on the activities of the Codification Commission in the field of private law and the Commission's drafting output, regardless whether a given draft managed to be enacted into law before the outbreak of World War II (e.g. the Code of Obligations, Commercial Code and Code of Civil Procedure) or provided the basis for legislation enacted after the war, especially the General Provisions of Civil Law, the Personal Law of Marriage, the Law of Matrimonial Property, the Real Law and the Law of Succession, all enacted as piecemeal statutes between 1945 and 1946, entering into force on 1 January 1947. The fundamental research question concerning the aforementioned legislative texts and their preparation concentrates on the ideological premises underlying the draft bills and their rejected alternatives, including the reasons leading to their rejection.
2. The period of the 'people's democracy' (1944–1989), in which we focus primarily on the ideological modalities of the legal reform carried out in the aftermath of World War II (the unification decrees of 1945–1946), the partial reforms of private law accomplished in 1950 (the new General Part of Civil Law and the new Family Code),[4] and, finally, the ground-up reconstruction of private law in 1964 (with its three codes: Civil Code, Code of Civil Procedure, Family and Guardianship Code).

---

3 Jerzy JODŁOWSKI: *Les principes de la procedure civil polonaise,* Revue internationale de droit comparé, 12 (1960)/2, 369–384.

4 Jerzy JODŁOWSKI: *Nowe drogi polskiego procesu cywilnego. Założenia ideologiczne reformy postępowania cywilnego* [The new ways of Polish civil procedure. The ideological basis of the reform of civil proceedings], Wydawnictwo Ministerstwa Sprawiedliwości, Warsaw, 1951; Anna STAWARSKA-RIPPEL: *O politycznych założeniach procedury cywilnej w Polsce Ludowej* [On the political foundations of civil procedure in People's Poland], in Marian MIKOŁAJCZYK, Andrzej DROGOŃ (eds), *Między I a III Rzecząpospolitą: kształtowanie europejskiej kultury prawnej. Prace ofiarowane prof. zw. dr. hab. Adamowi Lityńskiemu w czterdziestolecie pracy naukowej* [Between the First and Third Republics. The shaping of a European legal culture. Works dedicated to Professor Adam Lityński on the fortieth anniversary of his academic career], Miscellanea iuridica 7 (2005), 252–264.

We focus on the foundations and assumptions that enabled the drafters and the legislative decision-makers to reach a consensus as to the basic principles the codes of 1964 would embody.

3. The period of systemic transformation following after the events of 1989, when the decommunization of private law – the 'purging' of it of communist leftovers – was coupled with falling back on the pre-war traditions so as to modernize the country's private law on the basis of Western models, with emphasis on Europeanization of private law.

In each of these periods, our studies explored the premises underlying the bills and the surrounding or preceding debates unfolding in the legal circles (especially the codification commissions), on the one hand in academia and on the other hand in political circles desirous to achieve defined goals through a suitable constellation of legislative drafts. The successive codification commissions, however, did not operate in a vacuum. They were recruited from academics and practitioners whose opinions reflected the ideology and world view of Polish legal elites. Accordingly, our presentation of the ideology and axiology of the narrower circles directly responsible for the design and preparation of reforms of Polish private law juxtaposes and compares them with the academic voices of Polish legal scholars touching on the choice of directions for the evolution and transformation of private law and goals to be attained by the selection of institutions and legal principles. In this context, we also needed to account for the general trends prevailing in the individual periods in political and social thought and philosophy of law, because of their impact on the axiological and ideological layer. Furthermore, we took note of the views expressed by the political elites, their ideology, and doctrinal stances, which, however, we analysed only succinctly. Nevertheless, the ideology of the ruling elites marks an important point of reference for the principal focus of our research that is the axiology and ideology of the legal circles. Therefore, our intention was to analyse the network of mutual interdependencies between political and legal circles, focusing on parallel aspects and differences on points dealing with the fundamental characteristics of private law, as well as to analyse the mutual influence between the two groups.

As the main research hypothesis, we took the premise that, regardless of the changing political reality, the fundamental and generally understood paradigm of thinking about the role of law did not change over the course of the 20th century. This is because the axis of the debate on the construction and transformation of private law within each of the analysed periods was determined by:

(1) on the one hand, the national ideology seeking the fulfilments of needs connected with strengthening Poland's national identity and furthering

the interests of the Polish nation, which could be achieved by creating laws closely tailored to Poland's national characteristics or 'specificity';

(2) on the other hand, modernization tendencies prompting the use of foreign models and the emulation of those other countries whose directions of development of law and legal culture was deemed to be worth pursuing.[5]

Both the national interest and the modernizing occidentalism could each be very differently defined, depending on the method of description used; especially, however, depending on the period during which the debate was taking place and the concomitant changes in the political and socio-economic conditions. This is a factor that distinguishes, in particular, the period of 'People's Poland' from the other periods that we will be investigating.

The pressure to pursue modernization manifested itself in the fact that, whatever the chronological period, the legislators finding themselves under that pressure aspired to design a 'progressive' draft or, to be more precise, a draft corresponding to their own notion of modernity.[6] In pursuit of that goal, lawyers and jurists often created specific modernization models. Usually, those models were inspired by foreign solutions, often originating from a different cultural circle. On the one hand, they included the most up-to-date legislative achievements, such as whatever codes, principles and institutions were considered to be particularly progressive in a given historical period, as well as concepts and theoretical constructs developed and elaborated by academics and not necessarily tested in practice. On the other hand, and in a different perspective, they reflected the desired directions of social, economic and political changes. Those, the law sought to further by establishing development-stimulating institutions, while at the same time allowing for the adaptation of the legal system that was being created 'here

5 Rafał Mańko: *Relikty w kulturze prawnej: uwagi metodologiczne na tle pozostałości epoki socjalizmu realnego w polskim prawie prywatnym* [Relicts in legal culture: methodological remarks against the background of remnants of real socialism in Polish private law], in Mariusz Jabłoński, Michał Paździora (eds), *Postanalityczna filozofia prawa* [Postanalytical philosophy of law], Przegląd Prawa i Administracji 102 (2015), 185–208; Rafał Mańko: *Legal Survivals: A Conceptual Tool for Analysing Post-Transformation Continuity of Legal Culture*, in *Tiesību efektivitāte postmodernā sabiedrībā* [Effectiveness of law in postmodern society], Jānis Rozenfelds et al. (eds), LU Akadēmiskais apgāds, Riga, 2015, 16–27.

6 Wojciech Witkowski, Andrzej Wrzyszcz: *Modernisierung des Rechts auf polnischem Boden vom 19. bis Anfang des 20. Jahrhunderts*, in Tomasz Giaro (ed.), *Rechtskulturen des modernen Osteuropa. Traditionen und Transfers*, vol. 1: *Modernisierung durch Transfer im 19. und frühen 20. Jahrhundert*, Vittorio Klostermann, Frankfurt am Main, 2006, 249–274.

and now' to what its drafters anticipated to follow in the future. A modernization trend in this sense was a somewhat universal notion for the era, whether it was rooted in liberal or socialist slogans and in whatever way it happened to understand and represent the canon of democratic values or, on the contrary, perhaps advocate for its abandonment. For the aforementioned reasons, the aforesaid paradigm of modernization and progress informs our studies both for the part relating to the interwar era and for the part dealing with the period of radical ideological change in the aftermath of World War II (the socialist transformation), as well as after 1989, with Poland returning to the Western world and values. In all three examined periods, we focused on the criteria determining the path chosen for the pursuit of modernization ideas, which constituted a determinant of progress.

One factor achieving significant autonomy within, but nonetheless remaining part of, the modernization current was the aspiration of Polish scholars to take global inventory of the development of international legal scholarship, thereby tracing the progress of studies done abroad and ultimately attaining a general view. For this aspect of the problem, our research covers the dominant trends in the legal community, beginning from the convictions held by Polish academic circles about the direction legal developments should take, as well as the world views and ideologies espoused by the experts tasked with preparing the legal reforms at hand.

In the entire analysed period (and, as a matter of fact, also before it), the conservative-national world view was placed in opposition to modernization trends; upon this world view an ideology was built according to which traditional, indigenous values should be respected, as well as reflected, protected and cherished in the legal regulations. This world view and the ideology founded upon it were strictly correlated with a certain canon of principles and institutions (national characteristics) genetically connected with the historical tradition of each individual country, nation or cultural area; this canon changed depending on the perspective taken and the historical moment. In the lens of this tendency, we tried to analyse how the elements constituting Polish national identity, tradition and legal culture were defined, and what specific rules of Polish social, economic and political life determined, in each period, the development trends in private law. Finally, we examined how this was influenced by the various pressure groups, beginning with the pursuit of political goals by the power apparatus, through other organizations and movements whose ideologized approach to law made an imprint on the shape of solutions adopted and their subsequent evolution in the process of judicial interpretation of the law.

The principal goal of this book was thus to determine the values the reformers of Polish private law in the 20th century were pursuing in their efforts. If they perceived the institutions of private law as an instrument that could be deployed in order to effect a change in the socio-economic or political reality, then in what directions and according to what premises were the reforms supposed to proceed? Applying to the individual periods the paradigm of goals informed by either the national or the modernization ideology, we found ourselves able to discern:

(1) for the interwar period:
   a. legal instruments aimed to strengthen the national identity, in keeping with the assumption that a uniform private law, contained in modern, coherent and linguistically attractive codes, would constitute a symbol of national unity and showcase of restored Polish legal culture to the outside world, as well as an important factor genuinely consolidating the nation, although there were differences in the understanding of both the concept of a nation and the way to consolidate it;
   b. instruments aimed to achieve a 'capitalist' modernization of the legal system on the basis of models and ideas considered to be the most modern (referring to the creations of other legal cultures, their legislative and academic achievements), as well as the modernization of socio-economic and political circumstances in line with social, economic and political ideas considered to be progressive;

   in both cases, the axis of our analysis was the degree of fascination with Western achievements and the capacity for their critical evaluation, as well as the criteria to be followed;

(2) for the socialist period:
   a. instruments aimed to achieve a socialist modernization of the country, with socio-economic engineering based on communist and socialist inspirations, Soviet models and directives coming from the USSR, on the assumption that civil law was to be included in the process of 'socialism-building' and therefore take was intended to contribute to the creation of legal foundations for the dominance of 'socialized property,' along with a legal framework for contracts formed between 'socialized economic units' (literally: 'units of socialized economy') in a centrally planned system, and the development of a centralized co-operative sector;

b. the policy of socialization (i.e. socialist transformation) of the law, particularly visible through civil-law instruments limiting the exercise of individual ('subjective') rights, which were required to conform to their socio-economic purpose; this was specifically manifest in certain rules of co-operative law, housing law and law of perpetual lease (also known as emphyteusis or – in literal translation – 'perpetual usufruct').

3 Methodology

Our research was based on the analysis of source texts, in particular materials produced by the various legislative circles involved in the reforms of private law in Poland – especially the codification commissions directly responsible for the drafting – as well as the scholarly writings discussing and responding to such drafting activities, in particular by authors speaking from a clearly ideological perspective on the role and significance of private law, as well as its principles and institutions:

(1) materials of the Codification Commission of the Second Polish Republic;
(2) materials of the Ministry of Justice dealing with reforms of private law, available in the Central Archives of Modern Records in Warsaw;
(3) explanatory memoranda attending the government bills instituting the reforms;
(4) writings by private-law scholars published in leading legal journals.

When focusing on the issue of the instrumental use of private law with a view to the achievement of specific long-term ideological and axiological goals (in particular national- and modernization-oriented), we firstly analysed the sphere of world views and value systems professed by the drafters of the private-law codes and other participants of the debate surrounding the reforms of private law. Accordingly, we used axiological and functional methods in our approach to the main research problem, namely how law functions as an instrument and the goals that such an instrument can be expected to achieve. When comparing the two periods under examination, we relied on the comparative method; among the things we compared were the modes of argumentation used to promote or advocate for specific solutions. We also looked for similarities in the presentation of the rationales and arguments invoking the various principles and institutions of private law, as well as characterizations of the system as a whole.

Furthermore, we employed classic methods of historical research to analyse the problems connected with the shaping of codification drafts. The descriptive method enabled us to reconstruct – with precision and in chronological order – the historical events, especially of political and socio-economic nature, that accompanied the discussions surrounding the private-law reforms and thus may possibly have influenced the course and outcome of the debate. By application of the doxographic method, we were able to present the leading views from in particular the perspective of their conceptual apparatus, which in turn allowed us to identify certain currents of legal thought and bring them to the front and centre.

The research also employed classic theoretical methods used in the humanities. We followed the inductive method. Since this is based on the analysis of specific facts in order to form general conclusions, we used it to extrapolate judgements on specific institutions, mechanisms and legal principles onto reasons for their application or non-application, especially in the context of their being *national* or *modern*. This method led to general findings concerning the methods of thinking and categorization of social and legal reality in the analysed texts. We also applied the deductive method, based on reasoning referred to specific phenomena in a situation in which certain general principles and mechanisms are already known. This method was employed in particular on the basis of the assumption that Polish legal thought had relied on a certain canon of general rules taken from Western legal scholarship as a reference point but, on the other hand, also assumed certain values to be specifically Polish or treated them as such. Such texts relating to private law with its various branches and subdisciplines as were of particular utility in the application of this method were analysed by us from a general perspective involving the conceptualisatation of law as a certain system (normative network) capable of changing the reality towards a certain direction.

Incidentally, the following methods would have been inadequate for our research project:

(1) classic formal-dogmatic method, as it seeks to reconstruct the content of legal norms, whereby any extranormative (e.g. ideological) functions of law are out of scope;

(2) the method of legal philosophy, as our aim was to analyse not the philosophical foundations of private-law reforms but rather their ideological instrumentalization;

(3) methods of empirical sociology of law, such as those inspired by P. Bourdieu's critical sociology, as our aim was not to analyse the societal impact of reforms of private law.

4 Structure

We divided this monograph into four main parts:

(1) General remarks about ideology in private law in a chapter by Rafał Mańko.

(2) The history of Polish private law and its ideology in the interwar period in a chapter by Michał Gałędek.

(3) The ideology of the authors of Polish private law after World War II until 1989. This part contains three chapters (3–5) by Anna Machnikowska and Michał Gałędek.

(4) The last chapter, covering the period from the transformation of 1989 to 2000, by Anna Machnikowska.

The purpose of the first part was to make a strong argument in favour of fostering the intellectual collaboration of historians of private law with critical legal theorists. The outcome of such collaboration could be an ideological history of private law (i.e. ideological analysis of elements of history of private law), where – in a transdisciplinary (or even postdisciplinary) fashion – the tools of critical legal theory would be employed by historians of private law, as well as critical legal theorists would benefit from the insights of private-law historians into the historical unfolding of ideological struggles in the field of private law.

Analysing the interwar period (1919–1939) in the second chapter, we attempted to test the hypothesis that, in the course of the drafting of a new system of private law by the Codification Commission and in the course of the public debate, there was a clash between – on the one hand – modernization ideas implying a search for models and determinants of modernity in comparative research into various legal systems in Europe and the rest of the world and – on the other hand – calls for the expectations of society, its customs and respect for a certain canon of traditional ways of social and economic life to be considered. In the latter vision, the law should address national needs, strengthen the nation, and conform to certain traditional features of the nation.

On the basis of the research material we had selected, we tried to analyse the reasons for the adoption of certain solutions and rejection of their alternatives, as well as why a given solution was deemed to be the best, especially on the basis of its purportedly native Polish origin, so that it could foster the national values and consolidate the nation or, on the contrary, on the basis of its being progressive, so that it could help drive the modernization of society. We analysed the problem of what values and aims were providing the point of reference for the actors engaged in the process of building a system of private law for Poland.

As for the law of obligations, commercial law and civil procedure, we analysed the relationship between the individual actors and the then-dominant tendency towards the international unification of those legal areas. We were interested in how this process of unification was envisaged especially in the context of the need for the protection of certain specific national customs, features and interests. The key research questions we saw the need to address for these fields are: what conditions a given code had to fulfil in order to be considered modern (i.e. the hallmark factor of modernity) or to satisfy the criteria for being a work adapted to the Polish reality, one based on local traditions and meeting the expectations of Polish society. We will be paying special attention to the ideological battles fought in the course of the drafting works, along with the futility of the attempts to adopt the draft Matrimonial Law. The general assumption to be analysed is that within family law, the sphere of protection of national identity, the imagined features of the nation, as well as methods for strengthening this identity were to a greater extent opposed to modernization trends fuelled mainly by Western standards.

For the postwar period until 1989, which will be described in the later chapters, our attention focuses on legal institutions being newly introduced to Polish private law often in the emulation of Soviet models, and in particular new general clauses (principles of community life, socio-economic purpose),[7] the stratification of ownership and its functional definition;[8] the rules for special legal capacity of legal persons; the civil-law aspects of the functioning of socialized economic units (prescription, planned contracts, etc.), new rules governing the inheritance of farms; newly created property rights (perpetual lease; co-operative proprietary right to an apartment); new legal institutions in the law of obligations (contract for the provision of agricultural produce; contract of supply; co-operative tenancy right in an apartment; new rules in

7 Józef NOWACKI: *Niektóre zagadnienia zasad współżycia społecznego* [Certain issues regarding the principles of social co-existence], PiP 12 (1957)/7–8, 99–113; Anna STAWARSKA-RIPPEL: *O klauzulach generalnych w pierwszych latach Polski Ludowej słów kilka* [*A few words on general clauses in the first years of People's Poland*], Miscellanea Iuridica 6 (2005), 117–129.

8 Anna MACHNIKOWSKA, *Prawo własności w Polsce w latach 1944–1981. Studium historyczno-prawne* [The right of ownership in Poland between 1944 and 1981: a study in legal history], WUG, Gdańsk, 2010; Jan WASILKOWSKI, Marek MADEY: *Prawo własności w PRL. Zarys wykładu* [The law of ownership in the Polish People's Republic: outline of a lecture], PWN, Warsaw, 1969.

housing law) or, last but not least, the legal regime for co-operatives were treated as part of the 'socialized' sector of the economy.

We looked for common motives linking the three periods in the development of Polish private law in the 20th century but also searched for specifically Polish – or perhaps Central and Eastern European (semi-peripheral) – aspects of thinking about law, concentrating on the field of private law. To this end, we endeavoured to compare, for each of the analysed periods, the mental schemata, views on the nature of law, its social value and creational capacities, as well as value systems. Our research focused not so much on the approaches taken to any specific legal institutions individually (except to exemplify more general trends) but rather on the ideological premises intimated by the social actors (members of codification commissions, legal scholars, practitioners) in the course of the works on the reform of private law. Our attention was on such areas and aspects of private law as were undergoing a process of change and reformulation in a given period.

We were aware, and proceeded from the assumption, that the chronological period we had chosen for our research project was heterogeneous not only because of the dynamically changing realities of the 20th century, but first and foremost due to the fundamental reversal of the vectors in periods of country-building on the basis of a liberal model (1918–1939) and subsequently on the basis of the Soviet socialist model (1944–1989). However, this does not necessarily mean that the foundations of the socialist legal transformation were not, at least partially, founded on similar premises. To analyse this problem, we created a common comparative matrix for all three periods, based on a common paradigm of (usually opposing) national and modernization goals.

As a result, with our analysis grounded in this theoretical framework, we set out to analyse the extent to which in the post-transformation period the law was still perceived as an instrument used to strengthen or protect national identity, for instance through its adaptation to the specific characteristics of Polish society (its legal culture, customs, practices, characteristic features and various needs) determining to what extent similar practices with regard to similar legal principles and institutions had been applied not only in the interwar period, but also in the postwar period in the legislative projects of the 1950s and 1960s. This sort of approach and the underlying world view after 1989 could be exemplified by the misgivings of certain circles (political, judicial, academic or legislative) against the process of implementation of EU directives into Polish law, whereas in other historical periods corresponding resistance may have been the result of attempts to transplant legal models not tested in Polish conditions and not adapted to suit them, whether those ideas were Western European or Soviet in origin (in the interwar period and the postwar period, respectively).

Furthermore, we engaged in comparative scrutiny of the issue of what categories were considered by Polish legal and political elites to be modern. Even if the model was subject to radical change due to the differences between capitalist and socialist modernization, the question arises whether in Polish realities that truly meant a radical break with the previously accepted goals, ideas and values in the postwar period.[9] Conversely, even if the reinstatement of a capitalist and democratic-liberal axiology in the period after 1989 was similar in many respects to the first decade of the Second Republic, one could still ask whether indeed the views on modernization may have undergone fundamental changes not only as a result of civilizational progress but also because of a different method being used for determining the model of modernization to be followed (e.g. a different perception of the West).

---

9 Rodolfo SACCO: *The Romanist Substratum in the Civil Law of the Socialist Countries*, Review of Socialist Law 14 (1988)/1, 65–86.

CHAPTER 1

Towards an Ideological History of Private Law, or What Legal History Can Gain from Critical Legal Theory

> … those who are in ideology believe themselves by definition outside ideology (…) ideology never says 'I am ideological.'[1]
>
> Louis ALTHUSSER

•••

> … the condition of being free from ideological control would be wholly disabling because there would be nothing either to be free with or for.[2]
>
> Stanley FISH

•••

> … in its basic dimension [ideology] is a fantasy construction which serves as a support for our 'reality' itself: an 'illusion' which structures our effective, real social relations…[3]
>
> Slavoj ŽIŽEK

•••

1 Louis ALTHUSSER: *Ideology and the State Ideological Apparatuses (Notes towards an Investigation)* [1970], in Louis ALTHUSSER: *On Ideology*, Verso, London-New York 2008, 49.

2 Stanley FISH: *Doing What Comes Naturally: Change, Rhetoric, and the Practice of Theory in Literary and Legal Studies*, Duke University Press, Durham-London 1989, 518.

3 Slavoj ŽIŽEK: *The Sublime Object of Ideology* [1989], Verso, London, 2008, 45.

Note: The present chapter, written by Rafał Mańko in his academic capacity, presents exclusively his personal views.

 | DOI:10.1163/9789004730021_003

> … handled with care, the concept 'ideology' provides an indispensable and irreplaceable tool of analysis.
>
> Alan HUNT[4]

∵

1 Introduction

The reader of the present volume might be perplexed not only by the title, which introduces the notion of ideology,[5] but also by the presence of a purely theoretical chapter in a volume belonging essentially to the domain of history of private law. The neat separation not only of disciplines (such as legal studies vs. sociology, economics, political science etc.), but also within disciplines (such as legal theory vs. legal history, private law dogmatics, comparative law, etc.) still continues to be a fact of academic life, with specialised chairs, departments, journals, publishing series and conferences contributing to their entrenchment. On the other hand, however, one can see the opposite trend, namely towards pluridisciplinarity, or even postdisciplinarity. Within comparative law, Alexandra Mercescu has recently proposed to transcend all the multidsciplinary, transdisciplinary and interdisciplinary approaches by opting for an 'indisciplined' approach.[6] In her elaborate classification, Mercescu identifies and defines, as distinct from each other, three forms of 'pluridisciplinarity': (1) 'multidisciplinarity' (parallel use of tools from two or more disciplines); (2) 'interdisciplinarity' ('interpenetration of … disciplinary cultures [or communities]'); and (3) 'transdisciplinarity' ('synthesis of … various [bodies of] knowledge in a global theory, [leading] to a higher level of integration').[7] The integration of various approaches, rather than merely adding them to each other, leading to the abandonment of disciplinary boundaries in the name of a holistic approach is known as 'postdisciplinarity,'[8] which is

4 Alan HUNT: *The Ideology of Law: Advances and Problems in Recent Applications of the Concept of Ideology to the Analysis of Law*, Law & Society Review 19 (1985)/1, 31.

5 The authors omitted the notion axiology originally considered for the title.

6 Alexandra MERCESCU: *Pour une comparaison des droits indiscipliné*, Helbing Lichtehain Verlag, Basel, 2018. Translation mine.

7 *Ibidem*, 162–164.

8 Ruth WODAK: *Inter/trans/post-disciplinarity and the Study of Language and/in Politics*, Journal of Language and Politics 4 (2005)/2, 170.

synonymous with pursuing research beyond disciplinary borders.[9] Advocates of a postdisciplinary approach point out that: 'Notions of interconnection, of crossing boundaries, are central to post-disciplinarity,'[10] mentioning, as examples of postdisicplinary research fields ('post-disciplines') 'science studies, feminism, cultural studies, post-colonial studies, and post-Marxism"[11] Others, however, understand postdisciplinarity as 'abolishing academic specialisms,' adding that '[s]uch a development would remove many insights and could also bring unwelcome reductions of diversity in academic knowledge.'[12] In my view, neither postdisciplinary nor transdisciplinary are about 'abolishing specialisms,' but rather about *transcending* them or, in other words, removing the 'silos' in which academics of different disciplines and sub-disciplines (e. g. within legal studies) tend to isolate themselves. In this paper, I will invite legal historians (therefore, representatives of one of the sub-disciplines of legal studies, or a 'transdiscipline' at the interstices of law and history) to *transcend* the hitherto focus of their discipline and make use of some of the insights of their colleagues working in the area of critical legal theory (a 'transdiscipline' at the interstices of legal theory and critical theory, or perhaps even part of the 'postdisciplines').

More specifically, the aim of the present chapter, in line with its title, is to enquire about the relationship between *ideology and private law*, with particular reference to the historical dimension of private law. This is because I fully agree with Alan Hunt when he states that 'the concept "ideology" provides an indispensable and irreplaceable tool of analysis.'[13] At the same time, as Costas Douzinas highlighted, law 'is first and foremost an ideological practice, a way of understanding the world.'[14] I will approach this question predominantly from the perspective of critical legal theory. Nonetheless, in line with the approach advocated above, I will not limit myself to the internal point of view of that perspective, but rather take a holistic, postdisciplinary approach, making sure to provide insights which historians of private law can find useful and inspiring in their own research.

---

9 Shireen R. K. PATELL: *Disciplinarity*, Social Text 27 (2009)/3, 104.

10 Trevor J. BARNES: *Situating Economic Geographical Teaching*, Journal of Geography in Higher Education 30 (2006)/3, 407.

11 *Ibidem*, 406.

12 Jan Aart SCHOLTE: *Globalization Studies: Past and Future: A Dialogue of Diversity*, Globalizations 1 (2004)/1, 105.

13 HUNT: *Ideology of Law*, 31.

14 Costas DOUZINAS: *A Short History of the British Critical Legal Conference or, the Responsibility of the Critic*, Law and Critique 25 (2014), 188.

The chapter is structured as follows. In Section 2, entitled 'Legal history and critical legal theory: a much needed dialogue,' I lay the ground for the very idea of researching legal history from a critical legal perspective, in particular as regards the ideological dimensions of private law. In Section 3, I introduce the crucial concept of ideology, which is one of the cornerstones of critical legal theory, including critical legal theory. Section 4, in turn, seeks to analyse, in a theoretical manner, the possible relations between law (in general) and ideology. It is followed by Section 5, which makes some more specific theoretical claims concerning the interrelationship between private law and ideology. This section should not be treated as a comprehensive analysis of the history of private law from an ideological perspective. Rather, it is aimed at setting a theoretical framework for more detailed studies on the ideological history of private law. Therefore, the focus in Sections 4 and 5 will be put on *structural relations* between law and ideology, thereby helping to formulate possible research questions at the crossroads of legal history and critical legal theory. Finally, Section 6, entitled 'Conclusions: Towards an Ideological History of Private Law' sums up the argument, inviting historians of private law to embark upon the task of a critique of ideology as a new, trandisciplinary tool.

From a methodological perspective, the present paper should be seen as a *meta*methodological intervention, grounded in critical legal theory, aimed at proposing certain broad research questions at the interstices of legal history and critical legal theory. The main argument advanced in the paper is that the questions suggested by critical legal theory could be extremely relevant and topical for research undertaken by legal historians, and could help enlarge the scope of their enquiry beyond the traditional scope of research. Specifically, the chapter will put forward a certain typology of the ideological entanglements of private law (positing the categories of extra-juridical ideology, juridical ideology and legal ideology), and will argue that any analysis of the ideological dynamics of private law should ideally entail taking into account all three types of ideologies which interact with private law, focusing on all possible vectors of influence in a broad social, political and economic context.

2 Legal History and Critical Legal Theory: A Much Needed Dialogue

2.1 *Beyond a Mere Description of Past Law*

Legal history can be conceived of as *the legal dogmatics of the past*, applying the methods of legal dogmatics (i.e. doctrinal research on law), but just to a different point in time. This way, the historian of private law is doing the same work as a dogmatician of private law, but only wants to know 'what the law *is*' not in 2025, but rather 'what the law *was*' in 1848, 1935 or 1967. In this way of approaching things, the legal historian will use the 'normal' sources of legal dogmatics, albeit not contemporary ones, but those dating from a past moment, i.e. study past legal texts (and their preparatory materials), past case-law and past scholarly writings (commentaries, monographs, journal articles, case-notes etc.).

Whereas this approach is good as a starting point, it could certainly be taken further. One can therefore agree with Markus D. Dubber when he rejects 'antiquarian jurisprudence', whose task is to 'dust off shards of pure law from a particular, great "age" of (Roman) law', but rather argues that

> The point of historical analysis of law is to trace the genealogy of law, or legality, over the *longue durée* in a particular legal-political project in order to bring into clearer relief its normative features, which then drive the critical analysis of legal norms and practices with that (temporally and spatially limited) project.[15]

Let us then see what options – other than 'antiquarian jurisprudence' – are on the table. Whereas legal dogmatics (doctrinal analysis of law) is always focused with one time and one space (the law *hic et nunc*, as interpreted by the courts and scholars), comparative law overcomes the *hic* (changing it to a *hic et alibi*), while legal history overcomes the *nunc* (changing it to *nunc et tunc*). Needless it to add, comparative legal history combines the two approaches, studying the law *hic et alibi, nunc et tunc*. This way, the synchronic and diachronic elements can be combined, showing the evolution of legal institutions over time and in different jurisdictions, as in doctrinal legal history.[16] This already adds some value, nonetheless answers only the 'what?' question, stopping short of the much more interesting question of 'why?' If the legal historian wishes to go beyond mere description of past law, he or she needs a certain theoretical foundation upon which to base their enquiry. Whereas a meticulous description, based on hard work in the archives of the

15 Markus D. DUBBER: *Legal History as Legal Scholarship: Doctrinalism, Interdisciplinarity, and Critical Analysis of Law* in MARKUS D. DUBBER, CHRISTOPHER TOMLINS (eds): *The Oxford Handbook of Legal History*, Oxford University Press, Oxford, 2018, 114.

16 Joshua GETZLER: *Legal History as Doctrinal History*, in DUBBER, TOMLINS (eds): *Oxford Handbook*, 171–191.

law is necessary,[17] an external guiding idea may be helpful in producing research results that will be interesting and inspiring also beyond the realm of legal history and, most importantly, which will contribute to a deeper understanding of the juridical phenomenon and its evolution over time. I fully endorse the 'increased interest in using the past to understand the present', which has been dubbed by Elizabeth Dale as 'the New Presentism'.[18] In my view, if legal history as a field of scholarly enquiry is to have also contemporary significance, it absolutely must be 'relentlessly presentist',[19] to use the expression of Markus D. Dubber.

It is precisely here where different research perspectives, or modes of enquiry, can intervene. Sociology of law, applied historically, can ask about the interaction between social structures and legal rules, as well as about the actual functioning of legal institutions (in the spirit of legal realism and socio-legal studies, albeit applied to the past). The philosophy of law can enquire about the changing understandings of justice, as evidenced by past legislation and judicial decisions, as well as social views, as registered in the historical sources. The anthropology of law, perhaps most closely linked to legal history, uses historical materials to build its phenomenology of law in a diachronic dimension.[20] Legal historians can embark upon intellectual legal history, tracing the history of concepts and ideas.[21] Finally, legal historical research can benefit from the insights of economics and economic history.[22] Conceived in this way, historical enquiry into law 'is a distinct mode of inquiry, with distinct virtues and vices. But its distinctiveness need not be incompatible with other modes of inquiry, nor neither superior or inferior to them.'[23] This approach is well attuned to the proposal made by Markus D. Dubber, who explicitly advocates

17 Cf. Renisa MAWANI: *Archival Legal History: Towards the Ocean as Archive*, in DUBBER, TOMLINS (eds): *Oxford Handbook*, 291–309.

18 Elizabeth DALE: *Spelunking, or, Some Meditations on the New Presentism*, in DUBBER, TOMLINS (eds): *Oxford Handbook*, 311–321.

19 DUBBER: *Legal History as Legal Scholarship*, 99–118.

20 See e.g. Peter GOODRICH: *Law and the Unconscious: a Legendre Reader*, Palgrave Macmillan, London, 1997.

21 Assaf LIKHOVSKI: *The Intellectual History of Law*, in DUBBER, TOMLINS (eds): *Oxford Handbook*, 151–170.

22 *Cf.* DUBBER: *Legal History as Legal Scholarship*, 99.

23 Maksymilian DEL MAR: *Philosophical Analysis and Historical Inquiry: Theorizing Normativity, Law, and Legal Though* in DUBBER, TOMLINS (eds): *Oxford Handbook*, 21.

> an approach to legal history that regards historical analysis as one mode of critical analysis of law, along with other modes of 'interdisciplinary' analysis (economical, philosophical, sociological, literary, etc.) and 'doctrinal' analysis. … According to this view of legal history, it is a mode of jurisprudence (in fact, we might call it New Historical Jurisprudence), rather than a subspeciality of law or a form of applied history.[24]

Conceived in this way, legal history has a definite interest in exploring other jurisprudential research currents, not excluding critical legal theory (critical jurisprudence). True, there has not been much scholarship combining the approach of legal history with that of critical legal theory, although some attempts were made, especially in U.S. scholarship during the heyday of the North American 'Critical Legal Studies' movement.[25] Regardless of the reasons for this limited collaboration between the two disciplines,[26] the point can be made concerning the urging need for adopting such an approach. In what follows, I first provide a brief introduction to critical legal theory (Sub-Section 2.2 below) before making a statement in favour of its use in historical research on the juridical phenomenon (Sub-Section 2.3). Only once the scene has been set, I address more specific questions of ideology critique (Section 3), including law and ideology (Sections 4 and 5).

2.2 *A Very Short Introduction to Critical Legal Theory, or Why the Jurist should be a Critic*

To put the long story short, one could simply say that critical legal theory is the application of critical theory to the juridical phenomenon. Therefore, a more apt name for the theory should be 'critical theory of law,' but of course the shorter reference is more handy, and hence the term 'critical legal theory' and its synonym 'critical jurisprudence,' will be used throughout the present chapter. In line with this assumption, an explanation of what critical legal theory is

---

24 DUBBER: *Legal History as Legal Scholarship*, 115. The Common Law expression 'doctrinal', used by Dubber, is the equivalent to 'dogmatic' in German or Polish legal culture.

25 For an overview of the early attempts, see e.g. Robert W. GORDON: *Critical Legal Histories*, Stanford Law Review 36 (1984), 100–116. For a recent critical reappreciation see John Henry SCHLEGEL: *Sez who? Critical Legal History Without a Privileged Position*, in DUBBER, TOMLINS (eds): *Oxford Handbook*, 561–575 (focusing on historians of labour law).

26 I am not discussing here the benefits for legal theory, including critical jurisprudence, from adopting methods of historical analysis of law. On this issue see e.g. Maksymilian DEL MAR, Michael LOBBAN (eds): *Legal Theory and Legal History*, Ashgate, Farnham, 2014; Maksymilian DEL MAR, Michael LOBBAN (eds): *Legal Theory and Legal History: New Essays on a Neglected Dialogue*, Hart Publishing, Oxford, 2016.

will require two steps: firstly, a determination what *critical theory* is, and secondly, what are the effects of applying critical theory to the juridical.

Faithful to its Greek etymology (κρίνειν), critique is 'a diacritical or cutting force, a critical separation and demarcation. Its aim is to distinguish between the just manifestations of a phenomenon and their inauthentic counterparts', as Costas Douzinas and Adam Gearey point out.[27] Hence, critique is the social practice of distinguishing the good from the bad, taking an evaluative, rather than dogmatic (uncritical) stance towards social phenomena. The first scholar to use the concept of 'critical' in relation to theory was probably Immanuel Kant, founding what is referred to as 'critical philosophy,' expounded in his three Critiques: the *Critique of Pure Reason* (1781, 1787), *the Critique of Practical Reason* (1788), and the *Critique of the Power of Judgment* (1790). In the sense used by Kant, the object of critique are received and unverified claims about the world, which are subjected to a rational evaluation, thereby opposing 'critical science' to theology, a discipline based *par excellence* on the unconditional acceptance of certain views without any rational verification, only on the basis of faith.[28] Therefore, it is plausible to claim that critical theory is an 'anti-theology of everything,' as Adam Sulikowski points out, drawing on Leszek Kołakowski's metaphor.[29]

In his essay on *Traditional Theory and Critical Theory*,[30] Max Horkheimer famously opposed critical theory to its traditional counterpart by pointing to the former's emancipatory goal. Along these lines of reasoning, critical theory is not only descriptive and explanatory, but also aims at *changing the social reality* which is the object of its critical enquiry, therefore being nor-

27 Costas DOUZINAS, Adam GEAREY: *Critical Jurisprudence: The Political Philosophy of Justice*, Hart Publishing, Oxford-Portland, 2005, 38.

28 Rafał MAŃKO: *W stronę krytycznej filozofii orzekania. Polityczność, etyka, legitymizacja* [Towards a critical theory of adjudication: the political, ethics, legitimacy], Wydawnictwo Uniwersytetu Łódzkiego, Łódź, 2018, 25–26.

29 Adam SULIKOWSKI: *Law After the Death of God. Jurisprudence and Some Assertions of the Contemporary Philosophy*, in Andrzej BATOR, Zbigniew PULKA (eds): *A Post-Analytical Approach to Philosophy and Theory of Law*, Peter Lang, Berlin, 2019, 181–194, 193. The term 'anti-theology' in this sense is borrowed from the Polish philosopher Kołakowski. See Leszek KOŁAKOWSKI: *Kapłan i błazen. Rozważania o teologicznym dziedzictwie współczesnego myślenia* [The priest and the jester: on the theological legacy of our contemporary thinking], in Leszek KOŁAKOWSKI: *Nasza wesoła apokalipsa. Wybór najważniejszych esejów* [Our happy apocalypsis: selection of most important essays], Znak, Kraków, 2010, 62.

30 Max HORKHEIMER: *Critical Theory*, Continuum, New York, 1982.

mative.[31] The concept of emancipation should be read in its deepest etymological sense as the removal of the subject from the power of another, making the subject independent (emancipated). Hence, the emancipatory aim of critical theory, as its characteristic feature,[32] should be understood as a struggle to liberate individuals from the power and oppression inflicted upon them by others, especially by social structures, with the aim of giving them a maximum degree of freedom.[33] This is in line with the approach of emancipatory ethic which 'envisions the good life in terms of freedom; creative self-realization within a democratic community where the fulfilment is available to all and all have dignity.'[34] Emancipation, understood as freedom from oppression and violence, includes also removing all forms of alienation of human beings,[35] including the question of recognition (recognitive justice[36]), a necessary precondition of human dignity.[37] As Adam Sulikowski and Krzysztof Otręba point out, a critical approach in jurisprudence 'requires combining the description and postulate, explanation and struggle, research and emancipation.'[38]

---

31 James BOHMAN: *Critical Theory*, in Edward N. ZALTA (ed.): *The Stanford Encyclopedia of Philosophy* (Winter 2019 Edition), available at: <https://plato.stanford.edu/archives/win2019/entries/critical-theory/>.

32 Adam SULIKOWSKI: *The Crisis of Traditional Legal Theory. A Diagnosis and View to the Future*, in Andrzej BATOR, Zbigniew PULKA (eds): *Legal Theory and Philosophy of Law: Towards Contemporary Challenges*, Scholar Publishing House, Warsaw, 2013, 238.

33 MAŃKO: *W stronę krytycznej filozofii orzekania*, 26.

34 Lauren LANGMAN, Dan ALBANESE: *Political Economy and the Normative: Marx on Human Nature and the Quest for Dignity*, in Michael J. THOMPSON (ed.): *Constructing Marxist Ethics: Critique, Normativity, Praxis*, Brill, Leiden, 2015, 69.

35 Burns identifies four dimensions of alienation: the sociological dimension (alienation from the product of one's labour); the aesthetic dimension (alienation within the production process); the psychological dimension (alienation of humanity in general from its species being); and the ethical dimension (alienation of of man from man). See Tony BURNS: *The Idea of the 'Struggle for Recognition' in the Ethical Thought of the Young Marx and Its Relevance Today*, in THOMPSON (ed.): *Constructing Marxist Ethics*, 35–50.

36 BURNS: *Idea of the Struggle*, 49.

37 LANGMAN, ALBANESE: *Political Economy*, 65.

38 Adam SULIKOWSKI, Krzysztof OTRĘBA: *O potrzebie studiów krytycznych nad prawem konstytucyjnym* [On the need for critical studies in constitutional law], PiP 3 (2017), 5. Cf. Paweł SKUCZYŃSKI, *Typy myśli krytycznej w prawoznawstwie. Od krytyki poznania do walki o uznanie* [Types of critical thought in jurisprudence. From critique of cognition to struggle for recognition], in Tomasz BEKRYCHT et al. (eds): *Integracja zewnętrzna i wewnętrzna nauk prawnych* [The external and internal integration of legal sciences], vol. 1, WUŁ, Łódź, 2014, 34; MAŃKO, *W stronę krytycznej filozofii orzekania*, 77.

If critical theory's ultimate aim is emancipation, the means to achieving it have an epistemological character and can be described as a hermeneutic of suspicion.[39] This translates itself into a disbelief in official narratives and, more concretely, into the critique of ideology which will be addressed in greater detail in Section 3 below. In the words of Adam Sulikowski, critical legal theory:

> postulates a sensitivity to the narrative character (simultaneously telling the story and legitimising) of seemingly objective deductions and legal inferences, encouraging deconstruction, mostly through research into the genealogy and imperious entanglements of tacit assumptions, as well as unquestioned doctrinal premises and discursive constructions.[40]

However, before moving on to the notion of ideology, it will be necessary briefly to present critical legal theory's ontological presuppositions, i.e. a set of theses concerning social ontology.[41] I propose to enumerate three such presuppositions: *first of all*, the thesis of social constructionism, claiming that the world we inhabit is socially constructed; *secondly*, the thesis of the political nature of the social world, claiming that it is inherently conflict-ridden and permeated by antagonisms; and *thirdly*, the thesis of the existence of structural violence, which is derived from the very existence of hierarchies, allowing to inflict harm on other people.[42] I will unpack each of them in the following paragraphs.

The assumption that the social world is constructed (also by law)[43] means a rejection of the existence of some form of eternal plan or programme, such

39 Cf. Brian LEITER: *The Hermeneutics of Suspicion: Recovering Marx, Nietzsche and Freud*, The University of Texas School of Law. Public Law and Legal Theory Working Paper No. 72/2005, accessible at: http://ssrn.com/abstract=691002; Rafał MAŃKO, Jakub ŁAKOMY: *In Search of the Ontological Presuppositions of Critical Jurisprudence*, Critique of Law 10 (2018)/2, 474; Adam SULIKOWSKI: *Fundamental Rights from the Perspective of Critical Legal and Social Theory* in: Adam SULIKOWSKI, Rafał MAŃKO, Jakub ŁAKOMY (eds): *Legal Scholarship and the Political: in Search of a New Paradigm*, C. H. Beck, Warszawa, 2020, 118 –119.

40 SULIKOWSKI: *Crisis of Traditional Legal Theory*, 238.

41 MAŃKO: *W stronę krytycznej filozofii orzekania*, 37.

42 *Ibidem*, 37–46. *Cf.* MAŃKO, ŁAKOMY: *In search for the ontological presuppositions*, 469–486.

43 Damjan KUKOVEC: *Hierarchies as Law*, Columbia Journal of European Law 21 (2014)/1, 133.

as 'natural law' in the traditional sense, or 'human nature', or some form of atemporal 'reason'. Likewise, assuming that the world is socially constructed means to reject the thesis, proposed by cognitive science and other forms of naturalised jurisprudence, that there are certain 'laws' of biology (or psychology, or any other empirical science analysing human 'nature') which predetermine the way our societies are arranged. To the contrary, critical legal theory sees all such 'scientific truths' as pure 'social constructs, enmeshed in structures of power and domination'.[44] There is, of course, a clear connection between the assumption that the social world is socially constructed, and the proposal that it can be changed. The ontological and normative aspects of critical legal theory are, therefore, interdependent.

The second key ontological assumption of critical legal theory is that of the political (or conflict-ridden) nature of the social world. The notion of 'the political' is used here following the Schmittian tradition, but in the form given to it by Chantal Mouffe and elaborated in order to distinguish the political from 'policies' and 'politics'.[45] The first of these notions – the political (*das Politische*) – denotes a certain social antagonism which is built upon the foundation of collective forms of identification (we *vs.* they),[46] and therefore it is something collective, and not merely individual.[47] In contrast to Schmitt, who saw the political only in situations of outmost enmity,[48] in the agonistic (Mouffian) version we have opponents, rather than enemies, and the *agon* can be kept within the borders of a single political community.[49] The aim is, in that situation, the imposition of one's hegemony upon

---

44 Adam SULIKOWSKI: *Konstytucjamizm a nowoczesność: dyskurs konstytucyjny wobec tryumfu i kryzysu moderny* [Constitutionalism and Modernity: Constitutional Discourse towards the Triumph and Crisis of the Modern], Wydawnictwo Uniwersytetu Wrocławskiego, Wrocław, 2012, 204.

45 Adam SULIKOWSKI, Rafał MAŃKO, Jakub ŁAKOMY: *Introduction*, in Adam SULIKOWSKI, Rafał MAŃKO Jakub ŁAKOMY (eds): *Legal Scholarship and the Political*, XI–XIV; Rafał MAŃKO: *Judicial Decision-Making, Ideology and the Political: Towards an Agonistic Theory of Adjudication*, Law and Critique 33 (2022), 177–179

46 Chantal MOUFFE: *On the Political*, Routledge, Abington-New York, 2005, 14.

47 Carl SCHMITT: *The Concept of the Political* (trans. G. SCHWAB), University of Chicago Press, Chicago, 2007, 27. *Cf.* Łukasz ŚWIĘCICKI: *Carl Schmitt i Leo Strauss. Krytyka pozytywizmu prawniczego w niemieckiej myśli politycznej* [Carl Schmitt and Leo Strauss: the critique of legal positivism in German political thought], von Borowiecky, Warsaw, 2015, 189.

48 SCHMITT: *Concept of the Political*, 25–27.

49 MOUFFE: *On the Political*, 14; Chantal MOUFFE: *Agonistics: Thinking the World Politically*, Verso, London, 2013, Chapter 1.

the opponent and not, as in the Schmittian model, the physical destruction of the enemy.[50]

The presupposition on the political nature of the social world, closely linked to its legal reality, is supplemented and further developed in the third ontological presupposition of critical legal theory, namely that of the existence of structural violence, produced and perpetuated by existing social hierarchies. There are various conceptualisations of the phenomenon of violence. According to Lidia Rodak, we can identify 'psychological, symbolic, structural, hermeneutic, as well as aesthetic violence'[51] and according to Joanna Helios and Wioletta Jedlecka, there are eight types of violence: physical, psychological (emotional), sexual, economic, latent (in the form of neglect), structural, instrumental and symbolic.[52]

Of particular importance in the legal context is symbolic violence, which is based on two aspects: firstly, the act of imposing of certain meanings as the only legitimate and correct ones, and secondly, on concealing the power relationships in society.[53] As such, symbolic violence, in contrast to physical violence, is usually hidden and even invisible to its victims who treat is as granted.[54] This is because symbolic violence occurs at the level of creating categories and structures through which we think and perceive the world,[55] as well as schemata of thinking.[56] What is crucial in symbolic violence, is the imposition of a certain point of view (favourable to those in power) as a universal one, so that the victims of the symbolic violence are not even aware that

---

50 SCHMITT: *Concept of the Political*, 37ff.

51 Lidia RODAK: *Structural Violence in Law and Its Gender Dimension in Polish Law*, in Rafał MAŃKO, Cosmin CERCEL, Adam SULIKOWSKI (eds): *Law and Critique in Central Europe: Questioning the Past, Resisting the Present*, Counterpress, Oxford, 2016, 133. One can also speak of linguistic violence, as Martin Škop rightly points out; Martin ŠKOP: *The Importance of Being a Linguist: Critical Legal Thought in Central Europe*, in MAŃKO, CERCEL, SULIKOWSKI: *Law and Critique in Central Europe*, 32ff.

52 Joanna HELIOS, Wioletta JEDLECKA: *Współczesne oblicza przemocy: zagadnienia wybrane* [Modern faces of violence: selected topics], Prawnicza i Ekonomiczna Biblioteka Cyfrowa, Wrocław, 2017, 15–30; Wioletta JEDLECKA: *Formy i rodzaje przemocy* [Forms and types of violence], Wrocławskie Studia Erazmiańskie 11 (2017), 13–29.

53 Pierre BOURDIEU, J.C. PASSERON: *Reproduction in Education. Society and Culture*, SAGE, London, 1990, 4.

54 Pierre BOURDIEU: *Masculine Domination*, Stanford University Press, Stanford, 2001, 1.

55 Cristina NICOLAESCU: *Bourdieu – Habitus, Symbolic Violence, the Gift: 'You give me / I give you' Principle*, Euromentor Journal 1 (2010)/3, 6.

56 Hanna DĘBSKA, Tomasz WARCZOK: *The Social Construction of Feminity in the Discourse of the Polish Constitutional Court*, in MAŃKO, CERCEL, SULIKOWSKI: *Law and Critique in Central Europe*, 118.

what they accept as a universal perspective is in fact the particular perspective, protecting the interests of the dominant groups.[57] As such, symbolic violence can even be more effective than purely psychical violence, because it enters into the ways of thinking, acting and perceiving the world by its victims.[58] Abstract legal notions, completely detached from real life, can also be examples of symbolic violence. A classical example is the liberal concept of 'autonomy' and 'freedom' of private law subjects which, as it is very well known, are actually unequal, and the 'freedom' is available only to the members of the economically privileged classes.[59]

2.3 *What Critical Legal Theory can Offer to the Legal Historian?*

The ontological and epistemological presuppositions of critical legal theory, coupled with its methodological assumptions, could be a source of inspiration for the historical analysis of (private) law. Let us take, firstly, the assumption of social construction of reality. It redirects attention of the legal historian from attempts at uncovering some eternal patterns or 'iron laws' of legal history, towards the question of who (what social groups) have been shaping the social reality of law in a given direction. This act of shaping need not be conscious or planned, nonetheless the aspect to which critical legal theory points the legal historian is that of human agency. Hence the need to analyse the empirical historical material – archival documents concerning the preparation of codifications and other legislation, historical case-law, scholarly writings, literature and other cultural texts – from the point of view of how and in what way the social reality was shaped, what was the role of lawyers in it. It is here that the concept of ideology, discussed in greater detail in Section 3, will definitely come in handy, as well as the proposed framework for the study of the mutual interactions between law and ideology, rolled out in Section 4 and developed in Section 5.

57 Hanna DĘBSKA: *Legal Doxa as a Form of Neutralization of Values in the Law. The Case of Constitutional Tribunal Judgments*, in Krzysztof PAŁECKI (ed.): *Neutralization of Values in Law*, Wolters Kluwer, Warsaw, 2013, 310. Ivana RADAČIĆ: *Feminist Legal Education in Croatia: A Question of Fundamentalism or a Fundamental Question?*, in MAŃKO, CERCEL, SULIKOWSKI: *Law and Critique in Central Europe*, 109.

58 NICOLAESCU: *Bourdieu*, 6.

59 For an ideological critique of the concept of freedom in law (especially private law), see Paweł SNOPEK: *Neoliberalism, ideology, social (in)justice and post-politics* in Paulina BIEŚ-SROKOSZ, Rafał MAŃKO, Jacek SROKOSZ (eds): *Law, Space and the Political: an East-West Perspective*, Podobiński Publishing, Częstochowa, 2019, 144–156. See also Janusz REYKOWSKI, *Wolność gospodarcza jako ideologia* [Economic freedom as ideology], Studia Socjologiczne 210 (2013)/3, 7–29.

The second ontological presupposition of critical jurisprudence, namely that of the political (conflict-ridden) nature of the social world also has an interesting potential of for inspiring novel research questions within legal history, especially in the field of private law. The history of legal institutions and concepts (*Begriffsgeschichte*) and the history of legal ideas (*Ideengeschichte*) could be complemented by a history of struggles (*Konfliktgeschichte*) within the juridical field, conceived not only in economic, but also social and ideological terms. Changes in property law or contract law will inevitably be a long history of class struggles between the owners of capital and those who need to sell their own labour to earn a living. Changes in family law will reflect, above all, shifts in the relative power of conflicting ideologies (conservative, liberal) in a given society. Changes in civil procedure, structured along the antinomy of court activism vs. litigant activism, will also reveal ideological shifts between liberalism and a more social-justice-oriented approach. What is important, an antagonism-oriented history of private law complements the research agenda by drawing attention to law as the outcome of social conflicts, be they of an economic or symbolic nature. This approach can be applied not only to legislative drafting, but also to judicial decisions, on the assumption that judges, especially of higher courts, enjoy a certain degree of judicial discretion and, ultimately, face a choice of two or more possible legal interpretations, and have to make a choice between them. That choice is not fully determined by the legal sources, but is ultimately a *judicio-political decision* taken by the judge.[60] The stake would be to enquire about the possible alternative solutions and see which of them served what kind of interests, comparing the outcome (the solution chosen by the judge) with the possible interpretive alternatives.

The third ontological presupposition of critical legal theory, linked closely to the second one, directs the attention of the legal historian to all those social groups and individuals which, in a given historical epoch, have been suffering exclusion and oppression, denied the possibility to articulate and defend their interests within legal discourse. This is the classical topic of interest of critical legal historians who have been focusing on histories of indigenous people, victims of genocide inflicted by conquerors, histories of slaves, serfs, and workers, suffering economic and social violence, etc.

A combination of this external perspective on the law with the *internal* legal point of view of the legal sources studied by the legal historian may shed a new light on the histories of violence inflicted through the use of pri-

60 MAŃKO, *Judicial Decision-Making, passim.*

vate law upon oppressed classes and groups. The history of the law of succession and family in the 19th and 20th centuries can be seen through the lens of oppression against children born 'out of wedlock' and against women, and their progressive emancipation. The legal historian could look into the channels through which the ideology of feminism gradually gained hegemony within private law discourse, ultimately influencing the shape of institutions of family law and succession law. The methodology of ideology critique and analysis of mutual relations between law and ideology, discussed in Sections 3–5 below, could come in handy.

Finally, the *hermeneutic of suspicion*, typical for critical legal theory, could also be of interest to historians of private law. Reading sources not at their face value, but through the prism of what is repressed, omitted, distorted, absent from the text could be a very inspiring way of approaching the history of private law. The hermeneutic of suspicion is particularly useful when analysing the ideological entanglements of private law. Ideological commitments are very often hidden behind others or concealed altogether, and jurists creating, applying or interpreting the law are quite often even unaware of their ideological entanglements altogether which they treat as normal and natural, rather than political and ideological. Critically-inspired history of private law could have a clear emancipatory potential, either *per se* and directly, or, at the very least, as a source of research material for critical legal theory.

3 The Concept of Ideology

Legal historians are becoming increasingly aware about the importance of ideological factors in the shaping of legal institutions. For instance, as Michał Gałędek points out:

> The instrumental application of legal tools in the implementation of certain aims may be connected with the execution of various political, social and economic programmes, be they short- or long-term, simple or complex, opportunistic or ideological. Every programme is based on an idea, a thought, a doctrine, on ideology and axiology, i.e. on the factors decisive in the process of establishing aims and their valuation.[61]

61 Michał GAŁĘDEK: *Introduction: Modernisation, National Identity, and Legal Instrumentalism* in Michał GAŁĘDEK, Anna KLIMASZEWSKA (eds.): *Modernization, National Iden-*

Gałędek's approach places ideas, thoughts, ideologies and axiologies on an equal footing, treating them as basis of 'various political, social and economic programmes'. If I understand his approach correctly, he treats these four categories (ideas, thoughts, ideologies and axiologies) as a kind of meta-telos of various political socio-economic programmes which, in turn, define the telos of the legal provisions adopted to implement those programmes. Individual 'ideas' and 'thoughts' are usually part of a given ideological framework. From the point of view of critical legal theory, however, the concept of *ideology* is the umbrella concept which covers all the others and allows to be operationalised in an ideological analysis of law. Indeed, the notion of 'axiology',[62] frequently used especially in Polish legal literature (*aksjologia*)[63] is, in fact, only a stand-in for 'values',[64] or, to put it more precisely, for value judgments which are, as a matter of course, part and parcel of any ideological project.

Before embarking upon the elaboration of the concept of ideology for the purposes of a historical analysis of private law, we must be aware that defining this concept is not an easy task. As Alan Hunt warned:

> Ideology is and will remain a difficult, slippery, and ambiguous concept, and there is little to be gained by searching for a 'better' definition. Problems cannot be avoided, for ideology involves issues that go to the

tity and Legal Instrumentalism: Studies in Comparative Legal History, vol. 1: *Private Law*, Brill-Nijhoff, Leiden-Boston, 2020, 1.

62 According to the *Stanford Encyclopaedia of Philosophy*: 'Axiology can be thought of as primarily concerned with classifying what things are good, and how good they are. (...) [O]ne of the central questions of traditional axiology is that of what stuffs are good: what is of value'; Mark SCHROEDER *'Value Theory'*, in *Stanford Encyclopedia of Philosophy*, < https://plato.stanford.edu/archives/fall2016/entries/value-theory/>.

63 It is quite revealing that most legal papers using the word 'axiology' were written by Polish scholars, either directly in English, or were translated from Polish. It is probably Jerzy Wróblewski who vastly contributed to the popularisation of the expression 'axiology of law,' rather obscure in Anglo-American legal discourse. See e.g. Jerzy WRÓBLEWSKI: *Ambiguities of Idealism and Materialism Opposition in Legal Theory*, Archives for Philosophy of Law and Social Philosophy 75 (1989)/3, 834–847. I am speaking here, of course, about the term, and not the object of research (values in law, legal values) which, of course, is universal.

64 According to Polish legal theorist Aleksander Peczenik: 'A value can be defined as a certain ideal, i.e. a criterion of evaluation. A principle (more precisely, a value-principle) is a norm which establishes such an ideal. The ideal can be carried into effect to a certain degree, i.e. more or less. Each value is an abstract content (...). A particular fact (...) is valuable to the extent it corresponds to a value'; Aleksander PECZENIK: *Weighing Values*, International Journal for the Semiotics of Law 14 (1992)/5, 138.

> heart of the puzzling interrelationship between human subjectivity and social action. Yet, handled with care, the concept 'ideology' provides an indispensable and irreplaceable tool of analysis.[65]

Keeping Hunt's remark in mind, and especially being aware that perhaps there are 'better' definitions of ideology available, I nonetheless think that the optimal starting point for conceptualising ideology in the context of the juridical is the definition developed by Duncan Kennedy. Since the 1970s, Kennedy was an unquestionable intellectual leader of the American Critical Legal Studies movement[66] alongside Roberto Mangabeira Unger. His publications, and especially *A Critique of Adjudication {fin de siècle}*[67] have been very influential, inspiring researchers interested in analysing the ideological entanglements of the juridical. Therefore, I will make Kennedy's definition of ideology my starting point here:

> Ideology is a universalization project of an ideological intelligentsia that sees itself as acting 'for' a group with interests in conflict with those of other groups (...).[68]

In order to grasp the content of this definition, it is necessary to explain two further concepts to which the definition refers. These are, firstly, the concept of a 'universalization project' and the concept of an 'ideological intelligentsia.' Both are of crucial importance to Kennedy's understanding of the concept of ideology. The first of these two concepts (universalisation project) needs, in turn, to be defined by introducing its two components: project and universalisation. The concept of a project is understood by Kennedy as a

> a continuous goal-oriented practical activity based on an analysis of some kind (with a textual and oral tradition), but the goals and the

---

65 HUNT: *Ideology of Law*, 31.

66 On the American Critical Legal Studies (CLS) movement, see e.g. Roberto MANGABEIRA UNGER: *The Critical Legal Studies Movement: Another Times, A Greater Task*, Verso, New York, 2015; E. Dana NEACŞU *CLS Stands for Critical Legal Studies, If Anyone Remembers*, Journal of Law and Policy 8 (2000), 415–453. The movement existed, in a more or less organised form, from the late 1970s until the early 1990s, and was succeeded, inter alia, by the law and humanities movement; MAŃKO: *W stronę krytycznej filozofii orzekania*, 29–32.

67 Duncan KENNEDY: *A Critique of Adjudication {fin de siècle}*, Harvard University Press, Cambridge MA, 1997.

68 KENNEDY: *A Critique of Adjudication*, 39.

> analysis are not necessarily coherent or consistent over time. It is a collective effort, but the players can change over time, and people at any given moment can be part of it without subscribing to or even being interested in anything like all its precepts and practical activities.[69]

As an example of a 'project' Kennedy gives the 'left project' whose aim is to 'change the existing system of social hierarchy, including its class, racial, and gender dimensions' in order to provide for 'greater equality and greater participation in public and private government.'[70]

The concept of 'universalization,' in turn, refers to Habermas and is understood as 'a defining characteristic of normative discourse of the type Habermas calls 'practical reason'.[71] It seems that the notion of universalization should therefore be understood in the sense of a claim towards intersubjective validity,[72] as well as an element of engagement in changing the social reality.[73] Therefore, as I have claimed elsewhere, the concept of a universalisation project in Kennedy's understanding can be ultimately defined as 'a continuous, purpose-oriented and engaged activity based on an analysis with claims to intersubjective (i.e. universal) validity.'[74] Personally, I think that the Habermasian component of intersubjectivity and universalisation is the weakest element of Kennedy's understanding of ideology. In fact, many ideological projects *ex definitione* renounce universalisation claims, openly admitting that their aim is to promote the interests of one group over the interests of others. Thus, nationalist ideologies do not claim they are good for foreigners and minorities, socialist ideologies do not claim to further the interests of the bourgeoisie, etc. On the other hand, the two ideologies that Kennedy explicitly mentions in his book, i.e. liberalism (understood as democratic socialism) and conservatism,[75] indeed have such claims.

---

69 *Ibidem*, 6.

70 *Ibidem.*

71 *Ibidem*, 382.

72 Cf. Paweł SKUCZYŃSKI: *The Status of Legal Ethics* (trans. Katarzyna POPOWICZ), Peter Lang, Frankfurt am Main, 2013, 237.

73 Cf. Wojciech TORZEWSKI: *Hermeneutyka a kwestia rozumu* [Hermeneutic and the question of reason], Filo-Sofija 11 (2010)/2, 34–35.

74 MAŃKO: *W stronę krytycznej filozofii orzekania*, 54.

75 KENNEDY: *Critique of Adjudication*, 39. See also Duncan KENNEDY: *A Left/Phenomenological Critique of the Hart/Kelsen Theory of Legal Interpretation*, in Duncan KENNEDY: *Legal Reasoning: Collected Essays*, The Davies Group, Aurora CO, 2008, 162.

Let me now turn to the second concept used by Kennedy, namely that of an *ideological intelligentsia*. By this term Kennedy understands the people who operate the ideology, including its development and modification.[76] Kennedy is right in pointing out that an ideology cannot exist without a human substratum of those who manage it, especially public intellectuals, academics, but also publicists and other authors upholding the ideological project within public discourse. In other words, ideology has a 'material existence', as Althusser already noted.[77] The identification of the ideological intelligentsia is a very important sociological insight which should be paid special attention to by historians of private law. Whenever they speak of a given ideology influencing private law or being influenced by private law, it is crucial to identify who are the operators of the ideology. Ideologies do not exist in the vacuum or in the *Himmel der Begriffe* – there are always real people behind it, and the legal historian's task is to identify those people and study the sources produced by those people.

Kennedy's social ontology of ideology provides, therefore, for two categories of subjects: (1) the ideological intelligentsia; and (2) the beneficiaries of the ideology, i.e. the persons whose interests (economic, social, cultural, etc.) the ideology purports to represent. However, as Kennedy himself admits, the link between the ideology and its beneficiaries is not obvious, and ideologies tend to live their own lives.[78] Furthermore, also the ideological intelligentsia is quite independent from the apparent beneficiaries of the ideology, and it can even have its own interests, independent from the interests of those who the ideology purportedly defends and represents, and possibly even in conflict with those interests.[79] These are also aspects which are worth looking into when studying the ideological history of private law. The ideological intelligentsia, proposing certain solutions, is often detached from those, who are supposedly to benefit from those solutions. For instance, liberal ideologists propose solutions which are to benefit (all) businesspeople, but sometimes the true interest of (some) businesspeople might be better served by solutions offered by social democrat ideologists. Conversely, socialist solutions are to be beneficial to (all) workers, but (some) workers might benefit, in certain circumstances, from solutions proposed by liberals or conserva-

76 KENNEDY: *Critique of Adjudication*, 41.

77 ALTHUSSER: *Ideology and Ideological State Apparatuses*, 39–40.

78 KENNEDY: *Critique of Adjudication*, 41.

79 *Ibidem*, 41–42.

tives.[80] What is more, individual people may have more than one identity, each of them affected by different ideological projects. For instance, a person may be at the same time a worker ('taken care of' by socialist ideology), but at the same time a devout Catholic ('taken care of' by conservative ideology), and wish to become an entrepreneur ('taken care of' by liberal ideology). Therefore, the relationship between ideology, its operators and its beneficiaries can be, at times, very complex.

According to Kennedy, ideologies are in conflict with each other, they have a deeply contested character, and they struggle both *in concreto*, with regard to individual legal rules or court decisions, and *in abstracto*, regarding the general way in which a society should be organised.[81] The conflict between ideological projects is, therefore, practically interminable.[82] We can speak of an on-going war between conflicting ideologies, which is composed of subsequent stages – battles – fought within codification commission, parliaments, regulatory bodies, and courts, concerning the definition of legal rules and their interpretation.[83] Kennedy's conflict-focused approach, different from the consensualist visions of Jürgen Habermas, is consistent with the general vision of critical theory emphasising the importance of the political, i.e. the antagonism inherent in every society.[84] In effect, ideologies are in permanent conflict, rather than in a Socratic dialogue – their aim is to win (impose their hegemony), and not to persuade opponents to their reasons.[85] This is logical, given that the interests which are backed by ideological projects are also in a permanent state of conflict (think of workers vs. capitalists; consumers vs. traders; cultural progressives/liberals vs. cultural conservatives; ethnic minorities vs. ethnic majorities, etc.).[86]

So far I have been discussing Duncan Kennedy's notion of ideology. I propose to supplement it with certain elements taken from the understanding of ideology in the critical tradition, and especially in the works of Louis Althusser

80 See e.g. KUKOVEC: *Hierarchies as Law*, 144–145.

81 KENNEDY: *Critique of Adjudication*, 42–43.

82 *Ibidem*, 43.

83 *Ibidem*. *Cf.* Rafał MAŃKO: *Legislation and the Political: Towards a Critical Legisprudence*, in Paweł CHMIELNICKI, Adam SULIKOWSKI (eds): *New Perspectives on Legislation: A Comparative Approach*, Peter Lang, Berlin, 2020, 11–36.

84 MOUFFE: *On the Political, paasim.*

85 KENNEDY: *Critique of Adjudication*, 43–44.

86 Rafał MAŃKO: *Nauki prawne wobec problemu polityczności: zagadnienia wybrane z perspektywy jurysprudencji krytycznej* [Legal sciences and the problem of the political: the perspective of critical jurisprudence], Archiwum Filozofii Prawa i Filozofii Społecznej 3 (2018), 40–41.

and Slavoj Žižek. First of all, following Althusser, it is important to emphasise the practical role of ideology, as opposed to science. The French philosopher defined ideology as

> a system (…) of representations (images, myths, ideas or concepts, depending on the case) endowed with a historical existence and role within a given society. (…) [I]deology, as a system of representations, is distinguished from science in that in it the practico-social function is more important that the theoretical function (…).[87]

This understanding is compatible with Kennedy's, but it is at the same time broader. Kennedy focuses on the 'universalisation project,' but ideologies are broader than that, and Althusser rightly captures this aspect. Ideology is not only a project, but also a set of ideas and a form of consciousness (though not necessarily false). I think that Douzinas rightly captures this aspect when he writes that ideology 'is a constellation of beliefs, practices and values that define ways of living, give meaning to experience and define and uphold our place in the world.'[88]

For Althusser, ideology 'is not an aberration or a contingent excrescence of History: it is a structure essential to the historical life of societies.'[89] Just like in Kennedy's approach, it is not a state of pathology (a form of 'false consciousness'), but rather a state of normality, making it 'indispensable in any society'.[90] Ideology is an 'active'[91] factor in that it 'contributes to [the] […] moulding'[92] of society. At the same time, it is a force that is difficult to 'tame' or manipulate: 'the men who would use an ideology purely as a means of action, as a tool, find that they have caught by it (…) just when they (…) believe themselves to be absolute masters of it.'[93] In his famous 1969 work on *Ideology and Ideological State Apparatuses*,[94] Althusser introduced

87 Louis ALTHUSSER: *Marxism and Humanism* [1963], in Louis ALTHUSSER: *For Marx* [1965], Verso, London, 2005, 231.

88 DOUZINAS: *Short History*, 188.

89 ALTHUSSER: *Marxism and Humanism*, 232.

90 *Ibidem*, 235. See also David LEOPOLD: *Marxism and Ideology: From Marx to Althusser*, in Michael FREEDEN, Lyman Tower SARGENT, Marc STEARS (eds): *The Oxford Handbook of Political Ideologies*, Oxford University Press, Oxford, 2013, 33.

91 ALTHUSSER: *Marxism and Humanism*, 234.

92 *Ibidem*, 235.

93 *Ibidem*, 234.

94 ALTHUSSER: *Ideology and Ideological State Apparatuses*, *passim*.

the novel concept[95] of ideological interpellation. In the words of Althusser, all ideology 'hails or interpellates concrete individuals as concrete subjects'.[96] He metaphorically elucidates the notion of ideological interpellation by comparing it to 'recruitment' and 'transformation',[97] a process which sculpts the amorphic individual into the ideological subject. The notion of ideological interpellation is the key linkage between the human individual and ideology, or, to use Lacanian parlance, between the subject and the big Other. In sum, interpellation is the mechanism whereby a biological, pre-ideological human being becomes a subject of ideology. As Adam Sulikowski emphasized, for Althusser the 'notion of a human being as a subject (...) is not a neutral epistemic notion.'[98] To the contrary, as Althusser himself pointed out, this notion is in fact: 'The philosophical form of the bourgeois ideology that has dominated history for five centuries and that (...) still reigns in large sections of idealist philosophy and constitutes the implicit philosophy of psychology, morality and political economy.'[99] In French, the term coined by Althusser – '*interpellation*' – has interesting connotations, having essentially three meanings: (1) to refer to someone in a violent way demanding something; (2) to ask someone for their identity; (3) to cause an echo in someone.[100] Let me recall here Althusser's metaphorical definition of ideological interpellation which is very telling in this respect:

> ... ideology 'acts' or 'functions' in such a way that it 'recruits' subjects among individuals (it recruits them all), or 'transforms' individuals into subjects (it transforms them all) by the very precise operation which I have called *interpellation* or hailing, and which can be imagined along the lines of the most commonplace everyday police (or other) hailing: 'Hey, you there!'

95 *Cf.* Joseph VALENTE: *Lacan's Marxism, Marxism's Lacan (from Žižek to Althusser)*, in Jean-Michel RABATÉ (ed.): *The Cambridge Companion to Lacan*, Cambridge University Press, Cambridge, 2003, 169.

96 ALTHUSSER: *Ideology and Ideological State Apparatuses*, 47.

97 *Ibidem*, 48.

98 Adam SULIKOWSKI: *Posthumanizm a prawoznawstwo* [Posthumanism and jurisprudence], Wydawnictwo Uniwersytetu Opolskiego, Opole, 2013, 98.

99 Louis ALTHUSSER: *On Marx and Freud*, Rethinking Marxism: A Journal of Economics, Culture & Society 4 (1991)/1, 23–24.

100 Translator's note (21) in Louis ALTHUSSER: *Ideologie i aparaty ideologiczne państwa*, Studenckie Koło Filozofii Marksistowskiej UW, Warsaw, 2006, 22.

> Assuming that the theoretical scene I have imagined takes place in the street, the hailed individual will turn around. By this mere one-hundred -and-eighty-degree physical conversion, he becomes a *subject*. Why? Because he has recognized that the hail was 'really' addressed to him, and that 'it was *really him* who was hailed' (and not someone else).[101]

Althusser's metaphor compares ideology (i.e. the big Other) to a policeman, and the interpellated individual to a passer-by who, for some reason, considers himself to be addressed by the policeman's shout of 'Hey, you!' The act of consent towards the interpellation (metaphorically expressed by the fact that the passer-by turns *always-already* around) expresses the necessity of interpellation: the interpellated individuals could not have *not* turned around.[102] As Mladen Dolar pointed out, ideological interpellation is similar to an offer made by a thief in a dark alley who gives a passer-by a false alternative: 'money or life!'[103] This 'alternative' is obviously false, because we can only chose life (and give up the money). If we chose money, we will have to give up life, and therefore, having lost our subjectivity, we will not be able to enjoy the money. Dolar believes that the interpellated individuals' freedom to chose interpellation or renounce it is exactly the same as the freedom of the person asked by the thief. In line with that, Adam Sulikowski remarks that ideological interpellation can be compared to 'animal training (*tresura*) within the framework of accepted social practices which impose upon the individual a role, and in consequence also the status of a subject.'[104] Sulikowski's metaphor, in which the human subject is compared to a tamed beast subject to *dressage*, and the big Other to an animal trainer, is insightful in that it ironically captures the falsehood of our illusions of freedom and choice with regard to ideological interpellation on the one hand, and the ruthlessness of the process itself on the other hand. In that context it comes as no surprise that Althusser's notion of ideology is quite pessimistic, because subjects interpellated by ideology:

> 'work', they 'work by themselves' in the vast majority of cases, with the exception of 'bad subjects' who on occasion provoke the intervention of

101 ALTHUSSER: *Ideology and Ideological State Apparatuses*, 48.

102 Pierre MACHEREY: *Judith Butler and the Althusserian theory of subjection*, Stephanie BUNDY (trans.), Décalages 1 (2013)/2, 16.

103 Mladen DOLAR: *Beyond Interpellation*, Qui Parle 6 (1993)/2, 82.

104 SULIKOWSKI: *Posthumanizm a prawoznawstwo*, 98.

> one of the detachments of the (repressive) State apparatus. But the vast majority of (good) subjects work all right 'all by themselves', i.e. by ideology (...).[105]

The Althusserian subject is therefore a *subjugated* and *subjected* one, tamed and trained, automatised and obedient, unable (in the vast majority of cases) to oppose the hegemonic ideology.

A second theoretical innovation of Althusser's 1969 essay is the notion of 'ideological state apparatuses,' as distinct from 'repressive state apparatuses.' The latter 'function massively and predominantly by repression' and the latter 'function massively and predominantly by ideology.'[106] Among the ideological state apparatuses, Althusser enumerates religious groups, the school system, families, the legal apparatus, the political system, trade unions, the media and the cultural apparatus.[107] What is of utmost importance from the perspective of the legal field, is that the legal apparatus is treated as being both part of the repressive state apparatus and an ideological state apparatus.

Finally, Althusser's most important contribution to the theory of ideology is the claim that individuals usually are not aware that they are influenced by an ideology:

> ... those who are in ideology believe themselves by definition outside ideology: one of the effects of ideology is the practical *denegation* of the ideological character of ideology by ideology: ideology never says 'I am ideological.' (...) As is well known, the accusation of being in ideology only applies to others, never to oneself (...). Which amounts to saying that ideology *has no outside* (for itself), but at the same time *that it is nothing but outside* (for science and reality).[108]

Althusser's observation is particularly pertinent to jurists – legal scholars, legislators, attorneys and judges. Although they act ideologically (consciously or unconsciously),[109] they are almost always in denial, knowing that the legal

105 ALTHUSSER: *Ideology and Ideological State Apparatuses*, 55.

106 *Ibidem*, 19.

107 *Ibidem*, 17. Ralph Miliband observed that Althusser's 'listing seems a little superfluous, since it is difficult to think of anything that has been left out'; Ralph MILIBAND: *Marxism and Politics* [1977], Oxford University Press, Oxford, 1986, 54.

108 ALTHUSSER, *Ideology and Ideological State Apparatuses*, 49.

109 Rafał MAŃKO: *'Reality is For Those Who Cannot Sustain the Dream': Fantasies of Selfhood in Legal Texts*, Wroclaw Review of Law, Administration and Economics 5 (2015)/1, 26.

discourse will not accept openly ideologically framed arguments. Of course, there are exceptions, especially with regard to the hegemonic ideology. For instance, to propose a 'national codification' of private law in the age of nationalism could have been done openly, and mentioning elements of nationalist ideology could only help the ideological project. But Althusser's remark that 'those who are in ideology believe themselves by definition outside ideology' is also applicable to legal historians themselves: each and every one of us has been interpellated by one or more ideologies, with the effect of retroversion (i.e. we do not realise we have been interpellated). The stake is to make the effort and step out of one's ideology when analysing the ideological character of private law. Even if the ideology is a hegemonic one (like neoliberalism) and even if we subjectively think that the solutions are commonsensical. Critique of ideology requires to take a *scientific* approach (in the sense used by Althusser), and therefore make the effort of stepping out of ideology.[110] Nothing in the law can be treated as obvious and self-explanatory, not even *pacta sunt servanda*, private ownership or the institution of marriage. They are all contingent phenomena, and perhaps the comparative legal historian is best placed to notice it, for instance by pointing to the remarkable evolution of family law from Roman times to contemporary law. The experience of socialist private law, in itself, is also very telling and can serve as an important *tertium comparationis*, revealing how ideological *our law* is.

Returning to the concept of ideology, I consider that in order to arrive at a complete picture, I still see the need to refer to three innovative ideas put forward by Slavoj Žižek, the Slovenian critical theorist and philosopher. The first of these concepts is the notion of ideology as a 'support for our "reality",' rather than a 'dreamlike illusion'; the second is the notion of the cynical subject of ideology; and the third is the concept of the fetishistic (vs. symptomal) mode of functioning of ideology in our allegedly 'post-ideological' times.[111] Let me start from Žižek's famous and already established definition of ideology, which can be treated a useful addition to the definitions of Kennedy and Althusser, discussed above:

> Ideology is not a dreamlike illusion that we build to escape insupportable reality; in its basic dimension it is a fantasy construction which

---

110 ALTHUSSER: *Ideology and Ideological State Apparatuses*, 49.

111 But note that, as Douzinas correctly affirms 'the idea that ideology has ended and politics was about the management of economics came to an abrupt end in the 2008 economic crisis' (DOUZINAS: *Short History*, 196).

> serves as a support for our 'reality' itself: an 'illusion' which structures our effective, real social relations and thereby masks some insupportable, real, impossible kernel (conceptualized by Emesto Laclau and Chantal Mouffe as 'antagonism': a traumatic social division which cannot be symbolized). The function of ideology is not to offer us a point of escape from our reality but to offer us the social reality itself as an escape from some traumatic, real kernel.[112]

In this definition Žižek emphasises two elements. Firstly, that ideology is not a form of false consciousness, it is not a 'dreamlike illusion.' We must stop thinking about ideology as a state of consciousness (as it has been traditionally done), but we must look at ideology as a 'fantasy'. This psychoanalytical concept essentially refers to a 'defence mechanism of the ego, a scenario according to which the ego organises and interprets reality in its own way which gives it pleasure.'[113] The need for a fantasy stems from the fact that 'for reality to be bearable' it must be 'always filtered and deformed by the fantasy mechanism'.[114] Secondly, that this fantasy is not about escaping the reality, but about actually structuring it. What Žižek means here is that although ideology is not true, although it is a fantasy, nonetheless we actually *act as if it were true.* Think of the concept of money: we all know that today's money are just pieces of paper, without any backing by the gold standard. We know, therefore, that the fantasy of money's value is not true. However, despite this knowledge, we actually act *as if* it were true, accepting money in payments and paying with money ourselves.

This brings us to the second aspect of Žižek's theory of ideology, which I consider to be an important supplement of the definitions given by Kennedy and Althusser. In contrast to traditional accounts, which equated ideology with a form of 'false consciousness', Žižek proposes the concept of a cynical subject of ideology. Whereas the traditional formula of ideology would be 'they do not know it, but they are doing it' (false consciousness), the formula proposed by Žižek (inspired by Sloterdijk) goes: 'they know very well what they are doing, but still, they are doing it.'[115] Assuming that many, perhaps most, subjects of ideology, not excluding the ideological intelligentsias, are

---

112 ŽIŽEK: *Sublime Object*, 45.

113 Mateusz BURZYK: *Psychoanaliza a polityka: stawka podmiotu* [Psychoanalysis and politics: the stake of the subject], Diametros 35 (2013), 11–12.

114 *Ibidem*, 12, fn 48.

115 ŽIŽEK: *The Sublime Object of Ideology*, 24, 30.

in fact cynical subjects of ideology, it is necessary to redefine the very mode of functioning of ideology in society, which is the third aspect of Žižek's theory of ideology which I would like to introduce as a supplement to the conceptualisations put forward above.

Referring to well-known psychoanalytical concepts, Žižek opposes two modes of functioning of ideology: the traditional *symptomal* mode and the contemporary *fetishistic* mode.[116] I think that these concepts are crucial for an ideological critique of law, also in its historical dimension, and therefore I will briefly introduce them here. According to Žižek's definition, in the symptomal mode 'the ideological lie which structures our perception of reality is threatened by symptoms *qua* "returns of the repressed" – cracks in the fabric of the ideological lie.'[117] This is because in the traditional, symptomal mode, people still took ideologies seriously, and the exposure of symptoms, i.e. 'cracks' in the ideological fabric, 'exception[s] which distur[b] the surface of the false appearance,'[118] had the power to undermine the efficacy of ideology. In other words, people who found out that ideology is false stopped believing in it, abandoning the ideological project. Whilst this may, perhaps, still be true with regard to certain ideologies and certain rather naïve ideological believers, the main mode of functioning of ideology today is – according to Žižek – the fetishistic mode. In psychoanalysis, the fetish is 'the embodiment of the Lie which enables us to sustain the unbearable truth.'[119] As Žižek explains:

> in the case of a symptom, I 'repress' this death, I try not to think about it, but the repressed trauma returns in the symptom; in the case of a fetish, on the contrary, I 'rationally' fully accept the death, and yet I cling to the fetish, to some feature that embodies for me the disavowal of the death. In this sense, *a fetish can play the very constructive role of allowing us to cope with a harsh reality*: fetishists are not dreamers lost in their own private worlds, they are thoroughgoing 'realists' able to accept the way things are because by clinging to their fetish they are able to mitigate the full impact of reality.[120]

116 Slavoj ŽIŽEK: *First as Tragedy Then as Farce*, Verso, London, 2009, 65.
117 ŽIŽEK: *First as Tragedy*, 65.
118 *Ibidem.*
119 *Ibidem.*
120 *Ibidem.*

The concept of the fetishistic mode of ideological functioning is, in my view, particularly pertinent in the nodal point of law and ideology,[121] where – as I will argue in the next section – three distinct types of ideology come into play, all of which can be analysed using the fetishistic vs. symptomal dychotomy, put forward by Žižek.

4 Law and Ideology

4.1 *Three Ideological Registers of the Juridical*

As Ronald Weitzer rightly affirms: 'While the repressive features of the law are only too well known and experienced, law's ideological components are less palpable.'[122] Due to the juridical's specific position, highlighted notably by Althusser who pointed to the fact that the legal apparatus is *both* repressive *and* ideological,[123] the relationships between law and ideology are particularly complex. According to Andrew Halpin, among jurists there are four possible approaches to the law and ideology nexus: (1) that ideology is irrelevant from the point of view of the law; (2) that the political is irrelevant from the point of view of the law; (3) that ideology is relevant to law; (4) that the political is relevant to law, but ideology is not.[124] According to Halpin, the first position (ideology is irrelevant for law) is that of Brian Z. Tamanaha, the second one (the political is irrelevant for the law) is that of positivists like Joseph Raz and Herbert Hart, as well as for the school of Natural Law;[125] the third one (ideology is relevant for the law) is that of the critical legal schools, like Duncan Kennedy, and the fourth one (the political is relevant for law, but ideology is not) is characteristic of Ronald Dworkin's 'integral philosophy of law.'[126] Needless it to say that this paper adopts the position of critical legal scholarship and assumes that not only the political, but also

121 See the argument in MAŃKO: *Reality is for Those Who Cannot Sustain the Dream*, 34–37.

122 Ronald WEITZER: *Law and Legal Ideology: Contributions to the Genesis and Reproduction of Capitalism*, Berkeley Journal of Sociology 24–25 (1980), 138.

123 ALTHUSSER: *Ideology and Ideological State Apparatuses*, 17, fn 9.

124 Andrew HALPIN: *Ideology and Law*, Journal of Political Ideologies 11 (2006)/2, 156–159.

125 *Ibidem*, 164 (referring to Aristotle and John Finnis).

126 As Halpin points out, according to Dworkin, 'hard cases are not ideologically controversial but intellectually taxing. Hercules does not have to engage in ideological arguments, but to possess a superhuman intellected so as to work out the right answers which follow from the values which a particular society has adopted'; HALPIN: *Ideology and Law*, 157. See also Jeremy M. BALKIN: *Taking Ideology Seriously: Ronald Dworkin and the CLS Critique*, UMKC Law Review 55 (1987)/3, 392–433.

specifically ideology is relevant for the law. As Douzinas pointed out, law 'is first and foremost an ideological practice,' adding that the 'claim that the law is value free is perhaps the strongest ideological ruse of our time.'[127] However, this preliminary assumption which legitimises the present exploration will be proven in the course of the analysis, both in general (this section) and specifically with regard to private law (Section 5).

The interrelationship between the concepts of 'law' and 'ideology' can be described in many ways. First of all, ideology can influence the content of legal norms,[128] as when the Bolshevik decrees nationalised all land[129] or reintroduced, for the first time since Roman law,[130] the unrestricted freedom to end marriage by divorce.[131] Secondly, the law can shape the hegemonic ideology,[132] as when people believe that what is prescribed by legal norms is normal and appropriate.[133] For instance, human subjects interpellated by the law as consumers (*homines oeconomici passivi*) start feeling more like consumers (economic subjects) than citizens (political subjects).[134] Thirdly, law can possess its own 'guild ideology' or 'professional ideology' of *legalism*, which aims at justifying the interests of lawyers in society.[135]

---

127 DOUZINAS: *Short History*, 188.

128 Julie NOVKOV: *Law and Political Ideologies*, in *The Oxford Handbook of Law and Politics*, G.A. CALDEIRA, R. Daniel KELEMEN, Keith E. WHITTINGTON (eds), Oxford University Press, Oxford, 2008, 627.

129 Adam LITYŃSKI: *Prawo Rosji i ZSRR 1917–1991 czyli historia wszechzwiązkowego komunistycznego prawa (bolszewików). Krótki kurs* [Law of Russia and the USSR, 1917–1991], C.H. Beck, Warsaw, 2012, 216–219.

130 In classical Roman law marriage was a quaestio facti and lasted only as long as both spouses wanted it to last. Otherwise, it simply ceased to exist without any required formalities. See e.g. Verena HALBWACHS: *Die römische Ehe (iustum matrimonium)* in: Ulrike BABUSIAUX et al. (eds): *Handbuch des romischen Privatrechts*, Mohr Siebeck, Tübingen, 2023, vol. I, 841, 845–846

131 John QUIGLEY: *Soviet Legal Innovation and the Law of the Western World*, Cambridge University Press, Cambridge, 2007, 23–26; LITYŃSKI, *Prawo Rosji*, 248–256.

132 NOVKOV: *Law and Political Ideologies*, 627.

133 Hanna DĘBSKA: *Władza, symbol, prawo. Społeczne tworzenie Trybunału Konstytucyjnego* [Power, Symbol, Law: The Social Construction of the Constitutional Court], Wydawnictwo Sejmowe, Warsaw, 2015, 251–253.

134 Martijn W. HESSELINK: *European Contract Law: A Matter of Consumer Protection, Citizenship, or Justice?* European Review of Private Law 15 (2007)/3, 323–348; MAŃKO: *Koncepcja interpelacji ideologicznej*, 52.

135 HALPIN: *Ideology and Law*, 159. I contend that an example of this kind of ideology of legalism is Artur Kozak's jurisce ntrism, on which see Rafał MAŃKO: *Artur Kozak's juriscentrist concept of law: A Central European innovation in legal theory*, Review of Central and East European Law 45 (2020)/2, 334–375.

In order to account for all these phenomena, I have recently proposed to identify three types of ideology or, more precisely, three different ideological registers which one encounters within the juridical: extra-juridical ideology; intra-juridical ideology; and legal ideology.[136] My approach, therefore, is somewhat more complex that the one advocated by Weitzer, who was satisfied with a two-way typology, claiming that:

> The ideological dimensions of law can be differentiated into two categories: (1) legal ideology as a political instrument exercised by a dominant or an insurgent class and (2) the prevailing ideological consequences of legal arrangements, irrespective of the specific interests and influence of any particular class.[137]

My approach differs from Waltzer's not only in that it includes the additional category of the 'legal ideology', but also differentiates between general political ideologies and lawyers' guild ideology.

In line with that approach, the concept of 'extra-juridical ideology' refers to the general political and societal ideologies which impact upon the juridical and which the juridical can also reversely impact. I refer to it as 'extra-juridical' in order to emphasise that ontologically it exists outside of the juridical, that "*it is*" conceptually distinct from the juridical, and that it can enter into various interactions with the juridical. Examples of extra-juridical ideologies include socialism, social democracy, communism, orthodox (Soviet) Marxism-Leninism, nationalism,[138] liberalism, conservatism, neoliberalism,[139] neocon-

136 Rafał MAŃKO: *Legal Form, Ideology and the Political*, in SULIKOWSKI, MAŃKO, ŁAKOMY: *Legal Scholarship and the Political*, 36–39.

137 WEITZER: *Law and Legal Ideology*, 138.

138 On nationalist ideology and private law see especially Guido COMPARATO: *Nationalism and Private Law in Europe*, Hart Publishing, Oxford, 2014.

139 For a classical and received definition of neoliberalism, see David HARVEY: *A Brief History of Neoliberalism* [2005], Oxford University Press, Oxford, 2007, 2: 'Neoliberalism is in the first instance a theory of political economic practices that proposes that human well-being can best be advanced by liberating individual entrepreneurial freedoms and skills within an institutional framework characterized by strong private property rights, free markets, and free trade. The role of the state is to create and preserve an institutional framework appropriate to such practices. (…) State interventions in markets (once created) must be kept to a bare minimum (…).' See also Paweł SNOPEK: *Neoliberalism, ideology, social (in)justice and postpolitics*, 142–143.

servatism,[140] to name but a few.[141] Such ideologies impact upon the content of rules adopted in the process of legislation, but also on the process of adjudication, i.e. judicial interpretation, which includes law-making. I shall discuss the role of ideology in adjudication later on in this section. Furthermore, extra-juridical ideologies impact upon scholarly writings, which also engage in legal interpretation, although of a non-binding character.

By 'intra-juridical ideology,' in contrast, I mean the ideological beliefs and practices held and perpetuated by lawyers *qua* professionals of the juridical, i.e. what Alan Hunt called the 'professional ideology' of lawyers.[142] I will refer to it as 'intra-juridical' because this ideology is ontologically placed *within the juridical*, or, to put it in Althusserian terms, it is the *internal ideology* of the State Legal Apparatus, justifying the existence of this very apparatus, and providing it with a legitimising narrative. This intra-juridical ideology is quite different conceptually from the various extra-juridical ideologies, even if the State Legal Apparatus expresses, defends and possibly even develops them both. Examples of intra-juridical ideologies include positivism, normativism, hyperpositivism,[143] jusnaturalism, juriscentrism,[144] legal modernism,[145] legal pragmatism, legal traditionalism, and so forth. Indeed, on the

140 Quite apart from the U.S. political context, I understand 'neoconservatism' as a simple combination of neoliberalism (in the meaning given to it by Harvey) as an economic ideology, with cultural and moral conservatism (inspired by sectarian views), as a cultural ideology.

141 The *Oxford Handbook of Political Ideologies* offers a much longer list, including: conservatism, Christian democracy, liberalism, social democracy, communism, anarchism, economic libertarianism, green ideology, nationalism, fascism, populism, republicanism, ideologies of empire, feminism, Islamic political ideologies, as well as a number of regional ideologies: Latin American, African, Chinese, south Asian and southeast Asian. See *Oxford Handbook of Political Ideologies*, part III.

142 HUNT: *Ideology of Law*, 29.

143 Hyperpositivism, also known as 'ultra-formalism,' was the intra-juridical ideology prevalent in state-socialist countries, especially between World War II and the fall of the Berlin Wall. However, hyperpositivism has proven to be more durable, remaining as a 'legal survival' in certain legal cultures, including the Polish one. For a brief account of hyperpositism, see MAŃKO: *Weeds in the Gardens*.

144 Juriscentrism is the intra-juridical ideology created and propagated by Artur Kozak. For an exposition of the main tenets of juriscentrism in English, see MAŃKO: *Artur Kozak's juriscentrist concept of law*.

145 I am using the term 'legal modernism' in the sense given to this term by Antoni Peretiatkowicz, i.e. to encompass the anti-positivist legal movements of the wake of the 20th century, such as *Freie Rechtsschule*, *école des libre recherches scientifiques*, etc. See Antoni PERETIATKOWICZ: *Studia prawnicze*, Księgarnia Św. Wojciecha w Poznaniu, Poznań, 1938.

one hand, the juridical serves the hegemonic extra-juridical ideology on account of its determination, in the last instance, by the political;[146] but on the other hand, in order to maintain its distinctiveness and justify its existence, it needs an ideology of its own, an ideology praising and legitimising the *legal form as such*, i.e. intra-juridical ideology. Whilst the main thrust of the ideological operation of law is performed at the service of the hegemonic political ideology (the extra-juridical ideology), the intra-juridical ideology has a residual and formal character. Being nothing else than precisely the ideology of the legal form as such, the intra-juridical ideology exists quite apart from the lawyers' attachment to a particular extra-juridical ideology, although, as I note later on, the two can enter into interesting functional couplings.

Intra-juridical ideology is composed, on the one hand, of a series of empty signifiers[147] of the juridical, such as 'legality,' 'justice' or the 'rule of law'. They are empty in that they are purely formal and autopoietic. They do not refer to any substantive ideology (scil. extra-juridical), but only to the legal form. It is difficult to know what is justice, unless we have a specific concept of justice. The same applies to the rule of law, a concept which begs the question *what law*, in whose interest, how applied, etc. Indeed, as Alexandre Kojève claimed, each epoch has its own conception of justice, and the task of judges is to apply it in an impartial and disinterested way.[148] But the conception of justice is overdetermined by the hegemonic ideology. As an empty signifier, its content is fixed in the form of 'temporary signifieds' that 'are the result of a political competition.'[149]

The second set of elements of juridical ideology is focused on praising the legal form, claiming that only the legal form can guarantee 'security' 'predictability' or 'transparency'. In other words, juridical ideology is a system of beliefs, held by lawyers or, rather propagated by them as (possibly cynical) subjects of ideology, according to which the legal form *qua* form, with its abstractness, selectiveness, and exchangeability, is a necessary gift of the

146 Michał PAŹDZIORA, Michał STAMBULSKI: *Co może dać nauce prawa polityczność – przyczynek do dalszych badań* [What can legal scholarship gain from the political: notes towards further research], Archiwum Filozofii Prawa i Filozofii Społecznej 2 (2014), 58.

147 *Cf.* Ernesto LACLAU: *Emancipations(s)*, Verso, London-New York, 2007, 36: 'An empty signifier is, strictly speaking, a signifier without a signified.'

148 Alexandre KOJÈVE: *An Outline of the Phenomenology of Right*, Bryan-Paul FROST (ed), Robert HOWSE (transl.), Rowman & Littlefield, Plymouth, 2007.

149 LACLAU: *Emancipations(s)*, 35.

legal community to society which, otherwise, would end up in the abyss of a *bellum omnium contra omnes*.[150] To put it in Žižekian terms,[151] intra-juridical ideology is, therefore, a fantasy of the legal community, a fantasy which acts as a screen masking the impossible kernel of the Real – of lawyers' fundamental dependence upon the political, understood as the overdetermination, in the last instance, of the content of legal norms (legislative or judge-made) by the situation of struggles of opposing groups in society. This fantasy of the juridical's autonomy[152] structures the actual, everyday reality of lawyers' social practices, the way they reason and the way they plead. A critique of juridical ideology is not likely to change the lawyers' way of thinking. As cynical subjects of ideology, *they know very well what they are doing, but they are still doing it*,[153] to refer to the Sloterdijk-Žižek formula. If anything, a critique of juridical ideology could change the approach of non-lawyers, pierce the magical veil of the legal form, thereby opening the door for a critique of the substantive solutions proposed by law under the influence of the political and its hegemonic ideology.

As I have already highlighted above, concrete extra-legal ideologies and intra-juridical ones can enter into interesting points of coupling. For instance, as Michał Stambulski notes, there is a structural coupling between legal formalism and political liberalism. This is because:

---

150 Critical theorists maintain that exactly the opposite is true. As Klare affirms: 'Until lawmaking becomes a quest for justice in each concrete historical setting, until the "rule of law" ideal (the separation of law and ethics) is abolished and brought directly into daily life as a continuous, participatory practice of mediation and redefinition of relations among people who see in each other the possibility their own fulfillment, that is until lawmaking becomes a self-conscious, critical form of social practice, there be no hope of the emancipation of labor (…) the struggle to emancipate labor must also be a struggle to emancipate law itself'; Karl KLARE: *Juridical Deradicalization or the Wagner Act and the Origins of Modern Legal Consciousness*, Minnesota Law Review, 62 (1978), 338.

151 *Cf.* ŽIŽEK: *Sublime Object of Ideology*, 45.

152 The autonomy of the juridical vis-à-vis the structures of economic and political power is only relative. As Alan Hunt explains, relative autonomy signifies 'the partial independence of different social elements, such as the legal, political, and ideological, both from each other and, more importantly, from the general interests of a dominant class. This concept (…) acknowledges the fundamental importance of the economic base (albeit 'in the last instance') while allowing the ideological realm to be treated as an arena of struggle that is not simply the reflex of economic class conflict'; HUNT: *Ideology of Law*, 14.

153 ŽIŽEK: *Sublime Object of Ideology*, 30.

> Liberalism provides formalism with an axiological justification. Law should be observed not only because it is a formal system free from contradictions, but also because it protects the fundamental rights of individuals in contemporary Western societies. These rights are objective.[154]

Another structural coupling can be found between hyperpositivism and actually existing socialism. Lawyers in socialist countries, who wished to conceal their political preferences and escape any form of critique for being non-Marxist, preferred to justify their legal reasoning by resorting to purely linguistic, mechanistic arguments, parading as pure *Subsumptionsautomate*, free of any personal will, ideological preference or political subjectivity.[155] The popularity of hyperpositivism – an intra-juridical ideology – was structurally coupled with the prevalence of the hegemonic ideology of official, orthodox Marxism-Leninism. However, in contrast to the coupling between formalism and liberalism, described by Stambulski, which can be referred to as a 'direct coupling', the coupling between hyperpositivism and Marxism-Leninism can be described as a 'reverse coupling'. Lawyers opt for the intra-juridical ideology of hyperpositivism precisely because they *do not share* the hegemonic ideology of Marxism-Leninism and wish to look for a 'safe haven'[156] where they will be able to pretend that they are 'ideology-free.' Of course, this instance of being 'ideology-free' is a pure fiction, and hyperpositivism allows lawyers to *conceal their actual ideological preferences* under the convenient guise of 'linguistic interpretation' and other similar gimmicks. After all, as Douzinas underlines 'objectivity tends to become the best disguise for ideological partisanship.'[157]

Quite apart from the extra-juridical and intra-juridical ideologies, there is the *legal ideology*, i.e. the ideology expressed in law as such,[158] or, in the words of Alan Hunt, 'the ideologies embodied in the policy aspects of legal

154 Michał STAMBULSKI: *Polityczność w polskiej analitycznej teorii prawa. Zarys problematyki* [The political in Polish analytical jurisprudence: an outline], Archiwum Filozofii Prawa i Filozofii Społecznej 3 (2019), 69.

155 MAŃKO: *Weeds in the Gardens of Justice*, 222. For a comprehensive analysis of hyperpositivism against a comparative legal background encompassing Central Europe see especially Zdeněk KÜHN: *The Judiciary in Central and Eastern Europe: Mechanical Jurisprudence in Transformation?*, Martinus Nijhoff, Leiden-Boston, 2011.

156 MAŃKO: *Weeds in the Gardens of Justice*, 223.

157 DOUZINAS: *Short History*, 196.

158 The notion can be traced back to ALTHUSSER: *Ideology and the State*, 44– 46.

doctrine'.[159] This is the aspect which Weitzer refers to as the 'mystif[ication of] fundamental economic relations'.[160] I refer to it as 'legal' and not as 'juridical' ideology, in order to emphasise that it is expressed in the *lex* (in the positive law). Of course, there are strong links between the legal ideology and the two other ideologies of the juridical, nonetheless they need to be conceptually distinguished.

Keeping in mind Žižek's claim concerning the gap between the ideological narrative (which structures social action) and the actual social consciousness, we must admit that all legal texts – regardless of legal field – convey a certain vision of society – an ideological fantasy – which creates and sustains the social reality. Popular sovereignty, equality before the law, autonomy of the will or responsibility based on guilt/fault – all these concepts represent certain ideological fantasies (in the psychoanalytic meaning of the term). I call them fantasies precisely because, when confronted with actual social reality, they are, for most of the time, fictions. Despite the legal dogma of equality of legal subjects, everyone knows that there are 'equal' and 'equaler' legal subjects, especially those who are more well off and can impose their terms in a contract or enforce their claims in a court by hiring a more expensive lawyer. The list of ideological fantasies which *structure the law from within* could be multiplied, including the fantasy that judges 'apply' the law and do not 'make it' (still popular in Polish or French legal culture, but rejected a long time ago in the United States), the fantasy that all people 'know' the law, although with its contemporary complexity this is utterly impossible, or the fiction that behind legislative texts there stands some kind of 'rational legislator' (a fiction typical for Polish legal culture), although lawyers know very well that legislation tends to be irrational and inconsistent, and so forth.

Following Žižek I insist that these fantasies of legal ideology, so prominent in private law, are not points of 'escape from our reality,' but, to the contrary, they actually 'offer us the social reality *itself*.' This is because the social practice of lawyers (and conforming legal subjects) usually proceeds *as if* the fantasies of legal ideology were true (otherwise they could face dire consequences and experience the violence of the law to the fullest). Thereby, these fantasies – built into social practices – structure those practices, and contribute to the social construction of reality, at least with regard to legal reality (reality of the legal sub-world).

Assuming that legal ideology – in Lacanian terms the 'Symbolic order' – represents a set of fantasies, we must take the second step and enquire *what*

---

159 HUNT: *Ideology of Law*, 29.

160 WEITZER: *Law and Legal Ideology*, 147.

do these fantasies mask? In other words, a critique of legal ideology must aim at unmasking the Real, the 'impossible kernel', which is masked by the fantasy. The identification of the gap between the ideological fantasy, expressed in legal ideology (e.g. the equality or freedom of subjects of private law) is a crucial element of the critique of legal ideology. This critique can be internal, i.e. it can focus on inconsistencies in legal materials (e.g. that the law presumes the equality and freedom of legal subjects, but in another rule it assumes that subjects are actually forced to do something and enjoy no freedom). These internal inconsistencies of the legal ideologies (in Lacanian parlance – 'symptoms') would contribute to showing the points at which the Symbolic order breaks down. An external critique, in turn, could show the inconsistencies between the legal ideology and real life (the law says that people are equal, but in fact they are not) and between the legal ideology and other ideologies at stake (intra- and extra-juridical). For instance, one could point out that the hegemonic extra-juridical ideology of neoliberalism cherishes the free market, but in fact there are elements of a statist economy (e.g. public bailout of banks, provided by the law). As Weitzer poignantly observes:

> the outcomes of legal processes are biased against certain groups and classes in terms of the extrajuridical societal context of racial and class inequality. In such a context, unequal legal outcomes are experienced by the poor and minorities because of (1) economic barriers to equal legal treatment, (2) structural and organizational characteristics of the legal profession, (3) social-psychological barriers (e.g., lack of knowledge of laws and legal rights, distrust of legal institutions), and (4) unfavorable treatment during legal proceedings (…).[161]

This gap is, of course, not only still true, but it is steadily growing larger.

4.2 *Instrumentalization of Law by Ideology as a Viable Concept?*

Lawyers, including legal theorists[162] and legal historians,[163] tend to speak about the 'instrumentalization' of law, including its instrumentalization by ideology. I have doubts whether this notion remains conceptually correct

161 WEITZER: *Law and Legal Ideology*, 149.

162 See e.g. Artur KOZAK (ed.): *Z zagadnień teorii i filozofii prawa: Instrumentalizacja prawa* [From topics of theory and philosophy of law: instrumentalisation of law], Kolonia Limited, Wrocław, 2000; SULIKOWSKI: *Posthumanizm a prawoznawstwo*, 65.

163 See e.g. GAŁĘDEK: *Introduction: Modernisation, National Identity, and Legal Instrumentalism, passim.*

and preserves any explanatory value if we adopt the views on law and ideology taken by Duncan Kennedy, in the context of the concepts of ideology put forward by Louis Althusser and Slavoj Žižek, which I have presented above. This is because if we work with a concept of ideology proposed by these thinkers, we must *eo ipso* assume that law is *always already* instrumentalized by ideology.[164] Law, just like any other sphere of social activity *cannot escape* ideology (just like it cannot escape the political.[165] It is impossible to imagine a law which is not instrumentalized by *some* ideology (intra-juridical or extra-juridical), which does not serve *any* values, which has *no goal* external to it. One can speak, perhaps, of *l'art pour l'art*, but to imagine *le droit pour le droit* is an absurdity. At the very least, law will serve the interests of lawyers and conform to the intra-juridical ideology they put forward to legitimise their power in society. Therefore, I assume that when lawyers speak of 'instrumental law,' and assume that law may be non-instrumentalized, they simply disapprove of the ideological goals or interests that the law is currently serving and are masking their critique, pretending that what they propose is not an ideology. Thus liberals will criticise socialists for ideologizing the law, but will pretend that 'freedom of contract' or 'liability for damages' are not ideological constructs, whereas they patently are. Likewise, conservatives will bemoan the introduction of gay marriage as ideological (pointing to so-called 'gender ideology'), whereas they will claim that their conservative vision of the family is ideology-free, while – of course – it is not, it simply expresses a different ideology (Christian, conservative, religious, etc.). Exemplary in this respect are the critical views on instrumentalization of law put forward by the late Polish legal theorist and proponent of juriscentrist ideology, Artur Kozak. In his view, a crucial element of legal culture is a paradigm of legal interpretation which 'on the one hand protects us from the arbitrariness of individual lawyers, and on the other hand does not allow the political conjectures, guiding actual lawmakers, to be reflected in legal practice.'[166] Concerning the relations between

164 Therefore, I am not questioning the fact that law is instrumentalised by ideology. I am only claiming that one cannot imagine in a situation in which law wouldn't be instrumentalised by this or other ideology, extra-juridical or intra-juridical. The point I am making is that ideology is simply inescapable for law.

165 Evgeny B. PASHUKANIS: *Law and Marxism: A General Theory*, Barbara EINHORN (transl.), Pluto Press, London, 1983, 81; Michael G. SALTER: *Carl Schmitt: Law as Politics, Ideology and Strategic Myth*, 30; MAŃKO: *Critique of the Juridical*, 33.

166 Artur KOZAK: *Granice prawniczej władzy dyskrecjonalnej* [The limits of the discretionary power of lawyers], Kolonia Limited, Wrocław, 2002, 152.

law and other sub-worlds, especially politics, Kozak openly defended law's autonomy and opposed its instrumentalization:

> Lawyers have always enjoyed a certain autonomy vis-à-vis politics. This is because the ruler, externalising his will into a text, lost control over it. A royal edict was no longer the will of the ruler, but a product of this will, belonging to the world of scripture and subject to the rules governing that world. [...] No-one can control a text, not even its author. This is the most profound reason for the autonomy of law and independence of lawyers vis-à-vis politics. But one may control those who read the text. And this is the most profound reason for the conflict between the world of politics and the world of law. Every law-maker who wishes to influence social relationships directly by its will has to ensure the obedience of lawyers.[167]

The critique of instrumentalism, put forward by the father of juriscentrism, is very revealing in that is shows that what is at stake is not a concrete conception of justice or a concrete ideological project, but merely the 'autonomy' of law, understood as the power given to the legal community in a given society. How different are the concerns of Kozak when compared to those of Duncan Kennedy, who sees law as an opportunity to change society for the better,[168] rather than focusing on guarding the legal community's prerogatives in a way agnostic towards any specific values.

4.3 *Ideology in Adjudication and Scholarly Interpretation of Law*

Legal historians, when analysing the ideological character of the law, should not limit themselves only to parliamentary or governmental law-making. Ideology is present also and to the same extent in judicial law-making and in scholarly analysis of law. This is simply because any given judgment and any given paper of a legal scholar is *per se* and *ipso facto* an act of legal interpretation – the legal materials which a judge or scholars works with are not apprehensible *sine interpretatione*.[169] In a sense, all interpretation

167 Artur KOZAK: *Myślenie analityczne w nauce prawa i praktyce prawniczej* [Analytical thinking in legal scholarship and legal practice], Maciej PICHLAK (ed.), Wydawnictwo Uniwersytetu Wrocławskiego, Wrocław, 2008, 208–209.

168 KENNEDY: *Critique of Adjudication*, 157ff.

169 As Jakub Łakomy points out: 'No element of reality that we experience, including texts, literary and legal, is objectively accessible. We have not the possibility of experiencing them "as is." In this sense, one may say that we actually create reality rather than

is creative,[170] especially if we adopt the definition of hermeneutic universalists who claim that it denotes 'cognition relativized to the perspective of the cognizing subject'.[171] There is no 'textual or extra-textual reality' to which the interpreter can refer, but he or she 'actively creates [that reality] in the course of interpretation as such.'[172] On the other hand, the *degree* of creativity can be measured by referring to certain objective yardsticks. For instance, a given judge's interpretation of a given rule of the Civil Code (say, Article 5 of the Polish Civil Code which enshrines the abuse of rights doctrine) may be less creative (if it follows existing case-law and scholarly views) or more creative (if the judge's interpretation departs from earlier cases and scholarly views).[173] Creativity becomes, in this sense, a synonym for innovativeness. The more innovative an interpretation of a given judge or legal scholar, the more creative it is.

The relationship between ideology and legal interpretation is, therefore, most crucial with regard to creative (innovative) interpretation, especially if it is based on open norms (general clauses), balancing of principles or applying proportionality tests, which give judges relatively more freedom than

---

experience it'; Jakub ŁAKOMY: *Hermeneutic Universalism: A Post-analytical Inquiry into the Political of Legal Interpretation* in Andrzej BATOR, Zbigniew PULKA (eds): *A Post-analytical Approach to Philosophy and Theory of Law*, Peter Lang, Berlin, 2019, 51. For a historical perspective, see e.g. Władysław ROZWADOWSKI, *Etiam clarum ius exigit interpretationem*, in Agnieszka CHODUŃ, Stanisław CZEPITA (eds): *W poszukiwaniu dobra wspólnego. Księga jubileuszowa Profesora Macieja Zielińskiego* [In a search for the common good: a jubilee book to Professor Maciej Zieliński], WUSz, Szczecin, 2010, 37–48.

170 Jakub ŁAKOMY: *The Space of The Political in Legal Interpretation* (*Some Remarks On The Dworkin-Fish Debate*), in BIEŚ-SROKOSZ, MAŃKO, SROKOSZ (eds): *Law, Space, and the Political*, 133, 135. As Stanley Fish argues: 'To explain a work is to point out something about it that had not been attributed to it before and therefore to change it by challenging other explanations that were once changes in their turn. Explaining and changing cannot be opposed activities (although they can be the names of claims and counterclaims) because they are the same activities'; FISH: *Working on the Chain Gang*, 562.

171 ŁAKOMY: *Hermeneutic Universalism*, 43.

172 Jakub ŁAKOMY: *Polityczność (teorii) wykładni prawa. Perspektywa neopragmatyzmu Stanleya Fisha* [The political character of (the theory of) legal interpretation: the perspective of Stanley Fish's neopragmatism], Archiwum Filozofii Prawa i Filozofii Społecznej 3 (2018), 27–28.

173 According to liberal legal theorist Ronald Dworkin, interpreters should merely explain the existing law, but not create it. See Ronald DWORKIN: *Law as Interpretation*, Texas Law Review 60 (1982), 543–544; ŁAKOMY: *The Space of the Political in Legal Interpretation*, 130.

black-letter rules.[174] However, even 'conservative' interpretation (repetitive towards earlier interpretations, non-innovative) can be viewed in the light of ideology because it is, in all probability, repetitive and secondary towards the ideological choices more or less consciously made by earlier interpreters (judges and scholars). A civil judge who follows an established interpretation of Article 5 of the Polish Civil Code and refuses to grant broader protection to weaker parties, is, of course, being 'conservative' in the sense of following established interpretations, but at the same time he cannot claim to be 'ideologically neutral', precisely because – consciously or not – he is following the ideological inspirations which had lead – consciously or not – to the emergence of the hegemonic interpretation in the first place (which may seem as reflecting the 'common sense').[175] Such ideological interpretations can be, in light of the theory of the ideological dualism of the juridical, inspired both by non-legal ideologies (such as conservatism, liberalism, neoliberalism, socialism etc.) and by legal (juridical) ideologies (such as positivism, hyperpositivism, normativism, jusnaturalism, free law, etc.). These ideologies can coincide in producing determined results. For instance, a conservative interpretation of Article 5 of the Polish Civil Code, refusing to use it creatively in order to grant protection to weaker parties in a given case, will be justified both by the non-legal ideology of neoliberalism (or conservatism or neoconservatism) *and* by the intra-juridical ideology of hyperpositivism (or judicial restraint, or normativism, etc.). This does not mean that these two ideologies are paired in some essential way (neoliberalism with hyperpositivism). It rather means that *in casu* they work together to produce a given result, but it does not exclude a situation in which they will function in quite different pairs under different circumstances.

The question of the ideological dimension of legal interpretation is strictly connected to the question of the relationship between legal interpretation and the political.[176] This is not to say that the concepts of ideology and the political are in any way interchangeable, synonymic or that they denote the

174 Rafał MAŃKO: *Ideology and Legal Interpretation: Some Theoretical Considerations*, in Kalvis TORGĀNS et al. (eds): *Constitutional Values in Contemporary Legal Space*, University of Latvia Press, Riga, 2016, 122–123; Artur KOTOWSKI: *Argumentacja z tożsamości konstytucyjnej – celem podsumowania* [Argumentation based on constitutional identity: a summary], Studia i Analizy Sądu Najwyższego 4 (2017), 47.

175 Hugh COLLINS: *Marxism and Law*, Oxford University Press, Oxford, 1982, 73; MAŃKO: *Reality is for Those Who Cannot Sustain the Dream*, 26.

176 Rafał MAŃKO: *Critique of the 'Juridical': Some Metatheoretical Remarks*, Journal of the University of Latvia. Law 11 (2018), 33.

same phenomena. Ideology and the political are quite distinct concepts which denote distinct phenomena, yet their functioning remains closely interlinked. However, I fully agree with Jakub Łakomy when he claims that 'the space of [legal] interpretation belongs entirely to the space of the political'[177] and in consequence,

> whenever a legal interpreter undertakes the activity of 'reading the law', they inevitably enter into the space of the political, and each and every intellectual move they make is (...) *inherently political.* (...) In reality, the space of interpretation is nothing else than a province within the empire of the political.[178]

The link between the political (understood, following Mouffe, as a structural social antagonism) and ideology is to be found in the person of the interpreter and the interpretive community to which she belongs. This is because legal interpreters do not exist in a void but rather they all 'occupy a determined place in the structure of social conflicts which constitute the political.'[179] In fact, '[b]roader social antagonisms finding their place in specific court proceedings undertake the form of debates on the 'proper' interpretation of legal texts that are to shape the basis for the decision in the proceeding.'[180] Legal interpretation without any ideological influence is a fiction which has never existed and will never exist. In the words of Stanley Fish:

> ... the condition of being free from ideological control would be wholly disabling because there would be nothing either to be free with or for. There would be nothing to be free with because every preconception, acquired belief, assumed point of view, opinion, bias and prejudice removed from the mind, there would be nothing left with which to calculate, determine and decide; there is nothing to be free for, because a mind divested of all direction – a mind not already orientated towards this or that purpose or plan or agenda – could not recognize any reason for going in one direction rather than another, or, for that matter, for going in any direction at all.[181]

---

177 ŁAKOMY: *The Space of the Political in Legal Interpretation*, 136.

178 *Ibidem*, emphasis added.

179 ŁAKOMY: *Polityczność (teorii) wykładni prawa*, 26.

180 ŁAKOMY: *Hermeneutic Universalism*, 51.

181 FISH: *Doing What Comes Naturally*, 518.

Despite the rejection of the unchecked freedom of legal interpreters, we must admit that they are constrained, but above all by the legal community itself and its political environment, rather than by 'the law".[182] To quote once again Stanley Fish:

> Interpreters are constrained by their tacit awareness of what is possible and not possible to do, what is and is not a reasonable thing to say, what will and will not be heard as evidence, in a given enterprise; and it is within those same constraints that they see and bring others to see the shape of the documents to whose interpretation they are committed.[183]

Quite apart from the influences of other institutional sub-worlds, such as those of politics, economy or religion, legal interpreters – judges and legal academics – are constrained in their readings of legal texts by *hegemonic ideology*. If certain legal interpretations are more prevalent and treated as 'objective' by a given legal community, this is because of a shared 'cognitive structure of the members of a given interpretive community'.[184] This 'cognitive structure', is, arguably, determined mainly by the hegemonic ideology.

From the perspective of critical legal theory, the role of ideology not only in legislation, but also in adjudication (which is always to an extent creative as a form of interpretation) is a fact.[185] A judge who claims that she is 'ideology free' is either acting in bad faith, or simply is 'in denial' in the psychoanalytical sense.[186] A special area of ideological inroads into adjudication are, as I have already mentioned above, open norms or open-texture norms, especially general clauses and other value-laden legal rules.[187] Judges deciding what is 'good faith,' 'fair dealing', or what is in conformity with the 'principles of social life,' cannot escape ideology and must adopt a certain ideological stance quite openly, sometimes even to the extent of openly admitting that they will propagate 'Christian values'.[188]

182 MAŃKO: *W stronę krytycznej filozofii orzekania*, 107–110, 118–130, 146.

183 FISH: *Working on the Chain Gang*, 562.

184 ŁAKOMY: *Polityczność (teorii) wykładni prawa*, 33.

185 MAŃKO: *W stronę krytycznej filozofii orzekania*, 136.

186 KENNEDY: *Left/Phenomenological Alternative*, 163.

187 MAŃKO: *W stronę krytycznej filozofii orzekania*, 137.

188 See decision of the Polish Supreme Court of 26 February 2006, Case II CSK 101/05, LEX No. 180197.

General clauses, therefore, are not only 'safety valves',[189] as Andrzej Stelmachowski described them, but rather 'mouthpieces',[190] as Martijn Hesselink sees them, being fully fledged competence norms for judges, allowing them to make law in the full daylight and even inviting them to disclose some ideological commitments. Historians of private law, analysing case-law from the past, should be particularly sensitive not only to open ideological commitments, made in judicial decisions, but also should carefully compare the content of the legislation, on the one hand, and the judicial decision, on the other, and search for ideology *within this gap* separating the two legal formants.

5 Relations between Private Law and Ideology

5.1 *The Ideological Character of the Very Idea of Private Law*

The very *idea of private law* is a heavily ideological one, assuming the existence of a certain 'private' sphere which can and indeed should be closed off from the 'public'. The public vs. private divide itself, and the exact border where it should be delimited, are both ideologically and politically heavily laden questions.[191] As Turkel points out:

> The [public/private] dichotomy appears necessary for individual autonomy, the maintenance of social institutions, and the conduct of legal action; At the same time, it tends to legitimate and mystify patterns of inequality and structures of power through which individual autonomy, social institutions, and legal action are accomplished. (…) Institutional and legal practices supported by the public/private dichotomy both legitimate and block the recognition of patterns of inequality and power in the relationships among personal experience and public policy. Social dislocations are experienced as 'personal troubles' rather than formu-

189 Andrzej STELMACHOWSKI: *Zarys teorii prawa cywilnego* [An outline of the theory of civil law], PWN, Warsaw, 1998, 120.

190 Martijn W. HESSELINK: *The Concept of Good Faith,* in Arthur HARTKAMP et al. (eds): *Towards a European Civil Code,* Kluwer Law International, Alphen aan den Rijn 2010, 645.

191 Duncan KENNEDY: *The Stages of the Decline of the Public/Private Distinction,* University of Pennsylvania Law Review 130 (1982), 1349–1357; Karl E. KLARE, *The Public/Private Distinction in Labor Law,* University of Pennsylvania Law Review 130 (1982), 1358–1422; Gerald TURKEL: *The Public/Private Distinction: Approaches to the Critique of Legal Ideology,* Law & Society Review 22 (1988)/4, 801–823.

lated as public issues and psychological individualism dominates popular consciousness (...).[192]

To claim that the negation of this divide, and the so-called 'publicisation' of private law is ideological,[193] is of course true, but the opposite, namely that cherishing the 'autonomy' of private law and entrenching the private vs. public divide in law is also *per se* ideological. Both approaches simply corespond to different ideologies, especially extra-juridical ones (liberalism, neoliberalism and conservatism will tend to emphasise the 'autonomy' of private law, whereas socialism, social democracy, or feminism will tend to downplay it).

With this assumption in mind, let me now roll out a systematic account of the private law–ideology nexus, focusing on the impact of extra-juridical ideology upon private law first.

5.2 *The Impact of Extra-Juridical Ideology upon Private Law*

The first and most obvious area of links between private law and ideology is the impact of a given ideology upon private law.[194] By this I understand a

---

192 TURKEL: *The Public/Private Distinction*, 801–802.

193 See e.g. Marek SAFJAN, Aneta WIEWIÓROWSKA-DOMAGALSKA: *Political Foundations of European Private Law: Rethinking the East-West Division Lines*, in Roger BROWNSWORD et al. (eds): *The Foundations of European Private Law*, Hart Publishing, Oxford, 2011, 278: 'the Polish private law system ... survived the communist times buried under the cover of ideology ... the classic civil law basic constructions remained, sometimes hidden under the surface of the ideological ornament [therefore] [w]hen the ideological implant is removed [private-law treatises written under actually existing socialism can] serve as a source of great inspiration.' What is striking in this narrative, is that Safjan and Wiewiórowska assume that after 1989 law stopped to be ideological, as if there was no liberal or neoliberal ideology which provided the blueprint for legal reform following the abolition of state socialism. See also Marek SAFJAN: *European Law versus Private Law: Transformation or Deformation of the Paradigm?*, in Ulf BERNITZ et al. (eds): *General Principles of EU Law and European Private Law*, Kluwer Law International, Alphen aan den Rijn, 2013, 159: 'The tendencies to publicize private law, which seem to question its autonomous goals and values and to blur the division between private and public law, are nothing new in the history of the twentieth century. Being aware of all the differences, we must not forget an experiment carried out for decades in Eastern and Central Europe which systematically undermined the idea of private law and its status as a branch of law independent from public law. ... [T]o some extent the lesson learnt from that 'experiment' may be useful and instructive in as much as it shows that there is an impassable border to the interference with private law, beyond which there is a risk of damaging the core of its structures.'

194 *Cf.* Piotr ECKHARDT: *Socialism under Construction: Law and Ideology in Housing, Construction and Spatial Planning in Poland 1944–1989*, Scholar, Warsaw, 2024, 10.

situation in which law-making in the area of private law, be it legislative or judicial,[195] is conducted in a way which leads to the implementation of the goals set by a given ideology, such as conservatism, liberalism, neoliberalism, Marxism, socialism, nationalism, etc. The impact of a given ideology upon private law may be conscious, where the actors who implement the ideology are conscious members of the ideological intelligentsia (in the meaning used by Kennedy, see Section 3 above), or unconscious, when the actors implementing the ideology treat their actions as merely belonging to the sphere of common sense. For instance, a civil judge interpreting the Civil Code in a way favouring the idea of a formal 'freedom of contract', at the expense of protection of weaker parties, is usually not so much consciously pursuing a neoliberal or neoconservative socio-political project, but rather is acting in accordance with what she perceives as common sense (people should be responsible for their acts, people are free, if they enter into a contract, promises must be kept, etc.).[196] After all, most judges are not social philosophers or political activists.

Whenever the impact of ideology upon private law-making is conscious, it may be patent or latent. The patency or latency of ideological influence is a question of degree (it is a typology) rather than a classification (zero-one approach). Hence, some ideological preferences may be disclosed, whilst others will be hidden. The degree of ideological openness will depend on various factors, especially the quality of the actor (parliamentary legislator or judge), the quality of the ideological preferences (hegemonic or counter-hegemonic), and the prevailing style of legal discourse in a given legal culture (formalist or pragmatist). Hence, parliamentary or governmental legislators usually tend to be more open about their ideological inspirations than judges. This is especially so in formalist legal cultures, such as the Polish one. Whereas a member

195 By judicial law-making I understand the creation of new legal norms by judges, either deciding individual cases or proclaiming those norms in the abstract, as in the system of Guidelines on the Administration of Justice and Judicial Practice in socialist Poland, or the abstract resolutions, interpreting the law, adopted by the Polish Supreme Court today. The thin line between legal interpretation (within the remit of legislation, *secundum legem*), development of the law (*Rechtsfortbildung*, operating more or less *praeter legem*) and sheer law-making (*praeter legem* or even *contra legem*) is outside my interest here. What counts, is that judge or legislator produces a new legal norm which becomes part of the operative law. Whether this fits into one or another theory of sources of law is a question for analytical legal theorists and constitutionalists. For the purposes of the present publication I take law-making as a *social fact*, not as a theoretical category.

196 COLLINS: *Marxism and Law*, 73; MAŃKO: *Reality is for Those Who Cannot Sustain the Dream*, 26.

of parliament or the government may be more open about the ideological choices, a judge is usually more reticent. Nonetheless, the same judge, when interpreting parliamentary legislation, is, according to some theories of interpretation, expected to follow the legislature's intent or the purpose of the legislation, rather than focusing exclusively on the letter and systemic arrangement of the law. In such situations the judge is even expected to refer to the political – and therefore ideological – goals pursed by the legislature. In doing so, the judge is not promoting *her own* ideological project, but merely *following* the legislature's ideological project. For instance, a judge may refer to the protection of consumers or to the freedom of contract, in line with the ideological preferences of the legislature. These preferences may be quite apart from the judge's *personal ideological preferences*. However, often judges may have such personal preferences which they will not disclose, but cloak their arguments in objectivist or textual or systemic arguments. Duncan Kennedy refers to such judges as 'cause lawyers in denial', because they are pursuing a certain cause (an ideological project), but at the same time they are denying it.[197] This coincides with the opposition between hegemonic and counter-hegemonic ideological preferences: a judge wishing to pursue a counter-hegemonic ideology (e.g. democratic socialism, in a society where neoliberal ideology prevails) will rather tend to be a cause lawyer in denial, and hide his or her preferences. On the other hand, a judge who is pursuing a hegemonic project will have less reasons to hide his or her preferences, especially if they have been openly referred to by the legislature.

The situation is somewhat more complex with regard to legislatures. On one hand, they are political actors and hence they can be more open about their ideological motivations, be they more neoliberal (freedom of contract, private property), or more social democratic (protection of consumers, workers, tenants). On the other hand, however, legislators may wish to pursue quite different goals from which they officially declare and which they would like their constituents and the public opinion in general think they are pursuing. The governmental-parliamentary *iter legislativus* is not immune from the influence of various lobbyists, pressure groups or, in some weaker political cultures, outright corruption. If the lobbyists are not particularly popular in society (e.g. banks or foreign investors), the political legislators will prefer to cloak their legislative proposals in ideological garments concealing, rather than revealing the actual interests and ideological projects that are being pursued. In

197 Duncan KENNEDY: *The Hermeneutic of Suspicion in Contemporary American Legal Thought*, Law and Critique 25 (2015)/1, 131.

the Polish context, the research performed by Paweł Chmielnicki and his school of critical socio-legal research on legislation is particularly instructive. By analysing the actual beneficiaries of legislation, Chmielnicki has laid bare the cynicism of legislators who were officially trumpeting the protection of consumers but in fact had the interest of banks in mind.[198] In ideological terms, they were claiming to pursue a social-demoratic agenda (protection and empowerment of consumers), whereas in fact they were pursuing a purely neoliberal ideological agenda (state protection of banks). Therefore, the official ideological declarations of legislators, even if made much more openly than judicial ones, always need to be approached *cum grano salis*.

In 1976, Duncan Kennedy proposed an analytical tool which can come in handy when analysing the ideological commitments of (legislative and judge-made) rules of private law.[199] Originally devised from a critical legal standpoint, Kennedy's concept of an axis extending from individualism (autonomy) to altruism (solidarity) was subsequently re-elaborated, in a liberal spirit, by Chantal Mak.[200] The essence of this approach is to analyse the possible solutions to a legal question along an axis stretching from the most individualistic (autonomy-focused) to the most altruistic (solidarity-focused) one. Kennedy was interested in finding out whether standards (roughly the equivalent of continental general clauses) are more conducive to individualistic, or to altruistic legal solutions (when applied by judges). Mak, in turn, revised the original Kennedian idea by introducing into it the possibility of finding a 'neutral solution' between autonomy and solidarity.[201] To my mind, the very question of the existence of such a 'neutral ground,' say, between consumers and traders or company owners and workers is, in itself, an ideological issue. If, like Mak, we subscribe to a roughly liberal (in the European sense) view of the social world, then – as per Dworkin and Habermas – the one right answer can be

198 Paweł Chmielnicki: *Źródła i efektywność regulacji dotyczących nabycia lokalu lub domu od dewelopera. Ocena wstępna* [The sources and the effects of regulations concerning the purchase of an apartment or a house from a housing developer: preliminary analysis], Przegląd Prawa Publicznego 7–8 (2014), 141–153; Paweł Chmielnicki: *Nabycie lokalu lub domu od dewelopera. Wykładnia przepisów i efekty ich stosowania* [Purchase of an apartment or a house from a developer: interpretation of the legal rules and the effects of their application], Difin, Warszawa, 2014.

199 Duncan Kennedy: *Form and Substance in Private Law Adjudication*, Harvard Law Review, 89 (1976), 1685–1778.

200 Chantal Mak: *Fundamental Rights in European Contract Law: A Comparison of the Impact of Fundamental Rights on Contractual Relationships in Germany, the Netherlands, Italy and England*, Kluwer Law International, Alphen aan den Rijn, 2008.

201 *Ibidem*, 212–213.

found, especially as a result of an inclusive debate. If, however, we take the approach of critical legal theory, the idea of the neutral solution is unacceptable.

This is because if we imagine that one and the same legal question can be answered in, let us assume, six different ways, with solution S_1 being the most favourable to the consumer, and solution S_6 being the most favourable to the trader, I still cannot agree that solutions 'in the middle' offer a fair and neutral approach to the question.[202] Even if there would be seven possible solutions, I still do not think that the solution 'in the middle', i.e. S_4, will be some kind of proper equilibrium that we should adopt, whereas solutions $S_1 - S_3$ and $S_5 - S_7$ would be ideologically biased. To my mind, there can be no mechanic analysis of possible legal solutions, leading to the discovery of a neutral point because adjudication should not be about neutrality (e.g. between the bourgeoisie and the workers), but about the pursuit of the common good and fairness (*ars boni et aequi*). Obviously, if one takes a different ideological standpoint than myself, for instance a liberal one (Mak) or a conservative one, one will make different claims about the question of neutrality. But from the standpoint of critical legal theory which has strong ethical commitments, there can be no compromise when it comes to doing justice and ensuring the full attainment of fairness and the common good. However, taking a step back, I can simply argue that instead of insisting on blaming the other side to be ideological (and political), both sides should simply recognise that they are engaged in an ideological and political struggle in the field of private law and they represent opposed ideological projects. What is important, is to make one's ideological commitments clear.

Quite apart from the grand ideologies planning all aspects of social life, such as neoliberalism, conservatism, democratic socialism or communism, there are also piecemeal ideologies, which could also be called 'thin ideologies' in that they are not as comprehensive as the 'thick' ones mentioned above.[203] Nationalism and modernisation are examples of such thin ideologies which

202 Rafał MAŃKO: *The Centre–Periphery Antagonism in Adjudication: A Case Study on the Spatial Dimension of the Political*, Acta Universitatis Lodziensis. Folia Iuridica, 94 (2021), 121.

203 The concept of a 'thin ideology' is used especially to describe the ideology of populism. See e.g. Michael FREEDEN: *Ideology: A Very Short Introduction*, Oxford University Press, Oxford, 2003, 97–100; Ben STANLEY: *The thin ideology of populism*, Journal of Political Ideologies 13 (2008)/1, 106–107. I would like to thank Dr. Krzysztof Mularczyk for drawing my attention to the notion of 'thick' vs 'thin' ideology and pointing me to the literature proposing it.

have a special place in the history of the impact of extra-juridical ideologies upon private law. The ideology of nationalism posits, first of all, that people belong to historically formed and durable entities called 'nations' or 'peoples', and reify such entities. Famous examples of the ideology of nationalism influencing private law include the unification of private law in 19th century Germany (*Ein Volk, Ein Reich ein Recht*) and in interwar Poland, or resistance towards foreign law, for instance in the Kingdom of Poland (in personal union with Russia) against transfers of French law.[204] Prince Czartoryski, a main representative of legal nationalism, claimed that the introduction of 'foreign laws [...] and with them – of foreign customs and sentiments' would lead the Polish nation to 'lose its originality' and, along with that 'its good qualities', and that the reception of foreign legal transfers leads to the acquisition of 'foreign failings' with them.[205]

5.3 *The Influence of Private Law upon Extra-Juridical Ideology*

Whereas undoubtedly ideology influences private law (Section 5.2), there is also a reverse influence, in which private law impacts the ideological hegemonies in society. This is because private law benefits from a certain surplus of legitimacy and authority, stemming either from its democratic pedigree ('this is what we all agreed in a democratic procedure, so this is how things ought to be') or – in the case of private law, even more likely – from a historical and traditional pedigree ('this has always been so, already the Romans had this rule, so this is how things ought to be'). Private law, being derived from a long historical tradition, enjoys what Weber would call 'traditional authority.'[206]

In this sense, private law is generally conducive to (neo)conservative and (neo)liberal ideological projects, as its traditional core – derived from Roman law and the 19th century Grand Codifications – is conservative and liberal, rather than progressive, socialist or democratic. The traditional (initially unlimited) authority of the *pater familias* can justify conservative ideological projects based on a strong legal position of fathers and husbands. The

204 Michał GAŁĘDEK, Anna KLIMASZEWSKA: *A Controversial Transplant? Debate over the Adaptation of the Napoleonic Code on the Polish Territories in the Early 19th Century*, Journal of Civil Law Studies, 11 (2018)/2, 269–298.

205 All quotes after Michał GAŁĘDEK: *Dreams of 'Moving from the Napoleonic Code to the New Era of the Judiciary' on the Eve of Establishment of the Kingdom of Poland (1814–1815)*, Rechtskultur 8 (2019), 80.

206 Max WEBER: *The Three Types of Legitimate Rule*, Hans GERTH (trans.), Berkeley Publications in Society and Institutions 4 (1958)/1, 1–11.

Roman system of contracts, and especially the abstract *stipulatio*, can be used to promote liberal ideological projects, emphasising the formal 'freedom of contract' and shunning away from state intervention to correct 'free market' injustice. Finally, the Roman institution of property has been frequently used to justify projects of strengthening private property and doing away with social limitations thereof.[207] All this is possible because, as Paulina Święcicka notes

> Roman law (...) was for centuries, and may still be, the object of a certain monumentalization or sublimation (...) In general, the sublimation of the past (...) means, aside from a sense of nostalgia giving to particular elements from the past an unreal dimension – a sort of mythologization – in order to describe both the past and the present world. Through such sublimation (...) legal historians and lawyers, via their narratives, found themselves engaging in monumentalizing Roman law. As a result, today this law is considered to be the embodiment of eternal legal wisdom, the ideal of equitable law, the cornerstone of the European legal tradition, and/or the remedy for a weak European legal order insofar as it is seen as the basis for the creation of *a ius commune europaeum*, a new common legal pan-European system.[208]

In fact, Roman law can also be used to justify less controversial ideological projects, such as Poland's European character,[209] where Roman-law legal identity replaces the missing link of national legal identity, whereby this particular 'iusromano-gigantomania' is part of a broader ideological post-transformational policy pursued by lawyers for lawyers as well as for the rest of the society.[210]

However, also the opposite can be true, for instance with regard to Western European consumer law or family law, which can be used as arguments in favour of introducing certain ideologically progressive solutions in Central

207 See e.g. Witold WOŁODKIEWICZ: *Czy święta własność prywatna w prawie rzymskim?* [Did Roman law provide for sacred private property?] Palestra 60 (2015)/3–4, 223–227.

208 Paulina ŚWIĘCICKA: *From Sublimation to Naturalization: Constructing Ideological Hegemony on the Shoulders of Roman Jurists*, in MAŃKO, CERCEL, SULIKOWSKI (eds): *Law and Critique in Central Europe*, 180–182. Footnotes omitted.

209 *Ibidem*, 195–196. For a characteristic example see Bronisław SITEK: *Roma communis nostra patria est (D. 50.1.33), czy może Europa communis nostra patria est?*, Studia Prawnoustrojowe 12 (2010), 219–229.

210 ŚWIĘCICKA: *From Sublimation*, 202.

Europe. On a more general note, it can be said that comparative law can provide materials which can serve to promote alternative ideological projects, and question arguments based on uniqueness and identity.[211]

In sum, we can say that private law participates in law's legitimising function:[212] private law, through its ideological content (its *legal ideology*, which I discuss below, in Section 5.4) participates in granting legitimacy to the concrete socio-economic order which is expressed in the *corpus* of private law of a given time and place.

5.4 *Private Law as Ideology, or the (Internal) 'Legal Ideology' of Private Law*

Lawyers tend to perceive law from the internal point of view,[213] and if we consider law as a form of ideology (i.e. of *legal ideology*), it becomes obvious that Althusser's famous dictum that who is in ideology thinks he is not in ideology,[214] is *par excellence* applicable to lawyers. However, private law is not only about ordering society (dividing property and profit, organising family life), and about impacting the ideological convictions of society (private law as an ideological apparatus in Althusser's sense),[215] but it is also *itself an ideology*. To grasp this facet of private law's ontology it seems useful to resort to conceptual metaphor theory.[216] The latter is based on the assumption that human cognition occurs through conceptual metaphors, whereby more complex phenomena are understood by resorting to simpler ones. The operation of metaphor is through the pairing of source domains (simple phenomena) with target domains (complex phenomena). For instance, in the conceptual metaphor LIFE IS A JOURNEY, the complex reality of LIFE is conceptualised (and thereby, explained and interpreted) by resorting to the simpler reality

211 *Cf.* Alexandra MERCESCU: *What Kind of Critique for Central and Eastern European Legal Studies? Comparison as One of the Answers*, Folia Iuridica 89 (2019), 56–57.

212 *Cf.* HUNT: *Ideology of Law*, 25, who emphasises that law's ideological role is that of legitimising the given *status quo*.

213 KOZAK: *Myślenie analityczne w nauce prawa*, 84.

214 ALTHUSSER: *Ideology and the State Ideological Apparatuses*, 49.

215 *Ibidem.*

216 For a brief introduction into the theory see above all: George LAKOFF, Mark JOHNSON: *Metaphors We Live By* [1980], University of Chicago Press, Chicago-London, 2003 (the seminal classic); Zoltán KÖVECSES: *Metaphor: A Practical Introduction*, 2nd ed., Oxford University Press, Oxford-New York, 2010; Zoltán KÖVECSES, *Extended Conceptual Metaphor Theory*, Cambridge University Press, Cambridge, 2020 (a contemporary systematic exposure).

of A JOURNEY. Conceptual metaphors are very popular in the juridical domain.[217]

But not only law abounds with metaphors, law itself can be said to be a metaphor of social life. This is precisely the sense in which I speak of private law as an ideological project in its own right: private law of any given jurisdiction and historical period can and should be seen not only as a form of social ordering, and not only as a source of influence upon ideological hegemonies in society, but also as a metaphorical narrative aimed at explaining how society functions, how it is structured, in short, a narrative giving sense (meaning) to social life. Law, therefore, is a *metaphor of society*. In this sense, social life is a highly complex and difficult to grasp phenomenon (target domain). It has various dimensions: economic, ethical, social. Private law (the source domain), in contrast, is rather simple – it has only one dimension (the juridical one), which is selective and strives at providing easy answers to difficult questions. Even if the legal provisions are not clear, and even if legal scholars debate about the answer to a given question, there is always a supreme court which can *trancher le litige*, cut through the Gordian knot and make complex things simple, provide answers to unanswerable questions. This is how legal form operates, and private law is a privileged example of this mode of law's functioning.

What needs to be emphasised here is that legal form is not only characterised by abstraction and exchangeability, as pointed out by Pashukanis,[218] but also by its selectiveness: it treats as juridically relevant some facts, whereas as juridically irrelevant others.[219] Hugh Collins emphasised this point with regard to contracts and contract law:

> (…) the contract 'thinks' about the relation between people in a particular way. (…) The contract constructs an image of the human associa-

---

217 For applications of the conceptual metaphor theory in the juridical field, see e.g. Stefan LARSSON: *Metaphors and Norms: Understanding Copyright Law in a Digital Society*, Lund University, Lund, 2012; Alberto VESPAZIANI: *Towards a Hermeneutical Approach to Legal Metaphor*, in Thomas BUSTAMANTE, Oche ONAZI (eds): *Human Rights, Language and Law*, Franz Steiner Verlag, Stuttgart, 2012; Stefan LARSSON: *Conceptions in the Code How Metaphors Explain Legal Challenges in Digital Times*, Oxford University Press, Oxford, 2017; Monika ZALEWSKA: *Cognitive Theory of Metaphor and Jerzy Wróblewski's Concept of Legal Interpretation*, Hybris 39 (2017)/4, 56–73; Sylwia WOJTCZAK, Iwona WITCZAK-PLISIECKA: *Metaphors and Legal Language: A Few Comments on Ordinary, Specialised and Legal Meaning*, Research in Language 17 (2019)/3, 273–295.

218 PASHUKANIS: *Law and Marxism*, 109–133.

219 MAŃKO: *Nauki prawne wobec problemu polityczności*, 42–43.

> tion that reduces its complexity to the elements and trajectories that have significance within the contractual framework. The contract thinks about events, for instance, by examining human actions and words within a narrow time-frame; the prior pattern of the social relation between the parties and their sentiments of trust and loyalty are irrelevant to this construction of knowledge. The contract thinks, for instance, about a promise, whether it was made, what the promisor intended by the commitment, and whether the promise has been kept. This construction of the event ignores most of the context in which the promise was made, how it fitted into a prior relation between the parties, how it affects other people, and how performance of the promise serves the interests and aspirations of the parties. (...) The association marked by a contract consists of isolated or discrete commitments, which (...) tend to displace other normative standards derived from the social context of the contractual relation, including other forms of association such as friendship and status. Contract therefore reduces the complexity of human association, rendering social relations susceptible to management and reconstruction.[220]

What Collins writes about contracts (and their social effects following from contract law) is true, to my mind, to juridical form in general[221] and especially to private law. Private law is selective and reductionist – it programmatically 'ignores most of the context' 'tends to displace other normative standards', and 'reduces the complexity of human association'. Private law 'thinks' about the relation between people in a particular way.

The functioning of private law *qua* ideology takes place in various dimensions. First and foremost, private law-as-ideology interpellates human beings as subjects. After all, the *persona* is not only the foundation of private law, but also private law's most important ideological innovation.[222] The idea that human subjects are interchangeable and equal, just like things (*res*) are, is definitely a legal invention of Roman law.[223] Forgotten during the Middle

220 Hugh COLLINS: *Regulating Contracts*, Oxford University Press, Oxford, 2003, 15–16.

221 MAŃKO: *Legal Form, Ideology and the Political, passim.*

222 Costas DOUZINAS: *The Radical Philosophy of Rights*, Routledge, Abingdon, 2019, 11–86.

223 Yan THOMAS: *The Subject of Right, the Person, Nature: Remarks on the Current Criticism of the Legal Subject*, in Yan THOMAS: *Artifices: Ten Essays on Roman Law in the Present Tense*, Thanos ZARTALOUDIS, Cooper FRANCIS (eds), Chantal SCHÜTZ, Anton SCHÜTZ (trans.), Edinburgh University Press, Edinburgh 2020, 107–143; Gian Giacomo FUSCO, *Notes on the Person and the Anthropological Machine of Law*, in Thanos ZARTALOUDIS

Ages, when human beings are once again differentiated by estate (*Stand, stan*), it returns with great force in the epoch of the Grand Codifications of the 19th century, from the Austrian Civil Code right down to the Swiss Law of Obligations and Swiss Civil Code, ZGB. All these Grand Codifications are characterised by the presence of a uniform, unitary, abstract and interchangeable legal subject – the *persona*. This ideological legacy endures until today, although somewhat weakened by the rise of the notion of the consumer and its counter-party, the trader.[224] Other examples include the features of the person, such as 'free will' 'rationality', recently reconsidered in the notion of the 'average consumer', who is expected to be 'reasonably well-informed and reasonably observant and circumspect'.[225] In the words of Costas Douzinas:

> The distance between legal person and individual takes the form of excess and lack. Excess: the law ascribes to the person a surplus of reason, self-control and calculation. The legal person like the 'economic' or 'rational' man of choice theory is an 'abstraction from real people emphasising one side of human life – the ability to reason and calculate – at the expense of every social circumstance that actually brings individuals to reason and calculate in particular ways' [Alan Norrie]. The 'reasonable man' is such a key figure in law because reason – excessive hyperbolic reason – has been turned into the ultimate mark of humanity.[226]

(ed.): *Law and Philosophical Theory: Critical Intersections*, Rowman and Littlefield International, London, 2018, 81–96.

224 It is true that even in the epoch of the Grand Codifications the law provided for a special type of subject, the merchant (*Kaufmann*), whose legal relations were codified in a separate code – the Code of Commerce (*Handelsgesetzbuch, code de commerce*). Nonetheless, despite the undeniable differences in the merchant's legal subjectivity, all the rules of the general part of civil law remained applicable to him and the dichotomy was relegated to a separate legal act (the Commercial Code) in order not to distort the aesthetic harmony of civil law with its uniform subject. Today, the consumer has made its way into the general part, as is visible, for instance, in the German or Polish Civil Codes.

225 See e.g. Vanessa MAK: *The consumer in European regulatory private law. A functional perspective on responsibility, protection and empowerment*, in Dorota LECZYKIEWICZ, Stephen WEATHERILL (eds): *The Image(s) of the Consumer in EU Law: Legislation, Free Movement and Competition Law*, Hart Publishing, Oxford, 2016, 381–400; Lotte ANEMAET: *The Many Faces of the Average Consumer: Is It Really So Difficult to Assess Whether Two Stripes Are Similar to Three?*, International Review of Intellectual Property and Competition Law 51 (2020), 187–213.

226 DOUZINAS: *Radical Philosophy of Rights*, 44. References omitted.

As is well known, the concept of the 'reasonable man' or 'reasonable person' is a typical concept of the Common Law, but the same approach is also present in Civil Law jurisdictions. Even in Poland, the codification commission for civil law proposed to introduce the concept of 'reasonableness' directly into Polish law,[227] on the clear understanding that 'reasonableness' is a criterion different from ethics or morality, present in the socialist general clause of 'principles of social life'.[228]

The importance of the legal form of private law for the capitalist mode of production is obvious. As Douzinas puts it: 'Capital needs abstractions such as the legal person, the reasonable man and equality before the law in order to have products go to the marketplace and become commodities. (...) The fetishism of commodities is replicated in the fetishism of the legal form.'[229] Indeed, the operation of ideological interpellation within the legal ideology of private law is crucial.[230] According to Alan Hunt:

> Legal discourse transforms both human beings and social entities; for example, corporations become 'legal subjects'. Legal subjects as the bearers of rights and duties are the primary constituents of the 'form of law' (...). The creation of legal subjects involves the recognition of 'the law' as the active 'subject' that calls them into being. It is by transforming the human subject into a legal subject that law influences the way in which participants experience and perceive their relations with others. Thus, legal ideology provides a constituent of what Althusser called the 'lived relation' of human actors (...).[231]

Legal ideology, therefore, is not only an ideology 'in itself,' but also, through ideological interpellation, transforms the way in which human beings perceive themselves. This has, obviously, consequences also beyond the sphere of subjectivity: private law not only interpellates human individuals as legal subjects, as 'persons', but it also entangles them in various legal relationships. As Cosmin Cercel puts it:

---

227 See e.g. Anna PIASKOWY: *Klauzule generalne w projekcie nowego kodeksu cywilnego* [General clauses in the draft of the new Polish Civil Code], Transformacje Prawa Prywatnego 3 (2012), 49–67.

228 *Ibidem,* 52.

229 DOUZINAS: *Radical Philosophy of Rights,* 123.

230 Cosmin CERCEL: *Towards a Jurisprudence of State Communism: Law and the Failure of Revolution,* Routledge, Abingdon-New York, 2018, 91.

231 HUNT: *Ideology of Law,* 15.

> Enmeshed in the ideological veil of the positive legal framework and legal doctrines lies a social reality which is distinct from others and takes the form of the *legal relationship* (...). The legal relationship is the nexus between the normative dimension of law and the material forces within society, it is the specific social relation which renders legal alienation operative and supports the overall social order as an order founded on law (...).[232]

Among the legal relationships constituted by private law, among the ideologically most fundamental ones is the relationship of property. Private law, effectively, reifies and naturalises private property, which it elevates to one of its foundations, conflating, however, fundamentally different realities of consumption (satisfaction of actual needs) and exercising economic power. As Weitzer explains:

> The bourgeois (especially Continental) conception of property involves no more than the relationship between a person (*persona*) and a tangible thing (*res*). The right to property (the Roman *dominium*) entails the right to use and consume things as one desires. But bourgeois law collapses fundamentally different kinds of property into an undifferentiated *res* – not distinguishing (...) between 'property for use' (personal consumption) and 'property for power' (control of the means of production). (...) The title to dispose of material objects is, under capitalist production arrangements, inherently converted into a title to profit, power, and domination over the property*less* laborer (...).[233]

Even socialist codifications of law, despite providing for the privileged position of state property, did not manage to get rid of the concept of property altogether, just like they did not manage to get rid of the concept of the subject. This does not mean that constructing a legal system without the concept of property and subjectivity is not possible,[234] but merely shows how the legal ideology of the Soviet civil law was influenced by ideological survivals of the pre-revolutionary period.

232 CERCEL: *Towards a Jurisprudence of State Communism*, 90.

233 WEITZER: *Law and Legal Ideology*, 144.

234 *Cf.* David MARRANI: *Althusser in Avatar: Comparative Law as a Science and the Haunting of the Subject*, in Laurent DE SUTTER (ed.): *Althusser and Law*, Routledge, Abington, 2013, 95–110.

The law of obligations, in turn, reifies 'consent' as the foundation of the contractual obligation,[235] 'fault' as the basis of liability in tort, propagating an ideology of individual responsility, quite concomitant with such extra-juridical ideologies as liberalism, conservatism and, most recently, neoliberalism. Perhaps the single area of private law whose *per se* ideological character does not raise any reasonable controversy is family law.[236] It is also the single area of private law which, looking back to Roman times, has been subject to the most far-reaching modifications, in comparison to the law of obligations, or even property law or the law of succession. The ideological commitments of such institutions as *patria potestas* and *manus mariti*, or the notion of *filii naturales*, right down to the current introduction of gay marriage in most European legal systems are *per se* ideological, in that they convey a certain vision of normality. As Fran Olsen affirms:

> Family law both reflects and helps create an ideology of the family – a structure of images and understandings of family life. This ideology serves to deny and disguise the ways that families illegitimately dominate people and fail to serve human wants. Embedded within the ideology of the family are notions of (1) the kinds of roles that individual members should serve within the family and what they should get out of these roles, (2) the kinds of bonds that hold families together, (3) the actual and the proper role of families in society, and (4) what the state or law can and should do to encourage desirable family life.[237]

Contrary to what most lawyers would normally be prepared to think, company law is also highly ideological, especially in making us believe that companies are subjects, that they have an independent existence, their own property and – even! – their own personality rights.[238] In short, one can only agree with Weitzer when he affirms that

235 Peter GABEL, Jay FEINMAN: *Contract Law as Ideology*, in David KAIRYS (ed.): *The Politics of Law: A Progressive Critique*, 3rd ed., Basic Books, New York, 1998, 497–510. *Cf.* Richard AUSTEN-BAKER, Qi ZHOU: *Contract in Context*, Routledge, London, 2014, Chapter 4: *The ideological context of contract.*

236 Fran OLSEN: *The Politics of Family Law*, Law & Inequality: A Journal of Theory and Practice 2 (1984)/1, 1–19.

237 *Ibidem*, 3.

238 See e.g. Agnieszka KUBIAK-CYRUL: *Dobra osobiste osób prawnych* [Personality rights of legal persons], Wolters Kluwer, Warsaw, 2005.

> the abstract and formal texture of the legal rights of property and contract and of the equality and freedom of individuals before the law constitutes a juridical veneer which occludes the pervasive substantive inequality and domination that structure the potential realization of these legal rights.[239]

Whereas the problem of abstractness and formalism is typical for the legal form in its entirety, private law, on account of the fact that it regulates the fundamental economic relationships of ownership and exchange, is a particularly poignant case of legal ideology.

5.5 *Private Law and Intra-Juridical Ideologies*

In Section 4.1. I identified, apart from extra-juridical ideologies (such as liberalism, socialism, etc.) and legal ideology (the ideology of law), also intra-juridical ideologies, i.e. the ideologies of jurists as a social group (e.g. positivism, normativism, juriscentrism School of Free Law, economic analysis of law,[240] etc.). These intra-juridical ideologies serve, above all, to legitimise the juridical in society. Each of these ideologies takes a different legitimising strategy. Positivism and normativism externalise legitimacy, legitimising the juridical through an external reference to the 'law maker,' or the 'sovereign.' Lawyers are legitimate, because they 'apply the law,' which is legitimised by coming from a legitimate source. In a democratic regime, this will mean democratic legitimacy: lawyers are legitimate in what they do, because they simply apply the rules that have been democratically established. However, this legitimising narrative is not the typical one for private law. This is partly due to the practical circumstance that traditionally, private law has been perceived as 'technical' and 'apolitical' and not open to a politically charged debate. Of course, this is not always the case and provisions, for instance, of a Civil Code can also be subject to a democratic debate.[241] However, politicians still tend to perceive private law as 'technical,' and private lawyers tend to look for other forms of legitimacy for their power. These include, especially, the *ideology of legal traditionalism*, which legitimises existing solutions by their historical pedigree. The importance of this ideology cannot be underestimated, as

239 WEITZER: *Law and Legal Ideology*, 144–145.

240 *Cf.* C. Edwin BAKER: *The Ideology of the Economic Analysis of Law*, Philosophy and Public Affairs 5 (1975), 3–48.

241 HESSELINK, *European Contract Law*, 323–348; Martijn W. HESSELINK, *The Ideal of Codification and the Dynamics of Europeanisation: the Dutch Experience*, European Law Journal 12 (2006)/3, 279–305.

legal tradition has been a crucial legitimsing factor from the very origins of the *ius*. A philosophically sophisticated version of this ideology is Artur Kozak's juriscentrism,[242] whereby lawyers are necessary to other members of society because they possess certain resources (knowledge, methodology) which help to solve conflicts which, to the members of society themselves, would otherwise seem to be irresolvible. Hence lawyers' claims to power in society cannot be based on the legal sub-world's claim to cognitive, ethical or any other superiority, but may only be made by resorting to the idea metaphorically captured in Teubner's anecdote about the khadi's 12th camel.[243] According to this narrative, lawyers are capable of solving other people's disputes because they filter them through their own categories and by resorting to law's purely formal values. The solutions given by lawyers to economic or political disputes are cognitively incomprehensible to individuals inhabiting other sub-worlds; at the same time, however, they are not the product of an individual lawyer's whims, but of the legal sub-world as such, with its specific legal culture, legal tradition and legal methodology.

Yet another strategy adopted especially with regard to private law is the *ideology of legal economism*, present in the Economic Analysis of Law school.[244] This intra-juridical ideology enters into a symbiotic relationship with the extra-juridical ideology of neoliberalism, claiming that the values important to society are not so much social justice, equality and true freedom (from alienation), but rather efficiency, which can be achieved through the 'free market' and through legal institutions which uphold the market, such as especially property, contract and torts. Ideologists of economic analysis of law claim that private law is legitimate, because it upholds market efficiency. Of course, this intra-juridical ideology can also lead to the deligitimisation of those private law institutions which its proponents see as 'inefficient'.

Finally, in peripheral societies, private lawyers may build their claims to legitimacy on *ideology of modernisation through law*.[245] This specific ideology, which could develop only in societies which perceive themselves as 'backward,' is based on the belief that backwardness can be overcome through law. In other words, modernisation through law assumes that it is up to lawyers – including private lawyers – to change society (from peripherality to

242 For details: MAŃKO: *Artur Kozak's Juriscentrist Concept of Law*, 334–375.

243 Gunther TEUBNER: *Alienating Justice: On the Surplus Value of the Twelfth Camel*, in David NELKEN, Jiří PŘIBÁŇ (eds): *Consequences of Legal Autopoiesis*, Aldershot, Dartmouth, 2001, 21–44.

244 BAKER: *Ideology of the Economic Analysis of Law*, 3–48.

245 GAŁĘDEK: *Modernisation, National Identity*, 3.

centrality, from backwardness to 'modernity') by enacting and applying legal rules.[246] The ideology of modernisation through law rests on the assumption that backwardness of a peripheral society can be cured by the enactment of codes, in the spirit of 'normative optimism' assuming that legal rules will 'by themselves' change the economic and social relationships.

The intra-juridical ideologies, professed by jurists, are a very important potential object of historical research. Historians of (private) law could, for instance, pay special attention to the intra-juridical ideologies, either explicitly formulate or implicitly present in the work of drafters, judges and legal scholars. References to legal tradition (especially Roman law) in the justification of certain rules, claim to economic efficiency of given legal institutions, or broader claims to the possibilities of modernisation of society through law will be interesting reflections of the intra-juridical ideologies of the time.

6 Conclusions: Towards an Ideological History of Private Law

The analyses made in this chapter were aimed at fostering a strong collaboration between history of private law, on the one hand, and critical legal theory, on the other. There is certainly room for more dialogue between legal history and legal theory, and it seems that concepts developed within critical legal theory could be a source of inspiration for the formulation of research questions within the domain of the history of (private) law. As it was pointed out in Sections 2 and 3, one of the chief possible inputs of critical legal theory for history of private law could be the concept of ideology and its relations to law.

The questions that can be asked in this context are manyfold. Firstly, the legal historian can pose the question of the *ideological inspiration* of concrete private law institutions that were introduced in a given period in a given legal system. Secondly, the legal historian can take a step back and treat private law as such as a *manifestation of ideology*. This is especially true with nationalist ideology that had emerged in the 19th century, and lead to the creation of 'national' codifications of private law, on the assumption that one can imagine an 'Italian' 'German' or 'Polish' private law, rather than private law *as such*. The same goes for liberal and, today, neoliberal ideology, which is expressed through modern private law. Finally, the legal historian can venture into social

246 Manuel GUȚAN: *The Legal Transplant and the Building of the Romanian Legal Identity in the Second Half of the 19th Century and the Beginning of the 20th century*, Romanian Journal of Comparative Law, 8 (2017)/1, 64.

history and enquire about the *impact of private law upon ideology*, and attempt to trace the influence of private law (its norms, doctrine and case-law), and even its individual institutions, as well as even individual rules or court rulings upon ideological hegemony. How did private law, in a given period, impact upon social consciousness? How did it contribute to the feeling of what is normal and acceptable? Politically and ideologically sensitive areas, such as family law (think of divorce or extra-marital children) or law of persons (think of the legal status of the *nasciturus*), enforced by the judicial system, have a direct impact upon the life of millions of 'users' of private law. It would be fascinating if legal historians could uncover this influence in the rich source materials giving evidence to societal culture at a given time and place, such as press articles, novels, films or songs. It is precisely in such non-disciplinary approach, to follow Alexandra Mercescu's plea, that all forms of enquiry unite in order to study a given social phenomenon. In this vein, the historian of private law could focus not only on the study of codes, journals and law reports but also embark upon a broadened research agenda, combining cultural studies, legal anthropology, law and literature, to name but a few forms of inspiration that can be drawn from the rich methodological palette of contemporary humanities.

However, given the complexity of the phenomenon, I consider it useful to sum up the possible forms of 'operationalisation' – by historians of private law – of critical legal theory, and specifically the critique of ideology within the juridical, in the form of the following synthetic conclusions which form an outline of a 'protocol' for historical research of ideology in private law.

I consider that the first step for an ideological analysis of the history of private law should be to *identify the three modalities of ideology that are at stake*: (1) the extra-juridical ideologies (such as conservatism, liberalism, nationalism, socialism, neoliberalism, modernisation); (2) the intra-juridical ideologies (such as positivism, normativism, jusnaturalism, juriscentrism, legal traditionalism, legal modernism); and (3) the legal ideology (ideology expressed by the law at a given time and place).

Whereas extra-juridical ideologies are well described by political scientists and historians of political ideas, and intra-juridical ideologies are the object of research of historians of legal ideas, legal theorists and philosophers of law, *legal ideology* is the most challenging one to grasp. This is because legal ideology is precisely *hidden behind the screen of neutral and reified legal institutions*. Legal institutions such as legal personality, *pacta sunt servanda*, fault-based liability for delict, or inheritance by family members are so natural, neutralised that it is difficult to decipher the ideological content behind them. But they all correspond to a certain normalised vision of social reality which, ultimately is in itself a certain ideological construct. The task of the ideological critique of private law is precisely to disentangle these ideological assumptions from among the legal rules, principles and precedents that make up the fabric of the juridical.

No type of ideology – extra-juridical, intra-juridical or legal – is uniform, monolithic (homogenous), or monopolistic. To the contrary, the borders of ideologies are blurred; ideologies have cores and penumbra; ideologies overlap; ideologies can even merge and give birth to hybrid ideologies. As Alan Hunt points out, 'an ideology is not a unitary entity. It draws its power from its ability to connect and combine diverse mental elements (concepts, ideas, etc.) into combinations that influence and structure the perception and cognition of social agents.'[247] Nationalism and conservatism tend to overlap, but nationalism can also overlap or merge with socialism, communism and liberalism. The ideology of modernisation can have socialist, communist, but also liberal or even conservative overtones. Private law can express, within its legal ideology, contradictory narratives: some rules can be liberal (e.g. in general contract law) others can be conservative (e.g. in family law), yet others progressive (e.g. in tort law) or even social democratic (e.g. in consumer law). What is more, the rules can be subject to different ideological interpretations, for instance a ruled conceived of under the influence of conservative ideology could be reinterpreted by the doctrine and judiciary in an opposite direction. Ideologies not only overlap, but also struggle for hegemony, and law – conceived of as legislation, scholarship and adjudication – is but one of the terrains of their struggle. The task of the historian of private law working on an ideological analysis is not made any easier by the gap between official declarations, deeply held (yet concealed) beliefs and actual actions of legislators, judges and legal academics.

The second step is to *identify the ideological intelligentsias* operating the three ideologies. As a rule of thumb, one can expect that the operators of the extra-juridical ideologies are public intellectuals, academics and other public figures of the given period. The intra-juridical ideology is *ex definitione* operated by jurists, especially legal theorists. The legal ideology, present *in nuce* in legal provisions, unfolds in the works of judges and legal academics ('dogmaticians') who develop it in their judgments and scholarly writings.

In analysing the role of ideological intelligentsias and their impact upon jurists, legal historians should pay attention to two important caveats: firstly, that ideological discourse is, as a rule, presented as non-ideological given that

247 HUNT: *Ideology of Law*, 16

its ideological nature is by definition concealed (Althusser); secondly, that subjects (jurists, intellectuals) may not be aware of being within ideology, they may be unconscious of that fact; thirdly, that today the mode of functioning of ideology is usually cynical, in the sense that the subject is fully aware that the ideology is 'false', nonetheless he continues to act in a way as if the ideology were true (Žižek). This is linked to the fact that ideologies are not so much important as regards what we believe, but are crucial in the way they structure the way we act. Hence, what is important for the legal historian of private law ideology is not so much what the historical subjects (draftsmen, judges, academic, legislators) actually believed but what they wrote and said and, even more importantly, what they actually did (in the proposed Codes, legal treatises, judicial decisions). Ideology is not subjective, but objective. It is not a form of false consciousness, but a structure determining social behaviour.

A third step is to analyse the *ideological dynamics of private law* in a given period. This will entail taking into account all three ideologies, and all possible vectors of influence. Hence, the influence of extra-juridical ideologies upon private law, and of private law upon extra-juridical ideologies. The mutual influence of private law and intra-juridical ideologies, such as normativism, legal traditionalism or legal modernism. Finally, the changing shape of legal ideology of private law under the influence of both extra-juridical and intra-juridical ideologies hegemonic in a given period.

The link between the ideology and its purported beneficiaries should never be taken for granted (Kennedy). Historians of private law should be fully aware that what ideological intelligentsias or jurists claim need not be actually true. Rules officially presented as benefiting buyers may in fact benefit banks. Rules meant or declared to facilitate trade may in fact make it more difficult. The gaps between the stated purposes, the actual intent of the legislators and the actual effect of the rules in practice must be attentively studied, as they are the space in which the impact of ideology upon private law is most crucial, yet most difficult to grasp.

Ideology and the political (understood as the dimension of structural societal conflict) are closely interlinked, yet distinct from each other. Ideological struggle in the superstructure, and struggles for economic power, social prestige, recognition and justice in actual social life are closely interlinked. Yet, following Kennedy's caveat we must not take for granted the symmetry between the two, as ideological intelligentsias – those who operate ideologies – may have different interests from the beneficiaries of ideologies. And the beneficiaries may be heterogeneous groups with conflicting interests themselves. And finally, the real outcome of the application of legal provisions or judicial decisions may be different from what legislators and judges expected.

The concept of 'instrumentalisation of law', used by some legal historians and some legal theorists is redundant if we adopt the views on ideology put forward by critical legal theorists (such as Kennedy) and critical theorists, such Althusser or Žižek. This is because law is *always already* instrumentalised by ideology. Law, just like any other sphere of social activity cannot escape ideology. It is impossible to imagine a law that is not instrumentalised by some ideology, that does not serve any values, that has no goal external to it. When lawyers speak of instrumental law, they assume that law may be non-instrumentalised, but in that case it will anyway serve some intra-juridical ideology, it will express some legal ideology (such as liberalism or conservatism or socialism).

Combining ideology critique with the history of private law is certainly a challenging task, requiring the application of critical legal tools by legal historians, and the use of historical findings by critical legal theorists in developing their theory. The outcome – an ideological history of private law – can definitely tell us much more about the social bond symbolised by *ius privatum* than the mere study of legislation, case-law and scholarly writings as manifestations of the positive law of a given epoch and place. Even if, as Althusser famously claimed, 'ideology has no history,'[248] the juridical definitely has one. The historical epiphany of ideology can, therefore, be studied precisely by legal historians, revealing the contradictions of legal development.[249] Beyond doubt, the history of private law is one of the most fertile areas for such research.

248 ALTHUSSER: *Ideology and State Ideological Apparatuses*, 108.

249 *Cf.* HUNT: *Ideology of Law*, 29.

CHAPTER 2

The Ideology of the Polish Private Law during the Interwar Period

Debates on the Assumptions of Codification

1 General Remarks

In the history of Polish law, the 20th century was undoubtedly an exceptionally turbulent period with rapid political and cultural changes. Nonetheless, even against this background, the interwar period stands apart, primarily due to the peculiarity of the situation at its onset, i.e. the reacquisition of independence after more than a century of non-existence as a legal and political entity, with the country partitioned among its neighbours. In such circumstances, the work on creating a national legal system had to be done from the ground up. The result was a set of highly specific background conditions in which the strokes of the new legal order were being drawn. At the onset – in the first years of independence – the causes, reasons and impulses or stimuli affecting the reception of the normative solutions all had a very special meaning. The preceding lapse, more than a century long, of Polish statehood confronted the nation's legal elite with almost one-of-a-kind challenges, determining also the goals and methods for their achievement.

The context in which the works on the nation's legal system were underway also evolved over the twenty-year period. First of all, during the first years of building of a democratic state, the reality of the landscape emerging in the aftermath of World War I was not only different from the succeeding context of the thirties, the perceptions and perspectives also distinguished the drafters in both halves of the interbellum. Consequently, different goals were set and expressed in the day of the Codification Commission of 1919 and on the even of World War II. This holds equally true for the ideological goals that could be classified as the long range, with a broader temporal and horizontal perspective, as well as goals corresponding to the political expedients of the moment, or those whose authors were focusing more on the technical aspects with a view to improving the effectiveness of the operation of the law without loading it with an ideological context.

Concentrating our attention on the first-mentioned group, i.e. the ideological goals, whose formulation was always linked to the pursuit of broader

 | DOI:10.1163/9789004730021_004

visions and concepts, we already need to note right here that those were usually inspired by and tightly interwoven with the faith that the law is capable of serving as a successful tool for social engineering and a driver of change in a determined direction prompted by an ideology or by axiological assumptions. Perhaps even – and that would be typical of legal elites – the law's agency was overestimated. However, even when that estimation happened to be more realistic, the process of creation of law was founded on certain ideological underpinnings, as well as values held and views taken of the reality of the situation. All these factors were evolving dynamically in the interwar period. Hence, while attempting to offer a synthetic encapsulation of the period, one has to pay attention to the changing context and heterogeneous nature of the two decades leading up to the outbreak of World War II.

2 Separating Unification from Codification

With the end of World War I, a Polish state rose back to independence – the symbolic date is 11 November 1918. That gave the impulse to Polish legal elites to initiate the debate on the implementation of the closest legislative tasks on hand. Those elites were confronted with the fundamental conundrum of the reborn Polish state's make-up comprising different legal spheres. Different legal orders were inherited from the Prussian state, from the Austro-Hungarian monarchy and the Russian Empire with Congress Poland subsumed within the latter. As far back as late 18th century, those areas lost their legal links, developing differently within foreign state organisms.

Following the re-unification of Polish territories and re-emergence of a sovereign nation-state, such a state of affairs could not be allowed to persist. The need for unification amounted to a pressing problem and no small challenge. In the motion tabled by a group of members of Parliament on 1 April 1919 to establish the Codification Commission, we read:

> The four legal systems imposed on the Polish population by foreign states have carved profound dents in the unity of the Polish nation, imposed on her foreign ordinances and legal prescripts and created throughout more of a hundred years of their rule over the various portions of the former Polish State a deleterious legal heterogeneity within both public and private law. The united Polish State must eliminate this

> legal heterogeneity the most expeditiously and aspire to uniformity of legal norms in all Polish territories.[1]

'Poland has found herself in an exceptional position,' concluded in 1919 Wacław Makowski, an eminent scholar of criminal law and government representative.[2] In his view, the exceptionality of the situation was the result of distorted 'legal physiognomy'. In what he deemed a 'civilized' state, such physiognomy ought to be the 'product of the natural development of its legislative life commenced at a time when the original customs were taking shape,' such customs 'becoming enriched with each [passing] day with the new creative work of the present generations and legislative institutions.' By contrast, in Polish circumstances 'the proper, normal legislative creativity was interrupted for all of Poland's territory already upon the first Partition,' i.e. in 1772.[3] Since then 'vast areas and diverse questions stand in which Polish thought had for 100 years and then some not been able to say anything, and Polish life had been wrought into a sphere of foreign interests and foreign legal creation.'[4] In effect, as observed by the Codification Commission's first president, Franciszek Ksawery Fierich, the new Polish state inherited from the partitioning states a 'different culture, different economic circumstances in the various partitions, [and] moreover a different sense of law.'[5]

The pressing task of the moment was to commence immediate unification in the practical sense, applied to the requirements of everyday existence, which could not wait until the learned lawyers find the best solutions to com-

1 *Wniosek nagły posła Zygmunta Marka i tow. w sprawie powołania do życia komisji dla stworzenia jednolitego prawodawstwa w Państwie Polskim* [An urgent motion by deputy Zygmunt Marek and companions concerning the establishment of a commission to create a uniformity of legislation in the Polish State], Druki Sejmu Ustawodawczego Rzeczypospolitej Polskiej [Records of the Legislative Sejm of the Republic of Poland], record no. 298. The main signatory, Zygmunt Marek, was a practising lawyer from Galicia (i.e. the Austrian Partition) and a socialist deputy to the Legislative Sejm.

2 In 1917, Wacław Makowski, a professor of the University of Warsaw, was appointed the Deputy Director of the Department of Justice of the Interim Council of State; early in 1918 he even led the Ministry of Justice.

3 Makowski, however, stipulated the caveat that while 'partial independent legislative works were conducted, undertaken up to 1830,' first in the Duchy of Warsaw and then in the constitutional Kingdom of Poland, but their scope covered 'only one part of the state and only a fraction of legal affairs.' Wacław Makowski: *W sprawie ujednostajnienia ustawodawstwa* [Concerning the harmonization of legislation], GSW 2–3 (1919), 14–15.

4 *Ibidem*, 15.

5 Franciszek K. Fierich: *Rzut oka na najważniejsze zadania prac kodyfikacyjnych* [A glance at the most important tasks of the codification works], KPCiK 2 (1919)/1–4, 456.

plex legal dilemmas. From the perspective of a certain time, near the end of the thirties, Stanisław Bukowiecki, Poland's first justice minister (he served in that capacity until 1918) and subsequently the vice-president of the Codification Commission, took it upon himself to explain the situation: 'not the moments of theory but the moment of the state's great need was reckoned with, and to satisfy that need codes must come into being.'[6] The fruition of the codification idea was to satisfy the need of reunification following the Partitions. 'In a state made up of several jurisdictions governed by laws of foreign origin, the [primary need of the state] is to create a universal law encompassing all topics and thus being the matter of codes.'[7] The dream was to create an opus reflecting the 'national spirit' common to all Poles regardless of which part of the country they lived in and thus corresponding to the specific characteristics of Polish society as a whole and its needs. The codification was intended to constitute a platform on which to unify and bond the nation and at once provide a 'starting point, a springboard, for the future evolution' of Polish life and with it Polish law, and thus constitute an important instrument of modernization.[8]

However, the common opinion was that before one could set out in pursuit of the goals of codification, a legal unification transacted on provisional terms at the earliest possible opportunity was necessary. Both the government and parliament alike with the lawyerly elites were in agreement on this point of the agenda. Immediately upon the restoration of independence, the belief was that this would be a problem to be solved within the closest coming months, with the conviction that the deleterious legal parochialism was not sustainable any longer. For that reason, as observed, among others, by Franciszek Bossowski,[9] the tasks placed before the Polish legislature had to be divided among those of 'lesser and greater urgency.'[10] That meant separating the transitional reforms pending unification from the long-term

6 Stanisław BUKOWIECKI: *Założenia podstawowe kodyfikacji prawa w Polsce* [Basic foundations of the codification of law in Poland], Przegląd Notarialny 1 (1948)/4, 283.

7 Bukowiecki went on to add: 'The weight placed by the Government and the Sejm on the tasks of the Codification Commission is reflected by its position in the hierarchy of state authorities, its autonomy, and its organization in general.' *Ibidem*, 284.

8 *Ibidem*.

9 A professor of Roman and civil law, Franciszek Bossowski obtained his doctorate from Jagiellonian University in Cracow in the years preceding World War I. During the interwar period, on the other hand, he was linked to the University of Vilnius, where he served as the dean of the Department of Law and Social Sciences.

10 Franciszek BOSSOWSKI: *O naszych najbliższych zadaniach ustawodawczych* [About our legislative tasks at hand], KPCiK 2 (1919)/1–4, 119.

codification works.[11] Already in early 1919 did Wacław Makowski, a prominent official within the Ministry of Justice, distinguish 'two departments' of legal works – a practical and a theoretical one. He associated the former with the topic of legislative unification in Poland and the latter with the eventual codification.[12]

3 The Inadequacy of the Partitioning Powers' Codes

In code matters, especially those of civil law, the need for immediate unification could lead to thoughts of extending the application of one of the codes left behind by the partitioning powers onto the whole country. For that to happen, however, the prerequisite was to amend some of the provisions, especially those completely conflicting with the then-newly forming basic assumptions on which the expected Polish civil code would be founded. That was where the problem emerged. It was diagnosed by Stanisław Car,[13] who concluded that, with regard to both substantive and procedural civil law:

> there [was] a great diversity flowing not only from the source that each partition [was] governed by a civil code of different original but also for the reason that those codes [had] originated in different, often long-separated eras, as a result of which they [were] permeated each with the spirit of a different time.[14]

This meant that replacing one code with another would have triggered too great a shock for the inhabitants of regions accustomed to a different legal environment.

Moreover, the French and Austrian Civil Code were regarded as being too anachronistic, having come to life amid the realities of a long-bygone era,

11 *Cf.* Leonard GÓRNICKI: *Prawo cywilne w pracach Komisji Kodyfikacyjnej Rzeczypospolitej Polskiej w latach 1919–1939* [Civil law in the works of the Codification Commission of the Republic of Poland in 1919–1939], Kolonia Limited, Wrocław, 2000, 75.

12 MAKOWSKI: *W sprawie ujednostajnienia*, 13–14.

13 Stanisław Car, legal practitioner from Warsaw, senior civil servant in the Department of Justice (Civil Law Commission), and, since 1918, Head of the Civil Chancellery of the Chief of State.

14 Stanisław CAR: *Pilne zadania prawnictwa* [The urgent tasks before the lawyerdom], Orgerlbranda Synowie, Warsaw, 1918, 9; Stanisław GRODZISKI: *Komisja Kodyfikacyjna Rzeczypospolitej Polskiej* [The Codification Commission of the Republic of Poland], CPH 33 (1991)/1, 47.

founded on assumptions that were out of touch with the challenges of the 20th century. Car viewed the Code of Napoleon, applicable in the central part of Poland, i.e. the former Congress Kingdom of Poland, as a work 'founded upon the principles of rationalism, characteristic of the turn of the 18th century, as well as the liberal and unfettered freedom of contract'. In his view the Napoleonic instrument represented an obsolescent extreme liberal concept in which: 'the state's intervention in the sphere of private-law relationships [was] completely excluded.' He formed a similar assessment of the Austrian Civil Code applicable in Galicia – 'of very ancient origin (the year 1811), reflecting a world view shaped under the banner of the law of nature'.[15] Hence, not only Car but also other prominent lawyers and jurists, such as Władysław Jaworski, followed in his footsteps by Ignacy Koschembahr-Łyskowski, concluded: 'Were we to follow the opinion, intimated by some lawyers, that suffice to modify and adapt to Polish needs one of the prominent civil codes, we would create (...) a code that would be anachronistic since the inception.'[16]

The German Code, applicable in the North-West of the country, appeared to be a favourable exception. Nonetheless, the lawyers speaking in the debate were rather sparing in their praises. While Car described it as a modern code 'of entirely new origin', constituting a 'reflection of the social currents [also close to Polish elites] under the influence of which modern Germany took shape and flourished,' and profoundly well-thought as a 'synthesis of the philosophical thought of the German lawyerdom', at once, however, he noted that it reflected the 'spirit of the German nation', polarly distant from the customs and needs of the Poles.[17] Thus, regardless of the balance of their own advantages and disadvantages, each of the partitioning powers' individual codes was burdened with the same 'common negative trait of not being a native creation and failing to account for the individual characteristics of the Polish nation.' In effect, Car summarized: 'none of those codes has sufficient adaptable strength to be fit for being extended onto the whole territory of a unified Poland and phasing out the remaining codes.'[18]

For comparison's sake, it will be expedient to note that he reached different conclusions in criminal law. He believed that 'the change of the criminal code does not evoke so great a disturbance in the legal order of a country as does

15 CAR: *Pilne zadania*, 9–10.

16 Władysław L. JAWORSKI: *Nowożytny Kodeks Cywilny* [A modern civil code], Czasopismo Prawnicze i Ekonomiczne 20 (1922)/3–6, 1–2.

17 CAR: *Pilne zadania*, 10.

18 *Ibidem*.

the change of the civil code'; moreover, he pointed towards the positive experience with the extension of the Tagantsev Code of 1903 onto the whole of the Kingdom of Poland. Although he was far from regarding that instrument as a height of perfection, he still emphasized that it had been 'adapted to the needs of Polish statehood.' Accordingly, he was inclined to surmise that a similar move involving Poland's other partitions would also be, as far as criminal law was concerned 'easy to accomplish; one would thus obtain not only the uniformity of criminal legislation throughout the country, which in itself constitutes an important goal of the state.'[19] He did not, however, elaborate on that thought much further; he especially did not define any criteria he believed to be decisive to the better adaptation of a given code to Polish circumstances.

A concurring appraisal of the situation comes from Ludwik Domański. That eminent legal practitioner from Warsaw took the following position: 'The foreign laws, imposed on us by violence, applicable heretofore in the various partitions of Poland, fail to satisfy the whole of Polish society on account of both their divergence and obsolescence.'[20] Like Car, he also counted the Napoleon's Code and the *Allgemeines bürgerliches Gesetzbuch* among anachronistic codes, while also mentioning Russian civil law. As for the BGB, by contrast, Domański highlighted its 'discordance' with the other three systems of civil law applicable throughout Polish territories. He, too, failed to give us a more precise articulation of his thoughts. Beyond any doubt, the German Civil Code was the most modern and best adapted to the spirit of the new time and therewith disparate from the anachronistic codes in force in the other partitions. Domański did not discuss this fact, subscribing to the position that none of the codes applicable in parts of the country was fit for extension to the rest of the Republic's territory. In his mind, such a role could not possibly be played by any foreign code applicable elsewhere, such as the cherished Swiss Civil Code. The reason was not so much the specificity of Polish circumstances as the generally understood fundamental 'change of living conditions throughout the world', which – in Domański's opinion – had occurred at the beginning of the 20th century, notably in connection with the transformations unfolding in Europe during World War I.[21]

19 MAKOWSKI: *W sprawie ujednostajnienia*, 12–13.

20 Ludwik DOMAŃSKI: *O systemie przyszłego Kodeksu Cywilnego polskiego* [On the system of the future Polish civil code], Dziennik Urzędowy Ministerstwa Sprawiedliwości, 4–8 (1919), 170.

21 *Ibidem.*

FIGURE 2.1
Ludwik Domański, 1877–1952, lawyer (advocate), member of the Codification Commission, participating *in.al.* in the works on the draft Code of Obligations; President of the Supreme Bar Council in 1936–1939.

The reasons why the ZGB was not to be transplanted to Poland were expounded by the public prosecutor and scholar of criminal law, Józef Bekerman, in his response to the proposals of 'one of the celebrated civilists' in the *Gazeta Sądowa Warszawska*. Bekerman did not dispute the great merit of the Swiss civil law. He began by stating: 'There can be no doubt that the *Code civil suisse* and its far earlier predecessor, the *Code federal des obligations*, are one of the best European legislative creations both as to the substance and as to the very fortunate drafting.' Nevertheless, his position was:

> (...) one cannot separate civil law from life, and life in Switzerland, divided into such a considerable number of cantons, each with its own specific character, has taken a completely different course than our life [here]. The economic relations and the distribution of immovable property have shaped up differently. The true and deep democratization in Switzerland is no mere catchword; the people's psyche is different. And all of this finds reflection in the law. Therefore, the complete reception of that law by us here is hardly conceivable.[22]

One could expect very similar remarks in respect of the BGB. Still, the laws having for many a decade been followed in Polish lands, however anachronis-

22 Józef BEKERMAN: *Czy kodeks, czy nowele?* [A code or amendments?], GSW 7 (1920), 49–50.

tic such laws may have been, had manage to strike root in Polish legal culture. Bekerman explained this phenomenon on the example of the French Civil Code. Appreciating the obvious fact that the 'Code of Napoleon, by origin and history, [was] wholly foreign to us,' noted that not only had we become accustomed to it but even 'put a halo around it', even surround it with a 'cult in which political elements played a certain role,' so that 'we came to fancy it our own code.'[23]

Similar opinions prevailed also in the first conference of Polish lawyers and economists following World War I (and sixth in general). It took place in September 1920. In consequence, the Civil Law Section (on motion of Stanisław Gołąb) passed a resolution to the effect that one should not 'impose the civil statutes existing in one partition on the other partitions wholesale and without reservation.'[24] The reasons for such a decision probably coincided with those put forward by Car and Domański and – as was evident from the language – constituted the aftermath of the exacerbating inter-partitional antagonisms. Members of the Section voiced a fear of the negative consequence of the dominance of one of the regions above the others, had the application of its code to be so extended. The problem was more comprehensively explained by Stanisław Bukowiecki, who termed the regionalism a 'disease' having afflicted Polish territories only as late as the 19th century, being 'exclusively the product of the Partitions'. His belief was as follows: 'one cannot find the sources of the present regionalism in any such foundational characteristics or distant past as we might have.'[25]

The force of regional legal parochialism was so strong that no single code could be extended onto the whole country. In the opinion of Stanisław Car, shared by a broader if not necessary dominant circle of lawyers and jurists, the

23 *Ibidem*, 50.

24 *Zjazd prawników i ekonomistów polskich* [Polish Lawyers and Economists' Conference], RPEiS 1 (1921), 241.

25 Stanisław BUKOWIECKI: *Dzielnicowość w Polsce współczesnej* [Parochialism in modern Poland], Związek Sejmików Powiatowych RP, Warsaw, 1923, 22. See also Jakób GLASS: *Współpraca poszczególnych dzielnic w budowaniu Państwa Polskiego* [The collaboration of the individual zones in the construction of the Polish State], GSW 3 (1920), 19; GÓRNICKI: *Prawo cywilne*, 72–74. He also made a contradistinction with the 19th century: 'in the Old Republic, during the later period of its existence, there were no territorially centrifugal tendencies. The only stratum living a political life and forming the public opinion was the noble stratum, which could be said to have undergone a perfect coalescence, having become, during the last two centuries of [the state's] independent existence a [single] whole almost completely homogeneous in political and social, as well as moral terms.'

regionalism ought to be treated as a *malum necessarium* and 'despite serious inconveniences such as [were to] arise from tripartite legislation, the existing civil code [ought to] be left in each partition,' with only some amendments conducive to unification.[26] This is because Car believed that an impromptu intervention in selected areas of civil law with a view to the unification of the principles held throughout the country was necessary for the 'organic integration of the three partitions, each of which [had] for more than a century lived a separate political life and legal consciousness,' while for the remainder the partitional regionalism could be maintained pending a new codification fit for the needs of the Polish nation. In his opinion 'immediately or at least in the near future,' it would be necessary to harmonize whatever parts of civil law 'touch[ed] upon the public interest.' Although he did not provide a precise definition of the term, he included in it inheritance law, marriage and family law, as well as what he termed to be the 'rights of a married woman.'[27]

The members of Parliament, led by Zygmunt Marek, tabling the motion to establish the Codification Commission took a narrower view of the list of areas to undergo immediate unification. They, too, were aware that 'beside (...) the great [future] codification of civil and criminal law, there must already now be undertaken a work of harmonization of the legislation for the time being, i.e. until the coming to life of the great legislative reforms.' To them, it was beyond any doubt that 'the need of everyday life require[d] those glaring differences arising from the three different legal systems of the former partitioning powers to be eliminated forthwith.' The matters requiring immediate legislative intervention with a view to harmonization and modernization of the applicable rules were, according to movants, above all the personal law, as they noted the need for harmonization of the rules governing the age of majority, legal capacity and capacity for legal transactions, as well as the equal rights of

26 CAR: *Pilne zadania*, 10. *Cf.* BEKERMAN: *Czy kodeks*, 44.

27 CAR: *Pilne zadania*, 11. What Car had in mind was the draft bill being prepared by the Ministry of Justice to put the rights of women on an equal footing throughout all of the regions of Poland, which above all entitled the amendment of the Code of Napoleon and other provisions governing women's civil rights in the 'former Congress Kingdom.' See Roman KURATÓW-KURATOWSKI: *O zdolności prawnej mężatek według Kodeksu Cywilnego Polskiego* [On the legal capacity of married women according to the Polish Civil Code], GSW 39 (1919), 375–377; Michał GAŁĘDEK, Anna KLIMASZEWSKA: *'Crippled Equality': The Act of 1 July 1921 on Civil Rights for Women in Poland*, Acta Poloniae Historica 113 (2016), 231–260; Anna KLIMASZEWSKA: *Searching for National Components in Building Own Legal Culture: The Debate on the Legal Situation of Women in Interwar Poland*, Studia Iuridica 79 (2019), 169–180.

women and men.[28] A different list of legal areas calling for unification was put together by Franciszek Bossowski. On the one hand, he emphasized: 'Necessary for the economic consolidation of the Polish State is (...) the unification [only] of such part of private law as is covered by the civil code and the commercial code and contains areas of such import to economic circulation and credit as bonds, lien, etc.'[29]

The pressure for the fastest possible harmonization of certain areas of civil law, so characteristic of the first months following the reunification of 1919, appeared to abate with time. The elites, having obtained the practical experience of the various sorts of inconvenience occasioned by the continuation of the partitional parochialism, seemed to be getting accustomed to the *status quo* with the resulting belief in the possibility of its continued maintenance for a longer time than had originally been expected without as great damage to the country's social and economic co-existence as would have appeared to be looming. The lawyers and jurists, whose voices – for the obvious reasons – appeared to predominate the public debate on the legislative reforms, showed a natural inclination to overestimate the influence of legal instruments on life, and – as was soon to turn out – their catastrophic visions of colossal problems to be brought about by partitional parochialism were not guaranteed to come true. It seems that already in 1920 concepts of immediate unification, even only with regard to a selection of areas of civil law, began to give way to a new programme gaining support in the aforementioned 6th conference of lawyers and economists. The latter's conclusions contained the following declaration: 'The conference believes it to be a very urgent matter to introduce in Poland a harmonized inter-regional private law.'[30] The resolution was tabled by Professor Fryderyk Zoll, Jr., soon to be tasked by the Codification Commission with the creation of the appropriate draft.[31] Thus, the adoption of harmonized inter-partitional private law, which eventually came to be in 1926, became the accepted solution for the neutrali-

28 *Wniosek nagły posła Zygmunta Marka.*

29 Bossowski: *O naszych najbliższych zadaniach*, 125.

30 *Zjazd prawników*, 241.

31 A breakthrough in the perception of the unification question came with the article published by Fryderyk Zoll in the *Gazeta Sądowa Warszawska* in the summer of 1919. Fryderyk Zoll: *Nasze zadania najbliższe w dziedzinie międzynarodowego i międzydzielnicowego prawa prywatnego* [Our tasks at hand in the field of international and inter-partitional private law], GSW 21 (1919), 21.

zation of the most pressing problems generated by inter-partitional legal parochialism.[32]

4 National Consolidation and the Progressive Private Law

At the onset of independence, Polish lawyers and jurists strived to anticipate whatever problems the implementation of the ambitious challenges of modernization faced by Polish society could bring. They made the first attempts to define the direction to be taken by social modernization following World War I. Their assumption was that a new era had begun, the birth of which would be attended by groundbreaking ideas in social and legal sciences. Compounding this universal problem was another, not any less important one, linked to the society's need to learn its own psyche and define its needs in the new circumstances following independence and reunification. In such circumstances, the reasonable thing to do was to avoid excessive haste with the ultimate codification and first to determine the directions of evolution on all relevant levels.[33]

Although Wacław Makowski wrote: 'This task ought not to be taken lightly, for not only does it have to facilitate the normalization of legal, political and economic relations in the country, nor will it remain without influence on the nation's psyche and all of social life,'[34] there was no doubt that the drafting of a new civil code meeting the standards expected by Polish politico-legal elites could only be a long-term development. Already at the beginning of 1919 the highest-ranking officials in the Ministry of Justice made unequivocal pronouncements on this matter. Neither Stanisław Car, announcing that the drafting of a civil code could take 'perhaps even several decades of arduous work,'[35] nor Wacław Makowski harboured any delusions: 'This work must be calculated on the long-term; it will consume many efforts and skills, and we

32 For a more extensive discussion see Robert JASTRZĘBSKI: *Prawo prywatne międzydzielnicowe: zarys problematyki* [Inter-partitional private law: an outline of the problem range], Krakowskie Studia z Historii Państwa i Prawa 8 (2015)/3, 277–298; Leonard GÓRNICKI: *Prawo prywatne międzydzielnicowe z 1926 r.* [The Inter-partitional Private Law of 1926], in Jacek PRZYGODZKI (ed.): *Okresy przejściowe – ustrój i prawo* [Transitional periods – political system and law], E-Wydawnictwo. Prawnicza i Ekonomiczna Biblioteka Cyfrowa. WPAIE UWR, Wrocław 2019, 163–191.

33 *Wniosek nagły posła Zygmunta Marka.*

34 MAKOWSKI: *W sprawie ujednostajnienia*, 14.

35 CAR: *Pilne zadania*, 10–11.

can expect it at some point to lead to the creation of a new legal life in Poland.'[36] The President of the Codification Commission, Franciszek Ksawery Fierich did not have the slightest doubt that 'out of all codification works, and in particular the largest codes (...), the greatest difficulties are posed by the drafting of a civil code.'[37]

Coming to the fore in the first pronouncements revealing the initial foundations of the codification programme was the conviction of the necessity of preparation of a code 'conforming to the nation's spirit, its psyche and its needs.'[38] The quest for the nation's spirit and psyche sparked the temptation to reach into Polish legal tradition. Nothing of the sort, however, could be found in the preceding decades. One had to trace back if not to the customary law of pre-partitioning Poland, then at least to the attempts at codification undertaken in the Kingdom of Poland in years 1815–1830. No wonder, therefore, that in the Codification Commission not only no calls were made for the reinstatement of some ancient version of national law but attempts to draw upon the past were regarded as questionable in general. Among speakers addressing this problem during the celebrations of the tenth anniversary of the Codification Commission was Fryderyk Zoll, Jr: 'A search for native Polish roots for the civil code is doubtless a tempting thing, even somewhat desirable, but it would delay the codification for many years.'[39]

The topic, however, continued to resurface in the discussions, mainly due to external pressure for borrowings to be made from ancient Polish laws. A current aspiring to draw inspiration from Polish legal traditions began to crystallize under the influence of legal historians. Its principal advocate was the renowned professor, Przemysław Dąbkowski. In the closing paper of the 6th Conference of Polish Lawyers and Economists in Warsaw delivered on

---

36 Makowski: *W sprawie ujednostajnienia*, 13. *Cf.* the official communication from the Ministry of Justice stating that the codification of civil law was to require 'many years' of work. *Kontrprojekt Ministerstwa Sprawiedliwości* [Counter-bill of the Ministry of Justice], KPCiK 2 (1919)/1–4, 283.

37 Franciszek X. Fierich: *Unifikacja ustawodawstwa* [Legislative unification], in *Dziesięciolecie Polski Odrodzonej: księga pamiątkowa 1918–1928* [The decennary of Poland Reborn: a commemorative book 1918–1928)], Ilustrowany Kurier Codzienny, Krakow-Warsaw, 1928, 333.

38 Leonard Górnicki: *Pogranicza systemów prawnych, w szczególności pozaborowych, w pracach nad kodyfikacjami prawa cywilnego i handlowego w II RP* [Intersections of legal systems, especially post-partitioning systems, in works on codifications of civil and commercial law under the Second Polish Republic], Acta Universitatis Wratislaviensis. Prawo 324 (2017), 132.

39 *Komisja Kodyfikacyjna Rzeczypospolitej Polskiej. Dział ogólny*, vol. 1, is. 13, 22.

23 May 1920 he reproached the members of the Codification Commission for having taken a not so much unfavourable as 'the most completely indifferent' attitude to ancient Polish law. And that triggered his surprise, for he saw in their number a large group of scholars of Polish legal history, including Franciszek Ksawery Fierich, Henryk Konic and Jan Jakub Litauer. In Dąbkowski's opinion, the right thing to do was to draw not only from native terminology but also from specific customs grounded in popular tradition.[40] In a work published several years later, Dąbkowski was seconded by another professor of legal history, Jan Adamus, who, however, viewed the situa-tion in a markedly different light. He did not charge the codifiers with indifference, concluding instead that Dąbkowski's thought had been meet 'indubitably with due understanding by both the members of the Codification Commission and the broad legal and perhaps even social circles.'[41] The basis for his optimistic conclusions is anyone's guess, however.

The currency of such ideas was ensured by the prevailing belief of the interwar period that only a code 'conforming to the nation's spirit, its psyche and its needs' could possibly reflect the 'true intention of Polish citizens', as the members of Parliament moving to establish the Codification Commission in 1919 put it.[42] That intention, determined by the perspective of the national needs and psyche, still had to crystallize first. The quest for knowledge of the national psyche and spirit was not limited to borrowings from native tradition; its goal was also, or perhaps first of all, to determine the extent to which those had transformed during the 19th century and what the national needs were in the new reality following World War I. Following more than a century of disintegration of both the nation and the state, in 1919 the processes of socio-economic reintegration were only in their incipient stages. Polish elites did not immediately become experienced in the difficult art of leadership and administration of one's own independent state. This was not made easier by the threat to the state's existence brought by the Polish-Soviet war, ending

40 Przemysław Dąbkowski: *Dawne prawo polskie a zadania Komisji Kodyfikacyjnej: od-czyt wygłoszony na zamknięcie VI-go Zjazdu prawników i Ekonomistów Polskich w War-szawie 23 maja 1920 r. w sali obrad Rady Miejskiej* [The ancient Polish law and the tasks of the Codification Commission: a paper delivered in the closure of the 6th Conference of Polish Lawyers and Economists in Warsaw, 23 May 1920, in the City Council Session Hall], Jan Cotty, Warsaw, 1920, 2.

41 Jan Adamus: *W sprawie stosunku prawa ludowego do kodyfikacji prawa prywatnego* [Concerning the relationship of the people's law to the codification of private law], Lviv, 1925.

42 *Wniosek nagły posła Zygmunta Marka.*

only with the Treaty of Riga in 1921. During that time the state's political system decreed by the March Constitution of 1921 was established. Overlapping all this was the necessity of restoration of the country's material substance, which had to be pursued in circumstances of an extraordinarily grave economic situation. In the early twenties the normalization of the state of affairs was a far-off prospect as a *sine qua non* condition of commencement of works on a modern codification.

Works on a civil code for Poland had to be preceded by identifying the socio-economic needs in a stabilized political situation. This order of precedence was determined by the high expectations placed before such a codification. Stanisław Car observed that the purpose to be served by Polish civil law was to reinforce national unity, and 'the process of coalescence, as long as it is to wipe the trace of the stitches left by the former border cordons and have a lasting effect, ought to take place on the path of internal fusion, complete mutual diffusion of cultural, intellectual, economic and organizational-political values.'[43] Polish society was only at the beginning of that road, which meant – as Ludwik Domański wrote – that

> [the] planning out of (…) a wholly new system [of civil law] more suited to modern requirements of social life (…) [was] impossible, as it [was] still not known how the general breakthrough caused by the universal war would end, whether it would lead to the change of the social order or the old order would undergo only partial transformations, for which demands were made before the war and which are currently in gradual implementation. One thing appears to be certain,' according to Domański: 'the pre-war state of affairs will not be completely restored,' because '[o]ur country, exhausted by many years of warfare and impoverished, is calling for the betterment of its existence, and the vast majority of our society sees the only rescue in social reforms, transformation or even replacement of the [existing] social order.[44]

For all these reasons, Polish legal elites were, of course, of one mind concerning that 'the codification of civil law in as short a time as possible [was] desirable,' as they declared in the resolution passed in the Conference of Lawyers and Economists in 1920. However, they followed that immediately with the

43 CAR: *Pilne zadania*, 2.

44 DOMAŃSKI: *O systemie przyszłego Kodeksu*, 170. See also BEKERMAN: *Czy kodeks*, 49–50.

proviso that such codification must not take place 'to the detriment of the completeness and depth of the legislative works.'[45]

Several years later, in 1925, amid what would seem to be normalized political and socio-economic conditions, the dean of the Faculty of Law and Administration of Stefan Batory University in Vilnius, Alfons Parczewski, also spoke on the matter. In his own words: 'The codification of civil law reaches deeply into the substance of social life; as a result, it should pay attention to the whole of its organism and at once be the expression of the harmonious juridical thought of the nation.'[46] Despite the passage of time, however, he believed the following to remain a current question: 'Is the current era, the end of which is difficult to foresee at present, the right and proper one to produce such a monumental opus as a Polish civil code ought to be?.'[47] He had his doubts, noting that the 'juridical psychology of the era' could still not be 'sufficiently calm and balanced' to undertake such a work. He also appreciated somewhat different problems facing the young nation than did his colleagues having had their say in the debate several years prior. In his opinion, the codification work could be thwarted, on the one hand, by the 'insufficient unification in their juridical world view' among Polish jurists, and on the other hand, by the 'insufficiently prepared legislative factors in modern Poland.'[48] By contrast, a civil code, as a legal instrument 'reach[ing] deeply into the substance of social life (...) as a result (...) should pay attention to the whole of its organism and at once be the expression of the harmonious juridical thought of the nation.'[49] Parczewski's conclusions constitutes the reminiscences of the passionate political disputes tearing Poland at the time – a time just before the May Coup of 1926 – forestalling any consensus above political lines of division on matters of greatest importance. Such matters unquestionably included the civil code.

The polemic on whether the 'current era is at all favourable and suitable to the codification of civil law here' was entered by the veteran socialist senator

45 *Miscellanea. Zjazd prawników*, 241.

46 Alfons PARCZEWSKI: *Uwagi nad kodyfikacją prawa cywilnego w Polsce* [Remarks on the codification of civil law in Poland], Rocznik Prawniczy Wileński 1 (1925), 1.

47 Parczewski was reiterating a question he had posed already in 1920, which would appear to mean that he continued to regard it as a current question several years later.

48 *Ibidem*, 2. Cf. Zbigniew RADWAŃSKI: *Kształtowanie się polskiego systemu prawnego w pierwszych latach Drugiej Rzeczypospolitej* [The shaping of the Polish legal system in the initial years of the Second Polish Republic], CPH 21 (1969)/1, 39–41; GÓRNICKI: *Prawo cywilne*, 71–72.

49 PARCZEWSKI: *Uwagi nad kodyfikacją*, 1.

FIGURE 2.2
Alfons Parczewski, 1849–1933; lawyer (advocate) and socio-economic activist in the national movement prior to World War I. After 1918, an academic linked to the Stephen Báthory University in Vilnius, serving as the first dean of the Faulty of Law and Social Sciences, as well as Rector. Member of the Codification Commission.

and lawyer, Stanisław Posner. He argued, comparing the French and German case studies, that just how 'the French continued to codify, starting from the *coutumes* all the way to Pothier and Cambacérès,' the Germans, by contrast, dilly-dallying with their Civil Code for all of the 19th century, eventually released a code 'almost a hundred years younger than the French Code, full of interesting, new substance, fanned in by the development of economic life – how far behind the French Code it falls in line!.' It is the French who 'are the masters and exemplars of the art of codification to the entire world,' while the Germans, ever in wait for the opportune moment 'have unlearned how to work from the codification work in the area of civil law.' According to Posner,

> Professor Savigny had written the same of the 'ill-suitability' of the times as did Professor Parczewski! However, the Heidelbergian professor, Thibaut, was right when finding the object of his fascination in the Code of Napoleon. The Polish predecessors of Professor Fierich, too, were right in attempting the codification crowned with the Civil Code of 1825.

Nonetheless, Posner was of the opinion that Parczewski was isolated 'in the field of opposing the codification trends.' While the Codification Commission ought to 'work providently, skillfully and without overmuch haste,' it also should do so consistently and without undue delays in the work for which it had been appointed. For, in his mind 'the juridical thought in certain areas has ripened throughout the world,' and 'is homogeneous in the cultural zone of Europe.' 'So there is a source to draw from.' The picture of the codification of the civil procedure and commercial law was painting itself especially clearly. Civil law itself, by contrast, would occasion many more difficulties. The latter does not change the fact that Europe made a 'great work of ideas' in this field in the 19th century. The fruit of that work, on the one hand, was the strengthening of individual autonomy, and on the other hand, its limitation 'due to the interest of the generality.' That could be something to be guided by when undertaking the work of codification in Poland.[50]

Political antagonisms had split Polish elites earlier on. Disputes concerning the vision of a new Poland and the road it should take had polarized society already prior to the war; following independence and amid the struggle for power in one's own country, they could only intensify. The main axis of division went between the nationalist right and the socialists as the strongest two factions. While the nationalists focused on matters relating to national consolidation and the pursuit of a polonization policy with regard to ethnic minorities, the socialists concentrated their attention on social problems. In both cases, the civil code was to serve as an important tool for ideological purposes. Representative of the socialist canon of thought are e.g. the above-cited writings of Ludwik Domański, according to whom Poland was on the even of social and democratic changes constituting the effect of the 'break-

50 Stanisław POSNER: *Rocznik wileński* [The Rocznik Wileński], GSW 2 (1926), 29. Cf. Stanisław POSNER: *Nasza Komisja Kodyfikacyjna* [Our Codification Commission], Palestra 5 (1925), 782. Responding to Posner, Parczewski addressed only one of his adversary's assertions. Parczewski disputed the suggestion that he was isolated in his doubts concerning the 'ill-suitability' of the time for a civil code. He clarified that: 'the concern for the new civil law not to be infused by the legislative factors enacting it with elements contrary to the foundations of civil rule of law is among our lawyers and society a very widespread symptom. That concern is justified, as the country's economic ruin and general pauperization are linked precisely to the undermining of the right to own property. The violations of its foundations since re-establishment of the Polish State has become the demagogical motive of numerous statutes.' Moreover, in Parczewski's opinion, the debate carried the marks of primarily a political dispute, with internationalist socialists and nationalists on the opposing sides; the ageing Alfons Parczewski was not only a member of the Polish nationalist party but first of all a veteran regionalist. His somewhat younger adversary, Stanisław Posner, had also shaped politico-ideological path mainly prior to World War I. Alfons PARCZEWSKI: *Z powodu recenzji pierwszego 'Rocznika Prawniczego Wileńskiego' w 'Gazecie Sądowej Warszawskiej'* [On account of the review of the first issue of Rocznik Prawniczy Wileński in the Gazeta Sądowa Warszawska], Rocznik Prawniczy Wileński 2 (1928), 571–572.

through caused by the universal war.' The nationalists did not oppose such calls; a degree of convergence was possible. However, they believed the accents ought to be placed differently, so as for the national goals to gain priority before social goals. In that connection, they assiduously sought for the spirit of Polishness in historical tradition and among Catholic values.[51]

5 National Law

In the thirties, the calls for the revival of the national legal spirit were intensely linked to the radicalization of nationalist sentiments and outlooks. Aspirations to saturate the law with elements consolidating the nation, expressing its characteristic qualities, attuned to its customs and satisfying its needs, however, are not something to be associated exclusively with nationalist thought. Cultural consolidation around Polishness was the professed tenet of broader circles of those regarding it as a value to not only appreciate but also cherish. Among them were representatives of the young generation of lawyers aspiring to set a new tone with the debate on the characteristics of Polish law, including the ever-pending civil code. The formative moment for the new, expansive group of Young Lawyers was its nationwide congress in Cracow in 1932. The resolution passed there called for legislation always to be guided by 'principles drawn from the spirit of the nation.'[52] The development and popularization of that concept followed several years later, near the end of the thirties, on the pages of the *Współczesna Myśl Prawnicza* (Polish for 'Modern Juridical Thought').

Thinking about the law in thirties was especially dominated doctrines referred to as legi-social or juris-social. As Emil Stanisław Rappaport put it: 'the substance of the present day, if not in the eyes of all, then in any case of the prevailing, more politically formed part of Polish society, is precisely – despite everything – (...) unitaristic solidarism,' as the predominant legi-social current. Its aim was to create a legal construct out of a 'synthesis of currents and joint interests' and thus not based on the reconciliation of conflicting interests and aspirations but on a 'creative self-contained basis.'[53]

---

51 GÓRNICKI: *Prawo cywilne*, 83–85.

52 The motion was tabled by Michał Jerzy Kahl, the *spiritus movens* of the whole undertaking – Jan ADAMUS: *Elementy rodzime i obce w prawie polskim* [Elements native and foreign in Polish law], Rocznik Prawniczy Wileński 10 (1939), 360.

53 Emil S. RAPPAPORT: *W poszukiwaniu prawa narodowego samoistnego* [On the search for a spontaneous national law], Palestra 15 (1938)/5, 540–541.

Could similar assertions, such as those put forward by Rappaport did not hesitate to put forward in the context of criminal law be offered with respect to the drafts of private law underway? He emphatically argued that the Codification Commission had managed to create a criminal code being above all a 'harmonious expression of the concept of such a bio-social configuration as is the best fit for the realistic Polish psyche of today and the present solidaristic aspirations of Polish society and state.' That was the main goal of the drafters of the code, with adherence to some doctrinal tenets or other having only secondary importance and not deserving to be excessively highlighted while evaluating and characterizing the code. In other words, the eclectic nature of the work, drawing upon different schools of thought, assembled by authors representing different academic and political approaches, was not a goal unto itself but only a means to the achievement of a social goal. Rappaport stressed that probably for this reason the code, only several years after its enactment, managed to 'root out the former penal legislation of the partitioning powers not only from the practice but also from the memory.' This proves that the basic goal was achieved. In principle, the work did not encounter any problems with adaptation in the social sphere and thus it must have constituted the correct answer to the needs of the national psyche and of the time in which the code came to being. Writing of the 'needs and goals of the present Polish reality', to which the criminal code had been adapted so brilliantly, Rappaport had in mind its 'moral structure' and 'social composition'.[54]

The criminal code thus proved to be 'close to society' rather than 'some legal construct detached from life'. It would not have become ingrained so quickly, even had it been 'the most resourceful, reckoning with a number of academic postulates of the recent day.' That would have been too bold an experiment at codification. This is with the caveat that Rappaport distanced himself from regarding the then-contemporary era as a 'transient' or 'transitional' age. Such an approach only compounded the difficulty of the proper preparation of the codification work. It bore fruit in, on the one hand, attempts to delve excessively in the legacy of the past, and, on the other hand, attaching too much important to forecasts of the future in the drafting process. He believed that to be an inappropriate attitude, only fit to 'strip [the codification works] of all their creative impetus and practical value,' and a

54 Emil S. Rappaport: *Media via kodeksu karnego polskiego* [The via media in the Polish Criminal Code], Palestra 12 (1935)/4, 284–285, 287.

product of parts of the legal circles being 'out of touch with reality and modernity.'[55]

The fullest exposition of the nationalist concept with regard to private law was offered by Edward Muszalski. The latter, near the turn of the thirties, claimed that road had to be paved for a new trend in civil law, a nationalist trend; that would be the third such trend after liberalization and socialization. 'In the field of civil law, we are presently encountering the products of a long evolution, shaped rather by the personalist and individualist current of thought,' he noted, in connection with the universalist strength of the influence initially of Roman law and subsequently of the Code of Napoleon. He delineated the main guiding ideas of it – autonomy of individual will and 'its emancipation from possibly all bounds.'[56] Partial modification, however, followed later with the partial acquiescence in the socialization trend, opposed to the liberal school, in the newest codes such as the BGB and the ZGB, still essentially being liberal works. On this substrate, according to Muszalski, a new path was being carved by the nationalist idea, which 'as any great idea ha[d] the swing towards universality and towards the creation of its own concept of private law.' The postulates formulated by this school were founded upon the base assumption that 'the individual is a creation in the life of the nation.'[57] Muszalski observed that the characteristic feature of nationalist doctrines was the postulate of 'legal locality', expressed through the need to 'take into account the living conditions of a given (…) nation.' For that reason, nationalist could not *a priori* side with either the liberalizing or the socializing trend, because any position to be taken should at each time be determined by a given need of the nation according to the 'national economy'. From this principle of 'aprincipiality' Muszalski derived one important exception – irre-

55 *Ibidem*, 286.

56 Edward Muszalski: *O narodowe prawo cywilne* [For a national civil law], Współczesna Myśl Prawnicza 11 (1938), 27. In Muszalski's opinion, the drafters of the Code of Napoleon and other civil codes of its era 'probably had not yet been aware of the fundamental antagonism between freedom and equality,' and the copying over of their concepts made subsequent developmental tendencies in private law suffer from this original sin. Freedom ideas continued to develop throughout the 19th and 20th centuries. On the one hand, mainly as a result of democratization, rights and independence were extended to those persons who had so far been partially deprived: foreigners, women (especially married ones) and extramarital children. Freedom ideas became commonplace. On the other hand were the fields of protection of individual rights, encompassing not only the integrity of the body, good name and personal freedom but also the name, image, correspondence and intellectual-property rights. *Ibidem*.

57 *Ibidem*, 30.

spective of whichever nation, the foundation of nationalist doctrines had to lie in the subordination of individual rights to the need for the achievement of the overarching function of national life; accordingly, similarly to the socialist trend, this meant the primacy of the collective, albeit defined and distilled according to a completely different set of criteria. In terms of programme, the closest to nationalism was the solidaristic orientation, whereby the 'relative latitude of the individual's legal situation' manifested itself only in so far as the individual was acting for the 'welfare of the nation', where the principal accent had to be placed not on the sphere of the individual's rights under private law but on its obligations in that sphere,[58] as determined through the prism of the nation's needs. The national goals were to shape the nature of each legal institution. No ancient idea, derived usually from the tradition of Roman law, could be accepted without a critical assessment.[59] As he went on to explain:

> to a legislator or judge thinking in national terms, the most important of all is the social and national benefit, the possibility of achieving the welfare of the nation in the future, the assurance of the private-law order and its alignment with the public-law order, with the national common welfare.

Translating this into the language of a directional instruction as to the method of interpretation of the substance of contractual relationships, he proposed the introduction of a general clause forcing their examination primarily through the prism of 'national benefit and conformity of the contract with the public order', rather than the intention of the parties or the literal meaning of the contract.[60] The structure of the provision, therefore, would not change compared to the regulations arriving on the coat tails of the Code of Napoleon in the German Civil Code or Polish Code of Obligations. A different, wholly vague factor, however, was to determine the interpretation of contractual relationships.

The specifics, however, were missing. What was to be the nature of that better adaptation of Polish national law to the 'needs, characteristics and spirit' of the nation and to its 'socio-political realities'? The definitions were exceedingly vague and, in essence, of low explanatory value. One such defini-

58 In this regard, Muszalski invoked the 19th century thought of August Comte.

59 *Ibidem*, 30–31.

60 *Ibidem*, 31.

tion was attempted by Józef Stanisław Piątowski, according to whom Polish national law was the conceptualisation of such

> legal norms as would be in the most perfect way adapted to the social, economic, geo-political and at last psychic conditions of the Polish nation, as would be based on the natural tendencies and developmental dispositions residing within it and would employ such forces to the benefit of the nation and of the state.[61]

For that to happen, on the one hand such law should 'flow from Polish tradition and legal consciousness', and on the other hand from 'Polish needs of the present time,' while simultaneously serving the more generally defined 'overarching interests of the community of the Polish nation.'[62]

The importance of the national-heritage component was the result of the belief that Polish law ought to reflect 'the nation's mental experience of its historical development.'[63] Muszalski noted that while German lawyers and jurists 'somewhat frequently lament the break with good German traditions in their law and the excessive reception of Roman law, as well as yielding, in the last century, to the influence of foreign laws,' the situation in Poland was even worse due to the partitions, which had caused an even more distant break with our native tradition. Although there existed laudable exceptions, such as the retention of certain elements of Old Polish mortgage in the law of the Congress Kingdom, or the survival of certain inheritance customs or prenuptial agreements among peasant farmers, those elements 'did not have a sufficient strength of influence on the full picture of private-law relationships.' Muszalski's conclusion was not at all that 'the legacy of Polish private law was to be too hastily scrapped.' On the contrary:

> one ha[d] to cherish the teaching of Old Polish law and as far as possible in present circumstances borrow from more ancient institutions in new legislation. Of course, one cannot imagine direct and uncritical reception of ancient institutions, which had been broken from for several

61 Józef St. Piątowski: *Polskie prawo narodowe* [A national Polish law], Współczesna Myśl Prawnicza 12 (1936), 10.

62 *Ibidem.*

63 Maciej Wojtacki: *Idea prawa narodowego na łamach 'Prawa' (1928–1939) i 'Współczesnej Myśli Prawniczej' (1935–1939)*, Historia i Polityka 6 (2011), 77.

> decades or a dozen decades or which would be untenable in today's economic circumstances.

This does not change Muszalski's belief that 'many (...) guiding ideas or details could even presently find successful application.' In his opinion, the principle of 'good-heartedness' (*zasada poczciwości*), emphasized so heavily in ancient legal transactions, could certainly be restored, and so could certain rules relating to the dowry or the dower, or, in inheritance law, the principle of *materna – maternis, paterna – paternis*. It would be expedient to develop upon and instill order in such traditional customary rules as were 'still here and there surviving' (here, he cited the *litkup* as an illustrative example; cf. German *Litkauf*).[64]

The Codification Commission's failure to draw upon such traditional institutions was met with criticism. The latter was joined by Muszalski himself, noting that the Commission's attention was focused on the then-present state of affairs 'under the influence of the existing legacy of the partitioning powers'. Especially in the Code of Obligations, which remained within the current of liberal doctrines, Muszalski saw a faulty tendency to 'yield to foreign influences, usually German, from before the Great War.' In his opinion, that was an obstacle to the development of the law in a native, national spirit.[65]

Another leading writer of the same school of thought, Tadeusz Orlewicz, encapsulated those vague deliberations in concrete principal demands placed before the national private law. On the one hand, he specified that Polish law ought to reflect Christian values due to their importance to the many centuries of development of national identity. Those would provide the foundation for the awakening of 'the nation's psychic imperialism.'[66] On the other hand, he noted that the even more important task for Polish national law to meet should be the protection of employment, due to the latter's role in the nation's life. The starting point for that was the solidaristic assumption that a contract of employment 'is not only a personal matter between the employee and the employer but is an act whereby the employee enters the circle of national employment, taking charge of a scope of work entrusted to them on behalf of the national organization.' According to Orlewicz, the concept of property also ought to be configured towards the achievement of similar purposes,

---

64 Muszalski: *O narodowe prawo*, 34.

65 *Ibidem*, 34–35.

66 Tadeusz Orlewicz: *Z rozważań o narodzie i państwie* [From ponderings on the nation and on the state], Prawo 5–6 (1936), 173.

which would involve the imposition of limitations arising from the need to protect the national welfare, to which all individual or social activity was to be subordinated.[67] All of this was to serve the purpose – so characteristic mainly of national democrats and their thought – of reinforcing the national community through the use of legal instruments.

From these positions, the Young Lawyers launched an assault on the Codification Commission, discrediting its work done to date and especially the Code of Obligations of 1933 and the Commercial Code of 1934, which, because of reliance on foreign models, were – in their opinion – altogether bereft of a national character, resulting in failure to correspond to the Polish psyche and Poland's social, economic and geopolitical circumstances. The instrumental borrowings from Polish national heritage incurred censure from Jan Adamus. He reproached the advocates of the national-spirit idea for having founded their theses on a unilateral ethnological current of studies into legal history.[68]

The concepts of national law were sceptically received by lawyers of the older generation, predominating the composition of the Codification Commission and even played leading roles in the justice system. However, even the legal historian and former advocate of borrowing abundantly from the legal heritage of past centuries, Jan Adamus, regarded the criticism of the codification works as unfounded. He argued that 'from contacts with various older lawyers (including the members of the Codification Commission),' it occurred that 'they tried to do all they deemed possible, for example, to mend the broken thread of tradition and [re-establish] links with the old.'[69]

A civil code being the fruit of native legal thought based on traditional values setting it apart from foreign codifications could, therefore, serve as one of the fundamental adhesives cementing the nation. Private law had a special role to play in integration processes because, on account of the topics of its regulation, it 'reaches deeply [and on many levels] into the substance of social life.'[70] Parczewski noted this, commenting that the need for codification was not at all as clear as it could have seemed. He was of the following opinion: 'the most powerful (…) motive directly calling to life any codification attempts in general and thus also in the field of civil law have been and usually are considerations of political nature.' In his article, he cited historical examples from other countries, summarizing his description with the conclusion the

67 *Ibidem.*

68 ADAMUS, *Elementy rodzime*, 360.

69 *Ibidem*, 363.

70 PARCZEWSKI: *Uwagi nad kodyfikacją*, 1.

'idea of state unity' was usually the 'banner' and 'strongest factor behind the codification initiative.' Simultaneously, however, he believed codification to constitute only an 'external symbol of political unity and centralization.' He went on to explain:

> For if this is about an essential external political and even national coalescence, the state's power on the outside, and strong organization and consolidation on the inside, then all these advantages are feasible and in reality sometimes they occur in abundance despite the divergence and diversification of civil law through the state's territory.[71]

Parczewski considered it an error to believe that 'economic development in a great and rich society requires the civil law to be codified.' The contrary examples were those of the United Kingdom and the United States, neither having a national civil code and yet overpowering other European states in terms of wealth and economic growth. Thus, according to Parczewski, not only the national codification but even the 'uniform legal dispensation of social relations and economic circulation within the state', on which had preoccupied the attention of lawyers and jurists so heavily in the first years following the restoration of independence, contrary to their belief, was not at all a prerequisite for welfare and prosperity. The absence of a homogeneous code did not necessarily have to lead to 'complications and chaos in social relations' or to a 'breakdown of economic life at every step'.[72] As he believed: 'given the existence of other true factors conditioning or even causing the state's external power and favourable internal condition of society, the diversity of civil law throughout the state's territory presents no obstacle to the nation's political and social happiness.'[73]

6 The Integrative Function of Codification

Following the May Coup of 1926, the matter of the opportune moment for the codification of civil law did not cease to preoccupy certain lawyers. A debate on this topic was heralded in the press by a judge from the 'Eastern Borderlands', Adam Bobkowski, who pondered whether the codification of

71 *Ibidem*, 30.
72 *Ibidem*, 3.
73 *Ibidem*, 31.

civil law (but also criminal law) was 'in touch with the times' or perhaps its implementation at that particular time in history could be rather 'deleterious'. According to him, the codifiers were facing pressure from the 'impatience of broad circles of society [which 'extended also to lawyers, even their pinnacles'] to get rid, at least, in free Poland of the traces of bondage in the form of the different legislations of the partitioning powers retained on an interim basis in the various parts [of the country].' Nonetheless, Bobkowski continued – eight years after the establishment of the Codification Commission – that the then-present 'moment of state life' evaluated through the lens of the 'psychic, moral, economic and thus also political condition of society' was still 'premature' for a codification. In support of that he argued the simple juxtaposition of the textbook 'foundations' of legal science with the 'circumstances of time and place in today's Poland.'[74] He claimed that the time had definitely passed when 'following the bitter disappointments of the Enlightenment Age' it was believed that codification could be 'simply the result of completely unfettered individual creativity of extraordinary individuals who simply drag the drab, uncomprehending and all-susceptible masses along.' One ought not to subscribe without critical reflection to the thought that codification was to achieve an in-depth social transformation. Codification should be adapted to society's degree of advancement and correspond to its habits and expectations, rather than imposing new forms without reckoning with the former. In its essence, the overhaul of the legal order could only be accomplished in an evolutionary manner, with a new code enacted only at an opportune moment occurring with 'relative infrequency.' As Bobkowski put it, the timing of the creation of a code ought to depend on the internal dynamics of the events, while being 'completely independent' from any external circumstances 'even the most categorical' 'commands most agreeable to reason,' such as the need to introduce homogeneous national legislation. That did not at all mean one had to wait passively, allowing the existing law to become more and more anachronistic by the day. The existing law had to be amended always with a peek into the 'best [examples] of modern foreign codes', albeit partially 'statute by statute.' According to Bobkowski, Poland was still at that stage when 'society develops in such a way that, for a time, under the old, established forms

74 Bobkowski cited Montesquieu's universal maxim (from the *Spirit of Laws*) that 'laws are necessary relations arising from the nature of things' (*les lois sont les rapports nécessaires, qui dérivent de la nature des choses*).

there develops a new substance in the form of tiny and so far inconsiderable legislative amendments in the details,' where that 'substance' 'has not yet duly ripened.' Things having been so, the role for the author of a future codification during the period of waiting for an opportune timing ought to be the skillful gathering of the whole new 'legal material' and its 'systematization, instilling a certain external order'. Relying on that method and building a 'legacy of a number of years', one could thoroughly prepare and calmly wait for the advent of that rare moment of a 'lawyers' heyday' when out of all of the previously prepared elements it would at last be possible to assemble the 'synthetic legal whole under the form of a code', that 'magnificent edifice driven by a single thought' and 'duly meditated'. That would be a time – in the suggestive picture painted by Bobkowski – when 'the changes in their wholeness' finally begin to 'tear apart, as it were, the previous moulds.'[75]

Bobkowski's assertion that the law in then-modern Poland ought not to be codified, in line with the titular maxim *festina lente!* was, however, isolated and 'thus far unfamiliar'. A quick riposte was delivered by another eminent professor, member of the Codification Commission and justice of the Supreme Court, Emil Stanisław Rappaport, in 1927. He disputed the foundations of Bobkowski's rationale. First of all, according to Rappaport, the assumption of a necessity of society's slow maturing towards codification was anachronistic. The dynamism of the changes unfolding in the then-modern world opposed that thesis, which had been current in the 19th century and made the cornerstone of Friedrich Carl Savigny and Georg Friedrich Puchta's historical school of law. By contrast, it could find no support in the dynamic realities of the 20th century – a 'radio-cinema-auto-aeroplane era' and at once an era 'following the great turbulence of a war that fastened the Old World and the New World with a clamp of new, profound and very rapid [M.G.] evolutionary procession of transformations.' In Rappaport's opinion: 'the problem of codification of (…) laws of the Polish State is not only an emotional imperative, a prompting of patriotic "impatience", but the cardinal prerequisite of a proper state structure and power, internally and externally.' For a 'proper state structure' to be established required that the state be provided with a modern legal order. So one could not afford to tarry. Codification was a need of the moment in the face of an unprecedented dynamic of social and civilization change in every area, which, according to Rappaport, was characteristic of Poland at that time in her history – 'the live Poland, the Poland of our generation.' For that reason,

75 Adam Bobkowski: *Festina lente!*, GSW 41 (1927), 563.

the 'codification' landscape as painted in Bobkowski's strokes, would have been the 'negation of a modern Poland' aspiring together with the Great Family of Nations to modernity and 'cultural and civilization coordinateness'. In the face of those changes and new challenged, the 'Polish province' could not 'calmly and quietly continue to cherish the post-partitioning forms of its legal tri-structure,' by upholding partitional legal parochialism.[76]

That need for immediate adaptation of the law to the dynamic of transformative developments was something Rappaport exalted above everything else. To explain his perspective, he declared: 'I do not at all ignore the great import of the partitional differences within Poland and the differences in her cultural circumstances abroad.' Thus, he opposed both the mythologization of the alleged cultural exceptionality of the Polish nation and the conviction (founded upon the same intellectual canons) of the existence of difficulties in overcoming the post-partitional barriers having arisen among the Polish communities of the various regions together composing the reborn Polish state.

A more severe criticism of Bobkowski's thought was offered by Jerzy Stefan Langrod. According to Langrod, Bobkowski's inference was founded on a selective choice of assertions that generally held true but had not been confronted by Bobkowski with the realities of the interwar period. Langrod conceded the merit of Bobkowski's claim that substantive civil law 'require[d] a longer evolution, transformation of the various institutions in collective life,' as well as the unquestionable truth that the success of the codification undertaking hinged upon its good timing and choice of place. 'But what of that?,' he asked, imputing to Bobkowski that the latter did not deign to construct a

> positive and logical theory [responding to the question of] which exact epochs in the development of humanity are conducive to codification and what ones are not; what the perceptible boundary is between a bad period and another that is good; what the criterion is to define without reservations that there has now come an opportune timing for codification, that society has already, in its everyday experience, digested a certain legal institution so that it can be without hesitation placed in the code.

76 Emil Stanisław RAPPAPORT: *Czy kodyfikacja prawa cywilnego i karnego jest na czasie?* [Is a codification of civil and criminal law timely?], GSW 41 (1927), 566.

Thus, in his opinion, arose a *circulum vitiosum* 'in part, perhaps, theoretically justified, but practically baseless and harmful'.[77]

Langrod also responded to the part in which Bobkowski asserted that at the then-present time, codification could no longer be the 'result of completely unfettered individual creativity of extraordinary individuals' setting new trends and giving directions to social transformations through their work. He emphasized that such individual 'creativity' need not be 'something asocial, detached from the trends and currents circulating in society, but is precisely their manifestation, part of society, and, outside of exceptional incidents, corresponds to those internal causes amid which law ripens for codification.' True, though – as the Codification Commission did in Polish circumstances – it rather ought to be the product of the collective work of a group of eminent individuals comprising both theoreticians and practitioners. It was thus a mistake to set the codifiers against society, for 'life and law, practice and theory' are by no means separate fields; in the creativity of truly eminent individuals they constitute 'a single whole constantly and mutually complementing itself.' In Langrod's picturesque terms, that is when the codification endeavour, composed of 'external [legal] commands will arise from the deepest internal need, from the digestion of the problem in the conscience of society,' and cannot 'diverge from the internal commands of the epoch.'[78]

As he observed, the situation in 1927 had taken a different shape. In his words:

> the [already] dying issue of Poland's division according to partition lines is strong evidence of the necessity of codification. Because of this problem, it is fitting to regret most fervently that the Polish legislature did not accelerate this work in the first years of Polish statehood in whatever areas it had been possible to do so.

He argued: 'If (...) there truly exists different partitional psychology [which, as he wrote, ought rather to be termed 'psychosis'], then it must be counteracted, and not along the lines of *festina lente* but rather *periculum in mora*.' And continued: '[there are] sufficient examples in Poland how quickly personal differences blur out *ceteris paribus conditionibus*, how artificially created and

77 Jerzy Stefan LANGROD: *O kodyfikację w Polsce* (*z powodu artykułu p. Adama Bobkowskiego*) [For a codification in Poland (on account of the article by Mr Adam Bobkowski)], GSW 48 (1927), 665.

78 *Ibidem*.

sustained differences evanesce following the harmonization of legal affairs in a given field.'[79]

Similarly to Jerzy Langrod, the majority of representatives of Polish lawyerly elite involved in the codification were aware that their work could play an important integrative work, and that the integration could proceed in the direction deemed the most favourable by the codifiers themselves. In the former aspect, it was appreciated that only homogeneous regulation of social relations could coalesce Polish society, creating a defined social order that – if only it gains ground and wins universal acceptance – brings the members of a given community close together and stabilizes its functioning. In that context, the law was fit to serve an integrative and unifying role.[80]

7 Codification as an Instrument of Social Modernization

In the latter dimension, both those representatives of the lawyerly elite who perceived the law as instrument of social modernization and those who examined the same tool through the prism of the pursuit of national goals and reinforcement of the national spirit were conscious of how, by creating the codification, they were achieving defined goals and upholding a defined system of values, giving shape to social affairs and spearheading the processes of change towards such directions as they deemed to be desirable.

In the twenties, the paradigm of modernity was delineated primarily by lively tendencies for codifications rooted by their pedigree in the liberal and individualist 19th century to be socialized and infused with the ideals of social solidarism. Especially those lawyers for whom socialist ideals (in a reformist cast) were close to their hearts, such as Ludwik Domański, favoured a sociological approach to law, regarding it as the freshest and most modern outlook best fit to tackle the challenges of modernity. They felt especially close to the thought of Leon Duguit and his theory of social solidarity whereon the main assumptions of a future civil code could be based. Domański, as an adherent of those ideals, simultaneously appreciated the differences separating Poland from Western Europe. He pointed towards the 'individual freedom, deeply engrafted in the organism of Polish society already in times in which in the West it was still remonstrating for its rights; following the collapse of the Com-

79 *Ibidem.*

80 Grzegorz L. Seidler: *Z zagadnień filozofii prawa* [From topics of philosophy of law], Wydawnictwo Lubelskie, Lublin, 1984, 55.

monwealth, it became the property of all spheres of society.'[81] Combining solidarist with freedom ideals, Domański called for the basis for all future works on a civil code to be the consensus that, by its own nature 'the Polish nation desires [above everything else] social freedom and demands, especially from specialist lawyers, the development of means to ensure its security and growth.'[82] He did not narrow it down how such an amalgamation could translate into specific principles and characteristics of the various institutions of civil law. Nonetheless, he specified a list of further theoretical underpinnings that, in his opinion, future codifiers should constantly and consistently be guided by, defining the 'history of the existing development of civil law and (...) legi-social doctrines.' According to him, it should be maintained that: (1) the law is not an abstract construct but a 'creation of social relations' (concealed in this assertion was the veiled criticism of the method adopted by the authors of the BGB); (2) 'civil relations, thanks to individual freedom, guaranteed by the acts of the 19th century, have developed to such a degree that they currently represent a weave of diverse interlinked interests and aspirations'; (3) 'because of the interconnection and interdependence of the interests, it is no longer possible [in contradistinction to the 19th century practice] to regulated civil relations from the position of the individual freedom of the subject in detachment from the entirety of legal and social affairs'; (4) 'the legal junction in civil relations are mutual obligations rather than individual rights and obligations depending on them'; (5) 'the use of rights in the sense of the individual rights of a subject is conditioned on the performance of obligations.'[83] Preponderating in those points was the stress on the performance of social obligations by individuals, so characteristic of socialist thought. In such a context, individual freedom had to admit of limitations, even though Domański emphasized his respect for Polish society's attachment to liberal ideals.

Doubtless, therefore, the expectations set before the Polish civil code were high. It should constitute a 'monumental opus', wrote Alfons Parczewski, one destined to 'last for decades, perhaps even centuries'.[84] For that condition to be met, it was necessary not only to base the codification on the 'most recent achievements of legal science'[85] but also to embark on sociological and anthropological studies enabling the 'spirit' and 'psyche' of Poles to become

---

81 DOMAŃSKI: *O systemie przyszłego Kodeksu*, 170.

82 *Ibidem*.

83 *Ibidem*, 171.

84 PARCZEWSKI: *Uwagi nad kodyfikacją*, 1.

85 MAKOWSKI: *W sprawie ujednostajnienia*, 13.

known. Last but not least, the Codification Commission, besides paying attention to 'the promptings of science for the future' ought also to 'be guided in its works by the experience of the past'.[86]

It was realized that too radical an attempt to break with the partitioning powers' legislation in favour of a new code satisfying all demands of modern codification could lead to a creation 'artificial in a degree, for at once the regulations ingrained in society would become lost.' This was appreciated by the dean of the Faculty of Law and Administration of the University of Warsaw, Zbigniew Cybichowski, in a speech held in the inaugurating session of the Codification Commission on 10 November 1919. He noted that the introduction of a new code would in itself constitute a rapid change in legal affairs, capable of sending a shockwave through society. The new law, contrary to the intentions of its creators, could be perceived as foreign and imposed by elites disregarding society's expectations. As he noted, the 'history of enlightened states' provided examples of that.[87] The Soviet example was a particularly strong deterrent. In Cybichowski's opinion, the latter proved that a radical overhaul of the entire legal order leads to 'anarchy in private life and ruin of the national economy'.[88] He pointed out that writers have on multiple occasions warned against the adverse consequences of breaking continuity in the evolution of the law by the unprepared introduction of new forms, institutions and principles. In his opinion, the danger was real, even where the 'modern lawyer', through better knowledge of the structure and functions of the law 'now ha[d] more extensive knowledge', and 'better preparation for codification work than the codifier of old'. He also cautioned: 'Studies into the life of modern-age societies have shown that the modern individual is characterized by indifferentism and scepticism. The modern human being, despite beliefs and hopes, sometimes becomes indifferent to lofty appeals and the power of ideas.' Cybichowski feared that the noble ideal of a modern national codification might fail to rouse the nation. On the other hand, that general rule did not necessarily have to apply to Poles in the same degree as representatives of other nations, due to our particular national characteristics. 'For in Poland the feeling of love

86 Domański *O systemie przyszłego Kodeksu*, 170.

87 *Cf.* Michał Gałędek: *The Problem of Non-Adaptability of National Legal Heritage. Discussion on the Reform of Civil Law in Poland in the Course of Work of Reform Committee in 1814*, Romanian Journal of Comparative Law 1 (2017), 33.

88 Ignacy Koschembahr-Łyskowski: *W sprawie kodyfikacji naszego prawa cywilnego* [Concerning the codification of our civil law], Themis Polska, Warsaw, 1925, 13–14.

for the Motherland is supreme,' as though stronger than in the more 'sceptical and indifferent' societies.[89]

The Warsaw law dean's appraisal of the situation was not a lone voice. The President of the Codification Commission, Franciszek Ksawery Fierich, also warned against breaking with the past and 'contriving originality in the shaping of our legal affairs'. His point was to balance the proportions and reconcile several different goals, namely, as he put it 'so that our legislation, relying on the instructive experience of the past, reckoning with modern cultural needs, with our national character, our political system, could not only respond to the need of the moment but be capable also of glancing with a prudent eye into the future.'[90]

But could the avoidance of violent upheavals truly justify retaining the institutions and principles inherited from the partitioning powers? To this question, Fierich responded as follows: 'Take from foreign statutes what is good in

FIGURE 2.3
Franciszek Ksawery Fierich, 1860–1928, professor of civil procedure at Jagiellonian University; also Dean of the Faculty of Law and Rector, as well as editor-in-chief of the *Czasopismo Prawnicze i Ekonomiczne*. From 1919, President of the Codification Commission.

89 *Przemówienie Dziekana Wydziału Prawnego Uniwersytetu Warszawskiego. Posiedzenie inauguracyjne Komisji Kodyfikacyjnej w Pałacu Rzeczypospolitej w dniu 10 listopada 1919* [Speech by the Dean of the Law Faculty of the University of Warsaw: inaugurating session of the Codification Commission in the Palace of the Republic on 10 November 1919], in *Komisja Kodyfikacyjna. Dział Ogólny* [Codification Commission: General Section], 1920, vol. 1, is. 1, 22.

90 FIERICH: *Rzut oka*, 457.

them, whatever is fit for our affairs; take it after thorough deliberation.'[91] The motto of the undertakings of the Codification Commission ought to be the words of Adam Jerzy Czartoryski: 'It is no shame – on the contrary, it is a duty – to draw upon the experience of others, to draw everywhere whatever is good and learn improvements, additions and refinements (...).'[92] Although a hundred years old by that time, Fierich regarded the maxim as enduringly sound advice. Hence, he proceeded from the assumption that 'in a desire to create homogeneous Polish legislation,' the task before the Codification Commission will be to 'accomplish comparative studies, gather statistical materials, take advantage of the judicature and benefit from experience in the field of legal life.' This comes with the caveat that the goal was not to carry out a simple analysis of the partitioning powers' dead codes but to 'reckon with a living law, which by the force of factual relations, consistent or inconsistent with the existing applicable law, has given manifestation to the legal principles and norms ingrained in society.'[93] Fierich, therefore, had in mind not so much the provisions already in force throughout Poland as the legal cultures having taken shape in the country's former partition zones on the basis of those provisions. It would seem that his perception of the problem in the sociological aspect was characteristic especially of Galician circles.

The sociological dimension raised by Fierich was expounded in detail by the representatives of that region such as Władysław Leopold Jaworski and Ignacy Koschembahr-Łyskowski.[94] Jaworski's appeal was for the authors of the civil code first of all to ask themselves 'what the relations [were] that [were] to be regulated by the civil code,' and only later to ponder 'what the regulation [was] to be.'[95]

Koschembahr-Łyskowski argued that the maintenance of a certain developmental continuity of the law needed not be tantamount with upholding the partitioners' regulations or incorporating them in the future codification; this is all the more important considering that, in his opinion, there was no way to reconcile them with each other in a satisfactory manner. The point was for the future civil code to be founded not on then-existing legal affairs but on the 'present factual relations in our society,' in line with the assumption that 'the

91 *Ibidem.*

92 *Ibidem*, 457–458.

93 *Ibidem*, 458.

94 Ignacy Koschembahr-Łyskowski hailed from the Prussian partition and was educated in German universities, but in the early 20th century he cast his lot with the Faculty of Law of the University of Lviv.

95 Jaworski: *Nowożytny Kodeks Cywilny*, 22.

law arises from factual relations of life, and it is on their basis that it is to be interpreted.'[96] Only then can it be possible to 'take into account local needs and outlooks.'[97]

The main source of inspiration for Koschembahr-Łyskowski's observation of this fact came from the legacy of the German philosophy of law and Austrian sociology of law of the early 20th century.[98] He cited Philipp Lotmar (*Der Arbeitsvertrag*) and Eugen Ehrlich (*Grundlegung der Soziologie des Rechts*).[99] He also noted his closeness to the views on nature expounded by Władysław Leopold Jaworski.

Koschembahr-Łyskowski disputed the view that Polish factual relations had been predominated by the partitioning powers' legislative provisions. On the contrary, he believed that they did not at all follow the dictates of the foreign codes applicable in Polish territories. He argued:

> Our society in the four partition zones did have to adapt to the foreign law applicable in each of the regions, but on the other hand it also adapted the foreign law to its own needs and outlooks, widely taking advantage of the semi-imperative provisions of so-called *ius dispositivum*.

The flexibility of the existing codes was, in Koschembahr-Łyskowski's opinion, the crux of the matter. The vast field in which to shape the legal relationships freely made possible the evolution of a Polish practice of application of foreign codes, resulting in significant differences in their functioning in Polish territories from how they were applied in the homeland. The above prompted Koschembahr-Łyskowski's conclusion that the provisions of the codes themselves were not the proper object of analysis because the path to understanding the law applied in Polish territories went only through 'very arduous study of the judicature' in the former partitions, provided

96 KOSCHEMBAHR-ŁYSKOWSKI: *W sprawie kodyfikacji*, 14.

97 *Ibidem*, 16. See Aleksander GREBIENIOW: *Römisches Recht als Vergleichsfaktor: Ignacy Koschembahr-Łyskowski (1864–1945) und die Methodenfrage*, in Tommaso BEGGIO, Aleksander GREBIENIOW (eds), *Methodenfragen der Romanistik im Wandel: Paul Koschakers Vermächtnis 80 Jahre nach seiner Krisenschrift*, Mohr Siebeck, Tübingen, 2020, 181–190.

98 Also the achievements of the German Codification Commission provided Koschembahr-Łyskowski with a principal frame of reference for the comparative evaluation of the assumptions and achievements of the Polish Codification Commission.

99 KOSCHEMBAHR-ŁYSKOWSKI: *W sprawie kodyfikacji*, 14.

that even that could not in itself be sufficient, because 'not all relations reached the cognition of the courts, and even among those, not all were published in court reports.'[100] Since, however, the study of court cases from the time of the partitions is not sufficient to answer the question of the factual relations in the land, all the stronger emphasis must be put on the diligent study of the jurisprudence of the Second Polish Republic, especially if it is to be assumed, from a realistic perspective, that the codification works may take a while.

Hence, it would be a completely abortive attempt to undertake codification through the elimination of the divergence among the codes applicable in the various regions in order to work out a homogeneous code through such efforts. According to Koschembahr-Łyskowski, not even the choice of such a way could possibly lead to the intended goals. While he conceded that the codes applicable throughout Polish territories rested upon the 'common foundations of Western European law', he immediately followed that the 'expression' of such basic principles of legal terminology was so different that it would be impossible quest – resulting in 'the greatest confusion in the judiciary' – to apply the French Code in Austria or Germany, or the Austrian or German Code in France. In his opinion, that was best proved by the deliberations of the Polish Codification Commission, during which the lawyers from the French-law area interpreted the basic terms and concepts of Austrian or German law in a completely different manner from their colleagues schooled on those provisions. The *vice versa* held equally true. Thus, it was impossible to merge all the codes into a single whole. At most, it could be possible to make borrowings, even abundant borrowings, of selected institutions and mechanisms contained in 'individual provisions'.[101]

So what was the creation of a new, Polish codification to look like? The purpose of the study of jurisprudence was to supply basic material for the determination of what legal norms were functioning in practice. Besides, the catalogue of sources from which 'any knowledge of local affairs and customs' could originate ought not to be limited anyhow. A separate task was to consist on the 'building of native Polish legal terminology', considering that the differences in the understanding of the various terms inherited from the partitioning powers frustrated any consensus among the representatives of the law-

100 *Ibidem*, 15. These were the conclusions to which Koschembahr-Łyskowski was prompted by the experience of the works on the draft of the chapter governing the general rules of inheritance. *Ibidem*, 16.

101 *Ibidem*, 15.

yerly circles of the various regions.[102] He reiterated this particular demand in the footsteps of Stanisław Gołąb.[103] Secondly, sufficient leeway had to be left in the new civil code in which to shape factual relations freely, on the basis of the experience of the time of the partitions, casting the provisions in terms of the *ius dispositivum*, allowing a 'slow evolution' of legal relations and gradual blurring of distinctions among the regions, though not all and not for any price, to run its own course. The codifier's task, accordingly, ought to be first of all to determine certain boundaries dictated by basic principles. Next, the designs were to undergo critical verification through the 'sourcing of the opinions of a broader circle of lawyers' on drafts presented to them.[104]

The taking into account of the then-current factual relations also meant, in Koschembahr-Łyskowski's view, that direct borrowings from collections of ancient Polish laws (such as the Collection of Judicial Laws of 1776 written by Andrzej Zamoyski) made no sense because those were only fit to serve as monuments in commemoration of customs long-bygone, which, however, did not at all preclude the necessity of 'discerning the guiding legal ideas' contained in those selections or even going as far back as laws from the 16th century (Taszycki's *Correctura Iurium*, Prussian *Correctura* and Lithuanian Statutes), which could be of assistance as sources of cognition of certain universal characteristics of the Polish nation and its psyche. Koschembahr-Łyskowski was far from disputing the possibility of the existence of a link between the ancient generations of Poles and the national characteristics of Poles contemporary to him.[105]

Ultimately, the Codification Commission reached a compromise. The Code of Obligations of 1933 did not give up maintaining liberal-individualistic principles, but significantly corrected them in the gspirit of social solidarity.[106]

In this context, it will be fitting to return to the already-discussed unification concepts by invoking the opinion of Franciszek Bossowski. The latter

---

102 *Ibidem.*

103 Stanisław GOŁĄB: *Przed projektem polskiego Kodeksu cywilnego*, Czasopismo Prawnicze i Ekonomiczne 1 (1920), 23.

104 KOSCHEMBAHR-ŁYSKOWSKI: *W sprawie kodyfikacji*, 17–18.

105 *Ibidem*, 14–15.

106 Grzegorz NANCKA: *Próba wykorzystania prawa rzymskiego w międzywojennej kodyfikacji prawa rzymskiego? Ignacy Koschembahr-Łyskowski i 'koncepcja podstawowa prawa zobowiązań'* [An attempt to apply Roman law in the interwar codification of Polish civil law? Ignacy Koschembahr-Łyskowski and his 'basic concept of the law of obligation'], Zeszyty Prawnicze, 22 (2022), 114–115, 128–129; GREBIENIOW: *Römisches Recht*, 200–202.

insisted on the necessity of an 'economic consolidation' as a priority, demanding the harmonization, in the first order, of 'areas of such import to economic circulation and credit as bonds, lien, etc.' In that area, regulated by the provisions of the civil code and of the commercial code, the introduction of new regulations – initially solely for unification purposes – could be accomplished within a relatively short timeframe and without major social upheavals as in the case of other areas of civil law, of which too rapid amendment was not expedient, as the consequences of the population's long attachment to existing law could significantly hinder adaptation.[107]

The aspiration to base the civil code on the most modern currents in legal science gave rise to another difficulty, also noted by Domański. Offering in his article an overview of the then-most recent trends in global legal science, he arrived at the conclusion that there was no consensus as to the direction to be taken by the evolution of legal science, with different solutions being offered to the same problems. 'Some argue that civil law is undergoing a gradual socialization; others, on the other hand, assert that individual autonomy is expanding and in parallel the individuals' obligations to the collective are growing.'[108] The situation led Domański to the following conclusion: 'the great abundance of legi-social theories and doctrines, oftentimes diametrically opposed [to one another], makes any selection from among them exceedingly difficult.'[109]

In turn, in the opinion of the President of the Codification Commission, Franciszek Ksawery Fierich, the new provisions of private law should also be coherent with the regulations applicable in other countries, because one could not allow a situation to develop in which 'our Motherland' would be an 'isolated state', because,

> she is bound by treaties to other states and must therefore regulate its legal affairs in such a manner as to be able in economic and social terms and in terms of its own position as a state to satisfy as best she can her own national, social and universal human tasks.

That last remark and 'guiding thought on the matter of the establishment of legislation following similar principles to those of other states' was, in Fie-

107 Bossowski: *O naszych najbliższych zadaniach*, 125.
108 Domański: *O systemie przyszłego Kodeksu*, 170–171.
109 *Ibidem*, 170.

FIGURE 2.4
Ignacy Koschembahr-Łyskowski, 1864–1945, prior to World War I linked to the University of Fribourg, University of Lviv (*in.al.* as dean of the law faculties) and thereafter the University of Warsaw following its reactivation in 1918, where he also served as Rector. Vice-President of the Codification Commission involved in works on various areas of civil law.

rich's opinion, of especial importance and 'extraordinary significance' in the areas of commercial, maritime, promissory-note and cheque law.[110]

What were, therefore, the works on the code drafts to look like so that the set goals could be met? In 1919, when the key decisions were made, lawyers employed at the Ministry of Justice, such as Wacław Makowski, were of the position that 'the drafting of bills, their tabling and sponsorship in the Sejm, [was] evidently first of all the task of the government.'[111] Accordingly, it could not be left to the 'private initiative of scholars'.[112] Nonetheless, neither Makowski, nor the Ministry of Justice itself advanced the proposal that works on the future codification be left in the hands of the government, either in an institution reporting directly to the Prime Minister or in the Ministry of Justice. During the deliberations of January 1919, the ministerial officials pondering the

110 Fierich: *Rzut oka*, 3. He argued: 'such legislative uniformization will facilitate commercial transactions between the citizens of our state and foreign nationals. This will especially apply to provisions respecting large-scale commerce and bills of exchange, which can be first of all of great service to interstate trade (...) guardianship (...) employment (...) aeronautics (...) telegraphs, telephones, automobiles and railways (...).' And he added: 'this perspective is of decisive influence on the determination of the legal assistance in litigious and non-litigious proceedings and especially in the enforcement of judgments, and it further has influence on the determination of the jurisdiction of civil and criminal courts (a practical outlook).'

111 *Kontrprojekt Ministerstwa Sprawiedliwości*, 283.

112 Makowski: *W sprawie ujednostajnienia*, 14.

latter alternative arrived at the conclusion that they were unable 'in the ranks of their own personnel to amass such a large host of first-rate expert forces from all regions as [was] indispensable for the completion of such works.' For that reason, they were inclined to establish a 'separate organization (...) such as, unburdened with the tasks of everyday life, could be able to devote itself solely to that work, calculated on a succession of years.'[113] According to Makowski:

> The head of that institution must have close ties to the cabinet while not forming part of it (...) [he] ought to stand apart from its political character and accountability, standing solely on the guard of the juridical nature of the works and their continuity, notwithstanding the variable face and composition of the political government. Moreover, the unification institute or committee (...) ought to enlist the most eminent representatives of legal science and practice from all over Poland. It should include the most illustrious university professors, legal practitioners, judges and civil servants, as well as administrators.[114]

In the Ministry of Justice, there was thus a consensus that the codification work had to be the fruit of 'arduous labour and effort of the flower of Polish lawyerdom from all regions of Poland', outside of the government bureaux.[115] First of all, they should be entrusted with the so-called 'theoretical department' consisting in 'specifying the common guidelines and defining such ideal paths as [in the long haul] the general legislative reform in Poland would have to tread.' That was a 'work set for academic societies, universities and individual scholars'. For as a target, irrespective of the short-term unification intervention the government had to implement immediately 'without a doubt, the best and easiest way out of these five different legislative regimes would be to create new legislation, rising above each of the individual five and all together, based on the most recent achievements of legal science, adapted to the needs of the new Republic.' As Makowski noted: 'This work [which can be left up to the initiative of individual scholars] must be calculated on the long-term; it will consume many efforts and skills, and we can expect it at some point to lead to the creation of a new legal life in Poland.'[116]

113 *Kontrprojekt Ministerstwa Sprawiedliwości*, 283.

114 Makowski: *W sprawie ujednostajnienia*, 14.

115 Car: *Pilne zadania*, 10–11.

116 Makowski: *W sprawie ujednostajnienia*, 13–14.

Already in February 1919, which is when Makowski's article was printed, it was clear to the author that it should be Parliament's task to establish a unification institution working near the government and also to create a 'private' academic platform for codification works. However, he believed the Sejm would for the time being be too absorbed in other matters. He wrote:

> Had we not before us such a pressing current task as the Legislative Sejm, as building from the ground up the administration of the state, which has to be created a new, as learning the practical life of a state, which all of our state's authorities strive with great effort to accomplish by their own designs, then probably our normally functioning Parliament would commence unification works with the appointment of a special institute to prepare the material for [that] great legislative task.[117]

It seems, however, that there was no obstacle for the Ministry of Justice to bring a draft bill under the deliberation of the Sejm, of which the first session began on 10 February 1919. Nevertheless, for the next half again a month, even though the necessity of commencing forthwith the 'intense, harmonized preparatory labour in the area of legislative unification'[118] appeared to be self-evident, the government did not undertake any such initiative. The reason for the delay is not known.

8 The Parliamentary Codification Programme

In that situation, in circumstances that remain unexplained (due to the lack of source materials), the Council of Ministers and the Minister of Justice were outpaced by the deputies' initiative.[119] On 1 April 1919 an urgent motion was tabled with the signatures of several dozen members of Parliament led by the Galician lawyer, Zygmunt Marek, deputy of Polish Socialist Party and Chair-

117 *Ibidem*, 14.

118 *Ibidem.*

119 The source material fails to answer the question of why the government tarried with the publication of the programme of institutionalization and commencement of the unification works and of the reasons for the problem being dealt with by deputies bypassing the government. See Michał Gałędek: *The Beginning of the Debate on the Codification of Polish Law after the First World War: the Issue of the Codification Commission Autonomy in the Light of Political Declarations*, Studia Iuridica 78 (2019), 133.

man of the Sejm's Legal Committee, to establish by statute a permanent 'commission to create a uniformity of legislation in the Polish State'. The motion was represented as the outcome of a non-partisan consensus. The signatories were recruited from all parliamentary factions, thereby proving – as recapitulated by the Legal Committee, to which the motion was forwarded by the Sejm and of which Marek himself was Chairman –

> the concordant opinion of all political circles in the country that the great work of codification should be commenced as soon as possible in the interest of the legal uniformity of the entire State and that an appropriate statutory framework should be created for such codification work.[120]

According to the intention of Zygmunt Marek and other signatories of the motion of 1 April 1919, it was not the government but the Sejm to delegate powers to the Codification Commission and – as a political and partisan body – to abstain from interfering with the Commission's works.[121] In the explanatory memorandum, the sponsors of the bill clearly enunciated their intention that the Sejm 'preoccupied with building the foundations of the Polish State and therefore its constitution, basic civil rights and administration,' should not undertake codification works directly, rely instead for that

120 *Sprawozdanie Komisji Prawniczej w sprawie wniosku nagłego posła Zygmunta Marka i tow. w przedmiocie powołania do życia komisji dla stworzenia jednolitego ustawodawstwa w Państwie Polskiem (Druk N° 298)* (Legal Committee's report on the urgent motion by deputy Zygmunt Marek and companions concerning the establishment of a commission to create a uniformity of legislation in the Polish State), in *Druki Sejmu Ustawodawczego Rzeczypospolitej Polskiej* [Records of the Legislative Sejm of the Republic of Poland], record no. 298, KPCiK 2 (1919)/1, 279. The fact of a non-partisan consensus is also attested by the fact that the motion was sponsored in the forum of the Sejm by the socialist Marek on the one hand and the national democrat, Zygmunt Seyda, Chairman of Constitutional Committee, on the other hand.

121 The idea of the establishment of a codification commission as an autonomous non-government college of experts was, of course, nothing new. Especially the German case study attracted the attention of Polish legal elites. For more information see Michael JOHN: *Politics and the Law in Late Nineteenth-Century Germany: the Origins of the Civil Code*, Oxford University Press, Oxford, 1989; Franz WIEACKER: *Privatrechtsgeschichte der Neuzeit unter besonderer Berücksichtigung der deutschen Entwicklung*, Vandenhoeck & Ruprecht Verlage, Göttingen, 1967; Hans H. SEILER: *Geschichte und Gegenwart im Zivilrecht*, Carl Hermanns Verlag, Köln, 2005, 315–332. Compare for instance Brian J. YOUNG: *Politics of Codification: The Lower Canadian Civil Code of 1866*, McGill-Quinn's University Press, Montreal-Kingston-London-Buffalo, 1994, 107–120.

purpose on a permanent Codification Commission, so that 'no important and great work in Poland not to come to rest.'[122] In the draft bill enclosed with Marek's motion, the deputies suggested vesting the Commission with the status of an 'organ of the Sejm' and thus acting on its behalf on the basis of a delegation of powers belonging to the legislature. The powers granted to the Commission were not complete. They were limited to preparing draft codes and referring them to the Sejm for 'constitutional processing', including the possibility of modification or even rejection of any proposals submitted.[123] Acting in that capacity, the Codification Commission was, among its other tasks, to take care of the preparation of draft civil and criminal substantive and procedural codes, as well as any such other drafts as might be entrusted to it by the Sejm. The sponsors proposed that the members of the Committee be appointed by the Chief of State upon recommendation of the Minister of Justice, which was finally corrected by requiring the minister to act in agreement with the Speaker of the Sejm. Thereby, the government, represented by that minister, had guaranteed influence on the composition of the Commission and the Sejm would not lose control of the selection process. Furthermore, the justice minister, in making the recommendation, would be obliged to seek a consensus on the matter with the law departments of all Polish universities, as well as the Supreme Court and bar associations. Once appointed, the members would be unable to be recalled, which, together with the lack of any legal avenues for interfering with the Commission's works, constituted one of the two basic guarantees of the autonomy of its operation.[124]

In the explanatory memorandum, Marek emphasized (without mentioning the government) that it was the constitutional responsibility of the Sejm, as the legislature, to eliminate the 'legal heterogeneity'. He stipulated that the intention of his motion was to create a codification body to perform the task 'independently from political currents, with objectivity unmarred by anything' and that such a body consequently had to be the 'fruit of the eminent expert forces in Poland'. Only such composition of the Codification

122 *Wniosek nagły posła Zygmunta Marka.*

123 *Ibidem. Cf.* similar assumptions in the draft submitted by Franciszek Nowodworski and the Supreme Court, whereby the Codification Commission would constitute a 'permanent central state authority' acting 'in companionship to the Sejm' and as an 'organ of the Sejm', hence independently from the executive branch. *Projekt Prezesa Izby II Sądu Najwyższego Franciszka Nowodworskiego (w porozumieniu z Sądem Najwyższym)* [Draft bill by the President of the 2nd Chamber of the Supreme Court, Franciszek Nowodworski (in agreement with the Supreme Court)], KPCiK 2 (1919)/1, 284–287.

124 *Wniosek nagły posła Zygmunta Marka.*

Commission would be capable of ensuring that the works were pursued 'free of partisan obstinacy, in the calm gifted by the authority of science but with attention to social development'.[125] Those 'eminent expert forces' were to be represented solely by the lawyerly elite – 'men of learning' – legal theoreticians and practitioners, without the participation of representatives of other social sciences.[126] That could appear to be reasonable, given that the Commission's task was not only the redaction of the provisions but also to achieve an understanding of the 'true will of society' and base the spirit of the laws being created on the outcome of that discernment.[127]

9 The Government Concept

The motion sponsored by Marek and others was forwarded for further proceedings to the Sejm's Legal Committee. Other drafts kept arriving.[128] Those included the 'counter-bill' of the Ministry of Justice, which eventually took a more proactive stance and came up with its own initiative to regulate the matter.

The Ministry concurred on the merits of the establishment of a 'separate organization (...) such as, unburdened with the tasks of everyday life, could be able to devote itself solely to that work, calculated on a succession of years.'[129] Neither the ministry, nor the authors of the other drafts submitted

125 *Sprawozdanie Stenograficzne Sejmu Ustawodawczego* [Stenographic report of the Legislative Sejm], 44th session of 3 June 1919, p. XLIV-5.

126 The participation of sociologists appeared to be especially justified in the context of the necessity of implementation of basic social and economic integration purposes through the use of legal instruments. See Władysław JACHER: *Zagadnienia integracji systemu społecznego: studium z zakresu teorii socjologii* [Topics of integration of the social system: a study in the theory of sociology], PWN, Warsaw, 1976, 13; Bolesław WINIARSKI: *Polityka gospodarcza* [Economic policy], WN PWN, Warsaw, 2006, 115. The implications of legal integration in reference to the BGB in Germany, providing a potential source of inspiration, became the topic of broad public debate involving not only economists but also ideologues and representatives of various circles.

127 *Wniosek nagły posła Zygmunta Marka.*

128 The *Kwartalnik Prawa Cywilnego i Karnego* published the following drafts in addition to the ministerial counter-bill: By Henryk Konic, prepared in agreement with the Civil Rights Commission of the Ministry of Justice; by Jan Jakub Litauer as President of the Civil Procedure and Commercial Law Commission of the Ministry of Justice; and by Franciszek Nowodworski, in agreement with the Supreme Court; KPCiK 1 (1919)/1, 284–291.

129 *Kontrprojekt Ministerstwa Sprawiedliwości*, 283.

to the Legal Committee during the same period, such as Henryk Konic, had any reservations against the Codification Commission being composed of legal practitioners and theoretical jurists.[130] Nonetheless, the Ministry of Justice decided to act to avert its own complete loss of influence on the activities of the Codification Commission, because the proposed relationship between the Commission and the government represented by the Minister of Justice was 'inappropriate from the perspective of state law'. While the Ministry professed the desire to maintain the 'autonomy and separation' of the Commission, explaining that 'this is not at all to create a relationship of subordination but only to safeguard the principle that the executive power belongs to the government,' still, a 'Commission detached from the government would form a body difficult to place in an expedient manner within the modern structure of a constitutional state.'[131] Favouring the establishment of links between the Commission and the Ministry of Justice was the need for the harmonization of the drafting-legislative works done by the government in the regulation of matters related to those falling within the ambit of the Commission's parallel operation. For that reason, it was argued, the Commission ought not to act with complete independence free of any consultation with the government. Among other devices, co-ordination was to be ensured by the proposal for representatives of the Ministry of Justice to participate in the Commission's meetings. However, the Ministry's counter-bill went even further than that. According to the assumptions of the draft, the Commission was to operate in companionship to the Ministry of Justice, acting externally only through the Ministry's mediation, especially in submitting its own drafts to the Sejm, and the Ministry would take responsibility for the Commission's actions.[132]

Yet another solution was proposed by Henryk Konic, who, as the President of the Civil Law Commission of the Ministry of Justice prepared, in agreement with the commission over which he presided, a draft supportive of the concept of direct subordination of the Codification Commission to the Chief of State.[133] Therewith, his commission offered, in a way, a dissent from the official position taken by the ministry itself – its own counter-

130 *Projekt Przewodniczącego komisji prawa cywilnego Min. Spraw. Henryka Konica (w porozumieniu z komisją)* [Draft bill by the President of the Civil Law Commission, Minister of Justice, Henryk Konic (in agreement with the Commission], KPCiK 2 (1919/1–4, 287–288.

131 *Kontrprojekt Ministerstwa Sprawiedliwości*, 283–284.

132 *Ibidem.*

133 *Projekt Przewodniczącego (...) Konica*, 288.

proposal in opposition not only to the deputies' bill but also to the ministerial one.[134]

10 The Final Concept

Pronouncing on the merits of the urgent motion and of the other drafts, chief among them the counter-bill of the Ministry of Justice, the Sejm's Legal Committee – in its report dated 30 May 1919 – declared its complete support for and acceptance of the reasons stated by Marek and companions.[135] As a result, it submitted to the Sejm's deliberation a draft only insignificantly modifying the original proposal of 1 April. This is hardly surprising, considering that the motion, tabled by Marek as President of the Legal Committee, had already won the support of other political factions. Thus, *de facto*, a similar group tabled the motion as debated on it in the Committee. However, the deputies intended to address the counter-bill and the explanatory memorandum submitted by the government via the Ministry of Justice and respond to other proposals.

The task did not seem excessively difficult, considering that the drafts were in agreement on multiple issues. First and foremost, both the signatories of Zygmunt Marek's motion and the government in its 'counter-bill' agreed that there was a real need – 'felt by all elements,' as the Legal Commission noted in its report – for the establishment of a Codification Commission to 'taken upon its shoulders as soon as possible the enormity of the tasks awaiting Poland in the field of judicial legislation and, in the interest of a homogeneous legal life of the entire State, achieve legislative uniformity.'[136] In the Legal Committee's opinion, nor did the Ministry of Justice dispute the concept that the Commission was to perform the task by operating on behalf of the Sejm rather than the government. The consensus was also the Sejm

134 The drafts submitted by Konic and by another president of another ministerial commission, Jan Jakub Litauer of the Civil Procedure and Commercial Law Commission, identify the difficulties faced by the Ministry of Justice in the development of a common position; the above may have been the reason behind the government's tardiness with the submission of its own draft and institutionalization programme for the codification works.

135 *Sprawozdanie Komisji Prawniczej*, 279. The course of the Legal Committee's deliberations is not known. Its position on the matter can be reconstructed on the basis o the report and subsequent speeches delivered in plenary sessions by deputies having participated in its meetings (Marek and Seyda).

136 *Ibidem*.

itself was not in a position to carry out such works by the participation of the deputies, as it was exceedingly preoccupied with 'concerns of state-making' and unable to take on the workload of the 'vast field of uniformization of legal co-existence in Poland'.[137]

On the other hand, the Legal Committee granted some of the postulates submitted by the Ministry of Justice with regard to bringing the Commission closer to the Ministry and provide the Ministry with a limited influence on the Commission's activities. For that reason, the Legal Committee recommended a draft requiring the Codification Commission to stay 'in constant touch' with the Ministry of Justice. The justification of that decision was strictly pragmatic: given that the Ministry of Justice had its own Legislative Department already 'working on draft bills in the same scope', it was fitting to establish a permanent link.[138] Accordingly, the Minister of Justice was afforded the right to participate in person or send delegates to participate in the Commission's meetings. Furthermore, the Legal Committee modified the final draft to make the Minister of Justice the sole body empowered to submit the legislative drafts prepared by the Codification Commission.[139] However, as noted by the national democrat, Zygmunt Seyda, when speaking in the plenary forum of the Sejm following the presentation of the Legal Committee's report, although neither the contents of the report nor the text of the draft following the Committee's modifications,

> spell this out clearly, the Committee was of one mind in deeming it an unacceptable thing for the Minister of Justice, in referring to the Sejm the bills drafted by the Codification Commission, to make any changes to the Commission's works. The Committee believed that the Minister of Justice had to be conceded the right to refer the bills to the Sejm, as that constitutes a political action, of which the Codification Commission, being an altogether apolitical body, had to be completely freed. For it is to be an institution with such gravitas, a circle of persons of such high academic standing, that the product of their work ought to have the justice minister's unconditional adherence.[140]

137 *Ibidem*, 280.

138 *Ibidem*.

139 *Ibidem*, 281.

140 *Sprawozdanie Stenograficzne Sejmu Ustawodawczego* [Stenographic report of the Legislative Sejm], 44th session of 3 June 1919, p. XLIV-7.

Moreover, reporting on the position taken by the Legal Committee, Seyda emphasized that in his opinion the principle of 'complete independence and autonomy of the Codification Commission' was of 'first-rate importance'. Bearing that in mind, members of the Legal Committee pondered: 'whether to base the Commission solely on the Sejm or base it on the Ministry of Justice, or leave it independent from both of these institutions,' and ultimately 'entered the path of compromise',[141] which probably meant – and was attested by the text of the act – that, while providing the Codification Commission with a relative independence, they to some extent catered to the need to bring it close both to the Sejm and to the Ministry of Justice. As occurred from the Legal Committee's report, this was to be proved by those provisions of the modified draft in which the Commission was guaranteed the right to define independently its own internal organization, although the text of the act contains the proviso that it has to do so exclusively 'in agreement' with the Ministry of Justice. The Legal Committee, however, emphasized that the role of the government, acting through the Ministry of Justice, is only to provide the Codification Commission with assistance and technical support.[142]

The matter of the desirable qualifications was discussed more broadly in the memorandum published by the legal circles of Lvov around the same time as Marek's motion. The Galician adepts imagines that only eminent lawyers or jurists having a specified level of knowledge and skill could serve as codifiers. In their opinion, neither a theoretician nor a practitioner gave the guarantee of being a 'good codifier'. They emphasized that a practitioner entrenched in routine could create bad legislation if lacking the skill for synthesis and generalization, which is the prerequisite of proper lawmaking technique free of casuistry.[143] Likewise, a scholar could fail in their discharge of the role, because 'a statute is not literature', and even 'with the most exacting knowledge of the subject,' the scholar could lack the sufficient talent to 'narrow a thought down, put it in a form that is succinct and clear,'

141 *Ibidem*.

142 *Sprawozdanie Komisji Prawniczej*, 280–281.

143 *Memoriał Wydziału Prawa i Umiejętności politycznych Uniwersytetu, Towarzystwa Prawniczego i Związku Adwokatów Polskich we Lwowie w sprawie techniki ustawodawczej* [Memorandum of the Faculty of Law and Political Skill of the University, of the Law Society and Polish Bar Association in Lvov concerning the legislative technique], KPCiK 2 (1919)/1–4, 154. In other words, the authors of the Memorandum appreciated that a legislator attentive to the proper form of the provisions being drafted ought to express their intention in a 'clear' manner 'corresponding to the language of the provision', and the regulation itself 'cannot be self-contradicting', or 'generate difficulties in application'.

or to 'exhaust the fullness of the matter in short, terse sentences.' On the other hand, the scholars were who should constitute the core of the expert support for the redaction works, because the codification work, or at least its first stage, was expected to be a type of 'theoretical' work consisting in the 'specifying the common guidelines and defining such ideal paths as the general legislative reform in Poland would have to tread.'[144]

Concerning this method of codification works, the authors of the motion to establish the Codification Commission, submitted on 1 April 1919, had already spoken in a laconic manner. They had believed that the preparation and drafting of the future code would require, firstly 'a comparative collation of legal principles and provisions [t]hereunto applicable in Polish territories,' and, which is worth emphasizing, in their imagination it would be based solely on the legal systems inherited from the partitioning powers, while consisting in the 'consideration of which of the several provisions regulating the same legal issue to give priority before the others.'[145] This corresponds to the above-cited assumption of the authors of the Lvov memorandum, who, among the qualifications required for codification works, did not ask for familiarity with any legislation other than applicable in Polish territories. That is characteristic of the enunciations of lawyers and jurists of 1919, who usually assumed that the codification opus would be based on the analysis of the legislation of the partitioning powers, and the work on it would consist in – as Wacław Makowski poetically put it – 'creation out of that diverse mosaic of a single picture, single whole subjected to a guiding idea had in common and functioning uniformly.'[146] In later utterances, as well as during the works of the Codification Commission, analysis of post-partitioning codifications was not the sole topic, which is understandable in a way, considering the accusations of datedness and incompatibility.

Already the participants of the Conference of Lawyers and Economists in September 1920 no longer attempted to claim that the works ought to consist in the processing and amalgamation of already applicable codified regulation. Instead, they passed a generally worded resolution to the effect that the codification should be the fruit of 'thorough and deep' works, because 'the new civil code has to be built on independent foundations, in conformity with the essential needs of the nation.'[147] How to build the independent foun-

144 Makowski: *W sprawie ujednostajnienia*, 13.

145 *Wniosek nagły posła Zygmunta Marka*

146 Makowski: *W sprawie ujednostajnienia*, 14.

147 *Zjazd prawników i ekonomistów polskich*, 241.

dations, however? We find some vision already in the text of the motion to establish the Codification Commission. While the authors did assume that the work would only involve 'the consideration of which of the several provisions [inherited from the partitioning powers] regulating the same legal issue to give priority before the others,' they also stipulated that the evaluation should consider 'the meaning and significance of each legal provision to the present time and continued social development'.[148] Therefore, they desired the new law to be modern and adapted to the changing realities of the time following World War I. In their assessment, the codifier ought not to lose sight of the direction taken by 'the development of affairs [or relations] in the Polish State,' so that 'a given norm theoretically deemed proper should not stand in conflict with the true expression of the will of our society.' Here a problem arose, however, for as they observed: 'Today, we cannot yet say what social forms life is to take; it only appears to be doubtless that we are only at the beginning of social transformations.'[149]

As we know, a similar assessment of the dynamically changing realities was offered by Ludwik Domański, who from the same premises derived the conclusion that 'the Codification Commission ought to be guided in its works by the experience of the past and the promptings of science for the future.' Moreover, as already emphasized, he was of the conviction that the contemporary world was characterized by 'a great abundance of legi-social theories and doctrines, oftentimes polarly opposed;. For the above reason, the work on the civil code would be very difficult and complicated. He believed, however, that

> the Codification Commission, following the example of the authors of the most recent codes, ought to seek the way out of the labyrinth of modern currents and aspirations in a synthesis, and the method of the synthesis should be captured by examining the direction so far taken by the development of civil legislation in all countries and the expected direction of its continued development in general and especially in our [country].[150]

The fruition of such a vision depended on heavily extending the spectrum of comparative studies to include other countries and focusing not so much on the regulations in force in those countries as the processes of legal develop-

148 *Wniosek nagły posła Zygmunta Marka.*
149 *Ibidem.*
150 Domański: *O systemie przyszłego Kodeksu*, 170.

ment taking place. According to Domański, one could take the Swiss codification works preceding the *Zivil Gesetzbuch* as a role model. He also appreciated the need to draw upon the experience of the past, whereby he came closer to the concepts of Alfons Parczewski, who called for the preparation of the draft civil code to be 'not only in the illumination of comparative remarks' but also of the 'historical perspective wherein any work of codification in general is usually placed'.[151]

Those calls to examine the law in a dynamic perspective, focus on its historical evolution and attempt to identify, on the basis, the direction its expected future development would take, while at the same time appreciating the pending socio-economic transformations or discerning 'the spirit of the nation', all that required considerably more in-depth study than a mere collation of civil-law provisions in force in other countries. In this context, it becomes understandable why the authors of the Lvov memorandum believed that a good codifier 'must know the history of the law, native and foreign law, and a Polish codifier must know the elements of ancient Polish law and the legislation of the partitioning powers, so as to refer to the existing state of affairs while constructing the edifice of the new law.'[152]

It can be surmised that the above assessment of the situation was close to the President of the Codification Commission, Franciszek Ksawery Fie-rich. It led him to the following conclusion: 'it would be amiss to cherish the partitional legislations beyond the necessary need and thereby de-facto sustain the former political borders dividing our Motherland.' Hence, Polish legislation ought to be homogeneous.[153]

11 The Track Record of Codification in the Twenties

Already in 1928, Fierich, the President of the Codification Commission, observed that the German Civil Code deserved to be distinguished from other codes applicable in Polish territories, as it 'reckoned with the manifestations of social and economic life in a greater degree',[154] That was because it not only 'venture[d] deeply into all affairs of life,' but also aimed to 'provide the basis for the continued development of such affairs'. Accordingly, due to the impor-

151 Parczewski: *Uwagi nad kodyfikacją*, 1.

152 *Zjazd prawników*, 241.

153 Fierich: *Rzut oka*, 456.

154 Fierich: *Unifikacja ustawodawstwa*, 264.

tance of the matter 'all such consequences as arise from one or other formulation of the basic principles of the civil code must be foreseen in advance.'[155] Fierich also appreciated the added difficulty stemming from the dynamic development of the situation. He remarked:

> following the great shockwaves societies had undergone and, in part, were still undergoing, especially in Europe, in political, economic and social terms, the matters of social organization, and therefore also of civil law, have become the subject of deep consideration of all of the juridical world.

There was a lively climate especially in Western Europe.[156]

Fierich observed that if the prevailing assumption was that in an unstable situation not amenable to the complete prediction of whatever direction of social development would be the most desirable and by what modern legal instruments – still being developed by European legal sciences – such development should be achieved, a civil code had to be postponed with patience.[157]

Soon after Karol Lutostański's draft Marriage Law, Fierich, as the Commission's President, took note of the intensified interest of 'as broad social circles as possible' in the future marriage law. That happened even though the subcomittee had not yet completed its work and had been the forum of exchange for different views on the legal character of marriage – secular (based on a civil contract) and religious (seeing marriage as first of all a sacrament). The growing social pressure made the subcommittee's works all the more difficult, undermining its independence. However, the situation could not possibly have taken anyone by surprise, as marriage had also officially been recognized by the drafters as the 'foundation of social and state organization'. Guiding assumptions such as the following were made: 'respect for the individual equal rights of both spouses, especially their equal obligations to the family' 'recognition of the permanence of marital cohabitation as the chief requisite for the development of family', and, in consequence, the termination of marriage was expected only in exceptional cases defined by legislative provisions; last but not least, the children's best interest was allowed to come to the

155 *Ibidem.*
156 *Ibidem.*
157 *Ibidem.*

fore.[158] Dissenting opinions within the subcommittee were voiced by Stanisław Gołąb and Władysław Abraham.

In 1928, the works on marital property law had not yet been completed. Eventually, that law was to be combined with marital personal law (and – ultimately – parts on the parents' relationship with the children, on guardianship and tutelage, as well as civil registration, ultimately 'most probably' to be found in a single draft for all of family law), as prompted by the sameness of the guiding principles of both of the parts: the legal equality of the spouses, the obligation incumbent on both to contribute according to their ability towards bearing the family's burdens, the joint-and-several liability of the spouses for obligations incurred by each of them in the ordinary household management, and the education of children. It was also a decided matter that the marital property law would be founded upon the principle of separate property (albeit with certain modifications prompted by the 'necessity to account for the community of life and collaboration in the spouses' income').[159]

Fierich expected the Commission to rely on the draft compiled by Władysław Leopold Jaworski. Being an opponent of statism, the latter proposed that matters of guardianship be entrusted to the family or persons appointed by he family or specialized private guardianship organizations vested with suitable powers. He, therefore, supported the institution of *opiekun przydany* (nominated or subrogated guardian, serving as a sort of co-guardian). Guardianship was conceived as an independent role and not as an activity exercised on behalf of the court. Given that, the key task was the skillful design of a monitoring system. The idea was to entrust the monitoring to the court, which, however 'ought to have a comprehensive network of bodies on the one hand inspiring it to exercise that monitoring and on the other hand enabling its actual exercise.' In that system, the key role was to be played by a family council, headed by a guardianship judge, replacing the court. All members of the family council were to be held accountable. In Jaworski's opinion, that would clothe the family council in suitable gravitas and avert the harmful 'bureaucratization of guardianship by the court.'[160]

In Fierich's opinion, inheritance law called for 'as expeditious elaboration as possible', if only for the reason that all former partitions of Poland had adopted proximate principles governing this area. Nonetheless, he stipulated the vague proviso that such principles were of 'politico-social nature', with the

158 *Ibidem*, 265.

159 *Ibidem*.

160 *Ibidem*, 265–266.

result that 'the section would work amid difficult conditions, without taking into account the currents circulating within legislative bodies.' He probably had in mind the reservations that the general provisions of inheritance law drafted by Henryk Konic could incur from political circles. Those provisions were ready by 1926 and were referred to debate. The debate saw a critical evaluation of modern codes. Both in inheritance law and in other parts, they were found to be afflicted by the defects of 'excessive subjectivism'. Furthermore, it was noted that 'based on ancient systems many such provisions and even entire legal institutions ha[d] moved into modern codifications despite having no value in practical life.' For that reason, Konic's aspiration was to simplify the inheritance system, by 'examining the individual issues from the perspective of practical affairs of life'. He also supported the principle of limiting the freedom of disposition of the estate in favour of protecting the rights of the family. The assumption was also that, in the event of a lack of close family members (up to the fourth or fifth degree), the inheritance would go to the state rather than the commune.[161]

As far as real law (the 'law of things', property law) is concerned, the codifiers led by Fryderyk Zoll, Jr. were primarily absorbed by the matter of rights in intangible goods. The harmonization was achieved by statutes other than codes. The Act on the Law of Authorship was met with a positive reception in the international arena. The expansion of the protection of the authors' personal interests was hailed as a special achievement of that act. Similarly, the Act on Counteracting Unfair Competition won recognition abroad. Favourable reviews were also attracted by the Act on the Protection of Inventions (1924). By contrast, with regard to the brunt of real law referring to tangible goods, the Commission had by 1928 not yet progressed past the preparatory stage. The main problems to solve were the practically necessitated need to modify the principle of absolute registration adopted by certain codes, and the necessity of maintaining – at least for a dozen or so years – partitional differences with regard to the keeping of land-and-mortgage registers (due to the lack of a cadastre as a basis for mortgage lists in the Russian partition and the need for the revision of rural land books in Lesser Poland – *Małopolska*).[162]

The only part of the Civil Code successfully implemented in the interwar period was the Code of Obligations of 1933. The authors were Ernest Till and

161 *Ibidem*, 266.

162 *Ibidem*.

Ludwik Domański for the General Part, and the same Till together with Roman Longchamps de Bérier for the Detailed Part. Similarly to developments unfolding in Western European countries, the debate saw the clash of two fundamentally different views. One, individualistic, was represented by Longchamps de Bérier. He demanded to follow the footsteps of the great 19th century codes, as well as the Swiss law of obligations in the redaction of 1901. That was opposed by Ignacy Koschembahr-Łyskowski (supporting the position taken on the matter by the French Legislative Unification Commission in 1925, i.e. after the redaction of a new general part of the law of obligations), calling – in the interest of socialization of civil law – for the imposition of considerable limitations on the intention of the parties with a series of provisions kept in line with the principle that the law ought to aspire 'not so much to the fulfilment of the parties intention as to the realization of justice'. On that basis, Koschembahr-Łyskowski compiled a counter-draft of the specific part. The subsection's task was to choose either one draft or find compromise solutions. The latter could include reliance on court cases, proceeding from the assumption, as Fierich did, that the courts would be the most appropriate guardians of public interest. It was realized that a position had to be taken vis-à-vis the strong calls for international harmonization of the law of obligations as the 'best suited' for that purpose. The trend was associated primarily with the completion, in 1927, on the works of a joint Italian-French draft code of obligations (the accession of Greece, Romania and Canada, among other expected countries, was also noted). The expectation, as read by Fierich was that 'in the field of the civil code, awaiting the Codification Commission is a momentous task (...) not only for the codification itself of civil law but also the position to be taken by Poland in the family of civilized states.'[163] Ultimately, the Codification Commission reached a compromise. The Code of Obligations of 1933 did not give up maintaining liberal-individualistic principles, but significantly corrected them in the spirit of social solidarity.

In Commercial Code issued in 1934, too, similarly to earlier enacted Cheque Law and the Law of Bills of Exchange, the guiding thought was for Polish legislation to follow similar principles as foreign states did, notably the specific group having already harmonized their respective legislation and also having close commercial ties to Poland. The overarching goal was to create legal mechanisms to facilitate trade among the citizens, which could be

163 *Ibidem*, 266–267.

achieved by levelling the differences among the legal institutions and principles of each such state.[164]

The commercial-law subcommittee, featuring Aleksander Doliński and Józef Sułkowski among others, compiled a draft based on Antoni Górski's work. That meant the draft followed the Italian example but had been modified by the subcommittee with a view to the commercial codes applicable in Polish territories and the 'needs of commerce'. Attention was also paid to the most modern solutions, drawing inspiration from the Swiss amendments to the law of obligations, mainly with regard to business companies. By 1928, however, that work had not yet been harmonized with the unfinished draft of the law of obligations.[165] For example, when it came to regulating the limited-liability company, the subcommittee concluded that the best statute in that field to date was the Austrian one of 1906 (as confirmed by a poll survey among business organizations), which was regarded more highly than the German statute of 1898 or the 1919 decree of the Chief of State regulating the institution of the limited-liability company in the territory of the former Congress Kingdom, the proper course of action was to follow the recent trends reflected in the Italian and Swiss drafts and the French statute of 1925.[166]

With regard to civil procedure, the members of the Commission did appreciate that the procedures applicable throughout Polish territories were all derived from the same source (the canon of principles of oral and public procedure and liberal theory of evidence) under the influence of French law. At the same time, however, they noted the existence of 'numerous differences in the various partitions (...) especially as to the position of the judge in the trial, the shaping of the means of evidence and legal remedies.' The specificity of the procedure was also delineated by the so-called 'four guidelines points' of the adopted concept: (1) mandatory response to the action (statement of defence), allowing Polish procedure to be included among those aspiring to 'alleviate the burdens of the main hearing'; (2) replacement of the parties' oath (still functioning in French and German procedures) with the interrogation of the parties in line with the positive experience from Austria and Hungary; (3) appellate proceedings *cum benefitio novorum* in the footsteps of French, German, Russian and Hungarian procedures but with significant limitations compared to those; (4) mixed model of proceedings before the Supreme Court,

164 *Ibidem*, 271.
165 *Ibidem*, 272.
166 *Ibidem*, 271.

with cassation (reversal) as the rule and reformation (modification) as the exception.[167]

During the works on enforcement procedures, the guiding belief was that the flagrant conflict between the creditor and the debtor's respective interests in such proceedings must be addressed in the broader categories of conflict of 'different economic or social groups'. The chosen objective was – in line with the 'trend among more recent enforcement statutes' – to govern the procedure and resolve all issues relating to it (assumption of liabilities and burdens by the acquiror; moment of incurring public fees) 'independently, without paying regard to the provisions of civil law', and without regard to the ensuing differences in decision-making from one partition to the next as a result of differences in substantive civil law.[168]

With regard to insolvency proceedings, the following overarching principles were adopted: (1) the institution of insolvency would be universal, extending both to merchants and non-merchants; (2) insolvency was not to cause actions transacted while already insolvent but before the declaration of insolvency (bankruptcy) to be *eo ipso* invalid but only assailable by court action; (3) 'expansion of the scope of action of the court at the expense of the self-governed community of creditors'.[169]

12 Freedom of Contract Versus Exploitation

Moving on to matters what was referred to as civil policy, i.e. examination of the problems of codification of civil law not only through the lens of a formal need to regulate social and economic relations but also as an instrument intended to 'contribute to the resolution of social and economic issues', the initial vague or fragmentary programmes characteristic of the first years of the interwar period must be distinguished from the extensive and complex programmes arriving in the later period.

The group of post-World War I concepts referring to the transformation of civil law was predominated by calls for restriction of the liberal principle of freedom of contract, while upholding the principle of inviolability of private property. Those calls constituted the response to the even more radical postulates of replacement of the capitalist order with a socialist one. The inter-

167 *Ibidem*, 268–269.
168 *Ibidem*, 269.
169 *Ibidem*, 269–270.

ventionist instruments imposing limitations on the civil-law principle of freedom of contract as the basis of obligation relationships were intended to be mainly in the nature of administrative law and thus regulated outside of the civil code. Thus, although the general part of the law of obligations was to retain its central significance, the focus needed to shift considerably towards the legislation accompanying the code and administrative regulations overriding general civil principles where they conflicted with the social policy pursued by the state.

First and foremost, emphasis was placed on 'checking exploitation' and on 'giving effect to the principle of equivalence of benefits,' which ought to be found in the future Polish code 'after the fashion of other legislations.'[170] As Leopold Caro went on to describe:

> In the latter half of the 19th century, in lieu of the principle of commutative justice, opportunity and therewith the availability of disproportionate profits and unexpected calamities have come to rule commerce. In the cornfield of our economic life, the weed of exploitation of the weak in the form of usury, playing the stock exchange, speculating on exchange rates, periodic commercial crises, disloyal competition of all kinds, and price inflation beyond any limits. (…) During this period, the prices of goods, interest rates, rents and wages of work are decided by the unilateral will of the stronger party.

Commerce is usually ruled by the market balance of supply and demand, and 'ethics are losing their voice in the regulation of the principles of commerce', because inscribed in the logic of the system are the following mechanisms of exploitation: 'the greater and thus more painful the shortage, the higher the price'; 'the more working hands generate new value, the lower wage is paid to each'; 'the lower the supply, and thus the more work is invested in general in generating the sum of the given goods, the lower the price falls'; 'the more goods are manufactured by the factory operator, thus the better the operator

---

170 See more Jan ANDRZEJEWSKI: *Laesio enormis i wyzysk: tradycja prawna a przeciwdziałanie nieekwiwaletności świadczeń w prawie prywatnym Austrii, Niemiec i Polsk* [Laesio enormis and exploitation: legal tradition and countering the non-equivalence of benefits in the private law of Austria, Germany and Poland], PhD thesis, Poznań, 2015, 118–168; Jan ANDRZEJEWSKI, Witold BORYSIAK, Aleksander GREBIENIOW, Jędrzej KONDEK: *Instytucja wyzysku w prawie cywilnym: perspektywa krajowa i prawnoporównawcza* [Institution of exploitation in civil law a national and legal comparative perspective], Wydawnictwo IWS, Warsaw, 2022, 169–217.

satisfies the common need, the lower prices the operator can get'; and 'the more difficult the position of merchants threatened with a crisis, the higher the discounts they pay on their promissory notes.' In a word, Caro summarized 'the triumphant liberalism (...) has gone to battle against ethics (...), attempting to stake in their place the banner of the right of the stronger.'[171] Citing Friedrich Engels, he attempted to demonstrate that trade, by its very nature, was 'licensed fraud,' being based on a logic of profit, so as to sell as dearly and buy as cheaply as possible, permitting the use of immoral means towards that end and especially the concealment of such qualities of the goods as might lead to the depreciation of their price.[172] He believed, however, that in many European states suitable civil and criminal provisions had already been enacted, along with the 'establishment of co-operatives moralizing the trade.'[173]

Caro demanded an effective fight on exploitation, believing that the 'motive of the stronger group to impose its will on the weaker group' as the 'determinant of the price' had the 'decisive strength' in a period of free competition in the capitalist order. That was especially visible 'in a period of postwar chaos benefiting the economically stronger manufacturers enjoying the support of the capitalist state', and the 'trade mediating the supply of the necessities of daily life'. The methods by which to curtail the exploitation, however, were not of the nature of civil law. He proposed 'curbing it with penal repression' 'by establishing co-operatives of all kinds', and 'temporary opening of borders to the import of foreign goods without customs', as the two principal categories of means to achieve a fair price of purchase of goods. Those he placed, at the same time, within the broader group of instruments for the protection of the weak, among which he mentioned

> [the] establishment of trade unions, social-security system in the event of illness, fortuitous accidents, unemployment and old age; collective bargaining of employment contracts and participation of the workers in the profits of the industrial enterprise wherever that is possible without injury to the development of industry.

171 Leopold Caro: *Równomierność świadczeń w ustawodawstwie* [Equivalence of benefits in legislation], KPCiK 2 (1919) /1–4, 332.

172 *Ibidem*, 335.

173 *Ibidem*.

All of the above, in his opinion, would 'lead to the achievement of a fair wage of work without violent revolutions and with the maintenance of private property as a natural principle of today's social order, guaranteeing the progress of humanity.'[174]

Caro delivered a whole arsenal of historical argumentation, proving that the entire tradition of European ethics was based on the need of regulation of disturbances of the free market. In his opinion, the use of instruments imposing limitations on the principle of the freedom of contract, rather than its liberal absolute understanding borne of 19th century economic thought, was more in line with the tradition of Roman law. In support of that claim, he invoked the Roman maxim *in emendo et vendendo naturaliter concessum est, quod pluris sit, minoris emere, quod minoris sit, pluris vendere et ita invicem se circumscribere*.[175] He pointed out the seller's right to challenge a perfected sale if the goods were sold at less than half their value. Sources for inspiration were to be sought, however, not only in Roman law but also in ancient philosophy. He cited Aristotle's *Nicomachean ethics* to claim that relationships between individuals in society should be governed by the principle of equivalence of exchange in any commerce. He invoked Cicero. In the *Summa Theologica* of Thomas Aquinas he found maxims demanding that contracts between parties should be based on the eqivalence of the object exchange and prohibiting the exploitation of the counterparty's hardship through the elevation of the price. Following in Aristotle's footsteps, mediaeval scholastic philosophers consistently demanded fair pricing. In modern legislation, Caro noted that the principle of equivalence of exchange (benefits) underwent limitations both in the French and Italian Codes, as well as the Prussian *Landrecht* and even in the BGB, the authors of which offered an – unconvincing, in Caro's view – attempt to justify the abandonment of the *laesio enormis*. Thus, the principle of equivalence found the 'fullest effect' in the ABGB, but in Austria, too, he discovered defects in the interpretation of the code's provisions by Austrian judges. The above led him to the following conclusion:

> The principle of equivalence of exchange constitutes such a momentous foundation for a society ruled by law and such an effective counterbalance to the mischiefs of the spirit of speculation, threatening especially to the stability and certainty of the right of ownership, that above all the propertied classes will demand its retention and expansion and limita-

174 *Ibidem*, 333–334.
175 *Ibidem*, 335.

> tion of exceptions from it according to necessity and equity. By contrast, the insatiable Manchesterism has attempted to expand those exceptions as far as it has been able.[176]

Similar overarching ideas could be found in the programmatic speech of the Codification Commission's President, Franciszek Ksawery Fierich. Similarly to other lawyers speaking in the debate in the immediate aftermath of World War I, he was conscious of the dynamic changes in the legal landscape. He especially noted 'lively movement in legal life' in the area of civil law.[177] In reference to early 19th century, he remarked that 'the ancient foundations of civil law largely came down crumbling in the past century,' having in mind the end of the feudal era characterized by 'tying certain social classes to the land, imposing restrictions on individual freedom, freedom of commerce, etc.' In that place a new, capitalist order was established on the basis of 'freedom of trade in land', having 'led to land becoming a sort of commodity, a sort of investment of capital,' as well as personal freedom and 'freedom of trade', which 'found its external manifestation especially in the freedom of contracting, in the unrestricted disposal of property in the event of death, the freedom of association, and freedom of movement in the areas of industry and commerce.' However, those principles could not function without limitations, and in Fierich's eyes the history of law in the 19th century largely constituted the history of evolution of the capitalist order, so as for the scope of individual freedoms guaranteed by it to be restricted in the interests of social solidarity. He went to explain:

> It is an understandable thing that the latitude could not be without limits, and that its confinement within appropriate borders, prevention of its excesses and deformations, had soon to become the second problem [after the replacement of the feudal order with a liberal one] and almost equivalent in rank to the first.

As he noted, already in the 19th century: 'the thought to the protection of the weaker party found its right of abode in the legislation,' but only 'especially in the current [i.e., 20th] century', one could see 'numerous legislative interventions partially of repressive and partially of preventive nature', counted

176 *Ibidem*, 309.

177 FIERICH: *Rzut oka*, 459.

on the fruition of such new ideas and currents in socio-legal thought. They found expression, as Fierich went on to enumerate 'in the principle, espoused by certain Western European legal systems, that the complete capacity to act in the legal sphere must be ensured only to those who have a suitable personal boldness, a suitable toughness.' And although in that principle 'we ought to see far-reaching limitations on the freedom of legal transactions,' his opinion was that such limitations would 'doubtless be taken into advisement in our circumstances of economic life.' Among that group he mentioned those limitations which would 'touch upon persons indulging habitually in drunkenness or habitually using toxic drugs against nervous diseases, or even, within certain limits, persons who mismanage their own property and especially the household, although frittering their property away might not yet be the case.' In this area, his main source of inspiration was 'Swiss legislation', to which the aforementioned circumstances were 'familiar to a certain extent'.[178]

13 The Identity Dispute in Marriage Law

In the identity paradigm, issues of personal marriage law came to the forefront in private law.[179] The matter involved not only deeply entrenched habits but also the canon of ethical and moral rules tightly linked to the religion defining a given community and shaping its identity. In Polish circumstances, national consolidation required cohesion on the basis of Catholicism.

To several jurists from the Civil Law Section, especially Alfons Parczewski, Leon Petrażycki and Stanisław Wróblewski, who, in 1925, tabled a motion on this topic – the fact that the matter was so sensitive in nature and, irrespective of whatever decision is taken, will immediately trigger passionate political disputes between the right and the left, meant that decision-making ought to be avoided in the draft, with the drafters instead taking the position of a 'legal technician' who provides the Sejm with a number of variants to choose

178 *Ibidem*, 459–460.

179 On Polish marriage law in the interwar period see Piotr FIEDORCZYK: *Development of Family Law on Polish Lands 1795–1945*, in Piotr GUZOWSKI, Cezary KUKLO (eds): *Framing the Polish Family in the Past*, Routledge, New York, 2022, 165–180; Piotr FIEDORCZYK: *Polish Matrimonial Law 1918–1939: Regulations, Attempts to Unify and Codify*, in Martin LÖHNIG (ed.): *Kulturkampf um die Ehe: Reform des europäischen Eherechts nach dem Grossen Krieg*, Mohr Siebeck, Tübingen, 2021, 147–165.

from.[180] The lawyer's task should be to remain 'objective' and content oneself with 'sounding' the public opinion.[181]

As Stanisław Gołąb took it upon himself to explain:

> The ecclesiastical or civil form of the celebration of marriage, indissolubility or development, these are matters of principle, determined internally by almost any intelligent person, carrying, however, as experience teaches, the spark of protracted and inevitable conflicts in which the 'objective' lawyer has only very little to say, from which, however, they must sound and record at least the basis for the formulation of the relevant provisions of the civil code or of a separate statute governing marriage.[182]

The manner of regulation of those issue should thus not be detached from society's attitude to them, which Gołąb term to be 'iurismatrimonial moods' (i.e., prevailing public sentiments regarding marriage law). In that context, he noted what he perceived to be the mass eruption of divorce after the Great War, often preceding by religious conversion. For that reason: 'The new Polish marriage law ought to avert the evil, eliminate the trade of creed, the changing of it as though of gloves, the – insulting to law – selection of law better suited, sometimes to human unhappiness, sometimes to the passion of the senses.' He believed:

> [it] impossible with the vain glitter of alleged 'progressiveness', or even a true one, wipe the trace of the dogmas of the first Church in the State (…) Things being as they are (…) an enormous number of people in Po-

180 Stanisław Gołąb: *Zasady prawa małżeńskiego* (*z obrad Sekcji Prawa Cywilnego Komisji Kodyfikacyjnej*) [The principles of marriage law (from the deliberations of the Codification Commission's Civil Law Section], Palestra 2 (1925)/2, 599–600.

181 *Ibidem*, 593.

182 Gołąb was inspired by the work of Eugen Huben preceding the ZGB, identifying his attempts at analysis of the following issues in personal marriage law: '(1) how to limit the right to demand divorce, so as to prevent too frequent and improvident divorces; (2) whether and to what extent the capacity to marry should be limited with regard to age, so as to prevent improvident marriages, or rather (…) the begetting of children in poor material, hygienic and educational circumstances; (3) how to table today the matter of man's relationship to a woman in marriage in the face of the fact of her full emancipation, her assumption of a large part of the burdens of marriage and sometimes more abundant generation of income by the wife than the husband?' *Ibidem*, 593–594.

> land are firmly rooted in the principles of the Catholic faith, holding marriage to be indissoluble, once contracted.[183]

The point of departure for the works on marriage law (both personal and property) was the debate held on the 'Principles of marriage law'. As soon as 29 March 1920, those were submitted by the then-Chairman of Civil Law Section, Władysław Leopold Jaworski. He set the canon of debate that was to heat up only several years later in the context of the concordat and the expectation of the lack of the Catholic Church's consent to civil marriages. However, Jaworski's draft fell far short of the expectations of the hierarchs of that denomination. Changes were drafted under the motto that 'Poland should follow progress.' The conundrum did not come down solely to whatever was progressive at a given point in history but also, as Stanisław Gołąb put it, included the dimension that 'what today flashes the mirage of progress can tomorrow, with [the benefit of] experience and deliberation, prove to [have been] a step backwards or to have highly detrimental consequences.'[184] It was beyond any doubt that the proposals would trigger 'conflicts both within society and with the Apostolic See,' whereas 'the times of a social revolution in which we [we]re living [were] an atmosphere thoroughly dangerous to legislative initiatives,' and with that 'while attempting any legislative works one had to reckon before everything else.'[185]

In his draft (accepted with reservation by two members of the Civil Law Section – Aleksander Doliński and Henryk Konic), Jaworski proposed for the celebration of marriage to be achievable both in a civil form before a civil-registration official and, optionally, before a 'pastor of souls' (*duszpasterz*) in religious form. In both cases the certificates would carry equivalent force. On their basis the state (and not a religious denomination) was to determine the validity of the marriage, resulting in civil registration.[186] Registration was to be mandatory for the validity of marriage, and thus it was to be left up to the state whether it wanted to recognize the validity of a marriage celebrated in religious form.

The giving of effect to that idea, however, could encounter factual difficulties due to the 'lack of suitable official staff, which the Catholic Church, by

183 *Ibidem*, 595.

184 *Ibidem*, 604.

185 *Ibidem*, 600.

186 *Ibidem*, 596.

contrast, [did] have.'[187] That was noted by Władysław Abraham, and the eminent legal historian canonist and marriage specialist's opinion was shared by the majority of the members of the Civil Law Section (including Alfons Parczewski, Leon Petrażycki, Jakób Glass, Ernest Till, Stanisław Wróblewski, Antoni Górski and Ludwik Zachariasz Cichowicz), observing that 'the sanction of nullity would be an insult to religious marriages.'[188]

In his ponderation of what solution would be progressive, Abraham noted that on the eve of the concordat the Roman Catholic Church would not consent to civil marriages. In his opinion, Jaworski's proposal of 'optional marriage' (literally: 'facultative'), i.e., admission of both civil and religious form, marked 'great progress, for it exclude[d] coercion on the part of both religion and the state.' Abraham believed that the matter of civil marriages ought not to be identified with the 'separation of Church and State'. He cited the example of the United States 'where that separation has been consistent and the most far-reaching', and yet civil marriages continued to be only optional. That was, in his opinion 'the blooming of the practicality of the Anglo-Saxon race', which had understood that 'for the State, a certain degree of control will suffice', all the more so considering that 'the state, wanting to act rationally, must pay diligent attention to the importance of social insti-

FIGURE 2.5
Stanisław Gołąb, 1878–1939, an academic linked to Jagiellonian University; professor of civil law and civil procedure, Dean of the Faculty of Law. As a member of the Codification Commission, involved in numerous works on civil law and procedure.

187 *Ibidem.*
188 *Ibidem*, 601

tutions; it must be able to know that the institution of marriage also has spiritual significance.'[189]

An extreme position in the religious direction was taken by Professor Józef Brzeziński, a canonist from Jagiellonian University. He evaluated the proposed solutions not through the categories of progress but those of their harmfulness caused by incompatibility with the national tradition. From that perspective, he believed: 'in line with Polish traditions, one should wish for our legislation to adhere to the principles of ecclesiastic law having the most developed system [i.e. Catholic]. In any case, conflict and "cultural fight" have to be avoided.' Also: 'Civil marriages contradict the essential foundations of marriage as an institution based on natural law and having religious and moral character.' In consequence, the registration of a marriage ought never to have any relevance in the context of its validity but only its civil effects. Thus, Brzeziński was of the opinion that 'the institution of religious marriage ought to be moved to the fore.' He emphasized that was even 'in the interest of the freedom and equality of the woman', whereas 'through the optional civil marriage only latitude is given to those individuals who do not wish to satisfy the obligations they have incurred.'[190]

The opposing extreme called for mandatory civil marriages. Out of more than a dozen members the Civil Law Section had, that solution was supported only by the socialist lawyer, Zygmunt Marek, and the Supreme Court justice, Tadeusz Bujak. Mentioned among the arguments favouring that choice was first of all that the 'evolution of legal culture required the retention' of that solution, especially as it had already been adopted in the former Prussian partition. If even the Catholic Austrian legislature had taken the position of a civil contract, all the more so – in the face of continued evolution of social affairs – ought a 20th century Poland not to dispute that change. Secondly, civil marriages 'promote[d] a sense of citizenship', emphasizing the primacy of state affiliation. Thirdly 'the state had the right and obligation to regard marriage as a social institution.' Marriage was union establishing the family as the most basic social organization, whereas for religion such a foundation should only be found in faith. At last, optional civil marriages were an impractical solution, resulting in the creation of two types of registers. Only civil registrars should serve that role.[191]

189 *Ibidem*, 596.
190 *Ibidem*, 599.
191 *Ibidem*.

Those voices, however, were unconvincing to the vast majority of the members of the Section (including Professor Maurycy Allerhand, Ignacy Koschembahr-Łyskowski, Ernest Till and Fryderyk Zoll, Jr., Józef Skąpski and Jakób Glass), who supported the solutions proposed by Jaworski and Abraham. The starting point for that concept was that 'nothing was more harmful than coercion in matters of marriage.' Mandatory civil marriage could only be justified if neither party belonged to a legally recognized religious denomination or a religious marriage was refused to them for a reason unrecognized by civil law.[192] Accordingly, the majority of the Civil Law Section favoured so-called optional civil marriages and opted against making the validity of marriage conditional upon registration in civil registers.[193]

Back to Jaworski's draft Principles, he further proposed that for civil marriages celebrated before a civil servant no 'facts or relations of religious nature' be capable of serving as impediments to the celebration of marriage. Jaworski enumerated secular impediments to the validity of marriage, such as bigamy, consanguinity, affinity, and age (harmonized with exemption from criminal liability for felonies). Moreover, the general provisions of civil law should determine the grounds on which the defectiveness of a statement of will or lack or limitation of capacity for legal transactions could vitiate the validity of the celebration of marriage (with the proviso that the impediments should include 'impotence and premarital pregnancy, while excluding property affairs').[194] Even that proposal, in Abraham's opinion, was taking things too far. In his opinion, where a state at all recognized a certain religious denomination, the latter had to be guaranteed the right to have the validity of marriage be evaluated by the competent religious authorities, only with the provision that state law should be able to expand the list of grounds of nullity. Additional, Abraham remarked, the civil effects of marriage should be subject to the decision-making of the civil authorities.[195]

The essence of the matter was reducible to the admission of ecclesiastical jurisprudence, which, given the solutions proposed by Jaworski, would be out of the question. That concept, however, did not find many supporters in the Section. Only three members spoke clearly against allowing ecclesiastical courts. Tadeusz Bujak and Zygmunt Marek, as proponents of mandatory civil marriage and legal divorce, were joined by Wróblewski, who proposed

192 *Ibidem*, 601.

193 *Ibidem*, 603.

194 *Ibidem*, 596.

195 *Ibidem*, 598.

an original solution in which, although the validity or marriage and admissibility of divorce were to be regulated by ecclesiastical law, the cases would be decided in state courts.[196]

Jaworski believed that divorce ought to be allowed unconditionally with the mutual consent of the spouses, and by petition of one spouse 'for reasons of aggravated adultery, permanent mental disease or [disease] causing a lasting threat of infection; aggravated ill-treatement, and hard labour,' [the latter as a criminal sentence for certain felonies]. He would allow no exceptions for religious marriages, Catholic marriages or marriages of other religious denominations. Nor did his plans include allowing ecclesiastical jurisdiction in divorce cases.[197] Such extreme proposals were met with doubts, first by Abraham. In Abraham's opinion, the admissibility of divorce 'ought to be considered,' but limited to cases 'demanded by the public welfare', and – e.g. following the Italian example – only for civil marriages. In the contrary case, he feared the frustration of the concordat. Contrary to Jaworski, the believed that 'one ha[d] firmly to oppose divorces by mutual agreement of the parties,' as well as any divorces transacted 'for egoistic reasons'. Marriages of which children had already been born should be subjected to the most stringent restrictions on the admissibility of divorce.[198] That opinion was shared by the clear majority of members of the Civil Law Section (including Cichowicz, Górski, Kroshembahr-Łyskowski, Parczewski, Petrażycki, Skąpski, Till, Wróblewski and Zoll), opposing the proposal of voluntary divorce by mutual consent. It was argued that, on the one hand 'ethics require[d] that marriage be, in so far as possible, permanent, and divorce only a *malum necessarium*,' and on the other hand 'the experience of different times and countries strongly favours the farthest restrictions on divorce.'[199] Brzeziński was of a different opinion, believing that the state ought not to recognize the divorces of Catholics and allow divorces for non-Catholics only on an exceptional basis but never by mutual agreement of the spouses.[200] Two of the Section's members, Allerhand and Glass, concurring with Jaworski's position, argued further than the admission of voluntary marriages (with an extended time-frame for 'negotiation of settlement') was the only possible way of breaking from the 'immoral' practice of circumvention of the law (*in fraudem legis agere*) through

196 *Ibidem*, 601.
197 *Ibidem*, 596.
198 *Ibidem*, 598.
199 *Ibidem*, 601.
200 *Ibidem*, 599.

religious conversion.[201] Eventually, the Civil Law Section, by 'considerable majority of the vote', accepted the 'dissolubility of every marriage before the state' (because, as Jaworski put it 'the law must not force the population to lie,' and 'neither may it speak only for the affluent, who have the money to afford the process') but not the availability of divorce by simple agreement of the spouses. That signified a departure from the original assumptions of the draft Principles, according to which the nature of marriage was to be that of a (relatively simple) civil contract and registration to be decisive of the validity of the marriage (which was inferred from the recognition of marriage as a 'social union'). The scrapping of the latter proposal did not at all mean the abandonment of the mandatory registration of marriages. The matter was only the sanction for non-compliance with the duty.

Jaworski adhered to the principle that separate property ought to be the default statutory property regime. 'The extent and quality of the wife's contribution to the carrying of the burdens of the marriage, in the absence of an agreement, [was to] be determined by a judge'. The freedom of matrimonial property agreements was to be limited. Changes to the default regime were to be available by court decision.[202] The Section unanimously favoured the 'separation of property' and the wife's obligation to 'contribute to the carrying of the burdens of the marriage'.[203]

In private-law relations, the spouses were to be equal to each other, and the wife not to be subjected to any legal limitations due to being a married woman. However, in the matrimonial community regime, the decision on matters of the household and education of the children was to belong to the husband.[204] That aspect incurred the criticism of Abraham, who observed that just as the principle of equality and separation of property was correct, so the deviation made from it in the aforementioned matters 'incur[red] doubts, especially where a daughter [wa]s concerned.' In his opinion, in that regard, too, the spouses' rights should be equal, and in cases of disagreement the decision should belong to the guardianship council and not to the husband.[205] That opinion won the acceptance of the Civil Law Section, which unanimously voted for the absolute equality of the rights of the husband and of the wife.[206]

201 *Ibidem*, 601, 605.
202 *Ibidem*, 597.
203 *Ibidem*, 602.
204 *Ibidem*, 597.
205 *Ibidem*, 598.
206 *Ibidem*, 602.

In the summary of his account of the proceedings, Stanisław Gołąb concluded that on the road of progress one ought to act not only with great deliberation and caution but also with moderation and in search of compromise.

> Acute contrasts should be mitigated; each must concede something of their own. Just as the brilliant paradox of Anatol France that «*le catholicisme est la forme la plus acceptable de l'indifference religieuse*» [Catholicism is the most acceptable form of religious indifference] is not true, just as it is true that the Roman Catholic Church will not deviate from what it deems to be its dogma, on the other hand one cannot strike with one stroke of the pen all of the aspirations of the state or 'freedom' in the field of marriage.[207]

14 Civil Procedure

A leading role in the Codification Commission's preparation of a new civil procedure was played by Jan Jakub Litauer, Vice-President of the Civil Law Section. He expounded his concept of civil procedure in an article titled General overview of the essence and development of civil procedure. Litauer argued that the shape of civil procedure (having for some time been 'the objective of subtle philosophico-legal inquiry') was not an ordinary technical matter (and should not be 'specified in a mechanical manner'), but similarly to other areas of the law and especially of substantive law, it was organically linked to social life. That was dictated by its close links to substantive law. For, according to Litauer 'without the procedural statute', substantive law 'would be a mere abstraction', as it was the 'task of the civil procedure [and other procedural statutes] to (...) give substantive law its practical significance, to bring it to life.' That, of course, made 'civil procedure (...) an auxiliary institution of civil law'. The manner of 'giving effect' to substantive law had to be sophisticated, adapted to the time and place and to the characteristics of the nation for which it was designed. In Litauer's opinion, it had to be borne in mind that, for all its immanent links to substantive civil law, civil procedure was something separate 'as the core of the procedure is made up of coercive norms',[208] and

207 *Ibidem*, 604

208 Jan Jakób LITAUER: *Pogląd ogólny na istotę i rozwój procesu cywilnego* [A general overview of the essence and development of civil trial], KPCiK 1 (1919), 31. Litauer's views on procedural law were a response to the lack of popularity of the theory of civil procedure.

thus, in designing the procedure, one first of all needed to consider society's reaction to the coercion to which it is to be subjected, with attention to the specific circumstances of the place and time of application.

As he put it, civil procedure was 'one of the manifestations of state life,' having its own 'external side', composed of a 'social and psychological substrate' of the process, and its 'impact on economic affairs.' The economic significance of this instrument was due to the fact that civil procedure ought to be viewed as a 'complex of forms and maxims' or as a 'system of means' for the giving of effect to the substantive rights of an individual adequately to the specificity of 'a given territory in a given era'. Accordingly, especially when it is 'considered from a certain height, it is not at all the dry and soulless topic it is commonly [...] taken to be.'[209] Its structure ought to be strictly adapted to the current socio-economic needs. Just as a theoretical jurist would be interested in the 'mechanism [or] technical organization', so a politician or statesperson to whom 'the institution of the process has no less a sense,' the 'political, economic and social function' of the procedure will be of primary significance.[210] The conviction of the necessity of adaptation of the civil procedure to the specificity of the 'socio-economic moment' in which it is expected to apply is something Litauer borrowed from the eminent Austrian proceduralist, Franz Klein.[211] With Klein, Litauer held that the primary goal of civil procedure was to determine the 'judicial truth' and that the methods of searching for that truth were the 'reflection of the intellectual, political and economic circumstances of the era'.[212]

Following in Klein's footsteps, Litauer proceeded from the assumption that the law of civil procedure was an area undergoing evolution 'together with the eminent transformations of state life'. To capture the moment of historical evolution was of key significance to him. The creation of a modern procedure require the diligent study of its direction of development. According to Klein and Litauer, following the breakthrough of the Enlightenment Age, civil procedure had evolved primarily in connection with the adoption of the principle that 'the sole criterion for the discovery of the truth,' may only be the 'free, completely unfettered intimate conviction of the judge'. In the 19th century, in keeping with concepts of individuality and autonomy of the parties, with the

209 *Ibidem*, 36.

210 *Ibidem*, 36–37.

211 Litauer's main inspiration probably came from Klein's views expounded in the publication titled *Zeit und Geistesströmungen im Processe*. See Szymon RUNDSTEIN: *Nowe prądy w procesie cywilnym* [New currents in civil procedure], GSW 23 (1902), 359.

212 LITAUER: *Pogląd ogólny*, 32.

exclusion of any form of interference from the state, the principle of formal truth was retained; it meant that the fact-finding in court procedures could take place without the court's active involvement. However, because of the dynamic economic development of the later half of the century, the retention of that principle ceased to be sufficient in the light of 'increasingly prominent class differences' making 'the equality of the parties [at trial] (...) a mendacious fiction'. Litauer, after Klein, proceeded from the assumption that the economically stronger party was '*de facto* better armed' for the trial and thus gained the advantage. For that reason, the harmful principle of formal truth had to be replaced with the principle of material (or substantive, or objective) truth, turning the judge into an active actor 'actively searching for the truth', rather than stopping at the evidence gathered by the parties. Moreover, Litauer invoked Klein's argument that 'Manchesterism and the judge's lack of agency in civil procedure is out of touch with the judge's role recognized in substantive law.' They observed that 'the judge, after all, had the power to interfere with contractual relationships, such as to decide whether a contract was or was not opposed to the good mores, or whether a contractual penalty was or was not excessive, or whether or not the exploitation of the weaker party was taking place.'[213]

The paradigm of modernity, according to him, was delineated by the socialist thought, which is where he differed from Franz Klein and took his inspiration mainly from another Austrian scholar, the socialist theoretician, Anton Menger. Litauer stood on the position that 'from the history (...) of the evolution of the procedure to date the unmoved certainty flows that the reign of formalism having often barred the judge from learning the truth ha[d] irretrievably come to an end.'[214] Even though he used the term 'evolution' with regard to civil procedure, in his views Litauer appeared to be close to Ludwik Domański, expecting both Poland and the world at large, following the experience of the Great War, to be on the eve of a epoch-making (revolutionary) democratic and socialist breakthrough. However, invoking Anton Menger, he believed that 'not even the most radical socialists,' imagined the complete abolishment of the forms composing the court procedure.[215] In his opinion, the existing forms of procedure, admittedly 'some-

213 *Ibidem*, 33–34.

214 *Ibidem*, 35.

215 Litauer believed the Jacobin experiment of 1793 with the 'abolition of all judicial forms and the entire judicial procedure' as a complete failure (resulting in seven years of 'confusion and unprecedented arbitrariness'), and he regarded the similar dispensation in Soviet Russia as only a transitional revolutionary form. *Ibidem*, 34–35.

what heavy but durable', had become in ingrained in people 'for millennia'. Therefore, those habits and the force of tradition ought not to be completely thwarted, even in attempts at the construction of a socialist state 'a people's state of labour'. In Litauer's opinion 'especially (...) for the resolution of property and family disputes (...) the factors of the old procedure w[ould] inevitably be maintained.'[216]

Litauer adhered to the concept that 'the law [wa]s the sum of institutions expressing certain conditions of moral existence,' such as property, contract, marriage or 'concept of human honour'. According to him, civil procedure should be viewed as an instrument for the protection of such rights, hence a guarantee of fruition of those conditions of moral existence.[217] Moreover, he held the belief in which 'the gradual intensification of coercion even constitutes the characteristic feature of the evolution of the state through history to date on the path to the creation of a people's state of labour.' Litauer ends with the conclusion that the state's evolutionary path to socialism is marked with the growing intensity of protection of the laws by the state authority. That, according to him, is the correct and progressive direction, because the more modern the state, the more strongly it aspires 'through the use of coercion to

FIGURE 2.6
Jan Jakub Litauer, 1873–1949, lawyer (advocate), member of the Codification Commission involved in the works of the subsection on civil procedure; justice of the Supreme Court.

216 *Ibidem*, 35–36.

217 Litauer invoked Ihering's *The Struggle for Law*.

[achieve] in the end result the harmonious co-existence of people in a given territory'. For that reason 'the judicial process, as a method of coercive enforcement of individual rights with the assistance of the state',[218] constitutes an instrument of modernization. The proper exercise of the procedural function makes 'manifest the moral value of human existence'. Appropriately designed civil procedure is not only a socially useful tool 'reinforcing morality' (whereas 'making light of and waiving one's rights weakens both moral resilience [and] the mores' in society) but outright indispensable to the assurance of social order, as it prevented the abandonment of rights, which Litauer regarded as 'moral suicide'.[219]

One could form the impression that Litauer placed less emphasis on the specificity of the place than the historical moment in which the civil procedure was to apply. That appears to be reasonable, considering his inclination towards the universalist historical philosophy characteristic of socialist thought, of which he was a sympathizer. However, the aspect of fruition of a specifically national history, through a procedure adapted to the characteristics of the Polish nation, was not alien to him. In procedural law, being part of private law (containing the aforementioned institutions constituting the conditions of moral existence), rather than public law, he saw 'the essential school for the political education of the nation'. The protection of an individual's rights in private life was capable of transference to the collective; in this case, the nation. Where individuals are able to defend their own rights successfully, having the appropriate instruments to do so, the nation also grows stronger, acquiring the same ability to protect its rights.[220] Citing Ihering, Litauer asserted that the 'impartiality and conscientious of the judicial estate doubtless depends on the energy of the sense of justice in the nation,'[221] where that energy is determined by the inclination to protect one's rights.

Should procedural regulations reflect the national specificity of the state? Litauer's answer was in the affirmative. He proclaimed: 'the reform of procedural law (e.g. in our three former partitions) must not consist in the simple adoption of someone else's concepts, even the wisest, but it must be based on aptly capturing their link to political institutions and national outlooks, habits and customs.'[222] This conclusion he inferred from the assumption that 'the

218 *Ibidem*, 27–28.

219 *Ibidem*, 38–39.

220 *Ibidem*, 39.

221 *Ibidem*, 40.

222 *Ibidem*, 31.

procedural system of every free nation develops simultaneously and gradually together with its other institutions', and is thus inextricably linked to the specific development of a given community, where the 'procedural forms (...), given the passage of time, create a whole so tightly linked to the state's general organization that it acquires the character of political institutions.'[223]

223 *Ibidem.*

CHAPTER 3

The Ideology of Polish Private Law after the World War II (until 1955)

I Until 1947

1 Introduction

At the time of they assumed power Poland in 1944–1945, members of the new Polish Workers' Party (*Polska Partia Robotnicza*) did not have sufficient knowledge or conception of the legal system. They had not previously engaged in conceptual works on the topic, and their political position was the result solely of Stalin's decision to support them and, by wait of *faits accompli*, put in their hands the government of Poland.[1] Those circumstances, combined with the need quickly to obtain at least a minimal level of societal support for a new government, completely unknown to the citizens, dictated that a model of law consistent with the USSR's subordination of all countries deemed to be in its sphere of influence would be introduced in stages.[2]

'Representatives of the new regime, fully conscious of the negative connotations of the word 'communism' in Poland, almost never used it, instead calling the newly forming system 'democracy'.[3] While doing so, they emphasized their determination to restore to that term its true sense, for, according to them, the political organization of Poland during the interwar period had never been democratic due to the dominance of liberal doctrine. The adjective properly describing that democracy was to be 'social',[4] soon replaced with the 'people's democracy' (*demokracja ludowa*). Nonetheless, no specific substance was provided for the concept. Instead, there were only declarations of under-

1 'Did we realize our weakness? Of course we did. We knew we were an overwhelming minority and the majority were hostile to us' – interview with Ludwik Chajn, Vice-Minister of Justice in 1944–1949; Teresa TORAŃSKA: *Oni* [They], Omnipress, Warsaw, 1997, 316.

2 That sphere was delimited by the Yalta Conference and the territorial extent of the presence of the Soviet Army in Europe at the end of World War II.

3 Jerzy EISLER: *Zarys dziejów politycznych Polski 1944–1989* [An outline of the political history of Poland 1944–1989], Polska Oficyna Wydawnicza BGW, Warsaw, 1992, 15.

4 Wacław BARCIKOWSKI: *Od demokracji liberalnej do demokracji społecznej* [From liberal democracy to social democracy], Nowa Epoka, Warsaw, 1947.

 | DOI:10.1163/9789004730021_005

taking ambitious original projects meeting society's expectations,[5] along with assurances along the lines of: 'the noblest goals are guiding those standing today at the helm of government.'[6] That was expected to be the sufficient basis for a presumption of 'good faith' in 'all actions of the government'[7], declared by parliamentary deputies even when initially raising some doubts about the changes underway. They approved those *ex post*, as the new administration took advantage of the power abrogated to itself to issue decrees ranking as statutes.

Temporarily, ignoring designs of implementation of Marxist doctrine in its Soviet interpretation, the new regime and some of the legal circles described the condition of civil law as transitional.[8] An evolutionary speed of changes or a peaceful revolution was suggested.[9] The experience of the value of universal social solidarism having formed in Poland as a result of the occupying powers' anti-human-rights policies[10] successfully pre-empted the use of slogans of class struggle and complete abolition of private property. There did exist, however, social room for other changes, whether due to significant initiatives to modernize the law that were not completed under the Second

---

5 See Krystyna KERSTEN: *Narodziny systemu władzy: Polska 1943–1948* [The birth of a system of power: Poland 1943–1948], SAWW, Poznań, 1990, 154–156, *passim*. The organizational and doctrinal autonomy of the Polish Workers' Party was stressed in its 1st Conference on 6 to 13 December 1945 by Władysław Gomułka.

6 Wacław BARCIKOWSKI: *Demokracja a sądownictwo* [Democracy and the judiciary], DPP 5 (1946), 8–11. Concerning the social self-determination and constitution process, which – beside geopolitical and economic changes – was the cause of the transformations in Central and Eastern Europe ending the era of communist rule in the region, see Ulrich K. PREUSS: *Revolution, Fortschritt und Verfassung, Zu einem neuen Verfassungsvertändnis,* Fischer Wissenschaft, Berlin, 1994, 88–97. Among other analyses of the situation of Poland, see Timothy G. ASH: *Polska rewolucja. Solidarność 1980–1982*, ResPublica, Warsaw, 1989, 5–24, 67–70, *passim* [English version: *The Polish Revolution: Solidarity, 1980–82*, Scribner, 1984].

7 *Sprawozdanie Stenograficzne z 20 sesji Sejmu Ustawodawczego* [Stenographic report of the 20th session of the Legislative Sejm] of 24 June 1947], statement of Stanisław Gross, 62–65.

8 Information about the direction of change represented as a transition from capitalism to socialism began to surface in the public space in 1947; Stanisław EHRLICH: *Zagadnienia praworządności* [Topics of rule of law], Książka i Wiedza, Warsaw, 1947, 17.

9 More extensively Hubert IZDEBSKI: *Polska Rewolucja – pokojowa rewolucja: ze studiów nad terminologią polityczną pierwszych lat Polski Ludowej (1944–1948)* [The Polish Revolution – a peaceful revolution: from studies on the political terminology of the initial years of People's Poland (1944–1948)], CPH 37 (1985)/2, 301–326.

10 Events of the occupation included act of genocide that claimed the lives of millions of citizens of the Second Republic, especially those of Jewish ethnicity, but also more than 1 million of ethnic Poles.

Republic or the citizens' view of the reasons for which Poland again lost its independence in 1939, as well as the new dynamic in social relations as a natural consequence of the events of 1939–1945.

Therefore, the emphasis was placed on those elements of ideas and axiology of the new law with which Polish society of that time could identify. National values, values of justice and safety, as well as ethics were invoked, taking advantage of the weight those terms carried in 1945–1948. Examples included one of the three questions of the referendum of 30 June 1946 intended to resolve the issue of the most important principles of the political system. Respondents were asked if they desired the 'solidification, in the future constitution, of an economic organization achieved by agrarian reform and nationalization of the core sectors of the national economy with the preservation of the basic rights of private initiative?'

The transformation carried out in reality was based on completely different doctrinal foundations. Before the official announcement of those, put to the fore was the protection of those economic interests of the Motherland and of its citizens that required the state's intervention in the affairs of private law. The state began to dispose of property it did not own, taking advantage of extraordinary circumstances including the mass migration of the population and the physical absence of many owners of property as a result of warfare and territorial changes.[11] The legal basis was found in the need to protect the property. As a similar role was ascribed to adjective-free justice, justifying – in the name of responsibility for crimes against the Polish nation – the confiscation of property belonging to the German state and German citizens, as well as Polish nationals who had supported the occupiers.

The third justification for the changes, intended to proclaim their permanent direction, were the calls upon 'the people's democracy'. Many functions were attributed to it, beginning with the simultaneous designation of 'national tradition' and modernity. The use of the term 'people's democracy' was showcased as evidence of progressive thinking about law, assuming the reinforcement of the rights of the generality of society, as well as the individual rights of every member of the community. Such interpretations were advanced in connection with changes to real law. Those were described as a balancing act

11 More extensively about this particular process, among others, Zygmunt Dulczewski (ed.): *Tworzenie się nowego społeczeństwa na Ziemiach Zachodnich* [The formation of a new society in the Western Territories], Instytut Zachodni, Poznań, 1961; Zygmunt Dulczewski, Andrzej Kwilecki (eds): *Pamiętniki osadników ziem odzyskanych*, [Memoirs of the settlers of the recovered territories], Wydawnictwo Poznańskie, Poznań, 1963.

struck among several competing values. According to that thesis, state ownership was expanded and given more protection (nationalization of the industry and certain other types of property) but also private ownership was popularized through the agrarian reform. Nationalization was to ensure better management and use of the property, subjecting it to modern but also participatory mechanisms of governance, making better use of the collective work of labourers. On the other hand, the agrarian reform was painted as a manifestation of direct democracy and social justice, one of the forms of which was to be equitable access to the ownership of agricultural land and giving the ownership of it to those having toiled on farms for generations.

Here, too, reality diverged from the political declarations, though the knowledge only became public around 1949. The peasant farmers increased their individual landholdings, but the administration withheld the formal transfers of title to them. Labourers' participation in the management of enterprises was fictional, and the management model of state-owned enterprises (also denied legal autonomy), combined with the introduction of central planning, proved dysfunctional.

The specificity of the situation arising at the time was that, although in Stalin's plans the law was first and foremost to be an instrument of coercion, also used to deprive one society after another of the national and cultural heritage, in years 1944–1948 some of the legislative initiatives were leveraged in attempts to persuade Polish citizens that the new regime guaranteed to them, in a far greater degree than did the governments of the sovereign Second Republic (1918–1939), simultaneously the respect for the spirit of the Nation and accelerated civilizational development. The goal of that was to neutralize any societal resistance to significant changes being introduced in parallel, on the foundation of a different ideology, to the economy and to politics, as well as enlisting the collaboration of eminent lawyers and jurists in the transitional period and the years that followed.

One of the methods of achieving that goal was the reactivation of the institutions of the justice system and resumption of posts in civil courts by judges and justices having exercised the same office in the interwar period. The Code of Civil Procedure of 1930 was retained. That was to imply the continuity of the political order, especially considering that the principles of operation and personal compositions of the other branches of government – the legislative and the executive were replaced instantaneously.[12]

12 See more Anna MACHNIKOWSKA: *Wymiar sprawiedliwości w Polsce w latach 1944–1950* [The administration of justice in Poland in 1944–1950], WUG, Gdańsk, 2008, 10–39.

The reconstruction of the judiciary was accompanied with declarations that foreign law would be replaced with Polish law without any delays in those areas of substantive civil law in which the codifications of the 19th century still applied.

The implementation of that undertaking took place in circumstances enabling the new regime to present itself as an efficient pragmatic organizer capable of modernizing the legal system and abolishing anachronistic parochialisms while respecting the tradition. Such type of progress did in fact take place in areas such as marriage law, family law and inheritance law. The unification also extended to real law and to the general provisions of civil law, though their impact on the legal system was limited. A similar marginalization affected the Code of Obligations. This was because more and more special provisions were created and placed in parts of the legal system deemed key by the Soviet interpretation of Marxist ideology. Deviations from principle were explained away as temporary solutions, citing the aforementioned extraordinary circumstances of warfare and, afterwards, reconstruction. Those provisions were drafted by officials of the Ministry of Justice in the form of decrees and regulations, allowing the legislature to be bypassed. The deviations were all the more significant considering that numerous civil cases were removed from the jurisdiction of the courts and handed over to the administration or *quasi*-judicial bodies, with the rationale that the proceedings would be swifter.

Despite such disadvantageous circumstances to the development of private law, the conceptual and legislative works done by representatives of academic legal circles in 1945–1949 made a sizeable contribution to the development of the field. While updating and supplementing the drafts left behind by the Codification Commission, high-quality legal instruments were drafted and, in 1945–1946, the process of unification of civil law was completed. In 1947, part of the lawyers and jurists engaged in the preceding works began to work on a draft civil code. The latter was to be based on the foundations of Polish legal thought, including the legacy of the interwar period, as well as comparative analytical studies, without the primacy of Soviet law, with the public evaluation of the fruits of the codifiers' labours by a broad circle of lawyers and jurists. Those works were halted in 1949, when the authorities' approval for the evolutionary transformation of the legal system was withdrawn.

The new point of reference was only to be the Soviet theory of law. The political directive did not, however, see a full implementation, as a result of which the legacy of Polish science of private law of years 1945–1948 became, in the twenty years to come, the point of reference for the continued functioning of the principles of private law, despite further limitations. Some of the normative constructs dating from that time were also used in 1964, when the new Civil Code, still in force today, came into being. Therefore, the ideological and axiological arguments presented during the works on the unification of civil law and the first attempts at its codification merit all the more attention.

2 The Initiation of the Works

The Polish state resurrected following World War II and dependent on Soviet Russia distanced itself from the 'bourgeois' legacy of the Second Republic. It began the building of a new socialist order in a 'people's state'. Nevertheless, the legal order inherited from interwar Poland was – provisionally – retained. In the sphere of private law, that was tantamount to the continued recognition of all codes adopted to date – the Code of Obligations, Commercial Code and Code of Civil Procedure. Moreover, in the years immediately following the end of the war, there was initially no political programme for the continuation, in the changed conditions, of the predecessors' unfinished plans of a future codification of civil law. The idea itself of codification was not in dispute. However, re-activation of the prewar 'bourgeois' Codification Commission was off the table. The initiative was to be taken over by the Ministry of Justice. The latter's conduct was, at the beginning, somewhat chaotic. Time and staff resources were insufficient for more organized action.

Amid the organizational chaos in the aftermath of the war, it is difficult to find symptoms of intense pressure for the resumed works to be given a clear ideological direction. There were not many directives from a-high instructing the ministry on how to deal with the reopening of the codification works. Sources are silent on the subject. The Ministry of Justice led by Henryk Świątkowski did not have the intention of taking the independent initiative of putting the new ideology in action by creating drafts of new legislation. Restraint and prudence were exercised in that aspect, while awaiting further developments.

Still, the key decision was made to accomplish the immediate unification of civil law and at last abolish the bourgeois-capitalist relics of laws inherited from the partitioning powers. The decision was made by the Council of Ministers on 12 June 1945, and the expected time-frame for its implementation set to 10 months, until 1 April 1946. Given the works of the codification of civil law not having been completed before the outbreak of the war but also the convenient availability of ready drafts for almost all of the various parts of the future code, the Ministry of Justice decided to execute an expedited provisional codification. To that end, the legacy of the prewar

Codification Commission was deemed to require only some tweaking.[13] Although the ultimate redaction of every single instrument was to be preceded by the assessment of so-called socio-political theses, the practice showed that no ground-up reworking of prewar drafts was in the plans. Whatever the desires may have been, there was simply no time. The deadline set by the Council of Ministers left no room for any thorough work.

There was more than one way in which the need for unification could be satisfied, but the decision was made to borrow abundantly from the codification legacy of the Second Republic. No public debate was held on the matter, nor any behind the scenes, at least not in the light of surviving sources. The choice that was made comprised two significant political decisions: (1) the unification of civil law was a pressing need and could not be delayed; (2) the bourgeois legacy of the interwar period had be relied upon, as it had made a lasting imprint on the continued development of Polish civil law. The extent to which the decision-makers of the time were aware of the implications of their decision is anyone's guess.

The so-called unification of civil law was nothing else than a camouflaged decision for the capitalist opus of the interwar period at last to see the light of day and enter into life. It was a perfect fit with the broadly understood 'introduction of a uniform democratic native Polish law common to the entire state'.[14] In the area of civil law, three conditions had to be met. Firstly, the codification work could not deserve the name of a 'uniform civil code' because it suffered from the taint of capitalism. Even so, it was represented as the unquestioned success of the people's government, the fruit of the effectiveness of its governance, juxtaposed with the laziness of the predecessors. The fact of appropriation of someone else's work was disguised. No further steps, however, were taken. The decision was made that the contents of the prewar drafts, although subjected to some last-minute modifications, ought not to be

---

13 The decision-making during the earliest phase, in 1944, is best illustrated by the short dialogue between the deputy head of the justice ministry within the PKWN (Polish Committee of National Liberation), Leon Chajn, with the PKWN Chairman and future prime minister, Edward Osóbka-Morawski. In response to Chajn's inquiry concerning the political vision of the future organization of the judiciary, Osóbka-Morawski declared: 'You have read the PKWN manifesto, haven't you.' 'I did ...,' Chajn began to reply. So not people's courts.' The vague generalities of the manifesto had to suffice for direction. TORAŃSKA: *Oni*, 297.

14 Henryk ŚWIĄTKOWSKI: *Społeczna myśl prawnicza w Polsce: dawniej i dzisiaj (szkic historyczno-prawny)* [Social legal thought in Poland: formerly and nowadays (a historico-legal sketch)], DPP (1) 1945, 6.

represented as the Civil Code of People's Poland. Given the contents of the laws being so enacted, it was self-evident that ground-up amendments would be needed sooner than later. Thus, there was need to emphasize the provisional nature of the unification action, with the true socialist work of codification having to wait. The substantive matter of the extent to which it constituted a cohesive whole was of secondary importance in the propaganda game. Secondly, the provisional unification had to be represented as a response to a pressing need, successfully delivered by the people's government. Thirdly, the leftover drafts had to be hastily but deliberately edited so as at least partially to adapt them to the new reality, producing the impression of creative change. Expectations in that area did not mount up high, and especially none of them deformed the prewar work in a fundamental way. It is worth noting that there was no talk of any need of immediate modification of the already applicable Code of Obligations, even though there was plenty enough room for edits, starting from curtailment of the principle of freedom of contract justified not only on grounds of socialist ideology but also the practical expediency of the moment arising from difficulties with the introduction of a postwar order.

The result of the lack of strong ideologico-political pressure for the adaptation of private law to the new political realities was that the work of unification was accomplished almost on time. During the fifteen months from August 1945 to November 1946, more than twenty decrees were published, of which ten formed the brunt of the new Polish civil law. Those were the General Provisions of Civil Law, of 12 November 1946; Personal Law, of 29 August 1945; Marriage (Personal) Law, of 25 September 1945; Matrimonial Property Law, of 29 May 1946; Family Law, of 22 January 1946; Guardianship Law, of 14 May 1946; Civil-Registration Law, of 25 September 1945; Real Law and Law on Land-and-Mortgage Register Books – both of 11 October 1946; and Inheritance Law, of 8 October 1946. The codification of civil procedure was also completed, most importantly with the Decree of 18 July 1945 – Code of Non-Litigious Procedure.

All of them involved modernization across many fields. The fact alone that the codes of the early 19th century – Code of Napoleon in the former Congress Kingdom and ABGB in Galicia – were of great significance. Overlapping all of this, however, was the fact that the prewar codification drafts usually reflected the most progressive currents of European civilist thought of the interwar period. Nor were they devoid of creative and original solutions of their own.

The completion of the work at once marked the opening of a new phase, that of codification. On 18 February 1947, the Minister of Justice established a commission for the compilation of a uniform Polish civil code,[15] referred to as the Civil Law Codification Commission[16]. Świątkowski himself became its President, with Stefan Bancerz, Seweryn Szer and Aleksander Wolter as permanent deputies and Witold Czachórski as secretary. The other members were Jan Wasilkowski, Marian Lisiewski and Jan Witecki. In December 1948, thus shortly before the completion of that phase of the Commission's work, its number was enlarged by two justices of the Supreme Court – Maurycy Grudziński and Jerzy Marowski.[17]

3 Attitude to the Codification Commission of the Interwar Period

That was thus a modest commission with only a few members. The communist authorities made the decision against the reactivation of the Codification Commission in its extensive and structured form from the interwar period, let alone as a college of experts independent of the government.[18] A plethora of arguments providing a rationale for that decision was offered by representatives of the Ministry of Justice already in publications from 1945 and 1946. Minister Świątkowski's own laconic explanation was as follows:

---

15 *Zarządzenie Ministra Sprawiedliwości w sprawie powołania komisji do opracowania jednolitego polskiego kodeksu cywilnego* (Order of the Ministry of Justice concerning the establishment of a commission for the compilation of a uniform Polish civil code), in *Dokumenty archiwalne dotyczące organizacji prac nad unifikacją i kodyfikacją polskiego prawa cywilnego w latach 1945–1948* (Document archives from the organization of works on the unification and codification of Polish civil law in 1945–1948), Piotr Fiedorczyk (ed.), MHI 4 (2006), 166. The progress on the unification action was described by Stefan Grzybowski. According to his account, in the autumn of 1945, he – similarly to other participants in the unification project – was entrusted with the 'adaptation of the draft Real Law to the changed realities' ('among other works') and 'completion of necessary edits in said project, even unrelated to said problem.' Thus, he was essentially given complete leeway as to the scale and scope of the modifications. He was only limited by the time available. Stefan Grzybowski: *Własność w projekcie prawa rzeczowego* [Ownership in the draft Real Law], PiP 4 (1946), 92.

16 Minutes of the session of the Codification Commission's Substantive Civil Law Team on 23 April 1948, AAN, MS, 2380, 80; Piotr Fiedorczyk: *Unifikacja i kodyfikacja prawa rodzinnego w Polsce (1945–1964)* [Unification and codification of family law in Poland (1945–1964)], WUwB, Białystok, 2014, 286.

17 Przemysław Kowalski: *Z badań nad prawem spadkowym w projekcie kodeksu cywilnego z 1948 r.* [Studies on the law of succession in the Draft Civil Code of 1948], MHI 12 (2013), 265.

18 *Cf.* Gałędek: *Beginning of the Debate*, 119–134.

> In the new Polish reality, the Codification Commission with its work system and progress rate is no longer a suitable body for the planning and drafting of new legislation (...) works on the creation of new statutes must be concentrated within the circle of a smaller number of experts, with any doubts arising being resolved swiftly and without recourse.[19]

The Ministry's point of view was further expounded by the deputy minister, Ludwik Chajn, regarded as the *de facto* most important person in the justice ministry[20]. He openly admitted that in the unification works 'perfection was not expected'.[21] For above the lawyerly subtleties one had to place the 'interests of the democratic system and cohesion of the new Polish state', with the 'democratization of social, economic and political affairs becoming especially clear in a unified law', viz. family, marriage, guardianship, real, inheritance, civil-registration and matrimonial property law.[22]

Chajn was very distant from depreciating the achievements of the Codification Commission, emphasizing that he 'had no intention of belittling the work' of that body, on which sat 50 of the most prominent Polish lawyers, including many of world renown. The quality of its work was thus not disputable. Nonetheless, the Commission could and should be charged with 'tortoise pace'. Thus, representatives of the government focused solely on the technical aspect – the sluggish progress rate. Even for that, they blamed the capitalist system and not the individual members of the Commission or

19 ŚWIĄTKOWSKI: *Społeczna myśl prawnicza*, 11; the deliberate discrediting of the prewar Codification Commission is the subject of: Piotr FIEDORCZYK: *Z prac nad unifikacją osobowego prawa małżeńskiego w 1945 roku* [From works on the unification of matrimonial personal law in 1945], MHI 1 (1994), 67. As I will demonstrate below, that assertion is not confirmed by the sources from 1945–1948 I have been able to analyse. It is worth noting that during the initial period of years 1945–1946, the communist government focused on the technical aspect of the Codification Commission's works, i.e. the slow progress rate, while a full arsenal of other means of denigration of the Commission as a whole, its individual members and its work was readily at hand.

20 Concerning the importance of Chajn and his concepts see Anna KORZENIEWSKA-LASOTA, Michał LASOTA: *Leona Chajna poglądy na wymiar sprawiedliwości* [Leon Chajn's viewpoints on the administration of justice], MHI 15 (2016)/2, 319–321.

21 He recalled the severe criticism offered by Benjamin Constant and other luminaries to the authors of the Code of Napoleon – 'that flat and miserable compilation of Roman law and French customs.'

22 CHAJN: *Rewolucyjny czyn polskiego prawnictwa (rzecz o unifikacji prawa)* [The revolutionary effort of Polish lawyerdom (the matter of unification of law)], PiP 9–10 (1946), 4–5.

even its organization and working procedures, except perhaps for the rather sparingly censured inclination to vain abstract disputes. Some of the lawyers and jurists who had served on the Commission, such as Jan Wasilkowski or Emil Stanisław Rappaport, had continued to be active participants in the works following the war or in the debates, and others were regarded as the indisputable role models and mentors of the new generation of Polish lawyers. A whole arsenal of means was available to denigrate both the Commission as a whole and its members as individuals, as well as its work, and yet the achievements of the prewar period were either not distanced from at all or only sporadically and with moderation.

The 'grey eminence' of the justice ministry, Ludwik Chajn, set the trends with his pronouncement that the slow rate of progress imputed to the Codification Commission could not possibly have been the result of only a 'lack of time' or 'attention to the perfection' of the drafts underway. He noted that the 'there was sufficient time and zeal,' for the unification (he avoided the term 'codification') of commercial law and a number of other special laws or for the enactment of codes of judicial procedure 'in a greater degree intended for the use of legal practitioners rather than the broader masses of society'. According to Chajn, that was not a work of accident. He noted that the 'spirit' of the partitioning powers 'at the section of socio-legal issues', was not as 'foreign to the Polish landowner-capitalist spirit', of the Second Republic. For that reason, he surmised, the Codification Commission 'did not reach more deeply,' did not codify the socially sensitive areas of civil law, because 'it could not violate those principles (…) [followed in] prewar Poland by the ruling class, with its ethics, its social structure, and its economic affairs.' Invoking historical arguments, he observed that in slave-holding, feudal and capitalist states the law always had been the 'exponent of the interests of the ruling class.' Thus, in the Second Polish Republic, the ruling class 'was not so lively interested in the abolition of the partitioning powers' laws,' which were protecting its interests.[23]

That last argument was elaborated upon by the First President of the Supreme Court, Wacław Barcikowski, in his article titled *Cele i zadania prawnictwa demokratycznego* (*The goals and tasks of democratic lawyerdom*) opening the first issue of *Państwo i Prawo* in May 1946. He argued that the giving of effect to the democratic ideals adhered to by the people's state required a different understanding of the concepts of justice than in a state with a 'lib-

23 *Ibidem*, 3–4. Similarly Świątkowski: *Społeczna myśl prawnicza*, 9.

eral-economic political system'[24] (such as the Second Republic). Drawing inspiration from Marxist social theory, he observed that in a 'liberal-economic political system' justice was 'measured by the interest of the classes having gained the advantage over the working masses,' whereas in a democratic state it was achieved by the creation of a system of legal protection 'securing the interests of every citizen irrespective of their origin, creed or wealth.' For it had to be the task of a truly democratic state to level the class differences, which could not be achieved in a capitalist order 'conducive to the expansion of individual egocentrism to the detriment of the social interest.'[25] The First President of the Supreme Court was echoed by the Minister of Justice. Nonetheless, Świątkowski appreciated that during the interwar period there had existed a 'democratic-progressive' current within the Codification Commission, albeit it was 'oppressed' by the 'reactionary-clerical elements'.[26]

4 The Groundbreaking Moment: New Reality – New Social Law

Coming to the fore amid the propaganda catchwords of the new government was the assertion that only then had the time come for the fruition of progressive ideas, also those that had been developed by the Codification Commission during the interwar period. As elucidated by the justice minister, then there had at last formed the advantageous conditions for the creation of a law that would 'encapsulate (...) in strict juridical formulae the crystallizing politico-social and economic changes, secure the new social order against assaults from the demolishers of the democratic order,' and 'solidify the rule of law.'[27] During that epoch-making moment, Świątkowski argued 'Poland found itself at a historical turn,' and was 'entering a new historical period'. For a 'Third Republic – Poland Reborn' was coming and was to be marked by a 'spirit of new history' and 'spirit of new law.'[28] In those realities, the future

24 Of all sources from the relevant period I have been able to analyse, the 'capitalist-landowner spirit' was mentioned only by Chajn. The term had not yet gained currency. References to the 'bourgeois' character of the state were completely avoided. In the same journal, Minister Świątkowski wrote in far harsher tones of a 'sanation-fascist political system.' ŚWIĄTKOWSKI: *Społeczna myśl prawnicza*, 10.

25 Wacław BARCIKOWSKI: *Cele i zadania prawnictwa demokratycznego* [The goals and tasks of democratic lawyerdom], PiP 1 (1946), 5–6.

26 ŚWIĄTKOWSKI: *Społeczna myśl prawnicza*, 10.

27 *Ibidem.*

28 *Ibidem.*

civil code, similarly to other statutes, faced the challenge of 'meeting the increasing necessities of life' and dynamic 'creation of a new Polish reality'.[29] Then then-present historical moment was characterized by a 'surging current of life', which was 'racing with great swiftness'.[30] Leaving besides the true political situation, it will be expedient to note the similarity of those catchwords in their ideological layer with those used by the participants of the public debate on codification in the first years of the Second Republic, especially the circles linked to the Polish Socialist Party.[31]

Similar phrasing was in use by the Ministry of Justice. The political creed was expounded in the first issue of the *Demokratyczny Przegląd Prawniczy* (Democratic Law Review) published by the Ministry. The *Przegląd*'s editors emphasized the 'primacy of politics and its vigorous developments'. That was where the aforementioned intensification of the dynamics of social transformations was 'manifesting itself'. And such was the justification of the need for the ministry to establish a law journal that would become 'a platform of the public service.' In that role, the official law review would be responsible primarily for the 'profusion of new legislation and its motives,' as well as serving as a 'tribune for the interpretation and explanation of the new law'.[32]

In this context, however, it will be worth focusing some attention on the minister's declaration. Świątkowski proclaimed that even despite such great challenges facing the new government, civil law would not be instrumentalized. What he had in mind was the subjection of it to so-called 'social interpretation', i.e. one that 'by way of explanation and narrowing down of the provisions ensures the most certain and perfect exercise of their rights by the broad masses in whose interests such law has been enacted.' The norms of civil law, Świątkowski went on to expound his perspective, while 'important', were still 'in the background of society's political life'. Accordingly, the Ministry would not resort to the use of circulars to impose an official interpretation bending the provisions of the code to fit current political and ideological needs. 'For one cannot apply the 'tailor's measure' where the proper measure

29 *Ibidem*, 11.

30 *Założenia i zamierzenia centralnego pisma prawniczego* [The assumptions and intention of a central legal journal], DPP 1 (1945), 2.

31 *Cf.* Michał Gałędek, Anna Klimaszewska: *Involvement of Polish Legal Elites in Preparing a New Draft of the Civil Code, Seen as an Intellectual Feast – Menu à la Carte or Fast Food?*, in Salvatore Mancuso (ed.), *The Language of Law and Food: Metaphors of Recipes and Rules*, Routledge, New York, 2021, 59–61.

32 *Założenia i zamierzenia*, 2.

is 'the measure of Fidias' – such was the conclusion of Świątkowski's argument.[33]

5 Functionalism, not Dogmatics

As it was proclaimed, 'any doubts arising' had to be 'resolved swiftly and without recourse', there was no room for theoretical vagaries; this was a particularly frequent trope in the utterances of legal decision-makers in the immediate aftermath of World War II. The First President of the Supreme Court, Wacław Barcikowski, thundered: 'The idealist philosophy dealing in abstracts, void of any tests at the intersection with reality, has to give way to a different, more realistic world view'[34] – it had to yield before the necessity of searching for practical 'democratic' solutions and equalization of opportunities intended to level the advantage obtained by the privileged classes over the 'working masses'; in a word: 'securing the interests of every citizen irrespective of their origin, creed or wealth'. In his view, such was the essence of the aforementioned groundbreaking historical moment having just arrived.

Similarly in his foreword expounding the 'assumptions and intentions' of the editorial board of the *Demokratyczny Przegląd Prawniczy*, it was noted that the 'chief' task of legal journalism was, besides the interpretation of the law, 'the more or less in-depth academic theorization leading to the crystallization and refinement of legal institutions'. However, as was emphasized with full force, that goal did not apply to 'groundbreaking historical moments', in which 'there [wa]s no time,' for lawyerly vagaries or the 'subtletization' of terms and institutions.[35]

The above-discussed general declarations resounded in the utterances formulated during the performance of concrete, specific tasks. Among others, Seweryn Szer, in his article dedicated to the problem of real burdens (i.e. burdens in real law),[36] disputed the need for 'scrupulous observance of traditional academic theories' and care for the 'purity' of particular legal construct or theory. He took the position that 'the most appropriate criterion in the evalu-

33 Henryk ŚWIĄTKOWSKI: *Wykładnia prawno-społeczna (uwagi na tle okólnika w sprawie reformy rolnej)* [Legal-social interpretation (remarks in the context of the circular on the agricultural reform], DPP 1 (1945), 20.

34 BARCIKOWSKI, *Cele i zadania*, 5–6.

35 *Założenia i zamierzenia*, 2

36 Szer invoked the views of Jan Wasilkowski. See Jan WASILKOWSKI: *Prawa rzeczowe ograniczone* [In rem rights], Przegląd Notarialny 1 (1947)/2–3, 176.

ation of the concepts of the Polish lawmaker is the criterion of functionality.' From there, he argued that whether the matter was of the scope of meaning of terms such as 'in-rem right', 'real right' (the subject of a dispute during the works on the interwar draft Real Law), or 'individual rights', one ought not to lose sight of the fact that those were merely 'a means of legal technique facilitating the organization of a specific group of economic affairs'. The purpose of the forms of real (property) law was to satisfy specific social or economic needs, and to that purpose the considerations of theoretical 'purity' always should give way.[37] Accordingly, one could not apriorically criticize the fact that a solution adopted in the real-law decree 'approached the formulation', used in the German Civil Code universally criticized for its degree of abstraction and detachment from the realities of life.[38] Dogmatism, or even ideology, must be rejected to concentrate solely on the utility of a specific device for the achievement of specific goals.[39]

6 A Time of True Democratization

In the above-given quotations, the 'people's state' is represented as a democratic state at last capable, through the arrival of a 'groundbreaking moment of history', of giving effect to the full range of progressive social goals. Those had already been delineated by the progressive Polish elites in the preceding eras but could not see fruition before the war due to unfavourable political circumstances. By contrast, the new historical moment was conducive, in the words of Deputy Minister of Justice Ludwik Chajn, would put it, to the true 'democratization' of the country, being characterized at the same time by an exceptional dynamism of events not allowing the 'revolutionary action of Polish lawyerdom' (*rewolucyjny czyn polskiego prawnictwa*) to drag on piece by piece for years.[40] Chajn goes on to explain that the necessity of expedited forceful transformations arises from the sins of omission committed by the Second Republic, which proved to be incapable of breaking out of the capitalist system of protection of the interests of the ruling class. Thus, since now 'on

37 Seweryn SZER: *Ciężary realne wobec polskiego prawa rzeczowego* [Real burdens in the light of Polish real law], PiP 9 (1947), 61.

38 That was also noted by Fryderyk Zoll, Jr. Fryderyk ZOLL: *Prawo cywilne w zarysie* [Civil law in an outline], vol. 2, Księgarnia Powszechna, Krakow, 1947, 17.

39 SZER: *Ciężary realne*, 61.

40 Ludwik CHAJN: *Trzy lata demokratyzacji prawa i wymiaru sprawiedliwości* [Three years of democratization of law and administration of justice], Prasa Demokratyczna, Warsaw, 1947, 59ff.

the debris of Hitler's defeat, the ruling class in Poland has come to be the world of labour,' and the 'micro-capitalist strata' allowed a 'share in social, economic and political life', the law must immediately follow the 'processes of significant constitutional change' to reflect not only the 'formal political ideals of democracy' but first of all 'economic and social democracy'.[41] The writings of 1947, celebrating the 25th issue of the *Demokratyczny Przegląd Prawniczy*, struck a similar tone. The editing board specified that the journal's principal purpose was 'fighting for a democratic rule of law' and a 'democratic, popular face of the justice system in Poland'.[42] The absence of references to socialism or communism from such rhetorics is striking. The democratic ideals that were to be given effect by the new state and its legal order were juxtaposed with ideas often termed 'liberal'.[43]

The chorus of 'admirers' of democracy in that understanding included, of course, also prominent interwar lawyers now enlisted in the service of the new government and new ideology. For example, Emil Stanisław Rappaport (erstwhile member of the Codification Commission), in his enthusiastic review of Chajn's book, wrote that difficult challenges consisted in the ability to strike balancing act between 'boldly putting an axe to dated legal norms and dispensations' and 'moderation in the preservation of that which has passed the test of functionality in the practice of the prewar years and may be useful in the new Polish reality.'[44]

7 Harnessing the 'Progressive' Legacy of Interwar Period

The thesis of that a progressive current existed in the Codification Commission and its works was developed by Jan Wasilkowski and Witold Czachórski when presenting the new unified marriage law in the Decree of 7 November 1945. The latter embodied the ideas advanced during the interwar period by Karol Lutostański and accepted by the Codification Commission at the

41 CHAJN: *Rewolucyjny czyn*, 4.

42 Leszek LERNELL: *Nasz jubileusz: uwagi z okazji 50 zeszytu 'Demokratycznego Przeglądu Prawniczego'* [Our jubilee: remarks on the occasion of the 50th issue of the Demokratyczny Przegląd Prawniczy], DPP 12 (1949), 21.

43 See BARCIKOWSKI: *Cele i zadania.*

44 Emil S. RAPPAPORT: *Recenzja: Leon Chajn – Trzy lata demokratyzacji prawa i wymiaru sprawiedliwości* [Review: Leon Chajn – Three years of democratization of law and administration of justice], PiP 12 (1947), 74.

time.[45] Wasilkowski and Czachórski insisted that the 'full extent' of the principles of Lutostański's draft had been taken up by the 'legislators of postwar Poland'. Among those principles, they mentioned: '(1) regulating marriage as an object of state legislation; (2) putting the spouses on an equal footing with regard to their mutual rights and obligations and those relative to the family; (3) recognition of the supremacy of the family's interests above those of the individual.'[46] They also claimed to accept the guiding ideal of the prewar Codification Commission's Principles, which had been binding on Lutostański and with which he had identified fully in the works entrusted to him: 'Legal norms should, as far as possible, direct social institutions with a sense of the internal substance of those institutions, consistently with the principles on which the state's political system is founded.'[47] Minister Świątkowski was likewise generous in his praise of the existence of a 'democratic-progressive current' in the Codification Commission. That current, according to him, was manifest in the position taken by two of the Commission's members – Zygmunt Marek (notably the initiator of the Commission's establishment in 1919) and Tadeusz Bujak – in favour of mandatory civil marriage. The minister cited their arguments, which largely coincided with the ideological outlooks of postwar 'democrats', thus providing a supply of ready-made rationales. Among other things, they argued that: (1) the 'evolution of legal culture', being the equivalent of postwar progress, required the establish-

45 As Piotr Fiedorczyk observes: 'the layout of the first draft of the new law was copied over from the prewar draft,' and even despite subsequent modifications 'the final layout of the decree reflected that of the prewar draft.' Things were different, however, with the substantive contents. A different form of the celebration of marriage was chosen. The full laicization of the institution of marriage had been a dogma since the beginning, though nothing posed an obstacle to borrowing the majority of the solutions relating to the civil marriage from Lutostański's draft. The main differences came down to the elimination of the institution of banns and of the requirement of parental consent for the marriage of a minor. The acceptance of divorce did not at all render the prewar model useless in this particular regard. The postwar committee employed a device consisting in the retention of Lutostański's grounds of separation as grounds of divorce in the postwar decree. Banns, compensation for divorce due to the fault of one of the spouses, and impediments to marriage, all of those were institutions with a prewar pedigree. Thus, one ought to repeat after Fiedorczyk that the Marriage Law decree constituted nothing else than a 'creative' 'modification of K. Lutostański's draft', all the more so considering that the drafters had abandoned the most extreme solutions inspired by Soviet law. P. FIEDORCZYK: *Z prac nad unifikacją*, 79–90.

46 Witold CZACHÓRSKI, Jan WASILKOWSKI: *Wspomnienie o profesorze Uniwersytetu Warszawskiego Karolu Lutostańskim* [Reminiscence of Karol Lutostański, Professor of the University of Warsaw], PiP 12 (1947), 59.

47 *Ibidem*, 58.

ment of civil marriage; (2) the state – in line with the basic assumption of legal thought after 1945 – had the right and obligation to regard marriage as a 'social institution', as marriage was the foundation of family and thus also of the state; (3) civil marriage 'promotes the sense of citizenship,' confirming that the nupturients are first and foremost citizens.[48]

Let us note the existence of certain similarities in his approach when compared to the arguments offered by Seweryn Szer in the latter's exposition of the Marriage Law decree of 7 November 1945. Firstly, Szer emphasized the fact that the laicization of marriage was nothing else than the long-awaited entering on the path of progress. For at last 'the legal devices in Poland were raised to the universally accepted civilizational level, eliminating anachronisms that had long cast shadows over our democratic reality.'[49] Similar tones were struck by Szer's superior, Minister Świątkowski. Citing the examples of other Catholic countries of Western Europe in which laicized marriage law had already been introduced (France, Italy, Spain and Portugal), he concluded that those were the role models to follow. Against their background, the Congress Kingdom governed by the Law on Marriage dating from 1836 was a relic and a heritage park, in which – as Świątkowski put it – the legal provisions in force were of 'mediaeval character'. In such circumstances, he argued, likely not coincidentally echoing Szer's words, that the introduction of secular marriage law '[wa]s necessary for the legal devices in Poland were raised to the universally accepted civilizational level.'[50] The rhetoric of breaking out of a 'group of nations having allowed their marriage law to remain entrenched in the Middle Ages' was also used by Antoni Bądkowski: 'the new marriage law has given society a legal institution modern to the core, adapted to contemporary conditions of life and moral ideas.'[51]

Szer, for his part, emphasized that the laicization of marriage was demanded by 'broad strata of Polish society'. In order to prove that fact, in keeping with his own habit (cherished, albeit to a lesser degree, also by other participants of postwar debate, with Minister Świątkowski at the helm), he painted a Polish (national) history of struggle for the laicization of marriage, in order to demonstrate what the correct path was for the evolution of legal

---

48 In his research for that information, Świątkowski relied on Stanisław Gołąb: *Polskie prawo małżeńskie w kodyfikacji* [Polish marriage law in codification], Biblioteka Prawnicza, Warsaw, 1932, 27–28.

49 Seweryn Szer: *Nowe prawo małżeńskie* [The new Family Law], PiP 1 (1946), 29–31.

50 *Wobec nowego prawa małżeńskiego: oświadczenie Ministra Sprawiedliwości* [Towards a new marriage law: declaration by the Minister of Justice], DPP 1 (1946), 22.

51 Antoni Bądkowski: *Bilans nowego prawa małżeńskiego* [A reckoning of the new marriage law], DPP 1 (1948), 29.

culture. Narrating the history of the struggle between the 'reactionary' clerical-conservative circles with the 'enlightened and progressive circles', he went back to the early 19th century, describing the abolishment of the secular marriage law introduced by the 'modern' Code of Napoleon in the Polish Kingdom under the pressure of 'backwardness'. That was supposed to prove the assertion that, already from the Age of Enlightenment onward, if not in Polish society as a whole, then at least among its 'enlightened representatives' and 'progressive opinion', there prevailed a 'firm desire to laicize marriage'.[52]

The historico-national arguments were accompanied by those of politico-constitutional nature. Szer argued that the 'sacral' institution of marriage constituted a 'social organization' remaining at odds with the 'fundamental' principles of law on which a state is based, namely the principle of supremacy (sovereignty) of the state's authority.

> Especially in democratic constitutional orders, where law is created under the influence of the political, economic and social needs of broad masses, the admission of other sources, from outside the state, is incompatible with the essence and spirit of the laws and, in consequence, weakens that direct link which exists between the citizen and the state.[53]

While arguing from that position, he did not distance himself from the prewar Polish statehood. On the contrary, in attempting to prove the assertion of the incompatibility of denominational marriage law with the principle of a sovereign democratic state, he quoted from the text of the March Constitution (of 1921) and even the concordat of 1925.

This rationale was developed upon by the authors of the first draft unification of marriage law from early 1945. In the first of their guiding principles, they emphasized that it was the state (and not any of the religious denominations) that had the exclusive power to regulate the relationships of marriage law. In no way could one, therefore, not even in a supplementary manner, call upon canon law or especially define marriage relations in reliance on the concordat of 1925. The ecclesiastical courts' right to exercise jurisdiction over marital cases was also denied. The further exposition of those thoughts, for its part still somewhat timidly noted that participation in the sacred rites relating to the celebration of marriage should not be mandatory and no one

52 SZER: *Nowe prawo małżeńskie*, 29–31.

53 *Ibidem*, 31.

ought to be compelled to participate because doing so would be incompatible with the principle of freedom of conscience and religion. In all of those assertions, the provisions of the March Constitution were cited as the still-binding basic law, since the April Constitution of 1935 was not recognized.[54]

8 A Law Adapted to the Nation's Psyche

As illustrated by the example of Seweryn Szer's analysis of old marriage law, invocations of national tradition and the legacy of 'progressive' thought were the distinctive staples of the rhetorics used during the initial years following the end of World War II. The path was carved by Minister Świątkowski, who – in the first issue of the *Demokratyczny Przegląd Prawniczy* – published an article in which he argued that social values were deeply entrenched in Polish national legal tradition and juridical thought. The principal thesis of his publication was that 'the new Polish law [wa]s not breaking continuity with ancient Polish law'; on the contrary, it 'stemmed from the best Polish legal traditions, drawing from them its sap and inspiration.' He insisted that native thought had for centuries been home to a current of 'progressive lawyerdom', starting from the Renaissance luminaries – Jan Ostroróg and Andrzej Frycz Modrzewski – and ending with the lawyers of the interwar period. Among the last group, Świątkowski counted the no-longer-living practitioners having served as defence counsel in political trials, and not only those having ties to the communist movement (such as Teodor Duracz) but also others (such as Zygmunt Marek, Leon Berenson or Wacław Szumański). All of them, in an equal measure, were – according to Świątkowski – the 'pride of democratic lawyerdom'.[55]

The new law had to be adapted to the needs, customs and psyche of the Polish nation. The partitioning powers' laws did not meet these standards. Although they had been in force in Polish territories for a very long time, Świątkowski did not regard them as assimilated. On the contrary, he argued that a fully sovereign Poland could not possibly be governed by foreign laws. Moreover, in addition to charges of datedness and 'reactionary' character 'not corresponding to the spirit of democracy', they were reproached, also by

54 Stefan M. GRZYBOWSKI, Ignacy RÓŻAŃSKI: *Komentarz: wyciągi z motywów Komisji Kodyfikacyjnej – tezy polityczne – wzory* [Commentary. Extracts from the Codification Commission's rationales], Księgarnia Powszechna, Kraków, 1946, 21–23.

55 ŚWIĄTKOWSKI: *Społeczna myśl prawnicza*, 10.

Świątkowski, for their maladaptation to the 'Polish sense of law'.[56] During the initial years after the war, that angle was especially often raised by Seweryn Szer. When presenting the draft Law on Land-and-Mortgage Register Books, he observed that the solutions contained in it should correspond to the needs of the Polish population. From that perspective, he criticized the German concept of an entry constituting the statutory premise of acquisition, modification or loss of in-rem rights. Even though that device had already functioned in all regions of Poland for more than a century, he still did not hesitate to denounce it as being 'at odds with the psyche of the Polish population, with its customs and needs, especially as regard[ed] the overwhelming part of the Nation – the population of peasant farmers.' What circumstances did Szer invoke in his search for a rationale for that assertion? Focusing on the constitutive force of the entry – an excessive rigour, in his opinion – he believed that lessons had to be learned from the decisions of the prewar Polish Supreme Court (and earlier Austrian jurisprudence), which had made attempts to mitigate it in the social interest.[57]

When it came to the need for the preservation of compatibility of the law with the expectations, customs and psyche of the Polish nation, the new government avoided a confrontational stance on its own laicized marriage law. The problem was not trivial. 'To the Russian partition, and largely also to the Austrian one, the [new law] marked a true revolution,' assessed the Supreme Court prosecutor, Antoni Bądkowski, in 1948, i.e. two years after the introduction of the law. Immediately, however, he was eager to reassure:

> society has been able to evaluate the benefit of the new law quickly. (...) Considering that in such cases the parties are recruited from the broadest social strata, not excluding workers and peasant farmers, one can justifiably claim that the new law was the answer to the needs of society as a whole.[58]

Świątkowski also borrowed from the pan-Slavist idea. He termed the 'spirit of Poland's new history' the 'spirit of Slavdom'. Thus, once again, (after Szer's invocation of the Polish nation's psyche), the circle of luminaries of the new government puts emphasis on ethnicity and cultural characteristics, which stands in tension with the dogmatically understood internationalization of

56 *Ibidem.*

57 Seweryn Szer: *Nabycie własności nieruchomości według nowego prawa rzeczowego* [Acquisition of ownership of real estate in the new Real Law], PiP 11–12 (1946), 55–56.

58 Bądkowski: *Bilans nowego prawa*, 9.

the communist movement. The spiritual community of 'brotherly Slavic nations' – in Świątkowski's view – had been 'fraught with the experience of suffering' by yet another 'invasion of Germanic hordes'. The 'jointly shed blood of Slavs fending off their common enemies' thus became the opportunity to cement all of Slavdom under the lead of the Soviet Union, which was portrayed as the saviour from 'German bondage and physical annihilation', as well as forerunner in the economic achievements obtained in the new social order.[59] Świątkowski thus did not call upon the slogans of internationalist communist revolution, replacing them in a way with the ideal of 'Slavic democracy', whereby 'Poland [wa]s joined [in stages] to the democracy of the world in the latter's aspiration to make permanent the peace obtained by bloody struggle and to reinforce the 'people's rule.'[60]

9 Civil Law as Instrument for the Pursuit of Social Goals

In the new constitutional circumstances, the law was to serve the purposes of pursuing the social goals. The best example is that of the Decree of 11 October 1946 – Real Law, introduced together with the Decree – Law on Land-and-Mortgage Register Books. The person responsible for the preparation of the draft was Stefan Grzybowski, who – in 'preparing the draft Real Law to the changed realities' – was not bound by any narrow directives and took his own initiative to change the way property was defined. 'Today's reality mandates that property be seen as a social function,' he wrote.[61] Thus, one could not stop at regarding ownership as a purely formal relationship in which property is not linked to any specific scope of property rights and obligations are excluded from the essence of the right. Nonetheless, Grzybowski was in favour of a structure based on existing patterns, i.e. continuation of the concept of an individual right while 'merely attempting to infuse it with new substance' into it, rather than 'looking for a completely new form'.[62] Grzybowski's functionalism was close to the views of Polish lawyers of the interwar period, with Lud-

59 Świątkowski, *Społeczna myśl prawnicza*, 10.

60 *Ibidem.*

61 Cf. Anna Machnikowska: *Nowe prawo własności: przekształcenia w stosunkach własnościowych w Polsce w latach 1944–1950* [New prioprietorship: privatization transformations in Poland in years 1944–1950], Zeszyty Prawnicze UKSW 11 (2011)/2, 257–258; Anna Machnikowska: *Prawo własności*, 342–344. *Ibidem* concerning the 'doctrinal mythologization' and 'political adaptation' of ideological assumptions – 83–86.

62 Grzybowski: *Własność w projekcie*, 91–92.

wik Domański at the helm.[63] Nonetheless, unlike Domański, he did not intend to be inspired by the concepts of Leon Duguit and reject the concept of an individual right.[64] According to Grzybowski, that would have been excessive experimentation without any guarantee of success. That was not done even in the Soviet Civil Code of 1922.[65]

The increasing involvement of public authorities in civil-law relationships were also the characteristic feature of the draft Law on the Relationships of Parents and Children and Law on Guardianship and Tutelage. In the socio-political theses of the latter, a liberal state was cast in opposition to the democratic state. The people's state, as a democratic state, should be guided by the interests of all of society and 'especially its future generations'. Accordingly, in a democratic state, the purpose of legal guardianship could not be to 'secure the future inheritance rights of the family', but 'solely and exclusively the interests of the child alone and therewith of society as a whole'.[66] Offering a criticism of the relations prevailing in interwar Poland, it was noted that legal guardianship, of course 'formally' was in force under the legislation of the partitioning powers, and thus it was not a new institution, but in reality ('in many cases, especially with regard to the central voivodeships') it remain 'on paper rather than in life'. The need for the establishment of guardianship organs came to be considered only when 'the need arose to deal with a specific matter, usually dealing with property.' Thus, the fundamental change to be introduced was to be the creation of a situation in which everyone who truly 'needed guardianship would have it, whether rich or poor,' and 'whether there is a need at a given time to deal with a specific matter or not.' Guardianship was to be a legal instrument of universal availability (the principle of universality of legal guardianship) and not only – as used to be the case – in specific situations, mainly serving to achieve the property goals of the wealthy.

---

63 Cf. Gałędek, Klimaszewska: *Involvement of Polish Legal Elites*, 59–60.

64 Duguit – erroneously, in Grzybowski's opinion – attempted to reject the concept of individual rights only because it was derived from the iurisnaturalist assumption of the Enlightenment Age that there existed a supralegal sphere of 'natural rights.' In his opinion, the rejection of the idea of a law of nature did not need to entail the rejection of the construct of individual rights.

65 A similar approach to Grzybowski's was also presented by Seweryn Szer in his article titled *Instytucja własności w projekcie prawa rzeczowego* (*The institution of ownership in the draft of Real Law*), which appeared in the *Myśli Współczesna* (3–4), incurring criticism from J.P., published by the Tygodnik Powszechny, to which Stefan Grzybowski replied. J. P.: *Własność jako funkcja* [Ownership as a function], Tygodnik Powszechny 39 (1946), 7; Stefan Grzybowski: *Odpowiedź p. J. P. z 'Tygodnika Powszechnego'* [Answer to Mr J.P. of the Tygodnik Powszechny], PiP 9–10 (1946), 119–122.

66 *Projekt prawa o opiece i kurateli* [Draft guardianship and tutelage law], DPP 2 (1945), 30.

It was held that the principal goal of the statute was to be achieved by the principle that the parents have equal rights and obligations in exercising parental responsibility over their children, thus giving effect to the programmatic idea of equal rights for women, thus attesting to its progressive nature, because that idea 'achieved practical recognition, becoming an inviolable principle in democratic states, only at a late time.'[67] 'Any remnants of male predominance', and 'former requisites of pre-feminist era', were represented as 'failing to respond to modern needs', and 'putting the woman in all aspects on an equal footing with the man', was the fruition of the noble goal of progress.[68] In response to the question of whether marriage law, in giving the woman full formal equality of rights, also took care of her social equality, which constituted the second condition for the fruition of the democratic ideal, Antoni Bądkowski enumerated a number of provisions creating the right conditions for that. He argued that in those cases in which marriage law mentioned a woman or wife, it did so always to her benefit. A key role, however, had to belong to court decisions, and the true weight and significance of those provisions came to light – in Bądkowski's opinion – only in connection with the interpretation given to them by the Supreme Court. It became 'clear', he argued, that those constituted primarily the 'protection of the woman, wife and mother', who may even pursue the determination that the entire burden of the family's maintenance must be borne by the husband when she has to dedicate herself to the education of the children or for some other reasons cannot earn an income.[69]

The socio-political theses of the draft Law on the Relationships of Parents and Children emphasized that that object of regulation was 'significant' from the perspective not so much of private or public interest not so much a 'section of family life' as a matter of the 'education of the future generations'. That goal was highlighted by the second socio-political thesis of the draft, emphasizing that while the purpose of parental responsibility was to serve the interests of the child, that was only with the goal of 'educating them to be a citizen

67 *Projekt prawa o stosunkach rodziców i dzieci* (Draft Law on the Relationships of Parents and Children), DPP 1 (1945), 32.

68 BĄDKOWSKI: *Bilans nowego prawa*, 9.

69 In his opinion, such type of provisions included the prohibition against demanding the annulment of the marriage due to the lack of the requisite age where the woman was pregnant or the option to retain the family name. Most importantly, the encompassed regulations intended to protect the mutual obligations arising from marriage. As he argued: 'for those, although they formally give the same rights to each of the spouses and impose the same obligations on each, in reality they serve primarily the protection of the weaker party and thus of the woman.' *Ibidem*, 31.

conscious of their obligations to the State, Nation and Democracy'. Accordingly, the stipulation was made that the parents were required to exercise parental responsibility in a manner required not only by the interests of the child but also the 'interests of society', and the state had the power to supervise the exercise of that responsibility. Above all, that referred to the guardianship authority having the power to interfere by issuing such orders as were 'necessary in order to eliminate violations' in a situation of the parents allowing a 'serious threat' to the child's interests to take place. That was a vague clause amenable to flexible and instrumental use by the state authority. Of that, the authors of the draft were fully aware, justifying the leeway given to the guardianship authority in the decision to intervene and the choice of the remedial measures with the necessity of the adaptation of such measure to the 'circumstances of the specific case'.

The power to interfere, as we learn from the historiosophic rationale of the draft, was to constitute the 'final stage' of a civilizational evolution having taken more than two thousand years. The beginning of that evolution was to have been the time of the popularization of the Roman-law principle that the child, in principle, constituted 'only the object of the absolute power of the father, who was the master of life and death.' The new order was represented as the 'democratic' end of the civilizational evolution (thereby without distancing oneself from certain historical milestone achievements) commenced in ancient Rome and having led to a situation in which 'the Roman construct of paternal authority had long been defeated, but its remnants subside[d] to the [then-]present day in existing legal systems.' The characteristic feature of the period, as it was represented, was the overcoming of the conception of the children's education as a private matter for first the father and then both of the parents to decide. 'The parents' relationship with the children continues to be viewed as a certain sort of taboo not yielding to control by factors placed outside of the family.' However, one had to break with the existing principle that the state could interfere only when abuse by the parents was 'especially clear and colliding pretty much with the provisions of the criminal code'. It was argued: 'Today, the state has too serious and significant a stake in the education of the future generations of its citizens to fail to reserve to itself the right to interfere with the internal life of the family.'[70]

The authors of the draft took the position that the mother and child were to be able to bring an action to dislodge the legal force of the recognition of paternity where the recognition had resulted in a significant harm to the

70 *Projekt prawa o stosunkach*, 32.

child. The thesis intended to protect the interest of the child was represented as 'outright contrary to nature', and 'putting an end to the fundamental dogma of the family relationship being based on blood ties.' It thus appears that to the drafters, their own device appeared to be excessively bold, undermining the foundation of private relationships that had better not be interfered with. The decision to do so was nonetheless made, although reluctantly, as though out of necessity.

A reflection of those tendencies to increase the interference of the public authority with private relationships were the attempts to amend the Code of Civil Procedure of 1930. The eminent proceduralist, Marian Waligórski, a professor and practitioner from Galicia, noted that the need was entailed by the 'serious transformations having taken place in recent times in the factual configuration of socio-economic relations and general world view.'[71] He observed: 'the introduction into life of a whole slew of newly codified areas of civil law [e.g. marriage law] has entailed the necessity of amendment of the norms of civil procedure.' Waligórski especially appreciated that the object of regulation extended to new categories of cases, such as those from the relationship between the parents and the children, in which 'the public interest is more involved than in the usual civil cases.' For that reason, besides the principal type of civil procedure based on a limited principle of disposability (the parties as the masters of the dispute), a somewhat different type of civil procedure based on special norms had to emerge 'wherein, on account of the object, more intensified interference from the state factor is required and thereby further restriction of the limits of the parties' disposing power.'[72]

The issue of the primacy of the public interest over the private was, however, not always as strongly highlighted as could be expected given the aspirations of the new government. First and foremost, in marriage law, the assumption that a family based upon marriage is the 'fundamental social unit' was not disputed. That, however, was not at all tantamount with the necessity of regarding the marital bond as indissoluble. It sufficed to vest it with the qualities of permanence.[73] That was the position taken by the authors of the first draft

---

71 Władysław SIEDLECKI: *Istota procesu cywilnego z punktu widzenia interesów państwa i jednostki* [The essence of civil trial from the perspective of the interests of the state and of the individual], PiP 7–8 (1947), 46.

72 Marian WALIGÓRSKI: *Zmiany proceduralne w związku z ostatnią unifikacją prawa cywilnego* [Procedural changes in connection with the recent unification of civil law], PiP 5–6 (1946), 80, 82.

73 Differently Piotr FIEDORCZYK: *Z prac nad unifikacją*, 71 (fn. 27), who is of the position that the drafters *de facto* took the position of the principle of 'impermanence of the marital bond.'

unification of marriage law.[74] According to the explanatory memorandum's rationale for the admission of unlimited divorce, the concept found support in the fact that the court should be completely stripped of the power to evaluate the potential negative social consequences of the act and especially the question of possible adverse impact on the children's interests. In the latter situation, the drafters argue 'one cannot coerce the spouses, when they have children, to disclose a scandalizing secret of marital cohabitation.'[75] That approach to the matter, clearly justified by the exigency of regularizing the exceptional situation after the war, was considerably closer to extreme liberal views on the role of the state in the shaping of social affairs than to socialist doctrine.

Ultimately, however, the concept was abandoned. However, the unifiers of Polish civil law – more due to the immediate social needs than to any particular ideological considerations – believed that divorce had to be allowed but only as an exception from the principle of permanence, rather than prohibited by making the bond indissoluble. Szer wrote: 'Only should such factors have crept into the marriage as to make it unable to meet its [social] tasks,' and 'maintenance of the community would lead to socially negative consequences,' then 'the bond and the community itself should be broken.'[76] And thus the permanence of the marital bond constituted a value but not an absolute. Divorce should be allowed as a 'necessary evil' if the marriage failed to serve its social functions. Those were situations in which persons who were legally married *de facto* did not live in marital community. In those cases, the existence of the bond led, in Szer's view, to 'extraordinarily socially adverse results'. By contrast, the institution of divorce, albeit leading to the breaking up of the marital bond and of the matrimonial community, it nonetheless enabled the creation of a new family.[77] The argument was made that experi-

74 The initiative began in the first half of 1945. Among the drafters, the principal role to play probably already belonged to Seweryn Szer, and besides Minister Świątkowski and Stefan Bancerz, the Director of the Legislative Department, also Jan Wasilkowski and Aleksander Wolter were involved. There is, however, no mention of the involvement of Stefan Grzybowski in the works.

75 Grzybowski, Różański: *Prawo małżeńskie*, 21–23.

76 Seweryn Szer: *Trwałość związku małżeńskiego* [The durability of the matrimonial union], DPP 1 (1946), 23.

77 In the realities of the first months following the war, divorce was the intended *ad hoc* solution to the urgent problem of marriages *de facto* broken up during the occupation and the turmoil of war, and primarily to enable new marriages to be contracted so as better to tackle the problem of loss of population. Procreation policy, or even outright eugenic reasons, were placed in the foreground, before which Christian morality based on the maintenance of the sacred and inviolable marital bond had to yield. Moreover,

ence of other states, whether of capitalist Western Europe (the drafters mentioned the examples of England, Belgium and Switzerland) or Eastern (Russia), showed that divorce did 'not at all entail adverse consequences for the life of nations,' and did 'not diminish the moral ground of society'.[78] Theoretically, therefore, the importance of marriage as the foundation of family relationships and the need to found the institution of family on the marriage bond were not in dispute, but the maintenance of marriage was not a goal unto itself or an absolute value. It could play its role when it become 'in the hand of the state a measure towards to the proper education of the citizens', as we read in the explanatory memorandum's rationale for the third of the main principles of the draft.[79]

On the other hand, as Seweryn Szer argued, the assurance of the durability of the marital bond constituted 'one of the main goals of modern marriage law' and was the characteristic feature of the legislation of more than a dozen states (which the author of the article did not omit to list) in all regions of Europe, where only divorces by mutual agreement without serious reasons were not allowed. Szer continued by arguing that one had to take a cautious approach to the institution of divorce, as it could give 'the parties a wide field to break up the matrimonial community for trivial reasons, socially irrelevant, in cases not at all attesting to the disintegration of the community'.[80] For that reason, the position taken by the unification draft was that divorce could only be allowed by court decision, when 'the interests of the minor child do not constitute an obstacle to the pronouncement of divorce,' and 'facts occur attesting that the marriage is no longer capable of meeting its social tasks, as it is in a state of permanent disintegration.' Soviet law served as the role model. The evolution it had undergone was discussed by Szer. He noted that while the

the grounds for divorce at the petition of one party came to include such items as change of nationality or imprisonment, we will have the full picture of the complicated postwar situation in which politico-ideological reasons overlapped the exceptionality of the geopolitical situation.

From the perspective of two years' time, that policy was regarded as a success: 'Among divorce cases, a considerable number were those of the marriages separated by war. But at the same time, the courts were faced by cases in which the spouses asking for divorce had not cohabited for a dozen years or even several decades and whom the existing law had not given the opportunity to obtain divorce. Thanks to the new marriage law, it became possible to discharge those long-escalated, often tragic situations.' Bądkowski: *Bilans nowego prawa*, 29.

78 Grzybowski, Różański: *Prawo małżeńskie*, 21–23. *Cf. Wobec nowego prawa małżeńskiego*, 23.

79 Grzybowski, Różański: *Prawo małżeńskie*, 21–23.

80 Szer: *Trwałość związku małżeńskiego*, 24.

Soviet Code of Laws of Marriage, Family and Guardianship of 1926 allowed for the unrestrained dissolution of marriages, even unilaterally, the amendment of 1944 'put a radical end to the above liberalism.' Since then, the court made the decision, following the examination of both parties' reasons, which was 'dictated by the desire to protect the permanence of the matrimonial community.'[81] There existed, however, an alternative concept in which even concern for the interests of the children could not in any way be allowed to restrict the availability of divorce by mutual petition of both spouses.

Corresponding with those assumptions was the proposal for concubinage to be deemed marriage (under certain conditions specified in the draft) on the basis of a decision of the regional court, with retroactive effect. The source of inspiration in that regard came from the Soviet Code of Laws of Marriage, Family and Guardianship. Differently to the Soviet Union, however, the Polish drafters wanted the registration to be performed not by an administrative authority but by a court of law.[82]

II After 1947

1 Introduction

The decommissioning of classical principles of private law in Poland started in 1946, together with nationalization of the industry, commerce and parts of agricultural production. This was achieved through special provisions invoking values such as the people's democracy and social justice, while direct borrowings from Soviet theories of state and law were avoided. The situation changed in 1949–1956, when the transformation took the general provisions in its crosshair. Now, the transformation was carried out under strong political pressure, amid catchwords of the dictatorship of the proletariat and Marxist ideology. Such was the result of Stalin's decision to exercise his right to strengthen the position of the Soviet Union in states falling within its sphere of military and economic influence after World War II.

The proclamation was made that the legacy of Polish scholarship, which had codified part of the country's civil law prior to the war and unified the rest in 1945–1946, would be replaced with avant-garde norms. The source of

81 *Ibidem.*

82 GRZYBOWSKI, RÓŻAŃSKI: *Prawo małżeńskie*, 21–23. In subsequent versions of the draft – for reasons unknown (perhaps political influence) – the provisions dealing with concubinage were scrapped.

those were to be the assumptions of Soviet legal science. The latter claimed to have achieved a successful implementation of Marxist doctrine and created a law that, for the first time in history, was delivering on ambitious social and economic goals. That was a false thesis, albeit a difficult one to verify in circumstances of totalitarianism and censorship. Assertions about the progressive nature of Soviet law were also repeated without criticism by a number of scholars from the academic circles of Western Europe.

Similarly to other states of Central and Eastern Europe subordinated to the USSR, those representatives of Polish scholarship who remained publicly active in the country after 1949 did not directly challenge to Marxist philosophy. Instead, they usually confined themselves to declarations of improving the already applicable law so as to make it reflect the socio-economic changes underway.[83] What distinguished Poland in years 1945–1956 was a lower scale of economic transformation and a slower pace of revolution in civil law. Polish peasant farmers retained the individual ownership of the majority of agricultural land, resisting collectivization. Nor was there a reform of civil law, because the drafting works of 1950–1956 fraught the legislators with numerous problems.

In consequence, during the period in which in other countries sprang civil codes reflective of Marxist ideology in its Stalinist interpretation, in Poland no such legal act entered into force. This difference in the substance of the applicable law made a strong impact on the ideological and axiological perspective confronting Polish academia. Every scholar was conscious of the possibility of the authorities' making of an instantaneous decision – an easy task in a totalitarian system – to reject the native legal tradition irrespective of the stage of legislative progress on the new provisions and regardless of the consequences of such a legal revolution. Hence, the majority of lawyers and jurists, framing their utterances in terms of Marxist, internationalist modernization, simultaneously put forward a thesis that added value would come for such type of change from merging it with certain elements of native legal identity and from the verification of proposed changes according to criteria of everyday utility. In that manner, rationales were supplied for corrections to one draft of the code after another, protracting the drafting process and subsequently

83 By way of example see Jan GWIAZDOMORSKI, Maurycy GRUDZIŃSKI, Stefan KALETA, Aleksander WOLTER: *Założenia prawa rodzinnego w świetle konstytucji PRL* [Assumptions of family law in the light of the Constitution of Polish People's Republic], in Stefan GRZYBOWSKI (ed.): *Zagadnienia prawne konstytucji Polskiej Rzeczypospolitej Ludowej* [Legal topics of the Constitution of Polish People's Republic], vol. 3, PWN, Warsaw, 1954, 52–120.

preventing the completion of a civil code containing a comprehensive implementation of the doctrinal assumptions of Marxism or their vulgarized Soviet variant.

The frame of the debate and of the legislative works done in 1949–1956 was set by the following legal circumstances: presence of private property in a large part of the agricultural economy; unsolved problem of regulation of the rules for the exercise of state ownership; limitation of the functions of private law through the narrowing of the jurisdiction of common courts in civil matters; codification of one part of the law (Family Code of 1950), invoking the new ideology but in reality incorporating several different axiologies; as well as inclusion of new interpretative clauses in the existing civil law.

The authorities in Poland had to tolerate the independent ownership and management of privately owned farms by those peasant farmers who did not support collectivization, because stated-owned enterprises did not have the capacity to cover the food supply. The aforementioned lack of effectiveness was caused by the defective structuring of the norms governing legal transactions involving state-owned and co-operative property. The continued existence of private ownership justified the retention of numerous traditional contents of real law (i.e. law of things, property law), law of obligations, inheritance law and family law, as well as general principles of civil law. Hence, in the course of discussions as to the extent of adaptation of Polish legal system to Soviet models, the lawyers and jurists were in agreement that until such time as private ownership of property was to disappear – and the date for that was always moving – any variant of a civil code could only be a temporary instrument.

The question was asked of the sense of creating a code containing – anachronistic from the beginning, from the perspective of a socialist state – provisions on the protection of private property and its derivatives. In response, the authorities and some of the legal minds argued the temporary nature of the problem. The forecast was that the peasant farmers would soon submit to collectivization, because they would, through the assistance of the party, rise to the same ideological maturity as the labourers massively employed by state-owned enterprises. Asserting the inevitability of that social transformation, the authorities instrumentally employed an argument derived from the native tradition, claiming the existence of a permanent antagonism between the working class (peasant farmers and labourers) and the capitalist class. The narration conveniently ignored the fact that, as a result of nationalization of part of agricultural land, there were no longer any capitalists remaining in Poland's rural areas. The argument that it would be premature to regulate civil law was also identified with the legislature's failure to define the terms of the exercise of economic rights in the state-owned economy. There, too, declarations were made that the obstacle was soon to be eliminated, which, however, ultimately never happened. The reason for that failure came from the systemic defects in the theory of social ownership and in the theory of organization of the economic model authored by Soviet jurisprudence.

The creation and reinforcement of a myth of continued modernization – both ideological and normative – and of its great scale proceeded not only through the omission of a large number of facts but also through the showcasing of the individual pieces of new legislation. Those were hailed as creations of socialist legal thought. Such an innovative status was ascribed e.g. to the codification of family law in 1950.[84] Contrary to facts, the narration highlighted the alleged internationalist substance of the code, which was to be the result of the collaborative work of Polish and Czechoslovak drafters undertaken in response to a political demand.[85] The establishment of family law as a separate code, as opposed to the inclusion of the matter in the civil code, was represented as the witness of ideological process. It was claimed that family in Poland was ceasing to be an institution defined by property relationships and thus it required a new method of regulation, the original model of which was supplied by Soviet legal science, with a focus on the family's social bonds.[86] Simultaneously, announcements were made that the changes in family law would be extended also to other areas of the law, including inheritance law and property law. In reality, the conceptual framework and the structure of the Family Code of 1950 were grounded in the legacy of Polish legal science of the Second Republic.[87] The general provi-

84 Act of 27 June 1950 – Family Code, Dz.U.34.308.

85 Seweryn SZER: *Współpraca polsko-czechosłowacka w zakresie kodyfikacji prawa rodzinnego* [Polish-Czechoslovak co-operation on the codification of family law], in Wacław OSUCHOWSKI, Mieczysław SOŚNIAK, Bronisław WALASZEK (eds): *Księga pamiątkowa dla uczczenia pracy naukowej prof. K. Przybyłowskiego* [A commemorative book to honour the academic work of Professor K. Przybyłowski], PWN, Krakow-Warsaw, 1964, 357.

86 Dmitry M. GENKIN et al. (eds): *Sovetskoe graždanskoe parvo* [Soviet civil law], vol. 1, Gosjurizdat, Moskva, 1950, 15.

87 Piotr FIEDORCZYK: *Czechosłowacka droga do kodyfikacji prawa rodzinnego 1919–1949: z dziejów współpracy z Polską* [The Czechoslovak route to codification of family law 1919–1949: from the history of co-operation with Poland], in Adam LITYŃSKI (ed.): *Państwo, prawo, społeczeństwo w dziejach Europy Środkowej: księga jubileuszowa dedykowana Profesorowi Józefowi Ciągwie w siedemdziesięciolecie urodzin* [The state, law and society in the history of Central Europe: a jubilee book dedicated to Professor Józef Ciągwa on the seventieth anniversary of his birthday], Towarzystwo Słowaków w Polsce, Katowice–Krakow 2009, 184–196; Andrzej DZIADZIO: *Polsko-czechosłowacka współpraca*

sions of civil law derived from the same source also applied to it. In consequence, the contents of the Polish code ended up being substantially different from those of the Czechoslovak Family Code.

Explanations offered for the continued applicability, of numerous legal instruments from the Second Republic within the system of private law invoked the argument that the special properties of Marxist interpretation of the law. The latter was to have universal features enabling the comprehensive updating of any legal norm, enabling a faster flow of information between the legal system and its environment than in the case of action taken by the legislature. That was also the manner of responding to calls for the elimination of gaps and inconsistencies in the new law. Assertions were made that such defects were natural at the stage of refinement of socialist socio-economic relationships. A better alternative, compared to legislative corrections or ground-up creation of new provisions corresponding to the Marxist ideology, was to be the addition of general clauses to existing provisions of civil law.

The ideological interpretation of the law was elevated to the most important element of the reform was not only to give the 'bourgeois' legislation new substance and improve the functioning of socialist law but also to justify the indoctrination of lawyers and jurists done in a manner undermining the value of the principle of judicial independence (in formal terms, the principle of independence was retained). Catchwords of ideological modernization achieved by new ways of interpretation of existing provisions were also relied upon in order to limit the jurisdiction of common courts. Assertions were made that this was the result of judges' failure to apply an interpretation consistent with the doctrinal assumptions of Marxism, resulting in incorrect rulings and requiring part of civil cases to be referred instead to administrative and *quasi*-judicial bodies equipped with the capacity to interpret the law in line with Marxist doctrine.

The consequence of such arguments and organizational decisions was the simultaneous weakening of the positions of the courts and of private law. The new bodies entrusted with the resolution of civil cases made their rulings on the basis of specific provisions of public law. As a result, the lack of a civil code

---

nad kodyfikacją prawa rodzinnego w latach 1948–1950. Z dziejów sowietyzacji prawa [Polish-Czechoslovak co-operation on the codification of family law in 1948–1950], in Jerzy Malec (ed.): *Rozważania o nauce i dogmatyce prawa. Materiały konferencji naukowej zorganizowanej przez Wydział Administracji Krakowskiej Szkoły Wyższej im. Andrzeja Frycza Modrzewskiego* [Ponderings on the science and dogmatics of law. Materials of the academic conference organized by the Faculty of Administration of Andrzej Frycz Modrzewski University in Krakow], Krakowskie Towarzystwo Edukacyjne, Krakow, 2002, 141–151.

or new code of civil procedure posed no significant political problem from the perspective of the political powers.

The claim that judges were unable to apply the law correctly ruling on civil cases was a form of axiological blackmail both with regard to the judges themselves and the participants of the legislative drafting works. To the judges, the suggestion was made that their reluctance towards the political interpretation of the law made them responsible for civil cases being transferred out of the court system. The drafters, on the other hand, could be made to believe that the situation of the courts would be changed by the preparation of a legislative instrument containing a sufficient degree of Marxist ideology. Such provisions would no longer require judges to apply extraordinary methods of interpretation, such as *contra legem*. The argument of the anachronicity of the justice system (incorporating judges educated in a capitalist system and basing their rulings on similarly capitalist law) would then lose its basis, all the more so considering that a new generation of judges began to enter the court system since 1950.

The aforementioned circumstances, together with the factual transformations of certain social and economic affairs calling for legislative intervention, shaped the ideological and axiological rationales for changes to the Polish system of civil law in 1949–1956. Those transformations, however, outside of the Family Code and certain isolated amendments to other provisions, did not move past the stage of successive drafts of the civil code.

2 The 1st Codification Commission

Despite the swiftness with which the unification was accomplished, the need for codification continued to make itself strongly felt. Although initially, in 1946, Minister Świątkowski assumed that the exigent need was only the ultimate abolition of the partitioning powers' laws, whereas 'the codification work could be performed without haste and could take a number of years,'[88] that assumption soon ceased to be valid. A new codification commission – Commission for the Development of a Uniform Polish Civil Code (Civil Law Codification Commission) – was established by order of the Minister of Justice of 18 February 1947.[89] It was also strictly subordinated to that minister. The latter had full control of the Commission's internal organization and personal

88 ŚWIĄTKOWSKI: *Społeczna myśl prawnicza*, 11.

89 *Cf.* remarks opposing the establishment of a Codification Commission depending on the government from the beginning of the interwar period.

composition. He could dissolve it at any time. In the exercise of his powers, Świątkowski appointed himself the Commission's president and retained the right to appoint deputies from among the employees of the Ministry.[90]

Formally, the codifiers' *de facto* dependence on the political authority was complete. To what extent, however, could the leading role in the works be played by a minister of justice potentially being mainly the messenger of political will coming from above?[91] In our attempt to answer that question, let us note that, according to the minutes, Świątkowski's presence at the Commission's meetings was rare. Nor can he be counted among its most active members. Even so, we note examples of his imperious conducting during sessions, such as when answering the following question: 'Is it expedient to include a provision banning the celebration of denominational marriages before the celebration of marriage before a civil registrar?' – the minister's response that he believed such a provision to be 'necessary' ended the discussion.[92] The relatively low pressure from the main political decision-makers on the shape of the future codification was of key importance; this is compared to the pressure put on the codifiers after 1949. A key indicator of this situation was especially the attitude of Seweryn Szer, different in years 1947–1948 than after 1949, which coincided with the timing of the intensification of his activity in the field of ideological rationales constantly drawing – as was expected – from Marxism-Leninism and Stalinist model from the USSR.[93]

The composition of the Civil Law Codification Commission was dominated by judges and legal scholars. Out of the five members, Marian Lisiewski and Jan Witecki were justices of the Supreme Court and Doctor Aleksander Wolter combined academic work at a university with employment by the Ministry of Justice and also the position of a judge of a Court of Appeals. Representatives of the academic circles included Professor Jan Wasilkowski, the dean of the

90 Order of the Minister of Justice of 18 February 1947, AAN, MS, 2390, 1.

91 A different assessment is called for by the matter of the dependence of the Minister of Justice and of the Codification Commission on the Legal Bureau of the Central National Council. The 1944 amendment of the Soviet Code of 1926 consisting in restrictions on divorce opportunities resulted in a change of the Legal Bureau's approach to the question. Until the time, in its correspondence with the Ministry of Justice, the Bureau had insisted on expanding those opportunities. FIEDORCZYK: *Z prac nad unifikacją*, 78.

92 Minutes of the session of the Codification Commission's Substantive Civil Law Team on 23 February 1948, AAN, MS, 2380, 37.

93 Seweryn SZER: *Pojęcie i przedmiot prawa cywilnego* [The concept and object of civil law], DPP 2 (1950), 15; Seweryn SZER: *Kodeks rodzinny* [The Family Code], DPP 3 (1950), 3; SZER: *Współpraca polsko-czechosłowacka*, 22–28.

Faculty of Law and Administration of the University of Warsaw. The government was represented, besides the minister himself, by the Deputy Director of the Legislative Department of the Ministry of Justice, Doctor Seweryn Szer, who also combined his duties with an academic career. Wasilkowski as rapporteur and Wolter as co-rapporteur were entrusted with the works on the General Part and, in the same configuration, Witecki and Szer with family law, Szer and Witecki with inheritance law, Wolter and Lisiewski with the law of obligations, and Lisiewski and Wasilkowski with real law. Despite the smallness of the composition, the extent of the works was spectacular. Over the span of two years – until early 1949 – the Commission prepared the drafts of the majority of the divisions of the civil code. Nonetheless, as a result of changed political circumstances, the works were interrupted, and the almost ready draft, as a manifestation of 'rightist-nationalist deviations' could not, or at least not formally, serve as the basis and point of reference for the next stage of the codification works undertaken in 1949. The most active members of the first Civil Law Codification Commission – Jan Wasilkowski and Se-weryn Szer – were not recalled from its composition, and thus their achievements and experience gained during that stage of the works doubtless must have provided the cornerstone for the works done on the subsequent stages.

FIGURE 3.1 Jan Wasilkowski, 1898–1977. Linked to the University of Warsaw since the 20s; long-term chair of the Department of Civil Law, also Dean of the Faculty of Law Administration and Rector shortly after the war. Member of the Codification Commission under the Second Polish Republic and also after 1945; President of the Civil Law Codification Commission of 1956. First President of the Supreme Court (1956–1967); head of Legal Sciences at Polish Academy of Science; leader of the parliamentary Commission for the Administration of Justice as a deputy of the PUWP (PZPR).

3 The General Assumptions

As opposed to the unification work, the codification was to be characterized by the creation of a system based 'on certain consistently pursued general assumptions.'[94] While the unification was able to be accomplished at an expeditious rate, the works on the codification had to face a number of problems.[95]

The agenda was drawn by Jan Wasilkowski. Similarly to the first Polish codifiers of the interwar period twenty-five years prior, he took the position that a codification in the full sense of the word would be premature. The unified law first required 'animation', a 'baptism of fire', to – upon the crystallization of a certain decision-making line of the courts interpreting the new provisions, along with out-of-court practice of application – delimit the future directions of remodelling of the new law. In the shorter term, one could primarily make adjustments to the technical aspects of the unified law, and the 'codification action' should be limited to such interventions, essentially consisting in corrections to the unified law.

What intentions, exactly, were underlying such a solution? Let us once again allow Wasilkowski to speak, at this time from the perspective of time, three years later. In 1950, amid changed political realities, the celebrated article titled *Kodyfikacja prawa cywilnego w Polsce* (Codification of civil law in Poland) was printed. Wasilkowski wrote that the codifiers in 1947 held the view that:

> a radical overhaul of the legislation originating from 1945/1946 would be premature, although it was realized that many provisions of that legislation must incur significant ideological reservations (especially provisions dealing with real law). The rapid transformations in the country during the initial years following the cessation of hostilities, transformations arising primarily from revolutionary socio-economic

94 Witold Czachórski: *Przebieg prac nad kodyfikacją prawa cywilnego PRL* [Course of work on the codification of civil law in the People's Republic of Poland], Studia Prawnicze 26–27 (1970), 8.

95 By decision of the Codification Commission (made upon 'preliminary deliberations on the technique and layout of the draft'), reflective at least partially of the approaches taken by its members, a 'traditional' division of the whole into family law, law of obligations, inheritance law and real law was retained, with – which, at last, was not part of the traditional canon – separation of the provisions common to all of the code and other private-law statutes into a general part. Marian Lisiewski: *Projekt części ogólnej kodeksu cywilnego*, Przegląd Notarialny 1 (1948)/4, 287.

> transformations (agrarian reform, nationalization of core sectors of the national economy), enormous population movements (the settlement of the Western Lands, mass repatriation from the USSR and from Western countries) and the hectic progress rate on reconstruction, appeared to demand great caution in codification designs.

Are these, however, all of the reasons, or did other reasons exist the author was not allowed to mention? To this question we do not know the answer. Wasilkowski did not, however, hesitate to highlight that the 'most important reason for the half-finished nature of the reform was unquestionably the circumstance that in the discussed period (the year 1947), the correct view of the political system of people's democracy as an organization meeting the basis tasks of the dictatorship of the proletariat had not yet been properly crystallized among lawyers as a whole,' contrary to the expectations of 1950.[96]

The Civil Law Codification Commission, making in 1947 the decision setting the direction for all of the works, so as to limit them to the technical refinement of the existing law and systemic coalescence of the whole, was inspired especially by the thought of the eminent French civilist, François Gény.[97] Changes venturing outside that codification goal were undertaken only on an exceptional basis, namely in cases when 'the need arose to adapt certain texts to the principles of the existing political system' ('this refers mainly to the provisions originating from the interwar period,' Wasilkowski reassured), or 'when in the light of already available experience, the inadequacy of a certain norm of applicable law was deemed to be beyond any doubt for other reasons.' The latter case could be stretched quite far.[98] This appears to mean that it was

96 Jan WASILKOWSKI: *Kodyfikacja prawa cywilnego w Polsce* [Codification of civil law in Poland], Nowe Prawo 12 (1950), 4. Cf. Anna Machnikowska, *Wymiar sprawiedliwości*, 355–363, 394–396.

97 *Praca nad kodyfikacją prawa cywilnego*, DPP 5 (1947), 47. References were made to Gény's monumental opus, the *Science et technique en droit privé positif* (1914–1924),

98 As noted by Wasilkowski and Wolter, despite such a limitation of the scope, it was still relatively extensive but what he had in mind was essentially only the time-consuming technical work, especially with regard to the General Part and correction of the provisions of Real Law. 'The consolidation and systematization of the provisions in force alone requires a new wording to be given to numerous texts. In many cases, purely editorial corrections will not suffice. The 'technical refinement' must consist in the elimination of substantive defects, especially the rectification of defective constructs, filling of gaps and development of principles not expounded exhaustively enough in the already applicable law. This will entail the necessity of amendment of a considerable number of existing provisions and addition of new provisions. At last, there remains the matter of a homogeneous and correct redaction.' Jan. WASILKOWSKI, Aleksander WOL-

assumed *a priori* that the codifiers should restrain their urge to examine in detail every provision of the unified law.[99]

In truth, the adaptation of the provisions, of which the brunt had originated before the war, to the principles of the new political system required the reassessment of the foundations on which the existing civil law was built. For example, the principle of freedom of contract stipulated in the Code of Obligations had to be rejected in the drafting of the General Part. In their decision to do so, the authors of that part of the draft – Wolter and Wasilkowski – simply decided to delete it, with the rationale that it had 'essentially the character of a programmatic declaration not harmonious with the principles of the new political system'.[100]

Providing historical arguments in support of his thesis of the necessity of holding back the creation of the final codification opus, Jan Wasilkowski reinterpreted historical facts partially in an incorrect manner. He cited the experience of the adaptation of the Code of Napoleon in Polish territories in the former half of the 19th century. The fact alone is worth emphasizing because he was invoking the experience of the arch-liberal capitalist Code. It

---

TER: *Projekt kodeksu cywilnego. Część ogólna* [Draft Civil Code. General Part], DPP 1 (1948), 10.

99 The limits of what could or should be changed were fluid and up to the codifiers' discretion. And thus the authors of the draft General Part did not, for example, decide in favour of introducing the *ad probationem* requirement of form for specific legal transactions, which would mean the modification of the – defective, in their opinion – evidentiary principle followed by the Code of Obligations. Still, they viewed themselves as having the authorization to modify the provisions of the Code of Obligations, under which the court was not, in disputed cases, empowered to make a decision concerning the avoidance of the legal effects of a defective statement of will. 'At a time when the average ethical level has undergone a certain depreciation as a result of the protracted war and occupation, it appears to be expedient to avoid such solutions as might, even though only indirectly, weaken the authority of the principle of *pacta sunt servanda*,' we read in their rationale. Similarly, the 'care to the interests of minors', identified with 'care to the interests of society', justified the decision to modify the provisions of the Code of Obligations 'prompting the expansion of the powers of the guardianship authority with regard to withdrawing from a partially incapacitated person or a minor above the age of 13 the management of the wage of work earned.' Furthermore, in respect of the determination of the scope of capacity to act at law, the most 'radical change relative to the existing law' was deemed to be the raising the upper limit of the age of incapacity from 7 to 13 years.

'The change was decided by practical considerations,' according to the rationale. Namely 'it was almost universally felt that, given the vast scope of legal transactions the applicable law allowed perosns restricted in their capacity for legal transactions to make, the limit of 7 years was too low.' *Ibidem*, 15–16.

100 *Ibidem*, 14.

appears, therefore, that to Wasilkowski, as a representative of legal academia of the prewar period, the historical experience of codification held universal value. He distorted the reality, however, in claiming that the Code of Napoleon needed a longer time to become assimilated, despite relying largely on old laws. Ancient Polish customary law, feudal in nature, evidently did not have much in common with the Code of Napoleon. Despite that, the problem of assimilation of the Code of Napoleon indeed involved time.

The article penned by Wasilkowski, the erstwhile member of the prewar Codification Commission, concerning the need for codification and for the drawing up of an agenda was during that time practically the sole postwar statement. No one else gained the concession or mandate from the state authorities to speak in the public forum on the assumptions of the future codification. Perhaps not only fears but censorship was at play. The problem calls for studies. It should not be forgotten that by no accident the *Przegląd Notarialny*, less than a year later, reprinted Stanisław Bukowiecki's article, published before the war – in 1938 – also containing a certain codification agenda.[101] The editorial board of the *Przegląd Notarialny* appeared to support of Wasilkowski's views. It painted Bukowiecki as an 'eminent lawyer and great citizen,' and above all emphasized the enduring 'vital importance' of his 'outlook on the codification of civil law in Poland, in conjunction with the general assessment of the works of the Codification Commission'.[102] The words of an 'eminent citizen' were cited, and at once of someone who could, as it were, personify the Commission, though Bukowiecki was without any doubt counted among the progressives. The editorial board of the *Przegląd Notarialny* implied that the codification programme, so abruptly interrupted ten years prior ought to be resumed. The thing to do was not to distance oneself from the interwar Commission's achievements but to continue its thought and work and perhaps also return to other assumptions relating to its existence, such as by guaranteeing the codifiers' independent operation.

In reprinting Bukowiecki's article, the editorial board of the *Przegląd Notarialny* was acting to defeat the above-cited charge brought by prominent offi-

---

101 Contrary to Piotr Fiedorczyk's view that Bukowiecki's outlook – published in the Przegląd Notarialny – on the course of the codification works 'was only of historical significance.' Rather, it was a veiled attempt at recalling the legacy of the prewar Codification Commission. Piotr FIEDORCZYK: *O początkach prac nad kodyfikacją polskiego prawa cywilnego w 1947 r.* [On the beginnings of the works on the codification of Polish civil law in 1947], MHI 4 (2006), 113.

102 *Przed 10-ciu laty: 'Kwartalnik Prawa Prywatnego'* [Ten years ago: the Kwartalnik Prawa Prywatnego], Przegląd Notarialny 1 (1948)/4, 278.

cials in the Ministry of Justice that the Codification Commission had acted slowly and sluggishly.

> If there are in society people believing the Commission to have done too little during that time [eighteen years], then perhaps they are not completely in the right. It is probably possible to argue theoretically that more could have been done (...) and considering (...) the inability of the members of the Commission to dedicate themselves solely to the work of codification, as well as bearing in mind the fact that the members of the Commission, educated on very different statutory frameworks could only after a long period of collaboration mutually educate themselves, develop a common type of work and find common guidelines, it appears to me that the Commission's activity to date must be regard as having produced a rich harvest.[103]

These arguments correspond with those put forward by Jan Wasilkowski, who – during that period of 1947–1948 – played the first fiddle in the codification works.

4 Harnessing the Native Legacy of Interwar Period

To what extent were the works and legacy of the interwar Codification Commission relied upon in the preparations for a new code during the period? Concerning the works conducted in 1948 on the General Part, let us turn to the views of Adam Szpunar. Responding to the question of the expected attitude of the civil code to the then-presently applicable unified law arising from the drafts prepared by the interwar Codification Commission, Szpunar did not at all suggest a need for verification from the ground up. On the contrary, he argued: 'the majority of the provisions of the presently applicable civil law have withstood the trial by fire of criticism, and some of the provisions (...) have been very favourably received by foreign writers,'[104] definitely not necessarily socialist authors. That belief in the existence of universal criteria allowing the quality of legislation to be assessed without differen-

103 Bukowiecki invoked the unification experience of other states that had faced a similar problem following World War I and done a far worse job facing up to that challenge. *Ibidem*, 283.

104 Adam Szpunar: *Uwagi do projektu części ogólnej kodeksu cywilnego* [Remarks on the draft of the General Part of the Civil Code], AAN, MS, 2390, 42.

tiating it on the basis of whatever ideological goals it was supposed to serve constituted a characteristic staple of the legal discourse of the time. It is no exaggeration to say that Szpunar's view was controversial. He could easily have incurred the accusation of being an advocate of the maintenance of the old legal order, because that was indeed the logical conclusion to be drawn from his words.

Szpunar's above-cited comment about the majority of the interwar code provisions' having withstood the test of fire applied 'especially' to the Code of Obligations, even though that part was, after all, in the greatest degree tied to the capitalist political system. To Szpunar, the key aspect was the assimilation of certain legal provisions by society (provisions dealing with the option to avoid the legal effects of a statement of will or with exploitation). Despite being in the process of building a new socio-economic system in the country, one ought not to ignore the fact that society had become accustomed to such type of provisions and 'underst[ood] them well.' In that situation, their amendment or elimination from the general part 'w[ould] not be making a step forward.'[105] This interesting conclusion reduced a progressive change to whether it avoided violating societal habits and removing socially accepted institutions. Otherwise he denied its progressive character. He illustrated his claims with references to the 'long developments of French law'.[106]

Szpunar, ever the harsh critic of the German Civil Code – appeared to be closer to the views taken by the historical school of law, focusing on its organic development. He explained his perspective as follows: 'The creation of the system of the civil code was strongly influenced by the previous historical development, and the lawmaker ought not to discount that development,' not even in a situation in which 'the generated system sometimes fails to live

105 *Ibidem*, 41.

106 Szpunar argued that the evolution of French law had led to the 'creation' of the principle that the provisions on the requirement of form for evidentiary purposes (Articles 1341ff of the Code of Napoleon) belonged to substantive law. Similarly, the Polish lawmaker in the Code of Obligations (Article 110) created a provision from which 'it seem[ed] to follow' that the legislature 'share[d] the tradition position held by French scholarship.' The drafters, by contrast, ignoring tradition, intended to break with that principle and regulate the matter of evidentiary limitations in the Code of Civil Procedure. A similar case was the case of the classical approach taken by Polish civilists to combine legal capacity and capacity to act at law and discuss them jointly – to break with that tradition was, in Szpunar's opinion, misguided. MS, 2390, 42. Additionally, the drafters followed the example of the BGB in formulating the capacity to act in legal transactions altogether, which also incurred his criticism.

up to the strict requirements of logic.'[107] For that reason, he belonged to the group of lawyers who were desirous to continue to draw from Polish tradition, even when other important considerations spoke against doing that.

An important, if not key, role in the development of the law was, according to Szpunar, played by native academia. This is attested by the criticism with which he met the attempt at departure from the settled approach in Polish science of civil law consisting in the tight linking of capacity for acting at law to legal capacity and joint discussion of the two institutions. In his opinion, if something had become settled in native scholarship, one should not break from it without good reason. By contrast, not only did the drafters decide to 'tear asunder' that continuity, by defining the two capacities in different places of the code despite the close linking of the two definitions, they – even worse – intended to follow the German model used by the BGB, in transforming the capacity for acting at law into capacity for legal transactions (*Geschäftsfähigkeit*), which, in Szpunar's opinion, was more defective due to not extending to all manifestations of human activity.[108]

Proceeding from such assumptions, Szpunar appreciated that the authors of the draft General Part – Jan Wasilkowski and Aleksander Wolter – clearly were drawing their inspiration from the general provisions of the Polish Code of Obligations, even though, sometimes – without good reason, he believed – they abandoned certain well-tested solutions, choosing those he deemed to be worse and modelled on other, foreign Western codes.[109] On the other hand, borrowings, even excessive, from the Code of Obligations were also noted. And thus, Doctor Adam Kozaczka of Jagiellonian University

107 SZPUNAR: *Uwagi do projektu części ogólnej*, AAN, MS, 2390, 42. In this part of his utterance we once again find reminiscences of Szpunar's negative attitude on the excessive formal refinement of the code for the sake of formal correctness but against existing habits.

108 *Ibidem*, 42–43. Szpunar believed the German approach to be incorrect, arguing: 'Besides legal transactions, the statute knows a succession of human activity ("acts", using the terminology of Article 1 of the Code of Obligations, *Rechtshandlungen* in German terminology), for which no provisions exist defining the actor's personal capacity.' *Ibidem*, 46.

109 Recognizing the need to draw upon the legacy of Polish law of the interwar period (primarily the Code of Obligations) and the native scholarship already shaped on its basis, Szpunar embarked on a criticism of the general part's drafters from the principle adopted in the Code of Obligations that avoidance of the effects of a statement of will must be in writing, whereas the advantages of that solution had been 'forcefully' elucidated by Roman Longchamps de Bérier (*Zobowiązania*, 97); SZPUNAR: *Uwagi do projektu części ogólnej*, AAN, MS, 2390, 57. Moreover, Szpunar called for the retention of those solutions that had not been critically evaluated during the interwar period, e.g. the admissibility of an irrevocable power of attorney. *Ibidem*, 58.

noted the drafters' 'reception' of 'almost whole Article 37 CO' into the draft's provisions governing error. In his opinion, said reception was so far gone that in their construct 'they reckoned almost exclusively with bilateral acts, whereas the law kn[ew] [also] unilateral acts.'[110]

Szpunar's views, therefore, suggest that the lawyers and jurists asked to review the draft did not feel a sense of being directly bound by the promptings of the new ideology. On the contrary, they did not hesitate to evaluate the solutions referred to them in such a manner as if there had been no socio-economic evolution in progress or at least as thought the latter did not play a key role. Only in a single case did Szpunar include a reference to the socio-economic transformations being in progress, deeming it 'expedient' to include a general provision about the *res extra commercium* as a term of 'significant practical importance in the era of socialized economy', which is when certain goods are completely withdrawn from circulation and cannot be the objects of the rights of private individuals.[111]

Szpunar's remarks correspond with Jan Wasilkowski's assessment in – as he himself termed it – the so-called historical aspect. Wasilkowski delivered it during the session of the Civil Law Codification Commission on 22 April 1948 concerning the concept of matrimonial property regime proposed in Marian Lisiewski's draft of matrimonial property law. Two alternative proposals for the cessation of statutory community property were deliberated upon at the time. One of the drafts, by Jan Witecki, foresaw a change in the spouses' property relations with the cessation of the statutory regime, consisting in the in-kind division of articles falling within community property, whereas Marian Lisiewski's alternative draft 'did not introduce any "traffic" to property relations,' contenting itself with disposing of the matter of settlements between the spouses. Taking the first turn to speak, Wasilkowski promoted Lisiewski's draft[112] and praised it, among others, in the historical aspect, for refraining from imposing thorough changes on Polish habits already settled by the old legal order. Lisiewski's solution, in Wasilkowski's opinion, was the '[logical] consequence of the very idea of statutory regime in the existing law'. For that regime,' Wasilkowski went on to explain 'in a certain sense [wa]s

110 Adam Kozaczka: *Kwestia błędu w części ogólnej Kodeksu Cywilnego* [The topic of an error in the General Part of the Civil Code], AAN, MS, 2390, 75.

111 Minutes of the session of the Codification Commission's Substantive Civil Law Team on 5 April 1948, AAN, MS, 2380, 61.

112 When discussing the advantages of the draft, Wasilkowski identified the technical legal, historical, utilitarian and social aspects.

the emulation of the regime of community in the event of death, known in the former Kingdom.'[113] To him, therefore, the 'existing law' was the aforementioned 'Polish-French law', and the form of his utterance attests to the codifiers' (hailing mainly from the Congress Kingdom) regard of the provisions of the French Civil Code as the most 'native' and assimilated out of all of the partitioning powers' laws. That, however, certainly was not the reason for any uncritical favouritism. For the 'Polish-French law' was archaic in part and long subjected to criticism. This is attested, among others, by the fact that Wasilkowski decided to support a different proposal offered by Lisiewski, one to retain the principle of subrogation of personal property, which 'although unknown to the Code of Napoleon, has been introduced by French scholarship and court decisions.'[114] Thus, similarly to the earlier stage of unification, the government's political ideology did not exert a sufficiently strong pressure on the codifiers. They were not ordered to make a radical break with their capitalist pasts or to aspire to a revolutionary transformation of socio-economic affairs in their work on the codification drafts. This is also attested by the opposition to Aleksander Wolter's request to expand the applicability of Article 145 to mortgage once a divorce petition has been lodged, the motive being that the statutory regulation of the matter had already been known e.g. to French law after a 1936 amendment of the Code of Napoleon (Article 313). The proposal incurred Wasilkowski's objection, supported by all other members of the Commission, justified by Wolter's request 'not being in the child's best interests'.[115] The Code of Napoleon thus served as the main or even the most important point of reference. Due to its application to the central region – unlike the BGB and ABGB – it constituted, in a way, a surrogate Polish codification that had to be taken into account and included in the discussion, though largely, after its critical assessment, to select a different solution, more effective and modern. In that approach, the French-Polish law mainly served as a springboard for the selection of something else.

Wasilkowski also turned out to be the promoter of the legacy of the prewar Codification Commission in a different debate – one on personal marriage law. While tabling an alternative motion, to base the structure of the divorce provisions on the premise of permanent marital cohabitation and necessity

113 Minutes of the session of the Codification Commission's Substantive Civil Law Team on 21 April 1948, AAN, MS, 2380, 71.

114 *Ibidem*, 73. We do not know, however, whether that meant it was also introduced in the Congress Kingdom.

115 *Protokół posiedzenia Komisji Kodyfikacyjnej Sekcji Cywilnej z dnia 1. VI.1948 r.*, 124–125.

for the court to determine the causes of its disintegration, he specified that his proposal was 'after the same thought' as the prewar draft of divorce provisions. At that time, the prevailing view in the Civil Law Commission, with which he too agreed on the merits, was that 'even the shocking facts usually cited as the causes of the disintegration cannot always be recognized as independent grounds for divorce.'[116] The invocation of arguments used before the war did not perhaps have a decisive positive influence on the Commission's opinion, but it certainly did not have a negative one, either, considering that Wasilkowski's motion passed unanimously,[117] and the solutions from the draft were replaced with institutions transplanted by him from the text of the prewar draft. Wolter, in turn, did not hesitate to invoke settled determinations from 'existing legal literature' (with regard to the use of the term *użytkowanie* to describe the right to draw benefits from property, on which account he – successfully – demanded the modification of a draft having employed that term in that meaning).[118]

In this context, one must note that aspirations to universalization and omission of the specificity of Polish realities from the draft solutions appear to be a rare development. In Piotr Fiedorczyk's view, one of the manifestations of such a tendency was the 'detachment of marriage from native tradition',[119] which the authors of the first draft of Polish Marriage Law of 1945 proposed due to the extraordinary political situation. That revolutionary change comprised: (1) a broad spectrum of availability of divorce, despite the professed policy of 'permanence of marriage'; (2) official recognition of concubinage as marriage under Soviet influence; (3) deeming betrothal (engagement) to be a superfluous institution (its introduction was opposed by the Legal Bureau of the Central National Council), along with the 'time-wasting' institution of banns. However, as soon as the next revisions of the drafts, that policy of not reckoning with Polish tradition was curtailed– (1) options for divorce were diminished considerably; (2) the idea of converting concubinage into marriage without observance of the form of celebration of marriage was abandoned; and (3) betrothal was reinstated as an institution deeply entrenched in Polish society, especially in the countryside.[120]

116 *Protokół posiedzenia Komisji Kodyfikacyjnej Sekcji Cywilnej w dniu 23. 11.1948 r.*, 36.

117 *Ibidem*, 39.

118 *Protokół posiedzenia Komisji Kodyfikacyjnej Sekcji Cywilnej w dniu 29. v.1948 r.*, 107.

119 FIEDORCZYK: *Z prac unifikacyjnych*, 76–77.

120 *Ibidem*, 77–78.

5 Instrumentalization of Civil Law and Views on Technical Legal Matters

The key role in the codification works was played by the preparation of the General Part. To the codifiers, the homogeneity of the principles governing not only the entire Civil Code but also extending onto all statutes dealing with private law was a value unto itself, and the benefit of creating a separate part out of provisions of general importance were 'self-evident'. That, however, was not merely a purely technical value, because, as Marian Lisiewski attempted to explain 'by regulating the principles permeating the whole of civil law in a single collective location their harmonious understanding and application in their very essence is ensured.' Doing so was thus decisive to the cohesion of the system as a whole.[121]

In the literature, much controversy was sparked by Article 1 of the General Part of the draft Code.[122] It was of high significance from the perspective of the manner of diffusion of ideology to the text of the code. The provision demanded that the filling of a legal gap, i.e. of a situation in which neither the statute nor customary law could provide the basis for the solution of the case, be guided by the principles of the social order existing in the state. That left leeway for extra-normative decisions based on the interpretation of maxims of equity on the basis of socialist doctrine.

The matter was also addressed by Adam Szpunar, who observed that the 'principles of the social system existing in the state' were not sufficient for that goal, as they 'often fail[ed] to give answers to technical legal questions.' Not too rarely a judge who is filling a gap 'must create a provision harmoniously supplementing the applicable law,' which is of relevance in the ideological context. For those reasons, in Szpunar's opinion, not only the social system but also the legal system had to be references as a sort of more objective canon of universal principles decisive of the quality of 'good law'.[123]

---

121 Lisiewski stipulated the caveat that it was not at all the drafters' intention for those applying to code to 'adhere slavishly to a certain template'. On the contrary, they believed that the 'characteristics of the object regulated in each individual part of the code will imbue the principles contained in the general part with a specific colouring; it will demand the adaptation of the general principles to a given subject.'

122 Especially Jan Jakub Litauer's article titled *O metodzie wypełniania luk prawnych* [On the method of filling legal lacunae], published in the *Państwo i Prawo* (PiP 7–8 (1947), 14–22), elicited a response.

123 SZPUNAR: *Uwagi do projektu części ogólnej*, AAN, MS, 2390, 43. He illustrated the situation on the example of looking for an answer to the following question: 'can an attorney enter into a contract with himself? ' which, in the absence of code regulation, the judges

Szpunar recalled the classic assumptions of codification, along with simple, clear and intelligible language. '[It] should correspond to the democratic assumptions and goals of the Polish state and thus be intended for the people, not solely for the professional lawyer,' he argued. One had to draw from the experience of the past, taking the example of the BGB as a 'warning' against the danger of 'formulating overly general principles and definitions and resolving theoretical disputes', as well as 'doctrinal' ones. Reliance on the existing legacy of the scholarship of civil law should be limited by the extent of necessity. The role model for the Polish lawmaker to follow could be derived from the case of the ZGB, which had 'combined in a fortunate manner a high academic level with clarity and accessibility of the text'.[124] From that perspective, the draft General Part, in Szpunar's view, fulfilled the above requirements 'only in part'. In some of its provisions, the drafter unnecessarily engaged in the resolution of theoretical disputes (Article 38), and at a different time he repeated definitions taken from textbooks of civil law (Articles 34, 35 and 38), making excessive use of abstract expressions ('terminological distinctions with the scholastic breath of Windscheid or Regelsberger's textoobks'), whereas the relevant matter had better be left to academia to resolve. The above remarks and his aversion to the German Civil Code corresponded with his other reservation, against 'assigning excessive importance to logico-systematic considerations'.[125]

The rhetorics of creating a law for the people combined with mistrust of the legal elites was falling on fertile soil. After all, the legal elites, mostly belonging to the former establishment, could be painted in the categories of 'enemies of the people', implying that the law created by them did not serve the ideological purposes of the new state. In this perspective, Szpunar's argument corresponds to the assertions we can find in an article penned by Józef Litwin: 'It is not the people but the lawyers, the clan, who diligently conserve the law.'[126] On the other hand, the communist authorities did not hesitate to set the legal elites to work. Only, however, in the capacity of advisory expert bodies. That was the character of the 'opining commission' established already in 1945.[127]

had to provide, and, in his opinion, the principles of the social system were not useful in the slightest.

124 *Ibidem*, 41.

125 *Ibidem*, 42–43, 48, 54, 71.

126 Józef LITWIN: *Recepcja prawa polskiego na Ziemiach Odzyskanych* [Reception of Polish Law in the Recovered Territories], PiP 1 (1946), 23.

127 Stefan BANCERZ: *Dwa lata prac ustawodawczych* [Two years of legislative works], DPP 7 (1946), 20.

In 1948, in turn, the draft General Part was distributed to several dozen eminent lawyers – scholars and judges of the highest instances – for opinions.

The ideological goal of Article 1 of the draft, to fill gaps in the code along the ideological line of the new system, corresponded to the language of Article 3: 'A statute shall not be retroactive save where its wording or purpose suggests otherwise.' That, too, opened the path to the instrumental use of the code for the achievement of short-term goals by the bodies applying the law. That was noted by the justice of the Supreme Court, Aleksander Baziński, who observed that the drafters were attempting to create a general norm leaving the assessment of whether the purpose of a statute warranted its retroactive application to the court or other authorities. Baziński argued: 'The creation of a general rule that the statute shall have retroactive force if that is what its purpose suggests makes the impression that one has to reckon in advance with the future lawmaker not always being aware of the purpose of the law.' He believed that to be an unacceptable situation, because the lawmaker had to be 'acutely' aware of the purpose of the act due to 'enacting it precisely because the necessity or at least the need to enact it has emerged.'[128] One could wonder whether Baziński did not perhaps imply that the drafter, in creating such type of general norm, did not intend – for a time – to conceal his motives, counting on the possibility that the situation might soon change, or, in full awareness, to expand the field of instrumental use of the law by liberally extending the applicable norms onto situations having preceded it in time, even at the costs of a lack of certainty of the state of legal affairs. Special circumstances – such as a fundamental political change – appeared to justify such conduct on political grounds. Of that Baziński was completely aware. He appreciated that 'such type of general norm could lead to arbitrariness, depending on the individuality of the person tasked with deciding whether a statute is retroactive or not.' Such a situation would be harmful to the ideals of rule of law, because there can be not the slightest doubt that the 'consequence of ['anyone other than the lawmaker'] being left with decision-making discretion' as to whether a given act is to be retroactive, can only be the 'diverging application of the statute in individual cases, depending on the views of the person deciding the specific case.'[129] In particular 'leaving (…) the judicature

128 Aleksander BAZIŃSKI: *Uwagi do części ogólnej projektu Kodeksu Cywilnego uchwalonego przez Komisję powołaną do sparowania tego projektu w I czytaniu* [Comments on the General Part of the draft Civil Code adopted by the Commission appointed to pair this draft in the first reading], AAN, MS, 2390, 29.

129 *Ibidem*, 28–29. Justice Baziński was aware and did not hesitate to emphasize that the side effect of such a broadly open door would be the 'complete uncertainty whether the

to decide in a general way whether a statute is retroactive on account of its purpose would be (...) the improper shifting of a decision belonging to the lawmaker onto the uncertain and variable waves of the judicature.'[130] Even leaving aside the alleged fears of the instrumental use of the law by the political authority in the circumstances of building a 'New Poland', Baziński was far from borrowing from British models or even from giving effect to the demands of the school of free law. He deemed the very idea of leaving it to the courts to decide this matter to be dangerous. Baziński emphasized that although he was basing his assertions on documented academic theses (with regard to the 'theory of subjective interpretation of statutes', he was drawing his inspiration from Adam Szpunar), he himself 'did not have academic ambitions.' He cited 'professional experience', with the proviso that professional experience should not 'always be identified with professional conservatism or traditionalism.'[131] In a way, he was apriorically deflecting the charge of failure to think progressively and of his opinion being the expression of the position of the former elites and of an anachronistic way of thinking.

Baziński stressed the technical legal aspects of the future codification also in a different general matter. He observed: 'the lawmaker cannot predict all the complicated events of life [and] cannot create norms for all such cases as may happen.' One should harbour no delusions – that was the direction taken by the legislative technique. For that reason, legal drafters must rely on general norms and avoid casuistry and 'minuteness'. That was something he held to be an objective truth and sign of technical progress, decisive of the higher quality of the law being made. In order, however, for that to be so, another condition had to be met: a narrowed-down axiology: 'the lawmaker must be acutely aware of the purpose of the statute being created, due to enacting it precisely because the necessity or at least the need to enact it has emerged.'[132] The lawmaker can, however, conceal the motives for a time, reckoning with the possibility that the situation might soon change, or attempt to expand the field for the instrumental use of the law by extending its norms liberally onto situations preceding it in time, even at the cost of a lack of certainty. Special circumstances, such as a fundamental political change, appear to justify such conduct on political grounds.

---

statute is (or some of its provisions are) retroactive.' *Ibidem*, 29. While doing so, he insisted that he was not allowing himself to 'be guided by the principle of the pandects: *lex retro non agit*'; *ibidem*, 33.

130 *Ibidem*, 30.

131 *Ibidem*, 33.

132 *Ibidem*, 29.

Baziński, therefore, believed the use of general norms to be consistent with the spirit of progress.[133] He would allow the flexible application of legal norms, which he regarded as an advantage: 'The broad confines of a provision facilitate the avoidance of misunderstandings; they enable different sets of facts to be moulded into general frames.' Thus, one had to reckon with the possibility and regard it as expedient that 'the statute, upon entering into life, gains an autonomous "existence", independent even from its drafters; sometimes it happens that some of the provisions are interpreted contrary to the intention of their authors.'[134] He went on to argue: 'The purpose arising from the text is not something settled once and for all; views on that purpose may change together with economic and social progress,' i.e. he appeared to be touching on the essence of the matter, viz. the level of development of Polish territories that inevitably had to change with the completion of the process of reconstruction of the country and normalization of its affairs, as well as at the threshold of its Sovietization. That is the context for Baziński's continued reflections:

> The purpose of a statute can be conceived different even by its drafters at the time of enactment, and in connection with the [soon expected] transformation of the economic and social structure, that purpose can

133 His remarks correspond to the position taken by Jan Wasilkowski during the examination of drafts of personal marriage law on the use in the code of terms that 'sometimes' would not be 'clear to the courts'. Such an objection to a term proposed by Wasilkowski was offered by Jan Witecki. In response, however, he heard that in his adversary's opinion, the flexibility of a term was the advantage of the construct being used. Wasilkowski argued: 'The same fact, depending on the circumstances and circles from which the spouses are derived might or might not be recognized by the court as the cause of disintegration of marital cohabitation'; *ibidem*, 38. Wasilkowski was thus closer to the possibility of the expansion of interpretative opportunities by the courts and not desirous to bind them to casuistic regulation. Witecki, in turn, opposed excessive flexibility (which opposition he voiced e.g. on the occasion of the grounds of divorce), favouring instead the use of 'clearer language'. His intention was to leave 'less interpretative discretion' to the judges; *ibidem*, 50.

134 *Ibidem*, 29. Baziński invoked the – 'universally known' – 'theory of subjective interpretation of statutes', identifying as his source of inspiration the book published in 1947 by Adam Szpunar under the title of *Nadużycie prawa podmiotowego* (*Abuse of individual right*), where the author focused on the problem of interpretation of the law in academic literature and court decisions. After Szpunar (86–87), Baziński held that in line with the subjective ('traditional') theory of interpretation, the judge, in interpreting general clauses 'should rely on outlooks prevailing at the time of ruling. Then he acts within the limits of the delegation granted (...) by the lawmaker'; *ibidem*, 32.

> acquire a different light or character and in that new task of its the statute can be interpreted and applied.[135]

According to Baziński, the same conclusions had to be considered in the paradigm of modernization.

Baziński's assertions in this area confirm the thesis that both the lawyers of the interwar period (especially in its initial years) and to the lawyers involved in the codification work in the immediate aftermath of World War II, the starting point was the same. The latter had not yet actively involved themselves in the work of promoting socialist ideas by opposing them to, or distansing themselves from, the social-democratic achievements of capitalist states, including the Second Polish Republic. Thus, it appears that there was a *iunctim* in the outlook on the law and its social role in the modern world (i.e. evaluated in the modernization paradigm setting the expected trend in development of the law for the future). Let us allow Baziński to continue:

> Modern views on the task of the law are taking shape in the direction that the interests of the individual must be subordinated to the collective interest. The individualist and liberal tendencies of the legislation of the 19th century are giving place to new outlooks on the law in more recent legislation.

A large body of left-leaning lawyers of the interwar period would certainly have signed their names under Baziński's enunciations of 1948. They would probably also have cited the same examples as the justice of the Supreme Court of 'People's Poland', who identified Article 2 of the Swiss Code – 'abuse of a right shall not have legal protection' – as the example of a modern general clause.[136]

The technical-legal perspective was also noted by Jan Wasilkowski in his review of Marian Lisiewski's draft Marriage Property Law. Referring to the proposed method of abolition of the statutory community property, he evaluated the draft as being very good, on the one hand it was 'consistent and simple' (the formal aspect), and on the other hand (the substantive aspect) it did not unnecessarily modify the property affairs between the parties, whereas the 'settlement with the effect of obligation [as provided by the draft] usually d[id] not present practical difficulties.'[137] In other words, in

135 *Ibidem*, 32.

136 *Ibidem*.

137 *Ibidem*, 71.

the technical legal perspective, the measure of good law to Wasilkowski were such regulations as caused no problems in the application, whether on formal (structure of the legal norm) or on the substantive front (ease of achievement of the purpose served and lack of difficulties with implementation).

Wasilkowski also took it upon himself to assess a body of regulation from a 'legislative point of view' in a discussion of a different draft – Personal Marriage Law. He noted the use of 'not too fortunate' expressions 'from a civilist point of view' (such as the expression: '[triggering of] legal effects in the face of the State,' which 'is perhaps appropriate in the constitution but not in the civil code') and the lack of 'substantive merit'. The issue was the use of laconic language and sparing use of form, limitation of the normative utterance to the bare minimum, avoidance of repetition, etc., and thus (as one can surmise) avoidance of saturation of a legal text with the ideological layer. That line of argument – on the formal side, at least – resonated with Minister Świątkowski, who viewed it as logical. Nonetheless, he assigned a higher priority to the duty to invoke the values and goals held that had to be 'clearly set', such as in the case of the need to emphasize the secular form of the celebration of marriage other matters 'of great significance to the state'.[138]

6 The Modernization Ideology

The utterances of Szpunar and Baziński can be viewed in the categories of protecting the legal order from instrumental interference by the authorities. In that context, they focused on the technical legal aspects of the future codification. Notwithstanding that, however, the matter of the extent to which the code was to give effect to the principles of the new social system kept resurfacing in the discussions of details, although not with such frequency as one might have expected. From that perspective, a critique of the provisions on minors was undertaken by the then-departmental direction in the Ministry of Justice, Jerzy Jodłowski. In his assault on the draft, he offered a rationale touching both on ideological issues (anachronism of the world view; incompatibility with the socialist ideology as the constitutional foundation of the state) and axiological grounds (effective protection of minors as the supreme value). He observed that the draft's proposal of a system for the protection of minors and people with limited capacity could be 'incompatible with the principles of the state's political system' and at the same time 'out of touch with

138 Minutes of the session of the Codification Commission's Substantive Civil Law Team on 17 February 1948, AAN, MS, 2380, 8, 12.

the outlooks of a modern life'.[139] Accordingly, it was anachronistic due to the world view transformations generally in the postwar world but specifically and especially in a socialist system. For it came down to the prohibition against making transactions with minors and people with limited capacity, and thus 'the law demand[ed] only a passive attitude from every third [party] while entrusting the care of the minor to those so authorized.' Modern social outlooks, however, were different: 'they require[d] from the citizen an active attitude with regard to their fellow citizens.' Consequently, refusal to enter into a legal transaction with a minor 'if the minor's interest require[s] it,' was now 'regarded as an unethical and uncivic act'. The outcome of that reasoning was: 'The law should not deter the entering into transactions with minors by making the effects dependent on the arbitrary decision of the statutory representative,' i.e. legal guardian. Modern ideology of social activity should have the effect of introducing to the new law a 'moral element, more in touch with modern views'. With regard to minors, the outcome would be the introduction of a principle – which he strived to achieve – that anyone who had entered into a transaction with a minor should be able to seek to have its validity upheld upon proving that it was advantageous to the minor. At the same time, he realized that the establishment of such a rule would be tantamount with the adoption of a principle already present in the Code of Napoleon, except that the burden of proof would be shifted onto the minor's counterparty.[140]

Proposing his own system for the protection of minors, he described its assumptions as follows:

> Protection is needed primarily by those minors who lack statutory representatives or whose parents or guardians take no care of them. Therefore, the protection must be organized in such a way that every minor or even third [party] should be able to request assistance from the guardianship authority and for that authority to have a duty to apply suitable measures for the minor's protection.

139 Additionally, according to the critic, raising the age limit to 13 years found no reasonable basis. Not only did it fail to protect minors, it did the opposite – deprived them of legal protection. It would also result in detachment of the law from life. 'Here, children work, earn incomes and enter into a number of transactions – they purchase, sell, drive (…) The whole system of dividing minors into two categories appears to be warranted only if one wants to bar small children'; Jerzy Jodłowski: *Uwagi do projektu k.c.* [Remarks to the draft of Code Civil}, AAN, MS, 2390, 18.

140 *Ibidem*, 19.

The caring state should actively engage in the protection of minors. And that needs suitable legal mechanisms included both in the provisions of the civil code and in other regulations. In particular 'the role of the court as a guardianship authority ought not to be a formality but an official element that with the assistance of the social element is supposed to protect not only the minor's property but also the minor's person.'[141] The spirit of the time and the changed perspective on socio-economic affairs also required the inclusion in the civil code (e.g. Article 83) of a number of contracts made by minors in relation to employment and the collective organization of labour. By way of example, he mentioned accession to a trade union, labour co-operative or group insurance.[142] Similar emphasis on civilizational progress, taking place rather in general, without excessively highlighting the reference to the socialist word, the progress that required changes to the code, called for the deletion of Article 86(2) with its introduction of the *peculium* as a form of property. The latter was deemed 'out of touch with the conditions of modern economic life'. He only conditionally or reluctantly accepted 'emancipation' as a possibility.[143]

Considerations of modernization were reflected also in Jodłowski's other remark, suggesting the abandonment of a single place of residence as something 'outdated in the light of the development of means of communication'.[144] Similarly 'the development of means of communication and search (the press, radio),' warranted the shortening of the duration of the required search for missing people before recognizing them as legally deceased to 5 years (Article 21(1)).[145] He also regarded Articles 22 to 25 as 'unsuitable for the civil code' due to being 'casuistically adapted to the conditions of the last war and present communication conditions'. They failed to account for 'technical development and changes to means of warfare', which 'in a short time', could make them 'prove to be out of touch with life'.

Even clearer was the critical voice of Adam Szpunar with regard to contracts of adhesion. He also took it upon himself to carry out a critical review of the provisions on statements of will (especially in respect of the formation of contracts) contained in the 1948 draft of the General Part. He denounced them as dated, due to being 'based on principles adopted in the civil codes of

141 *Ibidem*, 20.

142 *Ibidem*, 19.

143 Ibidem, 19–20.

144 *Ibidem*, 17. Justice Aleksander Baziński also offered his own criticism of the provision, citing examples – characteristic of the realities of the time – situations of life in which the requirement of having only a single place of residence would not be compatible with the facts; Baziński: *Uwagi do części ogólnej*, AAN, MS, 2390, 31.

145 Jodłowski: *Uwagi do projektu k.c.*, AAN, MS, 2390, 17.

the Modern Age [and] derived from as far back as Roman law', which 'still proceed from the assumption that parties entering into contracts conduct [ed] negotiations.' By contrast 'in economic life, we are increasingly dealing with cases in which there is no question of such formation of a contract.' The progress of civilization has led to the efflorescence of contracts of adhesion, and thus models based on old solutions should be modified and adapted to the changed reality. As a result 'because contracts of adhesion have [gained] significance in all areas of private life (cf. e.g. insurance contracts), the question arises whether the Polish lawmaker ought not to dedicate at least one provision in the general part to such an important matter.'[146] Szpunar, however – which is telling, for it demonstrates either a lack of contacts and acquaintances or deliberate ignoring of the first products of the work done in postwar era – did not cite any examples of codification solutions from other countries having faced similar problems in the immediately preceding years. Instead, he noted that, in Polish circumstances, the problem was so new that he was only just introducing the term 'contract of adhesion', 'for the lack of another', transforming the French scholarly term *contrats d'adhésion* and drawing simultaneously on the legacy of German scholarship and the construct of 'mandatory contracting' for one of the parties – *Kontrahierungszwang*.[147]

7 The Social Function of Civil Law Versus the Scope of Interference of the Public Authority

In evaluating various legislative solutions, the lawyers and jurists participating in the discussion of the expected codification distinguished the broadly understood matter of the public interest. That was the term employed by Justice Aleksander Baziński when analysing the problem of stability of marriages.

> When it comes to divorce [he explained his point of view] the lawmaker always ends up facing the problem of how to safeguard the permanence of marriage, so that it could not be repudiated by one of the spouses and at the same time how to eliminate the fiction of the legal existence of those marriages out of which nothing but the legal bond has remained and which are only an obstacle to the foundation of new families. Find-

146 Szpunar: *Uwagi do projektu części ogólnej*, 54.
147 *Ibidem.*

> ing a formula to reconcile both these social interests, if at all possible, certainly is not easy to accomplish.[148]

Therefore, the social interest could be exposed to harm both by the possibility of 'arbitrary' repudiation of the marital bond and by the upholding of a marriage at all costs to the detriment of the possibility of starting a new family.

Jan Wasilkowski, too, distinguished the so-called social aspect in the assessment of a given regulation, referring it to the idea of social justice and equality. From that perspective, he took a positive view of Lisiewski's proposal to equalize the opportunity of the spouse who was given only a claim against the other spouse for a share in the property whereas the other received a 'share in things in kind'. In that situation, the option to establish a security interest would serve to strengthen the position of the spouse receiving only an obligation claim.[149] Furthermore, Wasilkowski noted that especially 'marriages from workers' circles would be sufficiently protected by 'the introduction (…) of community property of household items, as those would usually constitute the largest portion of the property.'[150]

Similarly to the previous unification period, one of the key problems in the codification works was the issue of the admissibility of the state's interference in social affairs. During the discussions on personal marriage law, the opportunity to exchange points of view arose from the draft's proposal of subjecting the matters touching on the mutual relationship of the spouses to judicial supervision. This was opposed by Aleksander Wolter, who regarded the intervention of the courts in such cases as 'unnecessary and dangerous'. He went on to argue: 'Unnecessary because the relations in marriage are personal in nature and should not leave openings to external intervention; dangerous because the court's intervention would be without any sanction.'[151] Lisiewski, however, defended the draft. In his opinion: 'The signifi-

148 Baziński: *Uwagi do części ogólnej*, 33.

149 Minutes of the session of the Codification Commission's Substantive Civil Law Team on 22 April 1948, AAN, MS, 2380, 71.

150 *Ibidem*, 72. Wasilkowski cited Article 3, which – 'in the [then] current state of urban socio-economic affairs' – was to be of basic importance to the regulation of the spouses' mutual affairs, as household property would be the largest of their assets; *ibidem*, 71–72. The 'lack of a social basis' with regard to the regulation of the effects of cessation of community property through divorce or annulment was discussed by Aleksander Wolter; Minutes of the session of the Codification Commission's Substantive Civil Law Team on 24 April 1948, AAN, MS, 2380, 91.

151 Minutes of the session of the Codification Commission's Substantive Civil Law Team on 17 February 1948, AAN, MS, 2380, 21.

cance of the court's intervention, however, is that the court enjoys a certain authority and in many litigious cases a basis would be created for conciliatory mediation. Otherwise the parties would immediately be led to divorce.' In keeping with that phraseology, not the communist state's justified right of interference in the private sphere but rather the more broadly understood authority of the judicial institution justified the possibility of intervention in defence of a higher value – marriage as foundation of the family, the latter recognized as the basic social organization. According to the programmatic intention, the nature of the intervention was to be limited. The state, acting through the court, would be entering the role of a mediator and would not be assuming the initiative.

What was the importance placed by the members of the Civil Law Codification Commission in 1948 on the institution of marriage? During that period, the exceptional circumstances of the first year after the war were beginning to lose their importance. Jan Wasilkowski spoke on the matter, arguing that in Polish law the family ought to based on the marital bond, while recognizing that such an assumption precluded supporting extramarital relationships. An exception should be made only in favour of improving the fates of extramarital children, which, though 'weakening the importance of a family based on the matrimonial bond', was justified by other considerations.[152]

The inclination to ideologize in a legal text was ill-received by Wasilkowski. To him, the *clou* of the problem was the fear that the spouses might seek the court's intervention in all matters, no matter how trivial. Thus, practical considerations (the utilitarian aspect) had to be taken into account first and foremost.[153] Moreover, in Wasilkowski's opinion, in Polish circumstances, the regulation proposed in the draft could not possibly be implemented. He noted that the court, especially the lowest municipal tier (*sąd grodzki*), staffed by 'young judges [not only inexperienced but also unqualified] [wa] s perhaps not qualified to mediate marital cases.'[154] The two arguments, al-

152 Minutes of the session of the Codification Commission's Substantive Civil Law Team on 25 February 1948, AAN, MS, 2380, 49.

153 Wasilkowski's own example of a utilitarian approach to the law was the regulation contained in Marian Lisiewski's draft marriage property law, establishing a property regime in which property affairs would not have to undergo any changes throughout the duration of the marriage, and which he, Wasilkowski, reviewed; Minutes of the session of the Codification Commission's Substantive Civil Law Team on 22 April 1948, AAN, MS, 2380, 71.

154 Minutes of the session of the Codification Commission's Substantive Civil Law Team on 17 February 1948, AAN, MS, 2380, 21.

beit different, had a common denominator. Wasilkowski observed that the expectation that the court (state) – following the annihilation of the elites – would be capable of successful performance of its tasks was a delusion, additionally unnecessarily exposing its image to harm. Due to known problems with the qualification of officials, that aspect had to be considered and perhaps even as a priority.

The importance of the authority commanded by state was also invoked, although in a different context, by Minister Świątkowski. He emphasized that the Civil Law Codification Commission should first of all examine the 'matter of the solemnity of the form of celebration of marriage'. Although it was supposed to be a secular ceremony, the symbolic underscoring of the gravity of marriage was of no less importance to the communists than to the Catholic Church. Świątkowski argued: 'The matter is not trivial; it is of great importance to the state and should be disposed by statute.'[155] Among other things, that involved the solemn reading by the civil registrar of the legal provisions governing the mutual obligations of the spouses and their obligations to their children.

Świątkowski's postulates were linked to the fact that one of the priorities of communist rule was to sever the institution of marriage from the ideological influence of the Catholic Church. The Minister was taking care of that personally. In a session of the Commission on 17 February 1948, he emphasized: 'The matter of the secular form of marriage must be set clearly,' recognizing the insufficiency of the laconic disposal in the draft personal marriage law.[156] The people's state had to be given the monopoly on the matter, and, accordingly, the rights of the Catholic Church (and other religious denominations) to the institution of marriage had to be negated. Even Wasilkowski's suggestion of decreeing that 'marriage contracted according to religious provisions shall not have legal effects,' incurred a negative response. That was because, according to Director Szer, the lawmaker would be imputing the recognition of the 'religious rite as marriage', whereas the already applicable marriage law stood on the position that only a bond contracted pursuant to the provisions of civil law could be marriage.[157]

155 *Ibidem*, 9.

156 *Ibidem*, 8.

157 *Ibidem*, 12. Eventually, the participants of the deliberation decided to accept Wasilkowski's proposal: 'a union other than contracted before a civil registrar shall not be marriage in the face of statute.' *Ibidem*. That stance, however, lacked consistency, because Minister Świątkowski demanded that the draft include regulation prohibiting religious marriages from being contracted before entering into a civil marriage before a civil registrar (Minutes of the session of the Codification Commission's Substantive Civil Law Team on

8 Ethics and Morality

Members of the Civil Law Codification Commission invoked ethical and moral rules as a certain universal canon of values. That was done especially by Marian Lisiewski in the case of the draft personal marriage law, when – among his other suggestions – he proposed deleting as 'immoral' the regulation (Article 32) allowing the guilty party to seek divorce. He argued: 'civil law protects the ordinary property contract by not allowing it to be repudiated by the non-performing party; by contrast, in the marriage contract, the contrary principle would be introduced. That is inequitable.'[158] Wasilkowski, too, was of the opinion that 'one cannot, by statute, uphold open immorality, let alone in a flagrant case,' and – in his view – such would be the obtaining of divorce by the spouse bearing the sole culpability in the separation.[159] Moreover, he believed the existing formula to be 'not good, and dangerous to the principle of permanence of marriage'.[160]

On the other hand, Wasilkowski's approach was sometimes marked with certain legal purism. From that perspective, he launched the criticism of Lisiewski's draft of personal marriage law preceded by a set of general principles expressing the lawmaker's ideals. According to Wasilkowski such a device was out of place because if something '[wa]s an ethical norm,' it was 'thereby a superfluous norm'. To that, the drafter responded that there were no 'obstacles to the inclusion in the civil code of ethical norms having the character

---

24 February 1948, AAN, MS, 2380, 37), i.e. a provision from which, *a contrario*, it could be inferred that contracting religious marriages was allowed by law on condition of taking place after marrying before a civil registrar.

158 Minutes of the session of the Codification Commission's Substantive Civil Law Team on 24 February 1948, AAN, MS, 2380, AAN, MS, 2380, 42. The search for solutions 'more beneficial to the child' during the deliberations on the draft Law on Families and Children had a similar nature. Citing that consideration, Lisiewski asked to restore the text of the existing law, opposing the draft's redaction (Article 145), which purported to amend the existing regulation by leaving out the qualified mention of 'evident improbability' that the mother's husband could possibly be the father of the child in favour of the simple phrase 'the claimant cannot be the father of the child.' Minutes of the session of the Codification Commission's Substantive Civil Law Team on 7 June 1948, AAN, MS, 2380, 174.

159 Minutes of the session of the Codification Commission's Substantive Civil Law Team on 22 April 1948, AAN, MS, 2380, 71.

160 Minutes of the session of the Codification Commission's Substantive Civil Law Team on 24 February 1948, AAN, MS, 2380, 42.

of postulates if they touched on such matters as Article 16 of the Code,' i.e. definition of obligations in marriage and family.[161]

9 Use of Soviet Inspirations

What were the sources of inspiration of the authors of the first postwar codification draft? First of all, one must note that, at the time, Soviet inspirations were still somewhat rare. One such exception from the rule was the 1926 Code of Laws on Marriage, Family and Guardianship providing inspiration to the drafters in 1945 with regard to enabling the recognition of concubinage as marriage on condition of registration before the competent authority.[162] It probably also served as an important point of reference for the broad legalization of divorce planned by the authors of the draft, where the ultimate amendment of the Soviet code of 1926 in 1944 may have contributed to the modification of the draft. A certain degree of pressure exerted on the Ministry and on the Commission itself by the Legal Bureau of the State National Council to adhere to Soviet solutions was probably not without its own significance.[163]

By contrast, in 1947–1948, i.e. before the Stalinist breakthrough, the codifiers of Polish civil law assumed that Polish law, being model in a system of people's democracy, without yet having the quality of socialist law, could still diverge significantly from Soviet model. Attesting to that was the view expressed by Wasilkowski and Wolter, whereby even the concept of private law could be retained, even though it had been rejected by Soviet scholarship.[164] For they

161 *Ibidem*, 25–26.

162 GRZYBOWSKI, RÓŻAŃSKI: *Prawo małżeńskie*, 21–23.

163 This is attested by the correspondence kept by the Ministry of Justice with the Legal Bureau of the CNC, which sought to convince the decision-makers that divorce should not be allowed on a wider scale (as had been expected by the Ministry itself in the first draft, perhaps under external pressure) and without the existence of a justified ground (in particular, not on the sole basis of the spouses' mutual agreement). The amendment of the Soviet code of 1926, which was enacted in 1944 and which consisted in limiting the availability of divorce, affected the fate of the Ministry's concept. FIEDORCZYK: *Z prac unifikacyjnych*, 78.

164 Wasilkowski and Wolter relied on the works of Andrey Vyshinsky and civilists led by Mikhail Agarkov, as well as the explanatory memorandum to the Soviet draft civil code of 1947, rejecting as incompatible with the principle of the socialist political order the so-called theory of 'bisectoral law' whereby civil law regulated the legal affairs of the private sector, while relationships between socialist organizations were regulated by administrative law.

noted that in the Soviet socialist political system the concept of private law as an area of law contraposed to public law did not exist because Soviet law was a 'socialist law in all stages of its development and all its areas'. The transplantation of that concept from Soviet law to the legislation of People's Poland did not strike Wasilkowski and Wolter as possible, because, as they argued 'Polish legislation d[id] not sanction the principal premise of the socialist political order that is the abolition of individual ownership of land and other means of production.'[165] In evidence, they cited a number of recent legal instruments in which the distinction between public and private law was expressly affirmed.[166]

That Polish law ought not yet fully to have the character of socialist law could provide an excuse not to borrow a number of institutions and principles from Soviet law, but a certain degree of latitude in this matter did not equal licence to avoid Soviet inspirations altogether or especially to avoid paying attention to the transformations unfolding in the legal systems of other people's democracies. Especially attention-drawing is the pressure exerted by Henryk Świątkowski during the works on personal marriage law to follow in their footsteps in the ideological promotion of the secular form of marriage. The minister observed that in some countries the matter had even been resolved constitutionally, citing examples from the constitutions of Yugoslavia, Bulgaria and Albania. That was one of the first signs in the course of the Polish codification works on civil law that the process of uniformization and Sovietization of the law in the satellite states had begun.[167]

---

165 Wasilkowski, Wolter: *Projekt kodeksu cywilnego*, 11.

166 That did not at all imply the necessity of rejection of Ulpian's concept of contraposing the norms of private to those of public law according to the criteria of the different purposes of such norms. According to Wasilkowski and Wolter, one had to determine such a *criterium divisionis* as could be 'duly harmonized' with the principles of the new system, for in a people's democracy the 'principle of unity of the essence and purposes of the law' had to obtain and 'there c[ould] not be any opposition between the principal goals of legal norms.' *Ibidem.*

167 Minutes of the session of the Codification Commission's Substantive Civil Law Team on 17 February 1948 AAN, MS, 2380, 8. Świątkowski's speech constituted a response to the draft's non-ideological encapsulation of the form of celebration of marriage, which – in Jan Wasilkowski's opinion – was 'sufficient from the legislative point of view'. The minister, however, disagreed and decided to insist on a modification by suitable redaction of Article 8(1) 'or even return to the wording of Article 12 of the existing marriage law'. *Ibidem.*

10 Use of Capitalist Inspirations

What may be surprising, the main point of reference for the drafts was the capitalist legislation of Western Europe. In 1947, following the establishment of the first Civil Law Codification Commission, Jan Wasilkowski tabled the motion, accepted by the other members, for the Commission to be provided with aids in the form of the texts of the Swiss law of obligations in the 1936 edition, Danish Property Law of 1926, materials relating to the amendment of the Code of Napoleon, and, last but not least, the Czechoslovak draft Civil Code of 1937. During later discussions, references to Western European inspirations were made by Justice Wolter, who insisted on the propriety of the regulation excluding the possibility of claiming a right to marriage on the basis of betrothal. He noted the possibility of that happening, citing the legislation of certain cantons in Switzerland that knew the 'action for marriage arising from betrothal.'[168] Wasilkowski similarly cited Swiss and Polish law as modern civil codes that did not 'entirely' exclude procedural elements from substantive law (as in the cases of provisions governing time bars or the *actio Pauliana*). That method, according to Wasilkowski, could be a model to follow, but Lisiewski disagreed, characterizing it as something to be avoided.[169]

Just as taking inspiration from the substance of the codes of capitalist states was, for ideological reasons, difficult but not impossible, Wasilkowski – drawing his inspiration mainly from French solutions – saw no obstacle to borrowing not only technical[170] but even doctrinal solutions.[171] Also to Minister

168 Minutes of the session of the Codification Commission's Substantive Civil Law Team on 20 February 1948, AAN, MS, 2380, 20.

169 Minutes of the session of the Codification Commission's Substantive Civil Law Team on 22 May 1948, AAN, MS, 2380, 112.

170 Among his other beliefs was the following: 'In the footsteps of French law one should move all provisions relating to spouses to marriage law, combining with them also those property provisions that are independent from the property regime existing between the spouses.' In his assessment: 'In general, the concept of marriage property law as a part separate from personal marriage law, is a German one and not very fortunate'; by contrast, the French concept proceeded from a better principle, only separating the provisions on property regimes from the other regulatory matter of marriage law. 26 In turn, speaking against the differing qualifications of the various forms of nullity of marriage, he argued: 'excessively complicated constructs lead to ambiguity.' In his opinion 'abundant French experience,' supplied the proof of that; Minutes of the session of the Codification Commission's Substantive Civil Law Team on 20 February 1948, AAN, MS, 2380, 27.

171 Among Wasilkowski's other demands was to follow the assumption of 'French theory, which st[ood] on the position that the debtor is always capable of worsening their position by incurring new obligations, as a result of which provisions governing the special protection of creditors, outside of the *actio Pauliana*, are not warranted'; Minutes

Świątkowski, the popularity of a given solution in European legislation even without distinction among capitalist versus socialist states was an argument in favour of implementing such a solution in the Polish code. That was the case with the prohibition of entering into religious marriage prior to marrying before a civil registrar, which, according to Świątkowski, existed in all European legal orders save for Italy, Czechoslovakia and Spain.[172]

The preparation of a new General Part of the Code was deemed to be key to the eventual success of the codification works.[173] The authors of that draft, Jan Wasilkowski and Aleksander Wolter, distanced themselves from any German inspirations, which could be the impression drawn from the existence of a separate general part in the BGB. The authors of the Polish draft, however, specified that the decision to include such a part in the civil code was based solely on specifically Polish approaches to civil law.[174] They had to fend off accusations of having followed the method of creating 'multi-level abstractions', cherished by the authors of the BGB and criticized after war.[175] Their explanation was as follows: 'this [does] correspond to the tendency to create abstract concepts,' but since it 'characterizes Polish legislative technique', it

of the session of the Codification Commission's Substantive Civil Law Team on 22 February 1948, AAN, MS, 2380, 77.

172 Minutes of the session of the Codification Commission's Substantive Civil Law Team on 24 February 1948, AAN, MS, 2380, 37.

173 In a letter of 23 July 1948, the Legislative Department request 'further critical remarks' on the draft provisions of the General Part from a group of several dozen representatives of the legal elite, including professors and other lecturers of Jagiellonian University (Tadeusz Dziurzyński, Jan Gwiazdomorski, Kazimierz Przybyłowski, Stefan Grzybowski, Marian Waligórski and Adam Szpunar), Commercial Academy in Poznań (Józef Górski), Universities of Poznań (Alfred Ohanowicz), Łódź (Ludwik Domański), Wrocław (Kamil Stefko, Adam Chełmoński and Józef Fiema) and Warsaw (Włodzimierz Kozubski), as well as Jerzy Jodłowski and various judges (including Justices Jan Namitkiewicz and Jan Jakub Litauer); the Legislative Department's cover letter attending the distribution of the draft Book II of the Civil Code of 23 July 1948, AAN, MS, 2390, 4.

174 As noted by the drafters themselves – Jan Wasilkowski and Aleksander Wolter – 'from the perspective of the systematics of the existing legislation' that was to be a 'completely new' division of the code. It was expected to include 'provisions removed from their existing configurations,' except for several articles of a decree of 12 November 1946, titled General Provisions of Civil Law. By contrast, the majority of the provisions intended for inclusion in the General Part, especially provisions governing statements of will and time bars, had previously been contained in the law of obligations, of prewar redaction, and 'preocuppied themselves mainly with the problems of that area of the law.' Hence, the indispensable requirement of 'generalization' of their contents required 'significant change in their presentation'. WASILKOWSKI, WOLTER: *Projekt kodeksu cywilnego*, 10.

175 In European scholarship, it was mostly characteristic of adherents and sympathizers of Roman legal thought and exemplified by the BGB.

ought to be embraced, all the more considering that it could be seen as corresponding to the newest challenges and most modern trends. As Wasilkowski and Wolter went on to explain: 'The tendency to [to]wards general and necessarily abstract formulations is becoming more and more visible also in many other legal systems and is probably explained, among others, by the fact that statutory regulation is extending to an ever wider scope of social affairs.' Above all, attention was drawn to the fact that among the most recent civil codes both the codes of the various Soviet republics and the Soviet draft of a civil code of 1947 also contained general parts.[176] Naming their source of inspiration, the drafters proved their familiarity especially with French scholarship (notably works from early 20th century, such as those by François Gény or Henri Capitant). Out of specific proposals, it is worth noting that Wasilkowski and Wolter decided to reject the analysed German solution and instead opted for the principle of a single place of residence. They specified that for the sake of certainty of the circulation they had chosen the principle adopted in the Swiss Civil Code and the French-Polish rule. The use of the latter expression commands some attention. This is because it betrays an inclination to offer privileged treatment to French law and scholarship because of the long years of application of the Code of Napoleon in the central lands of Poland, with the accompanying surge in Polish interest in French scholarship.[177]

From among foreign inspirations, the authors of the 1948 draft of the General Part were particularly eager to look to the provisions of the Swiss Civil Code, such as in the case of provisions governing the place of residence or those protecting the personal interest.[178] To a lesser extent they were ready to borrow from the German Code.[179] Explanations are frequently offered for why they rejected a solution functioning in the German Civil Code.[180] Similarly, to some of the draft's reviewers, such as Adam Szpunar, neither the identification of the Swiss Civil Code as the source of inspiration, nor the promotion of the retention of the existing Polish regulation presented any problem whatsoever. Szpunar, amid extensive references to various different solutions from abroad, especially relied on the authority of those he termed 'modern'. In that group he reckoned the Swiss Code but, on the other hand, also the Soviet Civil Code. The latter provided him mainly with a source of certain technical solutions, while he cited the Swiss Code incomparably

176 *Ibidem*, 10.

177 *Ibidem*, 12, 14.

178 Szpunar: *Uwagi do projektu części ogólnej*, AAN, MS, 2390, 47–48.

179 *Ibidem*, 46, 49, 51.

180 Wasilkowski, Wolter: *Projekt kodeksu cywilnego*, 16, 18.

much more often as a model to follow. For example, according to Szpunar, the Soviet Code – similarly to the Swiss Code – distinguished itself *in plus* by providing strict criteria for the influence of the lack of capacity or limited capacity to act at law on the matter of liability for torts.[181] For substantive matters, such as the proper setting of the age of majority, the necessity of having an assigned place of residence (domicile), as well as protection of personal interest, it was the Swiss Code and not the Soviet one from which Szpunar usually drew his inspiration.[182] He viewed its solutions as progressive when compared to the laws applicable in Polish territories – not only the partitional legislation but even the Code of Obligations. Similarly, though to a lesser extent, he drew inspiration from other Western European codes. He also knew, as he himself claimed, the Austrian and the French Civil Codes,[183] which, however, he did not regard as being 'modern'. As a result, he drew more often from the German Code, despite his criticism of it, and the Franco-Italian draft Code of Obligations of 1927,[184] as well as the views of Western scholarship (French, Austrian and Swiss with regard to the canon for defining the capacity to act at law,[185] as well as German and again French with regard to contracts of adhesion formed in mandatory circumstances for one of the parties, which was a novelty in Polish law).[186] Against this background, Szpunar distinguished himself by his aforementioned critical view of the German Civil Code, whether the general assumptions on which the BGB was founded or the individual solutions used in it. Quintessential to Szpunar's attitude to the Swiss and German Codes was his criticism of the lack of provisions on exploitation in the draft General Part of 1948. To Szpunar, that was a step backwards in the development of Polish law, as it was tantamount with the rejection of the Swiss construct (Article 21), which had served as the model for the solution introduced in the Code of Obligations (Article 41), in favour of the German solution viewing usury as an immoral activity, and thus invalid, whereas the indisputable – according to Szpunar – academic authority on German and Swiss law, Andreas von Tuhr, conceded the superiority of the ZGB above the BGB in that respect.[187] In other words, the substantive choice of the Swiss solution by the Polish codifier ought to be product of

181 SZPUNAR: *Uwagi do projektu części ogólnej*, AAN, MS, 2390, 46.

182 *Ibidem*, 47–48.

183 *Ibidem*, 59.

184 *Ibidem*, 58.

185 *Ibidem*, 48.

186 *Ibidem*, 54.

187 *Ibidem*, 57.

FIGURE 3.2
Adam Szpunar, 1913–2002. Member of the Civil Law Codification Commission of 1956 and Civil Law Reform Commission of 1986; long-term Head of Department of Civil Law and Rector of the University of Łódź.

the voice of German-Swiss comparative scholarship. Thus, also the drafters of the General Part in postwar Poland should follow in the same footsteps as in the interwar period (as exemplified by the solution adopted in the Code of Obligations), taking their inspiration from the best Western European models, the selection of which should be motivated by the opinions of scholars from those countries. That should be all the more the case after successful transplantation onto Polish soil with support gained from the work of native scholarship. The new social system or the codification works in the Soviet state or satellite states at the stage the works had been in 1948 were not paid heed by Szpunar at all.

11 Stalinization of the Law after 1949

The works of 1947–1949 on the draft civil code were interrupted. Under Soviet influence, political shifts took place under the banner of combating 'rightist-nationalist deviations,' as was made evident especially in the plenary session of the Central Committee of Polish Workers' Party in the August and September of 1948. That situation made a significant impact on the entire direction of the communist state's legislative activities. The authorities demanded a radical break from the native legislative heritage. On Moscow's initiative, forceful Sovietization of the countries of the Eastern Bloc was decreed.[188] Despite the

188 Adam LITYŃSKI: *O prawie i sądach początków Polski Ludowej* [On the law and courts of the beginnings of the People's Poland], Temida 2, Białystok, 1999, 226; Adam LITYŃSKI:

advanced stage of progress, the finished parts of the draft civil code were to go into the bin. Jan Wasilkowski, the central personality among the drafters of the civil code, published self-criticism,[189] explaining on the pages of the press that,

> in the face of the rapid social reconstruction towards socialism, it turned out (...) that the goal of the codification works had been improperly set and as a result of that a code based on the 1947 plan would be an anachronism already at the time of promulgation. It became self-evident that Polish civil law, if it were to be an agent of true progress, facilitating and accelerating the building of a socialist system, first of all required a substantial revision of its ideological foundations.[190]

Suspension of the Civil Law Codification Comnission's operations was not tantamount with a halt to all of its works. In the Civil Law Section of the Legislative Department of the Ministry of Justice, mainly under Seweryn Szer's direction, works continued on a joint Polish-Czechoslovak project in the codification of family law.[191] 'That required the creation of numerous further provisions such as were necessary in order to harmonize the draft with

Nowe ustawodawstwo w nowym ustroju: o prawie karnym i cywilnym w pierwszym dwudziestoleciu Polski Ludowej [New legislation in a new political system. On criminal and civil law in the first twenty years of the People's Poland], MHI 4 (2006), 135; MACHNIKOWSKA: *Wymiar sprawiedliwości*, 396–398; FIEDORCZYK: *Unifikacja i kodyfikacja*, 145–147.

189 The public admission of such a fundamental error in the codification work to date had no negative consequences for Wasilkowski's academic career whatsoever. After two years as dean of the Faculty of Law and Administration, he was elected rector of the University of Warsaw in 1949. With regard to the codification works, this tends to suggest rather a masquerade of distancing himself from the results achieved thus far under his own predominant influence. Things took a similar turn for Seweryn Szer, who not only suffered no consequences for his involvement in the codification works following 1948 but his position and responsibilities increased in the next stage of the works continued to climb. The redefinition of the foundations of the future codification with regard to property law (in the light of the acceleration of pro-socialist reorganization processes in the economy) was a decision imposed from the outside, of such gravity that it was decided a public explanation was called for, which took the form of admission of responsibility and public representative of the project; in this case, Wasilkowski. Nevertheless, the political authority was not inclined to take advantage of the moment to sideline the most important, experienced and successful codifiers in the figures such as Wasilkowski and Szer, as well as their ministerial patron, Świątkowski.

190 WASILKOWSKI: *Kodyfikacja prawa cywilnego*, 4.

191 FIEDORCZYK: *Unifikacja i kodyfikacja*, 145–251.

other areas of civil law.' In parallel, works were initiated on the drafting of new general provisions of civil law in order to create a common superstructure, adapted to the current political, economic and social situation, for all areas of private law.[192] Last but not least, the Civil Section had works pending on civil-registration law and a reform of civil procedure.[193] The drafts compiled in the Civil Law Section were forwarded to a special Legal Commission detached from the Ministry of Justice and attached directly to the Praesidium of the Council of Ministers.

Full-scale resumption of codification works, however, required a new opening. That was taken care of by the resolution of the Praesidium of the Cabinet of 27 September 1950, assigning priority to the drafting works on the civil and criminal codes. The Ministry of Justice was ordered to complete the drafts at an expeditious rate by 1 September 1951.[194] In reality, the impulse for the resolution came from the Ministry of Justice itself, in the form of a letter mentioning 'the matter of the codification of civil law as an urgent matter and one significant from the perspective of the adaptation of that legislative area along with the practice of the justice system based on it to the needs and tasks of our political system.' In line with the expectations of the main political decision-makers, the ideological substrate of the reform was emphasized. The Ministry highlighted that 'the reform w[ould] also have significant importance for the development of Marxist legal science,' and the codification of civil law would become 'doubtless a breakthrough in the development of the Polish science of that area of the law, shifting it firmly onto Marxist tracks'. Such type of phraseology tended to be a rarity during the preceding period.

The scope of the codification works did not include the already enacted Act of 27 June 1950 – Family Code (the separate regulation of family law was decided by political reasons 52) and General Provisions of Civil Law, adopted three weeks later, on 18 July. Attention was focused on the remaining areas under the umbrella term of 'economic civil law', given that personal relationships had already been regulated through the aforementioned two instruments.

First and foremost, the enactment of the general provisions meant that there was no complete break from the codification works of the preceding

192 Quarterly report of the Legislative Department on the implementation of work from April to June 1951, AAN, MS, 5633, 16.

193 Quarterly report of the Legislative Department on the implementation of work from July to September 1951 AAN, MS, 5633, 51.

194 *Uchwała Prezydium Rządu w sprawie kodyfikacji* [Resolution of the Praesidium of the Cabinet], Nowe Prawo 10 (1950), 2.

period. The enactment took place so as to combine the general provisions of civil law of 1946 with the Personal Law enacted in 1945, based on Book I of the Civil Code drafted between 1947 and 1949. That also meant the borrowing of certain concepts and solutions adopted during the interwar period in the Code of Obligations of 1933. At the same time, the new general provisions of civil law were enacted also intended modify the General Part of the still-binding Code of Obligations. As Seweryn Szer endeavoured to explain:

> The separation of the totality of the provisions organizing family relationships into a standalone family code entails the necessity of a certain reconstruction of existing norms of civil law governing legal transactions. Such norms, so far contained in the Code of Obligations and thus in a legislative instrument from the scope of real law, bore by necessity the marks of that law and only with great difficulty could they and can they be applied in our reality to family relationships in the broadest sense of the word.[195]

Jan Wasilkowski added:

> The task of the statute at hand was not only the systematization and correct ordering of a number of issues significant to the whole balance of civil and family law but also – or even first of all – to set the proper, progressive direction for the application of the existing provisions of civil law [especially the Code of Obligations], which are insufficiently harmonized and partially outdated provisions.[196]

Key importance among the general provisions of civil law belonged to two directives – the former demanding that all 'provisions of the law be interpreted and applied in line with the principles of the political system and goals of the People's State,' and the latter prohibiting the use of one's right in a manner violating the principles of social coexistence in that state. The tone of those provisions was clear, especially following the entry into force of the 1952 Constitution defining the goals of the People's State as being to 'safeguard the achievements of the Polish working people of the towns and villages', 'protect its rule and freedom from forces hostile to the people', and 'restriction, phasing out and elimination of the social classes living off of the

195 SZER: *Kodeks rodzinny*, 4.

196 WASILKOWSKI: *Kodyfikacja prawa cywilnego*, 5.

exploitation of labourers and peasant farmers'. Even earlier on, however, Jan Wasilkowski harboured no doubts that the possibility of the moderation of the manner of exercise of civil rights violating the principles of social cohabitation in a People's State proceeded from a principle of which the 'class essence was altogether clear.' As for the directive of interpreting all provisions of the law through the prism of the constitutional principles and goals of the People's State, while that was 'self-evident' (or self-explanatory) 'still, given the insufficient level of ideological formation of part of the lawyers in Poland and the associated tendency towards formalistic interpretation, an express statutory mention appeared to be necessary in the present period.' For as one should constantly emphasize:

> The law of the People's State (…) expresses – irrespective of the time of origin of the individual provisions – the intention of the working class and other people of labour, serving the goals of building socialism by phasing out the remnants of capitalism in the national economy, in the living conditions and consciousness of the citizens.

In such a context, the circumstance that 'some provisions (…) had retained their outdated form c[ould] not have any impact on the application.'[197]

In such atmosphere of intensification of the front of ideological class struggle, already in 1949 was the Civil Law Codification Commission reactivated. New Commission, headed by Minister Świątkowski, was joined by two of the most actively involved members of the previous Commission – Jan Wasilkowski and Seweryn Szer – as well as Jerzy Marowski, who did not involve himself in the works, and Jan Topiński (President of the Chief Arbitration Committee). Wasilkowski was tasked with designing real law and coordinating the work on the law of obligations, as well as directly designing the part on torts. Ultimately, it was he who, outside of the redaction of the draft Real Law – again – acted as the editor of the entire draft of the civil code. Szer's domain was to become inheritance law, not counting the issue of economic plans as a source of obligation, also entrusted to him. Jan Topiński's share was to be the topic of state enterprises, contribution of socialist circulation to obligations, and the 'legacy' of commercial law in connection with plans of abrogation of the Commercial Code.[198] A motion was quickly tabled to expand the composition. That was done by Wasilkowski. This ra-

197 *Ibidem.*

198 Progress report of the codification work in 1951, AAN, MS, 2382, 52–56.

FIGURE 3.3
Jan Winiarz, 1923–1994. Linked to the Polish Academy of Sciences, working in several academic centres such as Gdańsk and Toruń; Vice-Rector of the Nicolaus Copernicus University of Toruń. Active participant in codification works.

tionale can be surprising in the context. He claimed that the Commission had become 'predominated by members of the judiciary'. Accordingly, there was need to co-opt representatives of socialist economy circulation.[199] The new members included Adam Chełmoński, who would prepare the preliminary draft of the law of obligations, and Jan Winiarz as secretary.[200]

The deadline – still in 1951 – appeared to be out of reach, especially considering that an in-depth reconstruction of the existing system in the Marxist spirit was expected. The Ministry of Justice, therefore, had to work under enormous time pressure. One could think that the boastful promise of codification could be kept only given a transplant from one of the existing codes of socialist countries or only superficial edits to the existing unified law, or the incorporation of the product of the codification works of 1947–1948. In the latter case, however, at least the appearance of a major overhaul had to be created. It appears also that the point was to combine the foundations of a traditional civil code with the new elements arising from the reorganization of the country's economic life – in 1949 and 1950 economic state arbitration was established, along with so-called plan contracts in the socialist economy, exchange of money with almost absolute principle of nominalism, as well as essentially unlimited options for expropriation without any realistic compensation; compulsory state management was also imposed on a wide scale. This is attested especially by the scope of works assigned to Topiński. In this sense,

199 *Ibidem.*
200 CZACHÓRSKI: *Przebieg prac*, 12.

the codification works of 1947–1948 could indeed at least partially fail to accommodate the country's reorganized economic system.

On the other hand, Wasilkowski observed that People's Poland was in a transitional phase. The socio-economic transformation could not be accomplished overnight. The country would necessarily have to reconcile for a time a socialist system developing faster in industry and commerce with the need to retain the principles of small-scale capitalist economy in agriculture. The collectivization of the countryside would require time.[201] As a result, the civil code, too, would have to bear the marks of a provisional solution adapted to the received reality of the transitional period. Wasilkowski harboured no delusions as to the possibility of creating a code for a 'longer period of time' in the circumstances. The very need to enact a civil code, however, was something he neither could nor wanted to dispute. He justified it nebulously with the need to 'break out of the "traditional" lagging behind on the developments of social life.'[202]

Until December 1950, efforts were concentrated on the gathering and analysis of informational materials, especially statistics and academic studies. During the same year, a set of general theses was created for real, inheritance and obligations law.[203] Polish translations were commissioned of the most recent civil codes from the Eastern Bloc – Soviet (1947), Czechoslovak (1950), with the explanatory memorandum, and Bulgarian Code. The theses were formulated before the translations of potentially model regulations were ready, which suggests that those were probably not the main source of inspiration when setting the principal directions for the codification.[204] This does not change the fact that the codifiers, even without the translations, still had some knowledge of the codes of other people's democracies, with the Soviet one at the helm, having cited it sporadically during the codification works of the preceding period.[205]

The new course of action and new pattern of reasoning for the rationales to follow was set by Seweryn Szer during the works on the Family Code. Let us quote his words published in early 1950:

201 WASILKOWSKI: *Kodyfikacja prawa cywilnego*, 22.
202 Progress report of the codification work in 1951, AAN, MS 2382, 53.
203 AAN, MS 5605, 30–33; MACHNIKOWSKA: *Prawo własności*, 351
204 Anna MOSZYŃSKA: *Prace nad kodyfikacją majątkowego prawa cywilnego w latach 1950–52*, MHI 14 (2015)/2, 171.
205 See the preceding section of this chapter.

> the future Family Code gives effect to the concept under which the full picture of family relations should be set apart as a separate discipline of the law. Given this assumption, the future civil code will cover only matters of property law, i.e. obligations, real law and inheritance. This is the concept followed by the legislation of the Soviet Republics (...) It would be impossible not to recognize the merit of the position taken by Soviet scholarship.
>
> As Professor D.M. Genkin would say: "In a capitalist society, matters of marriage, family, relationships between parents and children are primarily matters of property relations, matters of private law. In a socialist society, by contrast, those matters could not possibly be reduced in their principle to property relations. Members of the Soviet family fulfil the most diverse mutual obligations of non-economic nature imposed on them by the state." (...) The above premises of Soviet law also justify a fundamental change in the current systematization of Polish civil law, which constitutes a type of socialist law.[206]

One could scarcely find similar references to Soviet scholarship in the preceding period. Such type of assertions could lead one to assume, preliminarily, that the Family Code of 1950 was based on Soviet legal scholarship and the USSR code derived from it, which would operate to justify the thesis of the accelerated Stalinization of the country. Unquestionably, Genkin's work, Soviet Private Law, eventually saw publication, but only in 1955. Let us note that the code denied the right to seek divorce to a spouse having contributed to it, consistently with the existing line of court decisions shaped on the basis of the 1946 Decree. Attention is drawn, however, to the fact that the reasoning provided in support of this solution emphasized also (or perhaps primarily) its consistency with the direction taken by decisions made in the USSR. Let us see the conclusions of Piotr Fiedorczyk's specialist studies into this problem.[207]

Similarly, citing Soviet solutions and indeed borrowing from them, a specific (strict) regime of community property was adopted. That was different from real-law co-ownership in ideal parts. A spouse was not granted a share in community property. In consequence, unlike in real law, the spouses were not entitled to dispose each of their own part (which was not distinguished and

206 SZER: *Kodeks rodzinny*, 3.

207 Piotr FIEDORCZYK: *Radzieckie prawo rodzinne jako przedmiot recepcji w Polsce i innych państwach Europy Środkowo-Wschodniej*, Acta Universitatis Wratislaviensis 3154 (2009), 355.

set apart into a specific share) without the previous abolition of community property, which was possible only in exceptional situations, similarly to the availability of prenuptial property contracts.[208]

As the works, in line with the cabinet resolution of 27 September 1950, were to involve broad circles of 'employees of the judiciary and academia',[209] the Ministry of Justice conducted a survey among the courts, notaries and praesidia of national councils and held Polish-Czechoslovak conferences for the purpose of sourcing information about the codification experience. Active support was to be provided by the – having existed since 1949 – Consultative Academic Commission created at the Ministry of Justice. Its task was to provide 'consultation and theoretical assistance with in matters of legislation and codification' through the 'elaboration and in-depth study of legal issues (…) on the foundations of Marxist-Leninist science'.[210] The decision was made for academic sessions dedicated mainly to codification topics to be held monthly since March 1951.[211] The Consultative Academic Commission also managed to organize, for the benefit of its studies into real law, a conference of theoreticians and practitioners of law to discuss the basic problems of this particular discipline within civil law.[212]

The next stage of the codification works, inaugurated in early 1951, undertook to develop detailed theses elaborating on the general theses in the area of real, inheritance and obligations law.[213] Following the adoption of the theses, initial drafts were first redacted for each of the parts of economic civil law (April for inheritance, and May for real law and the general part of obligations),[214] subsequently to discuss them in the Civil Law Codification Commission and refer them to the Consultative Academic Commission. On that basis,

208 SZER: *Kodeks rodzinny*, 10–11.

209 *Uchwała Prezydium Rządu*, 2.

210 Piotr FIEDORCZYK: *Z dziejów stalinizacji polskiej nauki prawa. Komisja Konsultacyjno-Naukowa przy Ministrze Sprawiedliwości (1949–1951)* [From the history of Stalinization of Polish legal science: the Academic Consultative Commission to the Minister of Justice], in Robert KŁOSOWICZ et al. (eds): *Konstytucjonalizm, doktryny, partie polityczne: księga dedykowana Profesorowi Andrzejowi Ziębie* [Constitutionalism, doctrines, political parties: a book dedicated to Professor Andrzej Zięba], WUJ, Krakow, 2016, 257–268.

211 Minutes of the session of the Presidium of Academic Consultative Commission under the Ministry of Justice on 27 February 1951, AAN, MS 5465, 11.

212 AAN, MS 5604, 7; *Konferencja prawników-cywilistów* [Conference of civil jurists], Nowe Prawo 5 (1951), 54.

213 Monthly reports of the Civil Law Section of Legislative Department for March and April 1951, AAN, MS 2362, 67 and 80–83; 5605, 35.

214 Monthly reports of the Civil Law Section of Legislative Department for April and May 1951 AAN, MS 2362, 85, 87, 91, 100.

another version of the draft was created,[215] sent out to all ministries and referred to debate in the Polish Lawyers' Association.

The intensive works were accompanied by certain amount of press activity. On the one hand, *Państwo i Prawo* published articles written by Wasilkowski and Szer on topics of, respectively, real and inheritance law.[216]

In keeping with the expectations of the communist authorities, Wasilkowski proposed new forms of property relations adapted – as he believed – to the needs of the socialist economy; namely, he distinguished four categories of property: besides the individual ownership of means of production, means of consumption and articles of personal use, he distinguished the socialist ownership of means of production. He did not, however, intended to regulate the latter more extensively in the code, arguing that there would be frequent changes to it. For that reason, in his opinion, the real law in the code ought to concentrate on the creation of certain general frameworks and principles. Wasilkowski's concepts were already paving the way, as he assumed that the homogeneous understanding of property derived from the liberal and Roman traditions was eventually to be abandoned. The changes occurring to the legal concept of property affected not only civil law but also the entire legal system and were viewed as the 'most momentous phaenomena in the development of the law of People's Poland'. That, however, was only to be decided by the Constitution of 1952.

As for the law of obligations, Wasilkowski proposed its merger with commercial law and, of course, on the hand the elimination of 'anachronistic' provisions, i.e. inapplicable to a centrally planned economy, and on the other hand the introduction of new institutions (contracts) proper to the new system, such as plan or type contracts, *kontraktacja* ('contract forming') and *dostawa* ('supply').

Wasilkowski also suggested the necessity of relatively large-scale changes to inheritance law, thus far remaining under the 'significant influence of bourgeois ideology', which manifested itself in too broad a circle of those entitled to intestate inheritance, excessive testamentary freedom and insufficient share of the spouse in the estate.[217]

215 Quarterly report of the Legislative Department on the implementation of work from October to December 1952, AAN, MS 5633, 93.

216 Jan WASILKOWSKI: *Własność i inne prawa rzeczowe* [Ownership and other property rights], PIP (5–6) 1951, 854–876; Seweryn SZER: *Z zagadnień prawa spadkowego* [From topics of inheritance law], PIP 5–6 (1951), 910–924. MACHNIKOWSKA: *Prawo własności*, 353.

217 WASILKOWSKI: *Kodyfikacja prawa cywilnego*, 3–7.

In the *Nowe Prawo* calls were made for a public debate on codification.[218] Of course, given such a short time for the completion of the draft civil code, there was no chance for the voices in the debate to affect the shape of the solutions adopted in the code.

The evaluation of the drafts by the authorities was potentially of key importance. Remarks sent in by ministries and other state institutions did not, in the Ministry's opinion, provide grounds for any significant changes to be made to the draft. In the August report, Section Head Seweryn Szer announced success, noting that 'the final version of the draft Civil Code together with an explanatory memorandum' had been prepared on time.[219] Thereafter, it was submitted to the Praesidium of the Council of Ministers, but until the end of 1951 the Legal Commission assisting the Praesidium did not commence works on the draft.[220] Since September 1951, continued works in the Civil Law Section concentrate around the preparation of changes in civil procedure, especially intended for the adaptation of the provisions of the specific parts of the Code of Civil Procedure to the draft Civil Code.[221] With regard to substantive law, in November 1951, the Section also compiled a draft of implementing provisions for the Civil Code,[222] of which the second redaction was completed in December.[223] As of early 1952, meetings of the Civil Law Codification Commission of 1949 are still taking place, mainly dealing with the general part of civil law.[224] In the Civil Law Section, on the other hand, the action plan for 1952 was domianted by the codification of civil

218 *Uchwała Prezydium Rządu w sprawie kodyfikacji* [Resolution of the Praesidium of the Cabinet], Nowe Prawo 10 (1950), 2; *Szeroka dyskusja cenną pomocą w pracy kodyfikacyjnej* [A wide discussion as a valuable help in codification work], Nowe Prawo 4 (1951), 1–2; Jan KRAJEWSKI, Jan WINIARZ (eds): *Głosy praktyki sądowej: materiały do kodyfikacji prawa cywilnego* [Voices of judicial practice: materials for the codification of civil law], Nowe Prawo 5 (1951), 49–53.

219 Monthly report of the Civil Law Section of Legislative Department or August 1951, AAN, MS 2362, 111.

220 Quarterly report of the Legislative Department on the implementation of work from October to December 1951, AAN, MS 5633, 59.

221 Monthly report of the Civil Law Section of Legislative Department for September 1951, AAN, MS 2362, 113–114, 118.

222 Monthly report of the Civil Law Section of Legislative Department for November 1951, AAN, MS 2362, 123, 125.

223 Monthly report of the Civil Law Section of Legislative Department for December 1951, AAN, MS 2362, 129.

224 Monthly report of the Civil Law Section of Legislative Department for February 1952, AAN, MS 2362, 148; quarterly report of the Legislative Department on the implementation of work from January to March 1952, AAN, MS 5633, 65.

FIGURE 3.4 Seweryn Szer, 1902–1968. In legal practice before World War II. After the war, senior civil servant in the Ministry of Justice, member of codification commissions for civil law, and justice of the Supreme Court, as well as aspiring academic scholar. Affiliated successively with the Academy of Political Sciences and with the legal faculties of the Universities of Łódź and Warsaw; at the latter, in 1954–1965, head of the Department of Civil Law.

procedure. With regard to works on civil law, there were only plans for a meeting of theoreticians and practitioners dedicated to a discussion of the draft Civil Code to be organized.[225]

Translations were also commissioned of selected legal works. Although their publication had to wait, that did not mean the contents had not been familiar to at least some of the codifiers beforehand. Apart from the aforementioned work of 1953, the gargantuan work of Anatoly Venediktov, titled *State-Owned Socialist Property*, was published.

The works were conducted until 1955. The coming into force of the Constitution of 22 July 1952 and the academic congress held on its first anniversary were of fundamental importance to their continued course. That was, in a way, a turning point, at least partially closing the preceding period.[226] Family law, social property, personal property, and civil-law transactions in agriculture were established as separate topics within the scope of civil law. The

225 Work schedule of the Civil Law Section of Legislative Department for the year 1952, AAN, MS 2362, 133.

226 Cf. Henryk Rot: *Problemy kodyfikacji prawa PRL* [Topics of codification of the law of Polish People's Republic], Ossolineum, Wrocław, 1978, 30.

papers read and subsequently published constituted a sort of reopening of the debate surrounding the codification. With regard to topics of family law, speakers included Jan Gwiazdomorski as the principal rapporteur, Maurycy Grudziński, Aleksander Wolter and Stefan Kaleta. For social property, the main rapporteur was Jan Wasilkowski. He was accompanied by nearly all of the original members of the Codification Commission established in 1949 – Seweryn Szer, Adam Chełmoński, Jan Topiński and Kazimierz Przybyłowski. Topics of personal property were discussed by Stefan Grzybowski as the main rapporteur, Witold Czachórski, Adam Szpunar, Zbigniew Radwański and Zygmunt Nowakowski. The matter of civil-law transactions in agriculture was addressed by Henryk Świątkowski as the main rapporteur, Jerzy Ignatowicz, Józef Fiema and Franciszek Studnicki.

An order of the Minister of Justice of 27 July 1954 reorganized the body responsible for the functioning and appointments of the new codification commission which included a civil law section, assisting the Legislative Department of the Ministry of Justice. It was headed by Leszek Lernell, Director of the Legislative Department. During that period, two revisions of the draft Civil Code were published, of 1954 and 1955.[227] As a result of changes to the political situation, they were met with criticism.[228] There were, however, plans to continue the works without discarding the drafts in whole but instead recognizing them as valuable source material for subsequent drafting efforts.

---

227 Piotr FIEDORCZYK: *O powstaniu, strukturze organizacyjnej i trybie prac Komisji Kodyfikacyjnej z 1956 roku* [On the formation, organizational structure and procedure of the Codification Commission of 1956], in Marian MIKOŁAJCZYK et al. (eds): *O prawie i jego dziejach księgi dwie: studia ofiarowane Profesorowi Adamowi Lityńskiemu w 70-lecie urodzin* [On law and its history books two: studies dedicated to Professor Adam Lityński on the forty-fifth anniversary of his academic work and twenty-fifth anniversary of his birth], WUwB, Białystok, 2010, vol. I, 475.

228 LITYŃSKI: *O prawie i sądach*, 44.

CHAPTER 4

The Ideological Perspective of the Authors of the Codification of Civil Law (1956–1964)

1 Introduction

1.1 *The Three Layers of Private Law*

During the period of its functioning under the socialist regime, Polish private law had a three-layered structure. After 1964, the third layer achieved the greatest prominence. Attention is drawn to both its pedigree and substance, as well as the circumstances in which it came into being. The ideological and the axiological context of this calls for a brief description of the other two layers.

Composing the first of all three layers were norms originating either from the interwar period or enacted in the period immediately following World War II but on the basis of drafts or at least assumptions predating it. Among the latter, the codifications of the 30s of the 20th century were especially prominent – the law of obligations, commercial law, and civil procedure, as well as the part having entered the system in 1945–1946 as part of the process of finalizing the unification of substantive civil law. In 1948, the leadership of the ascendant Polish United Workers' Party (PZPR) pronounced upon that law as having a bourgeois character, which, in the linguistic convention of the politics of the time, was tantamount with a finding of irremediable defects.

Its swift and comprehensive replacement with a new codification was promised. That plan never came to fruition, though almost two decades later, in 1964, a Civil Code, Code of Civil Procedure and Family and Guardianship Code were enacted.[1] A significant part of their provisions retained their wording inherited from the previous political system or inspired by classic private law. This was a topic not discussed in the presentation of socialist law.

Certain statutes of the Second Republic remained on the book even after 1964. Those included the Commercial Code of 1934.[2] Its role was marginalized as part of the provisions were repealed following the entry into force of

1 Act of 23 April 1964 – Civil Code, Dz.U.16,93; Act of 17 November 1964, Code of Civil Procedure, Dz.U.43.296; Act of 25 February 1964, Dz.U.9.60.

2 Decree of the President of the Republic of Poland of 27 June 1934 – Commercial Code; Dz.U.57.502.

 | DOI:10.1163/9789004730021_006

the Civil Code and those that were retained, among them the ones on commercial companies, did not find application in practice due to the changes in the economy.[3] Commercial law was also removed from the curriculum in law schools. After the change of the political system, the surviving provisions would begin once again to be applied,[4] contributing to a cohesive and immediate reconstruction of this element of the legal system. A similar situation became the lot of other statutes, such as those on unfair competition, promissory notes and cheques. Modern scholarship still benefits from certain works predating World War II (e.g. the publications of the drafters of commercial law: Maurycy Allerhand, Tadeusz Dziurzyński and Zygmunt Fenichel).

Another characteristic element of postwar law were special provisions and executive legislation. In 1944–1947, those were relied on to address the exceptional problems caused by World War II. Those included the deaths of more than 6 million Polish nationals, changes to the country's border with the resulting migrations, and enormous destruction of property. However, norms introduced as exceptional measures remained on the books for several decades, changing their ratio and function. In enacting such instruments, the administration created a separated layer of law for use as a tool of legal nihilism. Their provisions imposed significant limitations on the exercise of *in rem rights* and on the sphere of the law of obligations.

Those provisions remain outside of the courts' or the Sejm's powers of review. They obtained their binding force on the basis of the broad delegation of legislative power to the executive branch. Part of them took the form of interpretations coming down from the high officialdom or the party leadership, referred to as 'copy-machine law'. The doctrinal sources of the provisions composing this layer of private law were diverse, often dictated by short-term political goals and pragmatism. The typical mechanism was to introduce provisions restrictively regulating the accessibility of a right in common use and thereafter eliminate or modify them for a short time. Examples included norms preventing the acquisition of the ownership of a house or apartment by individuals, which twice underwent incidental changes motivated by the

3 Several commercial companies were allowed to continue to exist for purposes such as foreign trade.

4 The Commercial Code was amended in order to adapt it to the new economic realities (such as the changes in 1990–1991; Dz.U.1990.17.98, Dz.U.1990.51.298; Dz.U.1991.35.155; Dz.U.1991.94.418). It was replaced with a new statute only in 2000, in the form of the Act of 15 September 2000 – Code of Commercial Companies, Dz.U.94.1037.

desire for the proceeds to be realized by the state from the sale of such property.[5]

It was also a form of avoidance of responsibility for the form and contents of the new law. If the damage done became public knowledge, the problem was depicted as an incidental error in the application of the law. Sufficed, therefore, to rectify only one of the many elements of the system, because the remaining ones always functioned correctly, including the principle from which the exception was made. The pursuit of modernization projects by means of a universally applied exception from the principle would be described as a temporary solution. Assurances were offered that the number of such provisions was to decrease with the impending codification of civil law.

The long wait for that to come was explained with the considerably labour-intensive nature of the drafting of an avant-garde code reflecting the substance and form of socialist law. Such an interpretation copied the popular Soviet myth of creation of a social order not thereunto known by our civilization.[6] According to the reforms, whatever kinds of costs were to be incurred towards the fruition of such an ambitious design should not be a concern.

The leadership of the PZPR benefited from the multiple deferrals of the advent of the new codification. The inability to propagate a new code as a testimony to the quality and efficiency of the socialist state was not as important as the power offered by existing legislative practices. Each day, they provided liberal access to just about any legal solution imaginable.

When in 1964 the Civil Code came to be but the various special provisions and executive instruments encroaching on matters reserved to statutes remained beside it, the announcement was made that the new code was to be a law for a 'transitional period'. The date for normalization was once again moved to unspecified future, described as a time when the development of Polish society has reached level achieved already by socialist legal theory. Throughout the next twenty-five years, from 1964 to 1989, the authorities, purporting to speak on behalf of the citizenry, claimed the condition had not been met. Accordingly, the role of the code for the time being was to set the direc-

5 For example, provisions permitting the sale to individuals of an administratively defined number of small houses and residential apartments in part of country but without full ownership of the land, transferred only as a limited-time leasehold excluded from economic circulation; see more note on funds needed to make up for shortages in goods mass in connection with the growth in the population's monetary incomes in 1957, AAN, BP KC PZPR 2831, 237.

6 Michaił HELLER: *Maszyna i śrubki. Jak hartował się człowiek sowiecki*, SIL Kultura, Paris, 1988, 9 [English version: Mikhail Heller: *Cogs in the Wheel: The Formation of Soviet Man*, Knopf, 1988].

tion of modernization and to regulate the majority of civil-law affairs, including the non-socialized economy. By contrast, the purpose of provisions located outside of the code and free of the burden of proximity to old legislation was to accelerate the progress of the transformation in new types of civil-law affairs, including those involving the state or other social entities.

The last of the three layers was also shaped by three codes – the Civil Code of 1964;[7] Code of Civil Procedure, having replaced the interwar codification of 1930,[8] and the Family and Guardianship Code of 1964,[9] with a predecessor dating from 1950. The scholarly pedigree of these statutes was as complex as the circumstances of their origin. The substance of the three codes was pervaded by ideas arising from classical tradition and two modernizing currents.

The first one bore no links to the assumptions of historical materialism. It had already been found in the provisions codified under the Second Republic (law of obligations, civil procedure) and subsequently incorporated into the Civil Code. This form of modernization took its source from the legacy of Polish legal scholarship, having in the 30s of the 20th century designed a model of balanced marriage between the individualism of the civilist tradition and the principle of socialization of the law.[10] The latter was assigned the role of a partial regulator of certain contracts with a view to preserving the principle of equality of the parties, which, due to the economic specificity of such contracts, was unable to be guaranteed by the principle of freedom of contract.

The nature of modernization is also present in the unification decrees of 1945–1946. The substance of those was also largely transposed into the two codes. Modification goals were also underlying the creative drafts prepared by Codification Commission estblished in 1956 mostly in reference to traditional legal institutions. This kind of continuity of the modernization process, still focused on the national identity, had for many years been ignored or discounted in the presentation of the 1964 law.[11]

---

7 Act of 23 April 1964 – Family Code, Dz.U.16.93 and 94.

8 Act of 17 November 1964 – Code of Civil Procedure, Dz.U.43.295, rectified Dz. U.1965.15.113.

9 Act of 25 February 1964 – Family and Guardianship Code, Dz.U.1964.9.59 and 60; Act of 27 June 1950 – Family Code, Dz.U.34.308.

10 See Leonard GÓRNICKI: *Zasada uspołecznienia pewnych stosunków umownych w Kodeksie Zobowiązań z 1933 r.* [The principle of socialization of certain contractual relationships in the Code of Obligations of 1933], in Marek PODKOWSKI (ed.): *Zasady prawne w dziejach prawa publicznego i prywatnego* [Legal principles in the history of public and private law], Kolonia Limited, Wrocław, 2015, 161–169.

11 Zbigniew RADWAŃSKI: *Ciągłość a reforma prawa w świetle doświadczeń unifikacyjnych Polskiej Rzeczypospolitej Ludowej (lata 1945–1964)* [Continuity and reform of law in the

The way in which the codes were described for the use of the public opinion and legal science highlighted the second modernizing current, i.e. the one invoking the doctrinal foundations of the socialist system. This was facilitated by the taxonomy of the Civil Code in highlighting the new principles of private law. Those introduced elements of public law, for example by establishing links with administrative law and with criminal law. On this basis, some members of the Codification Commission proposed the idea that in the process of socialist modernization a new form of civil law took shape, one with stronger links to other branches to the law than had previously been the case. That idea was expounded by Seweryn Szer: 'Civil law cannot be only the private law of the individuals, for its problem range, conditioned by our socio-economic system, has been made to include the important field that is the socialized circulation and to some extent also the organization of the units of the socialized economy.'

The law harnessed by this modernization current had to exhibit one of the two functionalities: supporting the development of new civil-law relationships (legal transactions with the participation of the state) or imposing restrictions on the development of certain non-socialist relationships of civil law (economic relations among individuals only). The Civil Code did not become the legal infrastructure for the first functionality. That role was taken by the provisions through which decodification was achieved. Those were given an inconsistent piecemeal redaction and sometimes contradicted the principle itself because the decodification was subordinated to short-term political goals. Bereft of modernization potential, the provisions of the executive legislation stunted rather than stimulating the development[12] of the legal relationships that were of key importance to the system. The implementation of the second of the two functionalities of the socialist modernization was divided into two spheres: codification and decodification.

This specific positioning within the legal system of the provisions responsible for the modernization of civil law in Poland was determined by factors to which no such key role had originally been ascribed. Those were the active taken by society – under the circumstances of the totalitarian system – in

light of the unification experience of the Polish People's Republic (1945–1964)], in *Dzieje kodyfikacji prawa: materiały na konferencję historyków prawa w Karpaczu* [A history of legal codification: materials for the conference of legal historians in Karpacz], PTH, Karpacz, 1974, 162.

12 *Problemy współczesnego prawa cywilnego (konferencja naukowa – Popowo)* [Problems in modern civil law (academic conference – Popowo)], Zeszyty Naukowe Instytutu Badania Prawa Sądowego 19–20 (1983).

defence of the national identity and rational modernization, and the consequent public discussion of the principles of the rule of law, the provisions applicable during the period immediately preceding the codification, as well as the ideological and axiological choices made by the authors of the new codes. A less important role fell to political decisions and theoretical problems faced by socialist jurisprudence as a whole.

In the post-1989 period our central object of interest was, on the one hand, legislative activities aimed at removing 'communist leftovers', e.g. abrogation of rules on stratification of ownership, on planned contracts, on farm inheritance, as well as a far-reaching liberalisation of the legal regime of socialist property rights (right of perpetual usufruct; co-operative proprietary right to an apartment). As the ending points of our research we adopt the three major reforms of the Civil Code (1990, 1996 and 2000), the major reform of the Code of Civil Procedure (1996) and the introduction of the new Code of Commercial Partnerships and Companies (2000). Finally, apart from the 'negative' aspect of post-1989 private law reforms (removal of legal 'survivals' of the socialist period), we also focused on the 'positive' reforms, i.e. on the introduction (or reintroduction) of legal principles and institutions unknown in the socialist period.

1.2 *Societal Resistance to the Communist Power and its Impact on the Codification*

The doctrinal rationale for the codification of 1964 took shape in the characteristic socio-economic circumstances of socialist states. Works on the code were initiated at a time when because of the resistance on the part of the citizenry, the state modified some of the principles of its own functioning, transforming from the totalitarian model given in this part of Europe the name of Stalinism to an era of authoritarianism retaining some of the elements of its predecessor system.[13] The direct impulse for the establishment

13 The thesis that the political system of the time transformed from totalitarian to authoritarian is a matter of dispute in Polish legal and political sciences. Arguments advanced in favour of the recognition of 1956 as the dividing point between totalitarianism and authoritarianism in Poland mention the presence in the political and legal system of the time of areas of relative independence, including private farms, see Lech Mażewski: *Cel doraźny – porządek autorytarny* [An extemporaneous goal – an authoritarian order], Przegląd Polityczny 11 (1988), 195–199; Hanna Świda-Zięba: *Stalinizm i społeczeństwo polskie* [Stalinism and Polish society], in Jacek Kurczewski (ed.): *Stalinizm* [Stalinism], Zakład Malej Poligrafii UW, Warsaw, 1991, 16; Leszek Kołakowski: *Główne nurty marksizmu: powstanie – rozwój – rozkład*, Aneks, London 1988 [English version: *Main Currents of Marxism*, OUP, 1978], 861. The contrary position cites the

of the Codification Commission[14] came from the mass demonstrations and strikes of 1956. Another, equally important factor was the determined attitude of society, continuing to protest in 1968, 1970, 1976, 1980 and 1988–1989.

The collective memory of sovereignty, freedom and democracy proved stronger than the economic and political coercion and ideological indoctrination into the universal benefits of the internationalist dictatorship. The long-term consequence of the confrontation was the downfall of the socialist system,[15] followed by breaking the legal system free from Soviet influence. Poland became the first of all countries in the same geopolitical position to achieve this, in 1989.

The cyclical outbreaks of societal protest set the boundaries for and determined the nature of the implementation of certain assumptions of the socialist system into the system of private law, primarily by blocking transformations going any further than the ones legislated into being with the codes of 1964. With minor exceptions, the codes retained their original wording until 1989, even though political plans had assumed the continued imposition of limitations on the functioning of some relationships of civil law.

The social circumstances in which the new works on the Civil Code had begun in 1956 is illustrated by the confrontation of the position taken by the protesting citizens with the response given by the leadership of the PZPR. The reasons for the strikes and demonstrations were the deteriorating material situation, lack of legal safety, marginalization of the national identity, as well as the ineffectiveness and window-dressing nature of the institutions touted as proofs of doctrinal progress. Accusations were levied that the party, while purporting to represent the proletariat, was divesting it of more rights than the non-socialist government had done in the interwar period. In streets and factories, slogans were chanted such as 'freedom', 'free elections under UN control', 'we want a Catholic, not a Soviet Poland',

retention of the single-party system even after 1956 and its mitigation only following repeat protests from the citizens, see Paweł Śpiewak: *Pamięć po komunizmie*, Słowo, Gdańsk, 2005, 15–16.

14 Order of the President of the Council of Ministers establishing a Codification Commission to assist the Minister of Justice, Monitor Polski 70.856.

15 There is a consensus in Polish legal scholarship as to the reception of the events of 1956: 'that was a great breakthrough. It was the acceleration of the diverse paths leading towards the relaxation of the dependence, towards sovereignty and freedom. The (…) process continued the whole time from 1956 (though it encountered slowdowns) all the way to 1989.' See Eugeniusz Duraczyński in *Dyskusja*, Polska 1944/45–1989. Studia i Materiały 3 (1997), 279.

'away with the Rushkies', 'away with the seventeen years of bondage', 'away with the red bourgeoisie'.[16]

The protests were curbed with the use of force, including the military. The ideological rationale for the decision was expounded by the prime minister, Józef Cyrankiewicz: 'Every provocateur or madman who dares raise a hand against the people's government may be sure to have that hand lobbed off by the government in the interest of the working class, in the interest of the working peasantry and of the intelligentsia (...).'

The protests, however, did not die down, although their form to some extent change, leading the participants' demands to become the topic of a universal debate that the censorship could not manage to lock out. The leadership of the PZPR decided in favour of a short-term tactical change also in legal policy. Certain special provisions restricting the exercise of private rights were repealed or amended and new principles were promised for the continued reform of civil law. The depositary of the latter was to be the Codification Commission appointed towards the end of 1956.[17]

The consequences of societal activism at the turn of 1956/1957 were not limited to the reopening of codification works. It also provided the inspiration for novel studies in legal sciences, along with nationwide debate in legal circles. Moreover, it led to the reinterpretation of the relationships among such notions as Polish national identity, legal culture, tradition and modernization. These circumstances shaped a new perspective for the codification works, of considerably more value than one informed by political decisions.

1.3 *The New Development Perspective of Private Law*

At the onset of its conceptual works, the Codification Commission had the benefit of a broader politico-legal sphere than available to lawyers and jurists in other socialist countries. Several factors were decisive to this. A code designed along the lines of a Stalinist interpretation of private law had not yet managed to come out in Poland at the time. Hence, the discussion on the codification did not have to involve, which would have been extraordinarily difficult to achieve in the circumstances of an authoritarian state dependent

16 Note concerning the events of 28 June 1956 – note of 18 August 1956, Poznań; Archiwum Instytutu Pamięci Narodowej [Archives of the Institute of National Remembrance], Po 570/86, 5–110, copy, see more Stanisław JANKOWIAK, Rafał KOŚCIAŃSKI, Edmund MAKOWSKI, Rafał RECZEK (eds), *Poznański czerwiec 1956: wybór dokumentów* [Poznań June 1956. Selection of documents], vol. 1, IPN, Poznań, 2012, 502–510.

17 See more FIEDORCZYK: *O powstaniu*, 473–484.

on the USSR, departure from Soviet jurisprudential theories. Where such a conflict emerged and triggered polemical debate, arguments of ideological nature did not predominate the discussion, or they were fused with other values. Such was the manner of discussing, for example, the form to be taken by the legislation on family law. The Codification Commission was faced with an existing Family Code of 1950, a product of decisions to introduce Soviet patterns to Polish private law, made at the turn of the forties and fifties.

Some of the Commission's members working at the turn of the fifties and sixties on a new codification of family and guardianship law were adamantly in favour of reincorporation of the matter into the draft Civil Code.[18] Others, explaining the rationale for the contrary decision taken by the Ministry of Justice, did not charge their opponents in that debate with the subversion of the ideological principles. They identified the characteristic features of socialist law, but they rounded their arguments out by accounting for the specificity of the social and economic affairs in the country.

Such was the rationale advanced by Seweryn Szer. The type of regulation of family law depended on the principles of regulation of economic relationships, he argued. Polish economic system, therefore, did not play such a strong role with regard to family law as either in bourgeois or in Soviet law. Accordingly, due to the private ownership of farms functioning alongside the socialized economy, the judgement on arguments in favour and against the separate codification of family law should be passed according to different criteria. 'I do not believe (…) the concept of economic law already having a history both in capitalist states and in the Soviet Union to merit implementation in our circumstances.'

Another factor conducive to a broad analysis of ideological and axiological rationales for a turn towards new or retention of existing norms of private law was the debate on the principles of the rule of law. That debate had been ongoing since the latter half of 1956, and the course it took was marked with intellectual ferment and universal interest from the legal circles. Participants included legal theorists, philosophers and historians, as well as representatives of economic sciences, and a great multitude of legal practitioners and judges. This exchange of information and opinions armed the Codification Commission with additional knowledge, making it properly

18 An example can be found in the statements offered in support of the principle of totality of the Civil Code, which was to include the reincorporation of family law into it and abandonment of separate regulation of the matter; see Aleksander WOLTER: *Kodeks cywilny a 'prawo rodzinne'* [Civil Code and 'family law'], PiP 3 (1957), 475–479.

equipped to judge the merits of the foundational assumptions of the codification and its detailed contents.[19]

The debate, interdisciplinary and societal as it was, persisted even at a time when the other debates initiated in 1956 had been extinguished due to the repetrification of the doctrinal foundations of the state's political system. This unique experience paid off in 1980, when a new debate was opened on the law as a result of the workers' strikes. The remarkable effectiveness with which the latter debate was conducted bore fruit in the compilation of high-quality private drafts of amendments to civil law in the space of several months.

In the meanwhile, at the turn of the fifties and sixties, legal theory and philosophy had set down to work on the key problems. The inspiration came from those disciplines' own critical analyses of the law, the social activism of those who had taken part in the strikes and demonstrations of 1956, as well as those who transposed their demands into the debate in the press and academic publications. The status of individual rights was among the topics of that debate. For reasons of the essence of a civil-law relationship, the importance of this to the discipline of civil law was fundamental. The hope was sparked for a return to a rational discourse on rights, rather than exclusively on obligations, of which the socialist lawmaker had been intent on introducing more and more into the system of private law.

The assumptions of historical materialism and of the interpretation of Marxist legal theory were among the topics subjected to debate. Referring to Karl Marx, the jurist, Konstanty Grzybowski, demonstrated the lack of a good foundation for the claim of unilateral dependence between the basis (production relationship) and the superstructure, previously relied upon to justify various types of legal and economic coercion. Thus, contrary to the doctrinaires, there was no bar to shaping legal relationships in a manner reflective of the social awareness.[20]

19 See Jan WASILKOWSKI, Aleksander WOLTER: *Wyniki dyskusji publicznej nad projektem kodeksu cywilnego* [Outcome of the public discussion on the draft Civil Code], PiŻ 22 (1961), 3; Piotr FIEDORCZYK: *Kilka uwag o publicznej dyskusji nad prawem rodzinnym w projekcie kodeksu cywilnego z 1960 r.* [Several remarks on the public debate on family law in the draft Civil Code of 1960], in Anna KRYNIECKA (ed.), *Filozofia Marii Szyszkowskiej* [The philosophy of Maria Szyszkowska], Kresowa Agencja Wydawnicza, Białystok, 2012, 360–380.

20 See Konstanty GRZYBOWSKI: *Z metodologii historii doktryn politycznych* [From the methodology of history of political doctrines], CPH 8 (1956)/1, 298.

The value in social participation, to be practised in multiple forms, was invoked by the philosopher, Leszek Kołakowski. Starting from the concept of democracy, he examined, among other things, the connection between economic democracy and political democracy. On that basis he argued convincingly for the need for institutional safeguards of societal participation trough suitable legislation. The socialist state, according to the philosopher, ought to employ different models of participation and safeguards, including those having a positive track record in other political systems.[21]

The works penned by the legal theorist, Jerzy Wróblewski, also discussed themes relating to the situation in which private law had found itself in Poland for the preceding decade. He asserted that for legal principles normative bases should be created with a suitable level of definiteness.[22] Another jurist, Zygmunt Izdebski, arguing from the definitional position of the rule of law, disputed the existing legislative policy consisting in the delegation of the power to make law to the bodies of the executive and the increasing trend for such bodies to enact provisions constituting exceptions from principle. A great many lawyers and jurists supported calls for putting an end to that practice, demanding the appropriate separation and narrowing down of the powers of the various organs of the state.[23]

In the course of the debate on the institutional strengthening of oversight of the administration, part of legal scholars asserted that laying down suitable administrative oversight would be a sufficient safeguard against administrative abuses of power. Others, by contrast, proposed farther-reaching changes, including the reactivation of the administrative judiciary or even provisions for the constitutional review of ordinary legislation.[24] Those were references to the state of legal affairs in interwar Poland[25] and the debate held on the

21 See Andrzej FRISZKE: *Polska: losy państwa i narodu 1939–1989* [Poland: the fate of the state and of the nation 1939–1989], Iskry, Warsaw, 2003, 136.

22 See Jerzy WRÓBLEWSKI: *Zagadnienia teorii wykładni prawa ludowego* [Topics in the theory of interpretation of the people's law], Wydawnictwo Prawnicze, Warsaw, 1959; Mieczysław MANELI: *Pojęcie funkcji państwa* [The concept of the state's function], PIP 1 (1957), 28.

23 See Stefan ROZMARYN: *Jakie zmiany należy wprowadzić do Konstytucji PRL?* [What changes ought to be introduced to the Constitution of Polish People's Republic?], Trybuna Ludu, 25 March 1957.

24 Wacław DAWIDOWICZ: *W sprawie sądownictwa administracyjnego*[Concerning the administrative-court system], PIP 1956/12, 1045; Kazimierz. BISKUPSKI: *Zmieniać czy nie zmieniać*? [To change or not to change?], PIŻ 8 (1957), 3–4; opposing view Konstanty GRZYBOWSKI: *Sądy a aparat władzy i Administracji* The courts and the apparatus of power and administration], PIŻ 8 (1957), 1.

25 Act of 25 November 1925 on the Competence Court, Dz.U.126.897.

subject in 1946–1948, prior to the transformation of the political system into a totalitarian model.[26]

The limits of executive legislation were an important topic for the codification works. The draft of the Civil Code provided for delegations of power to the executive branch to narrow down or independently regulate certain matters of potentially key importance to new civil-law relationships. In the absence of oversight safeguards, the move would eventually result in decodification.

From the perspective of the types of means by which the modification of the status of private law was pursued, attention is drawn to the analysis of the legislative practice of the addition of adjectives to basic legal concepts.[27] In collocations including the words 'democracy' or 'rule of law' on the one hand and 'people's' or 'socialist' on the other hand, the added words, rather than reinforcing the value of these concepts, had the effect of reducing their scope. The above was one of several methods of feigned modernization, as well as the impulse for the verification of the general clauses having appeared in civil law in the latter's new function in 1950,[28] of which there were to be even more in the new codes.

The input from economic scholars may also have contributed to the assessment of what had to be regarded as a necessary part of the codification.[29] Although some of it was intended solely for the eyes of the party leadership, the problems discussed came to the attention of broader circles. Economists, as well as management and organization specialists concentrated on diagnosing the underlying causes of the poor performance of the socialist economy and began to dispute the official line according to which that was a natural transitional stage in the initial phase of development of a socialist system. In reality, it was the result of the lack, on the part of the political decision-

---

26 See Andrzej MYCIELSKI: *Polskie prawo polityczne (Konstytucja z 17 III 2021 r.)* [Polish political law (Constitution of 17 March 1921)], Przełom, Krakow, 1947, 218.

27 For remarks on the contravention of the law with the use of the ambiguity of terms such as 'strict' and 'absolute' in relation to compliance with the law, as well as the Sejm 'generously' delegating its powers to civil servants see Zygmunt IZDEBSKI: *Rewizja pojęcia praworządności ludowej* [Revision of the concept of the people's rule of law], PiP 3 (1957), 443–454.

28 See Anna STAWARSKA-RIPPEL: *O klauzulach generalnych w pierwszych latach Polski Ludowej*, Miscellanea Iuridica 6 (2005), 117–129.

29 Letter of 3 May 1956 signed by a group of economists: Józef Pajestka, Zofia Morecka, Bohdan Gliński, Włodzimierz Brus, Henryk Fiszel and Kazimierz Łaski, submitted to the members of the Politburo of the Central Committee of the PZPR, AAN BP KC PZPR, 2829, 331–333.

makers, of an understanding of the laws of the economy and regulatory functions of the law, including their potential, as well as their limitations. This was confirmed by analyses of the deficient mechanisms used in other socialist countries – USSR, East Germany, Hungary, Yugoslavia and China – commissioned by the authorities.[30] The most important conclusion was that for the creation of new economic law, the mere replacement of private law with a centrally planned system based on orders and distribution would not suffice.

That too was an important topic to the codifiers. The codification was a chance to make partial adaptations to such a model of law, as postulated by some members of the legal circles. They pointed out the connection between the low effectiveness of part of the legal transactions undertaken in the state economy and the limitation of the scope of legal autonomy enjoyed by state-owned enterprises.[31]

Besides scholarly works, the ideological and axiological foundations of the norms on which the Commission was working may have also been influenced by the outlooks and analyses originating from hundreds of other lawyers and jurists. That was made possible also by the specific organization of the works of the Codification Commission providing for extensive public consultations. The legal circles also acted on their own initiative. The Polish Lawyers' Association debated in 1959 on the state of some private rights and the rule of law in the actions of the administration.[32] In cities and towns, numerous legal practitioners and scholars participated in meetings discussing the codification, during which they were given the opportunity to comment on the press articles on the subject[33] and fill in questionnaires designed by the Codification Commission.

The drafts referred to public consultations did not come with explanatory memoranda. That was a deliberate move in order to gather information, starting from opinions on the various solutions, through feedback on the redaction (whether the text is understandable) to information on the legal culture (de-

30 Input presented in a meeting of the Politburo of the Central Committee of the PZPR on 20 March 1957, AAN BP KC PZPR, 2831, 6–14 and 28–198.

31 Among others Stefan BUCZKOWSKI: *O właściwą rolę prawa cywilnego w gospodarce uspołecznionej* [For the proper role of civil law in the socialized economy], PiP 8–9 (1956), 249–262.

32 *Zjazd Krajowy Prawników Polskich* [Polish Lawyers' National Conference], Palestra 7–8 (1959), 146–147.

33 Examples include updates on the Commission's works, published in legal journals; see Aleksander WOLTER: *Wspólny majątek małżonków de lege ferenda* [Matrimonial community property de lege ferenda], PiP 10 (1957), 558–571.

gree of consistency between the legal awareness of the Commission itself and of the lawyers who would be applying the law).[34]

The feedback arriving from lawyers suggested that proposals respectful of the principle of continuity of civil law, Polish legal culture and the modernization current reflective of the social changes occurring at the time were met with acceptance. The assumptions of the ideology of a socialist state were not the dominant in those discussions, although they too were mentioned when values were being invoked in support of the solutions proposed. Information and opinions from public consultations were considered by the Commission. That led to a response in situations in which, for example, the language of the provisions was the subject of divergent or unwarranted interpretations. The weight given to the *vox populi* argument varied. For certain disputed matters, the invocation of social needs was countered by citing the expertise of the Commission members, albeit the latter did not reflect the opinion of the majority of society, as none of the members belonged to the worker or peasant-farmer class.

The thorough education enjoyed by the members was also relevant to the shaping of the proportions between the elements of the respective traditions of each of the two modernization currents.[35] They were well-versed in the contents and the practice of application of the law of the majority of European states. They also had the benefit of experience from previous codification works (Jan Wasilkowski and Kazimierz Przybyłowski) and unification works combined with judicial experience (Jerzy Marowski and Wasilkowski) or the function of President of the Chief Arbitration Committee (Jan Topiński). They were aware of the strong and weak points of the various aspects of codification in different countries, as well as the vulgarization the assumptions of historical materialism had undergone in the USSR. They had witnessed the socio-economic changes of the latter half of the 20th century, which, among other things, rendered obsolete a considerable part of the elements of the doctrine invoked in the constitutional foundations of the socialist state.

34 *Minutes of the session of the Substantive Civil Law Team of the Codification Commission on 7–12 September 1959 discussing the draft Civil Code passed in the first reading. Meeting on 7 September 1959*, AAN, MS 5415, 1.

35 Members of the Commission's team for substantive civil law included: Jerzy Marowski (chair), Witold Czachórski, Wacław Dawidowicz, Jan Gwiazdomorski, Jerzy Mayzel, Kazimierz Przybyłowski, Seweryn Szer, Adam Szpunar, Jan Topiński, Jan Wasilkowski and Aleksander Wolter, of whom Czachórski and Szpunar were late additions to the Committee's membership; Jan WINIARZ: *Sprawozdanie z prac Komisji Kodyfikacyjnej* [Report on the works of the Codification Commission], PiP 3 (1957), 622.

The codifiers were also mindful of the consequences of attempting to draw from doctrinarian views of the law, economy and society. Such had been the basis of the 1954 draft the Civil Code, the defects of which were broadly met with criticism among lawyers and jurists. That event was borne in mind also by those among the codifiers who were in favour of a far-reaching political modification of Polish law (such as Wasilkowski and Szer).

2 Between a Socialist and a Socialist-Nationalist Modernization of the Law

2.1 *'Modernization' of the Modernization Ideology*

The scale and tenor of social protests in 1956 undermined the legitimacy of the hegemonic PZPR, for which the modernization ideology was a tool. Until the time, the party had been invoking the assumptions of historical materialism, whereby change was taking place in the course of class struggle and the current stage was defined by the principles of the dictatorship of the proletariat. The method used in Poland to justify and subsequently maintain this model of governance, despite its inconsistency with the norms of Polish cultural identity, is noteworthy. This problem shows a direct connection to the ideology and axiology of a significant part of the changes visited on private law between 1944 and 1989.

The context here comes from the situation in which Polish society found itself at the conclusion of World War II. Its needs involved both the reconstruction of the economic system and the pursuit of the ideal of justice. In order to present itself as the depositary of both these values, a party unknown to society, the Polish Workers' Party (PPR, predecessor of the PZPR), imported into Poland by the Soviet power, began to highlight the experiences of the war and occupation, allegedly common to itself and the nation.

Simultaneously, however, it brought to the public space a narration – likewise counterfactual – describing and separating the two roles on account of responsibility for the war and its consequences. Out of the two states having occupied Poland during World War II under the Ribbentrop-Molotov Pact,[36] responsibility for the war and occupation was attributed to Germany. The elites of the Second Republic were also depicted as having contributed to

36 While highlighting the fact that is was Germany who initiated the war on 1 September 1939, no mention was made of the Ribbentrop-Molotov Pact whereby the USSR began the occupation of the eastern part of Poland, making it more difficult to defend the country.

the country's situation during and after the war by failing to prepare it for World War II due to creating a weak economic system and an unethical political system.

The USSR was cast in the role of the entity having defeated Germany and delivered justice to it on behalf of all nations wrong and enabled the latter to recover their independence and improve their economic situations through collaboration with the USSR. The abundance, success and morality of the USSR's actions was attributed to its power having emerged from socialist modernization implemented in line with the assumptions of historical materialism, including Marxist legal theory. The value of modernization in capitalist states was far less, as attested by the cases of Germany and Second Polish Republic. The preceding interwar period spanned only twenty-one years (1918–1939). Hence the necessity of a modernization guaranteeing social justice and material strengthening to Polish society to reduce the risk of another German occupation occurring in the future. The modernization in the USSR served as the model.

Such a synthesis of the course of history narrowed the room for development left to the citizens and to the party. Studies conducted by Antoni Dudek into this aspect show it to have served as a constant point of reference for justifications of a pro-Soviet stance 'which was accompanied by the conviction of an increasing threat to Poland from Germany.' The above contributed to the PZPR's rationalizations for its numerous missteps. The persistent refusal to guarantee the ownership of individual farms was regarded as conflicting with the principles of socialism and a betrayal of the 'friendship' with the USSR, where collectivization had been carried out.

Initially, information as to the new nature of the modernization was accompanied by highlighting the role of the agricultural reform[37] as a just solution to a social problem the Second Republic had failed to resolve. It was emphasized that the expropriated land would be used to give ownership to several million peasant farmers. On the same date as the act nationalizing the industry and other goods another act was enacted to allow the creation of private, small enterprises and providing for support for them.[38]

In 1948, the social rallying cry of solidarism was phased out by class struggle calling for accelerated modernization through increased coercion and rejection of the principle of legal continuity. In 1956, in the face of active social

37 Decree of 6 September 1944 on Carrying Out the Agricultural Reform, Dz.U.4.17.

38 Two Acts of 3 January 1946 – on the Nationalization of Core Branches of the National Economy, Dz.U.3.17, and on the Establishment of New Enterprises and Support for Private Initiative in Industry and Commerce, Dz.U.3.18.

resistance, in order to maintain political control and strengthen its legitimacy, the PZPR expanded the description of modernization by incorporating elements of national identity and respect for legal tradition. Simultaneously, the one party once again positioned itself as the sole interpreter of new social attitudes, as well as terms such as 'nation' and 'modernization'. The PZPR would take similar actions on several other occasions (1971, 1980 and 1989), at each time following protests from citizens against the goals and methods of the political power of the time.[39] The same arguments and counters were cited, though with the gradual addition of new 'constituent elements of Polish historical tradition'[40] which was at once intended to supply proof for the effectiveness of the ruling party, which modernized even its own assumptions.

Emphasizing that change consistent with the assumptions of historical materialism remained the goal of the socialist state, in 1956 the declaration was made that the party would follow calls to eliminate 'errors and distortions' committed during the implementation of socialist reforms. By distorting and downplaying the social and political dimension of the protests, the leadership of the PZPR acted to sustain the myth of infallibility of the assumptions of Marxist-Leninist doctrine. After an 'episode' of defective interpretation of the theory of class struggle, the party was returning to the 'healthy roots' of Leninism.

At the same time, the PZPR's new leader levied the charge of revisionism collectively against all other needs and proposals submitted during the period. He reduced it to the spreading of confusion among the citizenry through the propagation of bourgeois theories such as the theory of integral democracy. The latter was incompatible with the principles of the socialist system and not to be the subject of any analyses. In circumstances of lacking class uniformity in Polish society, there were extant sources of conflict linked to the remnants of the capitalist socio-economic formation (private ownership by farmers and

39 Marcin ZAREMBA: *Komunizm, legitymizacja, nacjonalizm. Nacjonalistyczna legitymizacja władzy komunistycznej w Polsce.* Wydawnictwo PAN, Warsaw, 2001; Jacek TARKOWSKI: *Sprawność gospodarcza jako substytut legitymizacji władzy w Polsce powojennej* [Economic efficiency as a substitute for the legitimization of power in postwar Poland], in Jacek TARKOWSKI: *Socjologia świata polityki* [Sociology of the world of politics], vol. 1: *Władza i społeczeństwo w systemie autorytarnym* [Power and society in the authoritarian system], Instytut Nauk Politycznych PAN, Warsaw, 1994, 67–84.

40 Antoni DUDEK: *Wybrane czynniki historyczne wpływające na politykę władz PRL* [Selected historical factors affecting the policy of the authorities of Polish People's Republic], in Paweł SKIBIŃSKI, Tomasz WIŚCICKI (eds): *Polityka czy propaganda PRL wobec historii* [Polish People's Republic politics or propaganda with regard to history], Muzeum Historii Polski, Warsaw, 2009, 35–36.

craftspeople).[41] Hence, the model of democracy could only possibly be a socialist one, to be replaced only in the future communist society.[42]

This type of axiological depreciation and ideological stigmatization[43] significantly narrowed the opportunities for holding a public debate on the methods and means of modernization. That happened even though the targets of the accusations of revisionism provided reassurances of their intentions: 'we are not fighting against Marxism but against its ossification and dogmatism,' 'criticism does not mean disputing the principles.'[44] The paradox was that the accusation was being levied in 1957 by an ideologue having himself in 1948 faced he charge of 'rightist-nationalist deviation'.

Tolerated by the authorities, the new political element referred to one of the characteristics of modernization. It was proclaimed that, in socialist law, there was room also for the 'progressive' elements of legal tradition and national consciousness. The socialist system would be combining them with the class awareness that is setting the direction of change. The remaining two components enhance the potential of the shared vision of the future.[45] Simultaneously, the warning came that propagation applied only to certain elements. The criterion for the selection was to be the contribution made to social development. The justification for that came from the purpose of the change, which continued to be the formation of a new socialist culture out of the 'progressive' national and internationalist elements.

The arbitrary fragmentation of the values of the national culture, including legal tradition,[46] was presented as being justified methodologically but also

41 Jerzy J. WIATR: *Przyczynek do zagadnienia rozwoju społecznego w formacji socjalistycznej* [A contribution to the topic of social development in socialist formation], Książka i Wiedza, Warsaw, 1979, 198.

42 Stanisław KOZYR-KOWALSKI, Jarosław ŁADOSZ: *Dialektyka a społeczeństwo: wstęp do materializmu historycznego* [Dialectics and society: an introduction to historical materialism], PWN, Warsaw, 1979, 320 and 246–247.

43 There is no need to prove that the enemy is wrong, but he must be destroyed. See Richard PIPES: *Komunizm*, Świat Książki, Warsaw, 2008, 21 [in English: Communism: the Vanished Specter, OUP, 1994].

44 Journalists' statements for the Central Party Control Committee, AAN, BP KC PZPR 2831, 101, 102, 105 and 115–116.

45 See Jerzy TOPOLSKI: *Tradycje i ich upowszechnienie* [Traditions and their propagation], Nowe Drogi 1 (1977), 111–112.

46 Legal tradition – 'set of deeply rooted, historically conditioned general outlooks on the origin, essence and function of the law, views on its relationship to politics, economics and the entire organization of social life, convictions as to the proper course of legislation, application, refinement and teaching of the law;' Roman TOKARCZYK: *Wstęp* [Introduction], in Roman TOKARCZYK (ed.): *Tradycja i postęp w prawie* [Tradition and progress in law], Wydawnictwo Lubelskie, Lublin, 1983, 11.

axiologically due to reinforcing the foundation of the power wielded by Polish workers and farmers in the national identity. In contradistinction to the elites of the preceding political formations, the PZPR was giving the voice back to those having made the greatest contribution to the nation's culture, including its history. In assisting to decode the constituent elements of the notions of the 'nation' 'culture' and 'tradition', the socialist modernization was also modernizing the development of the national elements. Hence the necessity to: 'distil and propagate the plebeian current in our history, emphasizing that only in the circumstances of socialism did the peasant farmers and the workers' class become fully enfranchised co-authors of the national culture and the main force of the Polish state.'[47]

The correct verification of the 'progressive' criterion was to be ensured by the 'perspective of the progressive class'.[48] The development realized by the socialist state thus far had already satisfied many of the needs of the workers' class and peasant farmers, so there was no need for the utility of the various elements of tradition to be judged solely by the principles of the dictatorship of the proletariat. The next stage of modernization was to proceed gradually, by 'building socialism'.

There was, therefore, no need to concentrate on a forced break with tradition, even though the latter contained elements such as the family,[49] the peasant farmstead, religiosity and strong position of the Catholic Church, although the latter stripped of its wealth.[50] One of the elements of the previous tradition was also the attitude taken by the intelligentsia in narrowing its conception of modernization to the Latin civilization circle. 'In such circumstances, social modernization is not an easy process,' as one of the of PZPR's leading ideologues, Jakub Berman, summarized; he was, however, of the belief that:

47 Cited after Bartłomiej NOSZCZAK: *Sacrum czy profanum? Spór o istotę obchodów Milenium Polskiego (1949–1966)* [The sacrum or the profanum? The dispute about the character of the celebrations of the Polish Millennium (1949–1966)], Towarzystwo Naukowe Warszawskie, Warsaw, 2002, 119.

48 See TOPOLSKI: *Tradycje i ich*, 111.

49 See Antonina KŁOSKOWSKA: *Wzory i modele w socjologicznych badaniach rodziny* [Patterns and models in sociological studies on family], Studia Socjologiczne 2 (1962), 52.

50 Piotr FIEDORCZYK: *Unifikacja i kodyfikacja prawa rodzinnego w Polsce Ludowej na tle stosunków Państwa z Kościołem katolickim (1944–1964)* [Unification and codification of family law in people's Poland against the background of the State's relations with the Catholic Church (1944–1964)], in Grzegorz GÓRSKI, Leszek ĆWIKŁA, Marzena LIPSKA (eds): *Cuius regio, eius religio: Zjazd Historyków Państwa i Prawa. Lublin, 20–23 IX 2006 r.* [*Cuius regio, eius religio*: conference of historians of state and law. Lublin, 20–23 September 2006], WKUL, Lublin, 2006, 415–431.

'the sum of our persistent actions will eventually bring results and create a new consciousness in Poles.'[51]

2.2 *The Codification Commission's Autonomy*

Of the theses and arguments entering the public space in 1956–1964, those referring to the modernization of the legal system and especially to the relationship between the modernization and the national character of the legal tradition, reinforced the Codification Commission's focus on what is a key aspect of any codification. The important things were the attitude of the citizens, the two-staged response of the authorities (corrections to certain principles, restricting the scope of such corrections), as well as the different meanings ascribed by society and party leadership to words and collocations such as: 'sovereignty', 'democracy', 'rule of law', 'progress', 'propagation of tradition', 'legal culture', 'socialism', 'socialized property', 'private law' and 'public law'.

For all its limitations, the PZPR's new position on characteristics to be taken by the modernization empowered the Codification Commission to adopt a broader perspective on matters linked to the spheres of ideology and axiology. Thus far, with certain exceptions, the government propaganda regarded tradition as a type of superstition. Now, exclusion was to be replaced with incorporating the 'progressive elements of tradition'. Potentially working in the Codification Commission's favour was an overinterpretation of the new collocation. In a search for confirmation of the thesis of a multi-century struggle fought by the Polish people against exploitation by the ruling classes, the government of the day invoked various events from Polish history, imbuing them with added significance according to need.[52]

At the opening of the activities of the Codification Commission, the announcement was made that its works would also borrow from the heritage of Polish jurisprudence. The inclusion of an element of national identity in the Commission's public presentation sent the message that the scope of its autonomy was being expanded, allowing legal sciences to leave the magical circle to which it had been confined under Stalinism. This is how the change was commented on by the deputy justice minister of the time, Tadeusz Rek:

---

51 Interview with leading ideologue of the PZPR party Jakub Berman, in TORAŃSKA: *Oni*, 417.

52 One of the examples from the seventies is the inclusion of one of the activities of the eminent mediaeval astronomer, Nicolaus Copernicus, among the socially 'progressive' elements. His main contribution to the development of science was the heliocentric theory (1543); however, for the purposes of linking together socialism with Polish national identity, his views on the functioning of the state were invoked.

'Gone are times of blindly following. Our legal thought will treat its own, Polish way to socialism. And this work will be informed by the struggle to rebuild the authority of the law and the respect commanded by the justice system.'[53]

To correct one of the existing directives of modernization was a decision prompted by the government's pragmatic approach. Previous attempts at extensive translation of Marxist doctrinal assumptions in their Soviet interpretation into the country's legal system encountered too many and too strong obstacles, beginning from ones of economic or social nature and ending with theoretical considerations. The selective use of quotations from Karl Marx, Friedrich Engels and Vladimir Lenin was not it itself enough to solve the problems. The ideological and legal goals set before the socialist lawmakers were mutually exclusive. Those in power expected greater material profit from the application of the new law than could be achieved in reliance on the provisions of classic civil law.

To reduce the scale of the problem, in 1956, the PZPR leadership made a correction to the thesis of the status of private property. To solidify the new, more stable legal position of individual farms, different statements were quoted from the publications of Marxist legal theorists and Soviet legal scholars than had previously been the case. On that basis, it was argued that such small acreages as family farms did not after all have a capitalist character.[54] With the small production scale as their distinctive characteristic, they could be allowed to exist within a socialist system. The caveat was, however, made that socialized farming represented a higher form of economic development. Thus, modernization would still envisage the gradual disappearance of even the smallest-scale private property.

The party leadership's doctrinal stance on the principles of functioning of state-owned property, on the other hand, did not change at all. The new regulation of that particular area of civil-law relationships was to become the new symbol of modernization in the system of socialist law.

In such multivarious circumstances the question arose of the factual scope of the ideological and axiological autonomy enjoyed by the Codification Commission. The matter of the Commission's autonomy had initially been highly accentuated in communicating with the public. It was also leverage to build a positive image of Poland abroad.

---

53 *Sprawozdanie z prac Komisji Kodyfikacyjnej*, PiP 3 (1957), 621–622.

54 The theory of Alexander Chayanov and Alexander Chelintsev; see more Jan K. SONDEL: *Granice kapitalizmu na wsi* [The limits of capitalism in the countryside], Przegląd ekonomiczny 11 (1934)/46–53, 92–103.

The invocation of the concept of autonomy in the presentation of the Commission's tasks was by many lawyers and jurists viewed as signalling the possibility of a real reform of civil law. Incoming proposals included those discussed in public in the context of the restoration of the principle of the rule of law. Two utterances from the period are representative of the expectation for the Commission to undertake that particular task. One referred to the terminology the codifiers should use. According to opinion volunteered by Maurycy Grudziński, a justice of the Supreme Court, it was necessary to: 'subject to thorough review a number of, one could think, immutable laws; therefore, there can be no doubt that it will become fitting to take a different look upon more than a few institutions of civil law.'[55]

Adam Podgórecki, by contrast, referenced the public debate on the 'omnipotence' of the administrative authorities taking advantage of executive legislation for such unacceptable practices. To prevent those from happening and at once to guarantee the preservation of the superior position of the codes and protect their potential through the appropriate quality of executive provisions, Podgórecki argued for the Commission to be allowed to enact 'binding guidelines as to the method of drafting and redaction of the instruments of small legislation,' (i.e. delegated legislation), also mentioning the need for the constant monitoring of the legislative technique.[56]

Dealing ambiguously with the problem of the Commission's autonomy was its own most active participant, justice of the Supreme Court and member of the PZPR, Jan Wasilkowski.[57] He emphasized the commencement of the works on the basis of the draft Civil Code of 1954, and in the case of the new codification of family law, he offered assurances that any changes would be narrow in scope because the existing regulation of family law, dating from 1950, was: 'certainly a law of the socialist type. The shortcomings of this code consist mainly in defects of legislative technique, not, in principle, involving the merits of its provisions.' With regard, on the other hand, to proposals of a new approach to the problem of terminology and fundamental institutions,

55 Maurycy Grudziński: *W przededniu kodyfikacji: list to redakcji* [On the eve of codification: a letter to the editors], PiŻ 12 (1956), 7.

56 Adam Podgórecki: *Założenia polityki prawa: metodologia pracy legislacyjnej i kodyfikacyjnej* [Assumptions of legal policy: methodology of the lawmaking and codifying work], Wydawnictwo Prawnicze, Warsaw, 1957, 55.

57 Jan Wasilkowski: *Zakres kodeksu cywilnego (streszczenie referatu wygłoszonego na posiedzeniu Wydziału Cywilnego Komisji Kodyfikacyjnej w dniu 19. XII.1956 r.)* [The scope of the Civil Code of the Polish People's Republic (summary of a speech delivered in the meeting of the Codification Commission's Civil Section on 19 December 1956], Nowe Prawo 2 (1957), 3–8.

Wasilkowski signalled the need for 'the utmost caution',[58] with the following warning: 'any constructs could have been altered with no trouble during the process of unification of the law. Presently, however, that the unified law has sunk in, the matter has become all the more complicated.'[59]

The context of the declarations of the Commission's relative independence began to change with the new legislative initiatives of the PZPR leadership. In parallel to the codification works, provisions were enacted from which one could infer that the 'new opening' in modernization policy was to be of short duration. Without backtracking from the emphasis laid on the community of the socialist state with the socialist nation, the party leadership leveraged a new thesis of the unity of the two categories to divert the attention back to the needs of the state. Private property continued to be nationalized,[60] and the exercise of private rights subjected to new restrictions, including in the inheritance law applicable to farms. Once again the socialization of farms was proclaimed as the ultimate target,[61] to be facilitated no longer by collectivization but by suitable provisions of civil law and their judicial interpretation.[62]

To increase the Commission's malleability to this change, the government confronted it with two dilemmas relating to the tenor of the modernization of the legal system.

The former accompanied the Commission from the onset. Its members were tasked with the responsibility for the reinstatement of the universal

---

58 *Minutes of the session of the Substantive Civil Law Team of the Codification Commission on 7–12 September 1959 discussing the draft Civil Code passed in the first reading. Meeting on 7 September 1959*, AAN, MS 5415, 1, 4–5 and 8.

59 *Ibidem*, 8.

60 Among others, the Act of 12 March 1958, nationalizing the property previously seized by the state in temporary control e.g. for the purpose of protecting it from destruction or damage.

61 Such was the goal formulated in a meeting of the Politburo of the Central Committee of the PZPR on 10 September 1958, AAN, BP KC PZPR, 2831, 138–139; its theses were reaffirmed by Władysław Gomułka on 19 March 1953 in the 3rd Congress of the PZPR; they were also incorporated in the Politburo's secret resolution of 1962; see more Antoni DUDEK, Zdzisław ZBLEWSKI: *Utopia nad Wisłą: historia Peerelu* [A Utopia at the Vistula-side: a history of the Polish People's Republic], PWN, Warsaw, 2012, 164.

62 Retention of the principle of limited development and *de facto* limited existence of peasant farm holdings was notified by circulars from the justice ministry, which were also followed by the courts, all the way up to the Supreme Court; see Supreme Court ruling of 13 June 1958, OSP.1958.12.311, and guidelines from the Supreme Court: I CO 34/59, resolution of 27 February 1960, OSN.1960.31; and III CO 33/62, resolution of 28 September 1963, OSNCP.1964.22. The practice was continued even after the new codification of civil law in 1964.

right to court in civil cases. Towards the end of 1956, representatives of government circles suggested that 'sufficiently socialist' civil code and code of civil procedure were to eliminate the need for resorting to special provisions. One of the characteristic features of such provisions was the exclusion of certain categories of civil-law relationships from the application of the principles of both substantive law and the procedure. The Commission was supposed to change that, by creating a uniform system of law, and therefore also the right conditions for returning the jurisdiction to the courts. Moreover, civil cases were to be heard by courts enjoying guarantees of judicial independence, as proclaimed in 1956 by the new Minister of Justice.[63]

In that manner, the Codification Commission was placed before a choice in which the stake was to be the legal safety of the citizens, some of whose cases had been waiting for access to a court of law since the mid-40s of the 20th century because of the special provisions.

The second dilemma facing the Commission surfaced near the end of the 50s and was linked to the party leadership's decision to return to the concept of marginalization of private law. That was accompanied by a charge of revisionism being levied against some of the proposed reforms. A considerable risk of political intervention undertaken with a view to gearing the Commission's works towards 'more socialist' outcomes became a reality. The consequence would be to squander much of the acquis of jurisprudence, with some of the drafted provisions being supplanted with the language of the existing special provisions because that was the only additional collection of norms available to the Ministry of Justice. Such a situation had already occurred once, in 1948, when the reformers' works were halted amid declarations of fighting the 'rightist-nationalist' deviation.

How the Codification Commission, operating in a landscape of progressing ideological petrification, took advantage of opportunities for the modernization of private law in keeping with Polish legal traditions, is the subject of the next chapter.

---

63 The Minister of Justice, Zofia Wasilkowska, (wife of Jan Wasilkowski, member of the Commission), highlighted the priority importance of the restoration – through legislative amendments – of the statutory safeguards of the independence of judges and uniformity of the judiciary, also promising the eventual fruition, continually deferred in time, of the constitutional principle of judicial nominations by election (not followed in practice under the People's Republic of Poland); *Rozmowa z Ministrem Sprawiedliwości – tow. Z. Wasilkowską* (Conversation with the Minister of Justice, Com. Z. Wasilkowska), AAN, MS 402, 14–19.

3 Civil Code

At the time the Codification Commission began its work, there was belief in the possibility of regulating civil-law relationships in a way that would serve to modernize the law of property and the law of contracts.

The new norms were also intended as a sufficient justification for administrative authorities not engaging in the functional-teleological interpretation of existing civil-law provisions or ignoring them. In its evaluation of the past state of affairs, the Codification Commission summarized such practices as a 'lack of legal culture', which: 'disregarded the law and overestimated the norms of criminal law as a regulator of social and economic life erroneously imagining that the concept of law can be fitted into the categories of expediency.'[64]

The modernization was to consist in the injection of new content into property rights and the introduction of differentiated rules for the exercise of certain rights depending on the categorization of the rights holder. The rationale for the changes, although invoking Marxist slogans, showed that the reformers' main intention was to put a measure of order and refinement in the regulation of the socialized economy[65] and adapt the existing institutions of private law to the socialist system, through suitable modifications. At the particular time, unlike in the Stalinist period, this was to be accomplished on the plane of private law. Previously, when the political powers interfered with many legal relationships through instruments of public law, the effect was harmful to the integrity of the legal system as a whole because of the low quality of such public law.

The Codification Commission's plan was to change the *status quo* by creating a common legal basis – a single code – for all entities, including natural persons and state-owned legal persons, such as the *przedsiębiorstwo państwowe* – literally a 'state enterprise'.[66] In order that political approval could

64 Meeting of the Codification Commission, 17 December 1956, Warsaw; Jerzy BAFIA, Leon CHEŁMICKI, Z. SZELIŃSKI (eds): *Z prac Komisji Kodyfikacyjnej* [From the works of the Codification Commission], BMS 2 (1957), 1–2.

65 Jan TOPIŃSKI: *Zarząd mieniem ogólnonarodowym* [The administration of national property], Książka i Wiedza, Warsaw, 1956, 60. The perceived degree of complexity of this problem was so high that the Codification Commission found it necessary to conduct the works on its regulation separately from its other business; Minutes of the session of the Codification Commission's Substantive Civil Law Team on 30 January 1957, AAN, MS, 5418, 16.

66 Proponents included Aleksander WOLTER: *Czy renesans koncepcji prawa gospodarczego?* [A renaissance of concepts of economic law?], Przegląd Ustawodawstwa Gospo-

be won for such a regulatory model, a certain degree of control over the drafting of legislative provisions was retained for the administrative authorities. This involved permission for some issues to be regulated below the statutory level.[67]

The first draft of the code already envisaged reference to administrative law[68] for civil-law relationships featuring state-owned legal persons on both sides of the transaction.[69] The second draft further expanded on that solution,[70] so as to include consumer transactions with a state-owned or socialized entity as counterparty. Because the economy had already been nationalized on a wide scale, the consequence was that administrative law became applicable to the majority of contracts citizens would enter into, from the purchase and sale of items of everyday use to the lease of residential apartments.

The choice of this method of regulation of legal issues previously governed by private law caused controversy within the Codification Commission,[71] as well as among lawyers and jurists at large. Some proposed to strengthen the status of private law by imposing restrictions on the passage of public law regulating private-law relationships different to the Civil Code. Some legal minds supported the concept of two codes – civil and 'economic' (i.e. business) – to make a clear distinction between the respective regulatory methods.

---

darczego, 3 (1957), 81–85 and Adam Chełmoński: *O znaczeniu zasad ogólnych w normowaniu prawnym gospodarki uspołecznionej* [On the importance of general principles in the legislative regulation of the socialized economy], Przegląd Ustawodawstwa Gospodarczego, 10 (1956), 359–363.

67 With regard to the regulation of the functioning of the socialized economy, such a position was espoused by e.g. Adam Chełmoński and Jan Wasilkowski; see Tomasz Dolata: *Adam Chełmoński (1880–1956) i jego udział w pracach Zespołu Prawa Cywilnego Materialnego Komisji Kodyfikacyjnej PRL* [Adam Chełmoński (1880–1956) and his participation in the works of the Substantive Civil Law Team of the Codification Commission of the Polish People's Republic], WUWr, Wrocław, 2023, 60.

68 Adherents included Wasilkowski and Chełmoński; Minutes of the session of the Codification Commission's Substantive Civil Law Team on 30 January 1957, AAN, MS, 5418, 16.

69 The original wording of Articles 1(2) and 342 of the draft bill; *Projekt kodeksu cywilnego Polskiej Rzeczypospolitej Ludowej* [Draft Civil Code in the Polish People's Republic], Wydawnictwo Prawnicze, Warsaw, 1960.

70 Articles 1(2) and 366 of the 1962 bill; *Projekt kodeksu cywilnego oraz przepisy wprowadzające* [Draft Civil Code and implementing provisions], Wydawnictwo Prawnicze, Warsaw, 1962; Articles 2 and 384 of the 1964 Civil Code.

71 The controversy surrounding the method of regulation of economic law was discussed when presenting the first and second versions of the draft. *Projekt kodeksu cywilnego,* 1960, 4; *Projekt kodeksu cywilnego,* 1962, 192–193.

In his opposition to these two proposals, Jan Wasilkowski did not resort to any ideological rhetoric.[72] The jurist did not regard the opposition to the introduction in the Code of an opening for the regulation of civil-law relationships by provisions not belonging to the system of private law as an example of *conservatism* and *fear of downgrading* the science of civil law. In his opinion, the source of objections to the hybrid model of regulation of private law came from excessive fears of the potential consequences of such practice, as well as the anticipation of a risk of excessive administrative rationing imposing limitations on the independence of economic actors. However, according to Wasilkowski, when it came to the dispute over the role of business law in the formation of the new principles of civil law, the expected benefits of the reform would outweigh the consequences of hypothetical errors. Hence the opinion that 'the view of the innovators seem[ed] to be closer to the truth.'[73] The argument the jurist regarded as having already settled the issue was the need for a new model of the law of obligations, made evident when the old law saw its application to the socialist economy.

Some of the Commission's members concurring with Wasilkowski decided that the classic law of obligations could in fact be modified to reflect the socialist theory of ownership. Those jurists marginalized the problem presented by the contradiction between the existence of a system of central planning on the one hand and the principle of equality of the subjects that was the cornerstone of private law on the other hand. They argued that both spheres would retain a common basis in the institution of contract. The contemplated modification would consist in the introduction of some contract types belonging to the structure of central planning.[74] The above was touted as an example of the innovative quality of socialist law, with intensive development of toolsets for co-operation and consolidation. That argument, however, failed to address a number of important concerns. The terms of contracts featuring state-owned entities on at least one side were dictated by administrative bodies, and the

72 Wasilkowski would sometimes resort to such arguments in the Commission's works on other problems. One example is his polemical dispute with Chełmoński. Chełmoński proposed the introduction of a defence of defective (vitiated) possession (*exeptio vitiosae possessionis*) in the code. Wasilkowski, on the contrary, cited that institution's pedigree going back to Roman law and early forms of capitalism as proof of its anachronicity and incompatibility with the needs of a socialist legal system; Minutes of the session of the Codification Commission's Substantive Civil Law Team on 9 September 1957, AAN, MS, 5418, 326.

73 Jan WASILKOWSKI: *Kodeks cywilny PRL a zagadnienia prawa gospodarczego* [The Civil Code of Polish People's Republic and problems of economic law], PiP, 3 (1962), 426.

74 *Projekt kodeksu cywilnego*, 1962, 191.

value of the obligations was determined by official price lists. State-owned entities did not have any independent right or power to refuse to enter into such a contract, and disputes arising from such contracts were resolved by quasi-judicial bodies[75] often dependent on the administration.

The drafts did not contain a safeguard against a situation in which the various administrative norms found outside the Civil Code but allowed by it to continue to exist would be moved from the sidelines as a set of mere subsidiary rules to the legislative foreground. This was a matter not only of the number of such provisions in existence, but above all their contents. The Code permitted administrative legislation to provide supplementary or even modified regulation of real law (i.e. the law of things; roughly property law) and the law of obligations, but did so without defining the terms on which that was to be done. It contented itself with imposing the obligation on socialist entities to perform their contractual obligations in line with the economic plans and refrain from exposing the national economy to loss.[76]

The lack of imperative force in the norms of the Civil Code respecting legal relationships with state-owned and social entities was confirmed by the Commission itself. During the presentation of the 1962 draft, it was noted that the new norms regulating this issue were merely guidelines espousing 'significant caution' in the formulation of rights and obligations. The explanation provided for this was that the Commission had encountered difficulties narrowing down the new economic needs for which the Code was intended to provide the legal basis.[77] Simultaneously, assurances were given that such was the natural course of things in a period of dynamic transition and transformation of the economy. By contrast, the propagandist claim of unity of socialist civil law asserted that the socialist lawmakers had accomplished the task of introducing to the legal system – through the Civil Code – a comprehensive and cohesive set of norms predominated by the new provisions governing the socialist economy.

In the opinion of a majority of the Commission's members, the innovative construct of property ownership became an instrument ensuring the integrity of a system of private law shaped also by numerous provisions of administrative law. At the same time, the change was intended as a stimulus for the

75 Article 397 of the 1964 Civil Code. The title of the subchapter regulating this group of legal transactions was: 'Mandatory contract formation between socialized economic units'.

76 Art. 386 of the Civil Code of 1964.

77 *Projekt kodeksu cywilnego*, 1962, 193.

modernization of other *in rem* rights, themselves being derivatives of ownership as the strongest of property rights.

The main change in private law was departure from the uniform concept of ownership.[78] The Commission shared the view that the existing structure did not take into account the subjective and objective differences pertaining to the exercise of this right, which had always existed. According to Jerzy Ignatowicz 'the formal concept of property mask[ed] its real class content' and ignored its social function.[79] Hence, a substantive definition distinguishing several types and kinds of ownership had to be introduced. The criteria for the distinction were the subjective characteristics of the owner on the one hand and the functions served by the items owned on the other hand.

The second change involved the definition of property rights. This was modified to include limits on the exercise of ownership, defined by statutes and two general clauses: the principles of social co-existence and the socio-economic purpose of the law.[80] This solution was presented as a departure 'to some extent', from the existing rules.[81] However, a more precise formulation of the concept was not offered. It was difficult to obtain this knowledge from the Commission member charged with the drafting of real law. According to Wasilkowski, the code only signalled some characteristics of the ownership property, since the latter always functioned within specific social relationships, which determined 'the form of appropriation of material objects.'[82] The use of language characteristic of Marxist-Leninist doctrine served to provide camouflage for some of the risks presented by retaining traditional principles of real law in the reformulated construct of ownership. This is because instead of the expected modernization, the realistic prospect was that the Code would achieve the formalization of the bureaucracy's power held over the vast resources of state-owned and, indirectly, private property.

Such was the consequence of the introduction of several solutions that the Codification Commission had been persuaded to adopt by ideological and subject-matter arguments. One of the new norms was the definition of ownership. Among the other consequences of this introduction, the new definition

78 The repealed Article 26 of Real Law reads: 'The owner may, within the limits set by the laws, use the thing to the exclusion of others and dispose of the thing.'

79 Jerzy IGNATOWICZ: *Prawo rzeczowe* [Real law], Warsaw, PWN, 1986, 42.

80 LITYŃSKI: *O prawie i sądach*, 248–268.

81 Jan WINIARZ (ed.): *Z prac Zespołu Prawa Cywilnego Materialnego Komisji Kodyfikacyjnej* [From the works of the Codification Commission's Substantive Civil Law Team], BMS, 4 (1958), 31–32.

82 Jan WASILKOWSKI: *Pojęcie własności we współczesnym prawie polskim* [The concept of property in current Polish law], Książka i Wiedza, Warsaw, 1972, 45.

enabled the marginalization of the rights of private owners through the imposition of boundless restrictions and obligations. The grounds for needing one more such new norm were expounded by reference to the special needs of a socialist economy. Namely, a provision enabling the arbitrary limitation of the legal capacity of state-owned and socialized entities, including legal persons, argued to constitute an innovation in the form of 'special' legal capacity. In reality, that was merely handicapped legal capacity stripping away the independence of entities such as state-owned enterprises, which were the most important type of entity in the socialist economy and with were thus distanced from ownership and other economic rights.

The Codification Commission appreciated the problem of the mounting effects of the new definition of ownership, handicapped legal capacity, and ability to delegate the powers to shape the terms of exercise of social ownership from the Code level to the level of administrative legislation.

At start, Aleksander Wolter believed in the possibility of normalization of civil-law relationships involving state-owned enterprises acting as legal entities.[83] Later, his initial concept was abandoned and the concept of 'incomplete' legal capacity was introduced, also without specifying its nature.[84] Some of the members of the Codification Commission, however, saw themselves persuaded by the argument that the optimal functioning of the socialist economy hinged on the availability of legal norms permitting the flexible management of the terms and formation of legal relationships. In the opinions of those jurists, the internal consistency of the new model of regulation of property was guaranteed by its ideological underpinnings. Jan Wasilkowski argued that the loophole created by the vagueness of the legal position of enterprises in civil-law relationships due to this omission was deliberate, given that enterprises could hold ownership title to state property. However 'the lack of regulation [was] apparent due to the principle of unity of na-

83 Minutes of the session of the Codification Commission's Substantive Civil Law Team on 28 March 1957, AAN, MS, 5418, 71. Original Article 37 of the draft: WINIARZ: *Z prac Zespołu*, 31.

84 A majority of the members of the Codification Commission supported the general principle expounded by Aleksander Wolter. On the other hand, they voiced certain reservations as to the detailed wording of the corresponding provision in the draft. In their opinion, it failed to account for the diverse spectrum of legal forms of organization and failed to enable the limitation of certain rights and obligations; Minutes of the session of the Codification Commission's Substantive Civil Law Team on 28 March 1957, AAN, MS, 5418, 71–89. The quest for a solution capable of accommodating political and administrative practice brought the opposite result to the intended – the terms *legal capacity* and *legal person* became distorted.

tional (state) property introduced into the Code. Socialist national (state) property shall vest indivisibly in the state.'[85] According to Wasilkowski, this accomplished the effective merger of two values – that of modernization, linked to the principle of economic planning, and that of socialist democracy. Under the principle of 'democratic centralism', the state consolidated the rights in its hand because it was acting on behalf of the public, which was entitled to all rights, including property rights.[86]

The above systemic assumption was so incomprehensible as to be beyond comprehensible interpretation and capacity for regulation. The Code accordingly contented itself with including referrals to other legislation. Doing so opened the way to the administrative normalization of the exercise of *in rem* rights and fulfilment of obligations by socialized economic units[87] in a manner the severed this principle from its links to private law.

The principle of protection of socialized property, which was incorporated into the draft, played a similar role. It was similarly vague but was presented as an example of progressive legal development, including the theory of the principles of *ex delicto* and *ex contractu* liability in a socialized economy. Meanwhile, judges gained knowledge of the new standard of civil liability through conversations with prosecutors.[88]

The Code was supposed to define new principles of real law, but it was also intended to establish the separate regulation of civil relationships of economic nature. Some of the contents of that part of the Code were intended as departure from the 'Romanist categories' of law,[89] and the knowledge of additional

85 Antolij W. WIENIEDIKTOW: *Państwowa własność socjalistyczna* [Socialist state property], Wydawnictwo Prawnicze, Warsaw, 1952.

86 Jan Wasilkowski described the principle of central planning as the 'main lever' for the performance of both economic and political tasks by states; see Jan WASILKOWSKI: *Metoda opracowania i założenia kodeksu cywilnego* [The drafting method and assumptions of the Civil Code], PiP 5–6 (1964), 741.

87 See Ryszard MALINOWSKI: *Węzłowe problemy prawa administracyjnego w zarządzaniu gospodarką narodową* [Seminal problems of administrative law in the management of the national economy], PWN, Warsaw, 1975, 43.

88 See Wacław MARKOWSKI: *Z zagadnień cywilnoprawnej ochrony własności społecznej* [From topics in the civil-law protection of socialized property], BMS 7–8 (1959), 31–36.

89 WINIARZ: *Z prac Zespołu Prawa Cywilnego*, 30. During the presentation of certain other draft provisions, their Roman pedigree was sometimes invoked. Any reaction to that only came when a different member was opposed to the particular proposal, on the stated grounds of its economic anachronism. An example can be found in Wasilkowski's polemic against the argument offered by Jerzy Marowski concerning some of the terms of enjoyment of possession; Minutes of the session of the Codification Commission's Substantive Civil Law Team on 9 September 1957, AAN, MS 5418, 326.

specialists working for the Commission was to be of assistance in this regard. The only type of legislation available to the Commission was special legislation.[90] At the same time, as Jan Wasilkowski acknowledged: 'The most debatable problem of economic law is the question of what is to constitute the subject matter of this branch of law.'[91]

In presenting their draft, the Commission members claimed to have fulfilled their original pledge to develop norms for a new economic law. The proof was to be found in the several rules governing the exercise and protection of socialized property, as well as a number of general clauses relating to property rights and to the formation of contracts between socialized economic units. The aforementioned principles, and more than a dozen Code provisions, were described as a mechanism for maintaining the principle of uniformity of civil law. Therefore, the members of the Commission argued, the Civil Code was placed in an overriding position within the legal system, thereby removing the need for a separate code of economic law – a solution used in other socialist countries such as Czechoslovakia and East Germany.[92]

On the other hand, the argument invoked to justify the Code's references in matters of economic circulation to provisions located outside of the Code was that in a modernized economy, the principle of completeness of the Code could not be observed. The overarching scope of the regulatory frameworks found outside the Code and their conlicts with provisions of the Code was not a topic of discussion. In 1964, to replace the situation in fact in which state-owned enterprises operated with the situation in law, declared in 1957, was forgotten.[93] Administrative bodies were given the independent power to issue regulations. The officialdom availed itself of that power on a large scale, squandering the potential of the codification and its capacity for stimulating economic modernization.

Opinions among Polish scholars on the latter issue were divided. Some lawyers who evaluated the merits of the Code from the point of view of its impact on the operation of socialized economic units argued that it helped to preserve some of the standards of classical law, as some of the provisions of the Code resorted to the use of state-operated arbitration boards to resolve

---

90 Winiarz: *Z prac Zespołu Prawa Cywilnego*, 31–32.

91 Wasilkowski: *Kodeks cywilny*, 431.

92 In that matter, the Codification Commission drew also from the example of those socialist states following a similar regulatory model to the Polish one, combining in a single legislative instrument the regulation of legal transactions involving natural persons and state-owned persons, as well as social entities, e.g. the 1961 Principles of civil legislation of the USSR and the 1959 Civil Code of Hungary; *Projekt kodeksu cywilnego*, 1962, 192.

93 Winiarz: *Z prac Zespołu Prawa Cywilnego*, 30.

business disputes.[94] However, a detailed analysis of this issue reveals that the selective and irregular application of the Code for legal transactions involving state-owned enterprises did not change the fact that many of those transactions were regulated in a manner contrary not only to the Code and to classical principles of law but even to common sense.[95]

The brunt of the Codification Commission's activities concentrated on the regulation of civil-law relationships involving individuals and non-socialized legal entities (the number of such entities in actual existence was negligible). Unable to create a large body of new norms governing tangible property, the Codification Commission focused on the protection of personal property, on tort liability,[96] and on the form of legal transactions. The consensus in the Commission regarding the aforementioned groups of legal relationships was that there was a need to improve their legal security. Some members favoured pursuing that goal through the incorporation of the provisions of the 1956 Act on the Liability of the State for Damages Inflicted by State Officials, introduced in response to social protests, into the Code. Towards the end of the 1950s, that became a matter of primary importance, concerning that strong authoritarian tendencies were resurfacing in the political system. When the proposal was tabled in 1959, the explanatory memorandum made various references to legal theory. Adam Chełmoński argued: 'civilists ought to aspire for important problems of civil law to be regulated by the civil code.'[97] Initially, he was met with a counterargument emphasizing the priority of achieving the Code's coming into force as soon as possible, posing a conclusive bar to the expansion of the originally planned scope of codification.[98] Ultimately, however, the Code did come to include some provisions addressing the liability of state officials.

In some cases, the Commission refrained from introducing new legal constructs and contented itself with modernizing the existing solutions, which had been developed during the interwar period or the unification efforts im-

---

94 Such a view was presented, for instance, by Józef SKĄPSKI: *Kodeks cywilny z 1964 r. Blaski i cienie kodyfikacji i jej perspektywy* [The Civil Code of 1964. The high and low points of the codification and its prospects], KPP 1 (1992), 75.

95 MACHNIKOWSKA: *Prawo własności*, 580–590.

96 For the Commission's work on this issue, see Alfred OHANOWICZ: *Odpowiedzialność za czyny niedozwolne w projekcie kodeksu cywilnego PRL* [Tort liability in the draft Civil Code of the Polish People's Republic], Ruch Prawniczy i Ekonomiczny 4 (1960), 53ff; Stanisław GARLICKI: *Przepisy o czynach niedozwolonych w projekcie kodeksu cywilnego* [Tort provisions in the draft Civil Code], Nowe Prawo 5 (1960), 656ff.

97 Minutes of the session of the Codification Commission's Substantive Civil Law Team on 17 February 1957, AAN, MS, 5411, 123.

98 *Ibidem*, 124–127.

FIGURE 4.1 Adam Chełmoński, 1890–1959. Member of the Codification Commission during the interwar period (head of Commercial Law Section and co-editor of the draft Commercial Code); academically linked to Vilnius. Lawyer (advocate), during the 30s Dean of the Bar Council in Warsaw and editor-in-chief of the *Palestra* bar journal. After the war, Head of Department of Civil Law of the University of Wrocław. Again involved in codification works in 1957.
SOURCE: PRIVATE COLLECTION OF THE CHEŁMOŃSKI FAMILY

mediately following the end of World War II. The decision was made when it became clear that a more ambitious programme of change would open the path to diverging interpretations, after which jurisprudence and scholarship would take several years to stabilize. Aleksander Wolter and Jan Wasilkowski explained that the Commission's method of moderate innovation made it possible for the development of the law to leverage the existing body of jurisprudence and judicature.[99] One example is the reasons the Commission gave for retaining the structure of tort liability from the 1933 Code of Obligations.

A difference of opinion as to the scale of innovation arose in no more than a dozen cases. One was the absolute requirement of the form of a notarial deed for the validity of conveyance of real estate, which ended up being introduced to the Code. Jerzy Marowski was unsuccessful in persuading the Commission of the fictitious nature of this provision with regard to transfers of farming land.[100] Farmers often failed to give formal notification of such transactions

99 WASILKOWSKI, WOLTER: *Wyniki dyskusji*, 3.

100 Minutes of the session of the Codification Commission's Substantive Civil Law Team on 25 May 1957 – away session in Osieczna, AAN, MS 5418, 225–232.

to a notary public because giving it entailed the risk of administrative confiscation of their property. Some farmers who had failed to formalize the acquisition of title to their land were given protection by the courts.[101] By proposing that this type of transaction should require simple written form, Marowski tried to avoid discrepancy between fact and law. Accommodating the existing practice, the first draft stipulated the qualified form of notarial deed, while also allowing written form in the implementation of a prior contract.[102] However, the majority of Commission members took the position that priority should be given to modernization goals, including the neat and orderly regulation of legal affairs in the country. The future sided with Marowski – oppressive agricultural policies frustrated some of the Commission's ambitions.

An example of divergent positions taken on the form of deeds transferring title to real estate can be found in the proposal, rejected by the Commission, to lift the prohibition on including a condition or stipulation of a time period in a contract transferring ownership of real estate. The argument was the resulting *pendente conditione* of the two owners. Also disputed was Jan Gwiazdomorski's view of the need for a form that would unambiguously communicate the transfer of the right, i.e. a contract covering the *causa* (cause of the transfer) and the *tradition* (delivery). The majority of the members considered such an expansion of the form to be unnecessary, on the grounds of the benefits of using legal constructs that are as simple as possible. Among those emphasizing this was Adam Szpunar, citing the French method and solutions[103] contributing favourably to the social acceptability of the law.

This value was invoked by the Commission in response to be public debate unfolding in 1960 on the draft Code. Initially, the General Part did not include the previous interpretative canon guiding the application of the provisions in the Code or a provision regulating the burden of proof, both deemed unnecessary. The provision on the abuse of individual rights was also eliminated. It was explained that the frequency of its invocation was prone to becoming a source of legal uncertainty. On the other hand, the lack of a formal basis for arguing the abuse of a right, according to the Codification Commission, would

101 Jan WINIARZ (ed.): *Z dyskusji w Zespole Prawa Cywilnego Komisji Kodyfikacyjnej nad prawem rzeczowym* [From the debate held in the Codification Commission's Civil Law Team on real law], BMS 5 (1958), 19–20.

102 Article 156 of the first draft; the second draft, of 1961, did nevertheless incorporate the absolute requirement of notarial form for the effectiveness of a transfer of title to real property – Article 157, see *Projekt kodeksu cywilnego,* 1960; *Projekt kodeksu cywilnego,* 1962.

103 WINIARZ: *Z dyskusji w Zespole*, 19.

motivate the courts to allow only exceptional resource to it.[104] The legal practitioners taking part in the public consultation disagreed, and all three institutions were as a result restored to the code. The above was a consequence of the Commission's previous announcement – while submitting the first draft for public evaluation – of its intention to compare its own position with the experience of the multitude of lawyers practicing throughout the country, with the formal correctness of the provisions not to be the sole criterion for reaching the final decision on the eventual contents of the Code.[105]

The Code's regulation of natural persons (individuals) drew heavily upon the norms of earlier legislation, including the 1933 Code of Obligations and the 1934 Commercial Code. The Commission's original output was everal additional elements of principles governing the implementation of contracts. However, simultaneously, a norm was added to allow contractual terms to be regulated by legislative provisions found outside the Code.[106] The latter was to achieve the submission of not only transactions involving business parties but also those involving consumers (standard-form contracts) subject to administrative law. Witold Czachórski's claims emphasizing the 'fundamental' nature of norms in the Code in relation to the entire system of law in the presentation of the draft[107] were not confirmed in commercial transaction practice.

However, some members of the Commission made efforts to retain the principle of freedom of contract, along with the innovative – compared to the BGB and ABGB[108] – addition of the *rebus sic stantibus* clause by the 1933 Code of Obligations, addressing the change of circumstances occurring after the conclusion of the contract.[109] Both were ignored on the alleged basis that they would be inapplicable in Poland's realities. The principle of *pacta sunt servanda* was invoked, along with the principle of central planning, to argue for the need of exacting enforcement of obligations. Contrary to ideological dogma, socialist economics still had need of classic institutions of the legal system. Things being so, scholars tried to achieve the partial reconstruction

104 Wasilkowski, Wolter: *Wyniki dyskusji*, 3.

105 *Projekt kodeksu cywilnego*, 1960, 3–6.

106 Article 385 of the Civil Code.

107 Czachórski, *Prawo zobowiązań*, 30.

108 For more on the original structure of these provisions, Kazimierz Danek: *Wpływ zmiany stosunków na zobowiązania umowne według Kodeksu zobowiązań na tle kodeksu cywilnego niemieckiego i austriackiego* [Farmers' views on the goals and consequences of the regulation of farm ownership: in the light of the Act of 26 October 1971], RPEiS 1 (1937), 14–29.

109 Skąpski: *Kodeks cywilny*, 75.

FIGURE 4.2 Witold Czachórski, 1915–1995. Lecturer of the University of Warsaw, involved in the unification works of 1948, subsequently in the Codification Commission operating from 1956. In 1986, President of the Civil Law Reform Commission. From 1971, member and later president of the Committee of Legal Sciences of Polish Academy of Sciences.
SOURCE: POLISH ACADEMY OF SCIENCES, ARCHIVES IN WARSAW, ZF XXI-235-001

of the *rebus sic stantibus* clause on the basis of the other provisions of the Code.[110] Equally, the members of the Codification Commission were not of one mind as to the form of regulation of the parties' freedom to shape the contents of their contracts. Some jurists, including Aleksander Wolter and Kazimierz Przybyłowski, declared themselves in favour of explicit proclamation of this freedom for all cases in which a Code provision did not stipulate its own mandatory application. Certain other codifiers argued that a general provision specifying the grounds of nullity of a legal transaction applicable to all legal relationships would suffice. Another argument followed from anticipated change in the status of certain norms (from imperative to semi-imperative or vice versa) on account of the rapid rate of the economic transformation.[111]

110 Including Józef SKĄPSKI: *Wpływ zmian stosunków na zobowiązania – klauzula rebus sic stantibus* [The impact of change in circumstances on obligations – the *rebus sic stantibus* clause], in Zbigniew RADWAŃSKI (ed.): *Studia z prawa zobowiązań*, PWN, Warsaw-Poznań, 1979, 305.

111 DOLATA: *Adam Chełmoński*, 87.

The reliance on classical principles of private law for the regulation of legal relationships between individuals (with the exception of farming land) and the references to non-Code provisions for the regulation of legal relationships involving socialized economic units bore fruit in the Codification Commission's design of a legal instrument in which most of the provisions still had their origins in Polish, and therefore European, legal tradition. In an attempt to disguise this fact, the chairman of the Codification Commission delivered a presentation of the Code from the perspective of the general clauses it contained. The goal was to convince the political decision-makers that the establishment of socialist private law was being achieved in Poland. One clause was assigned several roles, including that of a universal interpretative rule adapting every provision of the Code to the new regime, as well as that of a catalyst of social and economic development. Spinning the myth of socialist progress, Wasilkowski proclaimed:

> The nature of the principles of community life will undergo changes as socialist social relations develop and as changes occur in the consciousness of citizens that the development of these relations entails (...) the provisions of the Code will have the flexibility necessary due to the rapid transformation of our national economy. This close connection between the provisions in the Code and the social consciousness that is forming, at an increasingly high level, should be reckoned among the assumptions that will enable the Civil Code to play an active role as one of the factors in the construction of socialism in our country.[112]

The draft also incorporated a large part of the provisions of the 1946 Law of Succession.[113] An exception was made for farm inheritance, to which the authorities paid the most attention. The proposal additionally referred to the provisions of a special statute. This increased the number of types of restrictions on the exercise of the law governing private farms, as it was claimed that this would help modernize the agricultural economy.[114] However, the consequences of this change did not align with the political predictions.

---

112 Wasilkowski: *Metoda opracowania*, 741.

113 For more see Moszyńska: *Geneza prawa spadkowego*, 599–609.

114 More see Machnikowska: *Prawo własności*, 486–504.

As a result, from 1964 onward, the law of succession began to function with two different ideologies at its base.[115] The rules of inheritance were distinguished according to the type of estate, the range of grounds for disinheriting an heir was expanded, and so were escheats. Part of the law, prepared by the Codification Commission, drew upon classic institutions of the law of inheritance. Those included the circle of statutory heirs, freedom of testation, rules for the protection of statutory heirs, and liability for the debts of the estate. The source was a synthesis of the original body of Polish legal thought developed for the purposes and time periods of unification (1945–1946) and codification (1956–1961), and comparative analysis of more than a dozen legal systems, including non-European ones.[116] Such extensive research followed by the implementation of its findings distinguished the Polish legal system within Europe. Among the Polish projects of the time, there were some that came into effect only at the turn of the twentieth century, confirming their original modern potential.[117] Soviet law was also of interest to codifiers, but in contrast with the propaganda, only institutions that were also in use in Western European countries were included in the analysis; the law of succession in the USSR in the second half of the 20th century was not as avant-garde as the propaganda was wont to claim.

The remainder of the new law of succession was composed by provisions incorporated into the Code at the final stage of the legislative process and derived from the 1963 extra-code statute. They established far-reaching state interference in the inheritance of farms. Consequently, a very narrow group of qualified legal heirs, combined with the right of the Treasury to seize the inheritance in the absence of such heirs, was added to the classic rules. Moreover, the protection of the property rights of those who did not receive a share

115 See Józef Stanisław Piątowski (ed.): vol. 4: *Prawo spadkowe* [Inheritance law], in *System prawa cywilnego* [The system of civil law], ZN im. Ossolińskich, Wrocław-Warsaw-Krakow-Gdańsk-Łódź, 1986, 32.

116 For a detailed list of legislation of European and non-European countries analysed in the course of the unification and codification works, see Moszyńska: *Geneza prawa spadkowego*, 316 (fn 102). These included the provisions of the Swiss Code of 1907; the Italian Law of 1916 and 1942, the Portuguese Law of 1910, the Brazilian Code of 1916, the Belgian Law of 1919 and the French Law of 1917, as well as the Dutch Law of 1923, the Swedish Law of 1928, the Spanish Code of 1928, the Mexican Law of 1928, the Colombian Law of 1935, the Romanian Law, and several proposals for the law of succession of the 1930s. discussed in Germany, Italy, Greece and Latvia.

117 Examples include the return in 2003 to the concept of municipal inheritance and the limitation of inheritance by the Treasury to an inheritance whose owner lived abroad, and in 2015 to the concept of limited liability for inheritance debts, with the Act of 20 March 2015, Dz.U.519.2015.

in such inheritance was reduced, while heirs who did inherit a farm were subjected to a more favourable regime of liability for the debts of the estate. Simultaneously, the rules of procedure were transformed; although the proceedings were still conducted in court, they took on a judicial-administrative nature. The purpose of this was to the heighten the scrutiny of the strict criteria qualifying the heirs to inherit a farm. The public judged those criteria to be oppressive, entailing a high risk of *de facto* expropriation. Therefore, most village dwellers chose not to pursue inheritance proceedings and enjoyed the inheritance without ownership title.[118]

This dual model of succession law created an atypical state of legal affairs compared to the legislation of other socialist countries. There were three peculiarities. Firstly, the institutions of the law of succession commonly used in Western European countries continued to operate in Poland throughout the second half of the 20th century. At this point, it should be noted that the classic norms of the 1964 Polish Civil Code, in some cases, were more modern and more strongly implemented the ideas of liberalism than the legislation of Western Europe. The difference, however, consisted firstly in the smaller scale of use of such institutions. They applied to the inheritance of goods of lesser value, as more valuable production assets had been taken over by the State. The second distinction was in the illiberal restrictions imposed on farm inheritance, which were incompatible with the principle of equality before law. The circle of heirs and their rights also underwent limitations in other socialist countries, but since there was no widespread private ownership of agricultural land, Polish law on this issue was also atypical.

A third peculiarity, compared to other Central and Eastern European countries, arose from the marginal implementation of Soviet civil-law theory into Polish law of succession.[119] This was influenced by the public opposition in the face of the attempted Sovietization, and the associated short-lived abatement of forced indoctrination.[120] It was also affected by the attitude of legislators drafting the Civil Code, who, in the opinion of Anna Moszyńska, a researcher specializing in this particular issue, conducted 'real battles to maintain high standards of law (…) traditional canons of civil law.'[121] The public support ex-

118 For more see MACHNIKOWSKA: *Prawo własności*, 492.

119 For more see Anna MOSZYŃSKA: *Succession Law in People's Republic of Poland – Towards Western European or Soviet Standards?* in Danuta JANICKA (ed.) *Judiciary and Society between Privacy and Publicity*, WN UMK, Toruń, 2016, 259–276.

120 See Andrzej MĄCZYŃSKI: *Uwagi o stanie nauki polskiego prawa cywilnego*, PiP 6 (2011), 5.

121 MOSZYŃSKA: *Geneza prawa spadkowego*, 614.

pressed for these activities during the public discussion conducted in 1960 on some issues of the law on succession was another reason.[122]

The law of succession is a representative example of efforts to preserve the national cultural identity in a socialist system. Various arguments and a myth of creation of a socialist law of succession were used to further this goal. This was aided by selective presentation of elements of the new law, focusing – in addition to the special provisions governing the inheritance of private farms – on marginal issues, such as the inheritance of property of members of agricultural production co-operatives,[123] which covered less than 1% of all land in Poland after 1964.

At the same time, the Commission assured the political authorities that its work product was suitable for the stage of development of socialism in Poland at that time. Jan Wasilkowski argued that the changes would continue as the situation stabilized, stressing the previous high rate of socio-economic transformation.[124] Similar declarations were made by some members of the Commission to each other for example by Seweryn Szer: 'I think that the future historian of law (…) will not accuse us of being detached from the needs of this [socialist – AM] construction.'[125]

Many lawyers were aware of the fact that Polish law on succession after 1964 did not meet the ideological criteria set before it, and they pointed out as much during the public discussion in 1960 of the then-draft version of the Civil Code, of which many solutions old and new were met with acceptance. One could also learn from an analysis conducted on the date the new law came into force that the law on succession regulated by the Civil Code of

122 *A questionnaire presented for public discussion of the draft Civil Code*, including a questionnaire with questions on the law of succession, among other things: the scope of freedom of testation, the circle of statutory heirs including the order of inheritance of the testator's parents and siblings, and the choice between the system of legitimate portion and the system of reserve.

123 This is how the proposal for the law of succession was presented to members of parliament by the chairman of the Commission in 1959, see Jan WASILKOWSKI: *Fragmenty sprawozdania w Sejmowej Komisji Wymiaru Sprawiedliwości* [Fragments of a report to the Justice System Committee of the Sejm], PiP 1 (1959), 67–80.

124 Speech of Jan Wasilkowski in the *Sprawozdania Stenograficzne Sejmu PRL* [*Stenographic Reports of the Sejm of the Polish People's Republic*] from the 27th Session of the Sejm of the People's Republic of Poland, 1964, margin 49. Wasilkowski's status update on the Commission's works for the Justice System Committee meeting on 29 January 1963, in *Biuro Sejmu, Wydział Prawny, nr 319/III kad. Komisja Wymiaru Sprawiedliwości*, 29 January, 1963, III.

125 Minutes of the session of the Codification Commission's Substantive Civil Law Team on 22–24 May 1961. Meeting on 24 May 1961, AAN, MS 5420, 269.

1964 was a matter that, with the exception of the inheritance of agricultural land, had undergone the least change relative to the period of unification.[126] This was also indirectly confirmed by the legislature during reforms of the law of succession after the collapse of the socialist system. Repealing the special provisions on farm inheritance and adding a few minor adjustments was deemed sufficient because the provisions of the Civil Code for the most part reflected the classic institutions of the law of succession.

In reconstructing the progress of the codification works on the law of succession, it will be necessary to mention in a few sentences the Law of Succession of 1946, as it would provide the reference point for the 1964 Code. Several members of the Codification Commission participated in the unification of the Law of Succession in 1946. (Jan Gwiazdomorski and Kazimierz Przybyłowski), and even in the codification works undertaken during the interwar period (Przybyłowski and Wasilkowski).

The 1946 Decree on Law of Succession introduced the freedom of testation that would be retained by the Civil Code in 1964, with the exception of the special provisions dealing with farms. The much narrower circle of statutory heirs compared to the laws of other European countries also contributed to this freedom. In the 1946 legislation, those were the spouse, descendants, siblings and their descendants; of all ascendants only the parents. The explanatory memorandum invoked the strengthening of genuine family ties, the kind that usually existed between immediate family members. That argument had found support in international discussions held during the interwar period. Polish lawyers mentioned the resolution of the Second International Congress of Comparative Law,[127] reiterating in 1946 that the model of succession prioritizing distant relatives while marginalizing the spouse and extramarital children was anachronistic.[128]

---

126 Including Bronisław DOBRZAŃSKI: *Jakie zmiany w stosunku do prawa spadkowego z 1946 wprowadzi Kodeks cywilny* [What changes will the Civil Code introduce in relation to the inheritance law of 1946], Palestra 7 (1964), 4–21; Jan GWIAZDOMORSKI: *Prawa spadkowe w Kodeksie cywilnym PRL* [Inheritance laws in the Civil Code of the Polish People's Republic], PiP 5–6 (1965), 707–725; Władysław CHOJNOWSKI: *Niektóre zagadnienia z prawa spadkowego* [A few topics in inheritance law], Palestra 7–8 (1965), 37–50.

127 Stanisław PŁAZA: *Historia prawa w Polsce na tle porównawczym* [A history of law in Poland against a comparative background], vol. 3: *Okres międzywojenny* [The interwar period], Księgarnia Akademicka, Krakow, 2001, 147; Józef Stanisław PIĄTOWSKI, Agnieszka KAWALKO, Hanna WITCZAK: vol. 10: *Prawo spadkowe* [Inheritance law], in Zbigniew RADWAŃSKI (ed.): *System prawa prywatnego* [The system of civil law], C. H. Beck, Warsaw, 2015, 177.

128 Seweryn SZER: *Nowe prawo spadkowe* [The new Inheritance Law], Myśl Współczesna 9–10 (1947), 327.

FIGURE 4.3 Jan Gwiazdomorski, 1899–1977. In the 30s, Head of Department of Civil law, and, shortly after the war, also Dean of the Faculty of Law of Jagiellonian University. Transferred to the University of Wrocław after the war, serving as Head of Department of Civil law in 1948–1956; later, returned to Jagiellonian University, reaching and researching in 1956–1969. After 1945, actively involved in codification works, including membership in the Codification Commission of 1956. In 1956–1962, member of the Committee of Legal Sciences of Polish Academy of Sciences.
SOURCE: JAGIELLONIAN UNIVERSITY ARCHIVES

At the same time, the narrowness of the circle of statutory heirs increased the scope of the testator's freedom of disposition. Statutory inheritance occurred in the absence of a will, and a will could take a variety of forms. The 1946 law, however, precluded contracts on succession from being made *inter vivos*, which was justified on the basis of the principle of the freedom of the testator, who should always be left free to change their will. An original legal construct derived from the legacy of the Codification Commission of the Second Polish Republic[129] was developed for the absence of testamentary and statutory heirs. In such situations, the inheritance would go to the municipality or, if the testator resided abroad, the state (Treasury). The concept was deformed by extension of the Treasury's escheat rights to all landed

129 Henryk KONIC: *Spadkobranie z prawa* (*ustawowe*): *referat dla Komisji Kodyfikacyjnej* [Inheritance by law (statutory). paper for the Codification Commission], Gazeta Sądowa Warszawska 11–12 (1920), 98–99.

property,[130] and in 1950 the inheritance rights of municipalities ended with the abolition of local governments. The protection of statutory heirs omitted in the testament was based on the Law of Succession of 1946 and relied on a system of legitimate portion. The architects of this solution, however, had to persuade those of the reformers who favoured the reserve system, and only the need for rapid unification ultimately secured the conditional approval of legitimate portion.[131] The rules of liability for the debts of the estate were also a matter of disagreement. The principle introduced in 1946 was that of unlimited liability, which could be transformed into liability up to the value of the estate if the heir made a declaration of acceptance 'with the benefit of inventory' (*z dobrodziejstwem inwentarza*) within six months.

When in 1956 the Codification Commission again set down to work on the law of succession, the task of developing its basic constructs was entrusted to Jan Gwiazdomorski and Kazimierz Przybyłowski. Both presented their solutions in such a way as to demonstrate their usefulness to the then-socialist legal system in Poland, despite the fact that the new regulations in reality standardized, sometimes in a more modern variation, the classic institutions of the law of succession. Gwiazdomorski insisted that statutory inheritance was the default principle,[132] even though the provisions reproduced from 1946 gave priority to testamentary inheritance, actually used by the citizens only on a limited scale.[133] Przybyłowski, by contrast, argued that an effective solution would be to regulate the general rules in the Code and the exceptions outside of it, especially as the latter were anticipated to change frequently. The Commission also intended to approach the inheritance of private farms in the same manner, while professing to understand their exceptional status in the socialist economy. Until 1963, the Commission expected that significant changes to this type of inheritance would be avoided, allowing the succession regime to maintain its consistency.

---

130 Letter from the Ministry of Agriculture and Agrarian Reform of 23 July 1946 to Ministry of Justice, AAN, MS 4430, 145.

131 Kazimierz PRZYBYŁOWSKI: *Uwagi do tytułu IV projektu prof. Gwiazdomorskiego* [Remarks on Title IV of Professor Gwiazdomorski's draft], AAN, MS 4431, 170; *Uzasadnienie ważniejszych uwag merytorycznych do projektu prawa spadkowego* [Reasons for the more important comments on the draft inheritance law]; AAN, MS 4430, 206–213.

132 Jan GWIAZDOMORSKI: *Prawo spadkowe* [Inheritance law], PWN, Warsaw, 1959, 16.

133 Responses to a survey conducted in 1960 showed that the share of testaments as the basis of inheritance in different regions of the country did not exceed 10% to 30%. One should note that many farmers did not seek a court decision to formalize the inheritance, contenting themselves with informal possession. For more see MACHNIKOWSKA: *Prawo własności*, 486–497.

FIGURE 4.4 Kazimierz Przybyłowski, 1900–1987. During the interwar period, linked to the John Casimir University in Lviv, serving as Head of Department of Civil Law and Dean of the Faculty of Law and Administration. After the war, Head of Department of Civil and Private International Law of Jagiellonian University (1945–1970). Active participant in the Codification Commission of the Second Polish Republic and of the Codification Commission of 1956.
SOURCE: POLISH ACADEMY OF SCIENCES, ARCHIVES IN WARSAW, ZF XXI-132-001

Moreover, Jan Wasilkowski, who introduced parts of Soviet theory of property rights to real law, did not extend it to the law of succession (as established by Anna Moszyńska, who studied this particular issue).[134] The rationale provided in this case, not least by Wasilkowski, indirectly protected the classical institutions retained in the 1946 law, because in relation to the law of succession, the Codification Commission had no compelling reasons to change the law if it had become part of social tradition, especially as in the meantime – after partial nationalization – no new socio-economic relations even tangentially related to law of succession were created and simultaneously there still existed legal relationships demanding solutions not directly derived from the assumptions of the socialist system[135]. This position

134 Anna MOSZYŃSKA: *Politics and Inheritance Law. Endeavours to Keep Classical Rules of Inheritance Law in the Polish Civil Code*, Studia Iuridica Toruniensia 13 (2013), 131–147.

135 Minutes of the session of the Codification Commission's Substantive Civil Law Team on 12–16 May 1958 in Nieborów. Meeting on 25 May 1958, AAN, MS 5407, 171–181; Minutes of

was reinforced by Wasilkowski with the following argument: when 'there is no certainty that legislative change is needed, the rule adopted by the law [currently] in force should be maintained.'[136]

Tradition also justified the correction of some decisions, including the re-action of some of the provisions originally removed in 1946, if there were strong social reasons for their restoration, such as in the case of the allographic form of wills used by village dwellers.

The basic point of reference for many of the Codification Commission's decisions was the *de facto* state of affairs, including the slow progress on the development of the socialist economy. This, in turn, was coupled with the need to protect the heirs' small assets, which the vast majority of them had before and after the inheritance. The issue also painted a symbolic summary of the effects of implementation of the ideological premises of Marxist doctrine, including the fabricated economic argument of a leap in the living standards of the proletariat. The proviso was made that many of the proposed regulations needed to be evaluated in terms of the financial impact of their widespread application. The rationale was provided by Wasilkowski, who explained the reason for the change in views on the system of legitimate portion thus: 'in recent years in the USSR and other socialist countries, the argument that the monetary economy is fading in importance has been proved wrong.'[137]

Occasionally, and without influencing the most important decisions, members of the Commission referred to the possible strengthening, through a specific norm of the law of succession, of the 'remnants' of capitalist economy (including one voice critical of the institution of legitimate portion). There was a single reference to such categories as 'socialist morality' in the Commission's dispute over the number and type of grounds of an heir's unworthiness of inheritance.[138] More frequently, the argument of principles of social justice and equity was raised, as in the case of the discussion on abolishing the obli-

---

the session of the Codification Commission's Substantive Civil Law Team on 7–9 September 1959. Meeting on 7 September 1959, AAN, MS 5419, 74; See also Piotr FIEDORCZYK: *Dylematy socjalistycznego kodyfikatora. Dokument archiwalny o pracach komisji Kodyfikacyjnej w latach 1956–1958* [The dilemmas of a socialist codifier. Archive document on the works of the Codification Commission in 1956–1958]; MHI 8 (2009), 259–267.

136 Minutes of the session of the Codification Commission's Substantive Civil Law Team on 23 May 1961, AAN, MS 5420, 247.

137 *Ibidem*.

138 Minutes of the session of the Codification Commission's Substantive Civil Law Team on 22 May 1961, AAN, MS 5420, 204.

gation to repay those legal heirs who did not inherit the farm, having previously relied on its income to finance their education, for example.

When invoking the ideal of modernization, Commission members rarely added any doctrinal adjectives to it. In explaining why a particular institution was being abandoned, they pointed to its feudal pedigree[139] or to the complete absence from the socialist economy of any legal relationship that could be regulated by the relevant provision. Attention was also drawn to those statements by members of the Commission that emphasized the need to strengthen in private law, including the law of succession, the conditions for the emergence of scarce goods. This is because the national economy on its was incapable – temporarily, it was asserted – of providing a sufficient supply of food and housing. Therefore, the functioning of private law, including the law of succession, had become an important issue, facilitating private agriculture and the acquisition by citizens of land that could be used to build houses.

At the same time, they also emphasized the necessity of popularization of the law of succession and of avoidance of the need to work out interpretative doubts that always plagues new legislation for at least several years after its enactment. The means to this end was to simplify the regulation, even at the expense of partial distortion of classic legal constructs. This was done, for instance, with the rules governing financial settlement between multiple heirs.

This prioritized list of tasks concerning succession law focused the Commission's interest on the revision of existing law and resolution of longstanding controversies surrounding certain institutions of succession law in Polish and foreign scholarship. Those included the rules of protection of statutory heirs not receiving an inheritance and rules of liability for the debts of the estate. With regard to the general principles of protection of the rights of those statutory heirs who, as a result of the existence of a will, did not receive an inheritance, two issues were important: the choice between the systems of reserved portion and legitimate portion, and the selection of a settlement regime among the heirs including or excluding adjustments for events having taken place during the deceased's lifetime.

Kazimierz Przybyłowski advocated limiting both the circle of entities entitled to protection and the type of actions of the deceased person giving rise to adjustments in settlements among the heirs. He invoked both the principle of testamentary freedom and the small scale and size of the preceding donations *inter vivos*. A different position was advanced by Jan Wasilkowski. Seweryn

139 GWIAZDOMORSKI: *Prawo spadkowe*, 19.

Szer and some other members of the Commission, however, contested the narrowing and stressed the need to safeguard the equal rights of women keeping house and raising children, which was also expected to strengthen family relations as a whole.

There was also disagreement about the advantages and disadvantages of the system of legitimate portion in effect since 1946. Although this was the general rule applicable to all inheritance, it was seen primarily in the light of farm inheritance. Jan Gwiazdomorski supported its retention, citing macroeconomic arguments that it could help solve the problem of 'squaring the circle',[140] as he put it, with regard to the conflict between the interests of the national economy and the legitimate interests of the heirs. Replacing financial claims (in the system of legitimate portion) with claims in kind (the system of reserve) would entail according to him a high risk of fragmentation of farms, which was already occurring and reducing the efficiency of agriculture. On the other hand, protecting the farm's integrity also made it possible for the chosen heir to raise the funds to pay off the other heirs (mortgage). Additionally, the system of legitimate portion stimulated the relocation of the remaining heirs to the cities by providing them with the requisite money, with the effect of reducing the number of the population relying solely on rural labour for a living.

A different axiological perspective was adopted by the other members of the Commission, as a result of which the first version of the 1958 draft opted for the reserve system. Here, too, the rationale invoked economic considerations, pondered on an individual basis. According to Jan Wasilkowski, the obligation to repay in money often exceeded the financial capacity of the obliged heir, which increased the likelihood that the claims of the other heirs would go unsatisfied or alternatively that the condition of the farm would be worsened by the outflow of cash. Jerzy Marowski stressed the principles of community life and equity, citing the farmers' perception of the repayment obligation as an unfair and excessive burden. The system of reserve was also, according to its adherents, a mechanism that facilitated the acquisition by citizens of usually inaccessible land, which, while too small for farming, instead qualified as property on which a house could be built.[141] Supple-

140 Jan GWIAZDOMORSKI: *Rezerwa czy zachowek?* [Reserve or legitimate portion?], PiŻ 12 (1959), 3.

141 Minutes of the session of the Codification Commission's Substantive Civil Law Team on 12–16 May 1958 in Mądralin. Meeting on 13 May 1958, AAN, MS 5407, 68–69; Minutes of the session of the Codification Commission's Substantive Civil Law Team on 12–16 May 1958 in Mądralin. Meeting on 14 May 1958, AAN, MS 5412, 147–149.

menting this argumentation, Aleksander Wolter also drew attention to other types of inheritance estates (the inheritances of urban residents), where the system of reserve enabled the access of legal heirs to personal family items, which were usually the only items in the inheritance.[142] The system of reserve also had a supporter in Seweryn Szer, who emphasized its universality, given that it was found in French, Soviet and other legal systems.

The regime of liability for the debts of the estate was also a point of contention. Kazimierz Przybyłowski argued for the primacy of the principle of limited liability, citing examples from the legislation of both capitalist and socialist legal systems. Other members of the Commission, including Gwiazdomorski, Szer and Wolter, took a different view. They mentioned the realities of a socialist economy, in which only a few types of obligations incumbent on individuals could possibly arise, most of them capable of being fulfilled, as they were obligations relating to the acquisition of items included in the inheritance estate (loans for the purchase of household or farm equipment paid in instalments), and other obligations expired, such as maintenance.[143] The majority of the Commission's members concurred with this reasoning and opted for maintaining the existing model of unlimited liability for debts, with a potential deviation in favour of liability with the benefit of inventory, i.e. up to the value of the assets of the estate.

The Codification Commission's work on the law of succession involving farms proceeded at a different pace. It was halted in mid-1959, following news that administrative officials, without the Commission's involvement, had designed separate legislation.[144] In fact, only the provisions on the suspension of certain repayments of mutual obligations among heirs came into force at the time.[145] The practice of court proceedings was steered on the correct course by Supreme Court decisions. One such ruling negated the possibility of inheriting possession,[146] which had a negative impact mainly on farmers who often, as a result of the action of administrative authorities, did not have formal title to the property. The Supreme Court, of which Jan Wasilkowski was a member, also promulgated guidelines, binding on lower courts, to the effect of precluding interpretations leading to the deterioration of ad-

142 Minutes of the session of the Codification Commission's Substantive Civil Law Team on 11–14 May 1959. Meeting on 13 May 1958, AAN, MS 5415, 98–100.

143 Minutes of the session of the Codification Commission's Substantive Civil Law Team on 10–12 June 1958 in Mądralin. Meeting on 11 June 1958, AAN, MS 5407, 116–182.

144 Minutes of the session of on 11–14 May 1959. Meeting on 13 May 1958, AAN, MS 5416, 256.

145 Act of 18 June 1959 on the Suspension of Certain Inheritance Payments.

146 Supreme Court 26.03.1958, I CO 3/58, OSNC.1959.4.106; critical gloss by Andrzej Stelmachowski, PiP 4–5 (1960), 851–855.

ministratively specified standards.[147] It was not until 1963 that special legislation was introduced sanctioning the practice.[148]

In the political and legal climate, which had undergone another wave of changes, legitimacy was sought for the new restrictions by some representatives of the Commission, including Wasilkowski, in the different level of systemic protection of personal property and individual property for which farms were eligible.[149] Meanwhile, a few years earlier, a number of legal scholars, some of whom were also Supreme Court judges, extended the protection given to personal property also to small real estate, including residential dwellings,[150] which could be an argument for preserving their free inheritance as well.

On the other hand, ideological-axiological justification for depriving many statutory heirs of their right to inherit farms[151] was found in the argument of modernization, successfully leveraged by the legislature, relating to impeding fragmentation as a result of the application of the existing provisions on the division of inheritance.[152] Lawyers outside the Codification Commission argued in opposition, pointing towards other sources of low production coming from private farms. These were oppressive fiscal and administrative policies, for which evidence was provided from statistical and economic data. Aware of that fact, in the public discussion of the proposal for the code, lawyers stressed as early as 1960 that 'the law of succession [was] unfit to regulate agricultural policy.'[153] They advocated for the retention of the general principles of the law of succession also in relation to farms, pointing out that arguments favouring the legitimate portion should be referred to the new mechanism for calculating repayments[154] and that most inheritances, including those not involving farms, were too small to distinguish, in an economically rational way, a separate portion for the implementation of the system of reserve.

147 Guidelines on the Administration of Justice and Judicial Practice of the Civil Chamber of the Supreme Court of 27 February 1960.

148 Act of 29 June 1963 on the Restriction of the Division of Farms, Dz.U. 28.168.

149 Jan WASILKOWSKI: *Zagadnienia kodyfikacji polskiego prawa cywilnego* [Topics in the codification of Polish Civil Law], Nowe Drogi 11 (1960), 38.

150 Supreme Court 19.10.1951 C 1164/51, PiP 7 (1952), 129–132.

151 Including a new requirement of formal agricultural qualifications, which the vast majority of rural workers did not have.

152 SZER: *Prawo spadkowe*, 67.

153 For more see MOSZYŃSKA: *Geneza prawa spadkowego*, 614.

154 Józef Stanisław PIĄTOWSKI: *Rozdrobnienie gospodarstw rolnych a prawo spadkowe* [The fragmentation of farms and inheritance law], PiP 4–5 (1960), 676–677.

This position was cited by the Codification Commission in justification for abandoning its original proposal to introduce a system of reserve. However, a researcher on this issue, Anna Moszyńska, has established that the decisive factor in the final decision to maintain this practice was not the *vox populi*, but decisions taken outside the Commission, imposing restrictions on the inheritance of farms and thus automatically excluding the system of reserve.[155] Those decisions caused the Commision's inheritance model to disintegrate, rendering it incoherent (two separate sets of succession principles).

Developed outside the Commission, the political concept of modernization to be achieved by restricting the inheritance of private farms was criticized by only one deputy – Ludwik Stomma, describing the other new inheritance regulations governing farms as 'an important social experiment'.[156] Indeed, they placed a burden on the entire system. The far-reaching formal restriction of farm inheritance was accompanied by the simultaneous abandonment of inheritance proceedings by farmers in favour of informal succession divisions, systematically increasing the scale of fragmentation of agricultural production.

This was one example, also retained in the 1964 Civil Code, of the three-tier functioning of social relations and economic relations. The first, official tier was shaped by legal provisions still largely derived from classic legal institutions. New special norms were attached to them, often focused on deviations from the rules, and at this time these deviating norms were already contained directly in the Code or sanctioned by Code reference to non-Code provisions. The second level was the propaganda message touting the socialist characteristics of the new law. The authors of that propaganda were not only government officials but also sometimes the lawmakers themselves. The third tier was the actual state of affairs, often diverging from the laws and regulations and from the propaganda slogans.

4 Family and Guardianship Code

The source information on the day-by-day work carried out by the Codification Commission on the draft Family and Guardianship Code comes from several sources. These include the minutes of the Commission's team meetings, collected at the Archives of Modern Records, as well as the findings

155 See MOSZYŃSKA, *Geneza prawa spadkowego*, 453, 464.

156 Stenographic Sejm report of 1964, margin 116.

yielded by detailed research conducted on this particular issue, among which the work of Piotr Fiedorczyk stands out.[157] Some information is also provided by academic articles published in the 1960s, whose authors included Commission members Jan Wasilkowski, Aleksander Wolter,[158] Jan Winiarz,[159] Witold Czachórski[160] and Seweryn Szer.

The task of the Commission team charged with drafting the new Family and Guardianship Code was to modify the already codified law. The ideology invoking the values favoured by the socialist state did not in practice distort the principles of this element of codification. The propaganda aspects were mostly confined to the statements made by the authors of the code and commentators on the legislation, involving the implementation in the Code of the new constitutional principle of the state's care of family,[161] as well as values such as socialist morality, social interest and principles of social co-existence, all cited as evidence of a socialist pedigree.

Studies on this code conducted in the 21st century (including the work of Fiedorczyk) confirm that the most significant influence the Soviet model had on Polish family and guardianship law was its separate codification. Some of the norms of the Code, specified as examples of the implementation of doctrine, reflect content present in Soviet legislation but also in non-socialist legal systems.

The Codification Commission used norms dating back to the Second Polish Republic (the law unified in 1946) and the then-current Code (1950), which had been criticized for its poor editorial quality.[162] The drafters also had access to decisions of the Supreme Court[163] and several new scholarly works analy-

157 For more see FIEDORCZYK: *Unifikacja i kodyfikacja, passim.*

158 CZACHÓRSKI: *Przebieg prac*, 18; Aleksander WOLTER: *Nowy projekt kodeksu cywilnego* [The new draft Civil Code], PiP 2 (1962), 210–218.

159 Jan WINIARZ: *Socjalistyczne prawo rodzinne PRL: ewolucja – stan aktualny – perspektywy* [The socialist family law of the Polish People's Republic: the evolution, the current state and the perspectives], Studia Prawnicze 4 (1974), 57–97.

160 CZACHÓRSKI: *Przebieg prac*, 15–20.

161 Article 67: Marriage and the family are under the care and protection of the Polish People's Republic. Families with numerous offspring are given special care by the state; birth outside marriage does not diminish the rights of the child.

162 IGNATOWICZ: *Prawo rzeczowe*, 32.

163 Piotr FIEDORCZYK: *Wytyczne Sądu Najwyższego dotyczące wykładni przepisów kodeksu rodzinnego z 1950 r.* [Supreme Court Guidelines on the interpretation of the provisions of the 1950 Family Code], in Marian Małecki (ed.), *Świat, Europa, mała ojczyzna: studia ofiarowane Profesorowi Stanisławowi Grodziskiemu w 80-lecie urodzin* [The world, Europe, the little fatherland: studies dedicated to Professor Stanisław Grodziski on the

sing the design flaws of the existing law.[164] This collection of materials provided a solid foundation for the conceptual work to be undertaken.[165] The Commission was also able to compare its position on the various issues with the opinions of the legal community at large, as the draft was submitted to public consultation. It was family law, of all the civil law branches under discussion, in which there was the greatest public interest.[166]

The architects of the Family and Guardianship Code had differing views on the various institutions in this body of legislation, but the disputes and discussions held did not bear on the fundamental issues. Those had been regulated before the codification, and in a way that enjoyed broad acceptance. This included the equality of spouses, the equality of children, including children born out of wedlock, as well as the secular nature of marriage. Such changes resulted from the genuine transformation of community life in which war and industrialization strengthened the social role of women and accelerated changes in the family model.[167] At the same time, the political and legal marginalization of the Catholic Church did not reduce the high level of religiosity in society.

The architects of the Code maintained their independence with a substantive debate that took into account realistic social expectations and needs. This helped to objectively identify the legal problems that needed to be solved with codification. The new legislation was to be of higher quality than its predecessor, and the regulation of issues important to society was to confer legitimacy on the balancing act struck among the various competing values. The identifi-

---

80th anniversary of his birthday], Wyższa Szkoła Administracji, Bielsko-Biała, 2009, 627–638.

164 Józef Stanisław PIĄTOWSKI: *Stosunki majątkowe między małżonkami* [Property relations between spouses], Wydawnictwo Prawnicze, Warsaw, 1955; Zygmunt ZIEMBIŃSKI: *Podłoże społeczne przysposobienia dziecka w Polsce Ludowej* [The social underpinnings of the adoption of a child in People's Poland], Wydawnictwo Prawnicze, Warsaw, 1956; Andrzej STELMACHOWSKI: *Przysposobienie w polskim prawie rodzinnym* [Adoption in Polish family law], Wydawnictwo Prawnicze, Warsaw 1957; Jan GÓRECKI: *Unieważnienie małżeństwa* [The annulment of marriage], Uniwersytet Jagielloński, Krakow, 1958; Bronisław WALASZEK: *Uznanie dziecka w polskim prawie rodzinnym* [Recognition of parentage in Polish family law], PWN, Krakow, 1958.

165 Jacek BAGIŃSKI, Stefan GRZYBOWSKI, Jan IGNATOWICZ, Józef Stanisław PIĄTOWSKI, Andrzej STELMACHOWSKI, Edmund WENGEREK: *Prawo cywilne w XX-leciu PRL* [Civil law at the 20th anniversary of the Polish People's Republic], Studia Prawnicze 9 (1965), 72–73.

166 WASILKOWSKI, WOLTER: *Wyniki dyskusji*, 3; Piotr FIEDORCZYK: *Kilka uwag o publicznej*, 360–380.

167 KŁOSKOWSKA: *Wzory i modele*, 52.

cation of such values, the criteria for assigning weights to them, and the rationale for the compromise also characterizing the way in which the Commission members reached consensus on explanatory memoranda were important in the drafting works on issues such as grounds for and bars to divorce, the model of the matrimonial property regime, and the nature of parental authority (responsibility, custody), including its limits.

When first setting down to work, the Commission resolved to regulate family law in the Civil Code,[168] but it was later removed from the draft.[169] The Commission had previously discussed the advantages and disadvantages of separate codification of family law. The official argument of the proponents of separate codification invoked the changed nature of the future Civil Code due to including a new type of regulation of civil-law relationships in commercial matters, with socialized economic units, primarily state-owned enterprises, as the main actors. Therefore, according to Seweryn Szer, Jan Topiński, and others, the normalization of family relations had better be achieved by a separate code because of the differences between the two matters and the anticipation of frequent amendments to regulations dealing with economic affairs as a result of the rapid development of a socialist economy. This type of argumentation benefited from the Soviet theory of jurisprudence, which considered as one of the characteristic features of socialist civil law the extent of its regulation focused on property relations. In Poland, this argument was flawed in the eyes of a large part of the legal circles, since even in a socialist economy economic (property) rights were still related to non-economic rights. Moreover, in codification practice, the argument of saturation of the Civil Code with new 'commercial' content turned out to be untrue. There were very few such norms in the new code, and the entire regulation of socialist or socialized civil-law relationships involving, for example, state-owned enterprises, was transferred to legislation enacted by administrative bodies and located outside of the Code.

The connection between the two codes was to be ensured by the reference in family law to the provisions of the Civil Code.[170] When analysing this

168 *Projekt kodeksu cywilnego.*

169 *Projekt kodeksu rodzinnego i opiekuńczego oraz przepisów wprowadzających kodeks rodzinny i opiekuńczy* [Draft Family and Guardianship Code and draft implementing provisions for it], Wydawnictwo Prawnicze, Warsaw, 1962.

170 Jan Winiarz: *Kodyfikacja prawa rodzinnego i opiekuńczego w PRL* [The codification of family and guardianship law in the Polish People's Republic], in Jan Błeszyński, Jerzy Rajski (eds), *Rozprawy z prawa cywilnego: księga pamiątkowa ku czci Witolda Czachórskiego* [Dissertations in civil law: commemoration book in honour of Professor Witold Czachórski], PWN, Warszawa, 1985, 83ff.

solution, Piotr Fiedorczyk hypothesized that the model thus formed by the Codification Commission helped protect civil law from the excessive dispersion of principles and institutions demanded by political decision-makers. The formal separation was presented as an example of socialist progress, but the provisions of the Code still leveraged classic legal institutions. The above was, according to Fiedorczyk, an example of: 'a kind of camouflage against political pressure from the communist authorities'.[171]

Among the several issues subjected to such pressure was the matter of divorce grounds. According to the official narrative, the socialist state surrounded the family with care, thereby supporting the formation of a new morality that directed the attention of the individual to their activity in the social structure applicable to them. This structure, the family, as a rule, remained a private sphere, in contrast to the sphere of the labour activity of the citizens of the socialist state, which became a public sphere in which the state exercised control in the name of the interests of the working class.

And that was to be why the state would not ban divorce, because the principle of the permanence or at least durability or stability of marriage, while important, was not equivalent to the religious dogma of the indissolubility of matrimony. The state, by contrast, would make sure that a judicial decree of dissolution of marriage is not issued in situations that, in the eyes of the public (i.e. of the 'working masses') were incompatible with the morality of the new social order. Such a situation could arise when divorce was requested only by the spouse who was solely to blame for the breakdown of the marriage. Against this backdrop, divergent views emerged on whether such a ban ought to be absolute, and how any hypothetical exceptions should be handled. Each of these considerations involved the interpretation of concepts such as social interest, socialist morality, and principles of social co-existence.

Initially, the new law (1950) provided for exceptional situations in which there was greater public interest in the dissolution of a marriage than in its continuation (the principle of recrimination). However, other legal scholars pointed out that public interest as a divorce ground (this was the sense implied by the wording of the exception) did not correspond to the meaning of this concept.[172] The Codification Commission accordingly decided to modify

171 FIEDORCZYK: *Unifikacja i kodyfikacja*, 25.

172 Jan GÓRECKI: *Wina rozwodu a moralność (z rozważań nad zasadą rekryminacji)* [Culpability and morality (from discussions on the principle of recrimination)], PiP 1 (1965), 27–41, as well as a comprehensive study by the same author: Jan GÓRECKI: *Recrimination in Eastern Europe: An Empirical Study of Polish Divorce Law*, American Journal of Comparative Law 14 (1965–1966), 603–629.

the original draft compiled by Aleksander Wolter, justifying the change as follows: 'It is impossible without some mental acrobatics to justify as public interest the permissibility of a divorce demanded by a spouse solely responsible for the marital breakdown.'[173] In the final draft of the Code, the principles of social co-existence became the source of obstacles to divorce.

Some members of the Commission, including Seweryn Szer, argued that the legal protection of marriage was important but should not lead to the maintenance of artificial entities in society, namely those marriages in which the Code's prerequisites for divorce were not met but in which the marital relationship was irretrievably broken. Szer also invoked an argument from the practical application of the law, pointing out that under the existing provisions, which did not include such restrictions, the number of divorces being sought and granted was not high.

An additional socialist form, this time procedural, of securing the interests of the socialist family was a new principle invoked for this purpose, that of 'material truth' (also known as objective truth), in use since 1950. The codifiers assumed that the court's activity in pursuance of that principle, by means such as admitting evidence on the court's own motion, would reduce the number of cases, also contrary to the public interest, in which the consent of the other spouse had been obtained either by coercion or in an equally defective way.

The second bar to divorce came to be the welfare of a minor. This was emphasized by the Supreme Court, whereas the judges of the lower courts took it into account only sporadically. According to one legal scholar, Andrzej Stelmachowski, this rendered defunct the concept of 'the child's welfare'.[174] At the first stage of the Codification Commission's work, the status of the welfare of the child changed, becoming a 'positive premise' (ground as opposed to bar or obstacle) because the dissolution of marriage was to be permissible only when conducive to the welfare of the child – the author of this concept, Aleksander Wolter, abandoned it at a later stage.[175]

The socialist concept of the family as the basic unit ('cell') of society with intangible ties as its bond, and with the economic element either absent or

173 *Projekt kodeksu rodzinnego*, 47.

174 Andrzej STELMACHOWSKI: *Dobro dziecka w procesie rozwodowym* [The child's welfare in divorce litigation], Nowe Prawo 8–9 (1953), 59.

175 Aleksander WOLTER: *Kierunki zmian polskiego prawa rodzinnego* [Directions of change in Polish family law], PiP 8–9 (1958), 283. For more, see the criticism of the premise of the child's welfare so formulated: Wanda STOJANOWSKA: *Rozwód* [Divorce], in Zbigniew RADWAŃSKI (ed.): *System prawa prywatnego* [The system of private law], vol. 11: Tadeusz SMYCZYŃSKI (ed.): *Prawo rodzinne i opiekuńcze* [Family and guardianship law], C.H. Beck, Warszawa, 2009, 609.

playing a marginal role, also became a reference point for the works on the matrimonial property regime. A different draft, proceeding from the assumption of the existence also of economic ties between the spouses, which they were free to shape in whatever way they wished, was presented by Wolter, also disseminating his original concept in the press.[176] The base statutory regime was to be community property, which the parties would be able to change by contract and choose one of three options: separate property, community property and jointly acquired assets admitting of the expansion or narrowing of the community property.

The above model was criticized by Szer, who argued that it was an attempt at the restoration of provisions already repealed for their incompatibility with the tenets of socialist law, including the principle of social justice. Evidence in support of this was provided by the example, which could arise under the

FIGURE 4.5 Aleksander Wolter, 1905–1967. During the interwar period, an academic and judge linked to Cracow and Jagiellonian University. Active participant in works on the unification of civil law. After the war, employed by the Ministry of Justice, actively participating in the codification works after 1945, including the Codification Commission of 1956. Justice of the Supreme Court (1948–1951), Dean of the Faculty of Law of Marie Curie-Skłodowska University in Lublin (1950–1953); from 1963 member of the Committee of Legal Sciences of Polish Academy of Sciences.
SOURCE: THE MARIE CURIE UNIVERSITY IN LUBLIN ARCHIVES

176 Aleksander WOLTER: *Wspólny majątek*, 558–571.

model in question, of a spouse's independent management of the wage of their own work, even in matters exceeding the scope of ordinary management. Szer listed the consequences of such action including, in addition to reducing the scope of community property, an increase in mutual distrust between the spouses and the creation of conditions conducive to the breakdown of marital relations. Thus, there would be a risk of repeating the mistake made by bourgeois legislation, which was excessively focused on the regulation of economic matters.

The dispute also involved the assertion that some in the public did not understand the principles underlying the many variant regimes for community or separate property. The problem concentrated around wages, the main source of wealth creation in a socialist state. The exclusion of wages from joint property also excluded, by substitution, items financed with them. Therefore, it categorized the relevant items as different types of property. Jerzy Marowski addressed the differences in the property relations of married couples living in cities (small property, personal property) and married farmers, owning a private farm, to whom the specific property regime carried more relevance (the community-property model safeguarded women's rights). In this case, as always the case with farms, the Commission's attention also focused on concerns of the political correctness[177] of proposing a rule 'incidentally' accepting the premise of continued private ownership in agriculture.

The argument of Polish customs in rural social and economic relations (formal empowerment of the husband's rights, actual management of property by the wife) was invoked in order to neutralize this problem. Therefore, taking customs into account in this case would be a measurable factor in the application of the new regulations, if, in addition, they also permitted the use of a separate-property regime. That was because the conditions had not yet been created in Poland for the application of only one model of regulation of this issue, as was the case in other countries, such as France. At the same time, Jan Wasilkowski argued that taking the custom into account made sense in family law where there was a special relationship between property rights and non-economic affairs.[178] Legal historian Piotr Fiedorczyk stresses the importance of this particular discussion. Wasilkowski abandoned his position favouring a statutory regime and lent his support to the most extreme version of the prin-

177 Minutes of the session of the Codification Commission's Substantive Civil Law Team on 24 February to 1 March 1958 in Mądralin. Meeting on 24 February 1958, AAN, MS 5411, 208–212.

178 *Ibidem*, 217.

ciple of party disposition 'not even provided for in the legislation of most Western countries'.[179]

This decision caused further discussion by the Commission of this issue to take into account more and more consequences of the property-regime model under discussion, including the protection of the spouses' creditors and the position of women's advocacy organizations. Again, both sides of the debate also asserted that this copied the solutions of a capitalist system, and the counter-argument was that that some legal constructs changed their functions in the socialist system, so it was worthwhile to regulate some institutions flexibly. It was equally important to examine how useful they were in practice, which should not be narrowed down only to judicial practice, which in part focused on pathologies and highlighted them. Meanwhile, in the big picture of legal relationships, the same institution was functioning properly. The topic of the two property regimes continued to undergo analyses for which the point of reference was constantly changed by the Commission members themselves (including the interpretation of the interests of the working class and their protection through the norms of matrimonial property law).[180] The reasons for departure from the original concept of the two-system model were stated as follows: 'it is juridically unnecessary and politically flawed, giving the statutory community a sort of subsidiary character.'[181] This was one example of when the party considered acceptable only those solutions that were necessary for the existence of private property in agriculture. Other proposals for change were blocked on the pretext of conferring a preferential status on those entities, whether in family law, inheritance law, or even real law.

When examining this stage of the Commission's work, however, Fiedorczyk highlighted the circumstances capable of confirming the Commission's commitment to work around doctrinal directives. Indeed, the later works concerned a construct that, under the guise of the 'community property regime', disguised the possibility of partial fulfilment of the original purpose – the right to create a separate property regime (wages still not included in community property, along with the right to allocate unequal shares in the joint property of the spouses). The proposal published in the 1960 version was therefore limited to a new normalization of the rules on divorce at the request of the spouse solely responsible for the marital breakdown and allowing a separate property regime to be established by agreement between the spouses.

179 FIEDORCZYK: *Unifikacja i kodyfikacja*, 306.

180 Minutes of the session of the Codification Commission's Substantive Civil Law Team on 14–19 April 1958 in Mądralin. Meeting on 14 April 1958, AAN, MS 5412, 5.

181 *Ibidem*, Meeting on 18 April 1958, 89.

Among the other issues discussed by the Codification Commission, attention is drawn to those concerning the limits of parental authority, the rules for the division of family responsibilities between spouses, and solutions excessive haste in concluding marriages. One area of controversy came from Aleksander Wolter's proposals including a provision mandating a child's obedience to their parents, combined with the parents' right to discipline the child, with the proviso that any such action must not cause harm to the child's 'physical and moral health'. This was firmly contested by Szer, who argued that the Code must not provide for only one educational measure, being the most drastic. Education was to be achieved by appropriate means, not by corporal punishment.[182] His argument was accepted by the Commission.

A dispute featuring arguments invoking both the permanence of marriage and the superiority of the legal principles of the socialist system over the capitalist system was sparked by the proposal to raise the legal age for marriage (21 for men, 18 for women). Wasilkowski considered that to be unnecessary and even likely to be met with public incomprehension and incur objections due to restoring the institutions of bourgeois law, in a situation when the reformers should be creating new rules and institutions. The above argument was reinforced by statements invoking the need to act in accordance with the actions of state authorities.[183]

Witold Czachórski, with support from other Commission members, argued against this position, citing divorce statistics distinguished by the age of the spouses. At the same time, he stated that acting in accordance with party policy did not mean exempting the Commission from the obligation to address problems demanding legal regulation. Wolter made a similar declaration, giving the reassurance that the interests of the socialist state would be respected, while explaining that until the then-present time the legal age for marrying had not been regarded as an essential element of the state system.[184]

An example of a dispute over the Codification Commission's right to introduce regulations not previously found in Polish law, citing the state of social mores, was the proposal to ban the conclusion of a new marriage within six months of the termination of the previous marriage. The proposal in this regard tabled by Jan Gwiazdomorski was rejected by the Commission, and one

---

182 Seweryn SZER: *Recenzja pracy I. Andrejewa, Oceny prawne karcenia nieletnich, Warszawa 1964, PWN, s. 130* [Review of I. Andreev, Legal assessments of the punishment of minors, Warsaw 1964, PWN, pp. 130], PiP 1 (1965), 122.

183 Minutes of the session of the Codification Commission's Substantive Civil Law Team on 10 December 1957, AAN, MS 5411, 117.

184 *Ibidem*, 122.

of the arguments invoked was that only those issues it was necessary to regulated should be covered by family law and many issues should remain unregulated.

The emotional maturity of the people marrying, in the context of the permanence of marriage, was also a matter of dispute, this time due to the comparison of secular state law and canon law. The topic arose due to a solution[185] that, according to Wolter as its sponsor, would reduce the rate of reckless marriages; another Commission member, Gwiazdomorski, argued that it would make bigamy more difficult. Some members of the Commission even agreed that the issue would be linked to the institution of banns.[186] Fiedorczyk described the decision of some members of the Commission as an attempt to make 'a spectacular return to the old institutions of family law'. This inspiration was not constantly maintained, as is exemplified by the refusal to introduce a provision establishing grounds for the annulment of marriage due to defects in the statements of will by which the marriage was contracted. One of the reasons cited was that there was no need for the legislature to resort to institutions of canon law, as well as the public reception of the frequency of legal changes.

References to the past, combined with the argument of Polish identity, were used repeatedly in the discussion. However, some involved highly controversial proposals. A noteworthy one for its content and rationale, as well as consistency, was authored by Gwiazdomorski. It sought to clarify some of the rights and obligations of the spouses in such a way that the husband would be 'primarily' obligated to provide resources for the family's needs, and the wife to raise the children and manage the household. The basis for this concept was to be that the socio-economic conditions in Poland required the reformers to think for themselves and the content and method of regulation should not be 'limited to the adoption of foreign models'.[187]

Therefore, the legislation of socialist states, which emphasized the formal entitlement of women, but ignored, according to Gwiazdomorski, the problem of the lack of realistic equality at that time,[188] should not be copied for

185 The proposal stipulated that marriages could not be solemnized until one month after the documents were filed with the office.

186 Minutes of the session of the Codification Commission's Substantive Civil Law Team on 12 December 1957, AAN, MS 5411, 158.

187 Minutes of the session of the Codification Commission's Substantive Civil Law Team on 13 December 1957, AAN, MS 5411, 171.

188 Jan GWIAZDOMORSKI: *Równouprawnienie kobiety w rodzinie jako problem kodyfikacyjny* [Equal right for the woman in the family as a codification problem], PiP 11 (1959), 754–772.

implementation in Poland. The paradox was caused by women working two jobs between the family home and the workplace. The victims of the situation were not only the women themselves but also their children, who were deprived of the benefit of proper conditions for spiritual development. Thus, it was expedient for the legislature to change the existing assumptions for the family model, so that the rights would be equal but not identical.[189] The author of this view stressed that his intention was not to depreciate the role of women. Responding to his argument, the other members acknowledged the difficulty of the situation of women in the workforce. However they argued that the solution under discussion could harm women instead of helping them. The principle of equality was a direction-setting norm, and the situation would improve as the socialist economy developed. It was also pointed out that the spouses were free to choose the terms of division of family responsibilities between them. For the members of the Commission other than the sponsor of the idea, the principles of family law were unambiguous: joint contribution of the spouses, to the extent of their strength and ability, to the development of the family and joint decision-making in important family matters.

5 Code of Civil Procedure

Initially,[190] the work of the Codification Commission's members on procedural law differed considerably from their work on substantive law. Judging by the provisional declarations, the intention was for the Civil Code to rely on the concepts developed in 1955, albeit modified to some extent. However, Supreme Court Justice Marian Lisiewski, a member of the Commission's subcommittee tasked with codifying the procedural law from a fresh start, expressed an opinion in late 1956[191] in which he disagreed with solutions invoking socialist jurisprudence. Lisiewski openly criticized the procedural changes enacted into law in 1950 and 1953, as well as the new code draft of

---

189 Minutes of the session of the Codification Commission's Substantive Civil Law Team on 13 December 1957, AAN, MS 5411, 177.

190 Some parts of this subchapter have been published in Anna MACHNIKOWSKA: *The Principles of the Code of Civil Procedure*, in Anna MACHNIKOWSKA, Anna STAWARSKA-RIPPEL: *The Principles of Civil Procedure in Poland in the Twentieth Century. Doctrine, Drafts and Law in a Comparative Perspective*, Comparative Law Review, 21 (2016), 122–148.

191 Deliberations of the general assembly of the Codification Commission on 18 December 1956, AAN, MS, 5411.

1955, and made a case for the restoration of the principles followed in 1930–1950. Modernization was admittedly necessary, but it would continue to respect the classic principles of private law. If his ideas had been implemented, the Polish model of trial would have been reinstated, bringing back the autonomy of the individual and the equality of the parties, in a complete about-face on the legislation enacted in the meanwhile.

Lisiewski specified three areas belonging to the essence of civil trial: the role of a judge, the role of the public prosecutor, and the system of remedies.[192] His proposal pivoted on the principle of equality of the parties, which remained topical as class struggle had disappeared from Poland by 1956. Therefore, provisions on adversarial procedure and free exercise by the parties of their rights ought to be reintroduced and inquisitorial elements of the procedure ought to be eliminated. He moreover advocated limiting the activity of the judge, which had been expanded in 1950, to offering guidance to the weaker party, as well as narrowing the participation of public prosecutors to only a few categories of matters.

Most of the members of the Codification Commission concurred with his position to varying degrees. Zbigniew Resich emphasized the necessity of limiting the court's powers so that civil trial would reflect only certain elements of the inquisitorial principle rather than putting the latter on an equal footing with the dispositive principle.[193] In turn, Edmund Wengerek and others, such as Władysław Siedlecki,[194] presented additional arguments in favour of a reduction in the new powers given to the prosecutors in 1950–1953. Among other problematic aspects, it was argued that the controversial powers constituted an excessive exception from the principle of equality of the parties,

---

192 Marian Lisiewski: *Podstawowe problemy struktury nowego postępowania cywilnego. Streszczenie referatu wygłoszonego 18 grudnia 1956 r. na posiedzeniu Wydziału Cywilnego Komisji Kodyfikacyjnej* [Core problems of the structure of the new civil procedure. Abstract of the paper delivered on 18 December 1956 in a meeting of the Civil Department of the Codification Commission], Nowe Prawo 3 (1957), 9–17.

193 Zbigniew Resich; *Zasada dyspozytywności i kontradyktoryjności w procesie cywilnym PRL* [The dispositive and adversarial principles in the civil trial of the Polish People's Republic], PiP 7–8 (1957), 58–60.

194 Edmund Wengerek: *Udział prokuratora w postępowaniu cywilnym w świetle polskiej literatury prawniczej* [The prosecutor's participation in civil procedurę in the light of Polish legal literature], Studia Cywilistyczne 3 (1963), 176–177; Władysław Siedlecki: *Przebudowa sądowego postępowania cywilnego w Polsce Ludowej* [The overhaul of judicial civil procedure in People's Poland], Ruch Prawniczy i Ekonomiczny 21 (1959)/3, 101; Włodzimierz Berutowicz: *Charakter zmian prawa postępowania cywilnego w Polsce Ludowej* [The nature of changes to civil procedurę in People's Poland], Zeszyty Naukowe Uniwersytetu Wrocławskiego, Seria A Prawo 3 (1958)/10, 208–209.

weakened the position of the court (which was barred from evaluating the merits or expediency of the prosecutor's independent decision to initiate civil proceedings) and lacked theoretical justification, with the prosecutors given the greatest range of powers compared to the laws of the other socialist states.[195]

Among Lisiewski's other demands was the abolition of the extraordinary appeal against a final judgment, motivated by the abuse of the institution by the authorities. This proposal was met with varied responses by the other members of the Commission. Those in favour of the *revision* (*rewizja*) system included Siedlecki, Adam Chełmoński, Bronisław Dobrzański and Jerzy Marowski. Support for the three-instance system came from Resich, Aleksander Wolter, Jan Gwiazdomorski, and some others.[196] There was more of a consensus as to the necessity of modification of the rules governing the functioning of the institution of *extraordinary revision* (*rewizja nadzwyczajna*).[197]

In support of his views, Lisiewski delivered an in-depth analysis of the changes to which the civil procedure was subjected under socialism and claimed that they resulted in a situation: 'where the parties were largely demoted from the decision-making position they justly deserved to that of a participant who no longer [was] in charge of the proceedings. Th[at], to some extent, distort[ed] the purpose of the trial.'[198] He further argued that, contrary to the claims of the reformers of 1950, the guarantees for the principle of truth were not enhanced at the time. Instead, political, and thus non-objective, interference in judicial proceedings was made easier. Alas, this justified opinion was only partially adopted by the Commission and only partially made the basis for its works.

The first draft of the new Code was presented in 1960.[199] The main difference between this document and the previous draft (1955) was that two types

195 During the first years of the Codification Commission's mandate, Soviet law had provisions (the statute of 1923) empowering the court to evaluate the public prosecutor's conduct of the proceedings; furthermore, the prosecutor's participation was excluded in certain family matters (those were not civil cases within the conceptual framework of the Soviet provisions of 1923).

196 Wasilkowski: *Sprawozdanie z prac Komisji*, PiP 3 (1957), 624, Zbigniew Resich: *Środki odwoławcze w kodeksie postępowania cywilnego* [Appellate remedies in the Code of Civil Procedure], in Jerzy Jodłowski (ed.): *Księga pamiątkowa ku czci Kamila Stefki* [Commemorative book in honour of Kamil Stefko], PWN, Warsaw, 1976, 272.

197 Wasilkowski: *Sprawozdanie z prac Komisji*, 623–624.

198 Lisiewski: *Podstawowe problemy*, 12.

199 Zbigniew Resich: *Projekt kodeksu postępowania cywilnego po pierwszym czytaniu* [The draft of the code of civil procedure after the first reading], Nowe Prawo 1 (1960), 3–16; Władysław Siedlecki: *Z prac Komisji Kodyfikacyjnej nad nowym kodeksem postępowa-*

of proceedings, litigious and non-litigious[200] were maintained, and that the adversarial and dispositive principles were subjected to moderate limitations in favour of the powers of the court and of the prosecutor.[201]

Resich, being the Chair of the Procedural Civil Law Section, advanced the position that the point of reference in the design and drafting of a new code should be derived from what was referred to as the social function of civil procedure. The principal social value linked to civil procedure was, according to him, the creation of the conditions for the discovery of the truth during the trial, and, consequently, for the making of a decision based on accurately determined facts. Simultaneously, one had to pay attention to the nature of civil procedure defined by the dispositive principle and the adversarial principle. Accordingly, the above-expounded two-stage argument should be informing the criteria for the examination of whether the law as it stood was correct, as well as the criteria for the choice of direction in which the legal reform should proceed and direction for shaping its contents, including by recourse to comparative studies.

Analysis of European legislation led Resich to the conclusion that the draft should be the product of Polish codifiers' independent work because of the necessity of striking a balancing act to achieve the right proportions between guarantees giving effect to the principle of material (objective) truth on the one hand and the principles of autonomy and equality of the parties in civil procedure on the other hand. In his opinion, the legislative provisions enacted by other states fell short of completely achieving such a purpose.[202] Some guarantees of the principle of material truth were too weak (some of the codes of Western Europe), and some too forceful, deforming the essence of civil procedure (the codes of certain socialist states).

When analysing the progress of the legislative works, the historian of Polish civil procedural law, Anna Stawarska-Rippel, demonstrated that Resich's intention was to imbue the adversarial principle with new substance derived from the legacy of Polish legal scholarship, including the proposals discussed by the Codification Commission of the interwar period, as well as the outcome of the debate abroad before and after World War II. The initiative of the par-

---

nia cywilnego PRL [From the works of the Codification Commission on the new code of civil procedure], Studia Cywilistyczne 1 (1961), 205–215.

200 See Marian LISIEWSKI: *Scalenie postępowania spornego i niespornego* [The consolidation of litigious and non-litigious proceedings], Zeszyty Naukowe Uniwersytetu Łódzkiego 14 (1959), 83.

201 See SIEDLECKI: *Z prac Komisji*, 302.

202 RESICH: *Zasada dyspozytywności*, 58.

ties was to remain the cornerstone of the trial. The court's activity should be focused on giving direction to the procedure in such a way as to prompt the parties to act, while the adduction of evidence on the court's own motion or the judicial review of the parties' dispositive acts, or the power to make awards in excess of the claim, should be exceptions sanctioned by suitable wording of the new provisions.[203]

What was important to Resich was to achieve a moderate limitation of the dispositive principle and the adversarial principle while safeguarding the principle of equality of the parties. The latter was to be guaranteed by endowing the court with the power to engage in supplementary activity in all types of cases, not only a closed list specified by the legislature. Resolving the matter differently would have had the effect of conferring a privileged position on one of the parties in the types of relationships selected by the lawmakers.[204]

Resich's position, argued during the Codification Commission's works in 1957, in which he emphasized the need for balancing the diverse values that should be giving shape to shape the model of civil procedure, would be reiterated in 1959 by another active member of the Commission, Władysław Siedlecki. His argument, too, drew upon on a comprehensive review of European legislation and jurisprudence,[205] as well as the entire legacy of native legal scholarship. He subscribed to the view of the adversarial principle as the cornerstone of civil procedure, consigning the inquisitorial principle to merely a subsidiary role in the hands of a court venturing to establish the facts relevant to the outcome of the dispute in the face of insufficient activity of the litigating parties. Siedlecki emphasized the need for 'prudent limits' to be observed in doing this – limits laying the groundwork for a harmonious co-operation between the court and the litigating parties.[206] The development of the ideal of collaboration, would in turn, facilitate the streamlining of all other aspects of

---

203 Anna Stawarska-Rippel: *Elementy prywatne i publiczne w procesie cywilnym w świetle prac kodyfikacyjnych w Polsce (1918–1964): studium historycznoprawne* [Private and public elements in civil trial in the light of codification works in Poland (1918–1964): a historico-legal study], wwś, Katowice, 2015, 229.

204 Resich: *Zasada dyspozytywności*, 66–67; Zbigniew. Resich: *Ocena założeń kodyfikacyjnych kodeksu postępowania cywilnego* [Evaluation of the codification assumptions of the Code of Civil Procedure], in Kazimierz Piasecki (ed.): *Funkcjonowanie kodeksu postępowania cywilnego w praktyce. Materiały na konferencje naukową Popowo 25–27 października 1984 r.* [Functioning of the Code of Civil Procedure in practice. Materials for the academic conference in Popowo, 25–27 October 1984], Zeszyty Naukowe Instytutu Badania Prawa Sądowego 25 (1987), 17.

205 For more on Siedlecki's comparative studies see Introduction to the volume devoted to Professor Władysław Siedlecki's academic work, Studia Cywilistyczne 25–26 (1975), 4.

206 Siedlecki: *Przebudowa sądowego postępowania*, 99.

civil procedure. Such was the perspective espoused, according to Siedlecki, by the first draft of the Code of Civil Procedure.

In 1957, he became the rapporteur for the first position taken by the Commission on the model of the system of ordinary and extraordinary appellate remedies. He supplied arguments in favour of retaining the two-instance system introduced in 1949–1950 along with the institution of revision.[207] He cited examples from numerous other states and outlined a construct of the functions of second-instance proceedings founded on the ability to test both the legality and the merits of the first-instance ruling and enter either a reformative or a cassatory ruling. In Siedlecki's view, this way of organization of the procedure ensured greater effectiveness and efficiency of the court system.

It was, however, necessary to abandon the broad availability of 'extraordinary revision,' which had been introduced in 1950. Instead, it should be only on points of law, and the Minister of Justice, as an administrative authority, should not have the standing to bring it. The proposal was thus a compromise preserving the features typical of the legislation of socialist states while also imposing some limits on the political aspects. This concept came to serve as the starting point for the Commission's later works on the appellate system.[208] Partial modification increasing the role of ordinary appeals was the topic of the Commission's later meetings in 1958,[209] also resulting in a ban on detrimental outcomes of appellate procedures (prohibition of *reformatio in peius*).[210]

In the opinion of Siedlecki, the conceptual works and legislative *travaux* from the interwar period to date, including the works of the Codification Commission of 1956, justified the assertion that there existed a measurable and valuable contribution of Polish legal thought to the development of European theory of civil procedure.[211] That was firstly because the views advanced by Polish legal scholars generally refrained from advocating for the practical implementation of extreme positions, and secondly because Polish proposals

207 Report from the meeting of the Procedural Civil Law Team on 21 March 1957, AAN, MS, 2225, 2; WINIARZ: *Sprawozdanie z prac Komisji*, 628; Władysław SIEDLECKI: *System zaskarżania orzeczeń sądowych w kodeksie postępowania cywilnego PRL* [The system of remedies against judicial decisions in the Code of Civil Procedure of the Polish People's Republic], PiP 6 (1957), 1123–1142.

208 Report from the meeting of the Procedural Civil Law Team on 21 March 1957, AAN, MS, 2225, 3.

209 Meeting of the Civil Procedure Team on 13–16 January 1958 in Nieborów and in 5–6 June 1958 in Obory, AAN, MS, 2224, 70–82.

210 SIEDLECKI: *Z prac Komisji*, 299.

211 SIEDLECKI: *Przebudowa sądowego postępowania*, 91.

also incorporated certain original legal developments. As a result, the Commission was able to struck the right balance of proportions between the guarantees protecting the interests of society and those of the individual. According to Siedlecki, the attitude and experience of Polish lawyers and jurists were a contributing factor to this achievement. Some of that experience went all the way back to the codification efforts of the interwar period, and some dated back to the works on the unification of the provisions on non-litigious procedures during the latter half of the 1940s.

Unlike the lawyers and jurists of some socialist states in which a quick recodification ensued, the Polish Codification Commission beginning its works in 1956 had access to multiple sources of information, as well as the benefit of knowledge about the functioning of several different models of civil procedure. Reports on completely effective application of new socialist law, as well as the contents of the law enacted in capitalist states and its evaluation by the lawyers applying it in practice (notably in Germany and France),[212] as well as the rationales expounded at the onset of the final stages of the legislative process undertaken in some states (France, Sweden, Finland and Yugoslavia) with a view to stronger embodiment of the social function of civil procedure in the 1950s, these were all analysed and used in the Commission's work.

Meanwhile, the Soviet system of civil procedure was being overhauled. Its consolidation was initiated in 1957,[213] and the new code, implementing ideological assumptions announced long beforehand,[214] was adopted in 1964. Some of the solutions used by Soviet legislation, including the limitations of the adversarial principle, were merely the creative adaptation of principles borrowed from other jurisdictions.[215] Members of the Codification Commission were familiar with the works on the new Soviet procedural law, but such information did not become the main determinant of the shape taken by their proposal of a new code for Poland. Only a handful of features derived from Soviet legislation were included.[216] It is a fact, however, that the Commission's

212 *Ibidem*, 96–98.

213 See Kazimierz Lubiński: *Tendencje unifikacyjne w rozwoju postępowania cywilnego* [Unification tendencies in the development of civil procedure], in Andrzej Marciniak (ed.): *Księga pamiątkowa ku czci Profesora Witolda Broniewicza* [A commemorative book in honour of Professor Witold Broniewicz], WUŁ, Łódź, 1998, 230.

214 See Anna Stawarska-Rippel: *O rekodyfikacji radzieckiego postępowania cywilnego* [On the recodification of Soviet civil procedure], Z Dziejów Prawa 4 (2011), 141–142.

215 Pointed out by Stawarska-Rippel: *Elementy prywatne*, 364.

216 The principles of the civil procedure of the USSR and the constituent republics – 1961. For more see Stawarska-Rippel: *Elementy prywatne*, 241–242, 388.

proposal underwent a second round of editorial review with resulting modifications. That happened in part because of the public criticism of the first draft by one of the Commission's own members, Jerzy Jodłowski. His contention concentrated on the Commission's failure to incorporate the full extent of the legacy of socialist legal scholarship and with it the function served by civil procedure in furthering the public interest. Jodłowski was supported by Stefan Rozmaryn, a jurist of eminent standing among scholars of constitutional and administrative law at the time.[217] The argument was that the separation of two dichotomous modes of trial – litigious and non-litigious – in the first draft led to unjustifiable distinctions in the scope of the court's powers, which should be broad in any type of judicial procedure. Jodłowski also called for the restoration of the public prosecutor's powers on the scale delimited by the provisions enacted in 1950–1953.[218] In his opinion, the draft required some revisions to guarantee the maximum protection of socialized property. The appellate model also incurred similar objections from Jodłowski and Rozmaryn.

The criticism, based on Jodłowski's views dating back to the Stalinist period,[219] resulted in the partial modification of certain provisions that were of key importance to the model of civil procedure. The other members of the Commission managed to defend the separation of litigious from non-litigious proceedings with the argument that a new link had been established between the two procedural modes, namely, the *mutatis mutandis* applicability of the provisions of litigious procedure to the other modes. However, any designs of significantly curbing the prosecutor's independence were dropped. Instead, the powers of the public prosecutor to bring civil proceedings were strengthened. Modifications were also made to create more avenues for political interference at the stage of appellate proceedings and proceedings before the Supreme Court. Zbigniew explicitly informed the Commission members responsible for the drafting of the Code of Civil Procedure that the relevant provisions had incurred political censure from the Praesidium of the Commis-

217 Maria JĘDRZEJEWSKA, Jerzy LAPIERRE: *Sprawozdanie z dyskusji w komitecie nauk Prawnych PAN nad referatem Zbigniewa Resicha 'Ochrona własności społecznej w projekcie kodeksu postępowania cywilnego'* [Report on the debate held in the Legal Sciences Committee of the Polish Academy of Sciences on Zbigniew Resich's paper 'Protection of socialized property in the draft code of civil procedure'], PiP 10 (1960), 623.

218 Jerzy JODŁOWSKI: *Podstawowe problemy kodyfikacji postępowania cywilnego* [Core problems of codification of civil procedure], PiP 8–9 (1960), 174.

219 Jerzy JODŁOWSKI: *Nowy etap przebudowy polskiego procesu cywilnego* [New stage of remodelling of Polish civil procedure], PiP 5–6 (1953), 690–694.

sion,[220] which expected the development of a common model for civil and criminal procedure.

Among his other points, he argued: 'The above considerations leave the team with only one way out – revision of the concept of the draft from the perspective of both the political and the substantive assumptions, and its reformulation.'[221] In consequence, the 'extraordinary review' model introduced in 1950 made a return with only slight changes. Once again, the explanatory memorandum invoked an extra-legal premise – violation of the interests of the people's state.

When the Codification Commission closed its activities, the government once again resorted to the rhetorics of socialist ideology.[222] Auditing the Commission's work, it found that the draft did not sufficiently embody political directives, leading to significant modifications, sometimes outside of the official legislative track.[223] The new draft increased judicial and prosecutorial powers and conferred a privileged position on socialized economic units,[224] as well as reducing the distinction between litigious and non-litigous proceedings.

Notwithstanding the above changes, a great number of civil-law relationships were not regulated by the provisions of the Code of Civil Procedure. Moreover, the Code sanctioned the extra-judicial cognition of actions brought between socialized economic units and empowered the government to issue special legal provisions to deal with the resolution of other civil cases in a procedure removed from the jurisdiction of the courts. In the circumstances of a nationalized economy, this reduced the impact of the new law.[225] The last stage of the works on the Code, in 1964, bore fruit in a strengthening of the position of provisions enabling civil cases to be decided by non-judicial bodies, as was demanded by the President of the Chief Arbitration Committee,

220 Report from the meeting of the Civil Procedure Team on 27 March 1961 in Obory]; AAN, MS, 285, 9.

221 *Ibidem*, 10.

222 For more see SKĄPSKI: *Kodeks cywilny*, 75.

223 *Inter alia* Article 539(1) and Article 831(1) of the Code of Civil Procedure; see Władysław SIEDLECKI: *Kilka uwag na temat wykładni i stosowania przepisów nowego Kodeksu postępowania cywilnego* [Several remarks on the interpretation and application of the provisions of the new Code of Civil Procedure], Studia Cywilistyczne 12–14 (1969), 291. More about the methods and contents of the amendments to the draft see STAWARSKA-RIPPEL: *Elementy prywatne*, 357–360.

224 See Jan KRAJEWSKI: *Gwarancje ochrony własności społecznej w postępowaniu cywilnym* (*rozpoznawczym*) [Guarantees of protection of social property in civil procedure (main proceedings)], PiP 7 (1965), 32–46.

225 MACHNIKOWSKA: *Principles of the Code*, 122–148.

which heard cases with socialized economic units on both sides of the dispute.[226] The language of the provision governing this was, however, vague enough so that even certain disputes involving citizens could still be decided by administrative and quasi-judicial authorities. The bodies of the executive branch would avail themselves of that opportunity quite extensively.

As a result of multiple rounds of revisions to the original draft, the new law incorporated elements of different legal traditions.[227] The principles of the Code of Civil Procedure of 1964, and above all the regulation of these principles in special provisions, were shaped by an amalgamation of certain standards of Polish civil procedure applied in 1930, principles and institutions incorporated into the system after 1950 to force the transformation of the political system, and the original achievements of post-war Polish legal doctrine. The high editorial quality of the Code also needs to be mentioned, as its purpose was to achieve as much precision as possible and thus mitigate the risk of instrumentalized interpretation and application.

The official presentation of the Code and the structure taken by its first part were intended to highlight the differences between the law of 1930 and the law of 1964 and the progress in between.[228] Accordingly, the new guiding principles were placed in the spotlight, starting with the principle of material truth (objective truth), which was treated as 'the principle of principles,'[229] through the principle of protection of social property, the principle of 'real' (*realna* – true, genuine, realistic) equality of the parties, and the principle of controlled ability to exercise rights relating to the object of the process, to the principle of moderate formalism.[230] The Code also took heed of the classical principles of the conduct of process: public openness of the proceedings, oral conduct of

226 Letter from the President of the Chief Arbitration Committee. AAN, MS, 3128, 39.

227 See STAWARSKA-RIPPEL: *Elementy prywatne*, 110–151; 168–189; 221–242; Anna STAWARSKA-RIPPEL: *Fundamental Principles in the Views of the Authors of the Drafts of the First and Second Polish Codes on Civil Procedure – a Comparative Procedure*, in MACHNIKOWSKA, STAWARSKA-RIPPEL: *Principles of Civil Procedure*, 107–122.

228 Stenographic report of the 29th session of the Sejm of the People's Republic of Poland on 16 and 17 November 1964, 76–136.

229 Jerzy JODŁOWSKI: *Zasady naczelne socjalistycznego postępowania cywilnego* [The fundamental principles of socialist civil procedure], in Jerzy JODŁOWSKI (ed.), *Wstęp do systemu prawa procesowego cywilnego* [Introduction to the system of civil procedure], Ossolineum, Wrocław, 1974, 75.

230 For more see Władysław SIEDLECKI: *Zasady naczelne postępowania cywilnego w świetle przepisów nowego kodeksu postępowania cywilnego* [The fundamental principles of civil procedure in the light of the provisions of the new Code of Civil Procedure], Studia Cywilistyczne 7 (1966), 3ff.

the proceedings, immediacy (direct examination of evidence), free evaluation of evidence, and the judge's control of the proceedings.

The principle of equality of the parties functioned in a limited way. This was because of the provisions empowering courts and prosecutors to take active measures on behalf of the principle of objective truth, as well as provisions conferring a privileged position on entities representing the interests of the state. At their source was another guiding principle of socialist civil procedure – the protection of socialized property and of state institutions not engaged in economic activity. Due to the *de facto* ownership structure in Poland, this principle was mainly applicable to state ownership. The courts' responsibilities in the proceedings in this regard were manifold, ranging from the precautionary notification of the prosecutor, through powers of control over the parties' dispositive actions, as well as the ability to summon a person to participate in a case as a defendant or to bring charges against additional defendants on the court's own motion, all the way up to the possibility of adjudicating on a subject matter not covered by the prayers of the action and beyond the limits of the dispute.

The first and foremost of all the guiding principles – that of objective ('material') truth – was established on two levels of implementation. The first level was the duty of the parties and participants to speak the truth. There were no penalties for the breach of this duty, but it was based on the grounds of procedural loyalty and prohibition of abuse of rights in the procedure.[231] The second level, addressed to the courts themselves, established a duty to investigate and clarify the true nature of the factual and legal relationships involved in the cases coming up for ruling. While the legislature employed the weaker modalities of 'should,' and 'may,' the later interpretation of this provision reflected the theory 'that in a particular case a power can turn into a duty.'[232]

The court's power to admit evidence *ex officio* and to consider facts not claimed by the parties, as stated in the Code, was directly linked to the principle of objective truth. These powers were not limited by any requirements to be met, and the court also held the power to order an investigation to determine the evidence necessary for arriving at a decision. The relevant provision of the Code did not reflect the Codification Commission's original

231 See Kazimierz PIASECKI: *Nadużycie praw procesowych przez strony* [The abuse of procedural rights by the parties], Palestra 11 (1960), 20.

232 The resolution of the Supreme Court of 27.06.1953, CIC/C Prez 195/52, OSN 1953.4.95; see Jerzy JODŁOWSKI, Kazimierz PIASECKI (eds): *Kodeks postępowania cywilnego z komentarzem* [The Code of Civil Procedure with a commentary], Wydawnictwo Prawnicze, Warsaw, 1989, 39.

intention of emphasizing that the court's use of that particular power should be confined to exceptional circumstances. The judicature emphasized the desirability of its use especially in cases involving the protection of the public interest, which was understood to mean the involvement of state entities or social and family relations.[233] However, for cases related to the 'rights of status' concerning the civil situation of a person, it was stipulated that the principle of objective truth 'd[id] not reign supreme.'[234]

The courts of the first and second instances were accorded the power to adjudicate on subject matter not covered by the prayers and in excess of the dispute or petition. The court was not bound by the scope of maintenance claims, claims for damages in tort actions, or any cases with socialized economic units as claimants. The power to adjudicate beyond the limits was also applicable to labour cases with employee claimants. The interpretation of this provision was far-reaching, demonstrating that the courts were obliged to determine the existence of conditions for such adjudication, and, in the affirmative, to issue a decision affording broader procedural protection to the claimant.[235]

The limitation of the dispositive principle[236] also applied to judicial control of actions such as withdrawal of an action, limitation or waiver of a claim, consent judgement, withdrawal of a revision appeal, objection to a default judgment, or defences to writs. The court was empower to refuse to allow those on the grounds of unlawfulness, conflict with the principles of social coexistence or flagrant violation of the interests of rights-holders. The scholars acknowledged the social significance of these provisions, although the need for their strict interpretation as exceptions from the general rule of the dispositive principle.

The principle of prosecutorial participation in civil proceedings was worded very broadly in the Code. The prosecutor had both the standing to bring proceedings and to accede to any action, but in non-proprietary cases in family law an action could only be brought by a prosecutor in cases provided by statute, which in practice made divorce petitions the only exception. The grounds for prosecutorial involvement, which limited the disposi-

233 Resolution of the Supreme Court of 15 July 1974, C/ZO/Kw Pr 2/74, OSNCP.1974.12.203; resolution of the Supreme Court of 9 June 1976, III CZP 46/75, OSNCP.1976.9.184.

234 Resolution of the Supreme Court of 7 April 1971, III CZP 87/70, OSNCP.1972.3.42.

235 See JODŁOWSKI, PIASECKI (eds): *Kodeks postępowania*. 38.

236 For more see Jerzy LAPIERRE: *Kontrola sądowa czynności dyspozycyjnych stron i uczestników w postępowaniu cywilnym* [The judicial control of dispositive actions of the parties and participants in civil proceedings], in *Księga pamiątkowa ku czci Kamila Stefki*, 183.

tive principle, were so conceptually capacious that they left prosecutors with full freedom to act in order to protect the rule of law, the rights of citizens, the public interest, and social property.

Against this background, there were also voices supportive of the principle of co-operation between participants in a civil procedure, relativizing even further the adversarial principle.[237] Jurists supporting the retention of the adversarial principle and its procedural traditions, even with the possibility of *ex officio* adduction of evidence, emphasized that the powers of the judge in the proceedings did not eliminate the burden of proof, which was primarily incumbent on the parties.[238]

The system of appeals in the Code of 1964 was formed in line with the arrangements introduced to the Polish legal system in 1950, with only slight modifications.[239] The main appellate remedy in the normal hierarchical course of judicial instances was revision (*rewizja*), regulated in broad strokes retaining the specific legal nature of the institution. There were numerous exceptions to the principle that courts were bound by the scope of the revision, relating to the type of defect identified by the appellate court, the type of case (claims for intangible rights, support, or compensation for damage caused by a tort) and type of appellant (socialized economic entity or employee).

A remedy against a final and binding judgment was available in the form of extraordinary appeal. That institution was distinguished by the narrow circle of entities equipped with the standing to bring it (it could not be brought by direct action of the parties), its legal grounds and political bases – a flagrant violation of law or of the interests of the Polish People's Republic – and its availability against any final decision concluding the proceedings.

---

237 Władysław SIEDLECKI: *Zasada kontradyktoryjności (sporności) czy zasada współdziałania podmiotów postępowania cywilnego* [The adversarial principle versus the principle of co-operation between participants in civil proceedings], PiP 6 (1975), 63.

238 See Witold BRONIEWICZ: *Zasad kontradyktoryjności procesu cywilnego w poglądach nauki polskiej (1880–1980)* [The adversarial principle in civil procedure in the views of Polish legal scholarship (1880–1980)], in Maria JĘDRZEJEWSKA, Tadeusz ERECIŃSKI (eds): *Studia z prawa postępowania cywilnego: księga pamiątkowa ku czci Zbigniewa Resicha* [Studies in civil procedural law. commemorative book in honour of Zbigniew Resich], PWN, Warsaw, 1985, 39.

239 See STAWARSKA-RIPPEL: *Elementy prywatne*, 364–381.

CHAPTER 5

Political Petrification of the Idea of Modernizing the Law (1965–1989)

1 Introduction

The coming of the codes into force in 1965 coincided with the petrification of the party's concept of the contents and the principles of the modernization. The above had a significant impact on the system of private law and the respective fates of its two modernization currents. For the authors created the conditions for both, albeit it remains to this day an object of dispute in modern legal scholarship whether those were the right conditions and whether the codifiers' intention was the harmonious development of both currents.[1] It is a fact, on the other hand, that the modernization processes involving the three codes took a direction that was unexpected both to political decision-makers and to a large part of the legal circles.

Until the eighties of the 20th century, no significant changes to the codes followed. Their interpretation in the adjudication of the courts and in scholarly works also was stable. An exception has to be made for a scholarly controversy as to the Civil Code's principle of unity of state property (national property). The generality of its language was interpreted by some commentators as the codifiers' having left room for the use of different solutions in the provisions giving effect to the principle. That proposition was not heeded. The consequences were of significant import, locking out the opportunity to reform that element of the system of private law which had proven to be the most defect.

The modernization in social and economic affairs pursued in accordance with the assumptions of Marxist-Leninist ideology suffered from methodological flaws. As a result, it failed to achieve it's purpose, and at the same it deformed whatever parts of the legal system it was supposed to reform. The modernization impaired the functioning of the instruments it attempted to leverage, among them the Civil Code and the Code of Civil Procedure (the processes discussed here did not affect the application of the Family and Guardianship Code. This is because the solutions introduced to the codes

1 See Grzybowski: *Zagadnienia kodyfikacji*, 103ff; Skąpski: *Kodeks cywilny*, 57–76.

 | DOI:10.1163/9789004730021_007

subjected the economic relationships governed by civil law not only to the provisions of the codes themselves but also to provisions located outside of the codes and disposing of the same matters differently.

The scale of the use of such extra-code provisions and the fact that those were provisions enacted by the bodies of the executive branch, had the result that the main effect of the codes on a considerable part of civil law was reducible to the existence of a code provision as a basis for a reference to other legislation. Accordingly, this was a not case, known to other legal systems of the 20th century, where the notion of decodification is associated with a weakening of the code's primacy in the hierarchy of sources of law through the enactment of detailed statutes regulating civil-law relationships, along with the development of a body of previous court decisions and the use of non-classic source of law such as in labour law.[2] Poland of the 1965–1989 period underwent a real, far-gone and far-reaching fragmentation of the country's system of civil law. The use of the term 'decodification' as a descriptor of the status and position of the civil code and code of civil procedure in the legal system of the time has a solid basis and is well documented by sources after 1990.

The majority of the extra-code legislation governing civil-law relationships was in the nature of administrative rather than civil law, even though the enacting administrative bodies used the terminology of civil law, for example by referring to contracts. In the absence of a free-market economy, such provisions applied to entities of any kind, as it regulated civil-law relationships between state entities, economic relationships between state entities and natural persons, as well as a certain part of civil-law relationships with natural persons on both sides.

The above led to the deformation of the legal character of a great portion of legal relationships. The developments did not at the time become the subject of academic studies in civil law.[3] Theoretical studies in civil law continued to emphasize the distinguishing characteristics of civil law, such as the equality of the parties, entitlements, and the lack of compulsion.[4] The attitude taken by the members of the Codification Commission, who continued their work as active scholars or in the justice system, was a possible contributing factor to

2 Izdebski: *Kodyfikacje cywilne*, 160–161.

3 Józef Litwin: *Z problematyki styku prawa cywilnego z administracyjnym* [From the topics of the intersection of civil and administrative law], PiP 2 (1965), 540.

4 Andrzej Stelmachowski: *Wstęp do teorii prawa cywilnego* [Introduction to the theory of civil law], PWN, Warsaw, 1969, 17, 30, 54 and 317.

this. In their publications, they analysed the legal system primarily through the perspective of code norms, leaving the surrounding legal environment out of the discussion. Another contributing factor could be the difficulty in researching the enormous collection of administrative provisions regulating civil law dispersed throughout the entire legal systems.

The codifiers' professed principle of uniformity of civil law was legal fiction already at the time of coming into life of the Civil Code and of the Code of Civil Procedure. Some among the codifiers did not directly address this fact, contenting themselves, as Aleksander Wolter did, with expressing their view that the economic relationships arising in a money-goods economy 'and therewith based upon the principle of the equality of the parties, viz. civil-law relationships, ought in principle to be subjected to the same legal regime, irrespective of whether socialized, individual or personal property underlies them.'[5]

Other lawyers involved in the codification, such Jan Winiarz, argued for the soundness of the law applicable at the time; according to their explanation, the principle of uniformity of civil law was for objective reasons unable to find full reflection in reality, for there always existed additional regulation of civil-law relationships outside of the code. Our jurist omitted from his train of thought the circumstance that the activities of the administrative bodies in pursuance of the lawmaking delegation from the code had resulted in the emergence of fundamental differences between the laws and obligations of the entities whose legal transactions continued to be regulated by the code on the one hand and those whose relationships were governed by other provisions, albeit the code also contained regulation applicable to them. Winiarz reduced this fact to the observation that: 'the principle of uniformity of civil law does not imply the homogeneity of its solutions for all legal relationships.'[6]

Jan Wasilkowski, by contrast, asserted that the principle of uniformity of civil law was upheld, arguing that alongside classic civil-law relationships there also existed a new type of relationships combining in themselves the characteristic features of civil and administrative law.[7] The source for his view was the inclusion of the unity of state property (national property) in the Civil Code, whereby socialized economic units were divested of legal autonomy in civil-law relationships and subjected to administrative law instead.

5 Aleksander WOLTER: *Prawo cywilne: zarys części ogólnej* [Civil law: an outline of the general part], PWN, Warsaw, 1967, 20.

6 WINIARZ: *Kodeks cywilny*, 9.

7 WASILKOWSKI: *Pojęcie własności*, 62.

The ideology derived from Marxist-Leninist assumptions introduced two characteristic solutions to the Civil Code. One of those was used in practice to consolidate in the hands of the central administration the exercise of the property rights held by the state, the other one to impose limitations on the exercise of the rights held by individuals. Politics, on the other hand, determined the marginalization of the impact of the Civil Code on private law, so that ideological goals would be pursued on the path of legislation pertaining to administrative law. The latter *de facto* regulated a considerable part of the contents of civil-law economic relationships (limitations on the exercise of private rights with regard to farms, contained directly in the Civil Code, were an exception, although even there, provisions located outside of the Code were also applicable). In the case of Code of Civil Procedure, the judicial path was excluded or restricted for some categories of civil cases. As a result, a considerable body of civil-law relationships were exempted from the application of the recodified norms of procedural civil law.

The joint outcome of all of these factors taken together was the taking of a stronger position within the legal system – on the authority of the codes – by legal solutions transforming civil-law relationships along with their regulation far more extensively than the codes did. The tenor of the change contradicted equally the classic principles of civil law, as well as Polish legal tradition.

The Polish United Workers' Party [PZPR] worked hard to build its image of a moderator of social and legal affairs. However, it failed to introduce legislation consistent with that image. The new provisions, billeted as socialist law, were oppressive (curtailment of private law) and economically irrational (regulation of civil-law relationships involving state-owned and socialized parties). The fact of their use attested to the emptiness of the constitutional promises of social justice, popular democracy and socialist rule of law. The socialist model of modernization through law entered on an idle run of sorts, demonstrating the full extent of its deficiencies.

In the Polish culture of private law, part of the broader Roman culture, the governing principles had been the equality of the parties and the ability to exercise rights accompanied by obligations and balanced in due proportion, as a consequence of the regulatory method used. Mentally associated with private law were the concepts of individual rights and freedoms, the sense of which was expressed by, among others, the principle of freedom of contract. By contrast, the law applied on the basis of the Civil Code, because of the references to provisions located outside of the Code, to which the codifiers set no limits, followed a different axiology.

That axiology was culturally foreign to Polish society. In the new law, obligations predominated over the rights, at times marginalizing them altogether, as was to be experienced both by state-owned enterprises and by subsistence farmers. The principle of equality of the parties was either completely or largely eliminated from the new pattern of regulation of civil-law relationships. The administrative bodies enacting the provisions governing this part of the legal system followed typically administrative methods, which were only partially adapted to meet the specificity of civil affairs as a new subject-matter to regulate, without substantial modifications to previous practice.

From the perspective of the citizens, such actions caused the majority of society – two thirds of it the large-industry working class – to contend on an everyday basis with the irrationally regulated functioning of state-owned enterprises; on the workers' leaving the workplace to become consumers, the errors in the legal system would become even more apparent. The remaining one third in the 70s of the 20th century were the former peasants, i.e. small-scale farmers daily confronted with far-reaching limitations on the exercise of their private rights already envisaged by the Code but in practice much more frequent due to the special provisions enacted by the administration.

In consequence, in social reception, the socialist law lacked the qualities promised by the PZPR. Although, classic civil law remained rational and continued to provide a sense of agency, its use was confined only to a limited scope of civil-law relationships. An important circumstance here was Polish society's historical experience of a diversity of legal systems imposed by the partitioning powers, uniquely positioning it to compare and evaluate the effectiveness of the new legislation. In that comparison, as far as civil-law economic relationships were concerned, the socialist law placed at the bottom. During the interwar period, before the unification of substantive civil law was completed, different parts of Poland were governed by the AGBG, BGB and Code of Napoleon, as well as Polish Law and Volume X of Digest of Laws of the Russian Empire, the latter of which with only a narrow scope of application.

The unification completed in the aftermath of World War II introduced a more modern private law compared to its predecessor, which was adapted to society's national identity – a task facilitated by society's homogeneity following the border changes and population transfers – as well as reflecting the social and economic transformations of the beginning of the latter half of the 20th century. Its 1964 replacement with a codification of substantive law and recodification of procedural civil law, as well as recodification of family and guardianship law could be regarded as a progressive development only for the last-mentioned part. The modernization potential of the two first-mentioned codes was originally significant but marginalized by decodification.

The cited circumstances were significant to the social reception of the codification and to such elements of legal culture as the level of confidence the citizens would place in the state, in the law and in each other. Certain scholars reduced the critical outlook of some of the citizens on the law of time to resentment. One such scholar, Andrzej Stelmachowski, who in 1989 would become involved in the reconstruction of the legal order, in 1969 suggested to the citizens that they should leverage the potential of the codified family law and of the provisions guaranteeing the protection of their personal property:

> Of course, the significant intensification of extra-economic coercion has its negative sides – it paralyses individual activity and inflicts a number of losses, triggered if only by the need for the constant overcoming of inhibitions. Hence the longing in many for the restoration of the old system (...). Personally, I do not think such a longing can be satisfied in the foreseeable future.[8]

In the seventies and eighties of the 20th century, the future ideological and axiological motivations of the new reformers were taking shape. The first, in 1980–1981, compiled partial drafts intended to restore at least some legal principles without dislodging the foundations of the socialist system. That was connected with the phenomenon of societal resistance to the government and its understanding of law at the time. Those developments were unfolding under the Aegis of the first independent mass social movement in the socialist states of this part of Europe, which was the Solidarity trade union. Attempts at reform were blocked by the establishment of martial law in 1981.

The aforementioned mixed positive-negative experience, together with the observation of continued deformation of the law in 1982–1988, would serve society in 1989 with the demanded change of the political system from socialism to liberal democracy. That led not only to amendments of the Civil Code and Code of Civil Procedure but also safeguards against the repetition of the brand of decodification remembered from the socialist system. A new system of Polish private law was thus prepared, adapted to societal expectations of the time but also to the stage of functioning of codes in the era of post-modern law in which the legal systems of states in other parts of Europe had already found themselves.

8 Stelmachowski: *Wstęp do teorii*, 318.

The later part of this chapter discusses more closely the various factors affecting the course taken by that process of change. Those show the influence of the legal circumstances resulting subsequently in a paradigm shift with regard to the limits of the reforms, in the eyes of the majority of society. For not only economic considerations but also the perception of the law[9] prompted the prevalent societal determination to face up to the challenge of systemic change as the first among all communities confronted with a similar situation. That occurred when the state still had not only its socialist system in place but also the USSR as an immediate neighbour, having responded militarily in 1956 in Hungary and in 1968 in Czechoslovakia to block any significant political or economic changes in its zone of influence.

It is also worth emphasizing the relationship between the consequences of the PZPR's handling of the codes and the position taken by scholars in private law, part of those the codifiers and part, gradually, the lawyers and jurists who would influence in different forms the changes enacted in the nineties of the 20th century.

2 The Modernizer in Need of Modernization

The leadership of the PZPR would often address society with progress updates on the building of the socialist foundations of the state and law.[10] The method of presentation implied the omnipotence of the party, as well as bilocation. The party had the ability to discern properly the laws of history and the determinants of socio-economic processes, it was claimed. That special type of knowledge, inaccessible to anyone else, justified the monoparty's position in the political and the economic system,[11] guaranteed the optimal protection of the interests of the proletariat and prevented the

9 The question of the law is worth emphasizing because in the course of recent debate on the political culture of the 1965–1989 period, some representatives of social sciences focus on economic matters, copying the self-presentation of the People's Republic along with the assumptions of historical materialism proclaiming the law as secondary to relations of production.

10 An example can be found in the resolution passed at the 7th Congress of the PZPR on 8–12 December 1975, see *VII Zjazd PZPR. Podstawowe materiały i dokumenty* [The 7th Conference of the Polish United Workers' Party. Basic materials and documents], Książka i Wiedza, Warsaw, 1975, 222.

11 This assumption formed the basis of some analyses of legal affairs; Zygmunt RYBICKI: *Administracja gospodarcza w PRL* [The economic administration in Polish People's Republic], WN PWN, Warsaw, 1978, 49.

party's alienation. There was to exist a direct link between the '(party – A.M.) apparatus and the working people exercising the oversight of the apparatus.'[12]

In reality, those in power persisted in imagining a metaphysical connection between the economy and politics,[13] understanding neither of the two spheres and ignoring the laws of sociology.[14] By multiplying economically defective reproduction patterns, they compounded the negative consequences of their actions[15] and failed to take lessons from similar problems occurring in other socialist states.[16] They kept returning to the same 'socialization' projects and using methods that failed to achieve the expected results. Amid the socio-economic crises, claims such as the following were still made even in 1981: 'the application of Marxist analysis to social processes is one of the main prerequisites for the party's correct political course.'[17]

---

12 In the 13th Plenum of the Central Committee of the PZPR in 1964, among other things Władysław Gomułka proclaimed: 'the socialist consciousness must be characterized by a socialist attitude to specific economic and political needs (…) and to the party as the avant-garde of the working class, and to the principal assumptions of its policy.'

13 Leszek NOWAK: *U podstaw teorii socjalizmu* [At the foundation of the theory of socialism], Nankom, Poznań, 1991, 149.

14 Andrzej WALICKI: *Marksizm i skok do królestwa wolności: dzieje komunistycznej utopii* [Marxism and the jump to the realm of freedom: the history of the communist Utopia], WN PWN, Warsaw, 1996, 476–479; Stanisław KOZYR-KOWALSKI: *Socjologia, społeczeństwo obywatelskie i państwo* [Sociology, civil society and the state], WN UAM, Poznań, 2004, 35, 127.

15 For more see concerning the errors and absurdities of the economic reality of the Polish People's Republic see Janusz KALIŃSKI: *Gospodarka Polski w latach 1944–1989: przemiany strukturalne* [The economy of Poland in 1944–1989: structural transformations], Państwowe Wydawnictwo Ekonomiczne, Warsaw, 1995; Zbigniew LANDAU, Wojciech ROSZKOWSKI: *Polityka gospodarcza II RP i PRL* [The economic policies of the Second Polish Republic and of the Polish People's Republic], WN PWN, Warsaw, 1995; Andrzej JEZIERSKI, Cecylia LESZCZYŃSKA: *Historia gospodarcza Polski* [An economic history of Poland], Key Text, Warsaw, 1998.

16 The leadership of the PZPR had access to information about the economic and political situation in other socialist states enabling it to determine the sources of their problems. Among examples of unused analyses is the documentation sourced at the onset of the seventies, concerning the USSR, East Germany, Hungary and Czechoslovakia; see more meeting of the Politburo of the Central Committee of the PZPR on 30 November 1971, AAN BP KC PZPR, 2920, 327–550.

17 *IX Nadzwyczajny Zjazd Polskiej Zjednoczonej Partii Robotniczej. 14–20 lipca 1981 r.: stenogram z obrad plenarnych* [The 9th Conference of the Polish United Workers' Party. 14–20 July 1981. Stenogram of plenary deliberations], Książka i Wiedza, Warsaw, 1983, 691.

The doctrinarian interpretations of the ideology were not changed by the introduction of new technologies to industry and the expansion of the 'social base'. It consisted in the creation of the image of the party leadership as an amalgamation of ideology with managerism, along with the frequent shifting of accents from catchwords of the dictatorship of the proletariat to symbols and gestures invoking the values of the national identity and the latter's harmonious symbiotic relationship with the socialist political system. That was still accompanied, however, by reminders of the monoparty's role of initiation and interpretation: 'The PZPR, being a class party, is simultaneously a whole-national force (...) cultivating the most precious threads of our history.'[18]

In the new narration, the previous co-existence of socialism only with the progressive elements of plebeian tradition, avoided a similar kind of selection in the official message of the seventies, amid assurances that the development of the socialist state was benefiting from traditions originating from a diversity of social origins:

> The cultural policy of People's Poland proceeds from the Leninist concept of the existence of two cultural currents in the national society. From the recognition of and respect for the progressive traditions of both the culture of the former ruling classes and the plebeian circles, as well as the need to put to advantage both of these currents of cultural heritage in the shaping of a new type of socialist society.[19]

The verbalized politico-social unity of the nation and the state implied an equally strong involvement of the party in the development of the economy, as well as the protection of the 'national imponderables'.[20]

The actions were neutral towards such elements of legal tradition as customary law[21] and customs. The former had next to no significance for Pol-

---

18 AAN, Komitet Centralny Polskiej Zjednoczonej Partii Robotniczej, V/341, document prepared by the Ideological Section of the Central Committee of the PZPR: *Zasady obchodów świąt i ważniejszych rocznic historycznych* [Principles for the celebration of holidays and major historical anniversaries], 63–64.

19 Józef Burszta: *Wartości kultury ludowej w społeczeństwie socjalistycznym* [The values of popular culture in a socialist state], Nowe Drogi 10 (1976), 137–146.

20 Janusz Rolicki: *Edward Gierek: przerwana dekada: wywiad rzeka* [Edward Gierek: a broken decade: extended interview], Fakt, Warsaw, 1990, 83.

21 The ideological interpretation of customary law changed (according to the assumptions of Marxist doctrine, any law, in order to be applicable, required the sanction of the state either in statutory form or expressed by court decisions); because of its lack of wide-

ish society, while the ability to invoke custom[22] was incorporated into the Civil Code, as well as the preceding legislation, but in practice the citizens availed themselves of the opportunity only sporadically. The conclusion drawn from studies conduct at the time into the interpretation of the law by society and by the courts was that dynamic interpretation prevailed and historical interpretation was absent from general practice.[23]

The economy was still managed through a model developed near the end of the fifties.[24] The associated paradigm incorporated not only historical materialism but also the assumption, adhered to by the PZPR leadership even in the seventies and the eighties, that the USSR would respond negatively to any changes to Poland's economic system. The PZPR associated calls for reform with a challenge to the principles of functioning of the central-planning system, regarded as the introduction of changes not only conflicting with the ideological assumptions but also changes expanding the already existing gap between Poland's socio-economic system and the systems of other socialist states (lack of collectivization; greater freedom of expression). Of characteristic significance here is the declaration of the bond between the USSR and the Polish People's Republic, formalized constitutionally in 1976 by an amendment professing friendship between the two states.[25] The motivation for blocking the reforms in the seventies was explained from a later perspective by the then-First Secretary of the PZPR as follows: 'I was convinced, which I never concealed, that our ideological and political links to the USSR were inviolable and served our national interests. I had no intention of repudiating them. I was neither an adventurer nor a suicide.'[26]

A doctrinal foundation for the continued functioning of private law was supplied by a handful of provisions of the Constitution of the Polish People's Republic of 1952,[27] unofficially redacted by Joseph Stalin before their enact-

spread presence in Poland, this type of modernization failed to exert an influence on Polish legal culture.

22 The ability to invoke custom was envisaged by the general provisions and by real law (i.e. the law of 'things'), law of obligations and inheritance law – Articles 56, 65, 69, 287, 298, 354, 385, 394, 994 and 1039 of the Civil Code.

23 WRÓBLEWSKI: *Zagadnienia teorii*, 167–175.

24 'It was eager to present itself as an environment of efficiently organized and open-minded socialist managers'; DUDEK, ZBLEWSKI, *Utopia nad Wisłą*, 228.

25 Article 6 of the Constitution of Polish People's Republic.

26 Edward GIEREK: *Smak życia: pamiętniki* [*Taste of life: memoirs*], BGW, Warsaw, 1993, 191.

27 The provision regulating the state's protection for peasant farms did not envisage property ownership (Article 10 of the Constitution of Polish People's Republic), and the provision enumerating the rights to own and inherit property stipulated that the

ment by Polish legislature.[28] Some of the provisions were repressive in their tenor, and others, capable of objective interpretation, were not followed in practice.[29] Although the party exerted less coercion in the everyday lives of the citizens than in the fifties, it still controlled numerous developments through the law. The constitutional basis for this type of activity was also added to the Constitution of the Polish People's Republic in 1976,[30] through reference to the PZPR as the 'guiding force in society'.[31] The rationale justifying this type of power drew upon – simultaneously proclaimed in the same instrument – civilizational progress taking the Polish state from the 'people's democracy' stage to the 'socialism' stage.

scope of protection of said rights was to be determined by ordinary statutes (Article 12 of the Constitution of Polish People's Republic). According to Article 10, the state 'extend[ed] its protection to the individual farms of the working peasants and assist[ed] them with a view to protection from capitalist exploitation, agricultural-technological development, and increased prosperity'; Article 12: 'Polish People's Republic recognizes and protects through the applicable legislation the individual ownership and inheritance of land, buildings and other means of production belonging to peasant farmers, craftspeople and cottage workers.'

28 Krzysztof PERSAK: *'Troskliwy opiekun i światły doradca Polski Ludowej': poprawki Józefa Stalina do Konstytucji PRL z 22 lipca 1952 r.* ['The attentive protector and enlightened advisor of the People's Poland': Joseph Stalin's corrections to the Constitution of the People's Republic of Poland of 22 July 1952], in Dariusz STOLA, Marcin ZAREMBA (eds): *PRL: trwanie i zmiana* [The People's Republic of Poland: persistence and change], WSPIZ im. Koźmińskiego, Warsaw, 2003, 187–209.

29 Among others, Article 48 of the Constitution of Polish People's Republic, whereby the courts were to: 'guard the political system of Polish People's Republic, protect the achievements of Poland's working population, safeguard socialist rule of law, socialized property and rights of the citizens and punish criminals.' This aspect is noted by Andrzej Ajnenkiel: 'Of these phrases, only the latter two (...) were of objectivized nature. All of the preceding ones concerned themselves with the (...) politico-repressive function of the judiciary as one of the organs tasked with the maintenance of the regime existing in Poland'; Andrzej AJNENKIEL: *Konstytucje polskie w rozwoju dziejowym 1791–1997* [Polish constitutions in historical development 1791–1997], Rytm, Warsaw, 2001, 307.

30 Act of 10 February 1976 amending the Constitution of Polish People's Republic, Dz. U.5.39.

31 Studies into the functioning of administrative bodies in the sphere of the relationships between the citizens and the state supplied the basis for the conclusion that a 'new totalitarianism' making the administrative practices following 1956 – no longer physically coercive but still oppressive; see Jerzy W. OCHMAŃSKI: *Administracja świadcząca: kształtowanie się idei organizatorskiej funkcji państwa w Polsce Ludowej (1944–1989)* [A providing administration: the formation of the ideal of the organizing function of the state in People's Poland (1944–1989)], WUAM, Poznań, 2006, 20–22.

While the discrepancies between theory and practice were mounting, society would be advised of the transitional nature of such cases,[32] one caused by the significant economic dynamic of socialist Poland. The accompanying caveat was that the inconsistencies would 'continue to appear for a longer time ahead.'[33] According to this narration, socialism presented greater challenges than capitalism. Although both of these systems derived from Roman law, the latter had to confront the outgoing feudal system; socialism was building a new legal tradition. An additional guarantee of the PZRP's sustained control of the 'logic of history' would be the flexible adaptation of the assumptions of Marxism to the Polish state and law – albeit always in keeping with ideological principles. Such activities were referred to as 'practical doctrine'.[34]

The realistic evaluation of the ideological foundation of the state's political system does not paint a healthy picture. Selective quotations from the works of the authors of historical materialism were used, and their very abundance was meant to imply that socialism continued to developed economic, legal and other theories. Meanwhile, the PZPR was in a state of intellectual stagnation. The philosopher, Leszek Kołakowski, dubbed the party's ideological contents a fossil. For the historian, Andrzej Friszke, who studied this aspect at a later time, it was a 'dead ritual'.[35]

Since the sixties, scholars in the social sciences[36] had been sounding the alarm that doctrinairism was thwarting any chance of realistic moderni-

---

32 Detailed analysis of the factors determining the views taken by the PZPR leadership, including the increasing role of the 'baggage of experience' of successive socio-economic crises, as interlinked with the Marxist-Leninist theory of historical process and hostility to the values represented by the Catholic Church, with the following reservation: 'In particular, it appears to be impossible to determine the extent to which the officially proclaimed motives and the decisions and propaganda activities resulting from them corresponded to the true consciousness of the holders of key positions in the party and the state'; DUDEK: *Wybrane czynniki*, 35–36.

33 *Referat Władysława Gomułki na IX Plenum: węzłowe problemy polityki partii* [Władysław Gomułka's paper for the 9th Plenary Session: seminal problems of the party's policy], Nowe Drogi 6 (1957), 4.

34 This is the term used by, among others, Stanisław KOZYR-KOWALSKI: *Struktura gospodarcza i formacja społeczeństwa* [Economic structure and the formation of society], Książka i Wiedza, Warsaw, 1988, 272–277; to Leszek Kołakowski, that was primarily a social philosophy containing no methods of practical regulation of the principles and functioning of institutions; KOŁAKOWSKI: *Główne nurty*, vol. 1, 427.

35 Leszek KOŁAKOWSKI: *Główne nurty*, 923, FRISZKE: *Polska: losy państwa*, 338.

36 Leszek Kołakowski's speech delivered on 21 October 1966: *Kultura polska w ostatnim dziesięcioleciu* [Polish culture in the last decade], in Zbigniew ROMEK: *Droga Leszka*

zation, for which there was a place in a socialist state. In 1979, a number of academics, social activists and representatives of culture compiled proposals for a reform, which preserved the constitutional principles of the system and which were ignored – *Report on the state of the Republic and the paths leading to its emendation.*[37] In 1980, following a wave of mass protests from the citizens on a scale greater than before, the government entered into an understanding with representatives of society, agreeing to initiate some reforms.[38] In 1981, the leadership of the PZPR, withdrew from the previous declarations. Martial law was imposed,[39] certain civil rights were suspended, intervention in economic affairs escalated,[40] and some of the subsequent 'ordinary' legislation sustained the restrictions.[41]

The rationales for the decisions claimed that the reforms were thus being protected from the deformation that could ensue in circumstances of social 'loosening'.[42] Continued modernization along Marxist-Leninist lines was the proper course, since the cause of the existing and prior crises was found not in the principles but in the fact of their violation.[43] Accordingly, the party

---

Kołakowskiego ku antykomunistycznej opozycji. Od ortodoksyjnej ideologii do wolności myślenia [Leszek Kołakowski's road to anti-communist oppposition: from orthodox ideology to freedom of thought], Dzieje Najnowsze 4 (1999), 147; Leszek KOŁAKOWSKI: *Tezy o nadziei i beznadziejności, in Czy diabeł może być zbawiony,* Aneks, London 1984, 293 [in English: *Theses on Hope and Despair*, Kevin Devlin (transl.), in Leszek Kołakowski: *Can the Devil Be Saved?* Encounter, 1974, 7–12].

37 *Raport o stanie Rzeczypospolitej i drogach wiodących do jej naprawy* [Report on the state of the Republic and the paths leading to its emendation], Nowa, Warsaw, 1979; compiled by a group of persons operating under the collective name of *Konserwatorium Doświadczenie i Przyszłość* [Experience and Future Seminar] sent to the Sejm on 19 May 1979. One of the authors of the Report was Jerzy Stembrowicz, a jurist specializing in constitutional law.

38 Szczecin Agreement, 30 August 1980; Gdańsk Agreement, 31 August 1980; Jastrzębie Agreement, 3 September 1980.

39 Decree of 13 December 1981, Dz.U.29.154. The use of provisions regulating martial law was the result of not having provisions regulating emergency powers. The assumptions of the socialist system did not foresee a conflict between the proletariat and the authorities of the socialist state.

40 Anna MACHNIKOWSKA: *Wpływ ustawodawstwa stanu wojennego na prawo cywilne* [The influence of Martial Law legislation on civil law], Studia nad Autorytaryzmem i Totalitaryzmem 39 (2017)/3, 23–47.

41 Act of 21 July 1983 on Detailed Legislative Regulation in a Period of Overcoming a Crisis.

42 Wojciech Jaruzelski's address in the Sejm on 6 May 1982, *Sprawozdanie stenograficzne z posiedzenia Sejmu* [Stenographic Sejm Report], 14.

43 *Sprawozdanie z prac Komisji KC PZPR powołanej do wyjaśnienia przyczyn i przebiegu konfliktów społecznych w dziejach Polski Ludowej* [Report on the works of the PUWP

remained 'active and creative', and the citizens should desist from protesting.[44] The party's motivation was consistent with that of the majority of society:[45]

> We desire a great Poland – great in its heritage, culture, forms of social life, and position in Europe. The only path to this goal is socialism accepted by society and continually enriched with the experience of life. Such is the Poland we will build. Such is the Poland we will defend,

announced the leader of the PZPR.

The doctrinal paradigm was confirmed by the Sejm: 'it is a matter of prime import to strengthen the state and its structures and for the socialist democracy to continue to grow.'[46] The Soviet interpretation of one of the theories of Friedrich Engels was thus being invoked. He expected the dying down of the state during the last stage of development of socialism.[47] The Soviet interpretation joined to it the necessity of reinforcing the state before its end comes. Hence, there was no contradiction between declarations of intensifying the dynamic of the socialization process on the one hand and the acquisition of new powers by the authorities of the state and its bureaucracy.

3 The Codes in the Shadow of Decodification

The codification completed in 1964 transformed the system of civil law. The change took on a smaller scope and partially different nature compared to the assumptions adopted by the Codification Commission or those inferred

---

Central Committee's Commission appointed to investigate the causes and development of social conflicts in the history of People's Poland], Nowe Drogi, Special Issue (1983).

44 'Despite errors made and bitter defeats, the party in the process of historical transformations is still an active and creative force; I address you, Polish workers: for the sake of the homeland, renounce your inalienable right to strike for such a time as may be necessary for overcoming the most acute difficulties'; speech delivered on 13 December 1981 by General Wojciech Jaruzelski, First Secretary of the PZPR.

45 The martial law was imposed not by the Sejm but by an organ of the executive branch – the Council of State.

46 Resolution of the Sejm of Polish People's Republic of 25 January 1982, Monitor Polski 5.20.

47 Friedrich ENGELS: *Pochodzenie rodziny, własności prywatnej i państwa* [The Origin of the Family, Private Property and the State], Książka i Wiedza, Warsaw, 1949.

from the language of the norms contained in the code. Part of the norms of the Civil Code were not used because the events regulated by the relevant provisions of the Code ceased to occur.[48] For the norms that were applied, some of the disputes were removed from the purview of the courts.

Apart from norms derived from native legal legacy, the Civil Code contained norms modelled on Soviet institutions. Those had been criticized by some legal thinkers already prior to codification, when discussed in the context of the draft Civil Code in 1954. During the life of the 1964 Code, a small number of norms[49] won more influence on the legal system. Their popularization relied on the norms of the Civil Code determining the scope of application. The submission of some of the relationships governed by the Code to other provisions, enjoying the status of *lex specialis* was also considered.

The authority to take legislative action exceeding the executive provisions that merely narrow down the implementation of a code norm was delegated to administrative bodies, either by express mention or by reference to 'applicable provisions'. The decision as to the use of the delegation, as well as the scope of the Code regulation to be deviated from, also was left up to the administrative bodies. They could omit to use the delegation or use it selectively, or leverage it fully. The third possibility was chosen.

Combining multiple elements in their structure, the exclusions were not always readily visible from the level of the Code and statutes dealing with civil-law relationships.[50] They extended to obligation relationships, as well as real relationships (i.e. relating to real law), involving state-owned and socialized entities,[51] as well as, to a lesser extent, legal relationships among individuals. The margin of discretion left to administrative bodies was large enough to put them in a position to change the law without amending the Civil Code. For any content of a mandatory contract, or the introduction of another limitation or restriction, it sufficed to invoke the principle of central planning. The activities unfolded in the absence of an administrative judiciary, and the judicial review provided by the common courts, even though civil-law relationships were at issue, was infrequent and often futile, because

48 This includes, among other examples, provisions incorporated from the Commercial Code and Code of Obligations.

49 In addition to provisions diversifying the rights and obligations in respect of the various types of property, those included a chapter dealing with mandatory contract formation among socialized economic units; Articles 397–404 of the Civil Code.

50 For examples of such dispersed regulation see STELMACHOWSKI: *Wstęp do teorii*, 28.

51 Production, services, trade, commerce and use of property suitable for commerce.

the Supreme Court did not have a homogeneous position as to the binding effect of a decision of the administrative court.[52]

Some members of the Codification Commission ignored this fact, noting, as Aleksander Wolter did, that the Civil Code 'correspond[ed] to the assumptions of socialist law', with the 'best proof of that' being the small number of amendments of the Code.[53] Taking into account legislative initiatives contrary to the rule of law, such a claim could even, *à rebours*, be confirmed. The Civil Code corresponded to the principles of the functioning of a socialist state, for it set no limits to its own non-applicability.

Some scholars not involved in the codification works downplayed the scale of the decodification and its results. The applicability of the principle of uniformity of civil law was emphasized. When discussing, in succession, each of the provisions enabling matters to be regulated outside of the code, phrasing suggesting a small scope of such a solution was used. For example, adverbs such as 'only', 'solely', 'exclusively', as well as blurring the lines between the terms 'homogeneity' and 'difference'.

This is how the principal characteristic features of the regulation of civil-law relationships was presented by Jan Winiarz, secretary of the Codification Commission. At a time of the administration's making of the maximum possible use of the Code's delegations, the most important ones, covering practically all of the economy outside of farming, was described as being applicable 'exclusively' to the 'operative sphere'. That sphere covered all types of contracts and *in rem* rights, while in the 'non-operative' sphere civil law was not used.[54] Wolter, in turn, explained that a socialist system of law constituted a single whole that 'could not possibly be divided with sharp lines into specific branches.'[55]

According to the authors of the Civil Code, the heterogeneity of regulatory principles under the rule of one and the same code was also justified by two objective circumstances of material nature. The first one was the state's constitutional foundation in the form of a heterogeneous structure of property, requiring separate regulation of socialized, as opposed to non-socialized property. Such national circumstances were said to include the specificity of Polish economic affairs. Those were the anachronicity of the contents of a certain part of legal relationships involving individuals, the level of social conscious-

52 Litwin, *Z problematyki styku*, 546.
53 See Wolter: *Prawo cywilne*, 56.
54 Among other things, this sphere included the use of real property.
55 See *ibidem* 22.

ness in some of the individuals being party to such relationships, as well as the high development dynamics of legal relationships involving socialized entities.

Legal relationships characterized by such unequal modernization levels required the use of a suitable regulatory model. Regulating all of them comprehensively in a single legal instrument would have required its redaction to take a complicated form. For that reason, a different structure was employed. The rationale alleged that the structure used served to preserve the autonomy of the regulation of civil-law relationships involving entities belonging to the socialized economy. In reality, however, the provisions located outside of the Code resulted in a separation between the legal relationships governed by them on the one hand and the Code on the other hand.

The argument of anachronicity of the contents of part of legal relationships was not applied to the assessment of the Codification Commission's regulatory method itself. To explain the retention of such type of norms in the new code, it was argued that they marked the legislature's response to such social needs as would soon expire on their own, precisely due to their anachronicity. That referred primarily to peasant farms. Their existence was described as a product of the social consciousness of the farmers, developing more slowly than that of labourers. In the sixties, the party's leader spoke of an immaturity hampering the farmers' acceptance of the modern organization models offered by the socialist system[56] (collectivization). In the seventies, the assessment was mitigated by noting that part of society remained susceptible to imperialist propaganda.[57]

The point of the rationale referencing a 'transitional period' was also to justify the non-codification of economic law. In that case, the obstacle was not too slow but rather too fast modernization. Such a high speed of change in the civil-law relationships in the state-owned economy[58] required differ-

56 According to the PZPR leader, Władysław Gomułka, the reason behind the failure of collectivization in Poland was the 'imposition on them of too many benefits that by no measure could be reconciled to the peasant intellect'; see Andrzej BURDA: *Polskie prawo państwowe* [Polish state law], PWN, Warsaw, 1962, 164.

57 Such was the analysis of the social situation presented, among others, by Adam ŁOPATKA: *Rozwój społeczeństwa socjalistycznego w Polsce* [The development of socialist society in Poland], Ruch Prawniczy i Ekonomiczny 4 (1964), 1–16.

58 The facts were different; Poland's economic system was not transforming in any significant ways, as opposed to the situation in certain other socialist states, for example, in the seventies of the 20th century. In Czechoslovakia, the state increased its influence on the economic rights of farming co-operatives, and in the GDR the few private enterprises still operating there were nationalized; see more Tadeusz SZYMCZAK: *Ustrój europejskich*

ent and oftentimes flexible methods of regulation that the Civil Code could not provide.

4 The Consequences of Decodification

4.1 *The Rights of the Entities Belonging to the State-Owned/National Economy could always be Replaced with Obligations*

The theory of ownership, and with it also other economic rights, presented as an autonomous one from the perspective of legal history, became the symbol of socialist modernization. The constituent parts of that theory were the principle of unity of state property (national property), the administrative management of material goods through a system of central planning, and the marginalization of private ownership simultaneously with the preservation of personal property.

The Civil Code regulated the status of state-owned property only with a few norms. Besides the universal duty to provide a higher level of protection for state-owned property,[59] identified as an interpretative directive extending to all provisions of the Civil Code,[60] the principle was introduced for state-owned enterprises to have only limited legal capacity within the limits of which they could exercise the right of management of their own affairs.[61] Neither the Code nor any other legal instrument defined the terms. At the same time, the Code authorized administrative bodies to lay down the rules for the exercise of the state's ownership.

According to some lawyers and jurists, the legislature introduced an innovative and effective institution to Polish legal order, whether in economic or in social terms. The terms identifying such types of property were to be the evidence of the fact.[62] A modernizing function was also attributed to the limita-

państw socjalistycznych [The political system of European socialist states], PWN, Warsaw, 1983, 324 and 421–422.

59 For example, Articles 4, 127 and 129 of the Civil Code.

60 Article 129: 'The construction and application of the provisions of this code must consider that socialized property, as the basis of the constitutional system (…), benefits from the special protection of the law.'

61 Not equivalent to the institution of management (administration) in civil law.

62 The fact alone of the classification of types and kinds of property was, according to some legal minds, an independent modernization factor, since it was conducive to the increased effectiveness of state ownership; Jerzy Ozdowski: *Problem własności w społecznej gospodarce rynkowej* [The problem of ownership in a social market economy], in

tion of the autonomy of state-owned enterprises.[63] Consolidating the rights in a single entity – the state – provided the optimum protection of the sovereign's rights. Jan Wasilkowski thus argued in favour of the concept: 'There can be no doubt that the legal holder of national property can only be the socialist state, as an organization encompassing the whole nation.'[64] His simultaneous presence in the Codification Commission and in the Supreme Court contributed to the copying of this position by court decisions, resulting in further difficulties for scholarly debate on the subject as referred to the functioning of civil-law relationships.

Other lawyers and jurists, such as Stefan Grzybowski, noted that in their opinion, the Commission had foregone the complete analysis of the consequences of the transplantation of the categories of constitutional law to civil law. Thus, it bypassed a problem 'manifesting itself so sharply that one could not possibly fail to see it.'[65]

The right of management, which was to replace multiple other rights, was so avant-garde that scholars and the judicature never succeeded at the narrowing down of its contents.[66] According to scholars, it did not pose a significant problem, because the new, limited legal capacity[67] set the framework for the civil-law relationships undertaken by the enterprises. Their task was to execute, together with the others, nationwide central economic plans taking advantage of suitable legal solutions such as mandatory contracts. The attribution of a lower number of rights and a greater number of obligations was explained by the lack of antagonisms and particular interests in a socialist economy. By contrast, new needs in the area of co-ordination and co-

---

Piotr KACZANOWSKI (ed.): *Własność i demokracja* {Property and democracy], Fundacja ATK, Warsaw, 1995, 34.

63 In that manner, theories embroiled for decades in internal contradictions were copied over; this included the problem of defining the principles of the economic circulation within the system of state property; see more Evgeny B. PASHUKANIS: *Ogólna teoria prawa i marksizm*, PWN, Warsaw, 1985.

64 Jan WASILKOWSKI: *Zarys prawa rzeczowego* [An outline of real law], PWN, Warsaw, 1963, 35.

65 Stefan GRZYBOWSKI: *Sytuacja prawna mienia ogólnonarodowego w kodeksie cywilnym* [The legal situation of national property in the Civil Code], PiP 2 (1965), 527.

66 For example, Supreme Court resolutions in I Co 20/61, of 16 October 1961, OSN 1962, 41; I C 336/63, of 14 June 1963, OSNCP 1964, 223; I CR 80/66, of 16 April 1966, 4 OSPiKA 1967, 101; TOPIŃSKI: *Zarząd mieniem*, 28; Jan TOPIŃSKI: *Niedostatki i braki teorii prawno-gospodarczej* [Deficiencies and shortcomings of legal-economic theory], Przegląd Ustawodawstwa Gospodarczego 16 (1963)/3, 153–156.

67 See more theses 1 and 2 to Article 36 of the Civil Code; *Kodeks cywilny z komentarzem*, vol. 1, 52.

operation surfaced in such an economy and called for new legal solutions also in respect of civil-law relationships.[68]

Combined with decodification, doctrinarian interpretations of the principle of unity of state property[69] deprived state-owned enterprises of rights in their civil-law relationships[70] and opened those relationships to administrative law. In the latter area of law, the enterprises held no rights whatsoever, only performing duties imposed by administrative bodies on the basis of provisions located outside of the Civil Code, to which the Code made reference. The result of such status of state-owned enterprises in civil-law relationships was that the workers, too, became the object of new administrative commands and prohibitions. According to the above-cited theory of property, the working class ought to be the owner of state property, whereas in reality, through the above-described mechanism, it itself became owned.

To provide an explanation for the various doubts relating to the links between civil-law relationships involving state property on the one hand and administrative law on the other hand, the principle of legal continuity was set aside. In line with the concept, the avant-garde nature of socialist property called for a research methodology as innovative as the law being analysed. Responding to the new economic circumstances, legal science ought to work out a different demarcation between private and public law, as well as civil law versus all other branches.

The traditional taxonomy of branches of law and legal sciences, dating back to a different socio-economic formation, was not fit to constitute an element of the legal superstructure of the socialist state. 'For socialism follows its own,

68 Society's collective memory has preserved the rationales for the defectively function-ing mechanisms of central planning. According to the authorities, the socialist modernization had to be evaluated from a broader perspective. An thus, every single year in the summer rope was missing for farming machines, immobilizing them in a time of harvest, but at the same time a modern steel foundry was materializing into existence. Yes, prices of food were rising, but simultaneously 'locomotives ha[d] become cheaper.'

69 Some writers noted the inconsistency between the principle of unity of state property and the principle of legal personality of the state's legal persons; see Jan GWIAZDOMORSKI: *Zasada jednolitej własności socjalistycznej a osobowość prawna przedsiębiorstw państwowych* [The principle of uniform socialist property and the legal personality of state-owned enterprises], PiP 4–5 (1967), 597.

70 The inability of the enterprises to make independent dispositions of property was introduced by the resolution of the Council of Ministers of 29 April 1950, Monitor Polski 43.197; eighteen years later, also by resolution, the enterprises were allowed a certain scope of chattel transactions; see resolution of the Council of Ministers no. 262 of 12 August 1968 concerning the disposition of movable assets by socialized economic units, Monitor Polski 35.245.

separate way,' according to Jan Wasilkowski.[71] That particular characteristic also enabled a focus on the methodology, for which the co-author of the Civil Code and principle author of the provisions governing ownership himself argued. In a likewise manner he responded also in the seventies to theoreticians' and practitioners' complaints of protracted difficulties with achieving a cohesive regulation of the rights and obligations of the entities put in charge of the socialist state's property.[72] The creation and further development of new types of synergies among civil, administrative, financial and criminal law was his example of the expansion of the research perspective that was to lead to the elimination of such type of problems.

The projects pursued by the socialist state were creative and self-contained, for which reason they used the law as an instrument but not in its existing models. Resorting to traditional terminology and concept and causation networks resulted in a developmental slowdown or even, as some lawyers and jurists argued, entrenched the errors of capitalist legal science, now also in socialist jurisprudence.[73] The effect of substantial difference or even contrast between the socialist legal system and the systems of the preceding formations, according to Wasilkowski, could only have the effect that 'there [was] no continuity in legal sciences.' Accordingly 'there [was] no need for the socialist lawyer, in their research work, to reach into the past in order to achieve the understanding and scientific cognition of their contemporary law.'[74]

The consequence of this path of reasoning was the adaptation of the theory of the modernization of the legal system to the pattern applied to the economic system. The essence of that pattern was summarized by the sociologist, Jadwiga Staniszkis, who noted that real socialism had borrowed the methodology of economic activity from capitalism while excluding the

71 See WASILKOWSKI: *Pojęcie własności*, 60–61.

72 Problems of this type and their negative consequences for the entire system of civil law were noted by, among others, GWIAZDOMORSKI: *Zasada jednolitej własności*, 591; Andrzej STELMACHOWSKI: *Czy kryzys osoby prawnej?* [A crisis of the legal person?], Ruch Prawniczy Ekonomiczny i Społeczny, 3 (1968); WOLTER, *Prawo cywilne*, 168–169. The last-mentioned author, himself another co-author of the Civil Code, highlighted the complicated structure of the norms relating to the principle of unity of state property.

73 The charge of drawing from 'bourgeois legal science' was levied against Soviet researchers by Andrey Vyshinsky; see more LITYŃSKI: *Prawo Rosji*, 210.

74 See more Juliusz BARDACH: *W obiektywie nauki i w lustrze pamięci (o uczonych, pisarzach i politykach XIX I XX wieku* [In the lens of science and in the mirror of memory (on scholars, writers and politicians of the 19th and the 20th centuries], C. H. Beck, Warsaw, 2004, 347.

'economic sense of the various actions and concepts composing that methodology.'[75]

This matter was viewed differently by some of the authors of the Civil Code. According to them, the foundations of a new methodology for the theory of state property that is at once national property were defined by the Constitution of Polish People's Republic of 1952.[76] Without contradicting the reference, some lawyers and jurists contended that stopping there without going any further would be of no assistance to solving the problems faced by the theory of civil law. Without, for political reasons, being able to state explicitly that invoking the propaganda contents of a constitution dating from the Stalinist period did not serve to develop the theory of ownership of property but to petrify it,[77] lawyers and jurists made attempts to shift the discussion onto the level of the instruments of administrative law and the Civil Code.

According to them, the first thing to be determined was whether the object of the analysis should be only the contents of the legal norms or also their ordering and association with corresponding concepts.[78] Taking the latter position, they pointed out that conceptual definition and systematization could help break the impasse confronting research studies into the theory of state ownership.[79] One of the examples of the emerging situation was the analysis revealing that the interpretation of the principle came down to creating a special type of abstraction, in which the state owed any obligations only to itself alone, as well as with regard to the everyday transactions of civil law.

They adduced examples to show that those authors who claimed that all matters had already been explained were failing to back such claims with evidence or frame proper conclusions, or even that in lieu of analysis of the

---

75 Maciej BAŁTOWSKI: *Gospodarka socjalistyczna w Polsce* [Socialist economy in Poland], PWN, Warsaw, 2009.

76 Constitution of Polish People's Republic of 22 July 1952, Dz.U.33.232.

77 Concerning the way in which constitutional language stalled the development of property law, see Małgorzata BEDNAREK: Przemiany własności w Polsce. Podstawowe koncepcje i konstrukcje normatywne [Ownership changes in Poland. Basic concepts and normative constructions] WN Scholar, Warsaw, 1994, 33; MACHNIKOWSKA: *Prawo własności*, 295–312.

78 Stefan RITTERMAN: *Charakter metodologiczny dyskusji nad podmiotem cywilistycznej własności państwowej* [The methodological character of the discussion of the rights-holder of national property], Studia Cywilistyczne 13–14 (1969), 267–288.

79 One of the problems was the determination of the nature of economic legal relationships (whether civil-law or administrative-law) arising among state-owned legal persons or between them and the state.

relevant institution they contented themselves with platitudes such as 'adaptation of old form to new content'.

The following is the summarization offered by Stefan Grzybowski, who, together with some other legal minds, made some efforts to discuss the crucial problem arising for all of the economic law of the time from the lack of clarity and consistency in the Civil Code: 'One cannot restrict the discussion of national property to the scarcely illuminating constatation that legal personality is nowadays no more than a relic of juridical conservatism. It is fitting for the problem of personality to be explained.'[80]

Some of the participants called for the verification of the bases for the concept of restricting the legal autonomy of state-owned enterprises. In their opinion, backed by the argument of the economic situation prevailing at the time, the modernization potential of a model relying solely on procedural centralization of legal transactions involving state-owned enterprises had already exhausted itself.[81] The rationale for according ownership also to the state's legal person came from the desire to strengthen the effectiveness of state-owned enterprises. The proponents argued that there was a space in the Civil Code for such a solution. They argued that the Codification Commission had deliberately redacted the general provisions on state property in such a way as to leave the path open to the modernization of the details.[82]

Critics included Jan Wasilkowski and Stefan Rozmaryn. Citing the Constitution of the Polish People's Republic and its supremacy over the Civil Code, they regarded the proposal as an attempt to modify the underlying principles of the political system. With that in mind, they cited not only the direct constitutional regulation of property but also the thesis identifying the principle of unity of state property (national property) with democratic centralism.

All important matters relating to the exercise of the owner's rights with regard to state property were resolved by the Civil Code, they argued. If the Code did not directly tie the new principle to the traditional institution of private law, one should not create such a link. Doing so would contradict the

80 GRZYBOWSKI: *Sytuacja prawna mienia*, 533.

81 The leadership of the PZPR, in their own analysis of the legal and administrative frameworks regulating state-owned enterprises, admitted that the solutions gave 'no impulse to any increase in production volumes or profitability. The forecast for 1971–1975 expected losses in the range of PLZ 34 billion; AAN, BP KC PZPR, 2914, 635.

82 This was the position taken by, among others, Stefan Buczkowski and Jan Gwiazdomorski. See GWIAZDOMORSKI: *Zasada jednolitej własności*, 571; some of their arguments were supported by GRZYBOWSKI: *Sytuacja prawna mienia*, 527.

ideal of progress guiding the Codification Commission in its drafting of the Civil Code.

It was not the task of jurisprudence, according to Wasilkowski and Rozmaryn, to transform the existing law in a way turning back its development. The Civil Code did not tie the principle of unity of state property (national property) to the classic civilist theory of ownership featuring such categories as legal personality, capacity for legal transactions or the triad of the owner's rights, which the owner can transfer to a possessor. Polish legal science, therefore, ought to develop the new theory of civilist unity of state property, with the state alone as the owner and the other entities only as holders of a right of operative management (administration).

The cited type of argument was characteristic of the criticism of the principle of legal continuity in private law in situations in which the defective functioning of the new institutions and principles became increasingly common knowledge. The invocation by some of the co-authors of the Civil Code of the necessity to reject the dogmata of bourgeois legal science, served their purpose well when they were arguing for the limits on change to be lifted and advancing the cause of legislative reform. However, when after the removal of whatever had been outdated the time came to create new institutions, they restricted themselves to merely setting the direction for change. They left that task of allegedly secondary importance to other lawyers and jurists. When other representatives of legal science took up the challenge and the results of their studies confirmed the existence of gaps and contradictions within the theory of unity of state property, Wasilkowski contented himself with citing passages from the Constitution of Polish People's Republic.

This is one of the examples of the treatment of the socialist property theory resting on historical materialism as a category of 'truth revealed'. Its ideological basis capable of providing an explanation for 'everything',[83] including rules governing changes to legal relationships, became the origin myth not only for the new quality of law but also its scientific foundations. The first study on ownership under the Constitution of 1952 was written in 1953 and, until the eighties, its theses had been successively reiterated not only by its author, Jan Wasilkowski,[84] but also by other scholars in civil

83 'Marxism, accordingly, was a dogma pretending to be science'; PIPES: *Komunizm*, 21 (quotation back-translated from the Polish).

84 The first one was Jan WASILKOWSKI Adam CHEŁMOŃSKI, Kazimierz PRZYBYŁOWSKI, Seweryn SZER, Jan TOPIŃSKI: *Własność społeczna w świetle Konstytucji Rzeczypospolitej Ludowej*, in *Zagadnienia prawne Konstytucji Polskiej Rzeczypospolitej Ludowej, Materiały sesji naukowej PAN 4–9.7.1953 r.*, vol. 1, PWN, Warsaw, 1954, 17–114; subsequently WASIL-

law. The contents of the works on the subject, taken together with the socio-economic situation known to the authors, warrant the assertion that the socialist theory of ownership led some research currents into a politico-legal trap. In the meanwhile, the same scholars produced valuable analytic and synthetic studies in substantive and procedural civil law concerning priniples and institutions other than state property. When researching this particular category of ownership, by contrast, they avoided embarking on the verification of its components relating to the economy because: 'economic criticism (of the socialist state – A.M.) is followed by criticism of all other possible fields of life.'[85]

Another element of the same trap was the simultaneous search for a solution to the existing problem without deviation from doctrinarian interpretations of the ideology. The result of these attempts led this part of the legacy of Polish jurisprudence to the same state in which Soviet legal science had already been. It was described as follows: 'rightly opposed to barren normativism, the theory spawned its own dilemmas not so easy to unravel.'[86]

The ideologically motivated elimination of all elements of classic legal tradition from the state-ownership theory, in a situation in which socialist legal science did not have alternative to offer, could not last as long as the political decision-makers assumed. The stagnation led to a succession of socio-economic crises.

Responding to both of the circumstances, some jurists, including Walerian Pańko and Czesława Żuławska, involved themselves in 1980–1981 in works on citizens' drafts of statutes to regulate the ownership of property. To their predecessors, those legal minds posed two questions: (i) Which criteria identify the characteristic features of national property if this cannot be determined on the basis of the Constitution of Polish People's Republic and Civil Code or learned from the jurisprudence? (ii) Is what is presented as national property in a socialist state a right of ownership at all?

KOWSKI: *Zarys prawa rzeczowego*; WASILKOWSKI, MADEY, *Prawo własności*; WASILKOWSKI. *Pojęcie własności*.

85 Note made in 1957 for the needs of the Politburo of the Central Committee of the PZPR; AAN, BP KC PZRP 2831, 251.

86 Evaluation of the problems of the Soviet theory of property rights with the participation of socialized economic units, Jan BASZKIEWICZ, Franciszek RYSZKA: *Historia doktryn politycznych i prawnych* [History of political and legal doctrines], PWN, Warsaw, 1984, 463.

FIGURE 5.1 Czesława Żuławska. Born in 1930, linked to the Kraków University of Economics; in 1981–1992, member and vice-president of the Social Economic Council; active participant of the Solidarity Centre for Citizens' Legislative Action in 1981; member of the Civil Law Reform Commission (from 1986) and Civil Law Codification Commission (from 1996); Justice of the Supreme Court (1991–1999). SOURCE: ARCHIVE OF THE ACADEMY OF ECONOMICS IN CRACOW

4.2 *Limitless Changes to Provide Law*

The decodification also had an impact on civil-law relationships between individuals. The basis for this area of legislative activity came from the intention to adapt private rights to two purposes not articulated with sufficient strength by the norms of the Civil Code. The first, ideological and long-term purpose, was the elimination of the existing private rights. The second, the need for the fragmentary elimination of private rights with the preservation of some of their economic or social functionalities. The aforementioned activities intermittently curtailed and short-term-reinforced a certain part of private rights depending on the authorities' needs of the moment and social responses.

The regulation of private rights on the level of the Civil Code was presented as the modernization current introducing solutions enabling some of the rights to be exercised with the protection of the public good also in mind. The above applied to small-scale commodity ownership and related *in rem* rights and obligational rights, as well as inheritance rights. The rights had already been divested of their capitalist nature on the basis of other legislation blocking their access to certain means of production. One of the members of the Codification Commission, Aleksander Wolter, when giving a presentation of the contents of the new norms, even went as far as distinguishing as one of the Code's principles the 'principle of consideration for the needs of individual property' and emphasized the importance of the interpretation of the applicable provisions including the 'protection extended by the state' to the individual farms owned by the working farmers. Albeit using the word 'still', he emphasized that this particular type of ownership 'play[ed] an important role' in Polish countryside.[87]

A different concept of modernization was pursued on the level of the provisions located outside of the Code. It was founded on limiting the rights and increasing the obligations of private owners so as for the *fructus* of a thing to be mostly seized by the state. Political decision-makers interpreted the definition of ownership as the strongest of rights *à rebours*, arriving at the conclusion that it was capable of retaining specific functionalities selected by the authorities irrespective of whatever modifications it may have undergone. In this case, the innovation came down to disputing the rules of economics and expanding onto rights relating to farms, trades and crafts and small-scale services, as well as rights applicable to buildings and apartments. The language of the provisions of inheritance law became so complicated that not only farmers but even scholarly jurists specialized in inheritance law experienced difficulties with the interpretations.[88]

The adopted assumptions were to be pregnant with consequences for society, the economy and law. This was attested by a brief overview of the condition in which legal relationships of key importance to private law had found themselves. The peasant farmers – beneficiaries of the socialist political system according to the propaganda – fought a daily struggle to retain the right to their land[89] and achieve a production volume sufficient to cover their minimal existential needs. The additional burdens and limitations imposed in the name of modernization of the countryside were an economic anachronism. The contents of the new private law on farming were always presented as an

87 WOLTER: *Prawo cywilne*, 54.

88 Ten years after the introduction of the provisions (originally in the form of a statute enacted in 1963), attention was called to the interpretative doubts arising, as well as the redaction of the norms; see Józef S. PIĄTOWSKI: *Prawo spadkowe. Zarys wykładu*, PWN, Warsaw, 1973, 25–26.

89 More extensively on farmers' attitude to agricultural policy see Krystyna DANIEL: *Poglądy rolników na cele i skutki regulacji własności gospodarstw rolnych: w świetle ustawy z dnia 26 października 1971 r.* [Farmers' perspectives on the goals and effects of the regulation of farm property: in the right of the Act of 26 October 1971], ZN im. Ossolińskich, Wrocław, 1987.

issue of 'particularly complex nature.'[90] The purpose of the provisions was to achieve the socialization of the agriculture – unanimously regarded as one of 'the most difficult tasks when building socialism'.[91]

The agricultural reform popularized the independent possession of land but, contrary to the provisions applicable at the time, did not entail the title.[92] In parallel, limitations were imposed on the size of real property (between 7 and 15 h depending on the region.),[93] already previously restricted by the provisions governing the agricultural reform, and the power to divest ownership or possession was expanded, now on the basis of an individual administrative decision interfering with every form of commerce (sale, inheritance and division). The abandonment of the principle of freedom of contract affected agricultural products and means used in agricultural production. The institution of mandatory supplies and standard-form contracts were used alternatingly. Official prices were lower than the costs of production,[94] while fiscal burdens[95] and financial penalties for non-compliance with any of the numerous obligations imposed on farmers were high.

The practical application of this set of provisions, only some of which were placed in the Civil Code, resulted in a gap between the legal and the factual states of affairs. Due to the restrictions, many of the farmers were unable to

---

90 See Rybicki: *Administracja gospodarcza*, 208.

91 Wasilkowski: *Prawo rzeczowe*, 45.

92 Grants or other certifications not providing the basis for an entry into a land-and-mortgage register book. An indirect proof of the defective management of the procedure for the transfer of ownership on the basis of the decree on the agricultural reform were the several enactments (seven in total until the nineties) of legislation to put the situation in order, e.g. the Decree of 6 September 1951, Dz.U.46.340; and Decree of 18 April 1955, Dz.U.18.107.

93 Among others, the Ministry of Justice Circular no. 12 of 20 October 1948, without any basis in generally applicable legislation, ordering notaries to require additional documents from transaction parties. The inability to comply with this condition, as well as other limitations have caused the number of the notarial deeds necessary for a transfer of ownership to drop to a symbolic number, see Dorota Malec: *Dzieje notariatu polskiego,* wuj, Krakow, 2007, 215.

94 Differences between the price received by the farmers for their products and the price of the means of such production have caused the phenomenon of 'price shears', making farming unprofitable and forcing farmers into extensive farming, translating in the longer term into a lasting decrease in agricultural performance.

95 The progression ratio, also reflecting other duties owed to the state, in some years became as high as 1:20 with regard to the largest farms in some years; see Antoni Hanusz: *Polityka podatkowa w zakresie zróżnicowania obciążeń dochodów rolniczych w Polsce* [Tax policy in the scope of differentiating the burdens on farming incomes in Poland], wumcs, Lublin, 1996, 89–90.

formalize their rights to their farms. The situation was regularized in part only in 1971 and 1982,[96] at each time following societal protests in the preceding year. The scale of the problem is illustrated by the number of more than 2 million farmers who obtained title to their land only after many years. The gap also occurred between ownership and independent possession, because farmers in physical control of real property were divested of the freedom to make disposals and collect the *fructus*, and sometimes even the use of the components of a farm.

As a result, extensive farming had to be used and farms consistently decreased their size, preventing the achievement of a rational production volume. That thwarted the political assumption of the cost-free achievement of large *fructus* by the state from the rights exercised by the farmers. This was noted by some legal scholars, including Jerzy Ignatowicz, who stated that some of the provisions governing transfers of farming land were having the opposite consequences to what had been intended, due to their 'drastic nature', some being 'too extreme'.[97]

A gap was also experienced by the theory of social progress. Farms were operated under the ideological and political pressure of constitutional assumptions making the existence of independent farms conditional. In categorical terms, Jan Wasilkowski proclaimed such farms to have no future, because even within the environment of the social economic system, they were not going to become a new economic and legal 'quality'.[98] Simultaneously, announcement were made of the modernization of the countryside through new legal provisions applied to them, some of which were subsequently withdrawn upon meeting the farmers' opposition.[99] The farms, meanwhile, re-

96 An opportunity for legalization come only on the basis of the Act of 26 October 1971 on Regularizing the Ownership of Farms, Dz.U.27.250. The ministry of agriculture provided an estimate of 1 million informal possessors – April 1971; AAN, BP KC PZPR 2915, 560; total number of applications submitted – 2.4 million, after DANIEL: *Poglądy rolników*, 149.

97 See more IGNATOWICZ: *Prawo rzeczowe*, 79.

98 WASILKOWSKI: *Pojęcie własności*, 171.

99 The practice is exemplified by the making of another public declaration in 1971 (the previous one hard occurred in 1959) that the material and legal situation of individual farms would be improved; see the resolution of the Politburo of the Central Committee of the PZPR and the Supreme Committee of the NSL (United People's Party), Trybuna Ludu, no 109, 19 April 1971, the proof of which was to come with the Act of 26 October 1971 on the Abolition of Mandatory Supplies, Dz.U.27.253, and, two years after these decisions, the passage of a resolution to accelerate the progress on the full socialization of agriculture; see resolution of the 1st National Party Conference of the PZPR, October 1973.

tained the possession of anywhere from three fourths to four fifths of the farming acreage.[100]

A symbol of the modernization, now combining private law with the ideal of social solidarism, was to be the regulation of the legal affairs involving buildings and apartments in the cities. Introduced in the postwar realities of the late forties,[101] the relevant provisions remained the law on the books until the end of the 80s of the 20th century. They imposed restrictions on the disposal of the property, as well as its use and the drawing of the *fructus*; they also abolished the principle of freedom of contract. At the time of their enactment, the rationale pointed toward the need for

> the rational utilization of the apartment resource, diminished as a result of the war, as well as methodical regulation of public housing needs until such time as the reconstruction of damaged cities and settlements may ensure sufficient space for public institutions and satisfy the needs of the citizens.[102]

Several decades later, the Civil Code regulated the ownership of housing properties and the lease contract, but the latter institution was not used at all. Its place was taken by the public administration of apartments,[103] still in use in 564 towns in 1970. In accordance with detailed provisions, the right of third parties to inhabit multi-apartment private houses and the value of payments to be made on this account were administratively regulated. The result was the lack of sufficient income to finance repairs. In the eighties, this type of property underwent economic decapitalization. Deprived of the use or benefit of their properties, in practice the owners could not even sell them, although

100 Some authors indicate 83.3% of arable acreage in 1970; see *Geografia gospodarcza Polski* [The economic geography of Poland], Stanisław Berezowski (ed.), PWN, Warsaw 1978, 369; others state a lower figure at 75.1%, which may be the result of exclusion of a certain part of land used by farmers on an informal basis; see Grażyna Gradzińska: *Chłopi wobec kryzysów społeczno-politycznych w Polsce (1944–1989). Studium historyczno-politologiczne* [The peasant farmers in the face of socio-political crises in Poland (1944–1989)], Abos, Poznań, 1993, 70.

101 Decree of 21 December 1945 on the Public Administration of Apartments and Lease Control, Dz.U.1946.4.27; Decree of 7 September 1944 on Housing Commissions, Dz.U.4.18.

102 See Supreme Court resolution in C. Prez 331/48, of 25 September 1948, PiP 1 (1949), 120–122.

103 Initially, it functioned in the proximity of the 'public control of lease', providing merely for the administration to approve contracts; however, as from 1950, the restrictions became more severe, leaving in place only the public administration of apartments.

there was no official prohibition.[104] According to one of the scholars of private law at the time, Andrzej Stelmachowski, the regulation of the rights of the owners of the houses subjected to the public administration of apartments provided the basis for *de facto* 'nationalization of income from property'.[105]

The legal provisions governing apartments[106] became one of the most complicated areas of legislation.[107] Numerous difficulties were encountered by their practical implementation,[108] as well as the scholarship analysing them in the light of the Civil Code. In this case, too, the jurisprudence made attempts to decode the essence of the legal relationship created by the provisions located outside of the Code. The search for innovation prompted observations such as that a new legal relationship occurred from the combination of the features of a civil-law relationship with those of an administrative-law one. The content of such a new relationship was to be emergence of a new form of economic organization, proximate to a partnership, characterized by a community of interest between the owner and the mandatory tenants, together interested in maintaining the property in good order.[109]

The trades and crafts, as well as small-scale commerce and services, were also subjected to restrictions on the exercise of economic rights. Their total

---

104 While admitting the absence of a direct prohibition against the sale of buildings or land, the caveat was made: 'the economic reality follows a different course'; see Jerzy IGNATOWICZ (ed.): vol. 2: *Prawo własności i inne prawa rzeczowe* [Ownership and other property rights], in *System prawa cywilnego* [The system of civil law], ZN im. Ossolińskich, Wrocław, 1977, 188.

105 Andrzej STELMACHOWSKI, Kamil ZARADKIEWICZ: *Modele własności i ich uwarunkowania społeczno-ustrojowe* Ownership models and their socio-political circumstances], in Zbigniew RADWAŃSKI (ed.): *System prawa prywatnego* [The system of private law], vol. 3: Edward GNIEWEK (ed.): *Prawo rzeczowe* [Real law], C. H. Beck, Warsaw, 2013, 101.

106 Act of 10 April 1974 – Apartment Law, Dz.U.14.84, and Act of 19 October 1975 on Certain Land Taxes and Fees, Dz.U.45.229.

107 For more see Andrzej MĄCZYŃSKI: *Dawne i nowe instytucje polskiego prawa mieszkaniowego*, KPP 1 (2002), 65– 114.

108 Witold NIECIUŃSKI: *Czterdzieści pięć i dziewięć lat polityki mieszkaniowej w Polsce* [Forty-five and nine years of housing policy in Poland], in Lucyna FRĄCKIEWICZ (ed.): *Przeszłość i przyszłość polskiej polityki mieszkaniowej* [The past and the future of Polish housing policy], IPiSS, Warsaw, 2005, 113–121.

109 Zbigniew RADWAŃSKI: *Najem lokali w świetle przepisów kodeksu cywilnego a prawo lokalowe* [Apartment lease in the light of the provisions of civil law versus apartment law], PiP 2 (1966), 216– 217; Jan GWIAZDOMORSKI: *'Najem' lokali jako problem kodyfikacyjny* [Apartment lease as a codification problem], PiP 4 (1956), 652–677; Józef SKĄPSKI: *Zagadnienia cywilistyczne prawa lokalowego* [Civil-law topics in apartment law], Nowe Prawo 7–8 (1957), 32–33.

share in this sector of the economy stabilized at 1.3% to 1.5%.[110] The execution of the related civil-law transactions was regulated by administrative law,[111] as well as criminal law[112] used under the banner of combating speculation. Within that small field, the certainty of the law and stability of legal transactions stopped to exist. In consequence, the application of Code norms regulating the basic contracts in economic transactions was deformed, mutual trust was lost, as well as confidence in the state, the law and the honesty of small, private entrepreneurs.

5 In Search of a National Identity – Citizens on the Reform of Private Law

5.1 *Introduction*

The many years of confrontation of social, economic, legal and political needs with the ideology and axiology invoked by the PZPR and its practice of administration of the state led to multiple protests from the citizens, of growing intensity and frequency: 1956, 1968, 1970, 1976, 1980–1981, 1988 and 1989. The assumptions adopted by the party in the practice of decodification and the societal consequences, surprising to the party, played their own part in this.

The narrowing of the scope of applicability of the Civil Code was explained with the insufficient saturation of the Code's norms with contents taken from the new ideology. Simultaneously, in an area highly sensitive to that ideology, the state economy, use was made of provisions bringing fewer economic and social benefits compared to the application of the norms of the Civil Code. The several decades of continuation of such a state of affairs produced one of the sources of the permanent crisis leading to the downfall of the socialist system in Poland.

What is paradoxical is also that the limitation of the applicability of the codes was intended to provide the party leadership and the administrative authorities with more control of the law, while in reality that control proved to be very limited. Yes, both gained undue discretion and room for arbitrary

110 DUDEK: *Utopia nad Wisłą*, 163.

111 Among others, the Central Authority for Small-Scale Production Activities (CUDW) – Act of 7 March 1950, Dz.U.10.104. Partial freedom was introduced in the seventies, also in response to the protests of 1970, though the activity continued to be subjected to restrictions – Act of 18 July 1972 on the Organization and Exercise of Trades and Crafts, Dz. U.23.164.

112 For more see MACHNIKOWSKA: *Prawo własności*, 443–468.

action in the regulation of a great number of legal relationships. By the same decision, the political decision-makers blocked their own access to part of the necessary information about the operation of the law. In consequence, they became unable to defend their own interests at a time when the state of the law created by them triggered problems threatening the very existence of the socialist order in Poland.

The limitations of the PZPR's knowledge of legal affairs was one of the consequences of the linked scope of exclusion of codified substantive and procedural law. The practice was initiated in 1944 and continued until 1964. In those civil-law relationships of importance to the economy and society that were not regulated in detail by the Civil Code and disputes concerning them were not resolved on the path of the Code of Civil Procedure, substantive evaluation (by courts and academia) was replaced with bureaucratic directives and equally bureaucratic monitoring of compliance (e.g. state arbitration for the various entities of the socialized economy).[113] A 'closed circulation' resulted for the creation, application, enforcement and evaluation of the law. The modernization in such circumstances consisted in the end of the modernizing entity's existence occurring sooner than that of the intended object of the modernization, being the new law.

5.2 *Civil Disobedience and the Constitutional Scope of Private Law*

After 1964, a characteristic element of the status of private law was its presentation through the lens of the principle of socialist rule of law. It was argued that there was no contradiction between limitations on the exercise of certain private rights and the claim that the legal system provided the citizens with realistic and broad access to rights and to the protection of rights they could not receive from a capitalist system. Social rights were to become the new rights, more valuable than the rest. The concept fit into the propaganda picture of socialist modernization characterized by, among others, the use of a modern and highly ethical method of regulation of social relations through law.[114] In reality, numerous social rights were not realistically available, and the principle of socialist rule of law was subjected to interpretations typical of

113 Many of the entities active in the public sphere were given not legal personality but only an incomplete capacity for legal transactions. Together with legal persons, those functioned under the collective umbrella of 'entities of the socialized economy'. In this book, the term is used interchangeably with 'social entity'.

114 Elena A. LUKASHEVA: *Socjalistyczna świadomość prawna i praworządność* [Socialist legal consciousness and rule of law], PWN, Warsaw, 1977, 31.

certain forms of totalitarianism.[115] It was associated with the term 'dictatorship of the proletariat', relativizing the principle of equality before law.[116]

In the Civil Code, many of its norms regulated the classic institutions of private law, preserving the equality of the position of the parties. Simultaneously, others provisions with in the Code and without imposed a variety of limitations on the exercise of private rights. The justification was drawn from the assumptions of historical materialism. Those downplayed the value of the economic rights exercised by the citizens, asserting that some of such rights had no social function. With regard to private ownership of property (except for personal property), that thesis was reiterated by Jan Wasilkowski, who claimed that the contribution made by such a right to the development of the social system was an 'illusion (if not demagogy)'.[117] Hence, in the jurist and codifier's opinion, the legislature ought to consider the differences in the effectiveness of the rights exercised by public and by private entities. Adequately to that premise, the legal system could stipulate additional protection for socialized property and impose limitations, even of lasting nature, on private property, so as to prevent its improper functioning. Less attention was paid in this rationale to the legal safeguards required by such a model of application of the law.

The subject itself, on the other hand, attracted the interest of other scholars, all the more so in the light of the studies, commencing in the mid-fifties, into the theories of rule of law and *Rechtsstaat* and their doctrinal underpinnings.[118] The focus of attention fell not only on Marxism[119] but also normati-

115 To Jerzy W, Ochmański, analysing the functioning of the administrative bodies in the sphere of citizen-state relations, the continuation of some of the system's original characteristics is visible through the continued use throughout the entire era of People's Poland of methods he terms a new totalitarianism 'founded not on ideology or direct physical terror' but on 'direction of the individual's life', where 'the measure of the totalitarian oppression here is going to be not the number of victims but the level of the individual's dependence on the state'; OCHMAŃSKI: *Administracja świadcząca*, 20–22; see more Carl J. FRIEDRICH, Zbigniew. K. BRZEZINSKI: *Totalitarian Dictatorship and Autocracy*, Praeger, New York, 1965.

116 The Constitution of Polish People's Republic did not contain a provision on equality before law; it proclaimed the existence of multiple social rights.

117 WASILKOWSKI: *Pojęcie własności*, 79.

118 Concerning, original elements of the analysis of Marxism, providing the basis for rational conclusions in the works of Polish scholars of the era; see more KOŁAKOWSKI: *Główne nurty*, vol. 3, 177ff.

119 Kazimierz OPAŁEK, Jerzy WRÓBLEWSKI: *Zagadnienia teorii prawa* [Topics of theory of law], PWN, Warsaw, 1969, Zygmunt ZIEMBIŃSKI, *Teoria prawa* [Theory of law], PWN, Warsaw-Poznań 1977.

vism, analytical jurisprudence and legal positivism.[120] Favourable to the critical analysis of legal theory were the works of, among others, Stanisław Ossowski and Oskar Lange, discussing the social structure in the light of its multiple layers and interconnections[121] not having antagonistic characteristics.

Among studies into the theory of the rule of law, works written by two legal theoreticians, Kazimierz Opałek and Józef Nowacki, distinguished themselves with originality of thought.[122] Drawing a distinction between law in the descriptive and in the normative sense, Opałek analysed the former, i.e. the ability to give effect to certain demands through legal norms.[123] That required the introduction into the applicable law also of guarantees of its enforcement, especially when the discussion came to the rights of the citizens.[124] During the year in which the codification of civil law took place, Opałek expounded thoughts on the formal as contrasted with the substantive concept of rule of law, providing arguments in support of the former.[125]

That position was met with accusations of propagating a concept followed in capitalist[126] or even fascist systems. It was argued that the formal concept of

---

120 Jerzy ZAJADŁO: *Leksykon filozofii i teorii prawa, 100 podstawowych pojęć*, C. H. Beck, Warsaw, 2007.

121 Oskar Lange distinguished social strata and classified labour as connected with production either directly or indirectly, the latter such as conceptual work. Stanisław Osowski defined strata as elements of the social structure separate from social classes, taking non-production work into account as well; see KOZYR-KOWALSKI: *Struktura gospodarcza*, 99, 166 and 169.

122 Concerning the many years of academic discourse involving the two theoreticians, see Sławomir TKACZ, Zygmunt TOBOR: *Problematyka praworządności w teorii prawa Kazimierza Opałka* [Topics of rule of law in Kazimierz Opałek's theory of law], RPEiS (1) 2020, 40–55.

123 See more Kazimierz OPAŁEK: *Praworządność* [Rule of law], in Marian CIEŚLAK (ed.): *Zagadnienia prawa karnego i teorii prawa: księga pamiątkowa ku czci profesora Władysława Woltera* [Topics of criminal law and theory of law: a commemorative book in honour of Professor Władysław Wolter], Wydawnictwo Prawnicze, Warsaw, 1959, 129–133.

124 See more Kazimierz OPAŁEK: *Spór o pojęcie praworządności* [The dispute about the concept of rule of law], PiP 10 (1959), 519–535.

125 See more Kazimierz OPAŁEK: *Formalne i materialne pojęcie praworządności* [The formal and the substantive concept of rule of law], in Wacław OSUCHOWSKI, Mieczysław SOŚNIAK, Bronisław WALASZEK (eds): *Rozprawy prawnicze: księga pamiątkowa dla uczczenia pracy naukowej Kazimierza Przybyłowskiego* [Legal dissertations: a commemorative book to honour the academic work of Kazimierz Przybyłowski], PWN, Krakow-Warsaw, 1964, 201–208.

126 Such a position was voiced by Andrzej BURDA: *Demokracja i praworządność* [Democracy and rule of law], ZN im. Ossolińskich, Wrocław-Warszawa-Kraków, 1965, 213–216; Adam

rule of law ignored the social injustice of the contents of the norms, such as was the case of the norms in capitalist systems. Thus, a different, substantive formulation of the rule of law was more appropriate, one being developed by the legal science of socialist systems. The lawyers and jurists criticizing Opałek were conscious of the fact that the problems of the Polish legal system came not only from the authorities' failure to comply with the applicable law but also the enactment of discriminatory and rights-depriving legislation. In 1971, directly following another wave of social protests, Andrzej Burda acknowledged: 'changes toward the better in this regard had continued for a certain time; later, practices incompatible with the principle of the rule of law followed.'[127] A different message, however, was addressed to the legal community: 'the shortcomings of the legal system are by necessity greater than in a static society (and require – A.M.) the cross-positioning of the letter and spirit of the law with the needs of social life, without deviating from the path of socialist rule of law.'[128] At the same time, it was emphasized that the principle of rule of law extended not only to compliance with the law by the authorities but also by the citizens.

Referring that particular definition of the rule of law, a different legal theoretician, Józef Nowacki, pointed out its structural defect resulting in the establishment of legal fiction. For there did not exist a state in which one could create the conditions for the achievement of such an ambitious purpose as the constant compliance with the law by the citizens and the authorities alike. Hence, the terms 'compliance with the law' (or: respecting the law, abiding by the law) and 'rule of law' had to be distinguished. The latter applied only to the conduct of the authorities – acting in accordance with and on the basis of the law.[129]

The influence of Polish legal theory on the ideological and axiological foundations of the development of private law in Poland manifested itself during the first attempts at citizen-sponsored reform of private law, initiated in 1980.

ŁOPATKA: *Wstęp do prawoznawstwa* [Introduction to jurisprudence], PWN, Warsaw, 1975, 172–174; LUKASHEVA: *Socjalistyczna świadomość* (Polish translation from the Russian).

127 Andrzej BURDA: *Instytucjonalne gwarancje praworządności i ich rola w państwie socjalistycznym* [Institutional guarantees of rule of law and their role in a socialist state], PiP 8–9 (1971), 216.

128 Address by Justice Jankowski, Chamber President of the Supreme Court, to presidents of voivodeship courts; BMS 5 (1964), 11.

129 See more Józef NOWACKI: *Praworządność: wybrane problemy teoretyczne* [Rule of law: selected theoretical topics], PWN, Warsaw, 1977, 78 and 87.

The latter undertaking bore references to Nowacki's emphatic calls: 'the *sine qua non* condition for the commencement of discourse on the rule of law is the existence of a legal order (law).'[130] The values invoked at the time by part of society, including the reformers speaking out on its behalf, their methods used during the 1980–1988 period,[131] and the circumstances, including legal affairs, amid which they acted, all taken collectively warrant the application of the term 'civil disobedience'. The purpose of society's taking of that stance was to achieve the restoration of the principles of a state ruled by law, with one of its elements being equality before the law, guaranteed e.g. by the language of the provisions regulating private rights.

5.3 *Solidarity in the Interest of a Good Law*

In 1980, Poland became the arena of developments exceptional not only in the country's own scale. From the historical perspective, Stefan Bratkowski aptly summarizes one of the characteristics of the period: 'society took socialism more seriously than did the government presiding under its catchwords.'[132]

In 1980, amid nationwide strikes, the demands of the protesters were met with enormous social support. Their foundation was a comprehensive list of reforms, including the restoration of the principle of equality before the law in civil-law relationships involving farms.[133] In order to strengthen its bargaining power, society created the first organization independent from the state – the Solidarity trade union.

Several months later, works commenced on issues recognized as demanding the most urgent attention, led by the Solidarity Centre for Citizens' Legislative Action,[134] spearheaded and co-ordinated by Judge Kazimierz Barc-

130 See *ibidem*, 66.

131 Małgorzata Michalewska-Pawlak: *Obywatelskość demokratyczna jako idea normatywna w koncepcjach polityczno-programowych polskiej opozycji w latach 1980–1989* [Democratic civilness as a normative ideal in the politico-programmatic concepts of the Polish opposition in 1980–1989], ECS, Gdańsk, 2010, 239–285.

132 This was the conclusion advanced by Stefan Bratkowski as a commentator of the events unfolding at the time; see more Ash, *Polska rewolucja*, 49.

133 The protocol documenting the agreement reached by the government committee and the Interfactory Strike Comitee on 31 August 1980 at Gdańsk Shipyard included calls for 'equality of the farming sectors in access to all means of production, including land.' Wojciech Giełżyński, Lech Stefański: *Gdańsk, Sierpień 80* [Gdańsk, August 1980], KIW, Warsaw, 1981, 215.

134 The Solidarity Centre for Citizens' Legislative Action was established on 28 February 1981, following the First Polish Forum of Employees of the Justice System (*I Ogólnopolskie*

zyk, in co-operation with the Social Legislative Council under the leadership of Stefan Grzybowski. Those were, among others: ownership,[135] including legislation on state-owned enterprises and farms,[136] popularization of the institution of land-and-mortgage register books and mortgages, consumer rights, rights of authorship (copyrights, moral rights), and civil-law protection of the environment.[137] The list was proof of universal social engagement with the reform of civil law, in which the voices of different communities were heard,[138] in line with the principle of pluralism. All such initiatives remained outside the government structure, as the government did not exhibit serious commitment to the cause of the reform. The lawyers and jurists analysing the presented materials and evaluating their contents, concluded as follows: 'the government's proposals proceed towards the creation of a façade instrument

Forum Pracowników Wymiaru Sprawiedliwości), held on 17 January 1981; Stanisław GRODZISKI (ed.): *Wkład krakowskiego i ogólnopolskiego środowiska prawniczego w budowę podstaw ustrojowych III Rzeczypospolitej (1980–1994): projekty i inicjatywy ustawodawcze, ludzie, dokumenty i oceny,* [The Contribution of the Krakow and national legal environment to the construction of the political foundations of The Third Polish Republic (1980–1994): legislative projects and initiatives people: achievements and evaluations], Księgarnia Akademicka, Krakow, 2018

135 *Uwagi dotyczące projektu ustawy o gospodarce terenami nierolniczymi* [Remarks on the draft bill on the administration of non-farming land, September–October 1981], in Kazimierz BARCZYK, Stanisław GRODZISKI, Stefan GRZYBOWSKI (eds): *Obywatelskie inicjatywy ustawodawcze Solidarności 1980–1990. Materiały i projekty ustaw Centrum Obywatelskich Inicjatyw Ustawodawczych 'S' i Społecznej Rady Legislacyjnej* [The citizens' legislative initiatives of Solidarity. Materials and legislative drafts of the Solidarity Centre for Citizens' Legislative Action and Social Legislative Council], Wydawnictwo Sejmowe, Warsaw, 2001, 419–422.

136 Stefan GRZYBOWSKI: *Notatka z posiedzenia Zespołu dla zagadnień prawa rolnego Centrum Obywatelskich Inicjatyw Ustawodawczych w dniu 29 października 1981 r.* [Note of the Team for the Issues of Farm Law of 29 October 1981], in BARCZYK, GRODZISKI, GRZYBOWSKI: *Obywatelskie inicjatywy*, 422–423, mentioning liberalization of transactions involving farming land, elimination of 'contractation' rules.

137 *Protokół z posiedzenia Komisji ds. reformy prawa cywilnego NSZZ 'Solidarność' odbytego w dniu 30. III.1981 r.* (Minutes of the meeting of the Committee for Civil Law Reform of NSZZ Solidarność held on 30 March 1981), in BARCZYK, GRODZISKI, GRZYBOWSKI: *Obywatelskie inicjatywy*, 335–338.

138 The tasks were separated – designing the general assumptions for certain elements of the reform was entrusted to the *Konwersatorium Doświadczenie i Przyszłość* (Experience and Future Seminar), which launched initiated to reinforce civil rights during the 70s of the 20th century. On the other hand, one of the variant drafts of a bill on state-owned enterprises and crew self-government was prepared by representatives of the largest sixteen state-owned enterprises, the so-called '16'.

FIGURE 5.2
Stefan Grzybowski, 1902–2003. During the interwar period, a judge and academic linked to Jagiellonian University. After the war, long-term Head of Department of Civil Law and Rector of Jagiellonian University. President of the Social Legislative Council (1981–1992) and of the Civil Law Commission within the Council; active participant in the works of the Solidarity Centre for Citizens' Legislative Action in 1981.
SOURCE: JAGIELLONIAN UNIVERSITY ARCHIVE

containing provisions with the status of declarations, hence an instrument of dubious practical utility.'[139]

Scholars, members of the judiciary and of the bar involved themselves in the conceptual and redaction works. Such participants included Stefan Grzybowski, Kazimierz Barczyk, Stanisław Włodyka, Józef Skąpski, Ewa Łętowska, Czesława Żuławska, Andrzej Mączyński, Alfred Klein, Walerian Pańko, Józef Stanisław Piątowski, and Tadeusz Zieliński.[140] Some of them followed the directions of development of the culture of civil law shaped by the eminent jurists of the Second Republic, including Ernest Till and Fryderyk Zoll, Jr. Each topic was preliminarily processed by a rapporteur and then became the subject of a debate bringing together the different experiences of theoretical jurists and legal practitioners, looking for a compromise where the views diverged. That was conducive to the integration of the legal circles, previously having functioned in circumstances of censorship and omnipres-

139 Ewa ŁĘTOWSKA, Czesława ŻUŁAWSKA: *Uwagi dotyczące projektu ogólnych warunków gwarancji jakości oraz związanego z nimi projektu karty gwarancyjnej* [Remarks concerning the draft of general terms of the quality guarantee and the draft warranty card associated thereto], in BARCZYK, GRODZISKI, GRZYBOWSKI: *Obywatelskie inicjatywy*, 339.

140 The team on civil-law topics also included Antoni Agopsowicz, Zygmunt Bidziński, Barbara Błachowska, Bogusław Gawlik, Andrzej Kopff, Andrzej Kubas, Maria Poźniak-Niedzielska and Andrzej Wasilewski; see Andrzej MĄCZYŃSKI: *Ustawa o Komisji Kodyfikacyjnej w pracach Społecznej Rady Legislacyjnej* [The Act on the Codification Commission in the works of the Social Legislative Council], in GRODZISKI: *Wkład krakowskiego*, 155–160.

ent surveillance. A change pregnant with multiple positive consequences was also experienced by those in the legal circles who had taken it on themselves to design assumptions for a future legal reform. The method of operation of the Social Legislative Council was described as follows:

> the unconventional collaborative formula of a melting pot of ideas and remedial workshop, with the confrontation of views and ideas of people having something to say and propose, irrespective of any academic title or formal position at a university (…)[;] with the sole verification being the utility, effectiveness and consonance with our imaginations of what the standards of a democratic state ruled by law ought to look like.[141]

Attention was focused on the quality of both the substantive content and the structural form of the future law, as evidenced by the establishment of an additional team for legislation, under the leadership of Tomasz Studnicki.

The measurable effects of that social action, though lasting only several months are worth emphasizing. Some of the results took the form of draft bills, including amendments of the Civil Code and Code of Civil Procedure. For other subject matters, basic assumptions were designed.

The lower scope of the initial works of the Social Legislative Council and of the Solidarity Centre for Citizen's Legislative Action in the area of civil law, as compared to other legal fields such as criminal law, was the consequence of the view of the Civil Code as an instrument not in need of an immediate and complete overhaul. This is what Kazimierz Barczyk had to say on the matter:

> the Civil Code, on which we have undertaken the preliminary works, had not been highly deformed ideologically under the Polish People's Republic, having retained the basic solutions of Roman law, as it had been neither instrumentally threatening nor of utility to the powers of the time, except for (…) limitation of the role of ownership.[142]

The most important value brought by the activities of the social reforms of civil law in 1981 was, on the other hand, the long-term axiological and norma-

141 Marek SAFJAN: *Wspomnienia o Społecznej Radzie Legislacyjnej* [Remiscences of the Social Legislative Council], in BARCZYK, GRODZISKI, GRZYBOWSKI: *Obywatelskie inicjatywy*, 550–552.

142 Kazimierz Barczyk, quote after Krzysztof SOBCZAK: *Budowa demokratycznego państwa prawa rozpoczęła się w 1981 roku* [The building of a democratic state ruled by law began in 1981], in GRODZISKI: *Wkład krakowskiego*, 583–584.

tive perspective adopted by them at the time: 'they saw a need the majority of Solidarity's enthusiasts did not see; they could answer the question of not only current affairs but also of, "what the new Poland should be like."'[143] For in calling for legislative changes, the citizens of the time had not yet been fully prepared for the legal consequences of the fruition of their social and economic demands.

With that in mind, the reformers emphasized the need for the popularization of details of their work, including specific, concrete proposals prepared and advanced by them, each with a rationale addressing the merits and discussing the impact of the incorporation of a given solution into the legal system. The purpose of such an approach was to reinforce the citizens' sense of subjecthood and agency, draw the attention and interest of some of them to the reform, source their opinions, but also assuage the societal tension. One of the inspirations came from the imagination of the new principles of functioning of enterprises, connected with improving their effectiveness: 'One cannot lose sight of the employees' concerns (...) transfers to other positions or even the possibility of unemployment. Awareness of this danger can put a serious obstacle on the path of the reforms.' Hence, it was emphatically stated: 'One must define the methods of implementation of the reform. On that its success depends.' The fundamental importance of this type of social communication is something the future reformers acting at the turn of the eighties and nineties experienced first-hand. At the time, they regarded the issue as a low priority; the consequences are felt to this day.

The ideological and axiological premises considered by the social reformers are of significant importance. From the statements of legal scholars one could deduce their attempts to strike a balancing act among competing values wherever that was expedient. Such was, for example, the manner of the selection of whatever issues required immediate response in the field of civil law on the one hand and issues that should not be approached hastily on the other hand, especially where the motivation would be solely to respond to the circumstances of the economic crisis prevailing at the time. Discussing this problem, scholars such as Alfred Klein encouraged the authors of the drafts of amendments to the Civil Code to maintain the internal redaction of the new provisions. They drew attention to cases in which the sole focus on the improvement of the merits of the regulation led to further compounding the complexity of its structure (e.g. changes to inheritance law).

143 Ryszard TADEUSIEWICZ: *Prawo nareszcie stanowione przez obywateli* [A law at last made by the citizens], in GRODZISKI: *Wkład krakowskiego*, 379.

A determination was also made with regard to the sequence of actions where an issue belonging to substantive civil law was regulated by separate legislation (e.g. intangible goods). The call to begin the amendment process, in such cases, from that legislation was advanced by Józef Skąpski.[144] Less coordination of the works was required by the amendment of the Code of Civil Procedure. Problems relating to its application related not to its contents – except for the system of appellate remedies with its restrictive impact on citizens' rights – but the fact of its applicability only to a subset of civil cases. Hence, the central demand was for the restoration, to the furthest extent possible, of the judicial path and strengthening of procedural safeguards with regard to the appellate remedies.[145]

However, in order to dispose of several other matters relating to the rules of procedure for the works on the reform of civil law, a dilemma had to be resolved. On the one hand, should one – for the sake of legal certainty and stability but also on account of the negative experience of the administration's lawmaking invention – define the principles in detail in the new provisions? Or perhaps, on the other hand, for the sake of the functionality of the legal text and faith in the new axiology of the exercise of power, should

FIGURE 5.3
Józef Skąpski, 1921–1998, lawyer (advocate), professor, linked to
Jagiellonian University, Head of Department of Civil and Private
International Law. In 1981–1992, member of the Social Legislative Council. Active participant in the works of the Solidarity Centre for Citizens' Legislative Action in 1981, and later Civil Law Reform Commission of 1986; secretary general of the Polish Academy of Learning (PAU) (1989–1994).
SOURCE: ARCHIVE OF POLISH ACADEMY OF ARTS AND SCIENCES

144 *Protokół z posiedzenia*, 336.
145 *Ibidem*, 338.

one also make use of references to executive legislation, subject to compliance with statutory form and openness to subsequent review, also on the merits of such executive provisions?[146]

With regard to this matter, on the occasion of the draft bill on state-owned enterprises, emphasis was put that: 'the statute must feature a higher degree of detail (...) it must contain safeguards for the enterprises' autonomy. The point, however, is not so much casuistic regulation as the predetermination of the shape to be taken by some of the solutions.'[147] While discussing the amendment of the Civil Code, the attention was focused on the provision dealing with the general terms of contracts and standard forms, delegating the details to executive legislation, which was of key importance to the socialist economy. The negative past experience with the use of such delegated authority by the administration motivated the reformers to design new mechanisms of control.

Of all works, those on consumer law reached the most advanced stage of progress. Against their background, the question surfaced of the relevant scope of the Civil Code. The drafters noted the increasingly common trend of 'escape from codes' in Europe in the regulation of the principles of the modern exchange of goods and services. 'Hence, one should rather accept the thought that the code is to remain a set of general structures of principles, with the bulk of the weight of immediate regulation to be carried by instruments of inferior rank.'[148]

The selection of this particular regulatory model called for the design of a solution to ensure the consistency of the Civil Code with other statutes, or at least the lack of a contradiction. Apart from ensuring suitable legislative quality of acts inferior to the Civil Code, one also had to make sure the new legislation was to pursue a 'conscious and socially approved legislative policy', as emphasized by Ewa Łętowska.[149] That, in turn, required a drafting and redac-

146 *Ibidem*, 336–338.

147 *II Zebranie Komisji Prawa Gospodarczego przy Centrum Obywatelskich Inicjatyw Ustawodawczych NSZZ 'Solidarność'* [2nd meeting of the Economic Law Committee of the Citizens' Legislative Action Centre of NSZZ 'Solidarność'], in Barczyk, Grodziski, Grzybowski: *Obywatelskie inicjatywy*, 392–395.

148 Ewa Łętowska: *Ochrona konsumentów: propozycja wzmocnienia mechanizmów ochronnych przewidzianych w kodeksie cywilnym* [Consumer protection: a proposal to strengthen the protective mechanisms provided by the Civil Code], in Barczyk, Grodziski, Grzybowski: *Obywatelskie inicjatywy*, 344.

149 *Ibidem*, 345.

tion intelligible to recipients other than lawyers and jurists, because legislation did not operate 'in a normative void.'

In addition to the matter of legislative quality standards, the reformers also appreciated ideological dilemmas. As recalled in his memoirs by Stanisław Włodyka, who had been in charge of the economic-law committee:

> All of its participants remember (…) the zeal with which the Committee commenced and continued its work, but also the limitations constraining its freedom (…) that was especially palpable, as the economic system of the time was strictly determined by the political system.[150]

One of such constraints was the principle of unity of state property. The suggested amendment extended both to the statute governing state-owned enterprise and the Civil Code, in which it was suggested to stipulate a clear guarantee of the individual exercise of proprietary rights by the enterprise. Time after time, the government firmly refused to acknowledge an enterprise as a 'full' legal person in civil-law relationships. The principle of unity of state property was to remain the binding concept, with the new Act on State-Owned Enterprises partially increasing their legal autonomy. Thus the potential of a social project anticipating the legal amendment that would follow ten years later, after the change of the political system, came to waste. What was regarded as important in the given situation by the reformers, including the Supreme Court justice, Czesława Żuławska,[151] was to empower 'not only on the juridical but also the psychological plane' the enterprise crews by vesting a set of powers in employee self-governments, which made it possible to sustain the subsequent social activity.

Much attention was paid also to the provisions of the Civil Code dealing with farms. Serious deliberation was necessitated in order to resolve the problems amassed in the preceding decades. The amendment of the Civil Code was enacted already during martial law.[152] Its contents followed part of the solutions designed for the purposes of Solidarity Citizens' Legislative Action's draft. The most important change was the elimination of certain limitations

150 Stanisław Włodyka: *Własność a reformy gospodarcze* [Property and economic reforms], in Barczyk, Grodziski, Grzybowski: *Obywatelskie inicjatywy*, 575.

151 Czesława Żuławska: *O początkach przekształcania systemu gospodarczego z perspektywy dwudziestu lat* [On the beginnings of the transformation of the economic system from twenty years' perspective], in Barczyk, Grodziski, Grzybowski: *Obywatelskie inicjatywy*, 576.

152 Act of 23 March 1982, Dz.U.11.81.

on transactions relating to the inheritance of farms. The farmers' motivation to step up their production was to come from the constitutional amendment redacted so as for the still-existing distinctions among the types of ownership according to the type of holder to be interpreted in a manner acknowledging the 'full protection' of the ownership of individual farms. A different approach was taken by the authorities to the draft amendment of consumer law; the printed materials were seized by the administration and disposed of.

CHAPTER 6

Between Freedom and Sovereignty, and Pragmatism (1989–2000)

1 Introduction

The imposition of martial law postponed the consolidation of grassroots resistance, which did not resurface until 1989, this time to a great effect and with calls for the reinstatement of classic principles of private law as one of its demands.[1] In the meantime, the work initiated back in 1981 by the 'Civil Lawmaking Initiative of Solidarity' on private-law reform was continued only informally due to the banning of Solidarity. The body that took over the task was the Grassroots Legislative Council,[2] which had been set up in 1981 by the legal community.

The first significant changes were political in nature and occurred in two stages. In April 1989, the Constitution of the Polish People's Republic was amended to include new institutions such as a second legislative chamber – the Senate – the office of president, and a National Council of the Judiciary, responsible for safeguarding independence of judges and courts. In December of that same year, the constitution was amended further with regard to the doctrinal foundations of Poland's political system, of which the newly adopted principles made Poland a democratic state ruled by law 'realizing social justice' and affording equal protection of property before the law.[3]

The first reform of the Civil Code, which had already occurred in the period of political transition in 1989, involved the repealing of several dozen provisions governing some of the principles introduced to civil law in 1964. The other provisions that were kept in force numbered a total of 1088 articles of the Civil Code at that time. The reformers believed that the overhaul had unlocked the potential of the Civil Code that had previously been suppressed due to two major reasons – first, the incorporation of solutions modelled on Soviet

1 See MICHALEWSKA-PAWLAK: *Obywatelskość demokratyczna*, 239–300.

2 Its full name was Grassroots Legislative Council at the Centre for Civil Lawmaking Initiatives; GRZYBOWSKI: *Zagadnienia kodyfikacji*, 109.

3 Anna RYTEL-WARZOCHA: *Reformy konstytucyjne w Polsce po 7 kwietnia 1989 r.* [Constitutional reforms in Poland after 7 April 1989], Toruńskie Studia Polsko-Włoskie 17 (2021), 75–86.

 | DOI:10.1163/9789004730021_008

theories of jurisprudence; second, the existence of numerous provisions regulating civil-law relationships but found outside the Civil Code, preventing the latter from having a role appropriate for an enactment of its type.

In this way, twenty-five years after codification, out of the two trends of modernization of the Civil Code, the one that was followed was derived from the native classic tradition of private law.[4] That trend guaranteed that the Civil Code, although enacted under a socialist regime, could survive the transformation ushering in a liberal-democratic system.

2 Unfinished Transformation of the Political System – Principles of Private-Law Reform

The 1990s witnessed the speedy announcement of the formation of a new political entity colloquially referred to as the 'Third Republic'. It embodied modernization ('Third') while safeguarding the national identity and its noble traditions ('Republic'). In the economic and social spheres, socialism was superseded by liberalism, while respecting social justice; in the political sphere, a single-party system and democratic centralism were replaced by a democratic state ruled by law and separation of powers. The nation once again became not merely nominally independent but also truly sovereign.

In such transformations, a crucial role belong to private law because one of the manifestations of change in the system of government is a redrawing of the demarcation line between public and private law along with laying down new principles governing the citizen's exercise of their rights. Under such circumstances, if one sets out to reform a legal system, facing profound social, economic and political transformations of the kind that Poland underwent after 1989, one has to confront at least three elements of such a reform.

The first element is a new definition of the nature of private law. Private law is relied upon by individuals to assert their rights more frequently and in a more direct way than other laws. The rights-holders enjoy autonomy, but the rights may be formulated differently with regard to their exact contents and limits. The second element, based on the first, is to specify the method of regulation of private law. In the course of a transformation, any such method should be functional enough to facilitate the fulfilment by private law of its fundamental role and simultaneously enable the use of additional instru-

4 Zbigniew RADWAŃSKI: *Kodyfikacja prawa cywilnego* [The codification of civil law], RPEiS 5 (2009), 134.

ments. The instruments are tailored to the circumstances, mainly social, of the reforms being introduced in the nation; they play an auxiliary role. The third element is to define the means to be used by the reformers.

Part of these tasks is to identify the ideological and axiological basis for further decisions. This includes the question whether the changes are to be pursued through a new codification of private law or merely its re-codification. A decision also needs to be made concerning the timeline for the changes – for example, whether they are to be implemented in gradual stages – and the legal position of the Civil Code during and after the amendments. This is because the Civil Code could either take precedence before other legislation regulating civil-law relationships or lack any such pre-eminent status while still providing the main standard for other statutes to follow, owing to the characteristics that make the Code special.

Whatever status the Code has in relation to other law, these special characteristics include: a broad scope of regulation covering key legal relationships and a special regulatory structure decisive of the significance of the provisions in the Code, as they include both norm-setting policies and principles prescribing ways of conduct. Therefore, any amendment process, regardless of its nature, must be carried out in such a way that after it is completed, it is still possible to identify the functions fulfilled by the particular norms of the Code.

In the case of the Polish system of private law, a reform concept was needed that would take into account the questions indicated above. The state of the law in 1989 called for a decision on whether the civil-law provisions found outside the Code should only be reformulated in line with the Code's provisions or repealed for the most part without being replaced. Repealing them would have the effect of strengthening the position of the Civil Code in the system and consolidating private law on the common foundation of its principles.

Making Poland a state ruled by law called for the reinstatement of the equal status and autonomy of the parties to civil-law relationships and re-establishment of the practice of resolving disputes concerning civil relationships by litigation. The extra-code provisions often did not provide for this, being the legacy of the previous political system.[5] They were numerous and

---

5 See *Rola prawników w państwie demokratycznym* [The role of lawyers in a democratic state], NRA, Warsaw 2005, 77; Marek SAFJAN: *Wyzwania dla państwa prawa* [Challenges to rule of law], Wolters Kluwer Polska, Warsaw, 2007, 22–36.

widely dispersed across the entire legal system. To make things worse, some contravened the fundamental principles of the Code.

The repeal of such provisions was a goal that could be achieved quickly in the circumstances. However, it meant having to co-ordinate the amendments so as to avoid creating new loopholes or contradictions between principles and ordinary provisions, as well as provisions defining the goals of the legislation and the policies pursued by it.

Another possibility was the more ambitious challenge of combining the changes described above with the modernization of the system of private law. Much more than marking a wholesale return of the legal system to Latin legal culture (in which it had for the most part remain embedded even under socialism), Polish private law could become part, and even the front line (because of lacking any norms that could slow down the process), of adaptation to new developments in global economy such as the transformation of industrial culture into financial culture. From the perspective of private law, that meant a reassignment of priorities, putting the law of obligations ahead of property law, with the increasingly prominent position of intangible goods (e.g. intellectual-property law).

This was also the historic moment when the national character of the goal of the changes underway could be legitimately emphasized.[6] The contents and the application of some parts of private law was a manifestation of the lack of nation sovereignty – a legacy of forcible implementation of a Soviet model of property law. Given the situation, the identification of modernization aspects relating to cultural identity could augment the sense of community and solidarity connected with it.[7] This kind of transformation carried a great risk of new rifts being opened in society. Economic reforms made private economy develop very quickly, while equally quickly reducing the workforce in state enterprises, leaving some workers initially unable to find new jobs.[8]

6 Anna Stawarska-Rippel: *Problemy kodyfikacji prawa prywatnego w państwach Europy Środkowo-Wschodniej z perspektywy stulecia* [Problems of codification of private law in Central and Eastern European countries from the perspective of the century], MHI 1 (2019), 49–51.

7 Krystyna Skarżyńska: *Człowiek a polityka. Zarys psychologii politycznej* [The human and politics. An outline of political psychology], Scholar, Warsaw, 2005, 121–125.

8 In the greatest numbers and with the greatest alacrity, jobs were lost in the state agricultural sector. This development revealed how badly the socialist economy had been mismanaged but also presented a major problem for the new socio-economic system because a considerable number of this sector's workers did not achieve economic independence.

The success of the reforms depended on their acceptance by the public at large. That could be attained by disseminating information on the reasons for the changes, the intended outcomes, and the rules for solving any ensuing problems. After all, state control and a culture of legal authoritarianism were to be replaced with the individual initiative of the citizens. All of this was important also due to the fact that Polish society was coming into contact with an environment that in itself was undergoing intensive changes, as illustrated by the new directions of European integration (multicentricity).

Consequently, the transformation of law involving a makeover of selected aspects of national identity should allow Polish society to judge freely the new social and ideological trends arising at that time, such as Euroscepticism and illiberal democracy, to name a few. The idea that one state of subjugation, to the USSR before 1989, was exchanged for another, this time to bodies representing the European Union on Poland's accession to the EU in 2004, called for reference to one's own law and identity.

Furthermore, the attitude of Polish society to law and rule of law gained in importance, as the nation had until then been subjected to an oppressive legal system that forced people to develop various survival strategies. For that reason, the legitimacy of the new law had to be particularly strong and have its source within the legal system. There was an opportunity for anchoring private-law principles not only to the traditions of the Second Republic of Poland but also to current elements of Polish identity. To assume that the foundations of the rule of good law would develop on their own would have been a risky thing. The process incorporated the restitution of guarantees of individual rights, originating with the Second Republic, and relied on the experience of the legal lawlessness of the non-sovereign Polish People's Republic that society had opposed by acts of civil disobedience. However, it also called for a present-day positive practice. That was easier to come by on an everyday basis with private law allowing the people to identify its principles and rules.

A broad discussion of the principles of present-day Polish private law was not undertaken until 2006, when the country was already a member of the EU (2004), and a new Polish Constitution (1997) and a new law governing the court structure (2000) had been in place for some years. Meanwhile, private law was frequently amended, but in a manner limited to selected parts, including the Civil Code and the Code of Civil Procedure.

In the meantime, major changes occurred in social attitudes towards law, administration of justice, the model of exercise of political power, and perception of the relationship between the individual and society. One reason for these changes was the nature of the transformation, as it created strong ties between the replacement of the socialist system of government with a liberal-democratic one and the expectation that the new law would be better for everyone. That expectation was further strengthened by the declaration of Poland's wish to accede to the European Union, which was at the time intensifying its harmonization of private law. Many citizens had a generally favourable idea of the future model of state and law, but some also had anxieties caused by the free-market economy (in the 1980s, the Polish public was extensively informed by the government media about some poor results of Margaret Thatcher's reforms in the United Kingdom).

Under these circumstances, private law could serve as a powerful mechanism regulating the process of change in some areas while setting a framework for it, with certain adjustments, in some others. Its effectiveness depended also on whether sufficient elements were to be introduced to the law to inform the people about the principles of the transformation and guarantees that the principles would be respected. Furthermore, it was advisable to publicize the reasons for any decisions made, specifically those ensuring that at least some of the rights and obligations the citizens found crucial would be upheld and fulfilled. However, any such efforts were only fragmentary and were in fact marginal in the case of publicization. The reformers were familiar with many publications written by legal historians, including historians of political and legal doctrines, which stressed the importance of strong popular legitimacy for legal norms applied in times of political and economic upheavals.[9]

A moderate interest in relevant research, illustrative of ignoring the relationship between private law and its politics on the one hand and individual and social attitudes on the other hand was not continued in the early 21st century. In fact, some in-depth analyses carried out in the 1990s, covering also attitudes towards law, were not repeated, making do with information on the attitudes and opinions of citizens with respect to courts. Nevertheless, even the results of such limited research ought to have made the reformers pause and reflect. When asked to assess the consequences of changes to the judiciary carried out in Poland, most respondents were unable to name any that were favourable.

However, the very same citizens were quite adamant that one of the main reasons for their unfavourable opinion of the way the justice system operated

9 See Konstanty GRZYBOWSKI: *Historia doktryn politycznych i prawnych: od państwa niewolniczego do rewolucji burżuazyjnych* [The history of political and legal doctrines: from the slave state to the bourgeois revolutions], PWN, Warsaw, 1968, 320.

was 'bad law.'[10] The number of negative responses grew in 1998, only to remain at a similar level in succeeding years. This unfavourable tendency kept resurfacing in spite of the new Polish Constitution (1997) having underscored the principles of equality before the law and the right to a fair trial and due process of law. A study of this tendency revealed that one of the reasons for the discrepancy between the norm and its interpretation was communication between courts and judges and society. It ignored social reality.

The search for the source of the problem, however, must be expanded into private law. It is there, despite many favourable changes, that the legal system lacked any guarantees of satisfying the urgent needs shared by most citizens in everyday life. This is illustrated by responses given in 1999, naming areas that allegedly were not properly protected in the new system. The first on the list was the recovery of a debt owed under a contract or in the form of damages.[11]

Importantly, in the opinion of judges at that time, the assessment of the law then in force was the chief source of the respondents' unfavourable opinion of the courts. They 'transferred' one opinion onto another,[12] not distinguishing or identifying certain causalities involving the administration of justice. People encountered law that they did not understand or that was ineffective in everyday life, and they usually only heard about corruption, considered to be one of the reasons for the unfavourable opinion of the courts, from other people.

Just one conclusion of that study needs to be highlighted: 'the conflict between the universal readiness to use the courts (the necessity of using them) and the relatively low opinion enjoyed by them makes demands for an overhaul of the courts and for the reform of the related law significant contributors to the overall social discontent.'[13]

Without identifying or focusing on this problem – deciding that the issue called for a separate study – during the period between 1993 and 2006 jurists for a long time discussed a regulatory model that would adhere to the princi-

10 Eighty-seven percent of respondents believed that the law was the cause of the poor effectiveness of the court system – see Janina CZAPSKA: *Wizerunek sądu w opinii publicznej* [The court's image in the public opinion], in MARIA BORUCKA-ARCTOWA, Krzysztof PAŁECKI (eds): *Sądy w opinii społeczeństwa polskiego* [The courts in the opinion of Polish society], Ratio, Krakow, 2003, 24.

11 For more see Michał STRZESZEWSKI: *Opinie o funkcjonowaniu wymiaru sprawiedliwości i walce z przestępczością: komunikat z badań* [Opinions on the functioning of the administration of justice and fight on crime: communication based on research], CBOS, Warszawa, 1999.

12 For more see Krzysztof PAŁECKI: *Społecznie oczekiwany wzorzec orzekania sądowego* [The socially expected model of judicial decision-making], in *Sądy w opinii*, 150.

13 *Ibidem*, 151.

ple of uniformity of civil law. Other topics of debate included the content and function of general clauses in the system of private law.

As far as the principle of uniformity of civil law is concerned, the discussion concentrated around whether the Civil Code should regulate civil law relationships between business parties and consumers, and whether it should incorporate family and guardianship law. Given the affirmative answer, the expectation was to lay down a common normative foundation for as many civil-law relationships as possible. Additionally, that foundation would be ideologically and axiology modernized and technically up-to-date. In 2000, however, a new Code of Commercial Partnerships and Companies was enacted. The Chairman of the Codification Commission discussed it as not putting a dent in the principle of uniformity of civil law, as the Code was limited in scope, regulating the status only of a specific group of entities, whereas the regulation of the transactions involving them was left in the Civil Code. Calling the new legislation a 'code' was meant to 'overcome the opposition from those who advocated that the old Commercial Code be kept in force.'[14]

In turn, the idea of individual freedoms and rights was to be reinforced by purging the restrictions on their exercise found in their Code formulations. Until then, such restrictions had been contained in general clauses forming parts of the definitions of the nature of the various rights and freedoms. In the new code, the general clauses were to be removed from the norms regulating these rights and form separate provisions, thus once again making an entitlement alone the nature of a right. Furthermore, the wording of the clauses was changed. The 'principles of community life' and 'socio-economic purpose of a right' were to be replaced with the criterion of 'good customs'. Another proposal was also considered: 'reasons of equity and principles of fair trading' but the notion of 'good customs' was found to be closer to the native culture.

Slowly, a dispute grew over how functional the 1964 Civil Code was in the new liberal-democratic system of government and new socio-economic conditions. This reflected different opinions on how the new codification was to be carried out. Jurists arguing for a slow approach claimed that the 1964 Codes could form the foundations of private law in Poland in the early 21st century. They believed that the Codes had preserved many classic legal institutions, including those inherited from the 1933 Code of Obligations, while their short-

14 See RADWAŃSKI: *Kodyfikacja prawa*, 137.

comings resulting from the implementation of Soviet models had already been eliminated.[15]

This description concentrated on only two characteristics of the Codes and ignored others coming into light after a few years of the transformation and beginning to determine the state of the entire system of private law. Those included deficiencies in the classic institutions of private law, resurfacing decodification, and failure to clearly articulate new or reinstituted principles of private law.

The first is the state of the classic institutions of civil law in the 1964 Civil Code after the amendments of 1989–2000. What is notable in this context is the discrepancy between the very existence of ownership of individual farms, which made the Polish legal system stand out from others in socialist times, and the enactment in the very same civil code, or sanctioning through its provisions, of restrictions on the operation of the provisions of real law and law of obligations. The legislators drafting the Code created, as far as they could, a cohesive piece of legislation. The original structure of the Code could not completely separate legal tradition from the elements of a socialist model of law derived from Soviet jurisprudence. Private ownership and freedom of contract were missing from most of them.

Consequently, the original content of the Civil Code featured departures from principles, including some departure from the principle of equal status and autonomy of the parties to civil-law relationships. On the other hand, they lacked any institutions supporting ownership of property and freedom of contract, such as provisions for various forms of security for a debt. For this reason, the elimination of norms directly derived from Marxist-Leninist ideology was only a partial solution to the problem.

The removal of the latter feature, in turn, called for the introduction of new content into the civil code. This was difficult to achieve,[16] as the new principles of private law had been left vague. A case in point was the regulation of ownership. Between 1989 and 1996, amendments purged the Civil Code of distinctions relying on criteria referring to the owner and to the item owned with regard to the rights and obligations relating to the ownership of property. However, in itself, the norm regulating ownership remained intact. It contained two general clauses, originating from Soviet legal theory: the principles of community life and the socio-economic purpose of the right. Both re-

15 *Ibidem*, 136.

16 For more on similar problems in other countries see STAWARSKA-RIPPEL: *Problemy kodyfikacji*, 50.

stricted the exercise of ownership. Some jurists believed that simply getting rid of them (which did not come to pass) was not the best way forward. It was necessary to decide first how to counter the abuse of ownership. The nature of ownership could be modified, or a single norm on abuse of rights in any civil law relationship could be enacted.

Such cases, as the advocates of the enactment of a new code believed, demonstrated that classic civil-law institutions included in the 1964 Civil Code helped the civil-law tradition survive under the socialist political system. However, at the beginning of the 21st century, they needed a major overhaul. This necessarily involved eliminating their background ties to the previous legal system, as well as adaptation to a reality of which many elements had not been known in the 1920s and 1930s when the classic institutions were first developed.

The second argument for new codification was the proliferation of decodification. This time, the legislature's intentions differed from those of its socialist predecessor, but the effect was similar. Between 1989 and 1996, the Civil Code was purged of provisions enabling administrative agencies to regulate civil-law relationships differently from the Code. In the meantime, and in the following years, many new or reactivated civil-law relationships were regulated by extra-code provisions, because their inclusion in the Code would have required too many fundamental changes. Other European countries struggled with the same problem.

The third argument was based on the fact that new codification would send a general, clear and easily understandable message to the citizens and society about the values that would be promoted by the provisions of public law and ways of giving effect to them, as well as the ideological and axiological reasons for the lawmaking decisions.

3 Reform of the Civil Code

From 1986 to 1996, amendments to the Civil Code were coordinated by the Civil Law Reform Commission that had been set up under the socialist political system. It was headed by Witold Czachórski – one of the drafters of the 1964 Civil Code. The very name of the Commission foreboded a limited scope of modernizing measures, for which the directions had been set in different circumstances from those in which the reforms were to be carried out. Admittedly, some fragmentary amendments were brought up to date, but without making changes to the paradigm of the Commission's work.

In its own words, the Commission's method was to make only where the system of private law was affected by the transformation of the political system (of which there were a few ways, for example the introduction of local government) or of the economic system. The Commission also stated that in its decisions it was taking into account the state of social consciousness, shaped by the existing law, and made it clear that its work focused for the most part on extra-code law. When carefully analysed, this information implied that the legal reform undertaken at the time only concerned the efficient administration of the normative infrastructure of the economic system. Moreover, any amendments should not go beyond the public expectations trained on the dispersed jurisprudential construct is originating from the previous political system.

This concept continued to provide the base frame of reference in the first half of the 1990s. This was a cause of disagreement with a group of jurists, who demanded the immediate beginning of comprehensive changes to the legal system. Before one could proceed with those, one first had to define their goals, methods, contents and instruments. The advocates of such a major overhaul argued that the reform should be completed in two stages. In the first stage, the pivotal elements of the private-law system should be modified quickly, provisionally and broadly, but in a single move. The determined goal was to stabilize the legal system and give it the first specific content. In the second and final stages, a new codification should be drafted over several years of careful interdisciplinary work, drawing on theory and practice.

Meanwhile, what the reformers did was amend the various provisions dispersed throughout the private law system, using for this purpose a diverse set of criteria for determining what and how to amend. Certain caveats were made that the amendments were fragmentary and sometimes only provisional. The legal changes were implemented in the course of and 'incidentally to' haphazard economic reforms. As a result, the legal reform slowed down and receded into the background, although it had begun from a widely understood and accepted, if only symbolic, amendment. Namely, it eliminated the principle of unity of state property with its related provisions from the Civil Code. Arguments for successive changes were laconic in terms of ideology and axiology. Scholarly publications from the era did not refer to these issues in any meaningful way, either.

In a critical response, Józef Skąpski warned and encouraged:

> You cannot live a normal life with a code that is continually being 'worked on'; that is in a state of permanent legal uncertainty. (...) Wherever possible, the old Polish solutions should be reached for, in this way

> breaking away from the bounds of Polish People's Republic law. Pragmatism should be the beacon to this work.[17]

Meanwhile, Stefan Grzybowski argued against delaying 'the introduction of a new legal system in full (...) even though (...) it were a legal system far from perfection.'[18] Additionally, he argued that the unreformed backlog grew with each successive year, causing legal problems such as the postponement of reprivatization.

Ewa Łętowska, in turn, judged the reformers' legislative activities at that time from yet another perspective: 'First and foremost, it is necessary to give up the principle underpinning much of legal reasoning by lawmaking bodies (and ones assessing if laws are correctly applied), namely the conviction that a legislator can do whatever they please.'[19]

Support for these aspirations was also voiced by other lawyers and jurists involved in the post-1989 continued works of Solidarity Citizens' Legislative Action and of the Social Legislative Council. They called for the reactivation of the Codification Commission from 1919–1939, to be tasked with the drafting of new codes, including for civil law. The suitable preparation of the procedural path to that end was presented as a guarantee of the quality of legislation expected to meet the standards of a modern democratic state ruled by law. With support from the law faculties of several universities, the appeal was addressed to the president, prime minister and speakers of both houses of parliament. In 1992, Kazimierz Barczyk sponsored the citizen bill in the Sejm.[20] The implementation of the idea was, however, blocked by the Legislative Council assisting the President of the Council of Ministers; that body, in the words of Andrzej Mączyński: 'apparently did not appreciate the need for any special organization of the works on the drafts.'[21] The result was that the best practices of Polish codifiers would not be leveraged by the Third Republic.

The position of codes during the transformation of the political system was supported by the Constitutional Court (*Trybunał Konstytucyjny*). Because of

---

17 SKĄPSKI: *Kodeks cywilny,* 85, 88.

18 GRZYBOWSKI: *Zagadnienia kodyfikacyjne,* 106.

19 Ewa ŁĘTOWSKA: *Konwencja Europejska w Polsce i nowe myślenie o prawie* [The European convention in Poland and the new thinking about law], KPP 1–5 (1992), 149.

20 Print of the Sejm no. 83, of 15 January 1992: amendment of the Act of 3 June 1919.

21 Andrzej MĄCZYŃSKI: *Ustawa o Komisji Kodyfikacyjnej w pracach Społecznej Rady Legislacyjnej* [The Act on the Codification Commission in the works of the Social Legislative Council], in GRODZISKI: *Wkład krakowskiego,* 158.

FIGURE 6.1 Andrzej Mączyński. Born in 1945. Linked to Jagiellonian University; Head of Department of Private International Law. In 1981–1992, member of the Social Legislative Council, participant in the works of the Solidarity Centre for Citizens' Legislative Action in 1981. Member of the Civil Law Reform Commission of 1986 and subsequently of the Civil Law Codification Commission of 1996; Justice and Vice-President of the Constitutional Court (1997–2006).
SOURCE: MĄCZYŃSKI'S PRIVATE ARCHIVE

the enactment of ever more new statutes, the question arose as to their relationship to the codes. The Constitutional Court invoked the special axiological status enjoyed by codes and reaffirmed the presumption of the existence of a duty to keep the concepts and terms used in legislation consistent with those of codes, which also applied to any new legislation:

> The essence of any code is [to be] the enactment of a cohesive and – as far as possible – complete and lasting regulation in a given field of law (...). For this reason, the terms and concepts used in codes are considered to be the model ones, and it is presumed that other statutes attach to them the same meaning.[22]

The year 1996 saw the establishment of a Codification Commission for Civil Law at the Ministry of Justice[23] headed by Zbigniew Radwański. Just as the

22 Decision of the Constitutional Tribunal of 18 October 1994, K 2/94, OTK 1994.2.36.
23 Resolution of the Council of Ministers no. 109/96, 17 September 1996.

previous one did, this Commission, too, focused on fragmentary amendments to the Civil Code and other statutes.[24] Arguing in favour of this method of modernization on private law, the 'high substantive value' of the Code was cited by the Commission's chair, who maintained that it could still serve as the foundation of Polish private law.[25] In the late 20th and early 21st centuries, this opinion continued to be held by the Commission, although an increasing number of jurists came to believe it was wrong.

At that time, only the choice of a regulatory model for commercial law was made. The rules for business parties were isolated and collected in the aforementioned new Code of Commercial Partnerships and Companies, enacted in 2000,[26] whereas the regulation of commercial transactions as such was left in the Civil Code. In this way, the principle of uniformity of civil law could be preserved. Two additional arguments adduced in favour of maintaining this model of normative structure were the need and ability to ensure the editorial cohesion of the two pieces of legislation, and the expectation that such an isolation of provisions would facilitate the regulation of newly emerging and changing types of obligations, transactions and other relationships in civil law, featuring business entities and consumers as parties.[27]

A separate codification was decided for family and guardianship law. Its corresponding code was praised by the Commission, who said that family law could be incorporated into the Civil Code in the event of a new codification.

Further codification work suffered many changes of fortune. As a result, a new civil code did not materialize (and has not materialized until the present day); any works on it were abandoned. The actual codification work did not begin until the 21st century. Codification preliminaries were published in 2006,[28] and a draft of the first of the five books of the Civil Code was presented

24 Zbigniew Radwański, *Trzy lata działalności Komisji Kodyfikacyjnej Prawa Cywilnego* [The three years of operation of the Codification Commission for Civil Law], PiP 4 (2000), 3.

25 Zbigniew Radwański: *Założenia dalszych prac kodyfikacyjnych na obszarze prawa cywilnego* [The assumptions for the continued codification work in the area of civil law], PiP 3 (2004), 5.

26 Act of 15 September 2000 – Code of Commercial Partnerships and Companies, Dz. U.94.1037, as amended.

27 Jerzy Rajski: *Kierunki rozwoju europejskiego prawa kontraktów* [Directions of development of the European law of contracts], KPP 1 (2002), 215.

28 Komisja Kodyfikacyjna Prawa Cywilnego działająca przy Ministrze Sprawiedliwości [Codification Commission for Civil Law at the Ministry of Justice]: Zbigniew Radwański (ed.), *Zielona Księga. Optymalna wizja Kodeksu cywil-*

to the public in 2009.[29] It was also then that a dispute arose over the methods and some of the content of modern-day private law. The controversy concerned fundamental issues, among which there were several moot points. One axis of division was opinions held of the 1964 codes of substantive and procedural law. Those who had a favourable opinion of them were against a new codification. In their opinion, a suitable adaptation of existing law had taken place both through amendments of the law and through the subjection of the application of the law to a new way of interpretation.

Another point at issue was the nature of changes in the environment of Polish private law. Some in the legal circles who had noticed the multitude and significance of the transformations (that awareness was by no means universal) considered them to be a sufficient reason for a new codification. However, there were also others who believed that the speed of the transformation was so high that it made necessary the use of other instruments to manage the legal system. The dispute pertains the axiological and ideological foundations of the present-day policy of the law, involving issues such as the interpretation of the Polish Constitution; purpose and functions of civil procedure; guarantees of judges and courts' independence;[30] and, consequently, also the method of codification and the content it should take.

Another object of controversy were the functions of a code. Some legal minds demanded that codes be given the role of delimiting and communicating the ideological and axiological foundations of private law, while others were against that, claiming that it would complicate the structure of the codes, decreasing their effectiveness.

Among the principal points of contention was also the use of solutions derived from foreign legislation. Some jurists were particularly wary of borrowings and transplants, maintaining that the constructs attracting the attention of the reformers functioned in a different environment in their native legislation compared to Polish socio-economic conditions.

---

nego w Rzeczypospolitej Polskiej [A green book. The optimal vision of a civil code in the Republic of Poland], Ministerstwo Sprawiedliwości, Warsaw, 2006.

29 Komisja Kodyfikacyjna Prawa Cywilnego działająca przy Ministrze Sprawiedliwości: *Księga pierwsza Kodeksu cywilnego. Projekt z uzasadnieniem* [Book I of the Civil Code. Draft and explanatory memorandum], C. H. Beck, Warsaw, 2009.

30 Anna Machnikowska: *O niezawisłości sędziów i niezależności sądów w trudnych czasach: wymiar sprawiedliwości w pułapce sprawności* [On judicial independence in difficult Times: the justice system in the trap of efficiency]. Wolters Kluwer Polska, Warsaw, 2017, 272–273.

In order to settle those disputes, it might have been helpful to return to the analyses of fundamental issues offered by some jurists in the early 1990s. In 1981, they were engaged in a grassroots initiative for legal reform under the auspices of Solidarity. Those included Stefan Grzybowski, Jerzy Skąpski, Ewa Łętowska and Andrzej Mączyński who, especially in 1991–1992, identified the various aspects of key topics for discussions of the transformation of private law unfolding at that time. One of the challenges was to find the appropriate criteria to guide the legislators in their current lawmaking activities, another was analogous but referred to the grander designs of a future codification. Both sets of criteria called for decisions to be made regarding the selection and interpretation of the ideological and axiological foundations to be underlying the new Polish private law.

It accordingly became necessary to conceptualize the relationship between the present and the future private law, as well as the situation of the addressees (recipients or affected parties) of the norms of the law. If the transformation was to be symbolized by notions such as equality before the law and equality and freedom of the parties to civil-law relationships, those had to be articulated in the new law. Such notions needed to be expressed in plain language and associated with the self-determination (self-guidance) of the individual and respect for their dignity. They also hd to conform to the new rules for the resolution of conflicts between individual rights and the wellbeing of society as a whole.

These considerations, however, were back-burned by reformers, who focused instead on draft new norms of specific rather than general nature, since the wording was becoming increasingly casuistic. In the system of private law, socialist fiction was superseded by complicated legalese, which achieved the status of a meta-language that spread to opinions to judgments. This fact indirectly contributed to the blocking of access for many citizens not only to the knowledge of specific legal solutions but even to the principles of fair resolution of conflicts using the law.

The source of the problem was not that the legal system had remained a compilation of three different systems for more than ten years. Some of its provisions had originated in the Second Republic, some were typical of a socialist political system, and some were new constructs geared to the needs of a market economy of the late 20th century. When analysed outside Poland, the odd compilation was even prematurely perceived[31] as a separate legal culture, different from that prevailing in Western Europe. It was tentatively believed to

31 For more see GIARO: *Legal Tradition*, 20.

comprise the legal systems of the former socialist countries.[32] In reality, however, it was an example of legal hybridization, dominated by the fusion of, on the one hand, a legal tradition sharing the same roots with the private law in Western Europe with, on the other hand, new legal solutions typical of the late twentieth century, also found in other European countries at that time. In this Poland was not unique against the background of the other states of Central and Eastern Europe. What did make Poland and some other countries different was the fast pace of hybridization. According to Kazimierz Braczyk's synthetic summary of the change: 'We were the precursors of transformation in Central and Eastern Europe, of a peaceful political, social and economic revolution; we moved from a totalitarian and badly organized state to a stable democracy and rule of law.'[33]

Moreover, a fact of significant consequence was the failure to convey to the general public which values would be promoted by the new private law from that time onward and why, what impact that would have on the individual and society, or where such values were to be found in the legal system and how they could be employed.

According to social scientists, the psychological reason for changing the political system in Poland in the late 1980s and early 1990s was the rise of an individualistic orientation,[34] which the reformers of private law adhered to as well. Commentaries on code proposals from 2006–2015, familiar mainly to lawyers and jurists, gave support to such values as autonomy of the parties, their agency, mutual trust between citizens and public institutions, and economic growth. The other actions taken by the reforms demonstrate that they were also guided by the belief that some new development processes would consolidate all by themselves. They also expected the gradual enhancement of social capital and increase in complex thinking about the functioning of the

32 This view was expressed, for instance, by Rudolf B. Schlesinger: *Comparative Law: Cases, Texts, Materials*, Foundation Press, New York 1998, 286.

33 Kazimierz Barczyk: *Centrum Obywatelskich Inicjatyw Ustawodawczych NSZZ 'Solidarność': spojrzenie po latach*, in Grodziski: *Wkład krakowskiego*, 446.

34 Jadwiga Koralewicz, Marek Ziółkowski: *Mentalność Polaków* [The Poles' mindset], Nakom, Poznań 1990; Janusz Reykowski: *Resolving Large-scale Political Conflict: The Case of the Round Table Negotiations in Poland,* in Stephen Worchel, Jeffry A. Simpson (eds): *Conflict Between People and Groups, Causes, Processes and Resolutions*, Nelson-Hall, Chicago, 1993; Krystyna Skarżyńska: *Czy jesteśmy prorozwojowi? Wartości i przekonania ludzi a dobrobyt i demokratyzacja kraju* [Are we prodevelopmental? The values and convictions of the people and the welfare and democratization of the country], in Marek Drogosz (ed.): *Jak Polacy przegrywają, jak Polacy wygrywają* [How Poles lose, how Poles win], Gdańskie Wydawnictwo Psychologiczne, Gdańsk, 2005.

legal system. They further assumed that the citizens would gain knowledge of the new law on their own initiative and by their own efforts, and use it to become economic beneficiaries of the new political system. Furthermore, in making use of the same law, the citizens were expected to expand the catalogue of values or tolerated by them, thus laying down the foundation for a civic society and liberal democracy. However, that anticipation was not verified, because attention was shifted to other issues.

The reformers appeared to mistake their own attitudes and experiences for the universal attitudes and experiences of society (false consensus effect). Their failure to communicate the fundamental issues at an early stage of the transformation of the legal system had consequences beyond the postponement of the decision to draft new codes. Risks arose and information gaps opened in the transition from a 'command-distribution' economic model to a free-market one. This also caused the structure of social relations to change.

The gaps were not bridged by the constitutionalization of private law. The new Polish Constitution of 1997 introduced new protections of individual rights against excessive interference from the legislative branch and doubled the protection of ownership of property by prohibiting such changes as would deprive it of its substance.[35] However, some lawyers, and what is to say of other citizens, did not view the Constitution as a direct signpost for legal changes. This problem was brought to the attention of the legal circles by certain jurists.[36] It also resurfaced with interpretations of the constitutional norm making judges subject to both ordinary statutes and the Constitution. Many judges did not regard it as a sufficient basis for the direct application of the Constitution, for instance in the event of conflict arising between an ordinary statutory provision and a constitutional one.

Ewa Łętowska had called attention to the problem earlier on in the context of the activity of the legal circles during the process of transformation of the legal system. In the case of legislation originating from the previous

35 The 1997 Polish Constitution, Art. 31(3) and 64.

36 Lech Morawski: *Stressing Relevancy and Admissibility*, paper – Copenhagen, December 2002, 2, quoted after Maria Borucka-Arctowa: *Komunikacja między sądami a społeczeństwem* [Communication between courts and society], in Borucka-Arctowa, Pałecki: *Sądy w opinii*, 73; Ewa Łętowska, Janusz Łętowski: *Co wynika dla sądów z konstytucyjnej zasady podziału władz* [What follows for the courts from the constitutional principle of separation of powers], in Janusz Trzciński, Adam Jankiewicz (eds), *Konstytucja i gwarancje jej przestrzegania. Księga pamiątkowa ku czci prof. Janiny Zakrzewskiej* [The Constitution and guarantees of its being respected: a commemorative book in honour of Professor Janina Zakrzewska], Wydawnictwa Trybunału Konstytucyjnego, Warsaw, 1996, 391–392.

political system, she signalled the commitment of the courts to interpretation encompassing the entirety of the legal system, including the Constitution and acts of international law. 'The goal is not to circumvent the law but to ask the question whether [its] existing interpretation should be revised and whether that can be achieved through the (proper) use of other methods of interpretation.'[37]

Freedom was always deeply embedded in Polish society's tradition and culture, but several decades of living under a socialist system of government and the trauma of World War II tinted it with mistrust of many institutions.[38] This attitude continued in the late 1990s and early 2000s, with the level of mistrust not only being higher than in other Central and Eastern European countries

FIGURE 6.2 Ewa Łętowska. Born in 1940. Linked to the Polish Academy of Sciences, head of the Civil Law Team in the Institute of Legal Sciences. Involved in the works of the Solidarity Centre for Citizens' Legislative Action in 1981. The first Civil Rights Ombudsman from the establishment of the office in 1987 to 1992; Justice of the Supreme Administrative Court (1999–2002) and Constitutional Court (2002–2011), member of the Civil Law Codification Commission.

37 Ewa ŁĘTOWSKA, Janusz ŁĘTOWSKI: *O państwie, administrowaniu i sądach w okresie przekształceń ustrojowych* [Of the state, administration and courts in a period of constitutional transformation], Scholar, Warsaw, 1995, 218.

38 Mirosława MARODY: *Oswajanie rzeczywistości. Między realnym socjalizmem a realną demokracją*, Instytut Studiów Społecznych UW, Warsaw, 1996.

(e.g. Czechia and Hungary), but also setting Poland apart from the rest of Europe.[39] In these circumstances, disappointment or indifference came easily when some changes were not carried out quickly enough or did not bring a benefit to all citizens. Similar feelings spread to more areas when it came to defining the relationship between freedom and equality, because sometimes – in private law as well – the two values come into conflict. As a result, some rules for resolving that conflict had to be agreed upon by society.[40]

In the 1990s and 2000s, only a portion of Polish society associated freedom of contract with achieving aspirations, exercising rights and having equal opportunities. Not all citizens, who in the past had not had the means of organizing their own life (control by the socialist state), became immediately active and successful. This, in turn, adversely affected their financial situation. Although there were several other reasons for the deterioration, some citizens believed that the primary culprit was the law. It was stereotypically held not to be equal for all, regardless of the political system. Studies conducted between 1990 and 2002 show that in spite of the change of the political system to liberal-democratic, next to the preference for maximum individual freedom, there also existed preferences for authoritarian attitudes. Interestingly, these two preferences were unevenly distributed among particular social groups. The former was stronger among workers than among the intelligentsia.[41]

Since preferences for an authoritarian attitude go hand-in-hand with the expectation of a specific social system, it can be presumed that the same was also true for the rules and scope of many civil-law relationships, whereas the legislators drafting the new private law, by contrast, stressed values more closely related to individualism and the advantages of multiple changes to the legal system. This choice of priorities was understandable, but certain circumstances ought to have been considered nonetheless. Those include the consequences of a situation in which the law was often amended in the

39 Czapska: *Wizerunek sądu*, 28, Michał Wenzel, *Zaufanie do instytucji publicznych w Polsce, Czechach i na Węgrzech. Komunikat z badań* [Confidence in public institutions in Poland, Czechia and Hungary. Communication based on research], CBOS, Warsaw, 2001.

40 John Rawls: *Political Liberalism*, Columbia University Press, New York, 1996, 212–230.

41 The studies concerned parental values or ones that respondents considered desirable in their children. Krystyna Skarżyńska explained the difference in results for workers and the intelligentsia by claiming that the former still accepted the ideological message that capitalism rewarded self-reliant individuals, while the latter had: 'now realized that capitalism in the form we encounter everyday is a system requiring from individuals not so much self-guidance (…) as conformism and obedience towards authorities'. For more see Skarżyńska: *Człowiek a polityka*, 57–58.

anticipation of a new codification. Moreover, society was undergoing deep transformations but was kept in the dark as to their relationship to the law.

A broad discussion on private law, although limited to the legal community, was initiated in the early 21st century after the publication of the first effects of the reformers' work. This time, more lawyers and jurists, including judges took part in the discussions, new arguments were voiced, and counters to them, and concrete proposals for amendments were discussed. The moderately favourable assessment of the works of the Codification Commission of 1996 had three underlying circumstances. The first one was the divergence of outlooks on the preliminary draft of some parts of the Code. Another one was the instability of such amendments to the codes of 1964 as were designed or opined on by the Commission. The third reservation touched on the organization of the Commission's activities, also viewed as a source of controversies about the quality of legislation. Criticisms included pointing out the excessive freedom for the Commission to choose its topics, the frequency of changes to its composition and transfer of part of the works to narrower non-member expert circles, as well as the lack of mandatory social consultations and verification of theoretical underpinnings against legal practice. Among the critical voices was Andrzej Mączyński: 'it seems that, sometimes, (...) the ambitions of the Commission's members prevailed rather than the true needs.'[42]

Some jurists were critical of plans for a new codification in any near future. Such plans were floated by the Civil Law Codification Commission after years of remaining silent. Criticisms directed at the plans had no common denominator. The opponents of a new code included those who considered the existing code to be the optimal solution, as well as others who claimed that it was already obsolete.

As for the first-mentioned group of debaters, the justices of the Supreme Court's Civil Chamber[43] claimed that the 1964 Civil Code had preserved its functionality. It owed its continued relevance, they believed, to the systematic amendments and new interpretations by the judicature since 1989. They were also convinced that the transformations undergone by civil-law relationships were not serious enough to necessitate further legislation on top of what was already in force at the time. Furthermore, they argued, there was no better alternative to the current Code because the principles of the new law presented in 2006–2009 raised serious doubts. So it was not reasonable, the Supreme Court justices argued, to give up values such as the stability and reli-

42 Mączyński: *Ustawa o Komisji Kodyfikacyjnej*, 160.

43 *Projekt kodeksu cywilnego: księga pierwsza* [Book I of the draft Civil Code] 104–123.

ability[44] of law and its interpretation only to make major changes, in the name of modernization, of which the beneficial effect was unknown. Once such a modernizing decision was made, the justices went on, a few years of destabilization would certainly follow. This would be due to the requirement for new interpretation standards and practice of application to accrue. Therefore, the legislature should continue the policy, pursued since 1989, of systematically amending the Code and any extra-code provisions.[45]

Hasty codification was also opposed by certain jurists who had a different opinion from the Supreme Court justices on the codes then in force and their socio-economic environment. Those believed[46] that the Codes had lost their functionality in confrontation with new economic, social, political and legal trends. Private law was undergoing constant modification conducted in a fragmentary 'patchy' and provisional manner. Meanwhile, change was proceeding so fast that new codification in the course of the changes would be unwise. This was due to two reasons: the need for the immediate introduction of diverse solutions into the various areas of the Polish legal system in response to new economic realities, and the need to respond to the process of harmonization of the European legal space. To make things worse, the harmonization proceeded in fits and starts, the principles of the harmonization were not cohesive, and myths were sometimes created about its achievements.[47] Until the system stabilized, it should not be managed in reliance solely on the codes, but also on legal principles developed by scholars and courts and adjusted to the changing conditions in which civil-law relationships were functioning.[48]

In response, another group of jurists, including the reformers,[49] adduced various arguments highlighting the defects and shortcomings of the codes

---

44 For the views of Polish authoritative literature on the reliability of law as a legal principle see Maciej WOJCIECHOWSKI: *Pewność prawa*, WUG, Gdańsk, 2014, 172–175.

45 Magdalena WRÓBEL: *Główne założenia projektu kodeksu cywilnego* [The main assumptions for the draft Civil Code], Monitor Prawniczy 13 (2007), 733–740.

46 Jan ANDRZEJEWSKI: *Czy nowa kodyfikacja prawa cywilnego jest potrzebna w czasie kryzysu prawa?* [Is a new codification of civil law needed in a time of legal crisis?], RPEiS 1 (2014), 77–89.

47 Fryderyk ZOLL: *Europejski kodeks cywilny – wokół wizji nowego prawa prywatnego dla Europy* [European Civil Code – A vision of new private law for Europe], Nowa Europa, Przegląd Natoliński 1 (2018), 28.

48 ANDRZEJEWSKI: *Czy nowa kodyfikacja*, 77–89.

49 Zbigniew RADWAŃSKI: *Uwagi do sprawozdania z dyskusji przeprowadzonej w izbie Cywilnej Sądu Najwyższego nad 'Projektem Kodeksu cywilnego. Księga Pierwsza'* [Comments on the report on the debate held at the Civil Chamber of the Supreme Court on the 'Draft Civil Code. Book One'], Przegląd Sądowy 5 (2010), 5–15.

then in force. The faults, allegedly, could not be remedied by successive amendments. Attention was also drawn to circumstances making a new codification a challenge for the 'here and now'.[50] Those included technological advances and Constitutional Court decisions.[51] Another circumstance that the reformers emphasized was the reforming efforts undertaken in some European countries in the late 20th and early 21st centuries.[52] Other former socialist countries decided in favour of successive codifications, but those were chiefly countries with small populations. A new Lithuanian Civil Code was adopted in 2000 and an Estonian one in 2002. Countries with larger populations – Czechia and Hungary – enacted new codifications in the next decade of the 21st century, in 2012 and 2013 respectively.[53] A sweeping recodification was carried out in the Netherlands between 1981 and 2008,[54] while France decided on a limited recodification.[55]

In the case of Poland, the number of economic relationships and related legal events prompting new regulation was very high in 1989–2000. In the first decade after the change of the political system, the Civil Code received fifty amendments and extra-code provisions were modified as well in response to the rapid and multidimensional overhaul of the economic system. Many new regulations were presented as legislation pre-determined by new economic practices encountered by an equally new legislator. The same argument of legal determinism justified limiting the scope of major reforms of substantive law because the legislator had to respect the other long-standing norms of the Code.

Even more amendments – over one hundred – were made to the Code of Civil Procedure. Those adapted the Code to its environment and tested, with varying results, the effectiveness of different procedural models. In this case,

50 Marian KĘPIŃSKI: *Czy w Polsce jest potrzebny nowy kodeks cywilny? Artykuł polemiczny* [Does Poland need a new civil code? A polemical article], RPEiS 2 (2014), 237–245.

51 RADWAŃSKI: *Kodyfikacja prawa cywilnego*, 134–135.

52 See Hector L. MACQUEEN: *Private Law's Revolutionaries: Authors, Codifiers and Merchants?* in Sarah WORTHINGTON, Andrew ROBERTSON, Graham VIGO (eds): *Revolution and Evolution in Private Law*, Bloomsbury, Oxford-Portland, 2018, 42.

53 Katalin KELEMEN, Balazs FEKETE: *How Should the Legal System of Eastern Europe be Classified Today*? in Attila BADO et al. (eds): *International Conference for the 10th Anniversary of the Institute of Comparative Law*, Universitätsverlag, Potsdam, 2014, https://ssrn.com/abstract=2614944

54 *Staatsblad van het Koninkrijk der Nederlanden* 2011, 272.

55 See Ilona KUSKA-ŻAK, Marcin ŻAK: *Kierunki proponowanych zmian francuskiego prawa zobowiązań* [Directions of proposed changes to the French law of obligations], KPP 4 (2008), 1071.

the multitude of amendments represented legal creationism[56] because the legislator did not take into account existing judicial and social practices.

In the opinion of the advocates of a new codification, despite such extensive activity on the part of the legislator, the Civil Code ceased to regulate an ever-increasing number of new types of legal relationships, leaving them to be regulated by provisions found outside the Code. At the same time, it had ceased to be internally coherent, because its principles of private law had not been modified, except in 1989–1997, while at the same time in some other statutes new terminology was used or existing concepts were interpreted in new ways. As a result, the system of private law began to lose those of its characteristics that had been viewed as inherent to it. As a rule, such principles are enshrined in codes because it is codes that systematize the content and hierarchy of legal provisions and articulate the fundamental principles of the law, being a beacon for other legislation.

In this situation, a new codification became necessary because the provisions of the Civil Code 'no longer provided information about significant elements,' of particular institutions of the legal system and hindered the implementation of EU law.[57] Irrespective of the rate of harmonization, the accompanying conceptual work and international collaboration of jurists supported the development of private law and its doctrine, providing inspiration for the national legislatures as well.[58] In turn, for the argument that the high speed of change made codification ill-advisable, the counter was that the more comprehensive and protracted the transformation of a political system is, the more important the existence of a code becomes for the reliability of law, provided that the transformation is sufficiently functional. That relationship, it was argued, could not be disregarded. The proposition to make the courts responsible for developing new principles as new questions arose did not meet that condition. Court decisions would then set precedents, and that would only destabilize the system further,[59] as the culture of judicial precedent was alien to Poland. Furthermore, the debate in authoritative literature is still alive on some of the fundamental tenets of new private law. Therefore, a new codification, if perhaps limited in scope, was necessary.

---

56 Maciej Chmieliński: *Legal 'dererminism' or/and legal 'creationism'? Conservative-communitarian versus contractarian approaches to legal change*, in Maciej Chmieliński, Michał Rupniewski (eds): *The Philosophy of Legal Change. Theoretical Perspectives and Practical Processes*, Routledge, Abingdon-New York, 2020.

57 Kępiński: *Czy w Polsce*, 241.

58 Mańko: *Unifikacja prawa*, 61.

59 Kępiński: *Czy w Polsce*, 244.

In anticipation of a new Polish private law, the legal minds stressed the importance of characteristics such as high quality of the content, social acceptance, practical usefulness, and multidimensional effectiveness. Opinions differed, however, as to the means for the achievement of such goals. Each and every participant in the debate preferred for the legislature to make the full use of a special favourable coincidence. For the first time, the reformers were working under the conditions of full sovereignty, when the law had already been codified and much experience accrued in its application, some of it unique. Moreover, one had the benefit of access to a substantial body of Polish private-law scholarship, including the study of modifications. Many years of conceptual and comparative work could be drawn upon, also relating reforms carried out in other countries, including reforms aimed at maintaining the appropriate proportions between the EU harmonization and the other factors at play in the modernization of private law. Carefully studied, the recodification work done in the Netherlands received praise not only from Polish reformers[60] but also from the legislators drafting new codes in Czechia and Hungary, who took advantage of the Dutch experience.[61] In both countries, however, jurisprudence stressed the native nature of the new legislation.[62]

Some jurists, with Zbigniew Radwański – the first Chairman of the Civil Law Codification Commission among them – first deferred the date of commencement of the works and later found it well-advised to assign some additional functions to the new codification. Some non-normative functions were added to the principal function that was the regulation of legal relationships between civil-law entities. Specifically, some Code provisions were supposed to articulate the ideas of (then-)present-day Polish private law, including its direct connection to rights, others to indicate the sources, specify the rules of interpretation and spell out the Code's position within the system of private law. Finally, the provisions of the Code ought also to resolve certain concepts

---

60 Komisja Kodyfikacyjna Prawa Cywilnego działająca przy Ministrze Sprawiedliwości: *Sprawozdanie Komisji Kodyfikacyjnej Prawa Cywilnego 2002–2006* [Report of the Codification Commission for Civil Law 2002–2006], 2–8.

61 Leonard Górnicki: *Kodyfikacja prawa prywatnego* [Codification of private law], in Zbigniew Radwański (ed.), *System prawa prywatnego* [The system of private law]: vol. 1: *Prawo cywilne: część ogólna* [Civil law: general part], C. H. Beck, Warsaw, 2012, 124–125; 142; Jerzy Pisuliński: *Struktura części ogólnej prawa zobowiązań (wprowadzenie do dyskusji)* [The structure of the general part of the law of obligations (introduction to the debate)], Transformacje Prawa Prywatnego 2 (2017), 43; Stawarska-Rippel: *Problemy kodyfikacji*, 50.

62 Petr Dostalík, Ondřej Horák: *Zmiany w czeskim prawie prywatnym* [Changes in Czech private law], Forum Prawnicze 4 (2014), 16.

FIGURE 6.3 Zbigniew Radwański, 1924–2012. Linked to the Adam Mickiewicz University in Poznań, long-term Head of Department of Civil Law, Dean of the Faculty of Law and Administration (1966–1972) and Rector (1982–1984). Vice-President of the Polish Academy of Sciences and President of its Committee of Legal Sciences. First President of the Civil Law Codification Commission of 1996. Editor-in-Chief of the *System Prawa Prywatnego* and of the Ruch *Prawniczy, Ekonomiczny i Społeczny* Journal.
SOURCE: POLISH ACADEMY OF SCIENCES, ARCHIVES IN WARSAW, ZF-XXXIII-183-001

interpreted divergently in authoritative literature (such as the regulation of statements of will made by parties to transactions in civil law).

The above-discussed multifunction model attracted criticism from some scholars, practitioners and judges. The critics argued that its adoption would be detrimental to the principal regulatory role played by the Code. Moreover, there was a risk of encroaching on matters reserved for the Constitution. The justices of the Civil Chamber of the Supreme Court emphasized that codes should not be used for the resolution of doctrinal controversies or for an educational role. The drafters should instead shift their interest to the regulation of problems encountered in the 'life of society and in business'.[63]

Another issue provoking their criticism was the inclusion of provisions modelled on foreign legislation. In the opinion of the justices of the Supreme

63 *Projekt kodeksu cywilnego księga pierwsza*, 104–123.

Court justices, similarities between the conditions in which a suggested provision functioned in its country of origin and the conditions in which it would operate in Poland was not always a sufficient justification for its inclusion.[64]

Due to the criticism and following on its own further conceptual work under the leadership of a new chairman, Tadeusz Ereciński, President of the Civil Chamber of the Supreme Court, the Civil Law Codification Commission came to the conclusion that the dissemination of knowledge about legal concepts and similar tasks were 'no doubt important', but in practice their performance weakened the cohesion of the Code's structure and hindered the identification of its most essential content. Goals related to the development of legal culture were left to jurisprudence, including the resolution of theoretical doubts and questions regarding validation. Accordingly, in the modified draft of Book One of the Code, the number of norms serving other functions than the primary regulatory function was reduced, while retaining some definitions.

After the incorporation of the above changes, the redrafted Book One saw light in 2010–2015. It differed from the existing Code, but there were fewer differences than in the 2008 draft in spite of the fact that the later revision reflected more recent changes in socio-economic relations and European Union law.[65]

Selected ideological and axiological foundations of present-day Polish private law were to be represented in a new formulation of the freedom of contract. This was worded so as to cover the broadest possible range of contractual relationships and types of goods, including intangible goods, as well as contracts regulated by property, succession and family law. Furthermore, the restrictions on freedom of contract were excluded from the normative foundation of freedom of contract and placed elsewhere, among the general provisions on unlawful transactions. The nature of the reasons given for this exclusion was 'technical but also fundamental – ideological'.[66] More specifically, restrictions did not have the same status as a principle. The intention of the Civil Law Codification Commission was to underscore the primacy of freedom of contract and treat the autonomy of the parties as the 'natural state'.

---

64 *Ibidem.*

65 Komisja Kodyfikacyjna Prawa Cywilnego działająca przy Ministrze Sprawiedliwości: *Kodeks cywilny. Księga I: część ogólna: projekt z objaśnieniami* [Civil Code: Book I: General Part: draft and explanation]. https://www.projektkc.uj.edu.pl/dokumenty/Projekt_Komisji_Kodyfikacyjnej_Ksiega_I_z_uzasadnieniem.pdf

66 *Ibidem.*

In the context of the new structure of the provisions establishing the principles of the freedom of contract, the regulation of unlawful transactions, including sanctions visited on them, aroused considerable interest. Those were separately grouped,[67] for which the stated reason was found in the new economic, social and legal conditions arising. The latter part – social and legal conditions – denoted a growing number of provisions of public law offering protection against potential violations of various protected interests, as well as a growing presence of provisions intended to protect the weaker party to a contract. Such developments expanded the scope in which unlawfulness court arise, but not every such violation would necessarily infringe or threaten the most crucial interests. Therefore, a gradual catalogue of sanctions would respect the principle of proportionality and provide the desirable flexibility. At the time, the only sanction available was that of nullity.[68] The Codification Commission was conscious of the legal uncertainty to which the implementation of the proposal would lead, but yet again invoked the primacy of the intention of the parties. More protection was needed against excessive interference.

Moreover, a regulatory concept was presented with regard to the legal effects of a transaction or act-in-law. The decision was made to strengthen the individual and subjective factors, citing not only the actual but also the hypothetical intentio of the parties. That means the consideration of the effects that could be attributed by the parties in the light of customs, reason, and equity. Those criteria were described as: 'taking into account the purpose of a transaction as intended by the parties and maintaining such a balance between the advantages, burdens and risks, originally envisaged by the parties, as it comprises.'[69] At the same time, a proposal was made to expand the regulation of the parties' statements (declarations) of will. In addition to them, the parties should also be allowed to make statements of knowledge and acts communicating emotions 'if those were relevant at law.'[70] The ex-

67 *Ibidem.*

68 STUDY GROUP ON A EUROPEAN CIVIL CODE, THE RESEARCH GROUP ON THE EXISTING EC PRIVATE LAW (ACQUIS GROUP): *Draft Common Frame of Reference: articles and comments*, in *Principles, Definitions and Model Rules of European Private Law*, Christian von BAR, Eric CLIVE, Hans SCHULTE-NÖLKE (eds), 2000, Book II: 7:301ff. https://www.ccbe.eu/fileadmin/speciality_distribution/public/documents/EUROPEAN_PRIVATE_LAW/EN_EPL_20100107_Principles__definitions_and_model_rules_of_European_private_law_-_Draft_Common_Frame_of_Reference__DCFR_.pdf

69 *Kodeks cywilny.*

70 *Ibidem.*

pansion of the foundations of common principles also extended to rights, so that as many principles as possible could be used to convey them, regardless of the object.

The work on the reform of private law proceeded no further. In late 2015, the government stopped the codification work and dissolved the Civil Law Codification Commission. Since then, the public have not been informed about any new model of substantive or procedural private law. The political formation led by the Law and Justice party chose other priorities. Any significant amendments were made only to statutes regulating the administration of justice, such as the removal of some guarantees of impartiality of judges and independence of courts. That, in turn, was the reason for the procedure under Article 7(1) of the Treaty on European Union being initiated by the European Parliament against Poland.[71] Amendments to substantive and procedural private law continued to be made, but they were drafted by a group of Ministry of Justice officials.

Collaboration with most of the lawyers, scholars and judges until then engaged in legal reforms was phased out. That was part of the officially announced designs to replace the existing intellectual elites with new ones and of an ideological and axiological dispute with a part of the political establishment and legal community. In 2016–2023, legal scholars discussed the future of private law within their own circles. An initiative then emerged to continue with the 'organic, positivist work on the improvement of the law'[72] in reliance on the conceptual legacy of the Civil Law Codification Commission disbanded in 2015. The situation changed towards the end of 2023, when environments favourably predisposed to the development of concepts of liberal democracy gained the parliamentary majority. In 2024, the Minister of Justice established codification commissions once again tasked with drafting a new civil code and code of civil procedure.[73]

71 Resolution of the European Parliament of 5 May 2022 on ongoing hearings under Article 7(1) TEU regarding Poland and Hungary (2022/2647(RSP); https://www.europarl.europa.eu/doceo/document/TA-9-2022-0204_EN.html.

72 Jacek Gudowski quote after SOBCZAK: *Budowa demokratycznego państwa*, 586. The initiative was pursued under the name of the Academic Draft Civil Code.

73 Regulation of the Council of Ministers of 5 March 2024 amending the Regulation concerning the establishment, organization and procedure of a Civil Law Codification Commission, Dz.U.357.

4 Failure Fraught with Consequences – Private Law and the Reform of the Justice System

Pursuant to Article 45(1) of the Polish Constitution of 1997, everyone has the right to 'a fair and public hearing of his case, without undue delay, before a competent, impartial and independent court'.[74] This was an unambiguous expression of the expectations of society at the time the consensus was reached on this issue, as well as a symbolic encapsulation of society's hopes and the legacy of the various acts of civil disobedience of the past and numerous efforts by the legal community in the period between 1944 and 1989 to make Poland once again a democratic state ruled by law. However, the question at stake was whether the change of political system would leave society in an era of the rule *of* law or rather rule *by* law.[75]

The 1997 Constitution strengthened the judiciary but did not restore it to its rightful position under the separation of powers. This fact had a substantial impact not only on developmental processes in the administration of justice but also on the discussion on the modernization of private law. The conceptual work and the related legislative processes avoided the topic of who is expected to apply the new law.

Meanwhile, that ceased to be of interest once the fundamental standards of a state ruled by law had been restored. The indifference could be seen in the guarantees of judges' and courts' independence being provided in legislation of a lower rank than the Constitution and the lack of clarification of the role of a judge in the legal system, such as the principles guiding a judge in case management and legal interpretation, including the right to apply the Polish Constitution directly.

The first amendments to the Code of Civil Procedure, including those of 1996,[76] were met with a positive reception, but according to some commentators, the Code did not achieve the expected level of cohesion, and in the opinion of some jurists it lost its cohesion altogether in the course of successive

74 *The Constitution of the Republic of Poland of 2 April,1997*. 3rd ed., Wydawnictwo Sejmowe, Warsaw, 2010.

75 This question is presented from a European, historical and present-day perspective by Tomasz Stawecki: *Kodeks: idea, urzeczywistnienie i ograniczenie* [The code: the idea, the realization and the limitation], in Paweł Grzegorczyk, Krzysztof Knoppek, Marcin Walasik (eds), *Proces cywilny: nauka, kodyfikacja, praktyka. Księga jubileuszowa dedykowana Profesorowi Feliksowi Zedlerowi* [Civil procedure: scholarship, codification, practice], Wolters Kluwer Polska, Warsaw, 2012, 47.

76 Act of 1 March 1996 amending the Code of Civil Procedure (...), Dz.U.43.189.

amendments. One of the consequences is the blurring of the relationship between judicial case management and the adversarial procedure and the principle of free exercise by the parties of their rights. Jurisprudence and court decisions hold that this relationship has been given the wrong proportions from the perspective of the necessary involvement of judges in the correct course of a trial.[77] At the same time, judges faced new challenges in connection with the harmonization of European law and the implementation of new achievements of the theory of procedural law.[78] The benchmark for this is Article 6(1) of the Convention for the Protection of Human Rights and Fundamental Freedoms.[79]

Failure to resolve these questions allowed the Minister of Justice, this time without the participation of political parties, to obtain more power over the courts. Successive cabinets, invoking the responsibility of the bodies of the executive for the efficient work of courts, without authorization from the Constitution of 1997, empowered the Minister of Justice to make decisions in matters reaching far beyond the provision of organizational support for the administration of justice. As a result, political practice followed by doctrinal justification took shape in contravention of the rule of law. Initially, the impact of these elements of the legal culture on the functioning of courts and private law remained in the background among other changes studied at the time by jurisprudence.

If advanced works on the reform of private law had continued at that time, in keeping with the principles discussed in the first section of this chapter, it would have been easier to halt the process of distortion of the functions of the

77 Critical views on this issue were presented for instance by Walerian SANTERA: *Ustrój sądów a rozstrzyganie spraw z zakresu prawa pracy i ubezpieczeń społecznych* [The court system and the decision-making in labour and social-insurance cases], Przegląd Sądowy 9 (2009), 5–25.

78 See Tomasz T. KONCEWICZ, *Poszukując modelu sprawiedliwości proceduralnej w prawie wspólnotowym: mit czy rzeczywistość?* [Searching for a model of procedural justice in Community Law: myth or reality?], CE Natolin, Warsaw, 2009; Maria BORUCKA-ARCTOWA: *Koncepcja sprawiedliwości proceduralnej i jej rola w okresie przemian systemu prawa – analiza teoretyczna i funkcjonalna* [The concept of procedural justice and its role in the proces of transformation of the legal system – theoretical and functional analysis], in Krzysztof PAŁECKI (ed.), *Dynamika wartości w prawie* [The dynamic of values in law], Księgarnia Akademicka, Krakow, 1997, 31.

79 For more see Katarzyna GONERA: *Przewlekłość postępowania w sprawach cywilnych* [Protraction of proceedings in civil cases], Przegląd Sądowy 11–12 (2005), 3–38; Czesław P. KŁAK: *Pojęcie przewlekłości postępowania sądowego* [The concept of protraction of judicial proceedings], Prawo i Prokuratura 12 (2008), 63–79.

judiciary and maintain reference to the new axiology, embedded in substantive and procedural law, with guarantees of individual rights among its constituent parts. The discontinuation of the reform between 1993 and 2000 and measures applied only in selected points deprived the new law governing the structure of the common courts of strong support from its natural allies. When that grew weaker, because very little valuable new content was introduced to either the substantive or the procedural code, both subjected to numerous amendments,[80] the courts adjudicating on private-law matters found themselves in double jeopardy.

The general public became aware of certain faults of the private law in force only when members of the public became party to court proceedings or the target of the enforcement of court decisions. When that happened, the institution that the citizens identified as the source of their problems was not the legislature but the court system. Unresolved problems engendered further problems or aggravated the problems already existing. The country's rapid economic development and growth of people's aspirations ended up being far ahead of the content and methods of the regulation of substantive private law, which survived unreformed into the 21st century. The institution identified by the citizens as the source of their problems once again became not only the legislature but also the court.

80 Piotr STEC: *Kodeks cywilny: między dekodyfikacją a rekodyfikacją* [The Civil Code: between decodification and recodification], in Piotr STEC, Mariusz ZAŁUCKI (eds), *50 lat Kodeksu cywilnego: perspektywy rekodyfikacji* [Fifty years of the Civil Code: prospects of recodification], Wolters Kluwer Polska, Warsaw, 2015, 31–40; Feliks ZEDLER: *Co dalej z kodeksem postępowania cywilnego?* [What more with the Code of Civil Procedure?] in Izabela RATUSIŃSKA (ed.) *Czterdziestolecie kodeksu postępowania cywilnego. Zjazd Katedr Postępowania cywilnego w Zakopanem (7–9.10.2005 r.)* [The fortieth anniversary of the Civil Code. Conference of departments of civil procedure in Zakopane (7–9 October 2005)], Zakamycze, Krakow, 2005, 178.

Conclusions

1 Modernization Pressure in the 20th Century Central and Eastern Europe

The headline goal of this book was to highlight the ideological aspects influencing the modern shape of private law in Poland. This selection rests on two premises. Poland is a representative example of a state located in Central and Eastern Europe due to the historical trajectory of the 20th century shared across the region. At the same time, Poland is characterized by a certain specificity that is relevant to the analysis of the evolution of legal systems in all of Europe.[1] On the development timeline of almost all countries in this cultural circle, we can identify three turning points arising from the political history they share in common. The first one is the acquisition of political independence or at least the autonomy to develop the country's own legal system. This usually follows after what are often centuries of nonexistence as a state, and thus in a historic moment in which the new state in the region is, in principle, left without a legal heritage of its own such as could be put to direct use in the creation from the ground up of a a new, national legal system. For some of the states in Central and Eastern Europe (including Poland), this coincides with the end of World War I. For others, it begins a little earlier, usually near the end of the 19th century. In both variants, the modernization needs resulting in a search for models to follow from Western Europe have clashed with the national ideology consolidating around the same time.

The second turning point is linked to the end of World War II and entering the zone of influence of the Soviet Union and communist ideology. The so-called people's democracies were vassalized and subjected to ideological coercion. The consequence was curtailing the development of native legal culture, especially in the area of private law, the existence of which – except for personal and family law – was negated by the new ideology. The third moment is the liberation of the countries from the culturally foreign political and ideological dependence after 1989, resulting in a repeated stage (similarly to before World War II) of decisions concerning the scale of the westernization processes gaining in intensity following to the region's accession to the European Union.

1 Rafał Mańko: *The Unification of Private Law in Europe from the Perspective of the Polish Legal Culture*, Yearbook of Polish European Studies, 11 (2007–2008), 109–137.

© ANNA MACHNIKOWSKA ET AL., 2025 | DOI:10.1163/9789004730021_009

The basic canon of thinking about law in each of these historical moments was set by modernization trends, of course – especially under the 'people's state' – defined differently in each of the three periods. First of all, the law was expected to be modern and to become an instrument and lever of progress; simultaneously, however, which is especially visible during the first of the periods, it was to be a national law. This ideological paradigm set the general trend of the 20th century as an era of forceful socio-economic modernization resulting in new visions for private law.

The aim of this book was also to create an universal comparative platform for analysing the development of Polish law in the 20th century. In our view, this kind of research could enable to reconstruct the characteristic features of an ideological perspective on private law, held by Polish legal elites despite the changing political and socio-economic conditions. The perspective covered the entire 20th century and seems to be cognitively valuable thanks to the fact that it is not homogenic. Indeed, according to our hypothesis, the radical political transformations in Poland in 1945 did not have to mean that the Polish legal elites equally fundamentally changed their views on the nature of private law and its capacity to influence the socio-economic reality in a selected direction.[2] In effect, even in the period of 'People's Poland' that direction did not have to differ that much from the direction selected in the 2nd Republic as it would have followed from a simple comparison of socialism and liberalism.

Our hitherto research led us to the conclusion that the community of views was determined by an ambivalent stance of the legal elites whose majority was not that keen on a total transformation of private law in a socialist spirit, or at least was sceptical about mechanically copying Soviet legal models. Likewise, there was a universal understanding with regard to the way of looking upon the law, its creative capacity and ideological role of serving the society, as well as with regard to the direction of development of legal scholarship. The modernisation pressure, constantly felt, independently of the period, determined, together with the need of taking into account national specificity, a certain extent of agreement on the aims and ideological assumptions. Throughout the 20th century there was no essential change in the conceptualisation of the nature of Poles, their customs, which need to be respected, as well as the specificity of Polish relationships, to which law can be adapted independently

2 Agata. A. Kozioł: *Organizacja prac nad prawem cywilnym w Polsce w latach 1945–1946* [The Organisation of Civil Law Drafting in Poland between 1945 and 1946], Z Dziejów Prawa 7 (2005), 174–186.

of officially declared ideologies. Likewise, autonomously from historical turbulences, within each of the periods under scrutiny we noted that the needs for transformation were usually identified with modernisation and that independently from the dominant political ideology, they were progressively oriented. The preservation and protection of features and values ascribed to the Polish society directed the reforms towards the realisation of national needs. If modernisation was oriented towards the West, it was in opposition to the conservative-national world-view but the road towards modernity that was embarked upon could, equally well, follow the national path, cutting itself off from foreign models as pseudo-progressive in the Polish context.

The authors relied on cognitive theories well-known in the West, focusing on mechanisms of civilizational development (social and economic) of the world and its individual regions. We made an attempt to present the history of Polish private law reforms, putting forward the hypothesis that many elements of the Polish perception of reality, looking upon the law as an instrument of transforming that reality, as well as convictions and conceptions regarding the method, according to which such an instrument should be constructed. It is not only specific for Poland, but also for other countries of the Central and Eastern Europe which followed the same path in the 20th century.[3] As a result, the perspective of looking upon Central and Eastern European countries and their societies was similar not only due to parallel histories.[4] The research problem could even be approached from a broader perspective by indicating that the question of legal development and its ideological foundations in Poland is proper for semi-peripheral countries, remaining under the constant, relatively strong influence of the direction of development of the Western world and the ideological premises of such development. In the latter context Poland, just like other semi-peripheral states, is a country partly build upon the Roman Law Tradition and the Western Legal Tradition

3 Gianmaria AJANI: *By Chance and Prestige: Legal Transplants in Russia and Eastern Europe*, American Journal of Comparative Law 43 (1995), 93–117; Gianmaria AJANI: *Le fonti non scritte nel diritto dei paesi socialisti*, Giuffrè, Milano, 1985; Tomasz GIARO: *Aufstieg und Niedergang des sozialistischen Zivilrechts: von der Ideologie zur Rechtsdogmatik der Pauschalenteignung*, in *Recht im Sozalismus: Analysen zur Normdurchsetzung in Osteuropaeischen Nachkriegsgesellschaften (1944/45 – 1989)*, Gert BENDER, Udo FALK (eds), Bd 1: *Enteignung*, Vittorio Klostermann, Frankfurt am Main, 1999

4 GIARO: *Legal Tradition*, 4–5; Tomasz GIARO: *Some Prejudices about the Legal Tradition of Eastern Europe*, in *Comparative Law in Eastern and Central Europe*, Bronisław SITEK, Jakub J. SZCZERBOWSKI, Aleksander W. BAUKNECHT (eds), Cambridge Scholars Publishing, Newcastle upon Tyne, 2013.

(especially with regard to Enlightenment and Positivism), but is also partly different due to civilization backwardness and world-view differences following from a different historical path of development.

For the countries in Central and Eastern Europe, the classic paths of dealing with the situation usually led through legal transplants and transfers of often entire Western European codes, with certain small exceptions. Such was the case with the decisions made in the twenties and thirties of the 20th century, as well as the turn of the 20th century (e.g. Romania) and 21st century (e.g. Czechia Hungary). In consequence, one often stopped at adapting one of the predominant currents in Western European thought (such as Romania's following the French models and modern Hungary and Czechia adapting Dutch solutions).

Against the backdrop of other regions of the world inclined to pursue a similar policy of legal modernization, Central and Eastern Europe could only to a certain extent be better positioned (mainly due to cultural proximity to Western Europe and relatively high degree of development of legal science in the region) for the creative adaptation of Western European legal heritage on native soil, as well as certain originality of approaches and development of novel concepts. It appears, however, that in this capacity for the creative transformation of Western European legal legacy to design original solutions, Polish legal elites were further distinguished against the background of other states in the region.

The problems that we analysed presumed the hypothesis that the ideological issues of building own legal orders in connection with a strongly perceived modernisation pressure is still a contemporary issue in the semi-peripheral states of Central and Eastern Europe. Those problems are also of relevance in the context of the accession of this group of states to the European Union, whose original legal identity was build by Western European states, obviously on the basis of their specific legal cultures. In the light of advanced plans to build a common European legal system, including private law, the problems should be looked upon from the perspective of a polarisation of the views of elites and society at large to Europeanisation and westernisation, ranging from a full affirmation of Western European models (which results in a full approval of EU law and plans for covering, by a common legal framework, the entire sphere of private law), right down to a ever stronger position of negation, oriented at cherishing of each country's own national identity and presenting Europeanisation a risk of losing that national identity. We will strive to include also this aspect in our research on the ideological foundations of Polish private law reforms.

2 Summarization of the Polish Case at the Background of Global Private Law Transformation Throughout the Long 20th Century

The first stage of development of modern Polish law coincided with years 1918–1939, which was when a new perspective took shape in Europe for the status of private law and its functions. Some states at that time and some several years prior (e.g. the ZGB in 1912; reforms to the ABGB in 1914–1916) opted to codify their law or amend codes dating back to the 19th century.[5] The legal culture of the period was characterized by the multi-directional – also including Turkey – flow of ideas, theories and information. One of the examples of joint projects undertaken at the time was the 1927 Franco-Italian draft Code of Obligations,[6] and another was the 1933 congress of lawyers in Bratislava. In the private laws of European countries, in parallel, though at varying rates, the presence of native traditions and of modern, universal legal constructs increased.[7]

In states winning back their independence, societies could, through the law, express their national identity and at once accomplish rapid modernization. The law could be coherent with the economy (e.g. the transition from free-market capitalism to monopolist capitalism) and strengthen the position of individual rights, so as to make room – beside the principles of individualism and egalitarianism – for social solidarism, the latter inspired, among others, by the theory of Leon Duguit. Characteristic of the codification projects of the time[8] were in-depth comparative studies and participation in the supranational debate on the future of the law.

Two facts were conducive to the adoption of a broad perspective by Polish lawyers. The former was the co-existence within our country of several different systems of private law with different outlooks on tradition and modernization (e.g. the Code of Napoleon, ABGB, BGB, Digest of Laws of the Russian Empire), as a result of the loss of our independence (1795–1918) associated

---

5 See more Katarzyna SÓJKA-ZIELIŃSKA: *Wielkie kodyfikacje cywilne: historia i współczesność* [The great civil codifications: history and the present], Liber, Warsaw, 2009; Hubert IZDEBSKI: *Kodyfikacje cywilne II wieku* [The civil codifications of the 20th century], vol. 1: *Kodyfikacja jako instrument reformy prawa* [Codification as an instrument of law reform], CPH 62 (1990)/1–2, 129–162.

6 See more Anna MOSZYŃSKA, *Endeavours for international unification of law in the interwar period*, Rechtskultur 6 (2017), 29–34.

7 See more Martin LÖHNIG, Stephan WAGNER (eds), *Nichtgeborene Kinder des Liber-alismus? Zivilgesetzgebung im Mitteleuropa der Zwischenkriegszeit*, Mohr Siebeck, Tübin-gen, 2018.

8 See Leonard GÓRNICKI: *Prawo cywilne*; Anna MOSZYŃSKA: *Polen: Codification of the civil law in interwar Poland*, in LÖHNIG, WAGNER: *Nichtgeborene Kinder*, 149–194.

with the partitioning of our territory among the three neighbouring powers (1772, 1793 and 1795). The second special circumstance was related to interest taken not only in the progress of law but also its regression taking place in Poland's immediate neighbourhood – Russia (1917)[9] and Germany (the 1930s). Polish legal scholars embarked on a critical analysis of the treatment of national identity and modernity by contemporary German (e.g. Justus W. Hedemann) and Soviet (e.g. Pēteris Stučka, Evgeny B. Pashukanis) legal science. They emphasized that one of the sources of deformation was the creation of politically motivated theory of 'opposition' serving short-term interests. Squeezed into its mould was the antagonism between historical and future law, private and public law, as well as natural and positive law, even though in reality the political powers of totalitarian states rejected every single one of those laws along with concepts of social solidarism.

Polish scholarship also had its interest piqued by the lack of consistency between the ideology and the normative practice of totalitarian states. The inconsistency involved the exclusion of more and more legal relationships from the general principles of law under the guise of creation of new legal institutions, of which the name alone and the fact of repeat regulation were intended to confirm the change and vesting of the law with a national or communist character. In both cases that was mere propaganda act. As for the state of civil law in Germany, Szymon Rundstein provided the following description: 'in reality, the alleged innovations intended to eliminate formalism and abstract terminological dialectics are ... a game of new terminology.'[10] Similar conclusions applied to Soviet law, because its arguments denying to private law the right to continue to exist precluded simultaneously the existence of public law, the body of which, in the USSR, would ever grow larger and larger. Wiktor Sukiennicki thus summarized that state of affairs: 'we could call those things norms of law and call them teleologico-technical norms, but with the change of name will their essence change?'[11] In describing the structural defects of that direction of change, the co-author of the Polish draft Civil Code, Stanisław Gołąb, wrote: 'When they (the reformers) grow disappointed

9 See more Adam Bosiacki: *Utopia, władza, prawo: doktryna i koncepcje prawne bolszewickiej Rosji 1917–1921* [Utopia, power, law: the doctrine and legal concepts of Soviet Russia 1917–1921], Liber, Warsaw, 2012, 289–330.

10 Szymon Rundstein: *W poszukiwaniu prawa cywilnego* [On the search for civil law], Księgarnia Powszechna, Warsaw-Krakow 1939, 40.

11 Wiktor Sukiennicki: *Marksowsko-leninowska teoria prawa* [Marxist-Leninist theory of law], Wileński Przegląd Prawniczy 5 (1935): 145–153; 6 (1935): 196–202.

in their experimentation, then assuredly even the 'wretched' liberalism in a modern form will come to the rostrum.'[12]

Another round of unique experience of the links between tradition and modernity, as well as the essence of private law and ideology, was gained by Polish science after World War II. At that time, a political and legal division broke out in Europe. States having retained their sovereignty continued in their use of the classic institutions of private law. Without violating the fundamental principles, they adjusted certain solutions in response to evolutionary chances to social and economic affairs. Central and Eastern Europe, on the other hand, including Poland, came under the military, political and economic influence of the USSR. That was followed by the mandatory implementation of certain doctrinal assumptions of Marxism and views of Friedrich Engels, such as the theory of class struggle and critique of private ownership of property. Those were subjected to a Soviet interpretation, taking advantage of both philosophers' having given wide berth to problems of theory of law. Lenin's thesis become the order of the day: 'whatever concerns the economy is of public law, not of private law.' That meant the liquidation of the essence of civil law, which included the replacement of the freedom of contract with a centrally planned economy and reservation of ownership of property to the state.[13]

Polish legal science found itself in a peculiar situation. On the one hand, it was aware – as a result of prior research – of the destructive results of the introduction of Soviet theories to the domestic legal system. On the other hand, the sentiment of the citizens opposed the loss of national identity, including individual freedom. That attitude was decisive to Polish civil-law system's ability to preserve the greatest share of its pre-existing elements, through the years 1945–1989, compared to the systems of private law of other states forced into socialism. What is interesting in this context is the use by Polish lawyers and jurists – in the circumstances of a totalitarian state,[14] and after 1956 of an authoritarian state – of ideological and axiological arguments in defence of cultural identity and human rights simultaneously with the implementation of reforms, including some that were grounded in the Soviet theory of law.

---

12 Stanisław Gołąb: *Prądy w prawoznawstwie III Rzeszy* [Currents in the jurisprudence of the Third Reich], Druk. Rolnicza, Warsaw, 1936, 21.

13 See more Adam Lityński: *Prawo Rosji.*

14 See more Anna Moszyńska: *Work on the Polish Civil Code in Stalinist period (1948–1956)*, Právněhistorické studie 2(49) (2019), 30–38.

The analysis of legal theorists and practitioners' positions taken on tradition and modernization in 1945–1989, including their interpretations of the two categories, also explains the causes of the fiasco of the social and economic transformations pursued during that time in Central and Eastern Europe. It is also a source of information about the circumstances that led to Poland's becoming the first nation to have its citizens reject the socialist order. The result of that individual and later collective change – as other countries followed Poland's example – was the return to the idea of European integration in its full scale. An important role was played by reforms of private law in states returning to sovereignty, along with thematic debate among legal dogmatists and historians.[15]

3 National Distinctions: Poland against the Background of the History of (Private) Law in Central and Eastern Europe

In the creative transformation of Western European legal heritage combined with the creation of original constructs, Polish jurisprudence was distinguished against the background of the other countries of the region by the creative synthesis of multiple different elements drawn from Western legislative achievements and legal thought. This approach to the creation of law was the leitmotiv of the Codification Commission established in 1919 and subsequently having played a key role in lawmaking processes. In particular, the search was for the most modern solutions possible, constituting the outcome of the pan-European exchange of the legal and social thought of the 20th century, especially after World War I. Polish legal circles had the benefit of first-hand experience of several different foreign codifications applicable in the various parts of the formerly partitioned country, combined with the widespread command of several leading languages, assisting the scholars not only to broaden the scope of their studies into European legislation but also to take an active part in the international circulation of legal thought. The result was a heightened interest in comparative studies and cross-border mobility of

15 Only after 1989 did it become possible to take up open studies, based on archive materials, into the Polish law applicable in 1944–1989; see Andrzej Gulczyński, Jacek Wiewiorowski: *Ogólnopolska konferencja katedr historyczno-prawnych w Zajączkowie (14–17.09.1995 r.)* [National conference of historico-legal departments in Zajączkowo (14–17 September 1995)], CPH 67 (1995)/1–2, 314. Works on basic topics of private law only began to arrive in the 21st century, e.g. Anna Machnikowska, *Prawo własności*; Piotr Fiedorczyk: *Unifikacja i kodyfikacja*; Anna Moszyńska: *Geneza prawa spadkowego*.

Polish legal elites involved in international legal initiatives whether of scholarly or practical nature.

The acquired knowledge and skills facilitated the use of a creative and flexible approach to the works on a new national law for Poland. The essence of the work done by the lawyers and jurists came down to the comprehensive, multifaceted evaluation of Western models and their potential applicability in Polish circumstances. This trend was informed by the conviction of the existence of a great dynamic of changes occurring in 20th-century Europe with the resulting necessity of adaptation to the needs of the new era (one of democracy and solidarism), which – as the elites of the time were persuaded – was arriving after 1918. On the other hand, freedom traditions had been firmly entrenched in Polish thought (sometimes going back to the Old Polish-Lithuanian Commonwealth), demanding the recognition of individual autonomy as the paramount ideal in the development of the new legal system, including its private law.

The codification works were often attended by exacerbated ideological disputes, especially in the area of marriage law, which was of the greatest significance from the perspective of identity and culture. The prevailing attitude, however, was that of striving to achieve a consensus. The ideological polarization of the legal elites involved in the codification works was not as extreme as to prevent them from being able to appreciate the need for finding compromise solutions. The paradigm of modernization was more uniting than divisive. This is providing that the overarching goal and axiologically superordinate value was seen in the expedited establishment of a homogeneous system responding to the challenges of modern times in lieu of the anachronistic patchwork of regionally applicable foreign systems inherited from the partitioning powers. Such was the prompting of the national interest to be pursued above ideological divisions. The agreement elicited for a given solution from the ideological opponents was, however, usually conditional. In spite of doubts, they were willing to grant the opportunity to test the effectiveness or ineffectiveness of the proposed solution in practice.

Not only in the area of private law did the Codification Commission's works bring fruit in the work of ready-made codes or drafts, for example in the majority of the parts of the Civil Code, Commercial Code and civil procedure. Those incorporated normative solutions designed as a synthesis of different elements of the Western European legal heritage creatively enriched with original solutions borne of native legal thought. The high-quality work achieved at the time determined the subsequent fate of Polish private law.

Poland continued to distinguish itself against the background of the other states of Central and Eastern Europe also after 1945. This is because the core institutions of the 'capitalist' legacy of the interwar Codification Commission managed to survive despite a single attempt being made at completely discrediting it under the post-war 'people's democracy'. That attempt coincided with the end of the totalitarian Stalinist rule at the break of the 40s and the 50s and was never repeated. In Polish circumstances, maintenance of continuity in the development of private law was facilitated by several factors. On the one hand, the solidarist constructs with which the Polish system of private law from the interwar period was enriched in relative abundance. Those were usually easily transplantable onto the substrate of a 'people's state' invoking similar concepts and ideas, not always as a mere propaganda façade. On the other hand, there was the prevailing belief among the communist legal (and partially also political) elites, partially derived from the prewar elite, in the necessity of preserving at least a part of the national heritage as an important element of identity conferring a minimum of legitimacy on *authorities* de facto dependent on the USSR. In consequence, the constructs of classical, native private law, officially retained only because of the incomplete status of the modernization of economic affairs, co-existed alongside borrowings from Soviet law, which, in Polish practical experience, notably demonstrated the fundamental flaws of its principal theoretical underpinnings. Furthermore, an obstacle to more in-depth legal transformation came from the specific features of Poland's economy not amenable to such profound transformation in the communist direction as in the other states in the region. No small a role was also played by social resistance, especially to collectivization in the countryside, as well as repeat protests from factory workers. Thus, the law inherited from the interwar period survived the most difficult Stalinist era until 1956, and the process of its Sovietization ground down to a halt for good. The 'thaw' wave was significant in Poland compared to other countries in Central and Eastern Europe, which influenced both the contents and the characteristics of the afterwar legal system. In the end effect, the formally new Civil Code and Code of Civil Procedure originating in the 60s could, in principle, be regarded as the product of the legacy of the interwar period and continuation of the development course on which Polish private law had entered in 1918, with several institutions of communist origin added to it.

Moreover, the intervening period of exceptionally strong social protests (especially during the so-called Carnival of Solidarity in the early 80s) paved the way for the comprehensive reactivation of Polish law (not only private law) in its classic shape (rooted in the ideas of the interwar period). On the one hand, the goal was for the strong solidarist currents once again to begin to co-exist harmoniously with elements resting on the foundation of individual autonomy. On the other hand, attempts were made to reconcile the desire for returning to the Polish legal heritage of the interwar period with the need for the modernization of the system in the fashion of the newest Western standards developed in the last decades of the 20th century. Just as during the interwar period the most frequently invoked model was the Swiss Civil Code or the Franco-Italian draft Code of Obligations of 1927, at the end of the 20th century the eager gaze was set on the Dutch Civil Code of 1992. Upon these foundations, the decision was made after 1989 for the codes of the preceding era to be retained with suitable adaptations. Works on a new codification, in turn, were deferred in time pending the stabilization of the directions taken by the processes of harmonization of private law within the European Union.

The full picture of the development circumstances of Polish private law demonstrates that viewing the legal systems of the 'people's democracies' simply as a separate group constitutes an excessive simplification if not an outright error (literature). The case study of Polish private law attests to the durability of the legal system shaped during the interwar era. Only a socialist growth was imposed on it, which could be successfully removed after 1989 without upsetting the solid classical basis. Accordingly, the primary conclusion to be drawn from this book is that Polish law is genetically based first and foremost on more-than-century-old native legal tradition linking it to the ideology and axiology of the legal systems of Western Europe. It is not, by contrast, as some believe, a post-socialist law.[16]

4 Entering the 21st Century with an Existing Legacy

The book aimed at broadening the cognitive perspective with regard to the paths of development of contemporary private law and create an impulse for a meta-reflection on private law or, to strictly speaking, to analyse more closely the ideological meta-reflection of its creators and reformers in the key moments of Polish legal transformation. Indeed, it seems that the experiences of the 20th century, the nature of ideological problems that were solved, have still not lost their contemporary significance, especially that it is precisely on this ideological ground that the contemporary system of principles and institutions of private law was built. As a result, the research could allow to look in a retrospective and summary manner upon various visions and convictions regarding the nature of private law principles and institutions, their functional utility and ability to transform the socio-economic reality. In particular, the book could raise the level of ideological self-consciousness of

16 SCHLESINGER: *Comparative Law*, 286; GIARO: *Legal Tradition*, 20.

legislators engaged in the process of creating and modifying private law, as well as its application by legal practitioners. It could also allow better to understand the perspective of contemporary private law scholarship on the socio-economic role of this legal domain, perhaps inviting it to undertake a meta-reflexion which is, by its very nature, the aim of historical and comparative research.

For these reasons the authors claim that the history of Polish private law in the 20th century records developments unfolding in more than one country. It reflects the multi-layered transformations of legal systems throughout Europe.[17] It has direct links to the three experiences, common to the entire Old Continent and having shaped its legal culture in years 1918–1939, 1945–1989 and 1990–2000. It is also of assistance to identify the context of contemporary debate involving law, held in the third decade of the 21st century, in which liberalism is confronted with the concept of illiberal democracy and the ideal of integration with euro-scepticism and the postulate of two-speed Europe (EU founders and new members).

Private law shapes social affairs on the foundation of the principle of equality of the parties of a legal relationship and their autonomy from the state.[18] Comparative studies into this area of law in the European legal space, including the legal history of Europe in the 20th century, acquire a new significance with the advent of the 21st century. They can be of assistance to a comprehensive in-depth analysis of at least four new groups of circumstances currently influencing the development of private law in Europe.

The first of the four groups are those circumstances which are presently informing the content and speed of the harmonization of legal relationships and co-operation of the various bodies of European justice systems. The development of this project does not proceed in a regular fashion. It is confronted in some states with the reactivated doctrine of illiberal democracy or Euroscepticism, compounded by the verification of the original designs of the founding states and new member states of the European Union with regard to the characteristics and consequences of integration.

Another important matter is that of the difficulties encountered by the theory of private law and by the conceptual works on the reform of substantive private law (discontinuation of the works on the European Civil Code). Despite certain new legislative instruments dealing e.g. with private law, this

---

17 See more Stanisław PŁAZA: *Historia prawa.*

18 Franz BYDLINSKI: *System und Prinzipien des Privatrechts*, Springer, Wien-New York, 1996, 79, 92.

continues to be a nascent stage, with much heterogeneity preserved to this day among the legal systems of the individual member states. The above is linked to the first-mentioned ideologico-social premise (the postulate of guaranteed protection of the native legal cultures of the member states) and to the legislative aspects starting from the diversity of regulatory models available for the regulation of private law.

The third point of reference is the multitude of solutions used by the jurisprudence and legislators of the various member states in the adaptation of their systems of private law to the new economic and social developments. Some have opted for new codification, others for recodification, others still for transformation achieved mainly by the use of legislation placed outside of the code. The latter, in turn, marks the opening of a new chapter in the discussion of the means of integrating and modernizing the legal order, as well as the hierarchy of the values modern private law should serve. One of the purposes of the European Union is to support balanced and lasting economic and social progress, in particular by creating a space without internal borders and developing a close co-operation in the area of the administration of justice (the 1st and 4th tirets or Article B EU), where this progress is founded upon ideals of freedom.[19]

The fourth determinant of the direction taken by the evolution of private law in the European continent is the situation of states facing the necessity of modifying their legal systems, including systems envisaged for transitional periods from political authoritarianism to democracy. There are still some states in Europe needing to face this particular challenge in the close future, as the experience of history would teach us (Belarus, Turkey and perhaps Russia).

These circumstances explain the usefulness of the study of the relevant ideological and axiological criteria.[20]

The ideological and axiological rationales invoked by Polish lawyers and jurists after 1989 provide an argument in favour of a presentation of their outlooks. They became interested, among other things, in the debates held in the

19 Tampere European Council 15 and 16 October 1999 Presidency Conclusions, paragraph 2.

20 Ole LANDO: *Salient Features of the Principles of European Contract Law: A Comparison with the UCC*, Pace International Law Review, 13 (2011), 339–369, Martijn W. HESSELINK: *The Principles Of European Contract Law: Some Choices Made By The Lando Commission*, Global Jurist Frontiers, 1 (2001)/1, article 4; Rafał MAŃKO: *The Unification of Private Law in Europe from the Perspective of the Polish Legal Culture*, Yearbook of Polish European Studies 11 (2007–2008), 109–137.

latter half of the 20th century with the participation of Herbert Hart, Ronald Dworkin and Lon Luvois Fuller, analysis solutions to make the law more impervious to ideological and political deformations expected in the future and to prepare private law for – discernible already at the turn of the 20th century – further social and economic transformations (e.g. proliferation of information technologies).

The re-acquisition of political independence accompanied by the introduction of parliamentary democracy was to be combined with a qualitative change in the provisions of private law, enjoying universal social acceptance. Following the elimination of norms linked to the ideology of the previous political system, a vast doctrinal-normative space was left open, which is usually inaccessible to legislators in such proportions. The same challenge faced other countries of Central and Eastern Europe.

The use of this opportunity in Poland was decided by the interpretation given to the concept of modernization and the reforms' subsequent inconsistent references to the original rationales for the changes underway.[21] The source of modernization was also identified in the respect of national identity, in which patriotism, liberalism and conservatism were placed. For each and every one of them contributed to the protection of traditional values and institutions, eliminated or threatened at the time of socialist rule. Calls were also made upon the new element of national identity that, since 1980, came to be the idea of solidarity, linked to the Polish social phenomenon of a mass-scale independent trade union. In opposition to the Marxist ideology and the theory of class struggle, that organization took to itself the name of 'Solidarity'. Although it was outlawed, it survived and achieved the downfall of the socialist regime in 1989. Among its members were also Polish lawyers who took numerous initiatives to give back to private the functions it had lost.

A special role became the lot of the concept of freedom. It was used to justify the thesis of mutual development within the framework of a new stage of European integration. The reformed domestic system of law, including private law, restored Poland's presence in the circle of Western civilization, and at the same time that return also modernized European legal culture by introducing to it a renewed ideal of freedom, combined with the ideal of solidarity and backed by Polish experience.

21 See more Wiesław LANG: *Aksjologia polskiego systemu prawa w okresie transformacji ustrojowej*, in *Zmiany społeczne a zmiany w prawie, Aksjologia. Konstytucja. Integracja europejska*, Leszek LESZCZYŃSKI (ed.), Wydawnictwo UMCS, Lublin, 1999.

The tide of the transformation was not as swift and regular as it had been expected to be. The benefits, for example linked to changes in private law, were smaller and unevenly distributed in society. Moreover, the loss by some of the citizens of their economic sense of safety was ignored, and, in Poland, additionally the consequences of denial of compensation to those unlawfully deprived of their property under the regime. In the search for the optimal model of private law, the works on the reform became protracted, bringing only partial changes in response mainly to certain current events such as the requirements of accession to the European Union. Critics of that legal policy put forward the thesis of the squandering of part of the original and valuable legacy of Polish legal thought.[22] They saw the causes for that in the automated – in their opinion – assignment of priority to the processes of European unification, for some of the reforms became mentally associated with it. Of equal significance was the failure to take the opportunity during the initial period of the transformation (1990–2000) to implement changes to private law so as to allow the citizens the benefit of relatively swift and comprehensive application of a law that articulated in a clear manner the axiology of the new political system, including the cultural identity, while being modern, intelligible to society at large and successfully enforced. Such changes, had they been achieved, would have resulted in reinforcing the foundations of a civic society along with a cohesive multifaceted modernization of the legal system and its preparation for functioning within the new politics and policies of the European Union, accounting for the variability of the circumstances relating to doctrinal priorities – something which manifested itself rather quickly after the year 2000 in Poland, as well as a number of other countries.

Calls for the revision of practice of slow and selective changes to private law, without disputing the principles of parliamentary democracy or membership in the EU, demanded first of all a greater degree of intellectual independence of the reformers, as well as suitable communication between the legislators and society as a whole. After a little longer than a decade, in some circles, this demand took the form of calls for expansion of the scope of freedom of EU member states to enact their own national legislation. The latter was a result of transition from a stage of euro-enthusiasm to one of euro-

22 The methodological approach to this phenomenon is not homogeneous in Polish scholarship; see Marek Cichocki: *Władza i pamięć* [Power and memory], Ośrodek Myśli Politycznej, Kraków, 2005.

realism but also of the fact that part of the political circles having previously opposed communism in unison now began to exhibit marked differences in their outlooks on the constitutional principles of the state. Part of the differences related to matters of morality and part to the standard of the relationship between the individual and the state, including social policy. Although finalizing the reform of private law would have led to significant improvements in the quality of the legal safety of the citizens, the matter was once again relegated to the background, while the legislature's activities, however numerous, continued to be dispersed and focused around private law. Similar developments were observed in several other states, albeit some in Central and Eastern Europe did manage to enact new codifications (e.g. Czechia and Hungary). In parallel, a dispute arose about the European standard of rule of law and its ideological foundations and legitimacy, for some important matters are viewed very differently in different states. The starkest element of this polemic is the status of the judicial branch (Poland, Hungary, Romania), but the confrontation of positions also extends to relationships and events regulated by private law (e.g.personal and family law). This contributes to a mutual (East/West) revaluation of the imaginations of the foundation of the European community[23] and conditions for the development of private law in Europe in the third decade of the 21st century.

The outlined circumstances, past and present, the dynamics of developmental processes of private law in Europe, and the presence there also of Polish legal thought justify the presentation of its attitude to national identity and modernity in the context of such legal ideals as equality before the law, individual autonomy, democracy, justice, rule of law and human rights. Equally important are the axiological arguments accompanying them, for such arguments are what co-determines the creation of the law, its interpretation, application, compliance and enforcement. This can provide the starting point for universal reflection in the debate on the law, especially when the debate is held in circumstances of highly accelerated transformations and simultaneously doctrinal disputes finding newer and newer points of reference. Suffice to mention only those occurring in 2023: protracted warfare in Ukraine resulting from Russian aggression; resurgence of the migration crisis;

23 See Jarosław Kuisz: *The two faces of European disillusionment. An end to myth about the West and the East,* in Lisjak L. Gabrijelčič, Ferenc Laczo (eds): *The Legacy of Division: East and West after 1989*, CEUP, Budapest-New York, 2020, 254–263; Jarosław Kuisz: *Ende eines Mythos. Polen, Ostmitteleuropa und das Bils vom Westen,* Osteuropa, 66 (2016)/1–2, 201–220.

Europe's rapidly deteriorating technological potential in competition with other economies of the world; still preliminary stage of regulation of the rights and obligations relating to the use of artificial intelligence; as well as a divergence of conceptual outlooks on continued collaboration within the structures of the European Union.

Bibliography

Archive sources

Collections of Archiwum Akt Nowych [AAN] [The Central Archives of Modern Records in Warsaw]

1. Ministerstwo Sprawiedliwości w Warszawie [MS] [Ministry of Justice in Warsaw]
   - 285: Report from the meeting of the Civil Procedure Team on 27 March 1961 in Obory
   - 402: Conversation with the Minister of Justice, Com. Z. Wasilkowska)
   - 2224: Meeting of the Civil Procedure Team on 13–16 January 1958 and 5–6 June 1958
   - 2225: Report from the meeting of the Procedural Civil Law Team on 21 March 1957
   - 2362: Monthly reports of the Civil Law Section of Legislative Department for March, April, May, August, September, November and December 1952 and February 1952
   - 2362: Work schedule of the Civil Law Section of Legislative Department for the year 1952
   - 2380: Minutes of the session of the Codification Commission's Substantive Civil Law Team on 17, 20, 22, 23, 24 and 25 February, 5, 21, 22, 23 and 24 April, 22 May and 7 June 1948
   - 2382: Progress report of the codification work in 1951
   - 2390: Order of the Minister of Justice of 18 February 1947
   - 2390: the Legislative Department's cover letter attending the distribution of the draft Book II of the Civil Code of 23 July 1948
   - 2390: BAZIŃSKI Aleksander: *Uwagi do części ogólnej projektu Kodeksu Cywilnego uchwalonego przez Komisję powołaną do sparowania tego projektu w I czytaniu* [Comments on the General Part of the draft Civil Code adopted by the Commission appointed to pair this draft in the first reading]
   - 2390: JODŁOWSKI Jerzy: *Uwagi do projektu k.c.* [Remarks to the draft of Code Civil]
   - 2390: KOZACZKA Adam: *Kwestia błędu w części ogólnej Kodeksu Cywilnego* [The topic of an error in the General Part of the Civil Code]
   - 2390: SZPUNAR Adam: *Uwagi do projektu części ogólnej kodeksu cywilnego* [Remarks on the draft of the General Part of the Civil Code]
   - 3128: Letter from the President of the Chief Arbitration Committee
   - 4430: Letter from the Ministry of Agriculture and Agrarian Reform of 23 July 1946 to Ministry of Justice

4430: *Uzasadnienie ważniejszych uwag merytorycznych do projektu prawa spadkowego* [Reasons for the more important comments on the draft inheritance law]

4431: PRZYBYŁOWSKI Kazimierz: *Uwagi do tytułu IV projektu prof. Gwiazdomorskiego* [Remarks on Title IV of Professor Gwiazdomorski's draft]

5407: Minutes of the session of the Codification Commission's Substantive Civil Law Team on 12–16 May, 10–12 June 1958 and 12–16 May 1958 in Nieborów

5411: Deliberations of the general assembly of the Codification Commission on 18 December 1956

5411: Minutes of the session of the Codification Commission's Substantive Civil Law Team on 12 December 1957, 17 February 1957, 24 February to 1 March 1959, 12 December 1957 and 13 December 1957

5412: Minutes of the session of the Codification Commission's Substantive Civil Law Team on 14–19 April 1958 and 12–16 May 1958

5415: Minutes of the session of the Substantive Civil Law Team of the Codification Commission on 7–12 September 1959 and 11–14 May 1959

5416: Minutes of the session of on 11–14 May 1959

5418: Minutes of the session of the Codification Commission's Substantive Civil Law Team on 30 January 1957, 28 March 1957, 25 May 1957 and 9 September 1957

5419: Minutes of the session of the Codification Commission's Substantive Civil Law Team on 7–9 September 1959. Meeting on 7 September 1959

5420: Minutes of the session of the Codification Commission's Substantive Civil Law Team on 22 May 1951, 23 and 24 May 1961

5465: Minutes of the session of the Presidium of Academic Consultative Commission under the Ministry of Justice on 27 February 1951

5604: Conference of civil jurists

5633: Quarterly reports of the Legislative Department on the implementation of work from April to June 1949, from October to December 1949 and from January to March, from July to September and from October to December to 1952.

2. Biuro Polityczne Komitetu Centralnego Polskiej Zjednoczonej Partii Robotniczej [BP KC PZPR] [Political Bureau of the Central Committee of Polish United Workers' Party]

2829: Letter of economists of 3 May 1956 to the Politburo of the Central Committee of the PZPR

2831: Journalists' statements for the Central Party Control Committee

2831: Meeting of the Politburo of the Central Committee of the PZPR on 20 March 1957 and 10 September 1958

2831: Note made in 1957 for the needs of the Politburo of the Central Committee of the PZPR

2914: The forecast for 1971–1975

2920: Meeting of the Politburo of the Central Committee of the PZPR on 30 November 1971

3. Komitet Centralny Polskiej Zjednoczonej Partii Robotniczej [Central Committee of Polish United Workers' Party]

V/341: *Zasady obchodów świąt i ważniejszych rocznic historycznych* [Principles for the celebration of holidays and major historical anniversaries]

Collection of Archiwum Instytutu Pamięci Narodowej [Archives of the Institute of National Remembrance in Warsaw]

Po 570/86: Note concerning the events of 28 June 1956, 18 August 1956, Poznań

Printed sources

Decision of the Constitutional Tribunal of 18 October 1994, K 2/94, OTK 1994 2.36.

Decision of the Supreme Court 1953 4.95

II Zebranie Komisji Prawa Gospodarczego przy Centrum Obywatelskich Inicjatyw Ustawodawczych NSZZ 'Solidarność' [2nd meeting of the Economic Law Committee of the Citizens' Legislative Action Centre of NSZZ 'Solidarność'], in *Obywatelskie inicjatywy ustawodawcze Solidarności 1980–1990: Materiały i projekty ustaw Centrum Obywatelskich Inicjatyw Ustawodawczych 'S' i Społecznej Rady Legislacyjnej* [The citizens' legislative initiatives of Solidarity. Materials and legislative drafts of the Solidarity Centre for Citizens' Legislative Action and Social Legislative Council], Kazimierz BARCZYK, Stanisław GRODZISKI, Stefan GRZYBOWSKI (eds), Wydawnictwo Sejmowe, Warsaw, 2001, 392–394

VII Zjazd PZPR. Podstawowe materiały i dokumenty [The 7th Conference of the Polish United Workers' Party. Basic materials and documents], Książka i Wiedza, Warsaw, 1975

IX Nadzwyczajny Zjazd Polskiej Zjednoczonej Partii Robotniczej. 14–20 lipca 1981 r. Stenogram z obrad plenarnych [The 9th Conference of the Polish United Workers' Party. 14–20 July 1981. Stenogram of plenary deliberations], Książka i Wiedza, Warsaw, 1983

Act of 25 November 1925 on the Competence Court, Dz.U.126.897

Act of 3 January 1946 on the Nationalization of Core Branches of the National Economy, Dz.U.3.17

Act of 3 January 1946 on the Establishment of New Enterprises and Support for Private Initiative in Industry and Commerce, Dz.U.3.18

Act of 7 March 1950 on the Central Authority for Small-Scale Production Activities, Dz.U.10.104

Act of 27 June 1950 – Family Code, Dz.U.34.308

Act of 18 July 1950 – General Provisions of Civil Law, Dz.U.34.311

Act of 29 June 1963 on the Restriction of the Division of Farms, Dz.U.28.168

Act of 25 February 1964 – Family and Guardianship Code, Dz.U.9.60

Act of 23 April 1964 – Civil Code, Dz.U.16,93

Act of 17 November 1964, Code of Civil Procedure, Dz.U.43.296

Act of 26 October 1971 on Regularizing the Ownership of Farms, Dz.U.27.250

Act of 26 October 1971 on the Abolition of Mandatory Supplies, Dz.U.27.253

Act of 18 July 1972 on the Organization and Exercise of Trades and Crafts, Dz.U.23.164

Act of 10 April 1974 – Apartment Law, Dz.U.14.84

Act of 19 October 1975 on Certain Land Taxes and Fees, Dz.U.45.229

Act of 10 February 1976 amending the Constitution of Polish People's Republic, Dz.U.5.39

Act of 23 March 1982, Dz.U.11.81

Act of 1 March 1996 amending the Code of Civil Procedure (…), Dz.U.43.189

Act of 15 September 2000 – Code of Commercial Partnerships and Companies, Dz. U.94.1037

Act of 20 March 2015, Dz.U.519.2015

BAFIA Jerzy, Leon CHEŁMICKI, Z. SZELIŃSKI (eds): *Z prac Komisji Kodyfikacyjnej* [From the works of the Codification Commission], BMS 2 (1957), 1–19

BARCZYK Kazimierz: *Centrum Obywatelskich Inicjatyw Ustawodawczych NSZZ 'Solidarność': spojrzenie po latach* [Solidarity Centre for Citizens' Legislative Action NSZZ 'Solidarity: from a perspective of years], in *Wkład krakowskiego i ogólnopolskiego środowiska prawniczego w budowę podstaw ustrojowych III Rzeczypospolitej (1980–1994): projekty i inicjatywy ustawodawcze, ludzie, dokumenty i oceny* [The Contribution of the Krakow and national legal environment to the construction of the political foundations of The Third Polish Republic (1980–1994): legislative projects and initiatives people: achievements and evaluations], Stanisław Grodziski (ed.), Księgarnia Akademicka, Krakow, 2018, 427–446

Biuro Sejmu, Wydział Prawny, *nr 319/III kad. Komisja Wymiaru Sprawiedliwości* [Commission of the Administration of Justice], 29 January 1963

Constitution of Polish People's Republic of 22 July 1952, Dz.U.33.232

The Constitution of the Republic of Poland of 2nd April 1997, 3rd ed., Wydawnictwo Sejmowe, Warsaw, 2010

Decision of the Constitutional Tribunal of 18 October 1994, K 2/94, OTK 1994.2.36.

Decision of the Supreme Court 1953.4.95

Decision of the Supreme Court, OSNCP 1972.3.42

Decision of the Supreme Court – Civil/Labor Law Chamber 1974.12.203

Decision of the Supreme Court – Civil/Labor Law Chamber 1976.9.184

Decision of the Supreme Court of 26 February 2006, II CSK 101/05, LEX No. 180197

Decree of the President of the Republic of Poland of 27 June 1934 — Commercial Code; Dz.U.57.502

Decree of 6 September 1944 on Carrying Out the Agricultural Reform, Dz.U.4.17

Decree of 7 September 1944 on Housing Commissions, Dz.U.4.18

Decree of 21 December 1945 on the Public Administration of Apartments and Lease Control, Dz.U.1946.4.27

Decree of 6 September 1951, Dz.U.46.340

Decree of 18 April 1955, Dz.U.18.107

Decree of 13 December 1981, Dz.U.29.154

GIEREK EDWARD: *Smak życia: pamiętniki* [*Taste of life: memoirs*], BGW, Warsaw, 1993

GRZYBOWSKI Stefan: *Notatka z posiedzenia Zespołu dla zagadnień prawa rolnego Centrum Obywatelskich Inicjatyw Ustawodawczych w dniu 29 października 1981 r.* [Note of the Team for the Issues of Farm Law of of the Solidarity Centre for Citizens' Legislative Action of 29 October 1981], in Kazimierz BARCZYK, Stanisław GRODZISKI, Stefan GRZYBOWSKI (eds): *Obywatelskie inicjatywy ustawodawcze Solidarności 1980–1990. Materiały i projekty ustaw Centrum Obywatelskich Inicjatyw Ustawodawczych 'S' i Społecznej Rady Legislacyjnej* [The citizens' legislative initiatives of Solidarity. Materials and legislative drafts of the Solidarity Centre for Citizens' Legislative Action and Social Legislative Council], Wydawnictwo Sejmowe, Warsaw, 2001, 422–423

Guidelines from the Supreme Court, I CO 34/59

Guidelines on the Administration of Justice and Judicial Practice of the Civil Chamber of the Supreme Court of 27 February 1960

JANKOWIAK Stanisław, Rafał KOŚCIAŃSKI, MAKOWSKI Edmund, Rafał RECZEK (eds): *Poznański czerwiec 1956: wybór dokumentów* [Poznań June 1956. Selection of documents], vol. 1, IPN, Poznań, 2012

JODŁOWSKI Jerzy. Kazimierz PIASECKI (eds): *Kodeks postępowania cywilnego z komentarzem* [The Code of Civil Procedure with a commentary], Wydawnictwo Prawnicze, Warsaw, 1989

Judgment of the Court of Justice of the EU of 20 September 2017, *Ruxandra Paula Andriciuc and Others v Banca Românească SA*, Case C-186/16

KOMISJA KODYFIKACYJNA PRAWA CYWILNEGO DZIAŁAJĄCA PRZY MINISTRZE SPRAWIEDLIWOŚCI [CIVIL LAW CODIFICATION COMMISSION UNDER THE

Minister of Justice]: *Kodeks cywilny. Księga 1: część ogólna: projekt z objaśnieniami* [Civil Code: book 1: General Part: draft and explanation]

Komisja Kodyfikacyjna Prawa Cywilnego działająca przy Ministrze Sprawiedliwości [Civil Law Codification Commission under the Minister of Justice]: *Księga pierwsza Kodeksu cywilnego: projekt z uzasadnieniem* [First book of the Civil Code: draft with motives], C. H. Beck, Warsaw, 2009

Komisja Kodyfikacyjna Prawa Cywilnego działająca przy Ministrze Sprawiedliwości [Civil Law Codification Commission under the Minister of Justice]: *Sprawozdanie Komisji Kodyfikacyjnej Prawa Cywilnego 2002–2006*

Komisja Kodyfikacyjna Prawa Cywilnego działająca przy Ministrze Sprawiedliwości [Civil Law Codification Commission under the Minister of Justice]: *Zielona Księga: optymalna wizja Kodeksu cywilnego w Rzeczypospolitej Polskiej* [A Green Book: the optimal vision of a Civil Code in the Republic of Poland], Zbigniew Radwański (ed.), Ministerstwo Sprawiedliwości, Warsaw 2006

Konferencja prawników-cywilistów [Conference of civil jurists], Nowe Prawo 5 (1951), 54

Konserwatorium Doświadczenie i Przyszłość [Experience and Future Seminar]: *Raport o stanie Rzeczypospolitej i drogach wiodących do jej naprawy* [Report on the state of the Republic and the paths leading to its emendation], Nowa, Warsaw, 1979

Kontrprojekt Ministerstwa Sprawiedliwości [Counter-bill of the Ministry of Justice], KPCiK 2 (1919)/1–4, 281–284

Krajewski Jan, Jan Winiarz (eds): *Głosy praktyki sądowej: materiały do kodyfikacji prawa cywilnego* [Voices of judicial practice: materials for the codification of civil law], Nowe Prawo 5 (1951), 49–53

Memoriał Wydziału Prawa i Umiejętności Politycznych Uniwersytetu, Towarzystwa Prawniczego i Związku Adwokatów Polskich we Lwowie w sprawie techniki ustawodawczej [Memorandum of the Faculty of Law and Political Skills of the University, of the Law Society and Polish Bar Association in Lvov concerning the legislative technique], KPCiK 2 (1919)/1–4, 153–228

Order of the President of the Council of Ministers establishing a Codification Commission to assist the Minister of Justice, Monitor Polski 70.856

Print of the Sejm no. 83, of 15 January 1992: amendment of the Act of 3 June 1919

Problemy współczesnego prawa cywilnego (konferencja naukowa – Popowo) [Problems in modern civil law (academic conference – Popowo)], Zeszyty Naukowe Instytutu Badania Prawa Sądowego 19–20 (1983)

Projekt Kodeksu cywilnego. Księga pierwsza. Sprawozdanie z dyskusji przeprowadzonej w Izbie Cywilnej Sądu Najwyższego [Draft Civil Code. Book 1. Report of the discussion in the Civil Chamber of the Supreme Court], Przegląd Sądowy 10 (2010), 104–123

Projekt kodeksu cywilnego Polskiej Rzeczypospolitej Ludowej [Draft civil code in the Polish People's Republic], Wydawnictwo Prawnicze, Warsaw, 1960

Projekt kodeksu cywilnego oraz przepisy wprowadzające [Draft civil code and implementing provisions], Wydawnictwo Prawnicze, Warsaw, 1962

Projekt kodeksu rodzinnego i opiekuńczego oraz przepisów wprowadzających kodeks rodzinny i opiekuńczy [Draft family and guardianship code and draft implementing provisions for it], Wydawnictwo Prawnicze, Warsaw 1962

Projekt prawa o opiece i kurateli [Draft guardianship and tutelage law], DPP 2 (1945), 30–34

Projekt prawa o stosunkach rodziców i dzieci [Draft Law on the Relationships of Parents and Children], DPP 1 (1945), 33–37

Projekt Prezesa Izby II Sądu Najwyższego Franciszka Nowodworskiego (w porozumieniu z Sądem Najwyższym) [Draft bill by the President of the 2nd Chamber of the Supreme Court, Franciszek Nowodworski (in agreement with the Supreme Court)], KPCiK 2 (1919)/1–4, 284–287

Projekt Przewodniczącego komisji prawa cywilnego Min. Spraw. Henryka Konica (w porozumieniu z komisją) [Draft bill by the President of the Civil Law Commission, Minister of Justice, Henryk Konic (in agreement with the Commission], KPCiK 2 (1919)/1–4, 287–288

Protokół z posiedzenia Komisji ds. reformy prawa cywilnego NSZZ 'Solidarność' odbytego w dniu 30 III 1981 r., in *Obywatelskie inicjatywy ustawodawcze Solidarności 1980–1990: Materiały i projekty ustaw Centrum Obywatelskich Inicjatyw Ustawodawczych 'S' i Społecznej Rady Legislacyjnej* [The citizens' legislative initiatives of Solidarity. Materials and legislative drafts of the Solidarity Centre for Citizens' Legislative Action and Social Legislative Council], Kazimierz BARCZYK, Stanisław GRODZISKI, Stefan GRZYBOWSKI (eds), Wydawnictwo Sejmowe, Warsaw, 2001, 334–338

Przemówienie Dziekana Wydziału Prawnego Uniwersytetu Warszawskiego: posiedzenie inauguracyjne Komisji Kodyfikacyjnej w Pałacu Rzeczypospolitej w dniu 10 listopada 1919 [Speech by the Dean of the Law Faculty of the University of Warsaw: inaugurating session of the Codification Commission in the Palace of the Republic on 10 November 1919], in *Komisja Kodyfikacyjna: Dział Ogólny* [Codification Commission: General Section] 1920, vol. 1, is. 1, 22

Raport o stanie Rzeczypospolitej i drogach wiodących do jej naprawy [Report on the state of the Republic and the paths leading to its emendation], Nowa, Warsaw, 1979

Referat Władysława Gomułki na IX Plenum: węzłowe problemy polityki partii [Władysław Gomułka's paper for the 9th Plenary Session: seminal problems of the party's policy], Nowe Drogi 6 (1957) 1–4

Regulation of the Council of Ministers of 5 March 2024 amending the Regulation concerning the establishment, organization and procedure of a Civil Law Codification Commission, Dz.U.357

Resolution of the Council of Ministers of 29 April 1950, Monitor Polski 43.197

Resolution of the Council of Ministers no. 262 of 12 August 1968 concerning the disposition of movable assets by socialized economic units, Monitor Polski 35.245

Resolution of the Council of Ministers no. 109/96, 17 September 1996

Resolution of the European Parliament of 5 May 2022 on ongoing hearings under Article 7(1) TEU regarding Poland and Hungary (2022/2647(RSP)

Resolution of the Politburo of the Central Committee of the PZPR and the Supreme Committee of the NSL [United People's Party], Trybuna Ludu, no 109, 19 April 1971

Resolution of the Praesidium of the Cabinet, Nowe Prawo 10 (1950), 2

Resolution of the Sejm of Polish People's Republic of 25 January 1982, Monitor Polski 5.20

Resolution of the Supreme Court of 25 September 1948, C. Prez 331/48, PiP 1 (1949), 120–122

Resolution of the Supreme Court of 19 October1951, C 1164/51, PiP 7 (1952), 129–132

Resolution of the Supreme Court of 27 June 1953, CIC/C Prez 195/52, OSN.1953.4.95

Resolution of the Supreme Court of 26 March 1958, I CO 3/58, OSNC.1959.4.106; critical gloss by Andrzej Stelmachowski, PiP 4–5 (1960), 851–855

Resolution of the Supreme Court of 13 June 1958, OSP.1958.12.31

Resolution of the Supreme Court of 27 February 1960, OSN.1960.31 and III CO 33/62

Resolution of the Supreme Court of 16 October 1961, I Co 20/61, OSN.1962.41

Resolution of the Supreme Court of 14 June 1963; I C 336/63, OSNCP.1964.223

Resolution of the Supreme Court of 28 September 1963, OSNCP.1964.22

Resolution of the Supreme Court of 16 April 1966, I CR 80/66, OSPiKA 1967.4.101

ROLICKI Janusz: *Edward Gierek: przerwana dekada: wywiad rzeka* [Edward Gierek: a broken decade: extended interview], Fakt, Warsaw, 1990

SAFJAN Marek: *Wspomnienie o Społecznej Radzie Legislacyjnej* [The remiscence of the Social Legislative Council], in *Obywatelskie inicjatywy ustawodawcze Solidarności 1980–1990: materiały i projekty ustaw Centrum Obywatelskich Inicjatyw Ustawodawczych 'S' i Społecznej Rady Legislacyjnej* [The citizens' legislative initiatives of Solidarity. Materials and legislative drafts of the Solidarity Centre for Citizens' Legislative Action and Social Legislative Council], Kazimierz BARCZYK, Stanisław GRODZISKI, Stefan GRZYBOWSKI (eds), Wydawnictwo Sejmowe, Warsaw, 2001, 550–552

Sprawozdanie Komisji Prawniczej w sprawie wniosku nagłego posła Zygmunta Marka i tow. w przedmiocie powołania do życia komisji dla stworzenia jednolitego ustawodawstwa w Państwie Polskiem (Legal Committee's report on the urgent motion by deputy Zygmunt Marek and companions concerning the establishment of a commission to create a uniformity of legislation in the Polish State), in *Druki Sejmu Ustawodawczego Rzeczypospolitej Polskiej* [Prints of the Legislative Sejm of the Republic of Poland], print no. 298, KPCiK 2 (1919) 1, 279–280

Sprawozdanie z prac Komisji KC PZPR powołanej do wyjaśnienia przyczyn i przebiegu konfliktów społecznych w dziejach Polski Ludowej [Report on the works of the PUWP Central Committee's Commission appointed to investigate the causes and development of social conflicts in the history of People's Poland], Nowe Drogi, special issue (1983)

Staatsblad van het Koninkrijk der Nederlanden 2011, 272

Stenographic report of the Legislative Sejm, 44th session of 3 June 1919

Stenographic report of the 20th session of the Legislative Sejm of 24 June 1947

Stenographic report of the 29th session of the Sejm of the People's Republic of Poland of 16 and 17 November 1964

Stenographic report of the Sejm of the People's Republic of Poland of 6 May 1982

STRZESZEWSKI Michał: *Opinie o funkcjonowaniu wymiaru sprawiedliwości i walce z przestępczością. Komunikat z badan* [Opinions on the functioning of the administration of justice and fight on crime: communication based on research], CBOS, Warsaw, 1999

STUDY GROUP ON A EUROPEAN CIVIL CODE, THE RESEARCH GROUP ON THE EXISTING EC PRIVATE LAW (ACQUIS GROUP): *Draft Common Frame of Reference: articles and comments*, in *Principles, Definitions and Model Rules of European Private Law*, Christian von BAR, Eric CLIVE, Hans SCHULTE-NÖLKE (eds), 2000

Szeroka dyskusja cenną pomocą w pracy kodyfikacyjnej [A wide discussion is a valuable help in codification work], Nowe Prawo 4 (1951), 1–2

TADEUSIEWICZ Ryszard: *Prawo nareszcie stanowione przez obywateli* [A law at last made by the citizens], in *Wkład krakowskiego i ogólnopolskiego środowiska prawniczego w budowę podstaw ustrojowych III Rzeczypospolitej (1980–1994): projekty i inicjatywy ustawodawcze, ludzie, dokumenty i oceny* [The Contribution of the Krakow and national legal environment to the construction of the political foundations of The Third Polish Republic (1980–1994): legislative projects and initiatives people: achievements and evaluations], Stanisław GRODZISKI (ed.), Księgarnia Akademicka, Krakow, 2018, 379–384

TORAŃSKA Teresa: *Oni* [They], Iskry, Warsaw, 2004

Uwagi dotyczące projektu ustawy o gospodarce terenami nierolniczymi [Remarks on the draft bill on the administration of non-farming land, September–October 1981], in Kazimierz BARCZYK, Stanisław GRODZISKI, Stefan GRZYBOWSKI (eds):

Obywatelskie inicjatywy ustawodawcze Solidarności 1980–1990. Materiały i projekty ustaw Centrum Obywatelskich Inicjatyw Ustawodawczych 'S' i Społecznej Rady Legislacyjnej [The citizens' legislative initiatives of Solidarity. Materials and legislative drafts of the Solidarity Centre for Citizens' Legislative Action and Social Legislative Council], Wydawnictwo Sejmowe, Warsaw, 2001, 419–422

WASILKOWSKI Jan: *Fragmenty sprawozdania w Sejmowej Komisji Wymiaru Sprawiedliwości* [Fragments of a report to the Justice System Committee of the Sejm], PiP 1 (1959), 67–80

WINIARZ Jan (ed.): *Kodeks cywilny z komentarzem* [The Civil Code with a commentary], vol. 1, Wydawnictwo Prawnicze, Warsaw, 1988

WINIARZ Jan: *Sprawozdanie z prac Komisji Kodyfikacyjnej* [Report on the works of the Codification Commission], PiP 3 (1957), 621–628

WINIARZ Jan (ed.): *Z dyskusji w Zespole Prawa Cywilnego Komisji Kodyfikacyjnej nad prawem rzeczowym* [From the debate held in the Codification Commission's Civil Law Team on real law], BMS 5 (1958), 19–22

WINIARZ Jan (ed.): *Z prac zespołu prawa cywilnego materialnego komisji kodyfikacyjnej* [From the works of the Codification Commission's Substantive Civil Law Team], BMS 4 (1958), 29–33

Wniosek nagły posła Zygmunta Marka i tow. w sprawie powołania do życia komisji dla stworzenia jednolitego prawodawstwa w Państwie Polskim [An urgent motion by deputy Zygmunt Marek and companions concerning the establishment of a commission to create a uniformity of legislation in the Polish State], in *Druki Sejmu Ustawodawczego Rzeczypospolitej Polskiej* [Records of the Legislative Sejm of the Republic of Poland], record no. 298

Wobec nowego prawa małżeńskiego: oświadczenie Ministra Sprawiedliwości (Towards a new marriage law: declaration by the Minister of Justice), DPP 1 (1946), 22–23

Zarządzenie Ministra Sprawiedliwości w sprawie powołania komisji do opracowania jednolitego polskiego kodeksu cywilnego (Order of the Ministry of Justice concerning the establishment of a commission for the complication of a uniform Polish civil code); in *Dokumenty archiwalne dotyczące organizacji prac nad unifikacją i kodyfikacją polskiego prawa cywilnego w latach 1945–1948* (Document archives from the organization of works on the unification and codification of Polish civil law in 1945–1948), Piotr FIEDORCZYK (ed.), MHI 4 (2006), 166

Zjazd Krajowy Prawników Polskich Polish Lawyers' National Conference], Palestra 7–8 (1959), 146–147

Zjazd prawników i ekonomistów polskich [Polish Lawyers and Economists' Conference], RPEiS 1 (1921), 237–245

Literature

ADAMUS Jan: *Elementy rodzime i obce w prawie polskim* [Elements native and foreign in Polish law], Rocznik Prawniczy Wileński 10 (1939), 331–369

ADAMUS Jan: *W sprawie stosunku prawa ludowego do kodyfikacji prawa prywatnego* [Concerning the relationship of the people's law to the codification of private law], Lviv, 1925

AJANI Gianmaria: *By Chance and Prestige: Legal Transplants in Russia and Eastern Europe*, American Journal of Comparative Law 43 (1995), 93–117

AJANI Gianmaria: *Le fonti non scritte nel diritto dei paesi socialisti*, Giuffrè, Milano, 1985

AJNENKIEL Andrzej: *Konstytucje polskie w rozwoju dziejowym 1791–1997* [Polish constitutions in historical development 1971–1997], Rytm, Warsaw, 2001

ALTHUSSER Louis: *Ideologie i aparaty ideologiczne państwa* [Ideology and the state ideological apparatuses], Studenckie Koło Filozofii Marksistowskiej UW, Warsaw, 2006

ALTHUSSER Louis: *Ideology and the State Ideological Apparatuses (Notes towards an Investigation)* [1970], in Louis

ALTHUSSER: *On Ideology*, Verso, London-New York 2008, 1–60

ALTHUSSER Louis: *Marxism and Humanism* [1963], in Louis ALTHUSSER: *For Marx* [1965], Verso, London, 2005, 219–248

ALTHUSSER Louis: *On Marx and Freud*, Rethinking Marxism: A Journal of Economics, Culture & Society 4 (1991)/1, 17–30

ANDRZEJEWSKI Jan: *Czy nowa kodyfikacja prawa cywilnego jest potrzebna w czasie kryzysu prawa?* [Is a new codification of civil law needed in a time of legal crisis?], RPEiS 1 (2014), 77–89

ANDRZEJEWSKI Jan: *Laesio enormis i wyzysk: tradycja prawna a przeciwdziałanie nieekwiwaletności świadczeń w prawie prywatnym Austrii, Niemiec i Polsk* [Laesio enormis and exploitation: legal tradition and countering the non-equivalence of benefits in the private law of Austria, Germany and Poland], PhD thesis, Poznań, 2015

ANDRZEJEWSKI Jan, Witold BORYSIAK, Aleksander GREBIENIOW, Jędrzej KONDEK: *Instytucja wyzysku w prawie cywilnym: perspektywa krajowa i prawnoporównawcza* [Institution of exploitation in civil law a national and legal comparative perspective], Wydawnictwo OWS, Warsaw, 2022.

ANEMAET Lotte: *The Many Faces of the Average Consumer: Is It Really So Difficult to Assess Whether Two Stripes Are Similar to Three?*, International Review of Intellectual Property and Competition Law 51 (2020), 187–213

ASH Timothy G.: *Polska rewolucja. Solidarność 1980–1982*, ResPublica, Warsaw, 1989 [English version: The Polish Revolution: Solidarity, 1980–82 (Scribner, 1984)]

AUSTEN-BAKER Richard, Qi ZHOU: *Contract in Context*, Routledge, London, 2014

BĄDKOWSKI Antoni: *Bilans nowego prawa małżeńskiego* [A reckoning of the new marriage law], DPP 1 (1948), 28–48

BAGIŃSKI Jacek, Stefan GRZYBOWSKI, Jerzy IGNATOWICZ, Józef Stanisław PIĄTOWSKI, Andrzej STELMACHOWSKI, Edmund WENGEREK: *Prawo cywilne w XX-leciu PRL* [Civil law at the 20th anniversary of the Polish People's Republic], Studia Prawnicze 9 (1965), 49–92

BAKER C. Edwin: *The Ideology of the Economic Analysis of Law*, Philosophy and Public Affairs 5 (1975), 3–48

BALKIN Jeremy M.: *Taking Ideology Seriously: Ronald Dworkin and the CLS Critique*, UMKC Law Review 55 (1987)/3, 392–433

BAŁTOWSKI Maciej: *Gospodarka socjalistyczna w Polsce* [Socialist economy in Poland], PWN, Warsaw, 2009

BANCERZ Stefan: *Dwa lata prac ustawodawczych* [Two years of legislative works], DPP 7 (1946), 20–27

BARCIKOWSKI Wacław: *Cele i zadania prawnictwa demokratycznego* [The goals and tasks of democratic lawyerdom], PiP 1 (1946), 5–11

BARCIKOWSKI Wacław: *Demokracja a sądownictwo* [Democracy and the judiciary], DPP 5 (1946), 8–11

BARCIKOWSKI Wacław: *Od demokracji liberalnej do demokracji społecznej* [From liberal democracy to social democracy], Nowa Epoka, Warsaw, 1947

BARDACH Juliusz: *W obiektywie nauki i w lustrze pamięci (o uczonych, pisarzach i politykach XIX i XX wieku* [In the lens of science and in the mirror of memory (on scholars, writers and politicians of the 19th and the 20th centuries], C. H. Beck, Warsaw, 2004

BARNES Trevor J.: *Situating Economic Geographical Teaching*, Journal of Geography in Higher Education 30 (2006)/3, 405–409

BASZKIEWICZ Jan, Franciszek RYSZKA: *Historia doktryn politycznych i prawnych* [History of political and legal doctrines], PWN, Warsaw, 1984

BEDNAREK Małgorzata: *Przemiany własności w Polsce. Podstawowe koncepcje i konstrukcje normatywne* [Ownership changes in Poland. Basic concepts and normative constructions], WN Scholar, Warsaw, 1994

BEKERMAN Józef: *Czy kodeks, czy nowele?* [A code or amendments?], GSW 7 (1920), 49–50

BENDER Gerd, Udo FALK (eds): *Recht im Sozalismus: Analysen zur Normdurchsetzung in Osteuropäischen Nachkriegsgesellschaften* (1944/45 – 1989), Vittorio Klostermann, Frankfurt am Main, 1999

BEREZOWSKI Stanisław (ed.): *Geografia gospodarcza Polski* [The economic geography of Poland], PWN, Warsaw 1978

BERUTOWICZ Włodzimierz: *Charakter zmian prawa postępowania cywilnego w Polsce Ludowej* [The nature of changes to civil procedurę in People's Poland],

Zeszyty Naukowe Uniwersytetu Wrocławskiego, Seria A Prawo 3 (1958)/10, 187–212

Bieniek Gerard: *W sprawie przyszłości użytkowania wieczystego* [Regarding the future of perpetual usufruct], in *Ars et usus. Księga pamiątkowa ku czci Sędziego Stanisława Rudnickiego* [Ars et usus: collections of essays dedicated to the memory of Judge Stanisław Rudnicki], Lexis Nexis, Warszawa, 2005, 53–69

Biskupski Kazimierz: *Zmieniać czy nie zmieniać?* [To change or not to change?], PiŻ 8 (1957), 3–4

Bobkowski Adam: *Festina lente!*, GSW 41 (1927), 563–565

Bohman James: *Critical Theory*, in *The Stanford Encyclopedia of Philosophy*, Edward N. Zalta (ed.), Winter 2019 Edition

Borucka-Arctowa Maria: *Komunikacja między sądami a społeczeństwem* [Communication between courts and society], in *Sądy w opinii społeczeństwa polskiego* [The courts in the opinion of Polish society], Maria Borucka-Arctowa, Krzysztof Pałecki (eds), Ratio, Krakow, 2003, 71–94

Borucka-Arctowa Maria: *Koncepcja sprawiedliwości proceduralnej i jej rola w okresie przemian systemu prawa: analiza teoretyczna i funkcjonalna* [The concept of procedural justice and its role in the proces of transformation of the legal system: theoretical and functional analysis], in *Dynamika wartości w prawie* [The dynamic of values in law], Krzysztof Pałecki (ed.), Księgarnia Akademicka, Krakow, 1997, 29–57

Bosiacki Adam: *Utopia, władza, prawo: doktryna i koncepcje prawne bolszewickiej Rosji 1917–1921* [Utopia, power, law: the doctrine and legal concepts of Soviet Russia 1917–1921], Liber, Warszawa, 2012

Bossowski Franciszek: *O naszych najbliższych zadaniach ustawodawczych* [About our legislative tasks at hand], KPCiK 2 (1919)/1–4, 119–124

Bourdieu Pierre: *Masculine Domination*, Stanford University Press, Stanford, 2001

Bourdieu Pierre, J. C. Passeron: *Reproduction in Education. Society and Culture*, SAGE, London 1990

Broniewicz Witold: *Zasad kontradyktoryjności procesu cywilnego w poglądach nauki polskiej (1880–1980)* [The principle of adversarial civil proceedings in the views of Polish legal doctrine (1880–1980)], in *Studia z prawa postępowania cywilnego: księga pamiątkowa ku czci Zbigniewa Resicha* [Studies on civil procedural law: commemorative book in honour of Zbigniew Resich], Maria Jędrzejewska, Tadeusz Ereciński (eds), PWN, Warsaw, 1985, 39–53

Brozi Krzysztof J., Lech Winiarski: *Czy 'własność ogólnospołeczna' jest własnością* [Is 'social property' property?], Studia Filozoficzne" (1980), 19–32

Buczkowski Stefan: *O właściwą rolę prawa cywilnego w gospodarce uspołecznionej* [For the proper role of civil law in the socialized economy], PiP 8–9 (1956), 249–262

BUKOWIECKI Stanisław: *Dzielnicowość w Polsce współczesnej* [Parochialism in modern Poland], Związek Sejmików Powiatowych RP, Warsaw, 1921

BUKOWIECKI Stanisław: *Założenia podstawowe kodyfikacji prawa w Polsce* [Basic foundations of the codification of law in Poland], Przegląd Notarialny 1 (1948) 4, 281–286

BURDA Andrzej: *Demokracja i praworządność* [Democracy and rule of law], ZN im. Ossolińskich, Wrocław-Warsaw-Krakow, 1965

BURDA Andrzej: *Instytucjonalne gwarancje praworządności i ich rola w państwie socjalistycznym* [Institutional guarantees of rule of law and their role in a socialist state], PiP 8–9 (1971), 215–230

BURDA Andrzej: *Polskie prawo państwowe* [Polish state law], PWN, Warsaw, 1962

BURNS Tony: *The Idea of the 'Struggle for Recognition' in the Ethical Thought of the Young Marx and Its Relevance Today*, in *Constructing Marxist Ethics: Critique, Normativity, Praxis*, Michael J. THOMPSON (ed.), Brill, Leiden, 2015, 33–58

BURSZTA Józef: *Wartości kultury ludowej w społeczeństwie socjalistycznym* [The values of popular culture in a socialist state], Nowe Drogi 10 (1976), 137–146

BURZYK Mateusz: *Psychoanaliza a polityka: stawka podmiotu* [Psychoanalysis and politics: the stake of the subject], Diametros 35 (2013), 1–20

BYDLINSKI Franz: *System und Prinzipien des Privatrechts*, Springer, Wien-New York, 1996

CAR Stanisław: *Pilne zadania prawnictwa* [The urgent tasks before the lawyerdom], Orgerlbranda Synowie, Warsaw, 1918

CARO Leopold: *Równomierność świadczeń w ustawodawstwie* [Equivalence of benefits in legislation], KPCiK 2 (1919)/1–4, 293–336

CERCEL Cosmin: *Le jus commune dans la pensée juridique contemporaine, ou le comparatisme perverti*, in *Comparer les droits, résolument*, Pierre LEGRAND (ed.), Presses Universitaires de France, Paris, 2009, 457–485

CERCEL Cosmin: *Towards a Jurisprudence of State Communism: Law and the Failure of Revolution*, Routledge, Abingdon-New York, 2018

CHAJN Ludwik: *Rewolucyjny czyn polskiego prawnictwa (rzecz o unifikacji prawa)* [The revolutionary effort of Polish lawyerdom (the matter of unification of law)], PiP 9–10 (1946), 3–11

CHAJN Ludwik: *Trzy lata demokratyzacji prawa i wymiaru sprawiedliwości* [Three years of democratization of law and administration of justice], Prasa Demokratyczna, Warsaw, 1947

CHEŁMOŃSKI Adam: *O znaczeniu zasad ogólnych w normowaniu prawnym gospodarki uspołecznionej* [On the importance of general principles in the legislative regulation of the socialized economy], Przegląd Ustawodawstwa Gospodarczego, 10 (1956), 359–363

CHMIELIŃSKI Maciej: *Legal 'Determinism' or/and Legal 'Creationism'? Conservative-Communitarian versus Contractarian Approaches to Legal Change*, in *The Philosophy of Legal Change. Theoretical Perspectives and Practical Processes*, Maciej CHMIELIŃSKI, Michał RUPNIEWSKI (eds), Routledge, Abingdon-New York, 2019, 77–95

CHMIELNICKI Paweł: *Nabycie lokalu lub domu od dewelopera. Wykładnia przepisów i efekty ich stosowania* [Purchase of an apartment or a house from a developer: interpretation of the legal rules and the effects of their application], Difin, Warszawa, 2014

CHMIELNICKI Paweł: *Źródła i efektywność regulacji dotyczących nabycia lokalu lub domu od dewelopera. Ocena wstępna* [The sources and the effects of regulations concerning the purchase of an apartment or a house from a housing developer: preliminary analysis], Przegląd Prawa Publicznego 7–8 (2014), 141–153

CHOJNOWSKI Władysław: *Niektóre zagadnienia z prawa spadkowego* [A few topics in inheritance law], Palestra 7–8 (1965), 37–50

CICHOCKI Marek: *Władza i pamięć* [Power and memory], Ośrodek Myśli Politycznej, Krakow, 2005

CIEMIENIEWSKI Jerzy: *O konstytucyjnych problemach ustroju społeczno-gospodarczego* [On the constitutional problems of the socio-economic system], PiP 11 (1988), 24–33

COLLINS Hugh: *Regulating Contracts*, OUP, Oxford, 2003

COMPARATO Guido: *Nationalism and Private Law in Europe*, Hart Publishing, Oxford, 2014

CZACHÓRSKI Witold: *Prawo zobowiązań w zarysie* [The law of obligations in an outline], PWN, Warsaw, 1970

CZACHÓRSKI Witold: *Przebieg prac nad kodyfikacją prawa cywilnego PRL* [Course of work on the codification of civil law in the People's Republic of Poland], Studia Prawnicze 26–27 (1970), 5–22

CZACHÓRSKI Witold, Jan WASILKOWSKI: *Wspomnienie o profesorze Uniwersytetu Warszawskiego Karolu Lutostańskim* [Reminiscence of Karol Lutostański, Professor of the University of Warsaw], PiP 12 (1947), 57–59

CZAPSKA Janina: *Wizerunek sądu w opinii publicznej* [The court's image in the public opinion], in *Sądy w opinii społeczeństwa polskiego* [The courts in the opinion of Polish society], MARIA BORUCKA-ARCTOWA, Krzysztof PAŁECKI (eds), Ratio, Krakow, 2003, 13–70

DĄBKOWSKI Przemysław: *Dawne prawo polskie a zadania Komisji Kodyfikacyjnej: odczyt wygłoszony na zamknięcie VI-go Zjazdu prawników i Ekonomistów Polskich w Warszawie 23 maja 1920 r. w sali obrad Rady Miejskiej* [The ancient Polish law and the tasks of the Codification Commission: a paper delivered in the closure of the 6th Conference of Polish Lawyers and Economists in Warsaw, 23 May 1920, in the City Council Session Hall], Jan Cotty, Warsaw, 1920

DALE Elizabeth: *Spelunking, or, Some Meditations on the New Presentism*, in *The Oxford Handbook of Legal History*, Markus D. DUBBER, Christopher TOMLINS (eds), OUP, Oxford, 2018, 311–321

DANEK Kazimierz: *Wpływ zmiany stosunków na zobowiązania umowne według Kodeksu zobowiązań na tle kodeksu cywilnego niemieckiego i austriackiego* [Farmers' views on the goals and consequences of the regulation of farm ownership: in the light of the Act of 26 October 1971], RPEiS 1 (1937), 14–29

DANIEL Krystyna: *Poglądy rolników na cele i skutki regulacji własności gospodarstw rolnych: w świetle ustawy z dnia 26 października 1971 r.* [Farmers' perspectives on the goals and effects of the regulation of farm property: in the right of the Act of 26 October 1971], ZN im. Ossolińskich, Wrocław, 1987

DAWIDOWICZ Wacław: *W sprawie sądownictwa administracyjnego* [Concerning the administrative-court system], PiP 12 (1956), 1041–1048

DĘBSKA Hanna: *Legal Doxa as a Form of Neutralization of Values in the Law. The Case of Constitutional Tribunal Judgments*, in *Neutralization of Values in Law*, Krzysztof PAŁECKI (ed.), Wolters Kluwer, Warsaw, 2013, 303–351

DĘBSKA Hanna: *Władza, symbol, prawo. Społeczne tworzenie Trybunału Konstytucyjnego* [Power, symbol, law: the social construction of the Constitutional Court], Wydawnictwo Sejmowe, Warsaw, 2015

DĘBSKA Hanna, Tomasz WARCZOK: *The Social Construction of Feminity in the Discourse of the Polish Constitutional Court*, in *Law and Critique in Central Europe: Questioning the Past, Resisting the Present*, Rafał MAŃKO, Cosmin CERCEL, Adam SULIKOWSKI (eds), Counterpress, Oxford, 106–130

DEL MAR Maksymilian: *Philosophical Analysis and Historical Inquiry: Theorizing Normativity, Law, and Legal Though*, in *The Oxford Handbook of Legal History*, Markus D. DUBBER, Christopher TOMLINS (eds), OUP, Oxford, 2018, 3–22

DEL MAR Maksymilian, Michael LOBBAN (eds), *Legal Theory and Legal History*, Ashgate, Farnham, 2014

DEL MAR Maksymilian, Michael LOBBAN (eds), *Legal Theory and Legal History: New Essays on a Neglected Dialogue*, Hart Publishing, Oxford, 2016

DOBRZAŃSKI Bronisław: *Jakie zmiany w stosunku do prawa spadkowego z 1946 wprowadzi Kodeks cywilny* [What changes will the Civil Code introduce in relation to the inheritance law of 1946], Palestra 7 (1964), 4–21

DOLAR Mladen: *Beyond Interpellation*, Qui Parle 6 (1993)/2, 75–96

DOLATA Tomasz: *Adam Chełmoński (1880–1956) i jego udział w pracach Zespołu Prawa Cywilnego Materialnego Komisji Kodyfikacyjnej PRL* [Adam Chełmoński (1880–1956) and his participation in the works of the Substantive Civil Law Team of the Codification Commission of the Polish People's Republic], WUWr, Wrocław, 2023

DOMAŃSKI Ludwik: *O systemie przyszłego Kodeksu Cywilnego polskiego* [On the system of the future Polish Civil Code], Dziennik Urzędowy Ministerstwa Sprawiedliwości 2 (1919)/4–8, 161–173

DOSTALÍK Petr, Ondřej HORÁK: *Zmiany w czeskim prawie prywatnym* [Recent changes in the contemporary Czech private law], Forum Prawnicze 4 (2014), 16–25

DOUZINAS Costas: *The Radical Philosophy of Rights*, Routledge, Abigdon, 2019

DOUZINAS Costas: *A Short History of the British Critical Legal Conference or, the Responsibility of the Critic*, Law and Critique 25 (2014), 187–198

DOUZINAS Costas, Adam GEAREY: *Critical Jurisprudence: The Political Philosophy of Justice*, Hart, Oxford-Portland, 2005

DUBBER Markus D.: *Legal History as Legal Scholarship: Doctrinalism, Interdisciplinarity, and Critical Analysis of Law*, in *The Oxford Handbook of Legal History*, Markus D. DUBBER, Christopher TOMLINS (eds), OUP, Oxford, 2018, 99–117

DUDEK Antoni: *Wybrane czynniki historyczne wpływające na politykę władz PRL* [Selected historical factors affecting the policy of the authorities of Polish People's Republic], in *Polityka czy propaganda PRL wobec Historii* [Polish People's Republic politics or propaganda with regard to history], Paweł SKIBIŃSKI, Tomasz WIŚCICKI (eds), Muzeum Historii Polski, Warsaw, 2009, 13–36

DUDEK Antoni, Zdzisław ZBLEWSKI: *Utopia nad Wisłą: historia Peerelu* [A Utopia at the Vistulaside: a history of the Polish People's Republic], PWN, Warsaw, 2012

DULCZEWSKI Zygmunt (ed.): *Tworzenie się nowego społeczeństwa na Ziemiach Zachodnich* [The formation of a new society in the Western Territories], Instytut Zachodni, Poznań, 1961

DULCZEWSKI Zygmunt, Andrzej KWILECKI (eds), *Pamiętniki osadników ziem odzyskanych* [Memoirs of the settlers of the recovered territories], Wydawnictwo Poznańskie, Poznań, 1963

DWORKIN Ronald: *Law as Interpretation*, Texas Law Review 60 (1982), 527–550

DZIADZIO Andrzej: *Polsko-czechosłowacka współpraca nad kodyfikacją prawa rodzinnego w latach 1948–1950. Z dziejów sowietyzacji prawa* [Polish-Czechoslovak co-operation on the codification of family law in 1948–1950], in *Rozważania o nauce i dogmatyce prawa. Materiały konferencji naukowej zorganizowanej przez Wydział Administracji Krakowskiej Szkoły Wyższej im. Andrzeja Frycza Modrzewskiego* [Ponderings on the science and dogmatics of law. Materials of the academic conference organized by the Faculty of Administration of Andrzej Frycz Modrzewski University in Krakow], Jerzy MALEC (ed.), Krakowskie Towarzystwo Edukacyjne, Krakow, 2002, 141–151

ECKHARDT Piotr: *Socialism under Construction: Law and Ideology in Housing, Construction and Spatial Planning in Poland 1944–1989*, Scholar, Warsaw, 2024

EHRLICH Stanisław: *Zagadnienia praworządności* [Topics of rule of law], Książka i Wiedza, Warszawa, 1947

EISLER Jerzy: *Zarys dziejów politycznych Polski 1944–1989* [An outline of the political history of Poland 1944–1989], Polska Oficyna Wydawnicza BGW, Warsaw, 1992

ENGELS Fryderyk: *Pochodzenie rodziny, własności prywatnej i państwa* [The Origin of the Family, Private Property and the State], Książka i Wiedza, Warsaw, 1949

FIEDORCZYK Piotr: *Czechosłowacka droga do kodyfikacji prawa rodzinnego 1919–1949: z dziejów współpracy z Polską* [The Czechoslovak route to codification of family law 1919–1949: from the history of co-operation with Poland], in *Państwo, prawo, społeczeństwo w dziejach Europy Środkowej: księga jubileuszowa dedykowana Profesorowi Józefowi Ciągwie w siedemdziesięciolecie urodzin* [The state, law and society in the history of Central Europe: a jubilee book dedicated to Professor Józef Ciągwa on the seventieth anniversary of his birthday], Adam LITYŃSKI (ed.), Towarzystwo Słowaków w Polsce, Katowice–Krakow 2009, 184–196

FIEDORCZYK Piotr: *Development of Family Law on Polish Lands 1795–1945*, in *Framing the Polish Family in the Past*, Piotr GUZOWSKI, Cezary KUKLO (eds), Routledge, New York, 2022, 165–180

FIEDORCZYK Piotr: *Dylematy socjalistycznego kodyfikatora: dokument archiwalny o pracach komisji Kodyfikacyjnej w latach 1956–1958* [The dilemmas of a socialist codifier: archive document on the works of the Codification Commission in 1956–1958]; MHI 8 (2009), 259–267

FIEDORCZYK Piotr: *Kilka uwag o publicznej dyskusji nad prawem rodzinnym w projekcie kodeksu cywilnego z 1960 r.* [Several remarks on the public debate on family law in the draft Civil Code of 1960], in *Filozofia Marii Szyszkowskiej* [Philosophy of Maria Szyszkowska], Anna KRYNIECKA (ed.), Kresowa Agencja Wydawnicza, Białystok, 2012, 360–380

FIEDORCZYK Piotr: *O początkach prac nad kodyfikacją polskiego prawa cywilnego w 1947 r.* [On the beginnings of the works on the codification of Polish civil law in 1947], MHI 4 (2006), 109–120

FIEDORCZYK Piotr: *O powstaniu, strukturze organizacyjnej i trybie prac Komisji Kodyfikacyjnej z 1956 roku* [On the formation, organizational structure and procedure of the Codification Commission of 1956], in *O prawie i jego dziejach księgi dwie: dtudia ofiarowane Profesorowi Adamowi Lityńskiemu w czterdziestopięciolecie pracy naukowej i siedemdziesięciolecie urodzin* [On law and its history books two: studies dedicated to Professor Adam Lityński on the forty-fifth anniversary of his academic work and twenty-fifth anniversary of his birth], Marian MIKOŁAJCZYK et al. (eds), WUwB, Białystok, 2010, vol. 2, 473–484

FIEDORCZYK Piotr: *Polish Matrimonial Law 1918–1939: Regulations, Attempts to Unify and Codify*, in *Kulturkampf um die Ehe: Reform des europäischen Eherechts nach dem Grossen Krieg*, Martin LÖHNIG (ed.), Mohr Siebeck, Tübingen, 2021, 147–165

FIEDORCZYK Piotr: *Radzieckie prawo rodzinne jako przedmiot recepcji w Polsce i innych państwach Europy Środkowo-Wschodniej* [The Soviet family law as a subject of reception in Poland and in other states of Central-Eastern Europe], Acta Universitatis Wratislaviensis 3154 (2009), 355–380

FIEDORCZYK Piotr: *Unifikacja i kodyfikacja prawa rodzinnego w Polsce (1945–1964)* [Unification and codification of family law in Poland (1945–1964)], WUwB, Białystok, 2014

FIEDORCZYK Piotr: *Unifikacja i kodyfikacja prawa rodzinnego w Polsce Ludowej na tle stosunków Państwa z Kościołem katolickim (1944–1964)* [Unification and codification of family law in people's Poland against the background of the State's relations with the Catholic Church (1944–1964)], in *Cuius regio, eius religio: Zjazd Historyków Państwa i Prawa. Lublin, 20–23 IX 2006 r.* [*Cuius regio, eius religio*: conference of historians of state and law. Lublin, 20–23 September 2006], Grzegorz GÓRSKI, Leszek ĆWIKŁA, Marzena LIPSKA (eds), WKUL, Lublin, 2006, 415–431

FIEDORCZYK Piotr: *Wytyczne Sądu Najwyższego dotyczące wykładni przepisów kodeksu rodzinnego z 1950 r.* [Supreme Court Guidelines on the interpretation of the provisions of the 1950 Family Code], in *Świat, Europa, mała ojczyzna. Studia ofiarowane Profesorowi Stanisławowi Grodziskiemu w 80-lecie urodzin* [The world, Europe, the little fatherland: studies dedicated to Professor Stanisław Grodziski on the 80th anniversary of his birthday], Marian Małecki (ed.), Wyższa Szkoła Administracji, Bielsko-Biala 2009, 627–638

FIEDORCZYK Piotr: *Z dziejów stalinizacji polskiej nauki prawa: Komisja Konsultacyjno-Naukowa przy Ministrze Sprawiedliwości (1949–1951)* [From the history of Stalinization of Polish legal science: the Academic Consultative Commission to the Minister of Justice], in *Konstytucjonalizm, doktryny, partie polityczne: księga dedykowana Profesorowi Andrzejowi Ziębie* [Constitutionalism, doctrines, political parties: a book dedicated to Professor Andrzej Zięba], Robert KŁOSOWICZ et al. (eds), WUJ, Krakow, 2016, 257–268

FIEDORCZYK Piotr: *Z prac nad unifikacją osobowego prawa małżeńskiego w 1945 roku* [From works on the unification of matrimonial personal law in 1945], MHI 1 (1994), 65–80

FIERICH Franciszek X.: *Rzut oka na najważniejsze zadania prac kodyfikacyjnych* [A glance at the most important tasks of the codification works], KPCiK 2 (1919)/1–4, 455–480

FIERICH Franciszek X.: *Unifikacja ustawodawstwa* [Legislative unification], in *Dziesięciolecie Polski Odrodzonej: księga pamiątkowa 1918–1928* [The decennary of Poland Reborn: a commemorative book 1918–1928)], Ilustrowany Kurier Codzienny, Krakow-Warsaw, 1928, 263–274

FISH Stanley: *Doing What Comes Naturally: Change, Rhetoric, and the Practice of Theory in Literary and Legal Studies*, Duke University Press, Durham-London 1989

FREEDEN Michael: *Ideology: A Very Short Introduction*, OUP, Oxford, 2003

FRIEDRICH Carl J., Zbigniew. K. BRZEZINSKI: *Totalitarian Dictatorship and Autocracy*, Praeger, New York, 1965

FRISZKE Andrzej: *Polska: losy państwa i narodu 1939–1989* [Poland: the fate of the state and of the nation 1939–1989], Iskry, Warsaw, 2003

FUSCO Gian Giacomo: *Notes on the Person and the Anthropological Machine of Law*, in *Law and Philosophical Theory: Critical Intersections*, Thanos ZARTALOUDIS (ed.), Rowman and Littlefield International, London, 2018, 81–96

GABEL Peter, Jay FEINMAN: *Contract Law as Ideology*, in *The Politics of Law: A Progressive Critique*, David KAIRYS (ed.), 3rd ed., Basic Books, New York, 1998, 497–510

GAŁĘDEK Michał: *The Beginning of the Debate on the Codification of Polish Law after the First World War: The Issue of the Codification Commission Autonomy in the Light of Political Declarations*, Studia Iuridica 78 (2019), 119–134

GAŁĘDEK Michał: *Dreams of 'Moving from the Napoleonic Code to the New Era of the Judiciary' on the Eve of Establishment of the Kingdom of Poland (1814–1815)*, Rechtskultur 8 (2019), 75–90

GAŁĘDEK Michał: *Introduction: Modernisation, National Identity, and Legal Instrumentalism*, in *Modernization, National Identity and Legal Instrumentalism: Studies in Comparative Legal History*, Michał GAŁĘDEK, Anna KLIMASZEWSKA (eds), vol. 1: *Private Law*, Brill-Nijhoff, Leiden-Boston, 2020, 1–25

GAŁĘDEK Michał: *The Problem of Non-adaptability of National Legal Heritage. Discussion on the Reform of Civil Law in Poland in the Course of Work of Reform Committee in 1814*, Romanian Journal of Comparative Law, 7 (2017) 1, 7–38

GAŁĘDEK Michał, Anna KLIMASZEWSKA: *A Controversial Transplant? Debate over the Adaptation of the Napoleonic Code on the Polish Territories in the Early 19th Century*, Journal of Civil Law Studies, 11 (2018) 2, 269–298

GAŁĘDEK Michał, Anna KLIMASZEWSKA: *'Crippled Equality': The Act of 1 July 1921 on Civil Rights for Women in Poland*, Acta Poloniae Historica 113 (2016), 231–260

GAŁĘDEK Michał, Anna KLIMASZEWSKA: *Involvement of Polish Legal Elites in Preparing a New Draft of the Civil Code, Seen as an Intellectual Feast – Menu à la Carte or Fast Food?*, in *The Language of Law and Food: Metaphors of Recipes and Rules*, Salvatore MANCUSO (ed.), Routledge, New York, 2021, 48–67

GARLICKI Stanisław: *Przepisy o czynach niedozwolonych w projekcie kodeksu cywilnego* [Tort provisions in the draft Civil Code], Nowe Prawo 5 (1960), 656–662

GENKIN Dmitry M. et al. (eds): *Sovetskoe graždanskoe pravo* [Soviet civil law], vol. 1, Gosjurizdat, Moskva, 1950

GÉNY Francois: *Science et technique en droit privé positif*, Recucil Sirey, Paris, 1922

GETZLER Joshua: *Legal History as Doctrinal History*, in *The Oxford Handbook of Legal History*, Markus D. DUBBER, Christopher TOMLINS (eds), OUP, Oxford, 2018, 171–191

GIARO Tomasz: *Aufstieg und Niedergang des sozialistischen Zivilrechts: von der Ideologie zur Rechtsdogmatik der Pauschalenteignung*, in *Recht im Sozalismus: Analysen zur Normdurchsetzung in Osteuropaeischen Nachkriegsgesellschaften (1944/45–1989)*, Gert BENDER, Udo FALK (eds), vol. 1: *Enteignung*, Vittorio Klostermann, Frankfurt am Main, 1999

GIARO Tomasz: *Legal Tradition of Eastern Europe: Its Rise and Demise*, Comparative Law Review 2 (2011) 1, 1–23

GIARO Tomasz (ed.): *Rechtskulturen des modernen Osteuropa. Traditionen und Transfers, vol. 1: Modernisierung durch Transfer im 19. und frühen 20. Jahrhundert*, Vittorio Klostermann, Frankfurt am Main, 2006

GIARO Tomasz: *Some Prejudices about the Legal Tradition of Eastern Europe*, in *Comparative Law in Eastern and Central Europe*, Bronisław SITEK, Jakub J. SZCZERBOWSKI, Aleksander W. BAUKNECHT (eds), Cambridge Scholars Publishing, Newcastle upon Tyne, 2013, 26–50

GIEŁŻYŃSKI Wojciech, Lech STEFAŃSKI: *Gdańsk, Sierpień 80* [Gdańsk, August 1980], Książka i Wiedza, Warsaw, 1981

GINSBURG George, Donald. D. BARRY, William B. SIMONS (eds): *The Revival of Private Law in Central and Eastern Europe*, Martinus Nijhoff, The Hague-London-Boston, 1996

GLASS Jakób: *Współpraca poszczególnych dzielnic w budowaniu Państwa Polskiego* [The collaboration of the individual zones in the construction of the Polish State], GSW 3 (1920), 18–20

GOŁĄB Stanisław: *Polskie prawo małżeńskie w kodyfikacji* [Polish marriage law in codification], Biblioteka Prawnicza, Warsaw, 1932

GOŁĄB Stanisław: *Prądy w prawoznawstwie III Rzeszy* [Currents in the jurisprudence of the Third Reich], Druk. Rolnicza, Warsaw, 1936

GOŁĄB Stanisław: *Przed projektem polskiego Kodeksu cywilnego*, Czasopismo Prawnicze i Ekonomiczne 1 (1920), 5–36

GOŁĄB Stanisław: *Zasady prawa małżeńskiego (z obrad Sekcji Prawa Cywilnego Komisji Kodyfikacyjnej)* [The principles of marriage law (from the deliberations of the Codification Commission's Civil Law Section], Palestra 2 (1925)/2, 593–606

GONERA Katarzyna: *Przewlekłość postępowania w sprawach cywilnych* [Protraction of proceedings in civil cases], Przegląd Sądowy 11–12 (2005), 3–38

GOODRICH Peter: *Law and the Unconscious: a Legendre Reader*, Palgrave Macmillan, London, 1997

GORDON Robert W.: *Critical Legal Histories*, Stanford Law Review 36 (1984), 100–116

GÓRECKI Jan: *Recrimination in Eastern Europe: An Empirical Study of Polish Divorce Law*, American Journal of Comparative Law 14 (1965–1966), 603–629

GÓRECKI Jan: *Unieważnienie małżeństwa* [The annulment of marriage], Uniwersytet Jagielloński, Krakow, 1958

GÓRECKI Jan: *Wina rozwodu a moralność (z rozważań nad zasadą rekryminacji)* [Culpability and morality (from discussions on the principle of recrimination)], PiP 1 (1965), 27–41

GÓRNICKI Leonard: *Kodyfikacja prawa prywatnego* [Codification of private law], in *System prawa prywatnego* [System of private law], Zbigniew RADWAŃSKI (ed.), vol. 1: *Prawo cywilne: część ogólna* [Civil law: general part], C. H. Beck, Warsaw, 2012, 77–155

GÓRNICKI Leonard: *Pogranicza systemów prawnych, w szczególności pozaborowych, w pracach nad kodyfikacjami prawa cywilnego i handlowego w II RP* [Intersections of legal systems, especially post-partitioning systems, in works on codifications of civil and commercial law under the Second Polish Republic], Acta Universitatis Wratislaviensis 324 (2017), 129–167

GÓRNICKI Leonard: *Prawo cywilne w pracach Komisji Kodyfikacyjnej Rzeczypospolitej Polskiej w latach 1919–1939* [Civil law in the works of the Codification Commission of the Republic of Poland in 1919–1939], Kolonia Limited, Wrocław, 2000

GÓRNICKI Leonard: *Prawo prywatne międzydzielnicowe z 1926 r.* [The Interpartitional Private Law of 1926], in *Okresy przejściowe – ustrój i prawo* [Transitional periods – political system and law], Jacek PRZYGODZKI (ed.), E-Wydawnictwo. Prawnicza i Ekonomiczna Biblioteka Cyfrowa. WPAiE UWr, Wrocław, 2019, 163–191

GÓRNICKI Leonard: *Zasada uspołecznienia pewnych stosunków umownych w Kodeksie Zobowiązań z 1933 r.* [The principle of socialization of certain contractual relationships in the Code of Obligations of 1933], in *Zasady prawne w dziejach prawa publicznego i prywatnego* [Legal principles in the history of public and private law], Marek PODKOWSKI (ed.), Kolonia Limited, Wrocław, 2015, 153–169

GRADZIŃSKA Grażyna: *Chłopi wobec kryzysów społeczno-politycznych w Polsce (1944–1989): studium historyczno-politologiczne* [The peasant farmers in the face of socio-political crises in Poland (1944–1989)], Abos, Poznań, 1993

GREBIENIOW Aleksander: *Römisches Recht als Vergleichsfaktor: Ignacy Koschembahr-Łyskowski (1864–1945) und die Methodenfrage*, in *Methodenfragen der*

Romanistik im Wandel: Paul Koschakers Vermächtnis 80 Jahre nach seiner Krisensschrift, Tommaso BEGGIO, Aleksander GREBIENIOW (eds), Mohr Siebeck, Tübingen, 2020, 165–210

GRODZISKI Stanisław: *Komisja Kodyfikacyjna Rzeczypospolitej Polskiej*, CPH 33 (1991)/1, 47–81

GRODZISKI Stanisław: *Prace nad kodyfikacją i unifikacją polskiego prawa prywatnego (1919–1947)* [The process of codification and unification of Polish private law (1919–1947)], KPP 1 (1992)/1–4, 9–56

GRUDZIŃSKI Maurycy: *W przededniu kodyfikacji: list to redakcji* [On the eve of codification: a letter to the editors], PiŹ 12 (1956), 7

GRZYBOWSKI Konstanty: *Historia doktryn politycznych i prawnych: od państwa niewolniczego do rewolucji burżuazyjnych* [The history of political and legal doctrines: from the slave state to the bourgeois revolutions], PWN, Warsaw, 1968

GRZYBOWSKI Konstanty: *Sądy a aparat władzy i administracja* [The courts and the apparatus of power and administration], PiŻ 8 (1957), 1

GRZYBOWSKI Konstanty: *Z metodologii historii doktryn politycznych* [From the methodology of history of political doctrines], CPH 8 (1956)/1, 297–310

GRZYBOWSKI Stefan: *Odpowiedź p. J. P. z 'Tygodnika Powszechnego'* [Answer to Mr J.P. of the Tygodnik Powszechny], PiP 9–10 (1946), 119–122

GRZYBOWSKI Stefan: *Sytuacja prawna mienia ogólnonarodowego w kodeksie cywilnym* [The legal situation of national property in the Civil Code], PiP 2 (1965), 527–539

GRZYBOWSKI Stefan: *Własność w projekcie prawa rzeczowego* [Ownership in the draft Real Law], PiP 4 (1946), 16–27

GRZYBOWSKI Stefan: *Zagadnienia kodyfikacji polskiego prawa cywilnego (Organizacja i wyniki pracy 1919–1992)* [Codification of Polish civil law: work organization and products 1919–1992], KPP 1 (1992)/1–4, 91–114

GRZYBOWSKI Stefan M., Ignacy RÓŻAŃSKI: *Komentarz: wyciągi z motywów Komisji Kodyfikacyjnej – tezy polityczne – wzory* [Commentary: extracts from the Codification Commission's rationales], Księgarnia Powszechna, Krakow, 1946

GULCZYŃSKI Andrzej, Jacek WIEWIOROWSKI: *Ogólnopolska konferencja katedr historyczno-prawnych w Zajączkowie (14–17.09.1995 r.)* [National conference of historico-legal departments in Zajączkowo (14–17 September 1995)], CPH 47 (1995)/1–2, 310–314

GUȚAN Manuel: *The Legal Transplant and the Building of the Romanian Legal Identity in the Second Half of the 19th Century and the Beginning of the 20th Century*, Romanian Journal of Comparative Law, 8 (2017) 1, 62–99

GWIAZDOMORSKI Jan: *'Najem' lokali jako problem kodyfikacyjny* [Apartment lease as a codification problem], PiP 4 (1956), 652–677

GWIAZDOMORSKI Jan: *Prawo spadkowe* [Inheritance law], PWN, Warsaw, 1959

GWIAZDOMORSKI Jan: *Prawa spadkowe w Kodeksie cywilnym PRL* [Inheritance laws in the Civil Code of the Polish People's Republic], PiP 5–6 (1965), 707–725

GWIAZDOMORSKI Jan: *Rezerwa czy zachowek?* [Reserve or legitimate portion?], PiŻ 12 (1959), 2–3

GWIAZDOMORSKI Jan: *Równouprawnienie kobiety w rodzinie jako problem kodyfikacyjny* [Equal right for the woman in the family as a codification problem], PiP 11 (1959), 754–772

GWIAZDOMORSKI Jan: *Zasada jednolitej własności socjalistycznej a osobowość prawna przedsiębiorstw państwowych* [The principle of uniform socialist property and the legal personality of state-owned enterprises], PiP 4–5 (1967), 591–610

GWIAZDOMORSKI Jan, Maurycy GRUDZIŃSKI, Stefan KALETA, Aleksander WOLTER: *Założenia prawa rodzinnego w świetle konstytucji PRL* [Assumptions of family law in the light of the Constitution of Polish People's Republic], in *Zagadnienia prawne konstytucji Polskiej Rzeczypospolitej Ludowej* [Legal topics of the Constitution of Polish People's Republic], vol. 3, Stefan GRZYBOWSKI (ed.), PWN, Warsaw, 1954, 52–120

HALPIN Andrew: *Ideology and Law*, Journal of Political Ideologies 11 (2006) 2, 153–168

HANUSZ Antoni: *Polityka podatkowa w zakresie zróżnicowania obciążeń dochodów rolniczych w Polsce* [Tax policy in the scope of differentiating the burdens on farming incomes in Poland], WUMCS, Lublin, 1996

HARVEY David: *A Brief History of Neoliberalism* [2005], OUP, Oxford, 2007

HELIOS Joanna, Wioletta JEDLECKA: *Współczesne oblicza przemocy: zagadnienia wybrane* [Modern faces of violence: selected topics], Prawnicza i Ekonomiczna Biblioteka Cyfrowa, Wrocław, 2017

HELLER Michaił: *Maszyna i śrubki. Jak hartował się człowiek sowiecki*, SIL Kultura, Paris, 1988 [English version: Heller Mikhail: *Cogs in the Wheel: The Formation of Soviet Man*, Knopf, 1988]

HESSELINK Martijn W.: *The Concept of Good Faith* in Arthur HARTKAMP et al. (eds), *Towards a European Civil Code*, Kluwer Law International, Alphen aan den Rijn, 2010, 619–649

HESSELINK Martijn W.: *European Contract Law: A Matter of Consumer Protection, Citizenship, or Justice?* European Review of Private Law 15 (2007) 3, 323–348

HESSELINK Martijn W.: *The Ideal of Codification and the Dynamics of Europeanisation: The Dutch Experience*, European Law Journal 12 (2006) 3, 279–305

HESSELINK Martin W.: *The Principles Of European Contract Law: Some Choices Made By The Lando Commission*, Global Jurist Frontiers 1 (2001) 1, 3–16

HORKHEIMER Max: *Critical Theory*, Continuum, New York, 1982

HUNT Alan: *The Ideology of Law: Advances and Problems in Recent Applications of the Concept of Ideology to the Analysis of Law*, Law & Society Review 19 (1985)/1, 11–38

IGNATOWICZ Jerzy: *Prawo rzeczowe* [Real law], Warsaw, PWN, 1987

IGNATOWICZ Jerzy (ed.): vol. 2: *Prawo własności i inne prawa rzeczowe* [Ownership and other property rights], in *System prawa cywilnego* [The system of civil law], ZN im. Ossolińskich, Wrocław, 1977

IZDEBSKI Hubert: *General Survey of Developments in Eastern Europe in the Field of Civil Law*, in *The Revival of Private Law in Central and Eastern Europe*, George GINSBURG, Donald. D. BARRY, William B. SIMONS (eds), Martinus Nijhoff, The Hague-London-Boston, 1996, 3–16

IZDEBSKI Hubert: *Kodyfikacje cywilne XX wieku* [The civil codifications of the 20th century], vol. 1: *Kodyfikacja jako instrument reformy prawa* [Codification as an instrument of law reform], CPH 62 (1990)/1–2, 127–162

IZDEBSKI Hubert: *Polska Rewolucja – pokojowa rewolucja: ze studiów nad terminologią polityczną pierwszych lat Polski Ludowej (1944–1948)* [The Polish Revolution – a peaceful revolution: from studies on the political terminology of the initial years of People's Poland (1944–1948)], CPH 37 (1985)/2, 301–326

IZDEBSKI Zygmunt: *Rewizja pojęcia praworządności ludowej* [Revision of the concept of the people's rule of law], PiP 3 (1957), 443–454

J. P.: *Własność jako funkcja* [Ownership as a function], Tygodnik Powszechny 39 (1946), 7

JACHER Władysław: *Zagadnienia integracji systemu społecznego: studium z zakresu teorii socjologii* [Topics of integration of the social system: a study in the theory of sociology], PWN, Warsaw, 1976

JANISZEWSKA Beata: *O potrzebie zmiany klauzuli zasad współżycia społecznego (głos w dyskusji)*, Przegląd Ustawodawstwa Gospodarczego 61 (2003) 4, 7–12

JANISZEWSKA Beata: *Pojęcie dobrej wiary w rozumieniu obiektywnym a zasady współżycia społecznego* [The concept of good faith in the objective sense and the principles of social coexistence], Przegląd Ustawodawstwa Gospodarczego 61 (2003) 9, 2–10

JASTRZĘBSKI Robert: *Prawo prywatne międzydzielnicowe: zarys problematyki* [Interpartitional private law: an outline of the problem range], Krakowskie Studia z Historii Państwa i Prawa 8 (2015) 3, 277–298

JAWORSKI Władysław L.: *Nowożytny Kodeks Cywilny* [A modern civil code], Czasopismo Prawnicze i Ekonomiczne 1–4 (1922), 1–18

JEDLECKA Wioletta: *Formy i rodzaje przemocy* [Forms and types of violence], Wrocławskie Studia Erazmiańskie 11 (2017), 13–29

JĘDRZEJEWSKA Maria, Jerzy LAPIERRE: *Sprawozdanie z dyskusji w komitecie nauk Prawnych PAN nad referatem Zbigniewa Resicha 'Ochrona własności społecznej w projekcie kodeksu postępowania cywilnego'* [Report on the debate held in the Legal Sciences Committee of the Polish Academy of Sciences on Zbigniew Resich's paper 'Protection of socialized property in the draft Code of Civil Procedure'], PiP 10 (1960), 614–625

JEZIERSKI Andrzej, Cecylia LESZCZYŃSKA: *Historia gospodarcza Polski*, Key Text, Warsaw, 1998

JODŁOWSKI Jerzy: *Nowe drogi polskiego procesu cywilnego. Założenia ideologiczne reformy postępowania cywilnego* [The new ways of Polish civil procedure. The ideological basis of the reform of civil proceedings], Wydawnictwo Ministerstwa Sprawiedliwości, Warsaw, 1951

JODŁOWSKI Jerzy: *Nowy etap przebudowy polskiego procesu cywilnego* [New stage of remodelling of Polish civil procedure], PiP 5–6 (1953), 689–715

JODŁOWSKI Jerzy: *Podstawowe problemy kodyfikacji postępowania cywilnego* [Core problems of codification of civil procedure], PiP 8–9 (1960), 207–227

JODŁOWSKI Jerzy: *Les principes de la procedure civil polonaise*, Revue internationale de droit comparé 12 (1960)/2, 369–384

JODŁOWSKI Jerzy: *Zasady naczelne socjalistycznego postępowania cywilnego* [The fundamental principles of the socialist civil proceedings], in *Wstęp do systemu prawa procesowego cywilnego* [Introduction to the system of civil procedural law], Jerzy JODŁOWSKI (ed.), Ossolineum, Wrocław, 1974, 47–123

JODŁOWSKI Jerzy, Kazimierz PIASECKI (eds): *Kodeks postępowania cywilnego z komentarzem* [The Code of Civil Procedure with a commentary], Wydawnictwo Prawnicze, Warsaw, 1989

JOHN Michael: *Politics and the Law in Late Nineteenth-Century Germany: the Origins of the Civil Code*, OUP, Oxford, 1989

KALIŃSKI Janusz: *Gospodarka Polski w latach 1944–1989: przemiany strukturalne* [The economy of Poland in 1944–1989: structural transformations], Państwowe Wydawnictwo Ekonomiczne, Warsaw, 1995

KELEMEN Katalin, Balazs FEKETE: *How Should the Legal System of Eastern Europe be Classified Today?* in *International Conference for the 10th Anniversary of the Institute of Comparative Law*, Attila BADO et al. (eds), Universitätsverlag, Potsdam, 2014, 197–223

KENNEDY Duncan: *A Critique of Adjudication {fin de siècle}*, Harvard University Press, Cambridge, MA, 1997

KENNEDY Duncan: *Form and Substance in Private Law Adjudication*, Harvard Law Review, 89 (1976), 1685–1778

KENNEDY Duncan: *The Hermeneutic of Suspicion in Contemporary American Legal Thought*, Law and Critique 25 (2015) 1, 91–139

KENNEDY Duncan: *A Left/Phenomenological Critique of the Hart/Kelsen Theory of Legal Interpretation*, in Duncan KENNEDY, *Legal Reasoning: Collected Essays*, The Davies Group, Aurora, 2008, 154–173

KENNEDY Duncan: *The Stages of the Decline of the Public/Private Distinction*, University of Pennsylvania Law Review 130 (1982), 1349–1357

KĘPIŃSKI Marian: *Czy w Polsce jest potrzebny nowy kodeks cywilny? Artykuł polemiczny* [Does Poland need a new civil code? A polemical article], RPEiS 2 (2014), 237–245

KERSTEN Krystyna: *Narodziny systemu władzy. Polska 1943–1948* [The birth of a system of power: Poland 1943–1948], SAWW, Poznań, 1990

KŁAK Czesław P.: *Pojęcie przewlekłości postępowania sądowego* [The concept of protraction of judicial proceedings], Prawo i Prokuratura 12 (2008), 63–79

KLARE Karl: *Juridical Deradicalization or the Wagner Act and the Origins of Modern Legal Consciousness*, Minnesota Law Review, 62 (1978), 265–340

KLARE Karl E.: *The Public/Private Distinction in Labor Law*, University of Pennsylvania Law Review 130 (1982), 1358–1422

KLIMASZEWSKA Anna: *Searching for National Components in Building Own Legal Culture: The Debate on the Legal Situation of Women in Interwar Poland*, Studia Iuridica 79 (2019), 169–180

KŁOSKOWSKA Antonina: *Wzory i modele w socjologicznych badaniach rodziny* [Patterns and models in sociological studies on family], Studia Socjologiczne 2 (1962), 35–56

KOJÈVE Alexandre: *An Outline of the Phenomenology of Right*, Bryan-Paul FROST (ed), Robert HOWSE (transl.), Rowman & Littlefield, Plymouth, 2007

KOŁAKOWSKI Leszek: *Główne nurty marksizmu: powstanie – rozwój – rozkład*, Aneks, London, 1988 [In English: *Main Currents of Marxism*, OUP, 1978]

KOŁAKOWSKI Leszek: *Kapłan i błazen: rozważania o teologicznym dziedzictwie współczesnego myślenia* [The priest and the jester: on the theological legacy of our contemporary thinking], in Leszek KOŁAKOWSKI: *Nasza wesoła apokalipsa: wybór najważniejszych esejów* [Our happy apocalypsis: selection of most important essays], Znak, Kraków, 2010, 49–82

KOŁAKOWSKI Leszek: *Kultura polska w ostatnim dziesięcioleciu* [Polish culture in the last decade], in Zbigniew ROMEK: *Droga Leszka Kołakowskiego ku antykomunistycznej opozycji: od ortodoksyjnej ideologii do wolności myślenia* [Leszek Kołakowski's road to anti-communist oppposition: from orthodox ideology to freedom of thought], Dzieje Najnowsze 4 (1999), 147–153

KOŁAKOWSKI Leszek: *Tezy o nadziei i beznadziejności*, in *Czy diabeł może być zbawiony*, Aneks, London, 1982, 285–299 [in English: *Theses on Hope and Despair*, Kevin Devlin (transl.), in Leszek Kołakowski: *Can the Devil Be Saved?* Encounter, 1974]

KONCEWICZ Tomasz T.: *Poszukując modelu sprawiedliwości proceduralnej w prawie wspólnotowym: mit czy rzeczywistość?* [Searching for a model of procedural justice in Community Law: myth or reality?], CE Natolin, Warsaw, 2009

KONIC Henryk: *Spadkobranie z prawa (ustawowe): referat dla Komisji Kodyfikacyjnej* [A few topics in inheritance law: paper for the Codification Commission], GSW 11–12 (1920), 81–84

KORALEWICZ Jadwiga, Marek ZIÓŁKOWSKI: *Mentalność Polaków* [The Poles' mindset], Nakom, Poznań 1990

KORZENIEWSKA-LASOTA Anna, Michał LASOTA: *Leona Chajna poglądy na wymiar sprawiedliwości* [Leon Chajn's viewpoints on the administration of justice], MHI 15 (2016) 2, 317–326

KOSCHEMBAHR-ŁYSKOWSKI Ignacy: *W sprawie kodyfikacji naszego prawa cywilnego* [Concerning the codification of our civil law], Themis Polska, Warsaw, 1925

KOTOWSKI Artur: *Argumentacja z tożsamości konstytucyjnej – celem podsumowania* [Argumentation based on constitutional identity: a summary], Studia i Analizy Sądu Najwyższego 4 (2017), 180–201

KÖVECSES Zoltán, *Extended Conceptual Metaphor Theory*, Cambridge University Press, Cambridge, 2020

KÖVECSES Zoltán: *Metaphor: A Practical Introduction*, 2nd ed., Oxford University Press, Oxford-New York, 2010

KOWALSKI Przemysław: *Z badań nad prawem spadkowym w projekcie kodeksu cywilnego z 1948 r.* [Studies on the law of succession in the draft Civil Code of 1948], MHI 12 (2013), 261–276

KOZAK Artur: *Granice prawniczej władzy dyskrecjonalnej* [The limits of the discretionary power of lawyers], Kolonia Limited, Wrocław, 2002

KOZAK Artur: *Myślenie analityczne w nauce prawa i praktyce prawniczej* [Analytical thinking in legal scholarship and legal practice], Maciej PICHLAK (ed.), WUWR, Wrocław, 2008

KOZAK Artur (ed.): *Z zagadnień teorii i filozofii prawa: instrumentalizacja prawa* [From topics of theory and philosophy of law: instrumentalization of law], Kolonia Limited, Wrocław, 2000

KOZIOŁ Agata A.: *Organizacja prac nad prawem cywilnym w Polsce w latach 1945–1946* [The Organisation of Civil Law Drafting in Poland 1945–1946], Z Dziejów Prawa 7 (2005), 174–186

KOZYR-KOWALSKI Stanisław: *Socjologia, społeczeństwo obywatelskie i państwo* [Sociology, civil society and the state], WN UAM, Poznań, 2004

KOZYR-KOWALSKI Stanisław: *Struktura gospodarcza i formacja społeczeństwa* [Economic structure and the formation of society], Książka i Wiedza, Warsaw, 1988

KOZYR-KOWALSKI Stanisław, Jarosław ŁADOSZ: *Dialektyka a społeczeństwo: wstęp do materializmu historycznego* [Dialectics and society: an introduction to historical materialism], PWN, Warsaw, 1979

KRAJEWSKI Jan: *Gwarancje ochrony własności społecznej w postępowaniu cywilnym (rozpoznawczym)* [The guarantees of the protection of social property in the civil proceedings (examination proceedings)], PiP 7 (1965), 32–46

KUBIAK-CYRUL Agnieszka: *Dobra osobiste osób prawnych* [Personality Rights of Legal Persons], Wolters Kluwer, Warsaw, 2005

KUISZ Jarosław: *Ende eines Mythos. Polen, Ostmitteleuropa und das Bils vom Westen*, Osteuropa, 66 (2016)/1–2, 201–220

KUISZ Jarosław: *The two faces of European disillusionment. An end to myth about the West and the East* in *The Legacy of Division: East and West after 1989*, Lisjak L. GABRIJELČIČ, Ferenc LACZO (eds), CEUP, Budapest-New York, 2020, 254–263

KÜHN Zdeněk: *The Judiciary in Central and Eastern Europe: Mechanical Jurisprudence in Transformation?*, Martinus Nijhoff, Leiden-Boston, 2011

KUKOVEC Damjan: *Hierarchies as Law*, Columbia Journal of European Law 21 (2014) 1, 131–193

KURATÓW-KURATOWSKI Roman: *O zdolności prawnej mężatek według Kodeksu Cywilnego Polskiego* [On the legal capacity of married women according to the Polish Civil Code], GSW 39 (1919), 375–377

KUSKA-ŻAK Ilona, Marcin ŻAK: *Kierunki proponowanych zmian francuskiego prawa zobowiązań* [Directions of proposed changes to the French law of obligations], KPP 4 (2008), 1071–1098

LACLAU Ernesto: *Emancipations(s)*, Verso, London-New York, 2007

LAKOFF George, Mark JOHNSON: *Metaphors We Live By* [1980], University of Chicago Press, Chicago-London, 2003

ŁAKOMY Jakub: *Hermeneutic Universalism: A Post-analytical Inquiry into the Political of Legal Interpretation*, in *A Post-analytical Approach to Philosophy and Theory of Law*, Andrzej BATOR, Zbigniew PULKA (eds), Peter Lang, Berlin, 2019, 39–56

ŁAKOMY Jakub: *Polityczność (teorii) wykładni prawa. Perspektywa neopragmatyzmu Stanleya Fisha* [The political character of (the theory of) legal interpretation: the perspective of Stanley Fish's neopragmatism], Archiwum Filozofii Prawa i Filozofii Społecznej 3 (2018), 24–37

ŁAKOMY Jakub: *The Space of The Political in Legal Interpretation (Some Remarks On The Dworkin-Fish Debate)*, in *Law, Space and the Political: an East-West Perspective*, Paulina BIEŚ-SROKOSZ, Rafał MAŃKO, Jacek SROKOSZ (eds), Podobiński Publishing, Częstochowa, 2019, 127–137

LANDAU Zbigniew, Wojciech ROSZKOWSKI: *Polityka gospodarcza II RP i PRL* [The economic policies of the Second Polish Republic and of the Polish People's Republic], WN PWN, Warsaw, 1995

LANDO Ole: *Salient Features of the Principles of European Contract Law: A Comparison with the UCC*, Pace International Law Review, 13 (2011), 339–369

LANG Wiesław: *Aksjologia polskiego systemu prawa w okresie transformacji ustrojowej* [Axiology of the Polish legal system in the period of systemic transformation, in *Zmiany społeczne a zmiany w prawie, Aksjologia. Konstytucja. Integracja europejska* [Social change and legal change: axiology, constitution, European integration], Leszek LESZCZYŃSKI (ed.), WUMCS, Lublin, 1999, 47–55

LANGMAN Lauren, Dan ALBANESE: *Political Economy and the Normative: Marx on Human Nature and the Quest for Dignity*, in *Constructing Marxist Ethics: Critique, Normativity, Praxis*, Michael J. THOMPSON (ed.), Brill, Leiden, 2015, 59–85

LANGROD Jerzy Stefan: *O kodyfikację w Polsce (z powodu artykułu p. Adama Bobkowskiego)* [For a codification in Poland (on account of the article by Mr Adam Bobkowski)], GSW 48 (1927), 665–669

LAPIERRE Jerzy: *Kontrola sądowa czynności dyspozycyjnych stron i uczestników w postępowaniu cywilnym* [The judicial control of dispositive actions of the parties and the participants in civil proceedings], in *Księga pamiątkowa ku czci Kamila Stefki* [Commemorative book in honour of Kamil Stefko], PWN, Wrocław-Warsaw, 1967, 163–183

LARSSON Stefan: *Conceptions in the Code How Metaphors Explain Legal Challenges in Digital Times*, OUP, Oxford, 2017

LARSSON Stefan: *Metaphors and Norms: Understanding Copyright Law in a Digital Society*, Lund University, Lund, 2012

LEITER Brian: *The Hermeneutics of Suspicion: Recovering Marx, Nietzsche, and Freud*, The University of Texas School of Law. Public Law and Legal Theory Working Paper 72 (2005), 74–105

LEOPOLD David: *Marxism and Ideology: From Marx to Althusser*, in *The Oxford Handbook of Political Ideologies*, Michael FREEDEN, Lyman Tower SARGENT, Marc STEARS (eds), OUP, Oxford, 2013, 20–37

LERNELL Leszek: *Nasz jubileusz: uwagi z okazji 50 zeszytu 'Demokratycznego Przeglądu Prawniczego'* [Our jubilee: remarks on the occasion of the 50th issue of the Demokratyczny Przegląd Prawniczy], DPP 12 (1949), 21–25

ŁĘTOWSKA Ewa: *Konwencja Europejska w Polsce i nowe myślenie o prawie* [The European convention in Poland and the new thinking about law], KPP 1–5 (1992), 147–160

ŁĘTOWSKA Ewa: *Ochrona konsumentów: propozycja wzmocnienia mechanizmów ochronnych przewidzianych w kodeksie cywilnym* [Consumer protection: a proposal to strengthen the protective mechanisms provided by the Civil Code], in *Obywatelskie inicjatywy ustawodawcze Solidarności 1980–1990: materiały i projekty ustaw Centrum Obywatelskich Inicjatyw Ustawodawczych 'S' i Społecznej Rady Legislacyjnej* [The citizens' legislative initiatives of Solidarity. Materials and legislative drafts of the Solidarity Centre for Citizens' Legislative Action and Social Legislative Council], Kazimierz BARCZYK, Stanisław GRODZISKI, Stefan GRZYBOWSKI (eds), Wydawnictwo Sejmowe, Warsaw, 2001, 344–345

ŁĘTOWSKA Ewa, Czesława ŻUŁAWSKA: *Uwagi dotyczące projektu ogólnych warunków gwarancji jakości oraz związanego z nimi projektu karty gwarancyjnej* [Remarks concerning the draft of general terms of the quality guarantee and the draft warranty card associated thereto], in *Obywatelskie inicjatywy ustawodawcze Solidarności 1980–1990: materiały i projekty ustaw Centrum Obywatelskich Inicjatyw Ustawodawczych 'S' i Społecznej Rady Legislacyjnej* [The citizens' legislative initiatives of Solidarity. Materials and legislative drafts of the Solidarity Centre for Citizens' Legislative Action and Social Legislative Council], Kazimierz BARCZYK, Stanisław GRODZISKI, Stefan GRZYBOWSKI (eds), Wydawnictwo Sejmowe, Warsaw, 2001, 339–342

ŁĘTOWSKA Ewa, Janusz ŁĘTOWSKI: *Co wynika dla sądów z konstytucyjnej zasady podziału władz* [What follows for the courts from the constitutional principle of separation of powers], in *Konstytucja i gwarancje jej przestrzegania. Księga pamiątkowa ku czci prof. Janiny Zakrzewskiej* [The Constitution and guarantees of its being respected: a commemorative book in honour of Professor Janina Zakrzewska], Janusz TRZCIŃSKI, Adam JANKIEWICZ (eds), Wydawnictwa Trybunału Konstytucyjnego, Warsaw, 1996, 383–395

ŁĘTOWSKA Ewa, Janusz ŁĘTOWSKI: *O państwie, administrowaniu i sądach w okresie przekształceń ustrojowych* [Of the state, administration and courts in a period of constitutional transformation], Scholar, Warsaw, 1995

LIKHOVSKI Assaf: *The Intellectual History of Law*, in *The Oxford Handbook of Legal History*, Markus D. DUBBER, Christopher TOMLINS (eds), OUP, Oxford, 2018, 151–170

LISIEWSKI Marian: *Podstawowe problemy struktury nowego postępowania cywilnego. Streszczenie referatu wygłoszonego 18 grudnia 1956 r. na posiedzeniu Wydziały Cywilnego Komisji Kodyfikacyjnej* [Core problems of the structure of the new civil procedure. Abstract of the paper delivered on 18 December 1956 in a meeting of the Civil Department of the Codification Commission], Nowe Prawo 3 (1957), 9–17

LISIEWSKI Marian: *Projekt części ogólnej kodeksu cywilnego*, [Draft General Part of Civil Code], Przegląd Notarialny 1 (1948) 4, 287–294

LISIEWSKI Marian: *Scalenie postępowania spornego i niespornego* [The consolidation of litigious and non-litigious proceedings], Zeszyty Naukowe Uniwersytetu Łódzkiego 14 (1959), 50–65

LITAUER Jan Jakób: *O metodzie wypełniania luk prawnych* [On the method of filling legal lacunae], PiP 7–8 (1947), 14–22

LITAUER Jan Jakób: *Pogląd ogólny na istotę i rozwój procesu cywilnego* [A general overview of the essence and development of civil trial], KPCiK 1 (1919)/1–4, 27–42

LITWIN Józef: *Recepcja prawa polskiego na Ziemiach Odzyskanych* [Reception of Polish Law in the Recovered Territories], PiP 1 (1946), 12–23

LITWIN Józef: *Z problematyki styku prawa cywilnego z administracyjnym* [From the topics of the intersection of civil and administrative law], PiP 2 (1965), 540–555

LITYŃSKI Adam: *Dwie wielkie transformacje prawa sądowego w Polsce XX wieku: koncepcje i ich realizacja* [The two great transformations of court-system law in the Poland of the 20th century. Concepts and implementation], in Andrzej AJNENKIEL (ed.), *W pięćsetlecie Konstytucji Nihil Novi: z dziejów stanowienia prawa w Polsce* [On the five-hundredth anniversary of the Nihil Novi Constitution: from the history of lawmaking in Poland], Wyższa Szk. Handlu i Prawa w Warszawie, Warsaw, 2006, 108–128

LITYŃSKI Adam: *Nowe ustawodawstwo w nowym ustroju: o prawie karnym i cywilnym w pierwszym dwudziestoleciu Polski Ludowej* [New legislation in a new political system. On criminal and civil law in the first twenty years of the People's Poland], MHI 4 (2006), 122–141

LITYŃSKI Adam: *O prawie i sądach początków Polski Ludowej* [On the law and courts of the beginnings of the People's Poland], Temida 2, Białystok, 1999

LITYŃSKI Adam: *Prawo Rosji i ZSRR 1917–1991* [Law of Russia and the USSR, 1917–1991], C. H. Beck, Warsaw, 2012

LITYŃSKI Adam: *Wydział Karny Komisji Kodyfikacyjnej II Rzeczypospolitej: dzieje prac nad częścią ogólną kodeksu karnego* [The Criminal Section of the Codification Commission of the Second Polish Republic: a history of the works on the general part of the Criminal Code], UŚ, Katowice, 1991

LÖHNIG Martin, Anna MOSZYŃSKA (eds): *Laboratorium für internationale gesetzgeberische Arbeit: Die Geburt der polnischen Rechtsordnung der Zwischenkriegszeit im europäischen Kontext*, Böhlau Verlag, Wien, 2021

LÖHNIG Martin, Stephan WAGNER (eds): *Nichtgeborene Kinder des Liberalismus? Zivilgesetzgebung im Mitteleuropa der Zwischenkriegszeit*, Mohr Siebeck, Tübingen, 2018

LONGCHAMPS DE BÉRIER Roman: *Zobowiązania*, Księgarnia Akademicka, Poznań, 1948

ŁOPATKA Adam: *Rozwój społeczeństwa socjalistycznego w Polsce* [The development of socialist society in Poland], Ruch Prawniczy i Ekonomiczny 4 (1964), 1–16

ŁOPATKA Adam: *Wstęp do prawoznawstwa* [Introduction to jurisprudence], PWN, Warsaw, 1975

LUBIŃSKI Kazimierz: *Tendencje unifikacyjne w rozwoju postępowania cywilnego* [Unification tendencies in the development of civil procedure], in *Księga pamiątkowa ku czci Profesora Witolda Broniewicza* [A commemorative book in honour of Professor Witold Broniewicz], Andrzej MARCINIAK (ed.), WUŁ, Łódź, 1998, 225–247

LUKASHEVA Elena A.: *Socjalistyczna świadomość prawna i praworządność* [Socialist legal consciousness and rule of law], PWN, Warsaw, 1977

MACHEREY Pierre: *Judith Butler and the Althusserian theory of subjection*, Stephanie BUNDY (trans.), Décalages 1 (2013) 2, 1–22

MACHNIKOWSKA Anna: *Nowe prawo własności – przekształcenia w stosunkach własnościowych w Polsce w latach 1944–1950* [New prioprietorship – privatization transformations in Poland in years 1944–1950], Zeszyty Prawnicze UKSW 11 (2011)/2, 256–276

MACHNIKOWSKA Anna: *O niezawisłości sędziów i niezależności sądów w trudnych czasach: wymiar sprawiedliwości w pułapce sprawności* [On judicial independence in difficult times. The justice system in the trap of efficiency], Wolters Kluwer Polska, Warsaw, 2017

MACHNIKOWSKA Anna: *The Principles of the Code of Civil Procedure*, in Anna MACHNIKOWSKA, Anna STAWARSKA-RIPPEL: *The Principles of Civil Procedure in Poland in the Twentieth Century. Doctrine, Drafts and Law in a Comparative Perspective*, Comparative Law Review, 21 (2016), 122–148

MACHNIKOWSKA Anna: *Prawo własności w Polsce w latach 1944–1981: studium historycznoprawne* [The right of ownership in Poland between 1944 and 1981: a study in legal history], WUG, Gdańsk, 2010

MACHNIKOWSKA Anna: *Wpływ ustawodawstwa stanu wojennego na prawo cywilne* [The influence of Martial Law legislation on civil law], Studia nad Autorytaryzmem i Totalitaryzmem 39 (2017) 3, 23–47

MACHNIKOWSKA Anna: *Wymiar sprawiedliwości w Polsce w latach 1944–1950* [The administration of justice in Poland in 1944–1950], WUG, Gdańsk, 2008

MACQUEEN Hector L.: *Private Law's Revolutionaries: Authors, Codifiers and Merchants?* in *Revolution and Evolution in Private Law*, Sarah WORTHINGTON, Andrew ROBERTSON, Graham VIGO (eds), Bloomsbury, Oxford-Portland, 2018, 52–65

MĄCZYŃSKI Andrzej: *Dawne i nowe instytucje polskiego prawa mieszkaniowego*, [New and old institutions of Polish housing law], KPP 11 (2002) 1, 65–114

MĄCZYŃSKI Andrzej: *Uwagi o stanie nauki polskiego prawa cywilnego* [Comments on the state of the Polish civil law science], PiP 6 (2011), 3–17

MĄCZYŃSKI Andrzej: *Ustawa o Komisji Kodyfikacyjnej w pracach Społecznej Rady Legislacyjnej* [The Act on the Codification Commission in the works of the Social Legislative Council], in *Wkład krakowskiego i ogólnopolskiego środowiska prawniczego w budowę podstaw ustrojowych III Rzeczypospolitej (1980–1994): projekty i inicjatywy ustawodawcze, ludzie, dokumenty i oceny*, [The Contribution of the

Krakow and national legal environment to the construction of the political foundations of The Third Polish Republic (1980–1994): legislative projects and initiatives people: achievements and evaluations], Stanisław GRODZISKI (ed.), Księgarnia Akademicka, Krakow, 2018, 155–160

MAK Chantal: *Fundamental Rights in European Contract Law: A Comparison of the Impact of Fundamental Rights on Contractual Relationships in Germany, the Netherlands, Italy and England*, Kluwer Law International, Alphen aan den Rijn, 2008

MAK Vanessa: *The Consumer in European Regulatory Private Law. A Functional Perspective on Responsibility, Protection and Empowerment*, in *The Image(s) of the Consumer in EU Law: Legislation, Free Movement and Competition Law*, Dorota LECZYKIEWICZ, Stephen WEATHERILL (eds), Hart Publishing, Oxford, 2016, 381–400

MAKOWSKI Wacław: *W sprawie ujednostajnienia ustawodawstwa* [Concerning the harmonization of legislation], GSW 2–3 (1919), 13–18

MALEC Dorota: *Dzieje notariatu polskiego* [The history of Polish notaries], WUJ, Krakow, 2007

MALINOWSKI Ryszard: *Węzłowe problemy prawa administracyjnego w zarządzaniu gospodarką narodową* [Seminal problems of administrative law in the management of the national economy], PWN, Warsaw, 1975

MANELI Mieczysław: *Pojęcie funkcji państwa* [The concept of the state's function], PiP 1 (1957), 10–28

MANGABEIRA UNGER Roberto: *The Critical Legal Studies Movement: Another Times, A Greater Task*, Verson, New York, 2015

MAŃKO Rafał: *Artur Kozak's juriscentrist concept of law: A Central European innovation in legal theory*, Review of Central and East European Law 45 (2020) 2, 334–375

MAŃKO Rafał: *The Centre–Periphery Antagonism in Adjudication: A Case Study on the Spatial Dimension of the Political*, Acta Universitatis Lodziensis. Folia Iuridica, 94 (2021), 121–140

MAŃKO Rafał: *Critique of the 'Juridical': Some Metatheoretical Remarks*, Journal of the University of Latvia. Law 11 (2018), 24–37

MAŃKO Rafał: *Ideology and Legal Interpretation: Some Theoretical Considerations*, in *Constitutional Values in Contemporary Legal Space*, Kalvis TORGĀNS et al. (eds), University of Latvia Press, Riga, 2016, 117–126

MAŃKO Rafał: *Is the Socialist Legal Tradition 'Dead and Buried'? The Continuity of the Certain Elements of Socialist Legal Culture in Polish Civil Procedure*, in *Private Law and the Many Cultures of Europe*, Thomas WILHELMSSON, Elina PAUNIO, Annika POHJOLAINEN (eds), Kluwer Law International, Alphen aan den Rijn, 2007, 83–103

MAŃKO Rafał: *Judicial Decision-Making, Ideology and the Political: towards an Agonistic Theory of Adjudication*, Law and Critique 33 (2022), 175–194

MAŃKO Rafał: *Koncepcja interpelacji ideologicznej a krytyczny dyskurs o prawie* [The notion of ideological interpellation and critical discourse on law], Archiwum Filozofii Prawa i Filozofii Społecznej 8 (2004) 1, 41–54

MAŃKO Rafał: *Legal Form, Ideology and the Political*, in *Legal Scholarship and the Political*, Adam SULIKOWSKI, Rafał MAŃKO, Jakub ŁAKOMY (eds), C.H. Beck, Warsaw, 2020, 17–40

MAŃKO: Rafał: *Legal Survivals: A Conceptual Tool for Analysing Post-transformation Continuity of Legal Culture*, in *Tiesību efektivitāte postmodernā sabiedrībā* [Effectiveness of law in postmodern society], Jānis ROZENFELDS et al. (eds), LU Akadēmiskais apgāds, Riga, 2015, 16–27

MAŃKO Rafał: *Legislation and the Political: Towards a Critical Legisprudence*, in *New Perspectives on Legislation: A Comparative Approach*, Paweł CHMIELNICKI, Adam SULIKOWSKI (eds), Peter Lang, Berlin, 2020, 11–36

MAŃKO Rafał: *Nauki prawne wobec problemu polityczności: zagadnienia wybrane z perspektywy jurysprudencji krytycznej* [Legal sciences and the problem of the political: the perspective of critical jurisprudence], Archiwum Filozofii Prawa i Filozofii Społecznej 3 (2018), 38–50

MAŃKO Rafał: *Orzekanie w polu polityczności* [Adjudication in the field of the political], Filozofia Publiczna i Edukacja Demokratyczna 7 (2018) 1, 65–95

MAŃKO Rafał: *Quality of Legislation Following a Transition from Really Existing Socialism to Capitalism: A Case Study of General Clauses in Polish Private Law*, in *The Quality of Legal Acts and Its Importance in Contemporary Legal Space* Jānis ROZENFELDS (ed.), University of Latvia Press, Riga, 2012, 540–561

MAŃKO Rafał: *'Reality is For Those Who Cannot Sustain the Dream': Fantasies of Selfhood in Legal Texts*, Wroclaw Review of Law, Administration and Economics 5 (2015) 1, 24–47

MAŃKO Rafał: *Relikty w kulturze prawnej: uwagi metodologiczne na tle pozostałości epoki socjalizmu realnego w polskim prawie prywatnym* [Relicts in legal culture: methodological remarks against the background of remnants of real socialism in Polish private law], in *Postanalityczna filozofia prawa* [Postanalytical philosophy of law], Mariusz JABŁOŃSKI, Michał PAŹDZIORA (eds), Przegląd Prawa i Administracji 102 (2015), 185–208

MAŃKO Rafał: *The Unification of Private Law in Europe from the Perspective of the Polish Legal Culture*, Yearbook of Polish European Studies 11 (2007–2008), 109–137

MAŃKO Rafał: *Unifikacja prawa prywatnego w Europie z perspektywy społeczeństwa polskiego* [Unification of private law in Europe from the perspective of Polish society], Nowa Europa – Przegląd Natoliński 2 (2008), 35–84

MAŃKO Rafał: *'We Do Not Recognise Anything "Private"': Public Interest and Private Law Under the Socialist Legal Tradition and Beyond*, in *Private Interest and Public Interest in European Legal Tradition*, Bronisław SITEK et al. (eds), Olsztyn, 2015, 31–65

MAŃKO Rafał: *W stronę krytycznej filozofii orzekania. Polityczność, etyka, legitymizacja* [Towards a critical theory of adjudication: the political, ethics, legitimacy], WUŁ, Łódź, 2018

MAŃKO Rafał: *Weeds in the Gardens of Justice? The Survival of Hyperpositivism in Polish Legal Culture as Symptom/Sinthome*, Pólemos: Journal of Law, Literature and Culture 7 (2013) 2, 207–233

MAŃKO Rafał, Jakub ŁAKOMY: *In search for the ontological presuppositions of critical jurisprudence*, Critique of Law 10 (2018) 2, 469–486

MARKOWSKI Wacław: *Z zagadnień cywilnoprawnej ochrony własności społecznej* [From topics in the civil-law protection of socialized property], BMS 7–8 (1959), 30–36

MARODY Mirosława: *Oswajanie rzeczywistości. Między realnym socjalizmem a realnądemokracją*, Instytut Studiów Społecznych UW, Warsaw, 1996

MARRANI David: *Althusser in Avatar: Comparative Law as a Science and the Haunting of the Subject*, in *Althusser and Law*, Laurent DE SUTTER (ed.), Routledge, Abington, 2013, 95–110

MAWANI Renisa: *Archival Legal History: Towards the Ocean as Archive*, in *The Oxford Handbook of Legal History*, Markus D. DUBBER, Christopher TOMLINS (eds), OUP, Oxford, 2018, 291–309

MAŻEWSKI Lech: *Cel doraźny – porządek autorytarny* [An extemporaneous goal – an authoritarian order], Przegląd Polityczny 11 (1988), 195–199

MERCESCU Alexandra: *What Kind of Critique for Central and Eastern European Legal Studies? Comparison as One of the Answers*, Folia Iuridica 89 (2019), 45–61

MERCESCU Alexandra: *Pour une comparaison des droits indisciplinė*, Helbing Lichtehain Verlag, Basel, 2018

MICHALEWSKA-PAWLAK Małgorzata: *Obywatelskość demokratyczna jako idea normatywna w koncepcjach polityczno-programowych polskiej opozycji w latach 1980–1989* [Democratic civilness as a normative ideal in the politico-programmatic concepts of the Polish opposition in 1980–1989], ECS, Gdańsk, 2010

MILIBAND Ralph: *Marxism and Politics* [1977], OUP, Oxford, 1986

MOSZYŃSKA Anna: *Endeavours for International Unification of Law in the Interwar Period*, Rechtskultur 6 (2017), 29–34

MOSZYŃSKA Anna: *Geneza prawa spadkowego w polskim kodeksie cywilnym z 1964 roku* [The origin of inheritance law in Polish Civil Code of 1964], WN UMK, Toruń, 2019

MOSZYŃSKA Anna: *Polen: Codification of the civil law in Interwar Poland*, in *Nichtgeborene Kinder des Liberalismus? Zivilgesetzgebung im Mitteleuropa der Zwischenkriegszeit*, Martin LÖHNIG, Stephan WAGNER (eds), Mohr Siebeck, Tübingen, 2018, 149–194

MOSZYŃSKA Anna: *Politics and Inheritance Law: Endeavours to Keep Classical Rules of Inheritance Law in the Polish Civil Code*, Studia Iuridica Toruniensia 13 (2013), 131–147

MOSZYŃSKA Anna: *Prace nad kodyfikacją majątkowego prawa cywilnego w latach 1950–52* [Works on the codification of the property civil law in the years 1950–52], MHI 14 (2015) 2, 165–180

MOSZYŃSKA Anna: *Succession Law in People's Republic of Poland: Towards Western European or Soviet Standards?* in *Judiciary and Society between Privacy and Publicity*, Danuta JANICKA (ed.), WN UMK, Toruń, 2016, 259–276

MOSZYŃSKA Anna: *Work on the Polish Civil Code in Stalinist Period (1948–1956)*, Právněhistorické studie 2 (2019), 30–38

MOUFFE Chantal: *On the Political*, Routledge, Abington-New York, 2005

MOUFFE Chantal: *Agonistics: Thinking the World Politically*, Verso, London, 2013

MUSZALSKI Edward: *O narodowe prawo cywilne* [For a national civil law], Współczesna Myśl Prawnicza 11 (1938), 27–34

MYCIELSKI Andrzej: *Polskie prawo polityczne (Konstytucja z 17 III 2021 r.)* [Polish political law (Constitution of 17 March 1921)], Przełom, Krakow, 1947

NANCKA Grzegorz: *Próba wykorzystania prawa rzymskiego w międzywojennej kodyfikacji prawa rzymskiego? Ignacy Koschembahr-Łyskowski i 'koncepcja podstawowa prawa zobowiązań'* [An attempt to apply Roman law in the interwar codification of Polish civil law? Ignacy Koschembahr-Łyskowski and his 'basic concept of the law of obligation'], Zeszyty Prawnicze, 22 (2022), 111–134

NEACŞU E. Dana: *CLS Stands for Critical Legal Studies, If Anyone Remembers*, Journal of Law and Policy 8 (2000), 415–453

NICOLAESCU Cristina: *Bourdieu – Habitus, Symbolic Violence, the Gift: »You give me / I give you« Principle*, Euromentor Journal 1 (2010) 3, 1–10

NIECIUŃSKI Witold: *Czterdzieści pięć i dziewięć lat polityki mieszkaniowej w Polsce* [Forty-five and nine years of housing policy in Poland], in *Przeszłość i przyszłość polskiej polityki mieszkaniowej* [The past and the future of Polish housing policy], Lucyna FRĄCKIEWICZ (ed.), IPiSS, Warsaw, 2005, 113–121

NOSZCZAK Bartłomiej: *Sacrum czy profanum? Spór o istotę obchodów Milenium Polskiego (1949–1966)* [The sacrum or the profanum? The dispute about the character of the celebrations of the Polish Millennium (1949–1966)], Towarzystwo Naukowe Warszawskie, Warsaw, 2002

NOVKOV Julie: *Law and Political Ideologies*, in *The Oxford Handbook of Law and Politics*, Gregory A. CALDEIRA, R. Daniel KELEMEN, Keith E. WHITTINGTON (eds), OUP, Oxford, 2008, 626–643

NOWACKI Józef: *Niektóre zagadnienia zasad współżycia społecznego* [Certain issues regarding the principles of social coexistence], PiP 7 –8 (1957), 99–113

NOWACKI Józef: *Praworządność: wybrane problemy teoretyczne* [Rule of law: selected theoretical topics], PWN, Warsaw, 1977

NOWAK Leszek: *U podstaw teorii socjalizmu* [At the foundation of the theory of socialism], Nankom, Poznań, 1991

OCHMAŃSKI Jerzy: *Administracja świadcząca: kształtowanie się idei organizatorskiej funkcji państwa w Polsce Ludowej (1944–1989)* [A providing administration. The formation of the ideal of the organizing function of the state in People's Poland (1944–1989)], WUAM, Poznań, 2006

OHANOWICZ Alfred: *Odpowiedzialność za czyny niedozwolone w projekcie kodeksu cywilnego PRL* [Tort liability in the draft Civil Code of the Polish People's Republic], Ruch Prawniczy i Ekonomiczny 4 (1960), 53–67

OLSEN Fran: *The Politics of Family Law*, Law & Inequality: A Journal of Theory and Practice 2 (1984) 1, 1–19

OPAŁEK Kazimierz: *Formalne i materialne pojęcie praworządności* [The formal and the substative concept of rule of law], in *Rozprawy prawnicze: księga pamiątkowa dla uczczenia pracy naukowej Kazimierza Przybyłowskiego* [Legal dissertations: a commemorative book to honour the academic work of Kazimierz Przybyłowski], Wacław OSUCHOWSKI, Mieczysław SOŚNIAK, Bronisław WALASZEK (eds), PWN, Krakow-Warsaw, 1964, 201–208

OPAŁEK Kazimierz: *Praworządność* [Rule of law], in *Zagadnienia prawa karnego i teorii prawa: księga pamiątkowa ku czci profesora Władysława Woltera* [Topics of criminal law and theory of law: a commemorative book in honour of Professor Władysław Wolter], Marian CIEŚLAK (ed.), Wydawnictwo Prawnicze, Warsaw, 1959, 129–133

OPAŁEK Kazimierz: *Spór o pojęcie praworządności* [The dispute about the concept of rule of law], PiP 10 (1959), 519–535

OPAŁEK Kazimierz, Jerzy WRÓBLEWSKI: *Zagadnienia teorii prawa* [Topics of theory of law], PWN, Warsaw, 1969

ORLEWICZ Tadeusz: *Z rozważań o narodzie i państwie* [From ponderings on the nation and on the state], Prawo 5–6 (1936), 167–176

OSAJDA Konrad: *Głos w obronie klauzuli zasad współżycia społecznego (głos w dyskusji)* [A voice in defence of the clause of the principles of social coexistence (a voice in the discussion)], in *Europeizacja prawa prywatnego* [The europeanisation of private law], Maksymilian PAZDAN et al. (eds), Wolters Kluwer, Warsaw, 2008, vol. 2, 113–116

OZDOWSKI Jerzy: *Problem własności w społecznej gospodarce rynkowej* [The problem of ownership in a social market economy], in *Własność i demokracja* [Property and democracy], Piotr KACZANOWSKI (ed.), Fundacja ATK, Warsaw, 1995, 34–38

PAŁECKI Krzysztof: *Społecznie oczekiwany wzorzec orzekania sądowego* [The socially expected model of judicial decision-making], in *Sądy w opinii społeczeństwa polskiego* [The courts in the opinion of Polish society], MARIA BORUCKA-ARCTOWA, Krzysztof PAŁECKI (eds), Ratio, Krakow, 2003, 149–162

PARCZEWSKI Alfons: *Uwagi nad kodyfikacją prawa cywilnego w Polsce* [Remarks on the codification of civil law in Poland], Rocznik Prawniczy Wileński 1 (1925), 1–69

PARCZEWSKI Alfons: *Z powodu recenzji pierwszego 'Rocznika Prawniczego Wileńskiego' w 'Gazecie Sądowej Warszawskiej'* [On account of the review of the first issue of Rocznik Prawniczy Wileński in the Gazeta Sądowa Warszawska], Rocznik Prawniczy Wileński 2 (1928), 571–573

PASHUKANIS Evgeny B.: *Law and Marxism: A General Theory*, Barbara EINHORN (transl.), Pluto Press, London, 1983

PATELL Shireen R. K.: *Disciplinarity*, Social Text 27 (2009) 3, 104–111

PAŹDZIORA Michał, Michał STAMBULSKI: *Co może dać nauce prawa polityczność: przyczynek do dalszych badań* [What can legal scholarship gain from the political: notes towards further research], Archiwum Filozofii Prawa i Filozofii Społecznej 2 (2014), 55–66

PECZENIK Aleksander: *Weighing Values*, International Journal for the Semiotics of Law 14 (1992) 5, 137–152

PERETIATKOWICZ Antoni: *Studia prawnicze* [Legal studies], Księgarnia Św. Wojciecha w Poznaniu, Poznań, 1938

PERSAK Krzysztof: *'Troskliwy opiekun i światły doradca Polski Ludowej': poprawki Józefa Stalina do Konstytucji PRL z 22 lipca 1952 r.* ['The attentive protector and enlightened advisor of the People's Poland': Joseph Stalin's corrections to the Constitution of the People's Republic of Poland of 22 July 1952], in *PRL: trwanie i zmiana* [The People's Republic of Poland: persistence and change], Dariusz STOLA, Marcin ZAREMBA (eds), WSPIZ im. Koźmińskiego, Warsaw, 2003, 187–209

PIASECKI Kazimierz: *Nadużycie praw procesowych przez strony* [The abuse of procedural rights by the parties], Palestra 11 (1960), 20–28

PIASKOWY Anna: *Klauzule generalne w projekcie nowego kodeksu cywilnego* [General clauses in the draft of new Polish Civil Code], Transformacje Prawa Prywatnego 3 (2012), 49–67

PIĄTOWSKI Józef Stanisław: *Polskie prawo narodowe* [A national Polish law], Współczesna Myśl Prawnicza 12 (1936), 8–11

PIĄTOWSKI Józef Stanisław (ed.): vol. 4: *Prawo spadkowe* [Inheritance law], in *System prawa cywilnego* [The system of civil law], ZN im. Ossolińskich, Wrocław-Waraw- Krakow-Gdańsk-Łódź, 1986

PIĄTOWSKI Józef Stanisław: *Rozdrobnienie gospodarstw rolnych a prawo spadkowe* [The fragmentation of farms and inheritance law], PiP 4–5 (1960), 661–678

PIĄTOWSKI Józef Stanisław: *Stosunki majątkowe między małżonkami* [Property relations between spouses], Wydawnictwo Prawnicze, Warsaw, 1955

PIĄTOWSKI Józef Stanisław, Agnieszka KAWALKO, Hanna WITCZAK: vol. 10: *Prawo spadkowe* [Inheritance law], in *System prawa prywatnego* [The system of private law], Zbigniew RADWAŃSKI (ed.), C. H. Beck, Warsaw, 2015, 67–212

PILICH Mateusz: *Zasady współżycia społecznego, dobre obyczaje czy dobra wiara? Dylematy nowelizacji klauzul generalnych prawa cywilnego w perspektywie europejskiej* [Principles of social community life, good customs or good faith? Dilemmas of amending the general vlauses of civil law in a European perspective], in *Europeizacja prawa prywatnego* [The europeanisation of private law], Maksymilian PAZDAN et al. (eds), 'Wolters Kluwer, Warsaw, 2008, vol. 2, 37–57

PIPES Richard: *Komunizm*, Świat Książki, Warsaw, 2008 [in English: Communism: the Vanished Specter, OUP, 1994]

PISULIŃSKI Jerzy: *Struktura części ogólnej prawa zobowiązań (wprowadzenie do dyskusji)* [The structure of general part of obligation law (introduction to discussion)], Transformacje Prawa Prywatnego 2 (2017), 37–51

PŁAZA Stanisław: *Historia prawa w Polsce na tle porównawczym* [A history of law in Poland against a comparative background], vol. 3: *Okres międzywojenny* [The interwar period], Księgarnia Akademicka, Krakow, 2001

PODGÓRECKI Adam: *Założenia polityki prawa: metodologia pracy legislacyjnej i kodyfikacyjnej* [Assumptions of legal policy: methodology of the lawmaking and codifying work], Wydawnictwo Prawnicze, Warsaw, 1957

POSNER Stanisław: *Nasza Komisja Kodyfikacyjna* [Our Codification Commission], Palestra 5 (1925), 780–794

POSNER Stanisław: *Rocznik wileński*, GSW 2 (1926), 28–30

PREUSS Ulrich K.: *Revolution, Fortschritt und Verfassung, Zu einem neuen Verfassungsvertändnis*, Fischer Wissenschaft, Berlin, 1994

PRUTIS Stanisław (ed.): *Przekształcenia własnościowe w Polsce (determinanty prawne)* [Reforms of property in Poland (legal determinants)], Temida2, Białystok, 1996

Przed 10-ciu laty: 'Kwartalnik Prawa Prywatnego' [Ten years ago: the Kwartalnik Prawa Prywatnego], Przegląd Notarialny 1 (1948) 4, 276–280

QUIGLEY John: *Soviet Legal Innovation and the Law of the Western World*, CUP, Cambridge, 2007

RADAČIĆ Ivana: *Feminist Legal Education in Croatia: A Question of Fundamentalism or a Fundamental Question?* in *Law and Critique in Central Europe: Questioning the Past, Resisting the Present*, Rafał MAŃKO, Cosmin CERCEL, Adam SULIKOWSKI (eds), Counterpress, Oxford, 2016, 90–105

RADWAŃSKI Zbigniew: *Ciągłość a reforma prawa w świetle doświadczeń unifikacyjnych Polskiej Rzeczypospolitej Ludowej (lata 1945–1964)* [Continuity and reform of law in the light of the unification experience of the Polish People's Republic (1945–1964)], in *Dzieje kodyfikacji prawa: materiały na konferencję historyków prawa w Karpaczu* [A history of legal codification: materials for the conference of legal historians in Karpacz], PTH, Karpacz, 1974, 162–175

RADWAŃSKI Zbigniew: *Kodyfikacja prawa cywilnego* [Codification of civil law], RPEiS 5 (2009), 131–142

RADWAŃSKI Zbigniew: *Kształtowanie się polskiego systemu prawnego w pierwszych latach Drugiej Rzeczypospolitej* [The shaping of the Polish legal system in the initial years of the Second Polish Republic], CPH 21 (1969) 1, 31–48

RADWAŃSKI Zbigniew: *Najem lokali w świetle przepisów kodeksu cywilnego a prawo lokalowe* [Apartment lease in the light of the provisions of civil law versus apartment law], PiP 2 (1966), 216–230

RADWAŃSKI Zbigniew: *Trzy lata działalności Komisji Kodyfikacyjnej Prawa Cywilnego* [The three years of operation of the Codification Commission for Civil Law], PiP 4 (2000), 3–10

RADWAŃSKI Zbigniew: *Uwagi do sprawozdania z dyskusji przeprowadzonej w izbie Cywilnej Sądu Najwyższego nad 'Projektem Kodeksu cywilnego. Księga Pierwsza'* [Comments on the report on the debate held at the Civil Chamber of the Supreme Court on the 'Draft Civil Code. Book One'], Przegląd Sądowy 5 (2010), 5–15

RADWAŃSKI Zbigniew: *Założenia dalszych prac kodyfikacyjnych na obszarze prawa cywilnego* [The assumptions for the continued codification work in the area of civil law], PiP 3 (2004), 5–13

RAJSKI Jerzy: *Kierunki rozwoju europejskiego prawa kontraktów* [Directions of development of the European law of contracts], KPP 1 (2002), 211–221

RAPPAPORT Emil Stanisław: *Czy kodyfikacja prawa cywilnego i karnego jest na czasie?* [Is a codification of civil and criminal law timely?], GSW 41 (1927), 365–366

RAPPAPORT Emil Stanisław: *Media via kodeksu karnego polskiego* [The via media in the Polish Criminal Code], Palestra 12 (1935) 4, 283–290

RAPPAPORT Emil Stanisław: *Recenzja: Leon Chajn – Trzy lata demokratyzacji prawa i wymiaru sprawiedliwości* [Review: Leon Chajn – Three years of democratization of law and administration of justice], PiP 12 (1947), 73–75

RAPPAPORT Emil Stanisław: *W poszukiwaniu prawa narodowego samoistnego* [On the search for a spontaneous national law], Palestra 15 (1938)/5, 422–441

RAWLS John: *Political Liberalism*, CUP, New York, 1996

REICH H.C. Norbert: *Transformation of Contract Law and Civil Justice in the New EU Member Countries: The Example of the Baltic States, Hungary and Poland*, Penn State International Law Review 23 (2005), 271–302

RESICH Zbigniew: *Ocena założeń kodyfikacyjnych kodeksu postępowania cywilnego* [Evaluation of the codification assumptions of the Code of Civil Procedure], in *Funkcjonowanie kodeksu postępowania cywilnego w praktyce: materiały na konferencje naukową Popowo 25–27 października 1984 r.* [Functioning of the Code of Civil Procedure in practice: materials for the academic conference in Popowo, 25–27 October 1984], Kazimierz PIASECKI (ed.), Zeszyty Naukowe Instytutu Badania Prawa Sądowego 25 (1987), 39–53

RESICH Zbigniew: *Projekt kodeksu postępowania cywilnego po pierwszym czytaniu* [The draft of the Code of Civil Procedure after the first reading], Nowe Prawo 1 (1960), 3–16

RESICH Zbigniew: *Środki odwoławcze w kodeksie postępowania cywilnego* [Appellate remedies in the Code of Civil Procedure], in *Księga pamiątkowa ku czci Kamila Stefki* [Commemorative book in honour of Kamil Stefko], Jerzy JODŁOWSKI (ed.), PWN, Warsaw, 1967, 271–285

RESICH Zbigniew; *Zasada dyspozytywności i kontradyktoryjności w procesie cywilnym PRL* [The dispositive and adversarial principles in the civil trial of the Polish People's Republic], PiP 7–8 (1957), 56–69

REYKOWSKI Janusz: *Resolving Large-scale Political Conflict: The Case of the Round Table Negotiations in Poland*, in *Conflict Between People and Groups, Causes, Processes and Resolutions*, Stephen WORCHEL, Jeffry A. SIMPSON (eds), Nelson-Hall, Chicago, 1993, 214–232

REYKOWSKI Janusz: *Wolność gospodarcza jako ideologia* [Economic freedom as an ideology], Studia Socjologiczne 210 (2013) 3, 7–29

RITTERMAN Stefan: *Charakter metodologiczny dyskusji nad podmiotem cywilistycznej własności państwowej* [The methodological character of the discussion of the rights-holder of national property], Studia Cywilistyczne 13–14 (1969), 267–288

RODAK Lidia: *Structural Violence in Law and Its Gender Dimension in Polish Law*, in Rafał MAŃKO, Cosmin CERCEL, Adam SULIKOWSKI (eds), *Law and Critique in Central Europe: Questioning the Past, Resisting the Present*, Counterpress, Oxford, 2016, 131–153

Rola prawników w państwie demokratycznym [The role of lawyers in a democratic state], NRA, Warsaw, 2005

ROT Henryk: *Problemy kodyfikacji prawa PRL* [Topics of codification of the law of Polish People's Republic], Ossolineum, Wrocław, 1978

ROZMARYN Stefan: *Jakie zmiany należy wprowadzić do Konstytucji PRL?* [What changes ought to be introduced to the Constitution of Polish People's Republic?], Trybuna Ludu, 25 March 1957

ROZWADOWSKI Władysław: *Etiam clarum ius exigit interpretationem*, in *W poszukiwaniu dobra wspólnego. Księga jubileuszowa Profesora Macieja Zielińskiego* [In a search for the common good: a jubilee book to Professor Maciej Zieliński], Agnieszka CHODUŃ, Stanisław CZEPITA (eds), WUSZ, Szczecin, 2010, 37–48

ROZWADOWSKI Władysław: *Tradycje rzymskie w polskim prawie cywilnym* [Roman traditions in Polish civil law], in *System prawa prywatnego* [The system of private law], vol. 1: *Prawo cywilne: część ogólna* [Civil law: the general part], Marek SAFJAN (ed.), C.H. Beck, Warsaw, 2007, 1–28

RUNDSTEIN Szymon: *Nowe prądy w procesie cywilnym* [New currents in civil procedure], GSW 23 (1902), 358–360

RUNDSTEIN Szymon: *W poszukiwaniu prawa cywilnego* [On the search for civil law], Księgarnia Powszechna, Warsaw-Krakow, 1939

RYBICKI Zygmunt: *Administracja gospodarcza w PRL* [The economic administration in Polish People's Republic], WN PWN, Warsaw, 1978

RYTEL-WARZOCHA Anna: *Reformy konstytucyjne w Polsce po 7 kwietnia 1989 r.* [Constitutional reforms in Poland after 7 April 1989], Toruńskie Studia Polsko-Włoskie 17 (2021), 75–86

SACCO Rodolfo: *The Romanist Substratum in the Civil Law of the Socialist Countries*, Review of Socialist Law 14 (1988) 1, 65–86

SAFJAN Marek: *European Law versus Private Law: Transformation or Deformation of the Paradigm?*, in *General Principles of EU Law and European Private Law*, Ulf BERNITZ et al. (eds), Kluwer Law International, Alphen aan den Rijn, 2013, 155–170

SAFJAN Marek: *Klauzule generalne w kodeksie cywilnym (przyczynek do dyskusji)* [General clauses in the Civil Code (a starting point of discussion)], Państwo i Prawo 11 (1990), 48–59

SAFJAN Marek: *Wyzwania dla państwa prawa* [Challenges to rule of law], Wolters Kluwer Polska, Warsaw, 2007

SAFJAN Marek, Aneta WIEWIÓROWSKA-DOMAGALSKA: *Political Foundations of European Private Law: Rethinking the East-West Division Lines*, in *The Foundations of European Private Law*, Roger BROWNSWORD et al. (eds), Hart Publishing, Oxford, 2011, 265–284

SALTER Michael G.: *Carl Schmitt: Law as Politics, Ideology and Strategic Myth*, Routledge, Abingdon-New York, 2012

SANTERA Walerian: *Ustrój sądów a rozstrzyganie spraw z zakresu prawa pracy i ubezpieczeń społecznych* [The court system and the decision-making in labour and social-insurance cases], Przegląd Sądowy 9 (2009), 5–25

SAWCZUK Mieczysław (ed.): *Czterdzieści lat kodeksu cywilnego* [Forty years of the Civil Code], Wolters Kluwer, Krakow, 2006

SCHLEGEL John Henry: *Sez who? Critical Legal History Without a Privileged Position*, in *The Oxford Handbook of Legal History*, Markus D. DUBBER, Christopher TOMLINS (eds), OUP, Oxford, 2018, 561–575

SCHLESINGER Rudolf B.: *Comparative Law: Cases, Texts, Materials*, Foundation Press, New York 1998

SCHMITT Carl: *The Concept of the Political*, G. SCHWAB (trans.), UCP, Chicago, 2007

SCHOLTE Jan Aart: *Globalization Studies: Past and Future: A Dialogue of Diversity*, Globalizations 1 (2004) 1, 102–110

SCHROEDER Mark: *'Value Theory'*, in *The Stanford Encyclopedia of Philosophy* (online), Edward N. ZALTA, Uri NODELMAN (eds)

SEIDLER Grzegorz L.: *Z zagadnień filozofii prawa* [From topics of philosophy of law], Wydawnictwo Lubelskie, Lublin, 1984

SEILER Hans H.: *Geschichte und Gegenwart im Zivilrecht*, Carl Hermanns, Köln, 2005

SIEDLECKI Władysław: *Istota procesu cywilnego z punktu widzenia interesów państwa i jednostki* [The essence of civil trial from the perspective of the interests of the state and of the individual], PiP 7–8 (1947), 46–58

SIEDLECKI Władysław: *Kilka uwag na temat wykładni i stosowania przepisów nowego Kodeksu postępowania cywilnego* [Some remarks on the interpretation and application of the provisions of the new Code of Civil Procedure], Studia Cywilistyczne 13–14 (1969), 289–304

SIEDLECKI Władysław: *Przebudowa sądowego postępowania cywilnego w Polsce Ludowej* [The overhaul of judicial civil procedure in People's Poland], Ruch Prawniczy i Ekonomiczny 21 (1959) 3, 91–106

SIEDLECKI Władysław: *System zaskarżania orzeczeń sądowych w kodeksie postępowania cywilnego PRL* [The system of remedies against judicial decisions in the Code of Civil Procedure of the Polish People's Republic], PiP 6 (1957), 1123–1142

SIEDLECKI Władysław: *Z prac Komisji Kodyfikacyjnej nad nowym kodeksem postępowania cywilnego PRL* [On the work of the Codification Commission on the new Code of Civil Procedure], Studia Cywilistyczne 1 (1961), 205–215

SIEDLECKI Władysław: *Zasada kontradyktoryjności (sporności) czy zasada współdziałania podmiotów postępowania cywilnego* [The adversarial principle or the principle of cooperation between the participants in civil proceedings], PiP 6 (1975), 63–75

SIEDLECKI Władysław: *Zasady naczelne postępowania cywilnego w świetle przepisów nowego kodeksu postępowania cywilnego* [The fundamental principles of the civil proceedings in the light of the provisions of the new Code of Civil Procedure], Studia Cywilistyczne 7 (1966), 3–43

SITEK Bronisław: *Roma communis nostra patria est (D. 50.1.33) czy może Europa communis nostra patria est?* Studia Prawnoustrojowe 12 (2010), 219–229

SKĄPSKI Józef: *Kodeks cywilny z 1964 r.: blaski i cienie kodyfikacji i jej perspektywy* [The Civil Code of 1964: pros and cons of the codification and its prospects], KPP 1 (1992), 57–76

SKĄPSKI Józef: *Wpływ zmian stosunków na zobowiązania: klauzula rebus sic stantibus* [The impact of change in circumstances on obligations – the *rebus sic stantibus* clause], in *Studia z prawa zobowiązań*, Zbigniew RADWAŃSKI (ed.), PWN, Warsaw-Poznań, 1979, 301–318

SKĄPSKI Józef: *Zagadnienia cywilistyczne prawa lokalowego* [Civil-law topics in apartment law], Nowe Prawo 7–8 (1957), 32–51

SKARŻYŃSKA Krystyna: *Człowiek a polityka: zarys psychologii politycznej* [Problems of codification of private law in Central and Eastern European countries from the perspective of the century], 2nd ed., Scholar, Warsaw, 2011

SKARŻYŃSKA Krystyna: *Czy jesteśmy prorozwojowi? Wartości i przekonania ludzi a dobrobyt i demokratyzacja kraju* [Are we prodevelopmental? The values and convictions of the people and the welfare and democratization of the country], in *Jak Polacy przegrywają, jak Polacy wygrywają* [How Poles lose, how Poles win], Marek DROGOSZ (ed.), Gdańskie Wydawnictwo Psychologiczne, Gdańsk, 2005, 69–92

ŠKOP Martin: *The Importance of Being a Linguist: Critical Legal Thought in Central Europe*, in *Law and Critique in Central Europe: Questioning the Past, Resisting the Present*, Rafał MAŃKO, Cosmin CERCEL, Adam SULIKOWSKI (eds), Counterpress, Oxford, 2016, 32–44

SKUCZYŃSKI Paweł: *The Status of Legal Ethics*, Katarzyna POPOWICZ (trans.), Peter Lang, Frankfurt am Main, 2013

SKUCZYŃSKI Paweł: *Typy myśli krytycznej w prawoznawstwie: od krytyki poznania do walki o uznanie* [Types of critical thought in jurisprudence. From critique of cognition to struggle for recognition], in *Integracja zewnętrzna i wewnętrzna nauk prawnych* [The external and internal integration of legal sciences], Tomasz BEKRYCHT et al. (eds), vol. 1, WUŁ, Łódź, 2014, 133–148

SNOPEK Paweł: *Neoliberalism, ideology, social (in)justice and post-politics*, in *Law, Space and the Political: an East-West Perspective*, Paulina BIEŚ-SROKOSZ, Rafał MAŃKO, Jacek SROKOSZ (eds), Podobiński Publishing, Częstochowa, 2019, 144–156

SÓJKA-ZIELIŃSKA Katarzyna: *Wielkie kodyfikacje cywilne: historia i współczesność* [The great civil codifications: history and the present], Liber, Warsaw. 2009

SONDEL Jan K.: *Granice kapitalizmu na wsi* [The limits of capitalism in the countryside], Przegląd ekonomiczny 11 (1934)/46–53, 92–103

ŚPIEWAK Paweł: *Pamięć po komunizmie* [The memory left behind by communism], Słowo, Gdańsk, 2005

STAMBULSKI Michał: *Polityczność w polskiej analitycznej teorii prawa: zarys problematyki* [The political in Polish analytical jurisprudence: an outline], Archiwum Filozofii Prawa i Filozofii Społecznej 3 (2019), 64–73

STANLEY Ben: *The thin ideology of populism*, Journal of Political Ideologies 13 (2008) 1, 95–110

STAWARSKA-RIPPEL Anna: *Elementy prywatne i publiczne w procesie cywilnym w świetle prac kodyfikacyjnych w Polsce (1918–1964): studium historycznoprawne* [Private and public elements in civil trial in the light of codification works in Poland (1918–1964): a historico-legal study], WUŚ, Katowice, 2015

STAWARSKA-RIPPEL Anna: *Fundamental Principles in the Views of the Authors of the Drafts of the First and Second Polish Codes on Civil Procedure: A Comparative Perspective*, in Anna MACHNIKOWSKA, Anna STAWARSKA-RIPPEL: *The Principles of Civil Procedure in Poland in the Twentieth Century. Doctrine, Drafts and Law in a Comparative Perspective*, Comparative Law Review, 21 (2016), 107–122

STAWARSKA-RIPPEL Anna: *O klauzulach generalnych w pierwszych latach Polski Ludowej słów kilka* [A few words on general clauses in the first years of People's Poland], Miscellanea iuridica 6 (2005), 117–129

STAWARSKA-RIPPEL Anna: *O politycznych założeniach procedury cywilnej w Polsce Ludowej* [On the political foundations of civil procedure in People's Poland], in *Między I a III Rzecząpospolitą. Kształtowanie europejskiej kultury prawnej: prace ofiarowane prof. zw. dr. hab. Adamowi Lityńskiemu w czterdziestolecie pracy naukowej* [Between the First and Third Republics: the shaping of a European legal culture. Works dedicated to Professor Adam Lityński on the fortieth anniversary of his academic career], Marian MIKOŁAJCZYK, Andrzej DROGOŃ. Miscellanea iuridica 7 (2005), 252–264

STAWARSKA-RIPPEL Anna: *O rekodyfikacji radzieckiego postępowania cywilnego* [On recodification of the Soviet civil procedure], Z Dziejów Prawa 4 (2011), 187–202

STAWARSKA-RIPPEL Anna: *Problemy kodyfikacji prawa prywatnego w państwach Europy Środkowo-Wschodniej z perspektywy stulecia* [The problem of private law codification in the countries of Central and Eastern Europe from the perspective of the past century], MHI 1 (2019), 43–53

STAWECKI Tomasz: *Kodeks: idea, urzeczywistnienie i ograniczenie* [The code: the idea, the realization and the limitation], in *Proces cywilny: nauka, kodyfikacja, praktyka: księga jubileuszowa dedykowana Profesorowi Feliksowi Zedlerowi* [Civil procedure: scholarship, codification, practice], Paweł GRZEGORCZYK, Krzysztof KNOPPEK, Marcin WALASIK (eds), Wolters Kluwer Polska, Warsaw, 2012, 39–56

STEC Piotr: *Kodeks cywilny: między dekodyfikacją a rekodyfikacją* [The Civil Code: between decodification and recodification], in *50 lat Kodeksu cywilnego: perspektywy rekodyfikacji* [Fifty years of the Civil Code: prospects of recodification], Piotr STEC, Mariusz ZAŁUCKI (eds), Wolters Kluwer Polska, Warsaw, 2015, 31–40

STELMACHOWSKI Andrzej: *Czy kryzys osoby prawnej?* [A crisis of the legal person?], Ruch Prawniczy i Ekonomiczny 3 (1968), 199–210

STELMACHOWSKI Andrzej: *Dobro dziecka w procesie rozwodowym* [The child's welfare in divorce litigation], Nowe Prawo 8–9 (1953), 58–66

STELMACHOWSKI Andrzej: *Przemiany polityczne 1989 r. a model prawa własności* [The political changes of 1989 and the model of the right of ownership], in *Przekształcenia własnościowe w Polsce (determinanty prawne)* [Reforms of property in Poland (Legal determinants)], Stanisław Prutis (ed.), Temida2, Białystok, 1996, 11–27

STELMACHOWSKI Andrzej: *Przysposobienie w polskim prawie rodzinnym* [Adoption in Polish family law], Wydawnictwo Prawnicze, Warsaw 1957

STELMACHOWSKI Andrzej: *Wstęp do teorii prawa cywilnego* [Introduction to the theory of civil law], PWN, Warsaw, 1969

STELMACHOWSKI Andrzej: *Zarys teorii prawa cywilnego* [An outline of the theory of civil law], PWN, Warsaw, 1998

STELMACHOWSKI Andrzej, Kamil ZARADKIEWICZ: *Modele własności i ich uwarunkowania społeczno-ustrojowe* [Ownership models and their socio-political circumstances], in *System prawa prywatnego* [The system of private law], Zbigniew RADWAŃSKI (ed.), vol. 3: *Prawo rzeczowe* [Real law], Edward GNIEWEK (ed.), C. H. Beck, Warsaw, 2013, 217–336

STOJANOWSKA Wanda: *Rozwód* [Divorce], in *System prawa prywatnego* [The system of private law], Zbigniew RADWAŃSKI (ed.), vol. 11: *Prawo rodzinne i opiekuńcze* [Family and guardianship law], Tadeusz SMYCZYŃSKI (ed.), C. H. Beck, Warszawa, 2009, 531–804

SUKIENNICKI Wiktor: *Marksowsko-leninowska teoria prawa* [Marxist-Leninist theory of law], Wileński Przegląd Prawniczy 5 (1935), 145–153; 6 (1935), 196–202

SULIKOWSKI Adam: *The Crisis of Traditional Legal Theory. A Diagnosis and View to the Future*, in *Legal Theory and Philosophy of Law: Towards Contemporary Challenges*, Andrzej BATOR, Zbigniew PULKA (eds), Scholar Publishing House, Warsaw, 2013, 227–246

SULIKOWSKI Adam: *Fundamental Rights from the Perspective of Critical Legal and Social Theory*, in: *Legal Scholarship and the Political: in Search of a New Paradigm*, Adam SULIKOWSKI, Rafał MAŃKO and Jakub ŁAKOMY (eds), C.H. Beck, Warszawa, 2020, 117–130

SULIKOWSKI Adam: *Konstytucjamizm a nowoczesność: dyskurs konstytucyjny wobec tryumfu i kryzysu moderny* [Constitutionalism and modernity: constitutional discourse towards the triumph and crisis of the modern], WUWr, Wrocław, 2012

SULIKOWSKI Adam: *Law After the Death of God. Jurisprudence and Some Assertions of the Contemporary Philosophy*, in *A Post-analytical Approach to Philosophy and Theory of Law*, Andrzej BATOR, Zbigniew PULKA (eds), Peter Lang, Berlin, 2019, 181–194

SULIKOWSKI Adam: *Perspektywy zastosowań metod Krytycznej Analizy Dyskursu w badaniach nad prawem. Kilka uwag* [Some remarks on the prospects for applying the research approach of critical discourse analysis to the study of law], Wrocławskie Studia Erazmiańskie 8 (2014), 99–111

SULIKOWSKI Adam: *Posthumanizm a prawoznawstwo* [Posthumanism and jurisprudence], WUO, Opole, 2013

SULIKOWSKI Adam: *Prawa a ideologia. Prawa jednostki z perspektywy krytycznej myśli prawniczej i społecznej (wybrane zagadnienia)* [Rights and ideology: individual rights from the perspective of critical legal and social theory (some remarks)], Roczniki Nauk Społecznych 7 (2015) 4, 17–32

SULIKOWSKI Adam, Rafał MAŃKO, Jakub ŁAKOMY: *Introduction*, in *Legal Scholarship and the Political: in Search of a New Paradigm*, Adam SULIKOWSKI, Rafał MAŃKO, Jakub ŁAKOMY (eds), C. H. Beck, Warszawa, 2020, I–XXII

SULIKOWSKI Adam, Krzysztof OTRĘBA: *O potrzebie studiów krytycznych nad prawem konstytucyjnym* [On the need for critical studies in constitutional law], PiP 3 (2017), 5–16

ŚWIĄTKOWSKI Henryk: *Społeczna myśl prawnicza w Polsce: dawniej i dzisiaj (szkic historyczno-prawny)* [Social legal thought in Poland: formerly and nowadays (a historico-legal sketch)], DPP 1 (1945), 5–11

ŚWIĄTKOWSKI Henryk: *Wykładnia prawno-społeczna (uwagi na tle okólnika w sprawie reformy rolnej)* [Legal-social interpretation (remarks in the context of the circular on the agricultural reform], DPP 1 (1945), 20–22

ŚWIDA-ZIĘBA Hanna: *Stalinizm i społeczeństwo polskie* [Stalinism and Polish society], in *Stalinizm* [Stalinism], Jacek KURCZEWSKI (ed.), Zakład Malej Poligrafii UW, Warsaw, 1991

ŚWIĘCICKA Paulina: *From Sublimation to Naturalization: Constructing Ideological Hegemony on the Shoulders of Roman Jurists*, in *Law and Critique in Central Europe: Questioning the Past, Resisting the Present*, Rafał MAŃKO, Cosmin CERCEL, Adam SULIKOWSKI (eds), Counterpress, Oxford, 2016, 176–205

ŚWIĘCICKI Łukasz: *Carl Schmitt i Leo Strauss. Krytyka pozytywizmu prawniczego w niemieckiej myśli politycznej* [Carl Schmitt and Leo Strauss: the critique of legal positivism in German political thought], von Borowiecky, Warsaw, 2015

SZER Seweryn: *Ciężary realne wobec polskiego prawa rzeczowego* [Real burdens in the light of Polish real law], PiP 9 (1947), 57–65

SZER Seweryn: *Kodeks rodzinny* [The Family Code], DPP 3 (1950), 3–15

SZER Seweryn: *Nabycie własności nieruchomości według nowego prawa rzeczowego* [Acquisition of ownership of real estate in the new Real Law], PiP 11–12 (1946), 49–57

SZER Seweryn: *Nowe prawo małżeńskie* [The new Family Law], PiP 1 (1946), 29–38

SZER Seweryn: *Nowe prawo spadkowe* [The new Inheritance Law], Myśl Współczesna 9–10 (1947), 327–329

SZER Seweryn: *Pojęcie i przedmiot prawa cywilnego* [The concept and object of civil law], DPP 2 (1950), 12–17

SZER Seweryn: *Igor Andrejew: Oceny prawne karcenia nieletnich, Warszawa 1964, PWN, s. 130* [Igor Andreev: Legal assessments of the punishment of minors, Warsaw 1964, PWN, pp. 130], PiP 1 (1965), 122–124

SZER Seweryn: *Trwałość związku małżeńskiego* [The durability of the matrimonial union], DPP 1 (1946), 23–24

SZER Seweryn: *Współpraca polsko-czechosłowacka w zakresie kodyfikacji prawa rodzinnego* [Polish-Czechoslovak co-operation on the codification of family law], in *Księga pamiątkowa dla uczczenia pracy naukowej prof. K. Przybyłowskiego* [A commemorative book to honour the academic work of Professor K. Przybyłowski], Wacław OSUCHOWSKI, Mieczysław SOŚNIAK, Bronisław WALASZEK (eds), PWN, Krakow-Warsaw, 1964, 22–28

SZER Seweryn: *Z zagadnień prawa spadkowego* [From topics of inheritance law], PiP 5–6 (1951), 910–924

SZPUNAR Adam: *Nadużycie prawa podmiotowego* [Abuse of individual right], PAU, Krakow, 1947

SZYMCZAK Tadeusz: *Ustrój europejskich państw socjalistycznych* [The political system of European socialist states], PWN, Warsaw, 1983

TARKOWSKI Jacek: *Sprawność gospodarcza jako substytut legitymizacji władzy w Polsce powojennej* [Economic efficiency as a substitute for the legitimization of power in postwar Poland], in Jacek TARKOWSKI, *Socjologia świata polityki* [Sociology of the world of politics], vol. 1: *Władza i społeczeństwo w systemie autorytarnym* [Power and society in the authoritarian system], Instytut Nauk Politycznych PAN, Warsaw 1994, 67–84

TEUBNER Gunther: *Alienating Justice: On the Surplus Value of the Twelfth Camel*, in *Consequences of Legal Autopoiesis*, David NELKEN, Jiří PŘIBÁŇ (eds), Aldershot, Dartmouth, 2001, 21–44

THOMAS Yan: *The Subject of Right, the Person, Nature: Remarks on the Current Criticism of the Legal Subject*, in Yan THOMAS: *Artifices: Ten Essays on Roman Law in the Present Tense*, Thanos ZARTALOUDIS, Cooper FRANCIS (eds), Chantal

SCHÜTZ, Anton SCHÜTZ (trans.), Edinburgh University Pres, Edinburgh 2020, 107–143

TKACZ Sławomir, Zygmunt TOBOR: *Problematyka praworządności w teorii prawa Kazimierza Opałka* [Topics of rule of law in Kazimierz Opałek's theory of law], RPEiS (1) 2020, 40–55

TOKARCZYK Roman: *Wstęp* [Introduction], in *Tradycja i postęp w prawie* [Tradition and progress in law], Roman TOKARCZYK (ed.), Wydawnictwo Lubelskie, Lublin, 1983, 11–36

TOPIŃSKI Jan: *Niedostatki i braki teorii prawno-gospodarczej* [Deficiencies and shortcomings of legal-economic theory], Przegląd Ustawodawstwa Gospodarczego 16 (1963) 3, 153–158

TOPIŃSKI Jan: *Zarząd mieniem ogólnonarodowym* [The administration of national property], Książka i Wiedza, Warsaw, 1956

TOPOLSKI Jerzy: *Tradycje i ich upowszechnienie* [Traditions and their propagation], Nowe Drogi 1 (1977), 106–116

TORZEWSKI Wojciech: *Hermeneutyka a kwestia rozumu* [Hermeneutic and the question of reason], Filo-Sofija 11 (2010) 2, 29–40

TURKEL Gerald: *The Public/Private Distinction: Approaches to the Critique of Legal Ideology*, Law & Society Review 22 (1988) 4, 801–823

URBANIK Jakub: *Formalność rozwodu w rzymskim prawie klasycznym: D. 24,2,9 i augustowskie divortiis modum imponere* [The formality of divorce in classical Roman law: D.24.2.9 and the Augustian divortiis modum imponere], Zeszyty Prawnicze UKSW 9 (2009) 1, 85–121

VALENTE Joseph: *Lacan's Marxism, Marxism's Lacan (from Žižek to Althusser)*, in *The Cambridge Companion to Lacan*, Jean-Michel RABATÉ (ed.), CUP, Cambridge, 2003, 153–172

VAN DIJK Teun A.: *Discourse and Power*, Palgrave MacMillan, New York, 2008

VESPAZIANI Alberto: *Towards a Hermeneutical Approach to Legal Metaphor*, in *Human Rights, Language and Law*, Thomas BUSTAMANTE, Oche ONAZI (eds), Franz Steiner Verlag, Stuttgart, 2012, 79–92

WALASZEK Bronisław: *Uznanie dziecka w polskim prawie rodzinnym* [Recognition of parentage in Polish family law], PWN, Krakow, 1958

WALICKI Andrzej: *Marksizm i skok do królestwa wolności: dzieje komunistycznej utopii* [Marxism and the jump to the realm of freedom: the history of the communist Utopia], WN PWN, Warsaw, 1996

WALIGÓRSKI Marian: *Zmiany proceduralne w związku z ostatnią unifikacją prawa cywilnego* [Procedural changes in connection with the recent unification of civil law], PiP 5–6 (1946), 80–93

WASILKOWSKI Jan: *Kodeks cywilny PRL a zagadnienia prawa gospodarczego* [The Civil Code of Polish People's Republic and problems of economic law], PiP 3 (1962), 413–433

WASILKOWSKI Jan: *Kodyfikacja prawa cywilnego w Polsce* [Codification of civil law in Poland], Nowe Prawo 12 (1950), 3–7

WASILKOWSKI Jan: *Metoda opracowania i założenia kodeksu cywilnego* [The drafting method and assumptions of the Civil Code], PiP 5–6 (1964), 737–745

WASILKOWSKI Jan: *Pojęcie własności we współczesnym prawie polskim* [The concept of property in current Polish law], Książka i Wiedza, Warsaw, 1972

WASILKOWSKI Jan: *Prawa rzeczowe ograniczone* [In rem rights], Przegląd Notarialny, 1 (1947)/2–3, 175–191

WASILKOWSKI Jan: *Własność i inne prawa rzeczowe* [Ownership and other property rights], PiP 5–6 (1951), 854–876

WASILKOWSKI Jan: *Zagadnienia kodyfikacji polskiego prawa cywilnego* [Topics in the codification of Polish Civil Law], Nowe Drogi 11 (1960), 27–38

WASILKOWSKI Jan: *Zakres kodeksu cywilnego PRL (streszczenie referatu wygłoszonego na posiedzeniu Wydziału Cywilnego Komisji Kodyfikacyjnej w dniu 19. XII.1956 r.)* [The scope of the Civil Code of the Polish People's Republic (summary of a speech delivered in the meeting of the Codification Commission's Civil Section on 19 December 1956], Nowe Prawo 2 (1957), 3–8

WASILKOWSKI Jan: *Zarys prawa rzeczowego* [An outline of real law], PWN, Warsaw, 1963

WASILKOWSKI Jan, Adam CHEŁMOŃSKI, Kazimierz PRZYBYŁOWSKI, Seweryn SZER, Jan TOPIŃSKI: *Własność społeczna w świetle Konstytucji Rzeczypospolitej Ludowej* [Socialized property in the light of the Constitution of Polish People's Republic], in *Zagadnienia prawne Konstytucji Polskiej Rzeczypospolitej Ludowej* [Legal topics of the Constitution of Polish People's Republic], vol. 1, PWN, Warsaw, 1954, 17–114

WASILKOWSKI Jan, Marek MADEY: *Prawo własności w PRL. Zarys wykładu* [The law of ownership in Poland: outline of a lecture], PWN, Warsaw, 1969

WASILKOWSKI Jan, Aleksander WOLTER: *Projekt kodeksu cywilnego (część ogólna)* [The draft Civil Code (General Part), DPP 1 (1948), 10–18

WASILKOWSKI Jan, Aleksander WOLTER: *Wyniki dyskusji publicznej nad projektem kodeksu cywilnego* [Outcome of the public discussion on the draft Civil Code], PiŻ 22 (1961), 3

WEBER Max: *The Three Types of Legitimate Rule*, Berkeley Publications in Society and Institutions 4 (1958)/1, 1–11

WEISS Gilbert, Ruth WODAK (eds): *Critical Discourse Analysis: Theory and Interdisciplinarity in Critical Discourse Analysis*, Palgrave MacMillan, New York, 2003

WEITZER Ronald: *Law and Legal Ideology: Contributions to the Genesis and Reproduction of Capitalism*, Berkeley Journal of Sociology 24–25 (1980), 137–157

WENGEREK Edmund: *Udział prokuratora w postępowaniu cywilnym w świetle polskiej literatury prawniczej* [The prosecutor's participation in civil procedurę in the light of Polish legal literature], Studia Cywilistyczne 3 (1963), 163–214

WENZEL Michał: *Zaufanie do instytucji publicznych w Polsce, Czechach i na Węgrzech: komunikat z badań* [Confidence in public institutions in Poland, Czechia and Hungary: communication based on research], CBOS, Warsaw, 2001

WIATR Jerzy J.: *Przyczynek do zagadnienia rozwoju społecznego w formacji socjalistycznej* [A contribution to the topic of social development in socialist formation], Książka i Wiedza, Warsaw, 1979

WIEACKER Franz: *Privatrechtsgeschichte der Neuzeit unter besonderer Berücksichtigung der deutschen Entwicklung*, Vandenhoeck & Ruprecht Verlage, Göttingen, 1967

WIENIEDIKTOW Antolij W. [Venediktov Anatoliy]: *Państwowa własność socjalistyczna* [Socialist state property], Wydawnictwo Prawnicze, Warsaw, 1952

WIERZBOWSKI Błażej: *O przydatności użytkowania wieczystego* [On the usefulness of perpetual usufruct], in *Honeste vivere ... Księga pamiątkowa ku czci Profesora Władysława Bojarskiego* [*Honeste vivere* ... Collection of essays in memory of Professor Władysław Bojarski], WN UMK, Toruń, 2001, 617–627

WINIARSKI Bolesław: *Polityka gospodarcza* [Economic policy], WN PWN, Warsaw, 2006

WINIARZ Jan: *Kodyfikacja prawa rodzinnego i opiekuńczego w PRL* [The codification of family and guardianship law in the Polish People's Republic], in, in *Rozprawy z prawa cywilnego: księga pamiątkowa ku czci Witolda Czachórskiego* [Dissertations in civil law: commemoration book in honour of Professor Witold Czachórski], Jan BŁESZYŃSKI, Jerzy RAJSKI (eds), PWN, Warsaw, 1985, 77–88

WINIARZ Jan: *Prawo użytkowania wieczystego* [The right of perpetual usufruct], PWN, Warsaw, 1970

WINIARZ Jan: *Socjalistyczne prawo rodzinne PRL: ewolucja – stan aktualny – perspektywy* [The socialist family law of the Polish People's Republic: the evolution, the current state and the perspectives], Studia Prawnicze 4 (1974), 57–97

WINIARZ Jan, Janusz GAJDA: *Prawo rodzinne* [Family law], Wydawnictwo Prawnicze PWN, Warsaw, 1999

WITKOWSKI Wojciech, Andrzej WRZYSZCZ: *Modernisierung des Rechts auf polnischem Boden vom 19. bis Anfang des 20. Jahrhunderts*, in *Rechtskulturen des modernen Osteuropa. Traditionen und Transfers*, Tomasz GIARO (ed.), vol. 1: *Modernisierung durch Transfer im 19. und frühen 20. Jahrhundert*, Vittorio Klostermann, Frankfurt am Main, 2006, 249–274

WŁODYKA Stanisław: *Własność a reformy gospodarcze* [Property and economic reforms], in *Obywatelskie inicjatywy ustawodawcze Solidarności 1980–1990: materiały i projekty ustaw Centrum Obywatelskich Inicjatyw Ustawodawczych 'S' i Społecznej Rady Legislacyjnej* [The citizens' legislative initiatives of Solidarity. Materials and legislative drafts of the Solidarity Centre for Citizens' Legislative Action and Social Legislative Council], Kazimierz BARCZYK, Stanisław GRODZISKI, Stefan GRZYBOWSKI (eds), Wydawnictwo Sejmowe, Warsaw, 2001, 574–575

WODAK Ruth: *Inter/trans/post-disciplinarity and the Study of Language and/in Politics*, Journal of Language and Politics 4 (2005)/2, 169–171

WOJCIECHOWSKI Maciej: Pewność prawa [The certainty of law], WUG, Gdańsk, 2014

WOJTACKI Maciej: *Idea prawa narodowego na łamach 'Prawa' (1928–1939) i 'Współczesnej Myśli Prawniczej' (1935–1939)* [The idea of national law on the pages of 'Law' and 'Contemporary Legal Thought'], Historia i Polityka 6 (2011), 53–73

WOJTCZAK Sylwia, Iwona WITCZAK-PLISIECKA: *Metaphors and Legal Language: A Few Comments on Ordinary, Specialised and Legal Meaning*, Research in Language 17 (2019) 3, 273–295

WOŁODKIEWICZ Witold: Czy święta własność prywatna w prawie rzymskim? [Sacredness of private property in Roman law?], 3–4 (60) Palestra 2015, 223–227

WOŁODKIEWICZ Witold: *I cambiamenti del codice civile polacco dopo 1989 possono essere trattati come segno del ritorno alla tradizione romanistica?*, in *The Roman Law Tradition in Societies in Transition*, Petr BĚLOVSKÝ, Martin SKŘEJPEK (eds), Právnická Fakulta Univerzity Karlovy w Praze, Praha, 2003, 129–142

WOLTER Aleksander: *Kierunki zmian polskiego prawa rodzinnego* [Directions of change in Polish family law], PiP 8–9 (1958), 269–291

WOLTER Aleksander: *Kodeks cywilny a 'prawo rodzinne'* [Civil Code and 'family law'], PiP 3 (1957), 475–479

WOLTER Aleksander: *Nowy projekt kodeksu cywilnego* [The new draft Civil Code], PiP 2 (1962), 210–218

WOLTER Aleksander: *Prawo cywilne: zarys części ogólnej* [Civil law: an outline of the general part], PWN, Warsaw, 1967

WOLTER Aleksander: *Wspólny majątek małżonków de lege ferenda* [Matrimonial community property *de lege ferenda*], PiP 10 (1957), 558–571

WOLTER Aleksander: *Czy renesans koncepcji prawa gospodarczego?* [A renaissance of concepts of economic law?], Przegląd Ustawodawstwa Gospodarczego, 3 (1957), 81–85

WRÓBEL Magdalena: *Główne założenia projektu kodeksu cywilnego* [The main assumptions for the draft Civil Code Monitor Prawniczy 13 (2007), 733–750

WRÓBLEWSKI Jerzy: *Ambiguities of Idealism and Materialism Opposition in Legal Theory*, Archives for Philosophy of Law and Social Philosophy 75 (1989) 3, 834–847

WRÓBLEWSKI Jerzy: *Zagadnienia teorii wykładni prawa ludowego* [Topics in the theory of interpretation of the people's law], Wydawnictwo Prawnicze, Warsaw, 1959

Wstęp, Studia Cywilistyczne 25–26 (1975), 3–5

YOUNG Brian J.: *Politics of Codification: The Lower Canadian Civil Code of 1866*, McGill-Quinn's University Press, Montreal-Kingston-London-Buffalo, 1994

ZAJADŁO Jerzy: *Leksykon filozofii i teorii prawa, 100 podstawowych pojęć* [A lexicon of philosophy and theory of law; 100 essential terms], C. H. Beck, Warszawa, 2007

ZALEWSKA Monika: *Cognitive Theory of Metaphor and Jerzy Wróblewski's Concept of Legal Interpretation*, Hybris 39 (2017) 4, 56–73

Założenia i zamierzenia centralnego pisma prawniczego [The assumptions and intention of a central legal journal], DPP 1 (1945), 2–3

ZAREMBA Marcin: *Komunizm, legitymizacja, nacjonalizm. Nacjonalistyczna legitymizacja władzy komunistycznej w Polsce* [Communism, legitimation, nationalism. The nationalist legitimation of communist rule in Poland], WPAN, Warszawa, 2001

ŻARYN Jan (ed.): Dyskusja [Discussion], 3 Polska 1944/45–1989. Studia i Materiały 1997, 257–288

ZEDLER Feliks: *Co dalej z kodeksem postępowania cywilnego?* [What more with the Code of Civil Procedure?] in *Czterdziestolecie kodeksu postępowania cywilnego: zjazd Katedr Postępowania cywilnego w Zakopanym (7–9.10.2005 r.)* [The fortieth anniversary of the Civil Code: conference of departments of civil procedure in Zakopane (7–9 October 2005)], Izabela RATUSIŃSKA (ed.), Zakamycze, Krakow, 2005, 309–329

ZIEMBIŃSKI Zygmunt: *Podłoże społeczne przysposobienia dziecka w Polsce Ludowej* [The social underpinnings of the adoption of a child in People's Poland], Wydawnictwo Prawnicze, Warsaw, 1956

ZIEMBIŃSKI Zygmunt: *Teoria prawa* [Theory of law], PWN, Warsaw-Poznań 1977

ŽIŽEK Slavoj: *First as Tragedy Then as Farce*, Verso, London, 2009

ŽIŽEK Slavoj: *The Sublime Object of Ideology* [1989], Verso, London, 2008

ZOLL Fryderyk, Jr: *Nasze zadania najbliższe w dziedzinie międzynarodowego i międzydzielnicowego prawa prywatnego* [Our tasks at hand in the field of international and inter-partitional private law], GSW 21 (1919), 261–264

ZOLL Fryderyk, Jr: *Prawo cywilne w zarysie* [Civil law in an outline], vol. 2, Księgarnia Powszechna, Krakow, 1947

ZOLL Fryderyk: *Europejski kodeks cywilny – wokół wizji nowego prawa prywatnego dla Europy* [European Civil Code: a vision of new private law for Europe], in Nowa Europa, Przegląd Natoliński 1 (2018), 16–34

ŻUŁAWSKA Czesława: *Dwadzieścia pięć lat reformowania prawa cywilnego materialnego: kronika – wspomnienia – refleksje* [Twenty-five years of reforming substantive civil law: chronicle, recollections, reflections], KPP 16 (2007) 2, 305–335

ŻUŁAWSKA Czesława: *O początkach przekształcania systemu gospodarczego z perspektywy dwudziestu lat* [On the beginnings of the transformation of the economic system from twenty years' perspective], in *Obywatelskie inicjatywy ustawodawcze Solidarności 1980–1990: materiały i projekty ustaw Centrum Obywatelskich Inicjatyw Ustawodawczych 'S' i Społecznej Rady Legislacyjnej* [The citizens' legislative initiatives of Solidarity: materials and legislative drafts of the Solidarity Centre for Citizens' Legislative Action and Social Legislative Council], Kazimierz BARCZYK, Stanisław GRODZISKI, Stefan GRZYBOWSKI (eds), Wydawnictwo Sejmowe, Warsaw, 2001, 575–577

Index of Names

Index of Subjects

www.ingramcontent.com/pod-product-compliance
Lightning Source LLC
Chambersburg PA
CBHW071336230926
51849CB00002B/410